# THE SOCIAL WORLD
Third Edition

# THE SOCIAL WORLD

**Third Edition**

**Edited by Ian Robertson**

Worth Publishers, Inc.

**The Social World,** Third Edition

Copyright © 1987, 1981 by Worth Publishers, Inc.

Printed in the United States of America

Library of Congress Catalog Card Number: 81-52912

ISBN: 0-87901-330-3

   3 4 5 – 93 92 91 90 89


Cover photograph: © Geoffrey Gove


Worth Publishers, Inc.

33 Irving Place

New York, New York 10003

# Preface

Because of limitations of space and time, introductory sociology textbooks and lectures generally focus on the basic principles of the discipline, with appropriate examples included where practicable. A book of readings, on the other hand, can serve a different and supplementary purpose: to acquaint students at first hand with a more detailed and leisurely mode of sociological analysis. My main goal in compiling this book of readings has therefore been to provide examples of good sociological writing which, in the main, illustrate the applications of sociological ideas, rather than repeat the exposition of principles found in texts and lectures.

Half of the articles in the book are new to this edition. In all, there are fifty-nine readings drawn from a variety of sources, ranging from book excerpts and popular-press articles to material from professional journals. I selected the articles according to three basic criteria: that they be readable and interesting to today's students; that they reflect the diversity of concerns and viewpoints in the contemporary discipline; and that they provide the necessary practical illustrations of sociological theories and principles. Each reading is preceded by an introductory note and is followed by questions designed to promote reflection and provoke classroom discussion.

Although this book may be used independently or in conjunction with any text, it provides a particularly appropriate supplement to my *Sociology*, Third Edition (Worth, 1987), since the sequence of topics parallels that in the text.

I am most grateful to David Gordon (State University of New York, Geneseo), Eva Havas (Northeastern University), Maynard Seider (North Adams State College), and Shelley Tenenbaum (Clark University), who reviewed the previous edition and made many valuable suggestions for its improvement.

August 1987                                          IAN ROBERTSON

# Contents

x     Contents

# THE SOCIAL WORLD
Third Edition

# UNIT 1

# Introduction to Sociology

C. Wright Mills

# 1. The Promise

*The sociologist looks at the social world in a special way, with a distinctive perspective that is quite unlike that of the lay person. C. Wright Mills referred to this particular mode of examining our social surroundings as "the sociological imagination." The promise of sociology to the novice, he claimed, is that it ignites that particular imagination, and its possessor never sees society in quite the same way again.*

*Essentially, the sociological imagination enables us, as it were, to step outside our immediate confines—to see ourselves not just as isolated individuals but rather as beings who exist within, and who are largely shaped by, the broader context of time and place, history and society. As an example, Mills offers his classic distinction between "private troubles" and "public issues"—the former, a problem whose solution lies within range of the individual, the latter, one that is of societal concern. For instance, if only one man in a community is unemployed, the personal characteristics of that individual are probably at issue; but if 15 million workers out of a labor force of 50 million are jobless, then we must look to social forces for an explanation. The point seems obvious enough, but in countless more subtle situations it is habitually overlooked.*

*In this article, Mills outlines the essence of "the sociological imagination" and its promise to those who take up sociology.*

Nowadays men often feel that their private lives are a series of traps. They sense that within their everyday worlds, they cannot overcome their troubles, and in this feeling, they are often quite correct: What ordinary men are directly aware of and what they try to do are bounded by the private orbits in which they live; their visions and their powers are limited to the close-up scenes of job, family, neighborhood; in other milieux, they move vicariously and remain spectators. And the more aware they become, however vaguely, of ambitions and of threats which transcend their immediate locales, the more trapped they seem to feel.

Underlying this sense of being trapped are seemingly impersonal changes in the very structure of continent-wide societies. The facts of contemporary history are also facts about the success and the failure of individual men and women. When a society is industrialized, a peasant becomes a worker; a feudal lord is liquidated or becomes a businessman. When classes rise or fall, a man is employed or unemployed; when the rate of investment goes up or down, a man takes new heart or goes broke. When wars happen, an insurance salesman becomes a rocket launcher; a store clerk, a radar man; a wife lives alone; a child grows up without a father. Neither the life of an individual nor the history of a society can be understood without understanding both.

Yet men do not usually define the troubles they endure in terms of historical change and institutional contradiction. The well-being they enjoy, they do not usually impute to the big ups and downs of the societies in which they live. Seldom aware of the intricate connection between the patterns of their own lives and the course of world history, ordinary men do not usually know what this connection means for the kinds of men they are becoming and for the kinds of history-making in which they might take part. They do not possess the quality of mind essential to grasp the interplay of man and society, of biography and history, of self and world. They cannot cope with their personal troubles in such ways as to control the structural transformations that usually lie behind them.

Surely it is no wonder. In what period have so many men been so totally exposed at so fast a pace to such earthquakes of change? That Americans have not known such catastrophic changes as have the men and women of other societies is due to historical facts that are now quickly becoming "merely history." The history that now affects every man is world history. Within this scene and this period, in the course of a single generation, one sixth of mankind is transformed from all that is feudal and backward into all that is modern, advanced, and fearful. Political colonies are freed; new and less visible forms of imperialism installed. Revolutions occur; men feel the intimate grip of new kinds of authority. Totalitarian societies rise, and are smashed to bits—or succeed fabulously. After two centuries of ascendancy, capitalism is shown up as only one way to make society into an industrial apparatus. After two centuries of hope, even formal democracy is restricted to a quite small portion of mankind. Everywhere in the underdeveloped world, ancient ways of life are broken up and vague expectations become urgent demands. Everywhere in the overdeveloped world, the means of authority and of violence become total in scope and bureaucratic in form. Humanity itself now lies before us, the super-nation at either pole concentrating its most co-ordinated and massive efforts upon the preparation of World War Three.

The very shaping of history now outpaces the ability of men to orient themselves in accordance with cherished values. And which values? Even when they do not panic, men often sense that older ways of feeling and thinking have collapsed and that newer beginnings are ambiguous to the point of moral stasis. Is it any wonder that ordinary men feel they cannot cope with the larger worlds with which they are so suddenly confronted? That they cannot understand the meaning of their epoch for their own lives? That—in defense of selfhood—they become morally insensible, trying to remain altogether private men? Is it any wonder that they come to be possessed by a sense of the trap?

It is not only information that they need—in this Age of Fact, information often dominates their attention and overwhelms their capacities to assimilate it. It is not only the skills of reason that they need—although their struggles to acquire these often exhaust their limited moral energy.

What they need, and what they feel they need, is a quality of mind that will help them to use information and to develop reason in order to achieve lucid summations of what is going on in the world and of what may be happening within themselves. It is this quality, I am going to contend, that journalists and scholars, artists and publics, scientists and editors are coming to expect of what may be called the sociological imagination.

## I

The sociological imagination enables its possessor to understand the larger historical scene in terms of its meaning for the inner life and the external career of a variety of individuals. It enables him to take into account how individuals, in the welter of their daily experience, often become falsely conscious of their social positions. Within that welter, the framework of modern society is sought, and within that framework the psychologies of a variety of men and women are formulated. By such means the personal uneasiness of individuals is focused upon explicit troubles and the indifference of publics is transformed into involvement with public issues.

The first fruit of this imagination—and the first lesson of the social science that embodies it—is the idea that the individual can understand his own experience and gauge his own fate only by locating himself within his period, that he can know his own chances in life only by becoming aware of those of all individuals in his circumstances. In many ways it is a terrible lesson; in many ways a magnificent one. We do not know the limits of man's capacities for supreme effort or willing degradation, for agony or glee, for pleasurable brutality or the sweetness of reason. But in our time we have come to know that the limits of "human nature" are frighteningly broad. We have come to know that every individual lives, from one generation to the next, in some society; that he lives out a biography, and that he lives it out within some historical sequence. By the fact of his living he contributes, however minutely, to the shaping of this society and to the course of its history, even as he is made by society and by its historical push and shove.

The sociological imagination enables us to grasp history and biography and the relations between the two within society. That is its task and its promise. To recognize this task and this promise is the mark of the classic social analyst. It is characteristic of Herbert Spencer—turgid, polysyllabic, comprehensive; of E. A. Ross—graceful, muckraking, upright; of Auguste Comte and Emile Durkheim; of the intricate and subtle Karl Mannheim. It is the quality of all that is intellectually excellent in Karl Marx; it is the clue to Thorstein Veblen's brilliant and ironic insight, to Joseph Schumpeter's many-sided constructions of reality; it is the basis of the psychological sweep of W. E. H. Lecky no less than of the profundity and clarity of Max Weber. And it is the signal of what is best in contemporary studies of man and society.

No social study that does not come back to the problems of biography, of history, and of their intersections within a society has completed its intellectual journey. Whatever the specific problems of the classic social analysts, however limited or however broad the features of social reality they have examined, those who have been imaginatively aware of the promise of their work have consistently asked three sorts of questions:

1. What is the structure of this particular society as a whole? What are its essential components, and how are they related to one another? How does it differ from other varieties of social order? Within it, what is the meaning of any particular feature for its continuance and for its change?

2. Where does this society stand in human history? What are the mechanics by which it is changing? What is its place within and its meaning for the development of humanity as a whole? How does any particular feature we are examining affect, and how is it affected by, the historical period in which it moves? And this period—what are its essential features? How does it differ from other periods? What are its characteristic ways of history-making?

3. What varieties of men and women now prevail in this society and in this period? And what varieties are coming to prevail? In what ways are they selected and formed, liberated and repressed, made sensitive and blunted? What kinds of "human nature" are revealed in the conduct and character we observe in this society in this period? And what is the meaning for "human nature" of each and every feature of the society we are examining?

Whether the point of interest is a great power state or a minor literary mood, a family, a prison, a creed—these are the kinds of questions the best social analysts have asked. They are the intellectual pivots of classic studies of man in society—and they are the questions inevitably raised by any mind possessing the sociological imagination. For that imagination is the capacity to shift from one perspective to another—from the political to the psychological; from examination of a single family to comparative assessment of the national budgets of the world; from the theological school to the military establishment; from considerations of an oil industry to studies of contemporary poetry. It is the capacity to range from the most impersonal and remote transformations to the most intimate features of the human self—and to see the relations between the two. Back of its use there is always the urge to know the social and historical meaning of the individual in the society and in the period in which he has his quality and his being.

That, in brief, is why it is by means of the sociological imagination that men now hope to grasp what is going on in the world, and to understand what is happening in themselves as minute points of the intersections of biography and history within society. In large part, contemporary man's self-conscious view of himself as at least an outsider, if not a permanent stranger, rests upon

an absorbed realization of social relativity and of the transformative power of history. The sociological imagination is the most fruitful form of this self-consciousness. By its use men whose mentalities have swept only a series of limited orbits often come to feel as if suddenly awakened in a house with which they had only supposed themselves to be familiar. Correctly or incorrectly, they often come to feel that they can now provide themselves with adequate summations, cohesive assessments, comprehensive orientations. Older decisions that once appeared sound now seem to them products of a mind unaccountably dense. Their capacity for astonishment is made lively again. They acquire a new way of thinking, they experience a transvaluation of values: in a word, by their reflection and by their sensibility, they realize the cultural meaning of the social sciences.

## II

Perhaps the most fruitful distinction with which the sociological imagination works is between "the personal troubles of milieu" and "the public issues of social structure." This distinction is an essential tool of the sociological imagination and a feature of all classic work in social science.

*Troubles* occur within the character of the individual and within the range of his immediate relations with others; they have to do with his self and with those limited areas of social life of which he is directly and personally aware. Accordingly, the statement and the resolution of troubles properly lie within the individual as a biographical entity and within the scope of his immediate milieu—the social setting that is directly open to his personal experience and to some extent his willful activity. A trouble is a private matter: values cherished by an individual are felt by him to be threatened.

*Issues* have to do with matters that transcend these local environments of the individual and the range of his inner life. They have to do with the organization of many such milieux into the institutions of an historical society as a whole, with the ways in which various milieux overlap and interpenetrate to form the larger structure of social and historical life. An issue is a public matter: some value cherished by publics is felt to be threatened. Often there is a debate about what that value is and about what it is that really threatens it. This debate is often without focus if only because it is the very nature of an issue, unlike even widespread trouble, that it cannot very well be defined in terms of the immediate and everyday environments of ordinary men. An issue, in fact, often involves a crisis in institutional arrangements, and often too it involves what Marxists call "contradictions" or "antagonisms."

In these terms, consider unemployment. When, in a

city of 100,000, only one man is unemployed, that is his personal trouble, and for its relief we properly look to the character of the man, his skills, and his immediate opportunities. But when in a nation of 50 million employees, 15 million men are unemployed, that is an issue, and we may not hope to find its solution within the range of opportunities open to any one individual. The very structure of opportunities has collapsed. Both the correct statement of the problem and the range of possible solutions require us to consider the economic and political institutions of the society, and not merely the personal situation and character of a scatter of individuals.

Consider war. The personal problem of war, when it occurs, may be how to survive it or how to die in it with honor; how to make money out of it; how to climb into the higher safety of the military apparatus; or how to contribute to the war's termination. In short, according to one's values, to find a set of milieux and within it to survive the war or make one's death in it meaningful. But the structural issues of war have to do with its causes; with what types of men it throws up into command; with its effects upon economic and political, family and religious institutions, with the unorganized irresponsibility of a world of nation-states.

Consider marriage. Inside a marriage a man and a woman may experience personal troubles, but when the divorce rate during the first four years of marriage is 250 out of every 1,000 attempts, this is an indication of a structural issue having to do with the institutions of marriage and the family and other institutions that bear upon them.

Or consider the metropolis—the horrible, beautiful, ugly, magnificent sprawl of the great city. For many upper-class people, the personal solution to "the problem of the city" is to have an apartment with private garage under it in the heart of the city, and forty miles out, a house by Henry Hill, garden by Garrett Eckbo, on a hundred acres of private land. In these two controlled environments—with a small staff at each end and a private helicopter connection—most people could solve many of the problems of personal milieux caused by the facts of the city. But all this, however splendid, does not solve the public issues that the structural fact of the city poses. What should be done with this wonderful monstrosity? Break it all up into scattered units, combining residence and work? Refurbish it as it stands? Or, after evacuation, dynamite it and build new cities according to new plans in new places? What should those plans be? And who is to decide and to accomplish whatever choice is made? These are structural issues; to confront them and to solve them requires us to consider political and economic issues that affect innumerable milieux.

In so far as an economy is so arranged that slumps occur, the problem of unemployment becomes incapable of personal solution. In so far as war is inherent in the nation-state system and in the uneven industrialization of the world, the ordinary individual in his restricted milieu will be powerless—with or without psychiatric aid—to solve the troubles this system or lack of system imposes upon him. In so far as the family as an institution turns women into darling little slaves and men into their chief providers and unweaned dependents, the problem of a satisfactory marriage remains incapable of purely private solution. In so far as the overdeveloped megalopolis and the overdeveloped automobile are built-in features of the overdeveloped society, the issues of urban living will not be solved by personal ingenuity and private wealth.

What we experience in various and specific milieux, I have noted, is often caused by structural changes. Accordingly, to understand the changes of many personal milieux we are required to look beyond them. And the number and variety of such structural changes increase as the institutions within which we live become more embracing and more intricately connected with one another. To be aware of the idea of social structure and to use it with sensibility is to be capable of tracing such linkages among a great variety of milieux. To be able to do that is to possess the sociological imagination.

## III

What are the major issues for publics and the key troubles of private individuals in our time? To formulate issues and troubles, we must ask what values are cherished yet threatened, and what values are cherished and supported, by the characterizing trends of our period. In the case both of threat and of support we must ask what salient contradictions of structure may be involved.

When people cherish some set of values and do not feel any threat to them, they experience *well-being*. When they cherish values but *do* feel them to be threatened, they experience a crisis—either as a personal trouble or as a public issue. And if all their values seem involved, they feel the total threat of panic.

But suppose people are neither aware of any cherished values nor experience any threat? That is the experience of *indifference*, which, if it seems to involve all their values, becomes apathy. Suppose, finally, they are unaware of any cherished values, but still are very much aware of a threat? That is the experience of *uneasiness*, of anxiety, which, if it is total enough, becomes a deadly unspecified malaise.

Ours is a time of uneasiness and indifference—not yet formulated in such ways as to permit the work of reason and the play of sensibility. Instead of troubles—defined in terms of values and threats—there is often the misery of vague uneasiness; instead of explicit issues there is often merely the beat feeling that all is somehow not right. Neither the values threatened nor whatever threatens them has been stated; in short, they have not been carried to the point of decision. Much less have they been formulated as problems of social science.

In the thirties there was little doubt—except among certain deluded business circles—that there was an economic issue which was also a pack of personal troubles. In these arguments about "the crisis of capitalism," the formulations of Marx and the many unacknowledged reformulations of his work probably set the leading terms of the issue, and some men came to understand their personal troubles in these terms. The values threatened were plain to see and cherished by all; the structural contradictions that threatened them also seemed plain. Both were widely and deeply experienced. It was a political age.

But the values threatened in the era after World War Two are often neither widely acknowledged as values nor widely felt to be threatened. Much private uneasiness goes unformulated; much public malaise and many decisions of enormous structural relevance never become public issues. For those who accept such inherited values as reason and freedom, it is the uneasiness itself that is the trouble; it is the indifference itself that is the issue. And it is this condition, of uneasiness and indifference, that is the signal feature of our period.

All this is so striking that it is often interpreted by observers as a shift in the very kinds of problems that need now to be formulated. We are frequently told that the problems of our decade, or even the crisis of our period, have shifted from the external realm of economics and now have to do with the quality of individual life—in fact with the question of whether there is soon going to be anything that can properly be called individual life. Not child labor but comic books, not poverty but mass leisure, are at the center of concern. Many great public issues as well as many private troubles are described in terms of "the psychiatric"—often, it seems, in a pathetic attempt to avoid the large issues and problems of modern society. Often this statement seems to rest upon a provincial narrowing of interest to the Western societies, or even to the United States—thus ignoring two-thirds of mankind; often, too, it arbitrarily divorces the individual life from the larger institutions within which that life is enacted, and which on occasion bear upon it more grievously than do the intimate environments of childhood.

Problems of leisure, for example, cannot even be stated without considering problems of work. Family troubles over comic books cannot be formulated as problems without considering the plight of the contemporary family in its new relations with the newer institutions of the social structure. Neither leisure nor its debilitating uses can be understood as problems without recognition of the extent to which malaise and indifference now form the social and personal climate of contemporary American society. In this climate, no problems of "the private life" can be stated and solved without recognition of the crisis of ambition that is part of the very career of men at work in the incorporated economy.

It is true, as psychoanalysts continually point out, that people do often have "the increasing sense of being moved by obscure forces within themselves which they are unable to define." But it is *not* true, as Ernest Jones asserted, that "man's chief enemy and danger is his own unruly nature and the dark forces pent up within him." On the contrary: "Man's chief danger" today lies in the unruly forces of contemporary society itself, with its alienating methods of production, its enveloping techniques of political domination, its international anarchy—in a word, its pervasive transformations of the very "nature" of man and the conditions and aims of his life.

It is now the social scientist's foremost political and intellectual task—for here the two coincide—to make clear the elements of contemporary uneasiness and indifference. It is the central demand made upon him by other cultural workmen—by physical scientists and artists, by the intellectual community in general. It is because of this task and these demands, I believe, that the social sciences are becoming the common denominator of our cultural period, and the sociological imagination our most needed quality of mind....

## QUESTIONS

1. Explain, with examples, what Mills means by "the sociological imagination."

2. How does sociology differ from psychology?

3. Children from middle-class families are more likely to attend college than children from working-class families. Why do you think this is so?

*Peter L. Berger*
*Brigitte Berger*

# 2. Why Sociology?

*Many newcomers to sociology—possibly most—are not entirely certain about why they are taking the course. The single-minded few, perhaps, are determined to become sociologists, but the motives of others vary a great deal, ranging from a keen interest in the subject to the hope of finding a soft option for a social science course requirement. In time, the inherent fascination of the study of social behavior should make enthusiasts of nearly everyone: but in the meanwhile, why sociology?*

*In this article, Peter and Brigitte Berger consider some reasons for undertaking the scientific study of society. One set of reasons, they suggest, is more immediately practical: making a living through sociology as part of the "knowledge industry," in education or in the various professional fields where the skills of sociologists are sought. The second set of reasons, which they consider at least equally important, has to do with personal and intellectual development: in ways that become apparent only over time, they claim, a sociological understanding of the world contributes to a greater awareness of self and others, to a deepened appreciation of human liberty and the human potential.*

From Peter L. Berger and Brigitte Berger, Postscript—Why Sociology? in *Sociology: A Biographical Approach*, Second, Expanded Edition (New York: Basic Books, 1975). Copyright © 1972, 1975 by Peter and Brigitte Berger, Basic Books, Inc., Publishers, New York.

There are, of course, different reasons why students take an introductory course or read an introductory book on sociology. These range all the way from earnest career plans to the tactical requirements of seduction, not to mention the campus reputation and grading habits of sociology instructors. We have no objections to the less than earnest motives. But, optimists by inclination, we assume that having finished the course . . . at least some students will be more rather than less interested in sociology. In that case the question, "Why sociology?" will also be more interesting to them than it was at the outset.

The question can be asked with two different senses: "What can one actually do with sociology?" And, more searchingly: "Is sociology worthwhile?"

## Making a Living in the "Knowledge Industry"

One thing that one can obviously do with sociology is to become a sociologist. Only a very small fraction of those who take sociology courses as undergraduates take this direction. For those considering this awesome option, a few words on its practical implications are in order here.

The discipline of sociology is today a well-established and well-organized profession in America. As of late 1969, the membership of the American Sociological Association, the major professional organization of the discipline, was 12,903 if one includes student members and 8,461 if one only counts the fully certified brethren—in either case, a number not to be sneezed at. The association has an impressive headquarters in Washington and holds conventions in enormous hotels.

The visible output of American sociologists is impressive, too. Large numbers of books are published in sociology every year. There are dozens of journals in the field, more than anyone can possibly read and do anything else besides, so that there is now (as in other disciplines) a journal *about* journals, *Sociological Abstracts*, which classifies and summarizes this vast and rapidly growing body of professional lore.

Sociology constitutes a significant division of what Fritz Machlup, an economist, has called the American "knowledge industry." What is probably more important, sociology occupies, and has occupied for a considerable period of time, a respected place on the American intellectual scene. Naturally, there are also detractors, like the sardonic commentator who said some years ago that a sociologist is a man who will spend ten thousand dollars to discover the local house of ill repute. By and large, though, statements about society by sociologists exercising their professional judgment widely command authority or at least gain a serious hearing. This is true in the mass media, in political debate over current issues, among decision-makers in government and business, and in broad segments of the general public. We would not be sociologists if we did not agree that, much of the time, this intellectual status of the discipline is merited. To mention only some of the problems currently troubling American society, sociologists have contributed both important information and clarifying insights to the public discussion of urbanism, of the racial situation, of education, of government measures against crime and against poverty.

American sociology continues to hold a pre-eminent position in the discipline, comparable, say, to the position held by German philosophy and German historical scholarship in the nineteenth century. Sociology in no other country compares with American sociology in terms of academic and intellectual status, the variety and sophistication of theoretical approaches and research technology, both the quantity and quality of output, and the sheer size of the professional establishment. American books and journals throughout the field are necessary reading for foreign sociologists, while the reverse is only true for limited aspects of sociology (as, for example, for sociological theory). Foreign sociology students, if at all possible practically, seek to spend at least some portion of their studies in an American university's sociology department. Not surprisingly, English (one is tempted to add, especially if one looks at the writings of British sociologists, *American* English) has become the lingua franca of sociologists everywhere.

All the same, there has been quite a remarkable upsurge of sociology abroad over the last two decades. Sizable sociological establishments have grown up in Western Europe, particularly in Germany, France, Britain, Holland and the Scandinavian countries. Although the attitude toward sociology by Communist regimes has vacillated between condemning it as a "bourgeois ideology" and gingerly accepting it as a useful instrument in social planning, sociology is now a going concern in the Soviet Union and in the socialist countries of Eastern Europe. The holding of the 1970 World Congress of Sociology in Bulgaria symbolized this new acceptability of the discipline in the "socialist camp" (at least the part of it that is within the Soviet orbit). In the countries of the Third World, sociology is very widely regarded as an important aid for development planning and policy.

What are American sociologists actually doing? The very great majority are engaged in teaching at colleges and universities. This means, quite simply, that anyone planning to become a professional sociologist should reckon with the fact that most jobs in the field are teaching jobs, and that teaching is very probably what he will be doing at least much of the time. The most important other activity of sociologists is research, though for many this is not a source of continuous employment but rather something that they do besides teaching or on occasional leaves from teaching jobs. All the same, there are a good number of full-time research jobs, some connected with university research programs, others in agencies or research institutes of the government, business, labor or other organizations (such as churches) with an interest in discerning societal trends. Thirdly, there is a scattering of sociologists in jobs of the most different sorts, ranging from advertising and personnel management to community action in this country or abroad. Whether interested in teaching or one of the other options, the aspiring sociologist should realize that graduate study, increasingly up to and including the doctorate, is a prerequisite for jobs that carry professional status (not to mention the pay that one associates with such status). Different graduate programs emphasize different aspects of the field and some thought ought to be given to the choice of school, especially since the American academic system does not encourage easy transfers from one school to another.

## "Establishment" and "Radical" Sociology

There has recently been much debate within the profession about its present conditon, the directions it has been taking and the directions that it should take in the future. There are strong differences of opinion among American sociologists both as to diagnosis and prescription. Political radicals in the field have attacked what they consider to be "establishment sociology" as an ideological tool of the status quo and have demanded a new conception of sociology as a discipline standing in the service of radical or even revolutionary politics. Black sociologists have called for sociological work designed to serve the interests of the black community, sometimes meaning by this nothing more than work that would be more sensitive to the black experience in America than that of (or so they claim) the work of many white sociologists, sometimes going much further by demanding a distinctively black sociology that would be part of and ideologically attuned to "black consciousness." Various movements concerned with "liberation," most recently (and very audibly so) the Women's Liberation movement, have sought to enroll sociologists and sociology in their ranks. Whatever one may think of these critiques and redefinitions of the field, they have greatly enlivened sociological discourse in recent years. All of this has taken place against the background of a much broader feeling that intellectuals and their disciplines should be involved in the agonies of our time and concerned with the solutions of our most agonizing problems. It is understandable that this feeling has been particularly strong among sociologists, proponents of a discipline that explicitly takes society as its object of inquiry.

Since only a small minority of those who take undergraduate courses in sociology goes on to professional work in the field, a rationale for these courses as nothing but pre-professional education (comparable, say, to a premedical curriculum) is hardly persuasive. There ought to be other things that one can do with sociology.

## Dealing with Men Directly: The Human Sciences and the Humanities

Information and perspectives provided by sociology have wide applicability to other fields. This is obvious in a variety of practical fields that, in one way or another, must take cognizance of social structures. These range all the way from social work to the law. Sociology, by its very nature, has relevance for most other sciences dealing with man (those that the French, very aptly, call "human sciences"). In many places ... we have seen the relation of sociology to other social sciences—political science, economics, cultural anthropology and social psychology, to name the major ones. But even in the humanities, where there has been a strongly ingrained animus against sociologists and their "barbarian" incursions into territory where they have no business, the recognition of the usefulness of sociological insights has grown. This is especially true among historians, but it may also be found today among scholars of religion and literature.

But what about the individual who has none of these professional or scholarly ambitions? Is sociology worthwhile for him? We think so. Anyone who wants to live with his eyes open will profit from a better understanding of his society and his own situation in it. But perhaps even more important is the ability to understand the situations and the social worlds of others. Contemporary society needs this ability more than ever.

## A Pluralistic Society: Is Love Really All You Need?

Good will is not enough. Let us take just one example out of many possible ones. A few years ago a group of white upper-middle-class young people from the New York suburban area decided that, in order to show their concern for the "ghetto" and its people, they would go into some of the black neighborhoods of the city and help in fixing them up. They did so, on one fine weekend, the first and the last of the experiment. They came in full of enthusiasm and started to paint houses, sweep the streets, clean up piles of garbage and engage in other "obviously" desirable activities. Before long they were surrounded by angry black teenagers, and a good many angry black adults, who yelled obscenities at them, threw disagreeable objects and generally interfered with the progress of operation uplift. There is no reason to impugn the good will of the young whites. At worst, they were guilty of naiveté, slightly spiced with self-righteousness. Even a whiff of sociological insight on their part, however, would have avoided the entire debacle. It hardly needs emphasizing that better insight into the social situation, and therefore the motives and meanings, of others can be very useful for blacks as well.

Contemporary society ... is becoming increasingly complex and variegated. This is what is commonly called "pluralism." What is more, contemporary society, or any conceivable variation of its present structure, will break down into howling chaos unless a plurality of social groups and social worlds succeeds in existing together with a measure of mutual understanding. Under these circumstances, the insights of sociology are anything but an intellectual luxury. This is especially so if there is a future for democracy in this society. Sociology, as the application of critical intelligence to society, has a particular affinity to democracy, that political form that is based on the assumption that social conflicts can be resolved and social problems alleviated by means of rational persuasion and without recourse to violence. Non-democratic regimes, whether of the "right" or "left," have an instinctive aversion to sociology. Conversely, sociology has developed best in situations where the political structure has some real relationship to democratic ideas.

## Awareness Expansion: A Sense of One's Possibilities

If sociology has a particular affinity for democratic types of government, it has another, more personal relation to liberty. Anyone who seriously immerses himself in the perspective of sociology will find that his awareness of society, and thus his awareness of himself, will have changed considerably. This changed awareness is not always or one-sidedly "liberating," in the sense of expanding the individual's sense of being free and being himself. Sociological insight may lead to a recognition of limitations that one was previously unaware of, and it may further lead to the sad conclusion that courses of action that one had previously regarded as capable of realization are, in fact, illusions and fantasies. Working hard in one's vocation is *not* the sure way to wealth and fame. Participating in a campus riot is *not* a step toward the revolutionary overthrow of the capitalist system. And so on and so forth. Also, sociological insight may lead to an understanding of the great fragility of all the things one holds dear, including one's notions as to who one is, because sociology shows their ongoing dependence on social processes of definition and redefinition. This understanding, more than any other provided by sociology, can be deeply upsetting, as it seems to shake the very ground on which one is standing.

Thus the relation of sociology to the individual's sense of his own liberty is not a simple or easy matter. Still, when all is said and done, the perspective of sociology, correctly understood, leads to a deepening of the sense of liberty. Long ago the Stoics declared that wisdom consists in knowing what I can and what I cannot do, and that freedom is only possible on the basis of such wisdom. There is something of this wisdom in sociologically formed awareness. Precisely because sociology teaches the limitations and the fragility of what the individual can do and be in society, it also gives him a better sense of his possibilities. And, leaving aside philosophical sophistication, perhaps this is as good an operational definition of liberty as any—having a sense of one's possibilities.

Politics has been described as the art of the possible. If so, in all modesty, sociology might be described as *a science of the possible.*

It is for these reasons, we think, that sociology has a place in a "liberal arts" curriculum. Whatever may be its uses for professional training or scholarly enterprises, sociology has a bearing on the growth of personal awareness of the world, of others and of self. There is much controversy today over the future of college and university education. Whatever this future may turn out to be, we hope that it will have a place for this "liberal" conception of education, and thus for the peculiarly "liberal" discipline of sociology.

## QUESTIONS

1. Why did you and other members of the class decide to study sociology? Do the members have much the same motivation and anticipation, or is there a good deal of diversity?

2. How good a case do you think the authors make for the study of sociology?

3. How might sociology enhance an appreciation of human liberty and the human potential? Is it particularly different from other disciplines in this respect?

*James T. Richardson*
*Mary W. Stewart*
*Robert B. Simmonds*

# 3. Researching a Fundamentalist Commune[1]

*One of the most fruitful methods of sociological investigation is the case study—a detailed record of some episode of social behavior, such as a riot, a political campaign, or the daily life of a high school. Although the particular case under consideration may have unique features, information gained from studying it can sometimes offer useful insights into other apparently similar cases.*

*Sociologists need not necessarily take part in the activities of the groups they study, but many researchers prefer to play the role of participant observer. Sometimes these researchers conceal their true identity from the group, usually because they fear that the subjects would not knowingly allow themselves to be studied by sociologists. This practice, however, raises the ethical problem that information is being obtained through the use of deceit. In other cases, the researchers make their identity clear from the outset, although their honesty can sometimes jeopardize their chances of gaining access to the group.*

*This article discusses some of the problems faced by sociologists who wanted to study a small religious sect, and who preferred to declare their identities and intentions at the beginning of the project. Their approach raised one recurrent problem: group members were determined to convert the visiting sociologists to the sect, but, as it happened, the research ultimately benefited as a result.*

We have been involved for almost seven years with research on a large youth, communal, evangelical, fundamentalist organization that originated in the late 1960s as a part of the so-called Jesus Movement (JM).[2] This research, which has resulted in some of the first published reports on the Jesus Movement [2,3], continues even now, and has furnished considerable information to scholars involved in studies of such movements and groups.[3] During the course of the study a number of different methods have been used to gather data, including survey questionnaires, personality assessment instruments, content analysis of organization documents and publications, structured and unstructured interviews with selected members and leaders, participant observation of many different activities of group members, and considerable interpersonal contact with key informants.

One question that arises quite often when we present results of our research to professional and lay groups concerns how we have managed to maintain rapport with the group for such a long period of time, and gain the sorts of information that we have. This question often derives from simple curiosity about how research is "really done." However, the question is fair and important, especially in light of a rather general feeling that long-term research on evangelical groups is difficult to accomplish unless one converts or does covert research (neither of which was done in the present case). This general belief in the difficulty of researching evangelical groups has gained support through the reporting in the scholarly literature of the apparently problematic research experience involving another JM groups . . . [22].

## I

The study of evangelical groups presents a difficult problem that affects both the method of investigation and the content of interpretations. The problem that concerns us here is the proselytizing behavior of members of the evangelical group that is directed toward members of the research team. Pressure to convert, which has taken both overt and covert forms, has been brought to bear on us throughout our study, although such pressure, which was also reported by Robbins, Anthony, and Curtis [22], has lessened somewhat in recent years. In many ways, the overt pressure was easiest to handle. In nearly every interview, early in the research, attempts were made to convert the interviewer. We warned interviewers about this, but even so, some were rather unprepared for the intensity of proselytization attempts. All of us were asked repeatedly what we believed and why we did not "believe in Christ." Open disdain was shown by a few members for the value of what we were doing. They simply defined our presence there as being sent to them by God for conversion. The "subject" often tried to reverse the usual respondent-interviewer relationship, making the interviewer the "subject" of an intense witnessing and conversion effort. Most interviewers were successful in handling such attempts, but problems arose as a result of this overt pressure. Some interviewers got caught up in the situation and wanted to argue with some particularly forceful respondents. We continually counseled against argument *per se,* but it was a problem, particularly for some of the more politically conscious and articulate of the interviewers, some of whom had very strong negative feelings about the apparent "dropout" type of existence being lived by members of the group. A few other interviewers had a different type of problem. They were influenced by the situation to consider converting, and staying in the group. One person in the 1972 interview team, in particular, was hard-pressed when it came time to decide whether or not to return home after interviewing was complete.

The last comment illustrates the more subtle pressures of such research situations. We, being somewhat aware of the possible problems, had chosen carefully among selected mature undergraduates for our interview teams. We talked with them about what to expect and tried to prepare them mentally for the interviewing. The fact that one considered staying with the group, and that a few others found themselves responding so strongly in a negative way only illustrates the problems caused by dropping people literally into a "new and different world."

This "new world" was one where life "outside" was viewed as worthless. The fundamentalist-oriented world view had everything defined and ordered in a way considerably different from the experience of most interviewers. The most compelling aspect of this new world was its total permeation with genuine peace and love. It was obvious to all of us that the people being studied enjoyed being where they were, and that they loved one another. *And,* they "loved" us as well, and treated us as "prodigal sons and daughters." We were welcomed with open arms (not withstanding some concern by a few group leaders), fed, and furnished with a place to sleep.

They constantly expressed great concern that we should come to share their "peace that passeth understanding." One has to be hard-hearted indeed not to be moved when his or her name is mentioned in earnest prayer before meals and during Bible studies. This loving and caring atmosphere was hard to ignore, and different people responded differently to it. Lofland has also reported the use of "love" by a new religious group [14].

As a group, we made serious and systematic attempts to maintain what Berger called the "thin thread of conversation" [15], so that our view of reality would be reinforced. In the June 1972 visit, the research team of seven met every evening and during breaks during the day in a large pickup camper, which was brought to serve as a "headquarters," and which was generally off limits to members of the group being researched (except by special invitation). In these essential meetings in the camper, we talked about the experiences of the day (and also drank a little wine and smoked a little, just for good measure). If we had not had the camper along, we would have been forced to seek refuge by withdrawing, and going to a nearby town, as the smaller interview team of summer, 1971, did. As it was, we had a "retreat" at the research site which allowed us to withdraw quickly if desired, but, at the same time, we were continually around to observe activities and record information.

Our basic approach to research such as this is to be open about our objectives. This does not mean that we explain every detail of our research plans, but it does indicate a basic posture of lack of deception. This contrasts sharply with the work of some past and present researchers who have seen fit to use overtly deceptive tactics [16,17,18]. We think that generally such deception is unnecessary, impractical, and unethical. A more open approach *appears* (and may well be) more humane, more ethical, and it certainly is a demonstration that the researcher *probably* takes the beliefs of the other seriously. From a practical point of view, such an approach seems more honest, and will usually bear the "fruits of honesty" in human interaction.[5] Also, much information may be directly gained in such discussions. In our own research, we discouraged interviewers from engaging in serious discussions (because we feared what Robbins, Anthony, and Curtis had feared, namely, that such might terminate the research project), but we did *not* totally rule them out. Some interviewers and all three of the authors took part in such exchanges on occasion, especially with some group leaders. It was obvious that we did not fear being questioned and entering into serious discussions, and this openness was appreciated by those on whom we were doing research. Thus, instead of being seriously hindered by group beliefs and practices, we think we actually gained considerable information from the willingness of respondents to share their beliefs.

We are aware that this apparently more honest approach is subject to misuse, which raises potential ethical problems. Someone could be "planted," because of his or her personal beliefs, in a group more open to such a person. This is neither what we suggest nor what we did. No member of the interview teams we have used was a "believer" in the tenets of the group studied, although the background of some of us made it easier to understand the jargon of the group and its practices. We simply felt that we wanted to be as open as possible in our research, and that it was possible to do sound research of this type under such conditions. This decision was made mainly out of respect for the people being studied, and it was implemented with some qualms. We were a bit surprised at the "success" of the decision when it became translated into a strategy of research. We found out through personal experience that, at least with the group being studied, a decision to be more open was a "tactical success," although this was not the reason for deciding to operate as we did.

Because of our experience (along with other successful, more open research experiences, such as that of Liebow [19]), we are now convinced that being open with certain kinds of groups is an extremely successful research tactic. And, although we do not recommend it, if one is willing to carefully select interviewers to "match" the characteristics of the group being studied, then researchers of "deviant groups" truly do have a "secret weapon" against which many such will have little defense. Thus, certain groups, such as sectarian religious organizations that have heretofore been studied "successfully" using deceptive practices [16,17,18], may now be studied easier and "better" using "true converts" (or reasonable facsimiles). The question is whether or not to use this technique, and the reason the question is asked derives from ethical considerations, *not* tactical ones. From a tactical point of view, such an approach may be actually easier, and possibly promises more "inside information."

We have suggested several times that group beliefs and practices actually aided (rather than hindered) our research. The following section will discuss this idea more systematically.

A usually unnoticed, or at least uncredited, item, sometimes of great importance to a research project, involves the openness of the "culture" of a group (or the "personality" of a specific subject) to the research and the researcher. It is obvious that normal rules of courtesy generally aid any researcher who asks permission to interview a potential subject. Chances are usually quite good that the potential subject will treat the researcher with courtesy, unless there is some special problem (such as using non-black interviewers with black respondents in a time of racial confrontation). This "rule of common courtesy" plainly gives an initial advantage to any researcher willing to intrude her- or himself into

another's life. Further, Milgram's research on obedience to authority [20] . . . has demonstrated that many people will obey some requests that go far beyond the realm of normal courtesy, if such requests are couched in certain terms. Also, it is just as obvious that sometimes research is allowed because it is thought to be advantageous by the one (or the group or group leaders) being researched. . . . [6]

However, when we talk of the value of group culture and/or personal attributes to our research, we mean something more overt—but in some ways more subtle—than the kinds of things just mentioned (all of which admittedly have operated in our favor). The group studied has an authoritarian structure of organization, a factor that may be based on necessity, but which is usually justified by the group reference to ideology through the medium of quoting certain Bible verses that support such an approach to group life. Because of this definite authority structure, we were not faced with having to justify our existence to every subject, in an attempt to convince them to grant us an interview. Instead, we had only to persuade the leaders (and only a few of them) that our project was worthy, and that it should be done. When they decided that our work was acceptable, they told the members to allow us to interview them. We had very high response rates (95–100 percent) because of this, and it is worth admitting that the response rate would probably have been virtually zero if we had not cleared the project with those in charge. This is plainly a place where some knowledge of the group ideology (gained through previous experience of one author and through the initial contacts with the group) helped a great deal. If we had not known or found out that the group was authoritarian in nature, we might have just tried to start interviewing selected subjects, a tactic that would have virtually guaranteed the failure of the project, since members would not have cooperated without the express permission of their leaders. So, in a sense, the group was easier to study than a group in which each individual could decide whether or not to be interviewed. This latter situation is, of course, analogous to just about any survey research where interviewers go from house to house, trying to interview as many members of a sample as possible. And the low response rates of some such studies evidences our point.

The actual interview situation . . . was also helped considerably because of group beliefs and practices. Because the subjects really believed that their past life had been "washed clean" by virtue of their conversion, they were very willing to talk about their personal histories. It seemed as if this past life could no longer harm them in any way, and they could treat it in a very objective fashion (the problem of sometimes making it sound worse than it really was notwithstanding).[7] Also, their new beliefs contained a strong emphasis on honesty in personal relations, and, especially since we were "approved" by the leaders of the group, the respondents were quite open to us. . . .

It is interesting to examine in more depth the decision of group leaders that we were to be welcomed, and to look at group beliefs in an effort to understand how and why the decision to be open to us was made. We, of course, do not have secret tape recordings of deliberations of the group leaders as they were trying to decide what to do with us. However, we do have enough knowledge of how the group functions *and* of its belief system to construct fairly well, we think, key elements of the probable scenario. And, here especially, we see the importance of group beliefs to be the success of our research.

Jesus Movement groups, including the one we are researching, generally adopted the traditional dualism of fundamentalist Christianity. This system of thought is one of few categories, and can be described as simplistic in nature [22]. Things are good or bad, black or white, the "work of Satan" or the "work of the Lord." We think that this lack of differentiation served us very well, especially when taken *in conjunction with* some other important group beliefs and practices.

The group is very evangelical, and defines as a (possibly *the*) major goal, the conversion of "sinners" (which, simply defined, means those who do not accept the basic tenets of the group). Also, the ideology of the group is very "God-centered" in that they believe that their God is omniscient and omnipotent, and takes an active role in the affairs of the world, including their personal and group life. According to group beliefs, God *at least* "permits" *all* that happens. These elements of belief combined to force an interpretation of every contact with a "nonbeliever" (including us) as being an opportunity, even responsibility, sent by God to them, so that the nonbeliever might be witnessed to by members of the group.

The dualism of fundamentalist Christianity does, of course, include the concept of an "anti-God" (Satan) who also can move in human history, but we were fortunate enough not to be categorized as being a part of this evil contingent. Instead, partially because of our real and honest interest in what was taking place in the group, and because the group members were sincerely concerned about us, we got classified in just about the only other possible category in this simplistic system of thought, with its inherent lack of differentiation. We were classified as potential converts—converts who obviously were to be "won to Christ" by members of this group. This situation was similar to that reported by Robbins, Anthony, and Curtis [22]; there were, however, important differences.[8] Members and leaders of the group were led by their own beliefs to assume that God had sent or directed us (potentially even against our own wills and

without our knowledge) to this group. The least they thought was that God had *permitted* us to come there, and had thereby given us over to this group as a part of their Christian responsibility. It is possible, of course, that we could have been considered a "test" sent from God in a manner akin to the boils visited upon Job, but if some seriously entertained this thought we were unaware of it. And even if some had this thought, *that interpretation would still have probably resulted in our getting to stay with the group,* simply because we desired to do this and intended to stay until asked to leave.

In short, the beliefs of the group rendered members somewhat *passive* in the face of a concerted effort to study them. We, the active agents in all this, were apparently assumed somehow to be tied up with the will of God. Which group member or leader was going to try to thwart that? At least partially because of such ideological considerations, we were welcomed with sincere concern, even relish, and feted (to the extent that group resources allowed). Their usual practices of making potential converts welcome (at least for a time) seemed to be carried to the extreme.

It seemed that there was an implicit contest going on among group members to see who could convert one of us first. As stated, for the first few years of our research, nearly every interview was a contest of wills (and patience—on both sides). We regularly heard our names mentioned in prayers in their public gatherings, and some members made continual efforts to "win us to Christ." The importance of this issue to the group members was graphically illustrated when rumors of the impending conversion of a member of the June 1972 interview team swept the camp. There was much premature rejoicing among group members, who plainly assumed that the only "real purpose" of our being there was to "get converted."[9] Apparently what had happened was that an interviewer had expressed to a respondent an interest in finding out more about the group ideas, and he had started to read the Bible during his spare time. Just the sight of him reading the Bible seemed to be enough to set the rumor mill in motion. In some of our later visits, people still asked about the interviewer, desiring to know if he finally decided to convert. The tenacity of such ideas demonstrates their importance to the group (just as the continued interest of this interviewer in the group evidences the effect the research experience had on him).

## II

As has been stated, we are continuing our research, and have been studying the group since early 1971. That is a long time for the group to labor without converting us, and this suggests that there has been some redefining, by the group members, of us and our role *vis-à-vis* the group. We agree that such has occurred, but would suggest that the new definition, while being more elaborate, still is congruent with the basic beliefs of the group. First, we believe that we are still looked at as potential converts and may even be potential converts of special "worth," since we are people of relatively high status *vis-à-vis* the group members. But the days of the "hard sell" seem to be over, and now the approach is much more subtle. We are being witnessed to "by example" instead of using forceful argumentation. Second, the worldview of the group members appears to have gotten more complex in that the basic two-category world (saved and unsaved) has become more differentiated. Perhaps our presence has even hastened the predictable differentiation process. Whatever the cause, there now seem to be several categories of nonmembers, some of whom are viewed much more positively than others. For instance, some of the group view us as people with a special relationship to the group. They apparently think our being associated with the group has some "higher purpose," which will be revealed in due course. The fact that some converts have been gained through our publication of results serves to support such a view. It is entirely possible that the group is coming to think that we have been sent to chronicle their history for the larger public. Group leaders have indicated that they realize someone will eventually write their history, but so far they think it should be done by a member. However, their generally positive (even if somewhat unexpected) reaction to the first publication from our research [2] has caused us to think that perhaps they are reevaluating their view of us and their position on who will "write their history." Thus, our relationship with the group continues, but for reasons that we think are largely "out of control." We give a great deal of credit to the "positive" (from our point of view) features of group culture that have helped us continue our research. . . .

There are, of course, other reasons (some of which may not be known to us) why our research has been allowed to continue. Plainly, some members of the group like the attention we have paid to them, and they like the "anonymous fame" that our publications have brought to them. We have developed some rather strong affective ties with some members over the years of our research, and this means that there is more trust shared by all of us. And the mere passage of time has had another effect, in that the group as a whole may be growing more *tolerant* of outsiders as it gains strength and self-confidence. We have also *invested hard work to maintain contact and rapport* with the group and some key members. We have had our share of good luck, as well. And, one key thing has been the totally unexpected fact that the *group has actually gained some members as a result of our research.* Our first publication of material on the group [2] resulted in well over fifty letters being sent to us by people who wanted to join the group.[10] After some discussion, we sent these queries to the group, since we were bound by our pledge of anonymity and thus could not respond ourselves with the requested information. The next time we visited the group, there were a few people there who had first heard of the group through our publication! This situation demonstrates that no matter how hard one may try to avoid influencing a group being studied, it is virtually impossible to stop all influences. The gaining of a few members through our publication seemed to demonstrate to some group leaders that somehow we were "agents of God."

## QUESTIONS

1. What are the advantages and drawbacks of the participant-observer method of sociological research?

2. Are there any situations in which a researcher is justified in hiding his or her identity from the subjects of the research?

3. Using the article as a case study, identify and discuss some of the difficulties, expected and unexpected, that might be faced in sociological research.

## NOTES

1. This is an expansion of part of a paper presented at the 1975 annual American Sociological Association meeting, which was derived from the research appendix of a forthcoming monograph, *Organized Miracles* (1978), by the same authors.

2. The organization we have been studying is fully described in our forthcoming book, *Organized Miracles* [1]. The group described desires to remain anonymous, thus we cannot report their name or location, as per our original agreement with them when the research started.

3. Our research is a relatively large study which has resulted in a dozen or so papers being read at professional meetings, along with numerous talks given by the three of us to other professional and lay groups, in the United States, Western Europe, and Scandinavia. Also, about ten papers have been published [2,3,4,5,6,7,8,9,10,11]. Two dissertations have resulted as well [12,13].

4. We, of course, are not claiming that our own research experience is necessarily any more generalizable, but we think that discussing both experiences together may result in some general conclusions of value.

5. We say "usually" because it is plain that certain kinds of research cannot be done without deception. The questions are whether or not such research should be done, and whether or not some professional body should perhaps be charged with allowing such endeavors (in a manner similar to the recent decision of some biologists to organize a review group, and, in the meantime, to refrain from certain kinds of research).

6. We are all aware of the problems brought about by the desire of some to be "studied," with the resulting tendency to volunteer for studies, or the so-called "Hawthorne effect" that can cause workers to continue to put together complex devices in near darkness. Such tendencies "compensate" some for the features of a group or person that make most research "easier" than might first be thought, and must be taken into account in any research.

7. This problem of "negative bragging sessions" seems a classic illustration of the "reconstruction of biography" mentioned by Berger [21]. While we do not think many subjects made deliberate attempts to mislead us, we were aware, because of previous knowledge of the fundamentalist subculture, of the tendency to claim a "more sinful" past than was really the case. In ways that are discussed at more length in the appendix to *Organized Miracles,* there seemed to be an assumption on the part of some respondents that the best Christians were the ones who had sinned the most in their "previous existence." Because of this possibility, we tried to double-check information that seemed especially prone to this "sinful reconstruction of biography."

8. This definition of researchers as potential converts seems an ultimate example of the benefits of the "outsider role," as discussed by Trice [23]. The problem, of course, is to maintain this privileged status for a long enough time to do the research (and resolve ethical problems inherent in the situation).

9. We should add that this incident led to much discussion among the interview team members so that none of us would do anything to encourage such interpretations of our activities.

10. Our first publication was in *Psychology Today* [2], which, we understand, printed 450,000 copies of that issue. Perhaps we should have expected such a reaction from some in such a large readership, but nonetheless we were a bit taken aback by what happened, and had to make a decision about what to do with the letters. Some will disagree with what we did, but we are still satisfied with the decision.

## REFERENCES

1. James T. Richardson, Mary White Stewart, and Robert B. Simmonds. *Organized Miracles.* Transaction Books, 1979.

2. Mary White Harder, James T. Richardson, and Robert B. Simmonds. "Jesus People." *Psychology Today,* 6 December 1972, pp. 45-50, 110-113.

3. James T. Richardson, Robert B. Simmonds, and Mary White Harder. "Thought Reform and the Jesus Movement." *Youth and Society* 4 (1972):185-200.

4. Mary White Harder. "Sex Roles in the Jesus Movement." *Social Compass* 21 (1974):345-353.

5. Mary White Harder, James T. Richardson, and Robert B. Simmonds. "Life Style: Sex Roles, Courtship, Marriage, and Family in a Changing Jesus Movement Organization." *International Review of Modern Sociology* 6 (1975):155-172.

6. James T. Richardson. "The Jesus Movement: An Assessment." *Listening: Journal of Religion and Culture* 9 (1974):20-42.

7. James T. Richardson and Robert Simmonds. "Personality Assessment in New Religious Groups: Problems of Interpretation." In preparation, 1977.

8. James T. Richardson, Robert B. Simmonds, and Mary White Harder. "Evolving Structures of a Jesus Movement Organization." *Journal of Voluntary Social Action Research,* in press.

9. James T. Richardson and Mary White Stewart. "Conversion Process Models and the Jesus Movement." *American Behavioral Scientist* 20 (1977):819-838.

10. Robert B. Simmonds, James T. Richardson, and Mary White Harder. "Organization and Structure of a Jesus Movement Community." *Social Compass* 21 (1974):269-281.

11. Robert B. Simmonds, James T. Richardson, and Mary White Harder. "A Jesus Movement Group: An Adjective Check List Assessment." *Journal for the Scientific Study of Religion* 15 (1976):323-337.

12. Mary White Harder. *The Children of Christ Commune: A Study of a Fundamentalist Communal Sect.* Ph.D. thesis, University of Nevada, Reno, 1972.

13. Robert B. Simmonds. *The People of the Jesus Movement: A Personality Assessment of a Fundamentalist Religious Community.* Ph.D. thesis, University of Nevada, Reno, 1977.

14. John Lofland. "Becoming a World-Saver Revisited." *American Behavioral Scientist* 20 (1977):805-818.

15. Peter Berger. *The Sacred Canopy.* Doubleday, 1967.

16. Leon Festinger, H. W. Reicker, and Stanley Schachter. *When Prophecy Fails.* University of Minnesota Press, 1956.

17. John Lofland. *Doomsday Cult.* Prentice-Hall, 1965.

18. Hiley Ward. *The Far-Out Saints of the Jesus Communes.* Association Press, N.Y. 1972.

19. Elliot Liebow. *Tally's Corner.* Little, Brown, 1967.

20. Stanley Milgram. *Obedience to Authority.* Harper & Row, 1973.

21. Peter Berger. *Invitation to Sociology.* Doubleday, 1963.

22. Thomas Robbins, Dick Anthony, and Thomas E. Curtis. "The Limits of Symbolic Realism: Problems of Empathetic Field Observation in a Sectarian Context." *Journal for the Scientific Study of Religion* 12 (1973):259-272.

23. H. M. Trice. "The 'Outsiders'' Role in Field Study." *In Qualitative Methodology,* pp. 77-82. Edited by W. J. Filstead, Markham, Chicago, 1970.

# UNIT 2

# The Individual, Culture, and Society

Horace Miner

# 4. Body Ritual Among the Nacirema

*The anthropologist Ralph Linton once remarked that a fish would be aware of water only if it found itself on dry land. His point as it applies to human culture is that we are so used to our own particular social environment that we take it for granted, remaining almost oblivious even to some of the most distinctive features of our way of life.*

*One of the advantages of a sociological perspective on the world is that it trains us to become, as it were, outsiders in our own society and culture: we are enabled, at least to some extent, to see ourselves as others might, and to focus on aspects of our cultural reality that we might otherwise have overlooked. We would see ourselves most clearly, in fact, if we could step apart from our culture and view it with the same detachment and curiosity that a visiting anthropologist might apply to an unfamiliar and even exotic culture.*

*Horace Miner tries to achieve that kind of viewpoint in this article. The subject of his study is a rather remarkable tribe, the Nacirema, and his particular focus is their unusual and compulsive rituals concerning the human body.*

Reproduced by permission of the American Anthropological Association from the *American Anthropologist*, 58:503–507, 1956.

The anthropologist has become so familiar with the diversity of ways in which different peoples behave in similar situations that he is not apt to be surprised by even the most exotic customs. In fact, if all of the logically possible combinations of behavior have not been found somewhere in the world, he is apt to suspect that they must be present in some yet undescribed tribe. This point has, in fact, been expressed with respect to clan organization by Murdock (1949:71). In this light, the magical beliefs and practices of the Nacirema present such unusual aspects that it seems desirable to describe them as an example of the extremes to which human behavior can go.

Professor Linton first brought the ritual of the Nacirema to the attention of anthropologists twenty years ago (1936:326), but the culture of this people is still very poorly understood. They are a North American group living in the territory between the Canadian Cree, the Yaqui and Tarahumare of Mexico, and the Carib and Arawak of the Antilles. Little is known of their origin, although tradition states that they came from the east. According to Nacirema mythology, their nation was originated by a culture hero, Notgnihsaw, who is otherwise known for two great feats of strength—the throwing of a piece of wampum across the river Pa-To-Mac and the chopping down of a cherry tree in which the Spirit of Truth resided.

Nacirema culture is characterized by a highly developed market economy which has evolved in a rich natural habitat. While much of the people's time is devoted to economic pursuits, a large part of the fruits of these labors and a considerable portion of the day are spent in ritual activity. The focus of this activity is the human body, the appearance and health of which loom as a dominant concern in the ethos of the people. While such a concern is certainly not unusual, its ceremonial aspects and associated philosophy are unique.

The fundamental belief underlying the whole system appears to be that the human body is ugly and that its natural tendency is to debility and disease. Incarcerated in such a body, man's only hope is to avert these characteristics through the use of the powerful influences of ritual and ceremony. Every household has one or more shrines devoted to this purpose. The more powerful individuals in the society have several shrines in their houses and, in fact, the opulence of a house is often referred to in terms of the number of such ritual centers it possesses. Most houses are of wattle and daub construction, but the shrine rooms of the more wealthy are walled with stone. Poorer families imitate the rich by applying pottery plaques to their shrine walls.

While each family has at least one such shrine, the rituals associated with it are not family ceremonies but are private and secret. The rites are normally only discussed with children, and then only during the period when they are being initiated into these mysteries. I was able, however, to establish sufficient rapport with the natives to examine these shrines and to have the rituals described to me.

The focal point of the shrine is a box or chest which is built into the wall. In this chest are kept the many charms and magical potions without which no native believes he could live. These preparations are secured from a variety of specialized practitioners. The most powerful of these are the medicine men, whose assistance must be rewarded with substantial gifts. However, the medicine men do not provide the curative potions for their clients, but decide what the ingredients should be and then write them down in an ancient and secret language. This writing is understood only by the medicine men and by the herbalists who, for another gift, provide the required charm.

The charm is not disposed of after it has served its purpose, but is placed in the charm-box of the household shrine. As these magical materials are specific for certain ills, and the real or imagined maladies of the people are many, the charm-box is usually full to overflowing. The magical packets are so numerous that people forget what their purposes were and fear to use them again. While the natives are very vague on this point, we can only assume that the idea in retaining all the old magical materials is that their presence in the charm-box, before which the body rituals are conducted, will in some way protect the worshipper.

Beneath the charm-box is a small font. Each day every member of the family, in succession, enters the shrine room, bows his head before the charm-box, mingles different sorts of holy water in the font, and proceeds with a brief rite of ablution. The holy waters are secured from the Water Temple of the community, where the priests conduct elaborate ceremonies to make the liquid ritually pure.

In the hierarchy of magical practitioners, and below the medicine men in prestige, are specialists whose designation is best translated "holy-mouth-men." The Nacirema have an almost pathological horror of and fascination with the mouth, the condition of which is believed to have a supernatural influence on all social relationships. Were it not for the rituals of the mouth, they believe that their teeth would fall out, their gums bleed, their jaws shrink, their friends desert them, and their lovers reject them. They also believe that a strong relationship exists between oral and moral characteristics. For example, there is a ritual ablution of the mouth for children which is supposed to improve their moral fiber.

The daily body ritual performed by everyone includes a mouth-rite. Despite the fact that these people are so punctilious about care of the mouth, this rite involves a practice which strikes the uninitiated stranger as revolting. It was reported to me that the ritual consists of inserting a small bundle of hog hairs into the mouth, along with certain magical powders, and then moving the bundle in a highly formalized series of gestures.

In addition to the private mouth-rite, the people seek out a holy-mouth-man once or twice a year. These practitioners have an impressive set of paraphernalia, consisting of a variety of augers, awls, probes, and prods. The use of these objects in the exorcism of the evils of the mouth involves almost unbelievable ritual torture of the client. The holy-mouth-man opens the client's mouth and, using the above mentioned tools, enlarges any holes which decay may have created in the teeth. Magical materials are put into these holes. If there are no naturally occurring holes in the teeth, large sections of one or more teeth are gouged out so that the supernatural substance can be applied. In the client's view, the purpose of these ministrations is to arrest decay and to draw friends. The extremely sacred and traditional character of the rite is evident in the fact that the natives return to the holy-mouth-men year after year, despite the fact that their teeth continue to decay.

It is to be hoped that, when a thorough study of the Nacirema is made, there will be careful inquiry into the personality structure of these people. One has but to watch the gleam in the eye of a holy-mouth-man, as he jabs an awl into an exposed nerve, to suspect that a certain amount of sadism is involved. If this can be established, a very interesting pattern emerges, for most of the population shows definite masochistic tendencies. It was to these that Professor Linton referred in discussing a distinctive part of the daily body ritual which is performed only by men. The part of the rite involves scraping and lacerating the surface of the face with a sharp instrument. Special women's rites are performed only four times during each lunar month, but what they lack in frequency is made up in barbarity. As part of this ceremony, women bake their heads in small ovens for about an hour. The theoretically interesting point is that what seems to be a preponderantly masochistic people have developed sadistic specialists.

The medicine men have an imposing temple, or *latipso*, in every community of any size. The more elaborate ceremonies required to treat very sick patients can only be performed at this temple. These ceremonies involve not only the thaumaturge but a permanent group of vestal maidens who move sedately about the temple chambers in distinctive costume and headdress.

The *latipso* ceremonies are so harsh that it is phenomenal that a fair proportion of the really sick natives who enter the temple ever recover. Small children whose indoctrination is still incomplete have been known to resist attempts to take them to the temple because "that is where you go to die." Despite this fact, sick adults are not only willing but eager to undergo the protracted ritual purification, if they can afford to do so. No matter how ill the supplicant or how grave the emergency, the guardians of many temples will not admit a client if he cannot give a rich gift to the custodian. Even after one has gained admission and survived the ceremonies, the guardians will not permit the neophyte to leave until he makes still another gift.

The supplicant entering the temple is first stripped of all his or her clothes. In everyday life the Nacirema avoids exposure of his body and its natural functions. Bathing and excretory acts are performed only in the secrecy of the household shrine, where they are ritualized as part of the body-rites. Psychological shock results from the fact that body secrecy is suddenly lost upon entry into the *latipso*. A man, whose own wife has never seen him in an excretory act, suddenly finds himself naked and assisted by a vestal maiden while he performs his natural functions into a sacred vessel. This sort of ceremonial treatment is necessitated by the fact that the excreta are used by a diviner to ascertain the course and nature of the client's sickness. Female clients, on the other hand, find their naked bodies are subjected to the scrutiny, manipulation, and prodding of the medicine men.

Few supplicants in the temple are well enough to do anything but lie on their hard beds. The daily ceremonies, like the rites of the holy-mouth-men, involve discomfort and torture. With ritual precision, the vestals awaken their miserable charges each dawn and roll them about on their beds of pain while performing ablutions, in the formal movements of which the maidens are highly trained. At other times they insert magic wands into the supplicant's mouth or force him to eat substances which are supposed to be healing. From time to time the medicine men come to their clients and jab magically treated needles into their flesh. The fact that these temple ceremonies may not cure, and may even kill the neophyte, in no way decreases the people's faith in the medicine men.

There remains one other kind of practitioner, known as a "listener." This witch-doctor has the power to exorcise the devils that lodge in the heads of people who have been bewitched. The Nacirema believe that parents bewitch their own children. Mothers are particularly suspected of putting a curse on children while teaching them the secret body rituals. The counter-magic of the witch-doctor is unusual in its lack of ritual. The patient simply tells the "listener" all his troubles and fears, beginning with the earliest difficulties he can remember. The memory displayed by the Nacirema in these exorcism sessions is truly remarkable. It is not uncommon for the patient to bemoan the rejection he felt upon being weaned as a babe, and a few individuals even see their troubles going back to the traumatic effects of their own birth.

. . .

Our review of the ritual life of the Nacirema has certainly shown them to be a magic-ridden people. It is hard to understand how they have managed to exist so long under the burdens which they have imposed upon themselves. But even such exotic customs as these take on real meaning when they are viewed with the insight provided by Malinowski when he wrote (1948:70):

> Looking from far and above, from our high places of safety in the developed civilization, it is easy to see all the crudity and irrelevance of magic. But without its power and guidance early man could not have mastered his practical difficulties as he has done, nor could man have advanced to the higher stages of civilization.

## QUESTIONS

1. Why is Miner's presentation more effective than if he had simply written a matter-of-fact account?

2. We take our bathrooms, dentists, and hospitals for granted, although they would be matters of great curiosity to the millions of people elsewhere in the world who are unfamiliar with them. Can you think of any particularly distinctive American cultural traits that would surprise outsiders?

3. Using Miner's approach, prepare a short account of some other Nacirema traits.

## REFERENCES

**Linton, Ralph.** 1936. *The Study of Man.* New York, D. Appleton-Century Co.

**Malinowski, Bronislaw.** 1948. *Magic, Science, and Religion.* Glencoe, The Free Press.

**Murdock, George P.** 1949. *Social Structure.* New York, The Macmillan Co.

*Marvin Harris*

# 5.  India's Sacred Cow

*The cultural practices of other people often seem strange, irrational, and even inexplicable to outsiders. In fact, the very members of the culture in question may be unable to give a rationally satisfying explanation of why they behave as they do: they may respond, perhaps, that the gods wish it so, or that "it is always done that way." Yet it is a fundamental assumption of social science that all human behavior, no matter how peculiar or even bizarre it may appear, can be explained.*

*One of the more apparently perplexing cultural traits in the modern world is the attitude of most people in India toward cows: Hindus regard the animals as sacred, and will not kill or eat them. In a nation where the vast majority of the people are hungry and malnourished, an exploding population of cows wanders freely through both rural areas and city streets, undisturbed by the millions of hungry—even starving—humans who surround them. Why?*

*In this article, Marvin Harris suggests a plausible answer. He maintains that Hindu cow-worship and a multitude of other cultural practices around the world can be understood through an ecological analysis: in other words, the practices must be explained in terms of the total environment—social, technological, and natural—in which they exist.*

News photographs that came out of India during the famine of the late 1960s showed starving people stretching out bony hands to beg for food while sacred cattle strolled behind them undisturbed. The Hindu, it seems, would rather starve to death than eat his cow or even deprive it of food. The cattle appear to browse unhindered through urban markets eating an orange here, a mango there, competing with people for meager supplies of food.

By Western standards, spiritual values seem more important to Indians than life itself. Specialists in food habits around the world like Fred Simoons at the University of California at Davis consider Hinduism an irrational ideology that compels people to overlook abundant, nutritious foods for scarcer, less healthful foods.

What seems to be an absurd devotion to the mother cow pervades Indian life. Indian wall calendars portray beautiful young women with bodies of fat white cows, often with milk jetting from their teats into sacred shrines.

Cow worship even carries over into politics. In 1966, a crowd of 120,000 people, led by holy men, demonstrated in front of the Indian House of Parliament in support of the All-Party Cow Protection Campaign Committee. In Nepal, the only contemporary Hindu kingdom, cow slaughter is severely punished. As one story goes, the car driven by an official of a United States agency struck and killed a cow. In order to avoid the international incident that would have occurred when the official was arrested for murder, the Nepalese magistrate concluded that the cow had committed suicide.

Many Indians agree with Western assessments of the Hindu reverence for their cattle, the zebu, or *Bos indicus,* a large-humped species prevalent in Asia and Africa. M. N. Srinivas, an Indian anthropologist states: "Orthodox Hindu opinion regards the killing of cattle with abhorrence, even though the refusal to kill the vast number of useless cattle which exists in India today is detrimental to the nation." Even the Indian Ministry of Information formerly maintained that "the large animal population is more a liability than an asset in view of our land resources." Accounts from many different sources point to the same conclusion: India, one of the world's great civilizations, is being strangled by its love for the cow.

The easy explanation for India's devotion to the cow, the one most Westerners and Indians would offer, is that cow worship is an integral part of Hinduism. Religion is somehow good for the soul, even if it sometimes fails the body. Religion orders the cosmos and explains our place in the universe. Religious beliefs, many would claim, have existed for thousands of years and have a life of their own. They are not understandable in scientific terms.

But all this ignores history. There is more to be said for cow worship than is immediately apparent. The earliest Vedas, the Hindu sacred texts from the Second Millennium B.C., do not prohibit the slaughter of cattle. Instead, they ordain it as a part of sacrificial rites. The early Hindus did not avoid the flesh of cows and bulls; they ate it at ceremonial feasts presided over by Brahman priests. Cow worship is a relatively recent development in India; it evolved as the Hindu religion developed and changed.

This evolution is recorded in royal edicts and religious texts written during the last 3,000 years of Indian history. The Vedas from the First Millennium B.C. contain contradictory passages, some referring to ritual slaughter and others to a strict taboo on beef consumption. A. N. Bose, in *Social and Rural Economy of Northern India 600, B.C.–200 A.D.*, concludes that many of the sacred-cow passages were incorporated into the texts by priests in a later period.

By 200 A.D. the status of Indian cattle had undergone a spiritual transformation. The Brahman priesthood exhorted the population to venerate the cow and forbade them to abuse it or to feed on it. Religious feasts involving the ritual slaughter and consumption of livestock were eliminated and meat eating was restricted to the nobility.

By 1000 A.D., all Hindus were forbidden to eat beef. Ahimsa, the Hindu belief in the unity of all life, was the spiritual justification for this restriction. But it is difficult to ascertain exactly when this change occurred. An important event that helped to shape the modern complex was the Islamic invasion, which took place in the Eighth Century A.D. Hindus may have found it politically expedient to set themselves off from the invaders, who were beefeaters, by emphasizing the need to prevent the slaughter of their sacred animals. Thereafter, the cow taboo assumed its modern form and began to function much as it does today.

The place of the cow in modern India is every place—on posters, in the movies, in brass figures, in stone and wood carvings, on the streets, in the fields. The cow is a symbol of health and abundance. It provides the milk that Indians consume in the form of yogurt and ghee (clarified butter), which contribute subtle flavors to much spicy Indian food.

This, perhaps, is the practical role of the cow, but cows provide less than half the milk produced in India. Most cows in India are not dairy breeds. In most regions, when an Indian farmer wants a steady, high-quality source of milk he usually invests in a female water buffalo. In India the water buffalo is the specialized dairy breed because its milk has a higher butterfat content than zebu milk. Although the farmer milks his zebu cows, the milk is merely a by-product.

More vital than zebu milk to South Asian farmers are zebu calves. Male calves are especially valued because from bulls come oxen which are the mainstay of the Indian agricultural system.

Small, fast oxen drag wooden plows through late-spring fields when monsoons have dampened the dry, cracked earth. After harvest, the oxen break the grain from the stalk by stomping through mounds of cut wheat and rice. For rice cultivation in irrigated fields, the male water buffalo is preferred (it pulls better in deep mud), but for most other crops, including rainfall rice, wheat, sorghum, and millet, and for transporting goods and people to and from town, a team of oxen is preferred. The ox is the Indian peasant's tractor, thresher and family car combined; the cow is the factory that produces the ox.

If draft animals instead of cows are counted, India appears to have too few domesticated ruminants, not too many. Since each of the 70 million farms in India requires a draft team, it follows that Indian peasants should use 140 million animals in the fields. But there are only 83 million oxen and male water buffalo on the subcontinent, a shortage of 30 million draft teams.

In other regions of the world, joint ownership of draft animals might overcome a shortage, but Indian agriculture is closely tied to the monsoon rains of late spring and summer. Field preparation and planting must coincide with the rain, and a farmer must have his animals ready to plow when the weather is right. When the farmer without a draft team needs bullocks most, his neighbors are all using theirs. Any delay in turning the soil drastically lowers production.

Because of this dependence on draft animals, loss of the family oxen is devastating. If a beast dies, the farmer must borrow money to buy or rent an ox at interest rates so high that he ultimately loses his land. Every year foreclosures force thousands of poverty-stricken peasants to abandon the countryside for the overcrowded cities.

If a family is fortunate enough to own a fertile cow, it will be able to rear replacements for a lost team and thus survive until life returns to normal. If, as sometimes happens, famine leads a family to sell its cow and ox team, all ties to agriculture are cut. Even if the family survives, it has no way to farm the land, no oxen to work the land, and no cows to produce oxen.

The prohibition against eating meat applies to the flesh of cows, bulls, and oxen, but the cow is the most sacred because it can produce the other two. The peasant whose cow dies is not only crying over a spiritual loss but over the loss of his farm as well.

Religious laws that forbid the slaughter of cattle promote the recovery of the agricultural system from the dry Indian winter and from periods of drought. The monsoon, on which all agriculture depends, is erratic. Sometimes it arrives early, sometimes late, sometimes not at all. Drought has struck large portions of India time and again in this century, and Indian farmers and the zebus are accustomed to these natural disasters. Zebus can pass weeks on end with little or no food and water. Like camels, they store both in their humps and recuperate quickly with only a little nourishment.

During droughts the cows often stop lactating and become barren. In some cases the condition is permanent but often it is only temporary. If barren animals were summarily eliminated, as Western experts in animal husbandry have suggested, cows capable of recovery would be lost along with those entirely debilitated. By keeping alive the cows that can later produce oxen, religious laws against cow slaughter assure the recovery of the agricultural system from the greatest challenge it faces—the failure of the monsoon.

The local Indian governments aid the process of recovery by maintaining homes for barren cows. Farmers reclaim any animal that calves or begins to lactate. One police station in Madras collects strays and pastures them in a field adjacent to the station. After a small fine is paid, a cow is returned to its rightful owner when the owner thinks the cow shows signs of being able to reproduce.

During the hot, dry spring months most of India is like a desert. Indian farmers often complain they cannot feed their livestock during this period. They maintain cattle by letting them scavenge on the sparse grass along the roads. In the cities cattle are encouraged to scavenge near food stalls to supplement their scant diet. These are the wandering cattle tourists report seeing throughout India.

Westerners expect shopkeepers to respond to these intrusions with the deference due a sacred animal; instead, their response is a string of curses and the crack of a long bamboo pole across the beast's back or a poke at its genitals. Mahatma Gandhi was well aware of the treatment sacred cows (and bulls and oxen) received in India. "How we bleed her to take the last drop of milk from her. How we starve her to emaciation, how we ill-treat the calves, how we deprive them of their portion of milk, how cruelly we treat the oxen, how we castrate them, how we beat them, how we overload them."

Oxen generally receive better treatment than cows. When food is in short supply, thrifty Indian peasants feed their working bullocks and ignore their cows, but rarely do they abandon the cows to die. When cows are sick, farmers worry over them as they would over members of the family and nurse them as if they were children. When the rains return and when the fields are harvested, the farmers again feed their cows regularly and reclaim their abandoned animals. The prohibition against beef consumption is a form of disaster insurance for all India.

Western agronomists and economists are quick to protest that all the functions of the zebu cattle can be improved with organized breeding programs, cultivated pastures, and silage. Because stronger oxen would pull the plow faster, they could work multiple plots of land, allowing farmers to share their animals. Fewer healthy, well-fed cows could provide Indians with more milk. But pastures and silage require arable land, land needed to produce wheat and rice.

A look at Western cattle farming makes plain the cost of adopting advanced technology in Indian agriculture. In a study of livestock production in the United States, David Pimentel of the College of Agriculture and Life Sciences at Cornell University found that 91 percent of the cereal, legume, and vegetable protein suitable for human consumption is consumed by livestock. Approximately three quarters of the arable land in the United States is devoted to growing food for livestock. In the production of meat and milk, American ranchers use enough fossil fuel to equal more than 82 million barrels of oil annually.

Indian cattle do not drain the system in the same way. In a 1971 study of livestock in West Bengal, Stewart Odend'hal of the University of Missouri found that Bengalese cattle ate only the inedible remains of subsistence crops—rice straw, rice hulls, the tops of sugar cane, and mustard-oil cake. Cattle graze in the fields after harvest and eat the remains of crops left on the ground; they forage for grass and weeds on the roadsides. The food for zebu cattle costs the human population virtually nothing. "Basically," Odend'hal says, "the cattle convert items of little direct human value into products of immediate utility."

In addition to plowing the fields and producing milk, the zebus produce dung, which fires the hearths and fertilizes the fields of India. Much of the estimated 800 million tons of manure produced annually is collected by the farmers' children as they follow the family cows and bullocks from place to place. And when the children see the droppings of another farmer's cattle along the road, they pick those up also. Odend'hal reports that the system operates with such high efficiency that the children of West Bengal recover nearly 100 percent of the dung produced by their livestock.

From 40 to 70 percent of all manure produced by Indian cattle is used as fuel for cooking; the rest is returned to the fields as fertilizer. Dried dung burns slowly, cleanly, and with low heat—characteristics that satisfy the household needs of Indian women. Staples like curry and rice can simmer for hours. While the meal slowly cooks over an unattended fire, the women of the household can do other chores. Cow chips, unlike firewood, do not scorch as they burn.

It is estimated that the dung used for cooking fuel provides the energy-equivalent of 43 million tons of coal. At current prices, it would cost India an extra 1.5 billion dollars in foreign exchange to replace the dung with coal. And if the 350 million tons of manure that are being used as fertilizer were replaced with commercial fertilizers, the expense would be even greater. Roger Revelle of the University of California at San Diego has calculated that 89 percent of the energy used in Indian agriculture (the equivalent of about 140 million tons of coal) is provided by local sources. Even if foreign loans were to provide the money, the capital outlay necessary to replace the Indian cow with tractors and fertilizers for the fields, coal for the fires, and transportation for the family would probably warp international financial institutions for years.

Instead of asking the Indians to learn from the American model of industrial agriculture, American farmers might learn energy conservation from the Indians. Every step in an energy cycle results in a loss of energy to the system. Like a pendulum that slows a bit with each swing, each transfer of energy from sun to plants, plants to animals, and animals to human beings involves energy losses. Some systems are more efficient than others; they provide a higher percentage of the energy inputs in a final, useful form. Seventeen percent of all energy zebus consume is returned in the form of milk, traction and dung. American cattle raised on Western range land return only 4 percent of the energy they consume.

But the American system is improving. Based on techniques pioneered by Indian scientists, at least one commercial firm in the United States is reported to be building plants that will turn manure from cattle feedlots into combustible gas. When organic matter is broken down by anaerobic bacteria, methane gas and carbon dioxide are produced. After the methane is cleansed of the carbon dioxide, it is available for the same purposes as natural gas—cooking, heating, electricity generation. The company constructing the biogasification plant plans to sell its product to a gas-supply company, to be piped through the existing distribution system. Schemes similar to this one could make cattle ranches almost independent of utility and gasoline companes, for methane can be used to run trucks, tractors, and cars as well as to supply heat and electricity. The relative energy self-sufficiency that the Indian peasant has achieved is a goal American farmers and industry are now striving for.

Studies like Odend'hal's understate the efficiency of the Indian cow, because dead cows are used for purposes that Hindus prefer not to acknowledge. When a cow dies, an Untouchable, a member of one of the lowest ranking castes in India, is summoned to haul away the carcass. Higher castes consider the body of the dead cow polluting; if they do handle it, they must go through a rite of purification.

Untouchables first skin the dead animal and either tan the skin themselves or sell it to a leather factory. In the privacy of their homes, contrary to the teachings of Hinduism, untouchable castes cook the meat and eat it. Indians of all castes rarely acknowledge the existence of these practices to non-Hindus, but most are aware that beefeating takes place. The prohibition against beef eating restricts consumption by the higher castes and helps distribute animal protein to the poorest sectors of the population that otherwise would have no source of these vital nutrients.

Untouchables are not the only Indians who consume beef. Indian Muslims and Christians are under no restriction that forbids them beef, and its consumption is legal in many places. The Indian ban on cow slaughter is state, not national, law and not all states restrict it. In many cities, such as New Delhi, Calcutta, and Bombay, legal slaughterhouses sell beef to retail customers and to the restaurants that serve steak.

If the caloric value of beef and the energy costs involved in the manufacture of synthetic leather were included in the estimates of energy, the calculated efficiency of Indian livestock would rise considerably.

As well as the system works, experts often claim that its efficiency can be further improved. Alan Heston, an economist at the University of Pennsylvania, believes that Indians suffer from an overabundance of cows simply because they refuse to slaughter the excess cattle. India could produce at least the same number of oxen and the same quantities of milk and manure with 30 million fewer cows. Heston calculates that only 40 cows are necessary to maintain a population of 100 bulls and oxen. Since India averages 70 cows for every 100 bullocks, the difference, 30 million cows, is expendable.

What Heston fails to note is that sex ratios among cattle in different regions of India vary tremendously, indicating that adjustments in the cow population do take place. Along the Ganges River, one of the holiest shrines of Hinduism, the ratio drops to 47 cows for every 100 male animals. This ratio reflects the preference for dairy buffalo in the irrigated sectors of the Gangetic Plains. In nearby Pakistan, in contrast, where cow slaughter is permitted, the sex ratio is 60 cows to 100 oxen.

Since the sex ratios among cattle differ greatly from region to region and do not even approximate the balance that would be expected if no females were killed, we can assume that some culling of herds does take place; Indians do adjust their religious restrictions to accommodate ecological realities.

They cannot kill a cow but they can tether an old or unhealthy animal until it has starved to death. They cannot slaughter a calf but they can yoke it with a large wooden triangle so that when it nurses it irritates the mother's udder and gets kicked to death. They cannot ship their animals to the slaughterhouse but they can sell them to Muslims, closing their eyes to the fact that the Muslims will take the cattle to the slaughterhouse.

These violations of the prohibition against cattle slaughter strengthen the premise that cow worship is a vital part of Indian culture. The practice arose to prevent the population from consuming the animal on which Indian agriculture depends. During the First Millennium B.C., the Ganges Valley became one of the most densely populated regions of the world.

Where previously there had been only scattered villages, many towns and cities arose and peasants farmed every available acre of land. Kingsley Davis, a population expert at the University of California at Berkeley, estimates that by 300 B.C. between 50 million and 100 million people were living in India. The forested Ganges Valley became a windswept semidesert and signs of ecological collapse appeared; droughts and floods became commonplace, erosion took away the rich topsoil, farms shrank as population increased, and domesticated animals became harder and harder to maintain.

It is probable that the elimination of meat eating came about in a slow, practical manner. The farmers who decided not to eat their cows, who saved them for procreation to produce oxen, were the ones who survived the natural disasters. Those who ate beef lost the tools with which to farm. Over a period of centuries, more and more farmers probably avoided beef until an unwritten taboo came into existence.

Only later was the practice codified by the priesthood. While Indian peasants were probably aware of the role of cattle in their society, strong sanctions were necessary to protect zebus from a population faced with star-vation. To remove temptation, the flesh of cattle became taboo and the cow became sacred.

The sacredness of the cow is not just an ignorant belief that stands in the way of progress. Like all concepts of the sacred and the profane, this one affects the physical world; it defines the relationships that are important for the maintenance of Indian society.

Indians have the sacred cow; we have the "sacred" car and the "sacred" dog. It would not occur to us to propose the elimination of automobiles and dogs from our society without carefully considering the consequences, and we should not propose the elimination of zebu cattle without first understanding their place in the social order in India.

Human society is neither random nor capricious. The regularities of thought and behavior called culture are the principal mechanisms by which we human beings adapt to the world around us. Practices and beliefs can be rational or irrational, but a society that fails to adapt to its environment is doomed to extinction. Only those societies that draw the necessities of life from their surroundings without destroying those surroundings, inherit the earth. The West has much to learn from the great antiquity of Indian civilization, and the sacred cow is an important part of that lesson.

---

## QUESTIONS

1. Why did American Indians not worship their buffalo, and Asian Indians not slaughter their cows?

2. Make a list of American cultural practices that might seem strange to outsiders (or even, on reflection, to yourself). Then try to find explanations (not necessarily ecological) for them.

3. Various practices that directly or indirectly limit population growth—such as birth control, abortion, and homosexuality—are far more socially acceptable in the modern United States than they were in the past. Provide an ecological explanation. Does this explanation seem adequate, or might other factors be involved?

Napoleon A. Chagnon

# 6. Yanomamö:
# The Fierce People

The Yanomamö of the South American jungle inhabit a
social world utterly unlike our own. They are an
essentially horticultural people, tending gardens that
they carve from the forest and then abandon after a few
years when the soil is exhausted. Their subsistence
strategy has important implications for their society, the
primary ones being that their settlements are necessarily
small and their social structure is a relatively simple
one.

It must also be admitted that the Yanomamö are, if
judged by the ethnocentric standards of our own
culture, one of the most singularly unappealing peoples
in the world: dirty, smelly, cruel, aggressive, dishonest,
and "primitive." Yet we must try to suspend such
judgments in reading about the Yanomamö. Their
society is only one in an immense and diverse range of
societal types, each adapted, for better or worse, to the
demands and opportunities of its own unique
environment. Within the context of their own society,
their behaviors, norms, and values form an intricate
system that "works."

This article was written by Napoleon Chagnon, an
anthropologist who lived among the Yanomamö and
studied them in great detail. His findings, summarized
here, provide an excellent example of the kind of
resources that sociologists can call on in making the
cross-cultural comparisons that can highlight aspects
not only of other societies but also of our own.

The Yanomamö Indians are a tribe in Venezuela and
Brazil who practice a slash-and-burn way of horticultural
life. Traditionally, they have been an inland "foot" tribe,
avoiding larger rivers and settling deep in the tropical
jungle. Until about 1950 they had no sustained contact
with other peoples except, to a minor extent, with another tribe, the Carib-speaking Makiritaris to the north-
east.

I recently lived with the Yanomamö for more than a
year, doing research sponsored by the U.S. Public Health
Service, with the cooperation of the Venezuela Institute
for Scientific Research. My purpose was to study Yanomamö social organization, language, sex practices, and
forms of violence, ranging from treacherous raids to chest-
pounding duels.

Those Yanomamö who have been encouraged to live
on the larger rivers (Orinoco, Mavaca, Ocamo, and Pad-
amo) are slowly beginning to realize that they are not
the only people in the world; there is also a place called
Caraca-tedi (Caracas), from whence come foreigners of
an entirely new order. These foreigners speak an incomprehensible language, probably a degenerate form of
Yanomamö. They bring malaria pills, machetes, axes,
cooking pots, and *copetas* ("guns"), have curious ideas
about indecency, and speak of a new "spirit."

However, the Yanomamö remain a people relatively
unadulterated by outside contacts. They are also fairly
numerous. Their population is roughly 10,000, the larger
portion of them distributed throughout southern Venezuela. Here, in basins of the upper Orinoco and all its
tributaries, they dwell in some 75 scattered villages, each
of which contains from 40 to 300 individuals.

The largest, most all-embracing human reality to
these people is humanity itself; Yanomamö means true
human beings. Their conception of themselves as the
only true "domestic" beings (those that dwell in houses)
is demonstrated by the contempt with which they treat
non-Yanomamö, who, in their language, are "wild." For
instance, when referring to themselves, they use an hon-
orific pronoun otherwise reserved for important spirits
and headmen; when discussing *nabäs* ("non-Yano-

mamö"), an ordinary pronoun is enough. Again, in one of the myths about their origin, the first people to be created were the Yanomamö. All others developed by a process of degeneration and are, therefore, not quite on a par with the Yanomamö.

In addition to meaning "people," Yanomamö also refers to the language. Their tribal name does not designate a politically organized entity but is more or less equivalent to our concept of humanity. (This, of course, makes their most outstanding characteristic—chronic warfare, of which I shall speak in detail—seem rather an anomaly.) Sub-Yanomamö groupings are based on language differences, historical separation, and geographical location.

For instance, two distinguishable groups, Waika (from *waikaö*—"to kill off") and Shamatari, speak nearly identical dialects; they are differentiated mostly on the basis of a specific event that led to their separation. The Shamatari, the group I know best, occupy the area south of the Orinoco to, and including portions of, northern Brazil. Their differentiation from the Waika probably occurred in the past 75 years.

According to the Indians, there was a large village on a northern tributary of the upper Orinoco River, close to its headwaters. The village had several factions, one of which was led by a man called Kayabawä (big tree). A notably corpulent man, he also had the name Shamatari, derived from *shama*, the "tapir," a robust ungulate found throughout tropical South America. As the story goes, Shamatari's faction got into a fight with the rest of the village over the possession of a woman, and the community split into two warring halves. Gradually the fighting involved more villages, and Shamatari led his faction south, crossed the Orinoco, and settled there. He was followed by members of other villages that had taken his part in the fight.

Those who moved to the south side of the Orinoco came to be called Shamataris by those living on the north side, and the term is now applied to any village in this area, whether or not it can trace its origin to the first supporters of Shamatari.

For the Yanomamö, the village is the maximum political unit and the maximum sovereign body, and it is linked to other villages by ephemeral alliances, visiting and trade relationships, and intermarriages. In essence, the village is a building—a continuous, open-roofed lean-to built on a circular plan and surrounded by a protective palisade of split palm logs. The roof starts at or near ground level, ascends at an angle of about 45 degrees, and reaches a height of some 20 to 25 feet. Individual segments under the continuous roof are not partitioned; from a hammock hung anywhere beneath it one can see (and hear, thanks to the band shell nature of the structure) all that goes on within the village.

The palisade, about three to six feet behind the base of the roof, is some ten feet high and is usually in various stages of disrepair, depending on the current warfare situation. The limited number of entrances are covered with dry palm leaves in the evening; if these are moved even slightly, the sound precipitates the barking of a horde of ill-tempered, underfed dogs, whose bad manners preadapt the stranger to what lies beyond the entrance.

A typical "house" (a segment under the continuous roof) shelters a man, his wife, or wives, their children, perhaps one or both of the man's parents, and, farther down, the man's brothers and their families. The roof is alive with cockroaches, scorpions, and spiders, and the ground is littered with the debris of numerous repasts—bird, fish, and animal bones; bits of fur; skulls of monkeys and other animals; banana and plantain peelings; feathers; and the seeds of palm fruits. Bows and arrows stand against housepoles all over the village, baskets hang from roof rafters, and firewood is stacked under the lower part of the roof where it slopes to the ground. Some men will be whittling arrow points with agouti-tooth knives or tying feathers to arrow shafts. Some women will be spinning cotton, weaving baskets, or making hammocks or cotton waistbands. The children, gathered in the center of the village clearing, frequently tie a string to a lizard and entertain themselves by shooting the animal full of tiny arrows. And, of course, many people will be outside the compound, working in their gardens, fishing, or collecting palm fruits in the jungle.

If it is a typical late afternoon, most of the older men are gathered in one part of the village, blowing one of their hallucinatory drugs (*ebene*) up each other's nostrils by means of a hollow tube and chanting to the forest demons (*hekuras*) as the drug takes effect. Other men may be curing a sick person by sucking, massaging, and exhorting the evil spirit from him. Everybody in the village is swatting vigorously at the voracious biting gnats, and here and there groups of people delouse each other's heads and eat the vermin.

In composition, the village consists of one or more groups of patrilineally related kinsmen (*mashis*), but it also contains other categories, including people who have come from other villages seeking spouses. All villages try to increase their size and consider it desirable for both the young men and young women to remain at home after marriage. Since one must marry out of his *mashi*, villages with only one patrilineage frequently lose their young men to other villages; they must go to another village to *siohamou* (to "son-in-law") if they want wives. The parents of the bride-to-be, of course, want the young man to remain in their village to help support them in their old age, particularly if they have few or no sons. They will frequently promise a young man one or more of the sisters of his wife in order to make his stay more attractive.

He, on the other hand, would rather return to his home village to be with his own kinsmen, and the tendency is for postmarital residence to be patrilocal (with the father of the groom). If a village is rich in axes and machetes, it can and does coerce its poorer trading partners into permitting their young women to live permanently with the richer village. The latter thus obtains more women, while the poorer village gains some security in the trading network. The poor village then coerces other villages even poorer, or they raid them and steal their women.

The patrilineages that maintain the composition of the villages, rich or poor, include a man and his brothers and sisters, his children and his brothers' children, and the children of his sons and brothers' sons. The ideal marriage pattern is for a group of brothers to exchange sisters with another group of brothers. Furthermore, it is both permissible and desirable for a man to marry his mother's brother's daughter (his matrilateral cross-cousin) and/or his father's sister's daughter (his patrilateral cross-cousin) and, as we have seen earlier, to remain in his parents' village. Hence, the "ideal" village would have at least two patrilineages that exchanged marriageable people.

There is a considerable amount of adherence to these rules, and both brother-sister exchange and cross-cousin marriage are common. However, there are also a substantial number of people in each village who are not related in these ways. For the most part they are women and their children who have been stolen from other villages, segments of lineages that have fled from their own village because of fights, and individuals—mostly young men—who have moved in and attached themselves to the household of one of the lineage (*mashi*) leaders.

Even if the sex ratio is balanced, there is a chronic shortage of women. A pregnant woman or one who is still nursing her children must not have sexual relationships. This means that for as many as three years, even allowing for violations of the taboos, a woman is asexual as far as the men are concerned. Hence, men with pregnant wives, and bachelors too, are potentially disruptive in every village because they constantly seek liaisons with the wives of other men. Eventually such relationships are discovered and violence ensues.

The woman, even if merely suspected of having affairs with other men, is beaten with a club; burned with a glowing brand; shot with a barbed arrow in a non-vital area, such as the buttocks, so that removal of the barb is both difficult and painful; or chopped on the arms or legs with a machete or ax. Most women over thirty carry numerous scars inflicted on them by their enraged husbands. My study of genealogies also indicates that not a few women have been killed outright by their husbands. The woman's punishment for infidelity depends on the number of brothers she has in the village, for if her husband is too brutal, her brothers may club him or take her away and give her to someone else.

The guilty man, on the other hand, is challenged to a fight with clubs. This duel is rarely confined to the two parties involved, for their brothers and supporters join the battle. If nobody is seriously injured, the matter may be forgotten. But if the incidents are frequent, the two patrilineages may decide to split while they are still on relatively "peaceable" terms with each other and form two independent villages. They will still be able to reunite when threatened by raid from a larger village.

This is only one aspect of the chronic warfare of the Yanomamö—warfare that has a basic effect on settlement pattern and demography, intervillage political relationships, leadership, and social organization. The collective aggressive behavior is caused by the desire to accent "sovereignty"—the capacity to initiate fighting and to demonstrate this capacity to others.

Although the Yanomamö are habitually armed with lethal bows and arrows, they have a graded system of violence within which they can express their *waiteri*, or "fierceness." The form of violence is determined by the nature of the affront or wrong to be challenged. The most benign form is a duel between two groups, in which an individual from each group stands (or kneels) with his chest stuck out, head up in the air, and arms held back and receives a hard blow to the chest. His opponent literally winds up and delivers a closed-fist blow from the ground, striking the man on the left pectoral muscle just above the heart. The impact frequently drops the man to his knees, and participants may cough up blood for several days after such a contest. After receiving several such blows, the man then has his turn to strike his opponent, while the respective supporters of each antagonist gather around and frenziedly urge their champion on.

All men in the two villages are obliged to participate as village representatives, and on one occasion I saw some individuals take as many as three or four turns of four blows each. Duels of this type usually result from minor wrongs, such as a village being guilty of spreading bad rumors about another village, questioning its generosity or fierceness, or accusing it of gluttony at a feast. A variant of this form of duel is side slapping, in which an open-handed blow is delivered across the flank just above the pelvis.

More serious are the club fights. Although these almost invariably result from cases in which a wife has been caught in an affair with another man, some fights follow the theft of food within the village. The usual procedure calls for a representative from each belligerent group. One man holds a ten-foot club upright, braces himself by leaning on the club and spreading his feet, then holds his head out for his opponent to strike. Following this comes his turn to do likewise to his adversary.

These duels, more often than not, end in a free-for-all in which everybody clubs everybody else on whatever spot he can hit. Such brawls occasionally result in fatalities. However, since headmen of the respective groups stand by with bows drawn, no one dares deliver an intentionally killing blow, for if he does, he will be shot. The scalps of the older men are almost incredible to behold, covered as they are by as many as a dozen ugly welts. Yet, most of them proudly shave the top of their heads to display their scars.

Also precipitated by feuds over women are spear fights, which are even more serious than club fights. Members of a village will warn those of the offending village that they are coming to fight with spears. They specify that they are not planning to shoot arrows unless the others shoot first. On the day of the fight, the attackers enter the other village, armed with five or six sharpened clubs or slender shafts some eight feet long and attempt to drive the defenders out. If successful, the invaders steal all the valuable possessions—hammocks, cooking pots, and machetes—and retreat. In the spear fight that occurred while I was studying the tribe, the attackers were successful, but they wounded several individuals so badly that one of them died. The fighting then escalated to a raid, the penultimate form of violence.

Such raids may be precipitated by woman stealing or the killing of a visitor (visitors are sometimes slain because they are suspected of having practiced harmful magic that has led to a death in the host's village). Raids also occur if a man kills his wife in a fit of anger; her natal village is then obliged to avenge the death. Most raids, however, are in revenge for deaths that occurred in previous raids, and once the vendetta gets started, it is not likely to end for a long time. Something else may trigger a raid. Occasionally an ambitious headman wearies of peaceful times—a rarity, certainly—and deliberately creates a situation that will demonstrate his leadership.

A revenge raid is preceded by a feast in which the ground bones of the person to be avenged are mixed in a soup of boiled, ripe plantains (the mainstay of Yanomamö diet) and swallowed. Yanomamö are endocannibals, which means they consume the remains of members of their own group. This ceremony puts the raiders in the appropriate state of frenzy for the business of warfare. A mock raid—rather like a dress rehearsal—is conducted in their own village on the afternoon before the day of the raid, and a life-size effigy of an enemy, constructed of leaves or a log, is slain. That evening all the participants march, one at a time, to the center of the village clearing, while clacking their bows and arrows and screaming their versions of the calls of carnivorous birds, mammals, and even insects.

When all have lined up facing the direction of the enemy village, they sing their war song, "I am a meat-hungry buzzard," and shout several times in unison until they hear the echo return from the jungle. They then disperse to their individual sections of the village to vomit the symbolic rotten flesh of the enemy that they, as symbolic carnivorous vultures and wasps, partook of in the lineup. The same thing, with the exception of the song, is repeated at dawn the following morning. Then the raiders, covered with black paint made of chewed charcoal, march out of the village in single file and collect the hammocks and plantains that their women have previously set outside the village for them. On each night they spend en route to the enemy they fire arrows at a dummy in a mock raid. They approach the enemy village itself under cover of darkness, ambush the first person they catch, and retreat as rapidly as possible. If they catch a man and his family, they will shoot the man and steal the woman and her children. At a safe distance from her village, each of the raiders rapes the woman, and when they reach their own village, every man in the village may, if he wishes, do likewise before she is given to one of the men as a wife. Ordinarily she attempts to escape, but if caught, she may be killed. So constant is the threat of raids that every woman leaves her village in the knowledge that she may be stolen.

The supreme form of violence is the *nomohoni*—the "trick." During the dry season, the Yanomamö do a great deal of visiting. An entire village will go to another village for a ceremony that involves feasting, dancing, chanting, curing, trading, and just plain gossiping. Shortly after arrival, the visitors are invited to recline in the hammocks of the hosts. By custom they lie motionless to display their fine decorations while the hosts prepare food for them. But now suppose that a village has a grudge to settle with another, such as deaths to avenge. It enlists the support of a third village to act as accomplice. This third village, which must be on friendly terms with the intended victims, will invite them to a feast. While the guests recline defenseless in the hammocks, the hosts descend on them with axes and sharpened poles, treacherously killing as many as they can. Those that manage to escape the slaughter inside the village are shot outside the palisade by the village that instigated the *nomohoni*. The women and children will be shared between the two accomplices.

Throughout all this ferocity there are two organizational aspects of violence. One concerns leadership: A man must be able to demonstrate his fierceness if he is to be a true leader. It is equally important, however, that he have a large natural following—that is, he must have many male kinsmen to support his position and a quantity of daughters and sisters to distribute to other men. Lineage leaders cannot accurately be described as unilateral initiators of activities; rather, they are the vehicles through which the group's will is expressed. For example, when a certain palm fruit is ripe and is particularly abundant in an area some distance from the village, everybody knows that the whole village will pack its belongings and erect a temporary camp at that spot to collect the fruit. The headman does little more than set the date. When his kinsmen see him packing, they know that the time has come to leave for the collecting trip. True, the headman does have some initiative in raiding, but not even this is completely independent of the attitudes of his followers, which dictate that a death must be avenged. However, when the purpose of a raid is to steal women, the headman does have some freedom to act on his own initiative.

As a general rule, the smaller his natural following, the more he is obliged to demonstrate his personal qualities of fierceness and leadership. Padudiwä, the headman of one of the lineages in Bisaasi-tedi, took pains to demonstrate his personal qualities whenever he could; he had only two living brothers and four living sisters in his group. Most of his demonstrations of ferocity were cruel beatings he administered to his four wives, none of whom had brothers in the village to take their part. Several young men who attached themselves to his household admired him for this.

Padudiwä was also responsible for organizing several raids while I lived with the villagers of Bisaasi-tedi, a village that was being raided regularly by some seven or eight other villages, so that the danger of being raided in return was correspondingly reduced. On one occasion, when three young men from Patanowä-tedi arrived as emissaries of peace, Padudiwä wanted to kill them, although he had lived with them at one time and they were fairly close relatives. The murder was prevented by the headman of the other—and larger—lineage in the village, who warned that if an attempt were made on the lives of the visitors he himself would kill Padudiwä.

Obviously, then, Padudiwä's reputation was built largely on calculated acts of fierceness, which carefully reduced the possibility of personal danger to himself and his followers, and on cunning and cruelty. To some extent he was obliged by the smallness of his gathering to behave in such a way, but he was certainly a man to treat with caution.

Despite their extreme aggressiveness, the Yanomamö have at least two qualities I admired. They are kind and indulgent with children and can quickly forget personal angers. (A few even treated me almost as an equal—in their culture this was a considerable concession.) But to portray them as "noble savages" would be misleading. Many of them are delightful and charming people when confronted alone and on a personal basis, but the greater number of them are much like Padudiwä—or strive to be that way. As they frequently told me, *Yanomamö täbä waiteri!*—"Yanomamö are fierce!"

## QUESTIONS

1. Discuss the concepts of ethnocentrism and cultural relativism with reference to the Yanomamö.

2. Could American society be so thoroughly described in so short a space as Chagnon describes the Yanomamö? Justify your answer.

3. Are we really all that different from the Yanomamö?

*Ernestine Friedl*

# 7. Society and Sex Roles

*The various societies that exist, and have existed in the past, can be roughly categorized according to the basic strategy used to meet economic needs: hunting and gathering, pastoralism, horticulture, agriculture, or industrialism and postindustrialism. Each of these subsistence strategies offers certain opportunities and imposes certain constraints: for example, hunters and gatherers could never form large, concentrated populations, for they could not collect enough food to support themselves; industrial societies can support huge cities, for most of their members work at jobs other than food production. A society's subsistence strategy has far-reaching implications for a variety of other aspects of social and cultural life as well.*

*As Ernestine Friedl shows in her article, a people's subsistence strategy also affects the relative status of men and women. In hunting and gathering societies, the sexes are virtually equal; in pastoral and horticultural societies, distinct inequalities emerge; in agricultural and early industrial societies, the inequalities are great; while in advanced industrial or postindustrial societies, women again begin to achieve equality with men. In each case, the crucial factor affecting the status of the sexes is an economic one: the greater the female contribution to the group, the higher the status of women becomes.*

"Women must respond quickly to the demands of their husbands," says anthropologist Napoleon Chagnon describing the horticultural Yanomamö Indians of Venezuela. When a man returns from a hunting trip, "the woman, no matter what she is doing, hurries home and quietly but rapidly prepares a meal for her husband. Should the wife be slow in doing this, the husband is within his rights to beat her. Most reprimands ... take the form of blows with the hand or with a piece of firewood. . . . Some of them chop their wives with the sharp edge of a machete or axe, or shoot them with a barbed arrow in some nonvital area, such as the buttocks or leg."

Among the Semai agriculturalists of central Malaya, when one person refuses the request of another, the offended party suffers *punan*, a mixture of emotional pain and frustration. "Enduring *punan* is commonest when a girl has refused the victim her sexual favors," reports Robert Dentan. "The jilted man's 'heart becomes sad.' He loses his energy and his appetite. Much of the time he sleeps, dreaming of his lost love. In this state he is in fact very likely to injure himself 'accidentally.'" The Semai are afraid of violence; a man would never strike a woman.

The social relationship between men and women has emerged as one of the principal disputes occupying the attention of scholars and the public in recent years. Although the discord is sharpest in the United States, the controversy has spread throughout the world. Numerous national and international conferences, including one in Mexico sponsored by the United Nations, have drawn together delegates from all walks of life to discuss such questions as the social and political rights of each sex, and even the basic nature of males and females.

Whatever their position, partisans often invoke examples from other cultures to support their ideas about the proper role of each sex. Because women are clearly subservient to men in many societies, like the Yanomamö some experts conclude that the natural pattern is for men to dominate. But among the Semai no one has the right to command others, and in West Africa women are often chiefs. The place of women in these societies supports the argument of those who believe that sex roles are not fixed, that if there is a natural order, it allows for many different arrangements.

The argument will never be settled as long as the opposing sides toss examples from the world's cultures at each other like intellectual stones. But the effect of biological differences on male and female behavior can be clarified by looking at known examples of the earliest forms of human society and examining the relationship between technology, social organization, environment, and sex roles. The problem is to determine the conditions in which different degrees of male dominance are found, to try to discover the social and cultural arrangements that give rise to equality or inequality between the sexes, and to attempt to apply this knowledge to our understanding of the changes taking place in modern industrial society.

As Western history and the anthropological record have told us, equality between the sexes is rare; in most known societies females are subordinate. Male dominance is so widespread that it is virtually a human universal; societies in which women are consistently dominant do not exist and have never existed.

Evidence of a society in which women control all strategic resources like food and water, and in which women's activities are the most prestigious has never been found. The Iroquois of North America and the Lovedu of Africa came closest. Among the Iroquois, women raised food, controlled its distribution, and helped to choose male political leaders. Lovedu women ruled as queens, exchanged valuable cattle, led ceremonies, and controlled their own sex lives. But among both the Iroquois and the Lovedu, men owned the land and held other positions of power and prestige. Women were equal to men; they did not have ultimate authority over them. Neither culture was a true matriarchy.

Patriarchies are prevalent, and they appear to be strongest in societies in which men control significant goods that are exchanged with people outside the family. Regardless of who produces food, the person who gives it to others creates the obligations and alliances that are at the center of all political relations. The greater the male monopoly on the distribution of scarce items, the stronger their control of women seems to be. This is most obvious in relatively simple hunter-gatherer societies.

Hunter-gatherers, or foragers, subsist on wild plants, small land animals, and small river or sea creatures gathered by hand; large land animals and sea mammals hunted with spears, bows and arrows, and blow guns; and fish caught with hooks and nets. The 300,000 hunter-gatherers alive in the world today include the Eskimos, the Australian aborigines, and the Pygmies of Central Africa.

Foraging has endured for two million years and was replaced by farming and animal husbandry only 10,000 years ago; it covers more than 99 percent of human history. Our foraging ancestry is not far behind us and provides a clue to our understanding of the human condition.

Hunter-gatherers are people whose ways of life are technologically simple and socially and politically egalitarian. They live in small groups of 50 to 200 and have neither kings, nor priests, nor social classes. These conditions permit anthropologists to observe the essential bases for inequalities between the sexes without the distortions induced by the complexities of contemporary industrial society.

The source of male power among hunter-gatherers lies in their control of a scarce, hard to acquire, but necessary nutrient—animal protein. When men in a hunter-gatherer society return to camp with game, they divide the meat in some customary way. Among the !Kung San of Africa, certain parts of the animal are given to the owner of the arrow that killed the beast, to the first hunter to sight the game, to the one who threw the first spear, and to all men in the hunting party. After the meat has been divided, each hunter distributes his share to his blood relatives and his in-laws, who in turn share it with others. If an animal is large enough, every member of the band will receive some meat.

Vegetable foods, in contrast, are not distributed beyond the immediate household. Women give food to their children, to their husbands, to other members of the household, and rarely, to the occasional visitor. No one outside the family regularly eats any of the wild fruits and vegetables that are gathered by the women.

The meat distributed by the men is a public gift. Its source is widely known, and the donor expects a reciprocal gift when other men return from a successful hunt. He gains honor as a supplier of a scarce item and simultaneously obligates others to him.

These obligations constitute a form of power or control over others, both men and women. The opinions of hunters play an important part in decisions to move the village; good hunters attract the most desirable women; people in other groups join camps with good hunters; and hunters, because they already participate in an internal system of exchange, control exchange with other groups for flint, salt, and steel axes. The male monopoly on hunting unites men in a system of exchange and gives them power; gathering vegetable food does not give women equal power even among foragers who live in the tropics, where the food collected by women provides more than half the hunter-gatherer diet.

If dominance arises from a monopoly on big-game hunting, why has the male monopoly remained unchallenged? Some women are strong enough to participate in the hunt and their endurance is certainly equal to that of men. Dobe San women of the Kalahari Desert in Africa walk an average of 10 miles a day carrying from 15 to 33 pounds of food plus a baby.

Women do not hunt, I believe, because of four interrelated factors: variability in the supply of game; the different skills required for hunting and gathering; the incompatibility between carrying burdens and hunting; and the small size of seminomadic foraging populations.

Because the meat supply is unstable, foragers must make frequent expeditions to provide the band with gathered food. Environmental factors such as seasonal and annual variation in rainfall often affect the size of the wildlife population. Hunters cannot always find game, and when they do encounter animals, they are not always successful in killing their prey. In northern latitudes, where meat is the primary food, periods of starvation are known in every generation. The irregularity of the game supply leads hunter-gatherers in areas where plant foods are available to depend on these predictable foods a good part of the time. Someone must gather the fruits, nuts, and roots and carry them back to camp to feed unsuccessful hunters, children, the elderly, and anyone who might not have gone foraging that day.

Foraging falls to the women because hunting and gathering cannot be combined on the same expedition. Although gatherers sometimes notice signs of game as they work, the skills required to track game are not the same as those required to find edible roots or plants. Hunters scan the horizon and the land for traces of large game; gatherers keep their eyes to the ground, studying the distribution of plants and the texture of the soil for hidden roots and animal holes. Even if a woman who was collecting plants came across the track of an antelope, she could not follow it; it is impossible to carry a load and hunt at the same time. Running with a heavy load is difficult, and should the animal be sighted, the hunter would be off balance and could neither shoot an arrow nor throw a spear accurately.

Pregnancy and child care would also present difficulties for a hunter. An unborn child affects a woman's body balance, as does a child in her arms, on her back, or slung at her side. Until they are two years old, many hunter-gatherer children are carried at all times, and until they are four, they are carried some of the time.

An observer might wonder why young women do not hunt until they become pregnant, or why mature women and men do not hunt and gather on alternate days, with some women staying in camp to act as wet nurses for the young. Apart from the effects hunting might have on a mother's milk production, there are two reasons. First, young girls begin to bear children as soon as they are physically mature and strong enough to hunt, and second, hunter-gatherer bands are so small that

there are unlikely to be enough lactating women to serve as wet nurses. No hunter-gatherer group could afford to maintain a specialized female hunting force.

Because game is not always available, because hunting and gathering are specialized skills, because women carrying heavy loads cannot hunt, and because women in hunter-gatherer societies are usually either pregnant or caring for young children, for most of the last two million years of human history men have hunted and women have gathered.

If male dominance depends on controlling the supply of meat, then the degree of male dominance in a society should vary with the amount of meat available and the amount supplied by the men. Some regions, like the East African grasslands and the North American woodlands, abounded with species of large mammals; other zones, like tropical forests and semideserts, are thinly populated with prey. Many elements affect the supply of game, but theoretically, the less meat provided exclusively by the men, the more egalitarian the society.

All known hunter-gatherer societies fit into four basic types: those in which men and women work together in communal hunts and as teams gathering edible plants, as did the Washo Indians of North America; those in which men and women each collect their own plant foods although the men supply some meat to the group, as do the Hadza of Tanzania; those in which male hunters and female gatherers work apart but return to camp each evening to share their acquisitions, as do the Tiwi of North Australia; and those in which the men provide all the food by hunting large game, as do the Eskimo. In each case the extent of male dominance increases directly with the proportion of meat supplied by individual men and small hunting parties.

Among the most egalitarian of hunter-gatherer societies are the Washo Indians, who inhabited the valleys of the Sierra Nevada in what is now southern California and Nevada. In the spring they moved north to Lake Tahoe for the large fish runs of sucker and native trout. Everyone—men, women, and children—participated in the fishing. Women spent the summer gathering edible berries and seeds while the men continued to fish. In the fall some men hunted deer but the most important source of animal protein was the jack rabbit, which was captured in communal hunts. Men and women together drove the rabbits into nets tied end to end. To provide food for the winter, husbands and wives worked as teams in the late fall to collect pine nuts.

Since everyone participated in most food-gathering activities, there were no individual distributors of food and relatively little difference in male and female rights. Men and women were not segregated from each other in daily activities; both were free to take lovers after marriage; both had the right to separate whenever they chose; menstruating women were not isolated from the rest of the group; and one of the two major Washo rituals celebrated hunting while the other celebrated gathering. Men were accorded more prestige if they had killed a deer, and men directed decisions about the seasonal movement of the group. But if no male leader stepped forward, women were permitted to lead. The distinctive feature of groups such as the Washo is the relative equality of the sexes.

The sexes are also relatively equal among the Hadza of Tanzania but this near-equality arises because men and women tend to work alone to feed themselves. They exchange little food. The Hadza lead a leisurely life in the seemingly barren environment of the East African Rift Gorge that is, in fact, rich in edible berries, roots, and small game. As a result of this abundance, from the time they are 10 years old, Hadza men and women gather much of their own food. Women take their young children with them into the bush, eating as they forage, and collect only enough food for a light family meal in the evening. The men eat berries and roots as they hunt for small game, and should they bring down a rabbit or a hydrax, they eat the meat on the spot. Meat is carried back to the camp and shared with the rest of the group only on those rare occasions when a poisoned arrow brings down a large animal—an impala, a zebra, an eland, or a giraffe.

Because Hadza men distribute little meat, their status is only slightly higher than that of the women. People flock to the camp of a good hunter and the camp might take on his name because of his popularity, but he is in no sense a leader of the group. A Hadza man and a woman have an equal right to divorce and each can repudiate a marriage simply by living apart for a few weeks. Couples tend to live in the same camp as the wife's mother but they sometimes make long visits to the camp of the husband's mother. Although a man may take more than one wife, most Hadza males cannot afford to indulge in this luxury. In order to maintain a marriage, a man must supply both his wife and his mother-in-law with some meat and trade goods, such as beads and cloth, and the Hadza economy gives few men the wealth to provide for more than one wife and mother-in-law. Washo equality is based on cooperation; Hadza equality is based on independence.

In contrast to both these groups, among the Tiwi of Melville and Bathurst Islands off the northern coast of Australia, male hunters dominate female gatherers. The Tiwi are representative of the most common form of foraging society, in which the men supply large quantities of meat, although less than half the food consumed by the group. Each morning Tiwi women, most with babies on their backs, scatter in different directions in search of vegetables, grubs, worms, and small game such as bandicoots, lizards and opossums. To track the game, they use hunting dogs. On most days women return to camp with some meat and with baskets full of *korka*, the nut of a native palm, which is soaked and mashed to make a porridge-like dish. The Tiwi men do not hunt small game and do not hunt every day, but when they do they often return with kangaroo, large lizards, fish, and game birds.

The porridge is cooked separately by each household and rarely shared outside the family, but the meat is prepared by a volunteer cook, who can be male or female. After the cook takes one of the parts of the animal traditionally reserved for him or her, the animal's "boss," the one who caught it, distributes the rest to all near kin and then to all others residing with the band. Although the small game supplied by the women is distributed in the same way as the big game supplied by the men, Tiwi men are dominant because the game they kill provides most of the meat.

The power of Tiwi men is clearest in their betrothal practices. Among the Tiwi, a woman must always be married. To ensure this, female infants are betrothed at birth and widows are remarried at the gravesides of their late husbands. Men form alliances by exchanging daughters, sisters, and mothers in marriage and some collect as many as 25 wives. Tiwi men value the quantity and quality of the food many wives can collect and the many children they can produce.

The dominance of the men is offset somewhat by the influence of adult women in selecting their next husbands. Many women are active strategists in the political careers of their male relatives, but to the exasperation of some sons attempting to promote their own futures, widowed mothers sometimes insist on selecting their own partners. Women also influence the marriages of their daughters and granddaughters, especially when the selected husband dies before the bestowed child moves to his camp.

Among the Eskimo, representative of the rarest type of forager society, inequality between the sexes is matched by inequality in supplying the group with food. Inland Eskimo men hunt caribou throughout the year to provision the entire society, and maritime Eskimo men depend on whaling, fishing, and some hunting to feed their extended families. The women process the carcasses, cut and sew skins to make clothing, cook, and care for the young; but they collect no food of their own and depend on the men to supply all the raw materials for their work. Since men provide all the meat, they also control the trade in hides, whale oil, seal oil, and other items that move between the maritime and inland Eskimos.

Eskimo women are treated almost exclusively as objects to be used, abused, and traded by men. After puberty all Eskimo girls are fair game for any interested male. A man shows his intentions by grabbing the belt of a woman and if she protests, he cuts off her trousers and forces himself upon her. These encounters are considered unimportant by the rest of the group. Men offer their wives' sexual services to establish alliances with trading partners and members of hunting and whaling parties.

Despite the consistent pattern of some degree of male dominance among foragers, most of these societies are egalitarian compared with agricultural and industrial societies. No forager has any significant opportunity for political leadership. Foragers, as a rule, do not like to give or take orders, and assume leadership only with reluctance. Shamans (those who are thought to be possessed by spirits) may be either male or female. Public rituals conducted by women in order to celebrate the first menstruation of girls are common, and the symbolism in these rituals is similar to that in the ceremonies that follow a boy's first kill.

In any society, status goes to those who control the distribution of valued goods and services outside the family. Equality arises when both sexes work side by side in food production, as do the Washo, and the products are simply distributed among the workers. In such circumstances, no person or sex has greater access to valued items than do others. But when women make no contribution to the food supply, as in the case of the Eskimo, they are completely subordinate.

When we attempt to apply these generalizations to contemporary industrial society, we can predict that as long as women spend their discretionary income from jobs on domestic needs, they will gain little social recognition and power. To be an effective source of power, money must be exchanged in ways that require returns and create obligations. In other words, it must be invested.

Jobs that do not give women control over valued resources will do little to advance their general status. Only as managers, executives, and professionals are women in a position to trade goods and services, to do other favors, and therefore to obligate others to them. Only as controllers of valued resources can women achieve prestige, power, and equality.

Within the household, women who bring in income from jobs are able to function on a more nearly equal basis with their husbands. Women who contribute services to their husbands and children without pay, as do some middle-class Western housewives, are especially vulnerable to dominance. Like Eskimo women, as long as their services are limited to domestic distribution they have little power relative to their husbands and none with respect to the outside world.

As for the limits imposed on women by their procreative functions in hunter-gatherer societies, childbearing and child care are organized around work as much as work is organized around reproduction. Some foraging groups space their children three to four years apart and have an average of only four to six children, far fewer than many women in other cultures. Hunter-gatherers nurse their infants for extended periods, sometimes for as long as four years. This custom suppresses ovulation and limits the size of their families. Sometimes, although rarely, they practice infanticide. By limiting reproduction, a woman who is gathering food has only one child to carry.

Different societies can and do adjust the frequency of birth and the care of children to accommodate whatever productive activities women customarily engage in. In horticultural societies, where women work long hours in gardens that may be far from home, infants get food to supplement their mothers' milk, older children take care of younger children, and pregnancies are widely spaced. Throughout the world, if a society requires a woman's labor, it finds ways to care for her children.

In the United States, as in some other industrial societies, the accelerated entry of women with preschool children into the labor force has resulted in the development of a variety of child-care arrangements. Individual women have called on friends, relatives, and neighbors. Public and private child-care centers are growing. We should realize that the declining birth rate, the increasing acceptance of childless or single-child families, and a deemphasis on motherhood are adaptations to a sexual division of labor reminiscent of the system of production found in hunter-gatherer societies.

In many countries where women no longer devote most of their productive years to childbearing, they are beginning to demand a change in the social relationship of the sexes. As women gain access to positions that control the exchange of resources, male dominance may become archaic, and industrial societies may one day become as egalitarian as the Washo.

## QUESTIONS

1. How can such apparently unrelated matters as a society's subsistence strategy and the relative status of the sexes be connected?

2. Marx maintained that the economic base of a society was of paramount importance in shaping the society's social and cultural forms. Cite any evidence (not necessarily restricted to this article) that throws light on this view.

3. What are the implications of Friedl's analysis for the future roles and statuses of the sexes?

D. Stanley Eitzen

# 8. The Structure of Sport and Society

*Sport is a subject of considerable and growing interest to sociologists. It is, after all, an important institution in American society: the great majority of people discuss sport regularly, and most are either participants in, or spectators of, some game or another. And like any other institution, sport is an integral part of the society, with its characteristics reflecting those of the surrounding social order.*

*The kinds of sport that are played can tell us a great deal about the society. American sport, for example, tends to be competitive, specialized, professionalized, profit-oriented, and diversified—all characteristic features of the society as a whole, and particularly of its economy. The values of sport and of the society at large are often identical: discipline, hard work, success, conformity, team spirit. Even social changes, such as increased participation by women and blacks in other areas, are faithfully reflected in sport.*

*In this article, Stanley Eitzen explores the relationship between American sport and the American social structure, placing particular emphasis on the implications of two sports that lay equal claim to being the great American pastime—baseball and football.*

From *Sport in Contemporary Society*, Second Edition, edited by D. Stanley Eitzen. Copyright © 1984 by St. Martin's Press, Inc., and used with publisher's permission.

An important indicator of the essence of a society is the type of sport it glorifies. The examination of the structure of a society's dominant sport provides important clues about that society and its culture. For example, answers to the following questions will greatly inform the observer about that society: Is the sport oriented toward a group (team) or the individual? Does the outcome depend essentially on strength, speed, strategy, deception, or the mastery of intricate moves? Is the activity cerebral or physical? Is the primary goal to win or to enjoy the activity?

Let us begin by looking at what Americans consider the essence of sport—winning—to show how other societies have a different view more consonant with their culture. Sport, as played in America, is an expression of Social Darwinism—a survival-of-the-fittest approach where everyone competes to be alone at the top. Players are cut from teams even in our schools if they are not considered good enough. Tournaments are organized so that only one team or individual is the ultimate winner. Corporations sponsor contests for youngsters such as "Punt, Pass, and Kick," where winners are selected at the local level and proceed through a number of district and regional contests until a winner is declared in each category. In 1974, for instance, there were 1,112,702 entrants in the Punt, Pass, and Kick contest, and only six youngsters ended as winners.[1]

In cooperative, group-centered societies, such sporting activities would seem cruel, even barbaric, because success is achieved only at the cost of the failure of others. These societies, rather, would have sports where the object is something other than winning. For instance:

The Tangu people of New Guinea play a popular game known as *taketak*, which involves throwing a spinning top into massed lots of stakes driven into the ground. There are two teams. Players of each team try to touch as many stakes with their tops as possible. In the end, however, the participants play not to win but to draw. The game must go on until an exact draw is reached. This requires great skill, since players sometimes must throw their tops into the massed stakes without touching a single one. *Taketak* expresses a prime value in Tangu culture, that is, the concept of moral equivalence, which is reflected in the precise sharing of foodstuffs among the people.[2]

This example demonstrates that a society's sports mirror that society. Cooperative societies have sports that minimize competition, while aggressive societies have high competitive sports. This raises a question about the nature of the most popular American sports. What do they tell us about ourselves and our society? Let us concentrate on the two most popular team sports—football and baseball—as they are played at the professional level.[3]

## The Differing Natures of Football and Baseball

Although there are some similarities between football and baseball, e.g., cheating is the norm in both,[4] these two sports are basically different. In many ways they are opposites, and these incongruities provide insightful clues about Americans and American society.

Two fundamentally different orientations toward time exist in these two sports. Baseball is not bounded by time while football must adhere to a rigid time schedule. "Baseball is oblivious to time. There is no clock, no two-minute drill. The game flows in a timeless stream with a rhythm of its own."[5] In this way baseball reflects life in rural America as it existed in the not-too-distant past compared to football's emulation of contemporary urban society, where persons have rigid schedules, appointments, and time clocks to punch.

The innings of baseball have no time limit, and if the game is tied at the end of regulation innings, the teams play as many extra innings as it takes to determine a winner. Football, on the other hand, is played for sixty minutes, and if tied at the end, the game goes into "sudden death," i.e., the first team to score wins. Thus, even the nomenclature of the two sports—"extra innings" compared to "sudden death"—illustrates a basic difference between them. There are other semantic differences. A baseball player makes an "error," but a football team is "penalized." The object of baseball is to get "home" while the goal of football is to penetrate deep into the opponent's "territory." In baseball there is no home territory to defend; the playing field is shared by both teams. There is no analogue in baseball for the militaristic terms of football, e.g., "blitz," "bomb," "trap," "trenches," "field general," "aerial attack," and "ground attack."

Such linguistic differences imply a basic discrepancy between baseball and football. Baseball is essentially a calm and leisurely activity while football is intense, aggressive, and violent. Football is foremost a form of physical combat, whereas baseball is one of technique. A baseball player cannot get to first base because of his strength, aggression, or ability to intimidate. His only way to get there is through skill. In football, however, survival (success) belongs to the most aggressive. Former football player George Sauer has suggested that aggression on the football field leads to success just as it gets one ahead in American society.

> How does football justify teaching a man to be aggressive against another man? Any how does it justify using that aggression for the ends that it has? I think the values of football as it is now played reflect a segment of thought, a particular kind of thought that is pretty prevalent in our society. The way to do anything in the world, the way to get ahead, is to aggress against somebody, compete against somebody, try to dominate, try to overcome, work your way up the ladder, and in doing so, you have to judge yourself and be judged as what you want to be in relation to somebody else all the time. Given the influence football has on young children, the immense influence it has as a socializing force in society, its impact should be rigorously examined. People learn certain values from watching football, from watching aggression, from watching it performed violently and knowing that these guys are going to get a big chunk of money if they do it well often enough.[6]

The two sports require different mentalities of their athletes. Football players must be aggressive while that is not a necessary ingredient for the baseball player. Also, baseball is a game of repetition and predictable action that is played over a 162-game schedule. The players must stay relaxed and not get too excited because to do so for every game would be too physically and emotionally draining over the six months of the season. Moreover, because the season is so long, players must pace themselves and not let a loss or even a succession of losses get them down. In football, though, losing is intolerable because of the short season (sixteen games). Thus, football players must play each game with extreme intensity. As a result the incidence of taking amphetamines ("uppers") has been much greater among football players than among baseball players. The intensity that characterizes football resembles the tensions and pressures of modern society, contrasted with the more relaxed pace of agrarian life and baseball.

One of the more interesting contrasts between these two sports is the equality of opportunity each offers. Baseball promotes equality while football is essentially unequal. This difference occurs in several ways. First, football originated among college elites and even today requires attending college to play at the professional level. Baseball has never been closely identified with college. Essentially, the way to make it in baseball is to work one's way through the minor leagues rather than by attending college (although that is one route).

A second way that baseball is more egalitarian than football is that it can be played by people of all sizes.

There have been small All Star players such as Phil Rizzuto, Bobby Shantz, Pee Wee Reese, Joe Morgan, and Freddie Patek. Football, however, is a big man's game. In football the good, big team defeats the good, small team, whereas in baseball, the good, small team has an equal chance of beating the good, big team.

Baseball is also more equal than football because everyone has the opportunity to be a star. Each position has its stars. Pay is divided about equally by position. Except for designated hitters, all players must play both offense and defense. Thus, each player has the chance to make an outstanding defensive play or to bat in the winning run. Stardom in football is essentially reserved for those who play at certain positions. Only backs, receivers, and kickers score points while others labor in relative obscurity, making it possible for the "glamor boys" to score. This is similar, by the way, to American society, where the richest "players" score all the points, call the plays, and get the glory at the expense of the commoners. There is also a wide variance in pay by position in football. In 1977 the average NFL quarterback received $89,354 while the average defensive back received $47,403.

A final contrast on this equality dimension has to do with the availability of each of the sports to the masses. The average ticket price for major league baseball in 1978 was $3.98 compared to $9.67 for professional football.[7] The cheaper tickets for baseball allow families to attend and provide live entertainment for members of all social classes. Football, however, excludes families (except for the rich) and members of the lower classes because of the high prices and the necessity of purchasing season tickets.

Another major dimension on which these two sports differ is individualism. Baseball is highly individualistic. Elaborate teamwork is not required except for double plays and defensive sacrifice bunts. Each player struggles to succeed on his own. As Cavanaugh has characterized it:

> Although there are teams in baseball, there is little teamwork. The essence of the game is the individual with or against the ball: pitcher controlling, batter hitting, fielder handling, runner racing the ball. All players are on their own, struggling (like the farmer) to overcome not another human being but nature (the ball). This individualism is demonstrated when the shortstop, cleanly fielding the ball, receives credit for a "chance" even if the first baseman drops the thrown ball. It is demonstrated when a last-place team includes a Cy Young Award-winning pitcher or a league-leading hitter. It is perhaps most clearly manifest in the pitcher-batter duel, the heart of the game, when two men face each other. Baseball is each man doing the best he can for himself and against nature within a loose confederation of fellow individualists he may or may not ad-

mire and respect. This reflects a society in which individual effort, drive, and success are esteemed and in which, conversely, failure is deemed the individual's responsibility.[8]

Football, in sharp contrast, is the quintessence of team sports. Every move is planned and practiced in advance. The players in each of the eleven positions have a specific task to perform on every play. Every player is a specialist who must coordinate his actions with the other specialists on the team. So important is each person's play to the whole, that games are filmed and reviewed, with each play then broken down into its components and each player graded. Each player must subordinate his personality for the sake of the team. The coach is typically a stern taskmaster demanding submission of self to the team. The similarity of the football player to the organization man is obvious. So, too, is the parallel between football and the factory or corporation, where intricate and precise movements of all members doing different tasks are required for the attainment of the organization's objective.

## Conclusion

Sociologist David Riesman in his classic book, *The Lonely Crowd,* noted a shift in American character since World War II.[9] Prior to that war Americans were what Riesman called "inner directed," which fit the demands of an essentially agrarian society. The farmer and the small entrepreneur succeeded on their own merits and efforts. "Rugged individualism" was the necessary ingredient for success. There was the firm belief that everyone was a potential success.

But since the war the United States and Americans have changed. Rural life is replaced by living in cities and suburbs. Individuals now typically are dominated by large bureaucracies, whether they be governments, schools, churches, or factories. In these settings Riesman noted that Americans have become "other directed." Rather than an "automatic pilot" homing the inner-directed person toward his individual goal, the other-directed person has an "antenna" tuned to the values and opinions of others. In short he is a team player and conformist.

Baseball, then, represents what we were—an inner-directed, rural-individualistic society. It continues to be popular because of our longing for the peaceful past. Football, on the other hand, is popular now because it symbolizes what we now are—an other-directed, urban-technical-corporate-bureaucratic society. Thus these two sports represent cultural contrasts (country vs. city, stability vs. change, harmony vs. conflict, calm vs. intensity, and equality vs. inequality). Each sport contains a fundamental myth that it elaborates for its fans. Baseball represents an island of stability in a confused and confusing world. As such, it provides an antidote for a world of too much action, struggle, pressure, and change. Baseball provides this antidote by being individualistic, unbounded by time, nonviolent, leisurely in pace, and by perpetuating the American myths of equal opportunity, egalitarianism, and potential championship for everyone.

Football represents what we are. Our society is violent. It is highly technical. It is highly bureaucratized, and we are all caught in its impersonal clutches. Football fits contemporary urban-corporate society because it is team-oriented, dominated by the clock, aggressive, characterized by bursts of energy, highly technical, and because it disproportionately rewards individuals at certain positions.

The uniquely American sports of football and baseball, although they represent opposites, provide us with insight about ourselves and our society. What will become of these sports as society changes? Will we continue to find football and baseball so intriguing as society becomes more structured? We know that in the future American society will be short of resources. We know that its citizenry will be older and more educated than at present. We also know that society will become more urban. What will these and other trends mean for society and for sport? One thing is certain—as society changes, so, too, will its sports. Does this mean that baseball and football will change? Will another sport emerge that is more attuned with the culture and structure of society? Or will baseball become even more popular as we become more nostalgic for the peaceful, pastoral past?

## QUESTIONS

1. In what ways are the values of sport—such as competition, winning, perseverance—reflected in other institutions, such as politics, education, or the economy?

2. Can you identify some respects, in addition to those listed in the article, in which American sport reflects characteristics of the society?

3. Can you think of any characteristic differences between American sport and the sports of any other society? Are these differences sociologically significant?

## NOTES

1. D. Stanley Eitzen and George H. Sage, *Sociology of American Sport* (Dubuque, Iowa: Wm. C. Brown, 1978), pp. 68–69.

2. George B. Leonard, "Winning Isn't Everything: It's Nothing." *Intellectual Digest,* 4 (October, 1973), p. 45.

3. Several sources are especially important for the material that follows: Gerald J. Cavanaugh, "Baseball, Football, Images," *New York Times* (October 3, 1976), p. 28; George Carlin, "Baseball-Football," *An Evening with Wally Londo* (Los Angeles: Little David Records, 1975); Leonard Koppett, "Differing Creeds in Baseball, Football," *Sporting News* (September 6, 1975), pp. 4 and 6; Murray Ross, "Football Red and Baseball Green," *Chicago Review* (January/February 1971), pp. 30–40; Richard Conway, "Baseball: A Discipline that Measures America's Way of Life," *Rocky Mountain News Trend* (October 19, 1975), p. 1; "Behind Baseball's Comeback: It's An Island of Stability," *U.S. News & World Report* (September 19, 1977), pp. 56–57; William Arens, "The Great American Football Ritual," *Natural History,* 84 (October, 1975), pp. 72–80; Susan P. Montague and Robert Morais, "Football Games and Rock Concerts: The Ritual Enactment of American Success Models," *The American Dimension: Cultural Myths and Realities,* William Arens (ed.) (Port Washington, New York: Alfred, 1976), pp. 33–52; and R. C. Crepeau, "Punt or Bunt: A Note in American Culture." *Journal of Sport History,* 3 (Winter 1976), pp. 205–212.

4. Cf. D. Stanley Eitzen, "Sport and Deviance."

5. Crepeau, "Punt or Bunt," p. 211.

6. Quoted in Jack Scott, "The Souring of George Sauer," *Intellectual Digest,* 2 (December 1971), pp. 52–55.

7. Tim Fedele, *Left Field,* 1 (April 1978), p. 1.

8. Cavanaugh, "Baseball, Football, Images," p. 25S.

9. David Riesman, *The Lonely Crowd* (New Haven: Yale University Press, 1950). The analysis that follows is largely dependent on Crepeau, "Punt or Bunt," pp. 205–212.

*Elin McCoy*

# 9. Childhood Through the Ages

*We generally think of the human life course as a series of stages, such as infancy, childhood, adolescence, adulthood, and old age. These stages seem at first sight to be purely a matter of biology, with each stage succeeding its predecessor as a natural part of the aging process. Yet the life course is actually as much a social as a biological phenomenon, for its "stages," content, and length are shaped by social factors. In some societies, for example, average life expectancy is around fifty; in others, it is seventy-five. Similarly, in some societies, children and old people may be expected to work; in others, it may even be considered inappropriate—and even illegal—for them to do so. And some societies have "stages" in the life course that other societies do not even recognize.*

*In advanced industrial societies children are highly valued. It may come as a surprise, therefore, to learn that our concepts of childhood and adolescence as distinct stages of life hardly existed in some societies in the past. The idea of the child as a special and vulnerable being, uniquely worthy of love and attention, is actually quite rare in human history. Indeed, child labor—in which boys and girls as young as thirteen worked in factories and mines—was common in the United States around the turn of the present century. The status and treatment of children are strongly influenced by the time and place in which they live.*

*In this article, Elin McCoy traces some social and historical changes in the meaning and experience of childhood.*

From *Parents*, January 1981, pp. 60–65. Reprinted by permission of Elin McCoy and her agents, Raines & Raines, 71 Park Avenue, New York, N.Y. 10016. Copyright © 1981 Elin McCoy.

A gentleman-in-waiting and the nurse of little Comte de Marle often amused themselves tossing the swaddled infant back and forth across the sill of an open window. One day one of them failed to catch him, and the infant landed on a stone step and died.

The surgeon of the newborn Louis XIII cut the "fiber" under his tongue a few days after he was born, believing that if it remained uncut, Louis would be unable to suck properly and would eventually stutter.

These aren't atypical examples of child rearing in the past. Recent historical research indicates that for most of the past 2,500 years, childhood was a brief, grim period in most people's lives, especially when judged against contemporary views of child rearing.

## A New Field—Family History

Through a new field of historical research, known as family history, we now know that family life and childhood in the previous centuries were startlingly different from what most people, including historians, had imagined them to be. Scores of historians are currently probing such questions as: How were children treated in the past? What concept of childhood did people have in different centuries? How important were children to their parents? Is there such a thing as "instinctual" parental behavior? What do the prevailing child-rearing beliefs and practices of the past tell us about the political, social, and psychological ideals of society? And what kind of adults resulted from such child-rearing practices?

"Family history is the most explosive field of history today," says Professor Lawrence Stone—director of Princeton University's Shelby Cullom Davis Center for Historical Studies—whose 1977 book, *The Family, Sex and Marriage in England 1500–1800*, came out in an abridged paperback last year. "In the 1930s only about 10 scholarly books and articles on the family and childhood in history were published each year, but incredibly, between 1971 and 1976 over 900 important books and articles were published on that subject, just covering

America, England, and France." Two scholarly journals devoted to the subject were also started in the 1970s.

Why, suddenly, have so many historians focused on the family? "A whole series of contemporary anxieties has contributed to this new interest," explains Professor Stone. "General anxiety about the state of the family and whether it's breaking down, concern about the rising divorce rate, anxieties about current permissiveness in raising children, and concern about what effects women's liberation will have on children, the family, and society. And underlying all of these anxieties are two questions: Are we really doing so badly? Was it better in the past?"

In addition, two other trends in historical research have focused attention on childhood and the family. The first is social historians' growing interest in the daily lives of ordinary people in history, which has meant a greater concern with children, parenting, marriage, disease, death, and aging. The second is historians' recent efforts to employ psychological concepts as a research tool in order to understand human motivations and experiences in the past.

Although all family historians agree that child-rearing patterns influence what happens in history, they disagree about how much and in what precise ways the treatment of children shapes history. Some researchers in the field, like Lloyd deMause, founder of *The Journal of Psychohistory: A Quarterly Journal of Childhood and Psychohistory,* go so far as to say that, in deMause's words, "child-rearing practices have been *the* central force for change in history." Along with some other psychohistorians, deMause believes that "if you want to understand the causes of historical events like the growth of Nazism, you have to look at how the children who became Nazis as adults were treated as children." But many scholars have reservations about attributing the character of a society solely to the relations between parents and children, pointing out that these relations must be understood in the context of the society as a whole and that such factors as economics must also be taken into account.

## Surprising Discoveries

Family historians have recently exploded many long-standing myths about childhood and the nature of the family throughout history. It's now clear that the functions and structure of the family have changed continuously over the years and that a variety of family types coexisted in each historical period in different regions and classes. Scholars have found, surprisingly, that the prevailing family mode in America today (the small nuclear family of parents and children living apart from other relatives)—a structure that is under much attack—

is not as new to our culture as they had previously thought. Even as long ago as thirteenth-century England, as many as half of all families consisted of only a mother and/or father and two to three children. In fact, the large loving extended families we tend to picture, with eight to ten children and several generations of relatives living under the same roof, were more the exception than the rule, even in Colonial America.

According to Professor Tamara Hareven—founder and head of the first History of the Family program in the country, at Clark University in Worcester, Massachusetts, and founding editor of the *Journal of Family History*—one of the great surprises for today's historians was "finding out that in the past, the concept of childhood and children was not the same in all centuries, classes, and countries. While the middle classes were 'discovering' childhood and becoming interested in children," she explains, "the working classes still regarded children as small adults with the same responsibilities. And in the past, childhood as we know it lasted for a much shorter time." In medieval England, for example, children as young as seven were sent to live in other households as apprentices, and for peasant children, childhood was even briefer—they joined their parents to work in the fields as soon as they could.

Infants were regarded in medieval times as unimportant, unformed animals, in the sixteenth century as "exasperating parasites," and even as late as the seventeenth century they were not seen as individuals with their own identities. Children were considered interchangeable, and frequently were given the same name as an older sibling who had died. Small children were not even viewed as interesting; Montaigne, the French essayist, summed up the prevailing attitudes of a few hundred years ago when he dismissed infants as having "neither movement in the soul, nor recognizable form in the body by which they could render themselves lovable."

Scholars tell us that infants and small children were important only insofar as they could benefit their parents. Considered possessions with no individual rights, they were used to further adult aims, and they ended up as security for debts, as ways of increasing property holdings through arranged marriages, as political hostages, and even as slaves sold for profit.

## Infancy in the Past

Throughout history, parents' treatment of infants and very small children has been characterized by psychological coldness and physical brutality that horrify most of us today. But this behavior becomes at least comprehensible when we realize some of the conditions of people's lives. The physical realities of life were oppressive.

And there were severe parental limitations as well: in addition to being influenced by unscientific medical knowledge and religious views about the nature of man, most adults had to concentrate so much of their energy on mere survival that they had little time to care for or worry about infants and small children. Abusive and violent behavior was common among adults and, therefore, not looked on with disapproval when it appeared in the treatment of children.

In view of the following facts, consider what your experience as a parent and your child's experience as an infant would have been if you had lived prior to the eighteenth century.

*Your child probably wouldn't have been wanted.* Lack of birth control meant that having children was not a choice. For poverty-stricken peasants, an infant meant another mouth to feed—and food was precious—as well as interference with the mother's role as a worker whose contribution was necessary to the family's ability to survive. In all classes, the high risk of maternal mortality made the birth of a child a traumatic event. Even in the relatively healthy conditions enjoyed by the inhabitants of Plymouth Colony, 20 percent of women died from causes related to childbirth (compared with under 1 percent today), and in seventeenth-century England and France, the rates were much higher. It's no wonder that most children were probably unwanted. In fact, Professor Stone suggests that the availability of birth control was probably one of the necessary conditions for the increase in affection for children that began in England and America in the eighteenth century.

*Your infant would have had a good chance of dying before his or her first birthday.* In medieval England and seventeenth-century France, for example, between 20 and 50 percent of all infants died within the first year after birth. Complications of childbirth, prematurity, diseases such as smallpox and the plague, and generally unsanitary living conditions, as well as such customs as baptism in icy water in freezing churches, took a heavy toll among vulnerable newborns. America was healthier for infants—in Plymouth Colony, infant mortality was only 10 to 15 percent (which is still ten times higher than it is in America today). The likelihood that one's infants would die discouraged parents from investing much affection or interest in them and from regarding them as special, unique individuals until it appeared more certain that they might live to adulthood.

Illegitimate infants and infants of poverty-stricken parents (and parents who felt they already had enough children) were often the victims of infanticide through deliberate murder, abandonment, or neglect. In ancient Greece, for example, infants who seemed sickly or didn't have a perfect shape or cried too much or too little were "exposed," or abandoned to die, a decision that was made by the father shortly after birth. In mid-eighteenth-century England, so many babies—both legitimate and illegitimate—were abandoned to die in the streets of cities and towns that the first foundling home established in London received several thousand babies a year. In early America, infanticide seems to have affected only illegitimate children.

*If you were well-off, your baby probably would have been breast-fed by someone else.* In spite of the fact that all medical advice since Roman times had stressed that babies breast-fed by their own mothers had a better chance of survival, for eighteen centuries any woman who could afford it sent her infant to a wet nurse.

Recuperation from a difficult childbirth prevented some women from breast-feeding, but many others thought it too demanding, especially since it was customary for infants to breast-feed for as long as two years. Also, many husbands would not allow their wives to breast-feed, partly because medical opinion held that women who were breast-feeding should not engage in sexual intercourse.

Underlying these reasons may have been parents' desire to distance themselves emotionally from their infants.

In Renaissance Italy, middle-class infants were delivered to the *bália*, or wet nurse, immediately after baptism—two or three days after birth—and, if they survived, remained there for two years. Rarely did mothers visit their infants, and thus a baby was returned home at the end of that time to a stranger.

Although some wet nurses moved in with the family, most women left their babies at the wet nurse's home, where the child was often neglected and starved because wet nurses commonly took on too many babies in order to make more money. Frequently wet nurses ran out of milk, and infants had to be sent to a series of different nurses and thus were deprived even of a single surrogate mother.

The first groups of middle-class women to change this 1,800-year-old pattern on a large scale were the Puritans in the seventeenth century. Eventually, in the eighteenth century, there was a widespread cult of maternal breast-feeding in both America and England. Scholars have suggested that this shift may have contributed substantially to the shift in parental feelings for infants that began in the eighteenth century; certainly it reduced infant mortality.

*Your infant would have spent little time with you.* In the past, parents spent much less time with their children than even working parents do today and clearly did not feel the need to arrange supervision for them. Peasant women commonly left their infants and toddlers alone all day at home while they worked elsewhere. In one area of England during the thirteenth century, for example, half the infant deaths involved infants in cradles being burned while no one was home. Unsupervised toddlers frequently wandered off and drowned. In the middle and upper classes, parental neglect took the form of turning toddlers over to the servants to raise.

*Your infant would have been swaddled in tightly bound cloths from birth to as old as eight months.* Emotional distancing, economic necessity, and faulty medical knowledge are also evident in another common practice—swaddling. In England this practice continued up to the eighteenth century; in France, the nineteenth century; and in Russia, into the twentieth century. Kept in tightly bound bandages, swaddled infants were totally isolated from their surroundings for the first four months or so. After that, only their legs were bound. They couldn't turn their heads, suck their own thumbs for comfort, or crawl. Swaddling that was too tight occasionally caused suffocation. Although doctors advocated changing the infant two or three times a day, this apparently was uncommon, and even Louis XIII developed severe rashes because of his swaddling bands.

Medical reasons for the practice included the beliefs that if free, the infant might tear off his ears or scratch out his eyes, that swaddling was necessary to keep infants warm in cold, draughty cottages, houses, and castles, and that it ensured that the infant's pliable limbs would grow straight so he would be able to stand erect. Even when the swaddling bands were removed from their legs, children were not allowed to crawl "like an animal," but were forced to stand with the help of bizarre contraptions. Convenience was another reason for swaddling: it caused infants to sleep more and cry less, so they could be left for long periods of time while mothers worked. Also, swaddled infants were easier to carry and could even be hung on a peg on the wall out of the way.

*Your infant or child would probably have received harsh beatings regularly—from you or a servant—even for such "normal" behavior as crying or wanting to play.* For many centuries, discipline and teaching of the infant and young child concentrated on "breaking the child's will," which meant crushing all assertiveness and instilling complete obedience. This was accomplished through physical and psychological maltreatment that today we would consider "child abuse." Susanna Wesley, mother of John Wesley, the founder of the Methodist Church, records her treatment of her children: "When turned a year old, and some before, they were taught to fear the rod and cry softly." Louis XIII was whipped every morning, starting at the age of two, simply for being "obstinate," and was even whipped on the day of his coronation at the age of nine. The Puritans believed that "the newborn babe is full of the stains and pollutions of sin" and saw the first strivings of a one- and two-year-old to independence—which we now recognize as es-

sential to a child's growing mastery of himself and understanding of the world—as a clear manifestation of that original sin. It was considered the duty of parents to use physical harshness and psychological terrorization—locking children in dark closets for an entire day or frightening them with tales of death and hellfire, for example—to wipe this sin out.

These child-rearing practices, as well as the difficult realities of life in the past, had important psychological effects on children's development. According to Professor Stone, the isolation, sensory deprivation, and lack of physical closeness that resulted from swaddling; the absence of a mother because of death in childbirth or the practice of wet-nursing; the common experience for small children of losing parents and siblings; and the suppression of self-assertion through whipping and other fear-producing techniques all resulted in an "adult world of emotional cripples."

## A Change for the Better

In the late seventeenth and eighteenth centuries, many of these child-rearing practices began to change among wealthy merchants and other groups in the upper middle classes of England and America. Some changes can be traced to the Puritans, who, even though they advocated harsh disciplinary measures, focused a new attention on children and the importance of their upbringing. By the late eighteenth century, among some groups, methods of contraception were available, swaddling had been abandoned, maternal breast-feeding had become the fashion, and "breaking the will" had given way to affection and a degree of permissiveness that seems extraordinary even by today's standards. In England the indulgent Lord Holland, for example, intent on gratifying his little son Charles's every whim, allowed him to jump and splash in the large bowl of cream intended for dessert at a grand dinner while the guests, a group of foreign ministers, looked on. Many adults feared the effect on society when these spoiled children reached maturity. And in fact, many of them did spend their lives in lifelong dissipation and often became followers of evangelical religions. While the Victorian era varied from harsh to permissive in the treatment of children, by the end of the nineteenth century the child-oriented family became a reality for all classes in Western society.

## What It All Means for Us

Were childhood and family life better in the past? The answer—obviously—is a resounding no. One is tempted to agree with Lloyd deMause that "the history of childhood is a nightmare from which we have only recently begun to awaken."

Nevertheless, Professor Hareven feels that there *were* some good aspects to childhood in the past, which we can learn from today. "Children were not so segregated from adults and responsibility," she points out. "The historical record shows children grew up in households that included servants, other workers employed by the family, lodgers, visiting relatives, and siblings of widely differing ages, as well as parents. They were exposed to a greater variety of adult roles than children usually are today and they interacted with a greater variety of people of all ages. They also knew more about their parents' work. And unlike today, children were working, contributing members of families and the society from an early age—as they are in contemporary China. Today's child-oriented family and the postponement of responsibility and work limit children's experience. The models are there in history for us to borrow and shape to today's ideals."

Historical research on childhood helps us view our own ideas about parenthood from a perspective in which it is clear that there are no absolutes. The new facts that are available to us show that assumptions behind child rearing change and that what we think of as parents' "instincts" actually depend on the beliefs and experiences of their society. The possessiveness and affection toward infants, which we take for granted, is a recent development. Even the "maternal instinct" to breastfeed one's own child was not instinctive for many women for over 1,800 years.

Family history also gives us an informative view of family structure. Those who are worried about the high divorce rate and the effect of parental separation on children, for example, should realize that in the past, approximately the same percentage of families were separated—only it was by the death of one of the parents instead of divorce.

Although problems with child rearing will probably always be with us, the very existence of family history means that we have come to the point where we are much more self-conscious about how we raise children, and, in turn, this may help us to be more thoughtful about the way we treat them. By examining childhood in the past, we become aware that our own attempts to do things differently—"nonsexist" child rearing, co-parenting, and different mixes of permissiveness and discipline—may have profound effects on society. If we can avoid the mistakes of the past, borrow what was good, and continue to examine our own aims and practices, the society our children make may be a better one than ours.

## QUESTIONS

1. Suggest some social factors that could influence the nature and experience of childhood.

2. "Adolescence" was not recognized as part of the life cycle until about a century ago. Why do you think this was the case?

3. Why are advanced industrial societies so relatively child-centered?

E. Richard Sorenson

# 10. Growing Up as a Fore

*To survive, every society must reproduce itself—not only biologically, but also socially. In other words, a society must socialize its young in such a way that they can effectively play the appropriate roles later in life. The content of the socialization process therefore differs greatly from one society to another, for each has a different way of life and its children must learn the behaviors, thoughts, and feelings that are expected, useful, and rewarding in a unique culture.*

*In modern industrialized societies, socialization occurs not only in the family but in such formal contexts as the school. In traditional, preindustrial societies, on the other hand, there is little or no formal schooling, and children are socialized informally in the course of routine interaction in the family and the community. Over the course of history, these societies typically changed rather slowly, and so the socialization process was much the same from generation to generation. But today even the most remote traditional peoples are exposed to modern technologies and ideas. The result is often devastating, for the younger generation finds itself on the brink of a world quite different from the one that previous generations have inhabited.*

*In this article, E. Richard Sorenson describes the socialization process in a traditional society, the Fore of New Guinea, and shows how that process has been affected by contact with the outside world.*

From *Smithsonian*, May 1977. Copyright 1977 Smithsonian Institution. Reprinted by permission.

Untouched by the outside world, they had lived for thousands of years in isolated mountains and valleys deep in the interior of Papua New Guinea. They had no cloth, no metal, no money, no idea that their homeland was an island—or that what surrounded it was salt water. Yet the Fore (for'ay) people had developed remarkable and sophisticated approaches to human relations, and their child-rearing practices gave their young unusual freedom to explore. Successful as hunter-gatherers and as subsistence gardeners, they also had great adaptability, which brought rapid accommodation with the outside world after their lands were opened up.

It was alone that I first visited the Fore in 1963—a day's walk from a recently built airstrip. I stayed six months. Perplexed and fascinated, I returned six times in the next ten years, eventually spending a year and a half living with them in their hamlets.

Theirs was a way of life different from anything I had seen or heard about before. There were no chiefs, patriarchs, priests, medicine men or the like. A striking personal freedom was enjoyed even by the very young, who could move about at will and be where or with whom they liked. Infants rarely cried, and they played confidently with knives, axes, and fire. Conflict between old and young did not arise; there was no "generation gap."

Older children enjoyed deferring to the interests and desires of the younger, and sibling rivalry was virtually undetectable. A responsive sixth sense seemed to attune the Fore hamlet mates to each other's interests and needs. They did not have to directly ask, inveigle, bargain or speak out for what they needed or wanted. Subtle, even fleeting expressions of interest, desire, and discomfort were quickly read and helpfully acted on by one's associates. This spontaneous urge to share food, affection, work, trust, tools and pleasure was the social cement that held the Fore hamlets together. It was a pleasant way of life, for one could always be with those with whom one got along well.

Ranging and planting, sharing and living, the Fore

diverged and expanded through high virgin lands in a pioneer region. They hunted out their gardens, tilled them while they lasted, then hunted again. Moving ever away from lands peopled and used they had a self-contained life with its own special ways.

The underlying ecological conditions were like those that must have encompassed the world before agriculture set its imprint so broadly. Abutting the Fore was virtually unlimited virgin land, and they had food plants they could introduce into it. Like hunter-gatherers they sought their sources of sustenance first in one locale and then another, across an extended range, following opportunities provided by a providential nature. But like agriculturalists they concentrated their effort and attention more narrowly on selected sites of production, on their gardens. They were both seekers and producers. A pioneer people in a pioneer land, they ranged freely into a vast territory, but they planted to live.

Cooperative groups formed hamlets and gardened together. When the fertility of a garden declined, they abandoned it. Grass sprung up to cover these abandoned sites of earlier cultivation, and, as the Fore moved on to other parts of the forest, they left uninhabited grasslands to mark their passage.

The traditional hamlets were small, with a rather fluid system of social relations. A single large men's house provided shelter for 10 to 20 men and boys and their visiting friends. The several small women's houses each normally sheltered two married women, their unmarried daughters and their sons up to about six years of age. Formal kinship bonds were less important than friendship was. Fraternal "gangs" of youths formed the hamlets; their "clubhouses" were the men's houses.

During the day the gardens became the center of life. Hamlets were virtually deserted as friends, relatives and children went to one or more garden plots to mingle their social, economic and erotic pursuits in a pleasant and emotionally filled Gestalt of garden life. The boys and unmarried youths preferred to explore and hunt in the outlying lands, but they also passed through and tarried in the gardens.

Daily activities were not scheduled. No one made demands, and the land was bountiful. Not surprisingly the line between work and play was never clear. The transmission of the Fore behavioral pattern to the young began in early infancy during a period of unceasing human physical contact. The effect of being constantly "in touch" with hamlet mates and their daily life seemed to start a process which proceeded by degrees: close rapport, involvement in regular activity, ability to handle seemingly dangerous implements safely, and responsible freedom to pursue individual interests at will without danger.

While very young, infants remained in almost continuous bodily contact with their mother, her house mates or her gardening associates. At first, mothers' laps were the center of activity, and infants occupied themselves there by nursing, sleeping and playing with their own bodies or those of their caretakers. They were not put aside for the sake of other activities, as when food was being prepared or heavy loads were being carried. Remaining in close, uninterrupted physical contact with those around them, their basic needs such as rest, nourishment, stimulation and security were continuously satisfied without obstacle.

By being physically in touch from their earliest days, Fore youngsters learned to communicate needs, desires and feelings through a body language of touch and response that developed before speech. This opened the door to a much closer rapport with those around them than otherwise would have been possible, and led ultimately to the Fore brand of social cement and the sixth sense that bound groups together through spontaneous, responsive sharing.

As the infant's awareness increased, his interests broadened to the things his mother and other caretakers did and to the objects and materials they used. Then these youngsters began crawling out to explore things that attracted their attention. By the time they were toddling, their interests continually took them on short sorties to nearby objects and persons. As soon as they could walk well, the excursions extended to the entire hamlet and its gardens, and then beyond with other children. Developing without interference or supervision, this personal exploratory learning quest freely touched on whatever was around, even axes, knives, machetes, fire, and the like. When I first went to the Fore, I was aghast.

Eventually I discovered that this capability emerged naturally from Fore infant-handling practices in their milieu of close human physical proximity and tactile interaction. Because touch and bodily contact lend themselves naturally to satisfying the basic needs of young children, an early kind of communicative experience fostered cooperative interaction between infants and their caretakers, also kinesthetic contact with the activities at hand. This made it easy for them to learn the appropriate handling of the tools of life.

The early pattern of exploratory activity included frequent return to one of the "mothers." Serving as home base, the bastion of security, a woman might occasionally give the youngster a nod of encouragement, if he glanced in her direction with uncertainty. Yet rarely did the women attempt to control or direct, nor did they participate in the child's quests or jaunts.

As a result Fore children did not have to adjust to rule and schedule in order to find their place in life. They could pursue their interests and whims wherever they might lead and still be part of a richly responsive world of human touch which constantly provided sustenance, comfort, diversion and security.

Learning proceeded during the course of pursuing interests and exploring. Constantly "in touch" with people who were busy with daily activities, the Fore young quickly learned the skills of life from example. Muscle tone, movement and mood were components of this learning process; formal lessons and commands were not. Kinesthetic skills developed so quickly that infants were able to casually handle knives and similar objects before they could walk.

Even after several visits I continued to be surprised that the unsupervised Fore toddlers did not recklessly thrust themselves into unappreciated dangers, the way our own children tend to do. But then, why should they? From their earliest days, they enjoyed a benevolent sanctuary from which the world could be confidently viewed, tested and appreciated. This sanctuary remained ever available, but did not demand, restrain or impose. One could go and come at will.

In close harmony with their source of life, the Fore young were able confidently, not furtively, to extend their inquiry. They could widen their understanding as they chose. There was no need to play tricks or deceive in order to pursue life.

Emerging from this early childhood was a freely ranging young child rather in tune with his older and younger hamlet mates, disinclined to act out impulsively, and with a capable appreciation of the properties of potentially dangerous objects. Such children could be permitted to move out on their own, unsupervised and unrestricted. They were safe.

Such a pattern could persist indefinitely, re-creating itself in each new generation. However, hidden within the receptive character it produced was an Achilles heel; it also permitted adoption of new practices, including child-handling practices, which did *not* act to perpetuate the pattern. In only one generation after Western contact, the cycle of Fore life was broken.

Attuned as they were to individual pursuit of economic and social good, it did not take the Fore long to recognize the value of the new materials, practices and ideas that began to flow in. Indeed, change began almost immediately with efforts to obtain steel axes, salt, medicine and cloth. The Fore were quick to shed indigenous practices in favor of Western example. They rapidly altered their ways to adapt to Western law, government, religion, materials and trade.

Sometimes change was so rapid that many people seemed to be afflicted by a kind of cultural shock. An anomie, even cultural amnesia, seemed to pervade some hamlets for a time. There were individuals who appeared temporarily to have lost memory of recent past events. Some Fore even forgot what type and style of traditional garments they had worn only a few years earlier, or that they had used stone axes and had eaten their dead close relatives.

Remarkably open-minded, the Fore so readily accepted reformulation of identity and practice that suggestion or example by the new government officers, missionaries and scientists could alter tribal affiliation, place names, conduct and hamlet style. When the first Australian patrol officer began to map the region in 1957, an error in communication led him to refer to these people as the "Fore." Actually they had had no name for themselves and the word, Fore, was their name for a quite different group, the Awa, who spoke another language and lived in another valley. They did not correct the patrol officer but adopted his usage. They all now refer to themselves as the Fore. Regional and even personal names changed just as readily.

More than anything else, it was the completion of a steep, rough, always muddy Jeep road into the Fore lands that undermined the traditional life. Almost overnight their isolated region was opened. Hamlets began to move down from their ridgetop sites in order to be nearer the road, consolidating with others.

The power of the road is hard to overestimate. It was a great artery where only restricted capillaries had existed before. And down this artery came a flood of new goods, new ideas and new people. This new road, often impassable even with four-wheel-drive vehicles, was perhaps the single most dramatic stroke wrought by the government. It was to the Fore an opening to a new world. As they began to use the road, they started to shed traditions evolved in the protective insularity of their mountain fastness, to adopt in their stead an emerging market culture.

## The Coming of the Coffee Economy

"Walkabout," nonexistent as an institution before contact, quickly became an accepted way of life. Fore boys began to roam hundreds of miles from their homeland in the quest for new experience, trade goods, jobs and money. Like the classic practice of the Australian aborigine, this "walkabout" took one away from his home for periods of varying length. But unlike the Australian practice, it usually took the boys to jobs and schools rather than to a solitary life in traditional lands. Obviously it sprang from the earlier pattern of individual freedom to pursue personal interests and opportunity wherever it might lead. It was a new expression of the old Fore exploratory pattern.

Some boys did not roam far, whereas others found ways to go to distant cities. The roaming boys often sought places where they might be welcomed as visitors, workers or students for a while. Mission stations and schools, plantation work camps, and the servants' quarters of the European population became waystations in the lives of the modernizing Fore boys.

Some took jobs on coffee plantations. Impressed by the care and attention lavished on coffee by European planters and by the money they saw paid to coffee growers, these young Fore workers returned home with coffee beans to plant.

Coffee grew well on the Fore hillsides, and in the mid-1960s, when the first sizable crop matured, Fore who previously had felt lucky to earn a few dollars found themselves able to earn a few hundred dollars. A rush to coffee ensued, and when the new gardens became productive a few years later, the Fore income from coffee jumped to a quarter of a million dollars a year. The coffee revolution was established.

At first the coffee was carried on the backs of its growers (sometimes for several days) over steep, rough mountain trails to a place where it could be sold to a buyer with a jeep. However, as more and more coffee was produced, the villagers began to turn with efforts to planning and constructing roads in association with neighboring villages. The newly built roads, in turn, stimulated further economic development and the opening of new trade stores throughout the region.

Following European example, the segregated collective men's and women's houses were abandoned. Family houses were adopted. This changed the social and territorial arena for all the young children, who hitherto had been accustomed to living equally with many members of their hamlet. It gave them a narrower place to belong, and it made them more distinctly someone's children. Uncomfortable in the family houses, boys who had grown up in a freer territory began to gather in "boys' houses," away from the adult men who were now beginning to live in family houses with their wives. Mothers began to wear blouses, altering the early freer access to the breast. Episodes of infant and child frustration, not seen in traditional Fore hamlets, began to take place along with repeated incidents of anger, withdrawal, aggressiveness and stinginess.

So Western technology worked its magic on the Fore, its powerful materials and practices quickly shattering their isolated autonomy and lifestyle. It took only a few years from the time Western intruders built their first grass-thatched patrol station before the Fore way of life they found was gone.

Fortunately, enough of the Fore traditional ways were systematically documented on film to reveal how unique a flower of human creation they were. Like nothing else, film made it possible to see the behavioral patterns of this way of life. The visual record, once made, captured data which was unnoticed and unanticipated at the time of filming and which was simply impossible to study without such records. Difficult-to-spot subtle patterns and fleeting nuances of manner, mood and human relations emerged by use of repeated reexamination of related incidents, sometimes by slow motion and stopped frame. Eventually the characteristic behavioral patterns of Fore life became clear, and an important aspect of human adaptive creation was revealed.

The Fore way of life was only one of the many natural experiments in living that have come into being through thousands of years of independent development in the world. The Fore way is now gone; those which remain are threatened. Under the impact of modern technology and commerce, the entire world is now rapidly becoming one system. By the year 2000 all the independent natural experiments that have come into being during the world's history will be merging into a single world system.

One of the great tragedies of our modern time may be that most of these independent experiments in living are disappearing before we can discover the implication of their special expressions of human possibility. Ironically, the same technology responsible for the worldwide cultural convergence has also provided the means by which we may capture detailed visual records of the yet remaining independent cultures. The question is whether we will be able to seize this never-to-be repeated opportunity. Soon it will be too late. Yet, obviously, increasing our understanding of the behavioral repertoire of humankind would strengthen our ability to improve life in the world.

## QUESTIONS

1. How would you describe the traditional childhood socialization of the Fore?

2. In what ways was childhood socialization among the Fore changed by contact with the outside world?

3. The construction of a road made the Fore much less isolated. Do you think they were better off?

*Harry L. Gracey*

# 11. Learning the Student Role: Kindergarten as Academic Boot Camp

*Socialization is the lifelong process by which people develop personality and learn the way of life of their society. Since virtually all human behavior is learned rather than inborn, the process is essential for both individual and society; neither could survive without it. The most important agency of socialization is, of course, the family; it is in this context that the child learns such basic skills as language and begins to acquire the norms and values of the culture. But in all modern industrial societies, the child soon experiences another vital agency of socialization, the school.*

*On the whole, children learn a great deal in school, although what they learn is by no means restricted to the formal curriculum. Equally important is the "hidden curriculum," for children also quickly learn how to fit in with a social system, how to follow rules, how to be punctual, how to respect authority, how to follow orders, how to compete, how to achieve success.*

*In this article, Harry Gracey compares kindergarten to a military boot camp. He first describes and then analyzes a typical day in a kindergarten classroom, showing that what the children are really learning is the student role—a role which, with various elaborations, they will play for many more years of their lives.*

## Introduction

... Education has been defined by sociologists, classical and contemporary, as an institution which serves society by socializing people into it through a formalized, standardized procedure. At the beginning of this century, Emile Durkheim told student teachers at the University of Paris that education "consists of a methodical socialization of the younger generation." He went on to add:

> It is the influence exercised by adult generations on those that are not ready for social life. Its object is to arouse and to develop in the child a certain number of physical, intellectual, and moral states that are demanded of him by the special milieu for which he is specifically destined.... To the egotistic and asocial being that has just been born, [society] must, as rapidly as possible, add another, capable of leading a moral and social life. Such is the work of education.

The educational process, Durkheim said, "is above all the means by which society perpetually re-creates the conditions of its very existence."...

...

Kindergarten is generally conceived by educators as a year of preparation for school. It is thought of as a year in which small children, five or six years old, are prepared socially and emotionally for the academic learning which will take place over the next twelve years. It is expected that a foundation of behavior and attitudes will be laid in kindergarten on which the children can acquire the skills and knowledge they will be taught in the grades. A booklet prepared for parents by the staff of a suburban New York school system says that the kindergarten experience will stimulate the child's desire to learn and cultivate the skills he will need for learning in the rest of his school career. It claims that the child will find opportunities for physical growth, for satisfying his "need for self-expression," acquire some knowledge, and provide opportunities for creative activity. It concludes, "The most important benefit that your five-year-old will receive from kindergarten is the opportunity to live and grow happily and purposefully with others in a small society." The kindergarten teachers in one of the elementary schools in this community, one we shall call the Wilbur Wright School, said their goals were to see that the children "grew" in all ways: physically, of course, emotionally, socially, and academically. They said they wanted children to like school as a result of their kindergarten experiences and that they wanted them to learn to get along with others.

None of these goals, however, is unique to kindergarten: each of them is held to some extent by teachers in the other six grades at the Wright School. And growth would occur, but differently, even if the child did not attend school. The children already know how to get along with others in their families and their play groups. The unique job of the kindergarten in the educational division of labor seems rather to be teaching children the student role. The student role is the repertoire of behavior and attitudes regarded by educators as appropriate to children in school. Observation in the kindergartens of the Wilbur Wright School revealed a great variety of activities through which children are shown and then drilled in the behavior and attitudes defined as appropriate for school and thereby induced to learn the role of student. Observations of the kindergartens and interviews with the teachers both pointed to the teaching and learning of classroom routines as the main element of the student role. The teachers expended most of their efforts, for the first half of the year at least, in training the children to follow the routines which teachers created. The children were, in a very real sense, *drilled* in tasks and activities created by the teachers for their own purposes and beginning and ending quite arbitrarily (from the child's point of view) at the command of the teacher. One teacher remarked that she hated September, because during the first month "everything has to be done rigidly, and repeatedly, until they know exactly what they're supposed to do." However, "by January," she said, "they know exactly what to do [during the day] and I don't have to be after them all the time." Classroom routines were introduced gradually from the beginning of the year in all the kindergartens, and children were drilled in them as long as was necessary to achieve regular compliance. By the end of the school year, the successful kindergarten teacher has a well-organized group of children. They follow classroom routines automatically, having learned all the command signals and the expected responses to them. They have, in our terms, learned the student role. The following observation shows one such classroom operating at optimum organization on an afternoon late in May. It is the class of an experienced and respected kindergarten teacher.

## An Afternoon in Kindergarten

At about 12:20 in the afternoon on a day in the last week of May, Edith Kerr leaves the teachers' room where she has been having lunch and walks to her classroom at the far end of the primary wing of Wright School. A group of five- and six-year-olds peer at her through the glass doors leading from the hall cloakroom to the play area outside. Entering her room, she straightens some material in the "book corner" of the room, arranges music on the piano, takes colored paper from her closet, and places it on one of the shelves under the window. Her room is divided into a number of activity areas through the arrangement of furniture and play equipment. Two easels and a paint table near the door create a kind of passageway inside the room. A wedge-shaped area just inside the front door is made into a teacher's area by the placing of "her" things there: her desk, file, and piano. To the left is the book corner, marked off from the rest of the room by a puppet stage and a movable chalkboard. In it are a display rack of picture books, a record player, and a stack of children's records. To the right of the entrance are the sink and cleanup area. Four large round tables with six chairs at each for the children are placed near the walls about halfway down the length of the room, two on each side, leaving a large open area in the center for group games, block building, and toy-truck driving. Windows stretch down the length of both walls, starting about three feet from the floor and extending almost to the high ceilings. Under the windows are long shelves on which are kept all the toys, games, blocks, paper, paints, and other equipment of the kindergarten. The left rear corner of the room is a play store with shelves, merchandise, and cash register; the right rear corner is a play kitchen with stove, sink, ironing board, and bassinette with baby dolls in it. This area is partly shielded from the rest of the room by a large standing display rack for posters and children's artwork. A sandbox is found against the back wall between these two areas. The room is light, brightly colored, and filled with things adults feel five- and six-year-olds will find interesting and pleasing.

At 12:25 Edith opens the outside door and admits the waiting children. They hang their sweaters on hooks outside the door and then go to the center of the room and arrange themselves in a semicircle on the floor, facing the teacher's chair which she has placed in the center of the floor. Edith follows them in and sits in her chair checking attendance while waiting for the bell to ring. When she has finished attendance, which she takes by sight, she asks the children what the date is, what day and month it is, how many children are enrolled in the class, how many are present, and how many are absent.

The bell rings at 12:30 and the teacher puts away

her attendance book. She introduces a visitor, who is sitting against the right wall taking notes, as someone who wants to learn about schools and children. She then goes to the back of the room and takes down a large chart labeled "Helping Hands." Bringing it to the center of the room, she tells the children it is time to change jobs. Each child is assigned some task on the chart by placing his name, lettered on a paper "hand," next to a picture signifying the task—e.g., a broom, a blackboard, a milk bottle, a flag, and a Bible. She asks the children who wants each of the jobs and rearranges their "hands" accordingly. Returning to her chair, Edith announces, "One person should tell us what happened to Mark." A girl raises her hand and when called on says, "Mark fell and hit his head and had to go to the hospital." The teacher adds that Mark's mother had written saying he was in the hospital.

During this time the children have been interacting among themselves, in their semicircle. Children have whispered to their neighbors, poked one another, made general comments to the group, waved to friends on the other side of the circle. None of this has been disruptive, and the teacher has ignored it for the most part. The children seem to know just how much of each kind of interaction is permitted—they may greet in a soft voice someone who sits next to them, for example, but may not shout greetings to a friend who sits across the circle, so they confine themselves to waving and remaining well within understood limits.

At 12:35 two children arrive. Edith asks them why they are late and then sends them to join the circle on the floor. The other children vie with each other to tell the newcomers what happened to Mark. When this leads to a general disorder Edith asks, "Who has serious time?" The children become quiet, and a girl raises her hand. Edith nods and the child gets a Bible and hands it to Edith. She reads the Twenty-third Psalm while the children sit quietly. Edith helps the child in charge begin reciting the Lord's Prayer, while the other children follow along for the first unit of sounds and then trail off as Edith finishes for them. Everyone stands and faces the American flag hung to the right of the door. Edith leads the pledge to the flag, with the children again following the familiar sounds as far as they remember them. Edith then asks the girl in charge what song she wants and the child replies, "My Country." Edith goes to the piano and plays "America," singing as the children follow her words.

Edith returns to her chair in the center of the room, and the children sit again in the semicircle on the floor. It is 12:40 when she tells the children, "Let's have boys' sharing time first." She calls the name of the first boy sitting on the end of the circle, and he comes up to her with a toy helicopter. He turns and holds it up for the

other children to see. He says, "It's a helicopter." Edith asks, "What is it used for?" and he replies, "For the army. Carry men. For the war." Other children join in, "For shooting submarines." "To bring back men from space when they are in the ocean." Edith sends the boy back to the circle and asks the next boy if he has something. He replies "No" and she passes on to the next. He says "Yes" and brings a bird's nest to her. He holds it for the class to see, and the teacher asks, "What kind of bird made the nest?" The boy replies, "My friend says a rain bird made it." Edith asks what the nest is made of and different children reply, "mud," "leaves," and "sticks." There is also a bit of moss woven into the nest and Edith tries to describe it to the children. They, however, are more interested in seeing if anything is inside it, and Edith lets the boy carry it around the semicircle showing the children its insides. Edith tells the children of some baby robins in a nest in her yard, and some of the children tell about baby birds they have seen. Some children are asking about a small object in the nest which they say looks like an egg, but all have seen the nest now, and Edith calls on the next boy. A number of children say, "I know what Michael has, but I'm not telling." Michael brings a book to the teacher and then goes back to his place in the circle of children. Edith reads the last page of the book to the class. Some children tell of books which they have at home. Edith calls the next boy, and three children call out, "I know what David has." "He always has the same thing." "It's a bang-bang." David goes to his table and gets a box which he brings to Edith. He opens it and shows the teacher a scale-model of an old-fashioned dueling pistol. When David does not turn around to the class, Edith tells him, "Show it to the children," and he does. One child says, "Mr. Johnson [the principal] said no guns." Edith replies, "Yes, how many of you know that?" Most of the children in the circle raise their hands. She continues, "That you aren't supposed to bring guns to school?" She calls the next boy on the circle and he brings two large toy soldiers to her which the children enthusiastically identify as being from "Babes in Toyland." The next boy brings an American flag to Edith and shows it to the class. She asks him what the stars and stripes stand for and admonishes him to treat it carefully. "Why should you treat it carefully?" she asks the boy. "Because it's our flag," he replies. She congratulates him, saying, "That's right."

"Show and Tell" lasted twenty minutes, and during the last ten, one girl in particular announced that she knew what each child called upon had to show. Edith asked her to be quiet each time she spoke out, but she was not content, continuing to offer her comment at each "show." Four children from other classes had come into the room to bring something from another teacher or to ask for something from Edith. Those with requests were asked to return later if the item wasn't readily available.

Edith now asks if any of the children told their mothers about their trip to the local zoo the previous day. Many children raise their hands. As Edith calls on them, they tell what they liked in the zoo. Some children cannot wait to be called on, and they call out things to the teacher who asks them to be quiet. After a few of the animals are mentioned, one child says, "I liked the spooky house," and the others chime in to agree with him, some pantomiming fear and horror. Edith is puzzled, and asks what this was. When half the children try to tell her at once, she raises her hand for quiet, then calls on individual children. One says, "The house with nobody in it"; another, "The dark little house." Edith asks where it was in the zoo, but the children cannot describe its location in any way which she can understand. Edith makes some jokes, but they involve adult abstractions which the children cannot grasp. The children have become quite noisy now, speaking out to make both relevant and irrelevant comments, and three little girls have become particularly assertive.

Edith gets up from her seat at 1:10 and goes to the book corner, where she puts a record on the player. As it begins a story about the trip to the zoo, she returns to the circle and asks the children to go sit at the tables. She divides them among the tables in such a way as to indicate that they don't have regular seats. When the children are all seated at the four tables, five or six to a table, the teacher asks, "Who wants to be the first one?" One of the noisy girls comes to the center of the room. The voice on the record is giving directions for imitating an ostrich and the girl follows them, walking around the center of the room holding her ankles with her hands. Edith replays the record, and all the children, table by table, imitate ostriches down the center of the room and back. Edith removes her shoes and shows that she can be an ostrich, too. This is apparently a familiar game, for a number of children are calling out, "Can we have the crab?" Edith asks one of the children to do a crab "so we can all remember how" and then plays the part of the record with music for imitating crabs by. The children from the first table line up across the room, hands and feet on the floor and face pointing toward the ceiling. After they have "walked" down the room and back in this posture, they sit at their table and the children of the next table play "crab." The children love this; they run from their tables, dance about on the floor waiting for their turns and are generally exuberant. Children ask for the "inch worm," and the game is played again with the children squirming down the floor. As a conclusion Edith shows them a new animal imitation, the "lame dog." The children all hobble down the floor on three "legs," table by table, to the accompaniment of the record.

At 1:30 Edith has the children line up in the center of the room; she says, "Table one, line up in front of me," and children ask, "What are we going to do?" Then she moves a few steps to the side and says, "Table two over here, line up next to table one," and more children ask, "What for?" She does this for table three and table four and each time the children ask, "Why, what are we going to do?" When the children are lined up in four lines of five each, spaced so that they are not touching one another, Edith puts on a new record and leads the class in calisthenics, to the accompaniment of the record. The children just jump around every which way in their places instead of doing the exercises, and by the time the record is finished, Edith, the only one following it, seems exhausted. She is apparently adopting the president's new "Physical Fitness" program in her classroom.

At 1:35 Edith pulls her chair to the easels and calls the children to sit on the floor in front of her, table by table. When they are all seated she asks, "What are you going to do for worktime today?" Different children raise their hands and tell Edith what they are going to draw. Most are going to make pictures of animals they saw in the zoo. Edith asks if they want to make pictures to send to Mark in the hospital, and the children agree to this. Edith gives drawing paper to the children, calling them to her one by one. After getting a piece of paper, the children go to the crayon box on the right-hand shelves, select a number of colors, and go to the tables, where they begin drawing. Edith is again trying to quiet the perpetually talking girls. She keeps two of them standing by her so they won't disrupt the others. She asks them, "Why do you feel you have to talk all the time?" and then scolds them for not listening to her. Then she sends them to their tables to draw.

Most of the children are drawing at their tables, sitting or kneeling in their chairs. They are all working very industriously and, engrossed in their work, very quietly. Three girls have chosen to paint at the easels, and having donned their smocks, they are busily mixing colors and intently applying them to their pictures. If the children at the tables are primitives and neorealists in their animal depictions, these girls at the easels are the class abstract-expressionists, with their broadstroked, colorful paintings.

Edith asks of the children generally, "What color should I make the cover of Mark's book?" Brown and green are suggested by some children "because Mark likes them." The other children are puzzled as to just what is going on and ask, "What book?" or "What does she mean?" Edith explains what she thought was clear to them already, that they are all going to put their pictures together in a "book" to be sent to Mark. She goes to a small table in the play kitchen corner and tells the children to bring her their pictures when they are finished and she will write their message for Mark on them.

By 1:50 most children have finished their pictures

and given them to Edith. She talks with some of them as she ties the bundle of pictures together—answering questions, listening, carrying on conversations. The children are playing in various parts of the room with toys, games and blocks which they have taken off the shelves. They also move from table to table examining each other's pictures, offering compliments and suggestions. Three girls at a table are cutting up colored paper for a collage. Another girl is walking about the room in a pair of high heels with a woman's purse over her arm. Three boys are playing in the center of the room with the large block set, with which they are building walkways and walking on them. Edith is very much concerned about their safety and comes over a number of times to fuss over them. Two or three other boys are pushing trucks around the center of the room, and mild altercations occur when they drive through the block constructions. Some boys and a girl are playing at the toy store, two girls are serving "tea" in the play kitchen and one is washing a doll baby. Two boys have elected to clean the room, and with large sponges they wash the movable blackboard, the puppet stage, and then begin on the tables. They run into resistance from the children who are working with construction toys on the tables and do not want to dismantle their structures. The class is like a room full of bees, each intent on pursuing some activity, occasionally bumping into one another, but just veering off in another direction without serious altercation. At 2:05 the custodian arrives pushing a cart loaded with half-pint milk containers. He places a tray of cartons on the counter next to the sink, then leaves. His coming and going is unnoticed in the room (as, incidentally, is the presence of the observer, who is completely ignored by the children for the entire afternoon).

At 2:15 Edith walks to the entrance of the room, switches off the lights, and sits at the piano and plays. The children begin spontaneously singing the song, which is "Clean up, clean up. Everybody clean up." Edith walks around the room supervising the cleanup. Some children put their toys, the blocks, puzzles, games, and so on back on their shelves under the windows. The children making a collage keep right on working. A child from another class comes in to borrow the 45-rpm adaptor for the record player. At more urging from Edith the rest of the children shelve their toys and work. The children are sitting around their tables now, and Edith asks, "What record would you like to hear while you have your milk?" There is some confusion and no general consensus, so Edith drops the subject and begins to call the children, table by table, to come get their milk. "Table one," she says, and the five children come to the sink, wash their hands and dry them, pick up a carton of milk and a straw, and take it back to their table. Two talking girls wander about the room interfering with the children getting their milk and Edith calls out to them to "settle down." As the

children sit, many of them call out to Edith the name of the record they want to hear. When all the children are seated at tables with milk, Edith plays one of these records called "Bozo and the Birds" and shows the children pictures in a book which go with the record. The record recites, and the book shows the adventures of the clown, Bozo, as he walks through a woods meeting many different kinds of birds who, of course, display the characteristics of many kinds of people or, more accurately, different stereotypes. As children finish their milk they take blankets or pads from the shelves under the windows and lie on them in the center of the room where Edith sits on her chair showing the pictures. By 2:30 half the class is lying on the floor on their blankets, the record is still playing, and the teacher is turning the pages of the book. The child who came in previously returns the 45-rpm adaptor, and one of the kindergartners tells Edith what the boy's name is and where he lives.

The record ends at 2:40. Edith says, "Children, down on your blankets." All the class is lying on blankets now. Edith refuses to answer the various questions individual children put to her because, she tells them, "it's rest time now." Instead she talks very softly about what they will do tomorrow. They are going to work with clay, she says. The children lie quietly and listen. One of the boys raises his hand and when called on tells Edith, "The animals in the zoo looked so hungry yesterday." Edith asks the children what they think about this and a number try to volunteer opinions, but Edith accepts only those offered in a "rest-time tone," that is, softly and quietly. After a brief discussion of animal feeding, Edith calls the names of the two children on milk detail and has them collect empty milk cartons from the tables and return them to the tray. She asks the two children on cleanup detail to clean up the room. Then she gets up from her chair and goes to the door to turn on the lights. At this signal the children get up from the floor and return their blankets and pads to the shelf. It is raining (the reason for no outside play this afternoon), and cars driven by mothers clog the school drive and line up along the street. One of the talkative little girls comes over to Edith and pointing out the window says, "Mrs. Kerr, see my mother in the new Cadillac?"

At 2:50 Edith sits at the piano and plays. The children sit on the floor in the center of the room and sing. They have a repertoire of songs about animals, including one in which each child sings a refrain alone. They know these by heart and sing along through the ringing of the 2:55 bell. When the song is finished Edith gets up and coming to the group says, "Okay, rhyming words to get your coats today." The children raise their hands and as Edith calls on them, they tell her two rhyming words, after which they are allowed to go into the hall to get their coats and sweaters. They return to the room with these and sit at their tables. At 2:59 Edith says, "When you have your coats on, you may line up at the door." Half of the children go to the door and stand in a long line. When the three o'clock bell rings, Edith returns to the piano and plays. The children sing a song called "Goodbye," after which Edith sends them out.

## Training for Learning and Life

The day in kindergarten at Wright School illustrates both the content of the student role as it has been learned by these children and the processes by which the teacher has brought about this learning or "taught" them the student role. The children have learned to go through routines and to follow orders with unquestioning obedience, even when these make no sense to them. They have been disciplined to do as they are told by an authoritative person without significant protest. Edith has developed this discipline in the children by creating and enforcing a rigid social structure in the classroom through which she effectively controls the behavior of most of the children for most of the school day. The "living with others in a small society" which the school pamphlet tells parents is the most important thing the children will learn in kindergarten can be seen now in its operational meaning, which is learning to live by the routines imposed by the school. This learning appears to be the principal content of the student role.

Children who submit to school-imposed discipline and come to identify with it, so that being a "good student" comes to be an important part of their developing identities, *become* the good students by the school's definitions. Those who submit to the routines of the school but do not come to identify with them will be adequate students who find the more important part of their identities elsewhere, such as in the play group outside school. Children who refuse to submit to the school routines are rebels, who become known as "bad students" and often "problem children" in the school, for they do not learn the academic curriculum and their behavior is often disruptive in the classroom. Today, schools engage clinical psychologists in part to help teachers deal with such children.

In looking at Edith's kindergarten at Wright School, it is interesting to ask how the children learn this role of student—come to accept school-imposed routines—and what, exactly, it involves in terms of behavior and attitudes. The most prominent features of the classroom are its physical and social structures. The room is carefully furnished and arranged in ways adults feel will interest children. The play store and play kitchen in the back of the room, for example, imply that children are interested in mimicking these activities of the adult world. The only space left for the children to create something of their own is the empty center of the room, and the materials at their disposal are the blocks, whose use causes

anxiety on the part of the teacher. The room, being carefully organized physically by the adults, leaves little room for the creation of physical organization on the part of the children.

The social structure created by Edith is a far more powerful and subtle force for fitting the children to the student role. This structure is established by the very rigid and tightly controlled set of rituals and routines through which the children are put during the day. There is first the rigid "locating procedure" in which the children are asked to find themselves in terms of the month, date, day of the week, and the number of the class who are present and absent. This puts them solidly in the real world as defined by adults. The day is then divided into six periods whose activities are for the most part determined by the teacher. In Edith's kindergarten the children went through serious time, which opens the school day, sharing time, play time (which in clear weather would be spent outside), work time, cleanup time, after which they have their milk, and rest time, after which they go home. The teacher has programmed activities for each of these times.

Occasionally the class is allowed limited discretion to choose between proffered activities such as stories or records, but original ideas for activities are never solicited from them. Opportunity for free individual action is open only once in the day, during the part of the work time left after the general class assignment has been completed (on the day reported, the class assignment was drawing animal pictures for the absent Mark). Spontaneous interests or observations from the children are never developed by the teacher. It seems that her schedule just does not allow room for developing such unplanned events. During sharing time, for example, the child who brought a bird's nest told Edith, in reply to her question of what kind of bird made it, "My friend says it's a rain bird." Edith does not think to ask about this bird, probably because the answer is "childish," that is, not given in accepted adult categories of birds. The children then express great interest in an object in the nest, but the teacher ignores this interest, probably because the object is uninteresting to her. The soldiers from "Babes in Toyland" strike a responsive note in the children, but this is not used for a discussion of any kind. The soldiers are treated in the same way as objects which bring little interest from the children. Finally, at the end of sharing time, the child world of perception literally erupts in the class with the recollection of "the spooky house" at the zoo. Apparently, this made more of an impression on the children than did any of the animals, but Edith is unable to make any sense of it for herself. The tightly imposed order of the class begins to break down as the children discover a universe of discourse of their own and begin talking excitedly with one another. The teacher is effectively excluded from this child's world of perception, and for a moment she fails to dominate the classroom situation. She reasserts control, however, by taking the children to the next activity she has planned for the day. It seems never to have occurred to Edith that there might be a meaningful learning experience for the children in re-creating the "spooky house" in the classroom. It seems fair to say that this would have offered an exercise in spontaneous self-expression and an opportunity for real creativity on the part of the children. Instead, they are taken through a canned animal-imitation procedure, an activity which they apparently enjoy but which is also imposed upon them rather than created by them.

While children's perceptions of the world and opportunities for genuine spontaneity and creativity are being systematically eliminated from the kindergarten, unquestioned obedience to authority and rote learning of meaningless material are being encouraged. When the children are called to line up in the center of the room they ask "Why?" and "What for?" as they are in the very process of complying. They have learned to go smoothly through a programmed day, regardless of whether parts of the program make any sense to them or not. Here the student role involves what might be called "doing what you're told and never mind why." Activities which might "make sense" to the children are effectively ruled out, and they are forced or induced to participate in activities which may be "senseless," such as the calisthenics.

At the same time the children are being taught by rote meaningless sounds in the ritual oaths and songs, such as the Lord's Prayer, the Pledge to the Flag, and "America." As they go through the grades children learn more and more of the sounds of these ritual oaths, but the fact that they have often learned meaningless sounds rather than meaningful statements is shown when they are asked to write these out in the sixth grade; they write them as groups of sounds rather than as a series of words, according to the sixth-grade teachers at Wright School. Probably much learning in the elementary grades is of this character, that is, having no intrinsic meaning to the children but rather being tasks inexplicably required of them by authoritative adults. Listening to sixth-grade children read social-studies reports, for example, in which they have copied material from encyclopedias about a particular country, an observer often gets the feeling that he is watching an activity which has no intrinsic meaning for the child. The child who reads, "Switzerland grows wheat and cows and grass and makes a lot of cheese" knows the dictionary meaning of each of these words but may very well have no conception at all of this "thing" called Switzerland. He is simply carrying out a task assigned by the teacher *because* it is assigned, and this may be its only "meaning" for him.

Another type of learning which takes place in kindergarten is seen in children who take advantage of the "holes" in the adult social structure to create activities of their own, during work time or out-of-doors during play time. Here the children are learning to carve out a small world of their own within the world created by adults. They very quickly learn that if they keep within permissible limits of noise and action, they can play much as they please. Small groups of children formed during the year in Edith's kindergarten who played together at these times, developing semi-independent little groups in which they created their own worlds in the interstices of the adult-imposed physical and social world. These groups remind the sociological observer very much of the so-called informal groups which adults develop in factories and offices of large bureaucracies. Here too, within authoritatively imposed social organizations people find "holes" to create little subworlds which support informal, friendly, nonofficial behavior. Forming and participating in such groups seems to be as much part of the student role as it is of the role of bureaucrat.

The kindergarten has been conceived of here as the year in which children are prepared for their schooling by learning the role of student. In the classrooms of the rest of the school grades the children will be asked to submit to systems and routines imposed by the teachers and the curriculum. The days will be much like those of kindergarten, except that academic subjects will be substituted for the activities of the kindergarten. Once out of the school system, young adults will more than likely find themselves working in large-scale bureaucratic organizations, perhaps on the assembly line in the factory, perhaps in the paper routines of the white collar occupations, where they will be required to submit to rigid routines imposed by "the company" which may make little sense to them. Those who can operate well in this situation will be successful bureaucratic functionaries. Kindergarten, therefore, can be seen as preparing children not only for participation in the bureaucratic organization of large modern school systems, but also for the large-scale occupational bureaucracies of modern society.

---

## QUESTIONS

1. Is Gracey's comparison of kindergarten with a boot camp justified?

2. What are the similarities between the student role in the kindergarten and the student role in college? What are the differences?

3. What is distinctively sociological about Gracey's view of the kindergarten classroom? How would his understanding of what was taking place differ from that of the teacher and the children?

*Sherry Turkle*                    # 12. The Intimate Machine

*An important part of the socialization process is cognitive development—the process of learning to think. It seems that all normal humans learn to think in a series of stages, beginning in infancy with simple physical interactions with the environment, and culminating years later in the ability to manipulate abstract ideas. This developmental sequence seems to be universal in all societies. The actual content of people's thought, however, depends very much on the society in which they live—for example, one society might explain the movement of the planets in religious terms, another in mystical terms, and yet another in mathematical terms. Additionally, the rate at which people progress toward abstract thinking is strongly influenced by social factors, such as the family environment or the availability of opportunities for formal education.*

*In a highly technological society, machines—such as television and, more recently, the computer—can also play a part in socializing children in what and how to think. Although there is general agreement that computers are revolutionizing many aspects of social and economic life, there is still surprisingly little factual research on the cultural impact of the new machines. This article reports some preliminary impressions by Sherry Turkle, who has a particular interest in the relationship between young children and computers.*

It is summer. Robert, seven, is part of a play group at the beach. I have been visiting the group every day. I bring a carton filled with small computer toys and games and a tape recorder to capture the children's reactions as they meet these toys. Robert is playing with Merlin, a computer toy that plays tic-tac-toe. Robert's friend Craig has shown him how to "beat" Merlin. There is a trick: Merlin follows an optimal strategy most of the time, and if neither player makes a bad move, every game will end in a draw. But Merlin is programmed to make a slip every once in a while. Children discover a strategy that will allow them to win, but then when they try it a second time, it usually doesn't work. The machine gives the impression of not being dumb enough to let down its defenses twice. Robert has watched Craig perform the "winning trick" and now he wants to try it himself. He plays his part perfectly but on this round Merlin, too, plays a perfect game, which leads to a draw. Robert accuses the toy of cheating. Children are used to machines being predictable. But this is a machine that surprises.

Robert throws Merlin into the sand in anger and frustration. "Cheater. I hope your brains break." He is overheard by Craig and by Greg, aged six and eight, who sense that this may be a good moment to reclaim Merlin for themselves. They salvage the by now very sandy toy and take it upon themselves to set Robert straight.

"Merlin doesn't know if it cheats. It doesn't know if you break it, Robert. It's not alive," says Craig.

"Someone taught Merlin to play. But he doesn't know if he wins or loses," says Greg.

"Yes, he does know if he loses," Robert says. "He makes different noises."

"No, stupid. It's smart enough to make the right kinds of noises," Greg says. "But it doesn't really know if it loses. That's how you cheat it. It doesn't know you are cheating."

The conversation is over. I found it a striking scene. Children stand in the surf amid their shoreline sandcastles and argue the moral and metaphysical status of a machine on the basis of its psychology: Does the machine

Excerpted from *The Second Self: The Computer and the Human Spirit,* Simon & Schuster, Inc., 1984. Copyright © 1984 by Sherry Turkle. Reprinted by permission.

know what it is doing? Does it have intentions, consciousness, feelings?

What is important is not the yes or no of whether children think computers cheat or even whether computers are alive. What is important is the conversation, both psychological and philosophical, that the object evokes.

It was Jean Piaget who discovered the child as a metaphysician. Beginning in the 1920s, Piaget studied children's emerging understandings of causality, life, and consciousness. Why does the stone roll down the slope? "To get to the bottom," says the young child, as if the rock had its own desires. In time the child learns the stone falls because of gravity; intentions have nothing to do with it. And so a dichotomy is constructed: Physical and psychological properties stand opposed to one another in two great systems. The physical is used to understand things, the psychological to understand people and animals. But the computer is a new kind of object, psychological, yet a thing.

Marginal objects, objects with no clear place, play important roles. On the line between categories, they draw attention to how we have drawn the lines. Sometimes they incite us to reaffirm the lines, sometimes to call them into question. They are the growing point for new learning, new theory building. Computers, as marginal objects on the boundary between the physical and the psychological, force thinking about matter, life, and mind.

Marginal objects are not neutral. Sit silently and watch children pulling the wings off butterflies. They are not simply thoughtless or cruel. They are not playing with butterflies as much as with their evolving ideas, fears, and fantasies about life and death, about what is allowed and not allowed, about what can be controlled and what is beyond control.

Laura is six years old. I have interviewed several other six-year-olds from her neighborhood in Boston. Most of them seem streetwise. Laura is an innocent. She watches very little television, some *Sesame Street* and her favorite, *Mr. Rogers' Neighborhood,* which she likes because "there is magic and Mr. Rogers is very kind." She has no mechanical toys, "nothing that winds up or has batteries," she tells me, "just dolls and storybooks."

Laura begins her play session calmly. She quickly checks out the toys and forms definite opinions. The toys have "minds," says Laura, but they are not alive because "they don't have a brain." When I ask Laura if her alarm clock "remembers" when to wake her up, she is firm about the answer. "No, you set it. And then it does it. But not by itself."

As Laura plays, she becomes less composed. Merlin's "tic-tac-toe mind" turns out to be a formidable opponent. "How does he win so much? It tries to make me lose."

Laura is completely engrossed. She doesn't look up. My presence is forgotten. I ask her if she thinks Merlin could lose if it made a mistake. Her "yes" is almost inaudible. She is not sure at all. Laura begins to turn Merlin off between games, a ritual whose intent seems to be to weaken the toy. Her efforts are in vain; Merlin continues to win. After five minutes of this frustration, she puts Merlin aside and picks up Speak and Spell, a toy that can talk. Laura spells out her name on its keyboard. The toy obediently calls out the letters and displays them on a small screen: L-A-U-R-A. She seems satisfied and relaxes. This is going to be more reassuring than Merlin. Then Laura puts Speak and Spell into "Say it" mode. This is designed for younger children who, like Laura, may not be able to spell much more than their names. In "Say it" mode the machine calls out the phrase "SAY IT" followed by one of the words in its several-hundred-word vocabulary. And the child is given time to repeat the word before being offered another.

Speak and Spell is designed so that you can turn it off at will. But the first version of Speak and Spell on the American market has a bug, a programming mistake. You can't turn it off while it is in its "Say it" mode. This mode offers 10 "Say it" commands, and it brooks no interruption until the presentation of the 10 words is finished. You cannot change modes, and you cannot turn the toy off.

The uninterruptible cycle takes long enough so that within the first few sessions with Speak and Spell most children try to turn it off while it is in "Say it" mode and discover they cannot. In a small way, they are meeting a situation that is at the heart of almost every science fiction movie ever made about a computer. It is the story of the machine out of control. As far as the child can tell, this machine has developed a mind of its own.

Halfway through the cycle, Laura wants to turn "Say it" off and get back to spelling her name. She presses the off button. She persists, pressing it again and again, then trying several other buttons. "Why isn't this thing coming off?" She tries four or five buttons in a row, then all of them at once. Now Laura is panicked. She puts one of her hands on as many buttons as it will cover. She tries both of her hands. The machine goes on until it is done. Laura is quite upset.

When Paul, seven, discovers the "Say it" bug, he is startled, but he doesn't say anything. His first reaction is to put Speak and Spell on the ground. Then, kneeling above the toy but keeping some distance, he presses "Say it" again. He presses all its buttons in turn and then uses the palms of his hands, trying to press all its buttons at the same time, trying to make it stop. The toy remains unobedient, but when its 10 words have come to an end it stops unexpectedly. Paul puts the Speak and Spell in "Say it" mode again, but this time, just as it is demanding its fourth word, Paul turns it over, opens its back cover, and removes its batteries. Paul has found the way to pull the plug. A group of children gather round and take turns doing Paul's trick. They put the toy in "Say it" mode and then take out the batteries, shrieking their delight about "killing the Speak and Spell." They allow the toy its autonomous behaviour and then, when it is like a living thing, kill it.

Speak and Spell in its "Say it" mode is on the border. It is not alive but seems to act willfully, of its own accord. It can be an occasion for an almost ritual exploration of life and death: pulling out the batteries and putting them back again.

When a child explains the descent of a rolling stone by its wish to get to the bottom of the hill, a very primitive psychological category substitutes for a deficient ability in physical thinking. As the child develops, this animism is undermined from two sides: There will be growing sophistication about what domains are appropriately described in psychological terms—the behavior of rocks will not be among these. There will be growing sophistication about how to think about the physical causality. Computers, however, don't easily fit into the category of physical objects whose behavior is to be described in physical terms. The world of traditional objects serves as material for a child's construction of the physical; the computer serves as a stimulus to the construction of the psychological.

While very young children puzzle over the physical and metaphysical status of the computer, grade school children grow more practical, focusing on mastery of the world around them and how the computer can be made to work for them. When children learn to program, one of their favorite areas of work is computer graphics—programming the machine to place displays on the screen. At a private school I shall call Austen, a school with a long tradition of open classrooms and flexible scheduling, children from preschool through fourth grade learn to program in the Logo computer language, which provides a powerful medium for computer graphics.

Thirty-two computational objects called sprites appear on the screen when commanded to do so. Each sprite has a number. When called by its number and given a color and shape, it comes onto the screen: a red truck, a blue ball, a green airplane. Children can manipulate one sprite at a time, several of them, or all of them at once, depending on the effect they want to achieve. The sprites can take predefined shapes, such as trucks and airplanes, or they can be given new shapes designed on a special grid, a sprite "scratchpad." They can be given a speed and a direction and set in motion. The direction is usually specified in terms of a heading from 0 to 360, where 0 would point the sprite due north,

90 would point it due east, 180 south, 270 west, and 360 north again.

The teachers think the manipulation of directions, involving the concept of angles, is too complex for second graders, so these children are introduced to the commands for making sprites appear, giving them shapes and colors, and placing them on the screen, but not for setting them in motion. Motion will be saved for later grades.

The curriculum works until one second grader, Gary, catches on to the fact that something exciting is happening on the older children's screens and knows enough to pick up the trick from a proud and talkative third grader. In one sense, the teachers are right: Gary doesn't understand that he is dealing with angles. He doesn't have to. He wants to make the computer do something and he assimilates the concept of angle to something he already knows—secret codes.

"The sprites have secret codes, like 10, 100, 55. And if you give them their codes, they go in different directions. I've taught the code to 14 second graders," Gary confides to a visitor. "We're sort of keeping it a secret. The teachers don't know. We haven't figured out all the codes yet, but we're working on it." Two weeks later, Gary and his friends are still cracking the code. "We're still not sure about the big numbers" (sprites interpret 361 as one, one full revolution plus one), but they are feeling very pleased with themselves.

Jeff, a fourth grader, has the widest reputation as a computer expert in the school. He is meticulous in his study habits, does superlative work in all subjects. His teachers are not surprised to see him excelling in programming. Jeff approaches the machine with determination and the need to be in control, the way he approaches both his schoolwork and extracurricular activities. He likes to be, and often is, chairman of student committees. He has an idea and he wants to make it work. At the moment, his preoccupation with computers is intense: "They're the biggest thing in my life right now.... When I program, I put myself in the place of the sprite. And I make it do things."

Jeff is the author of one of the first fourth-grade space shuttle programs. He does it, like he does most other things, by making a plan. There will be a rocket, boosters, a trip through the stars, a landing. He conceives the program globally; then he breaks it up into manageable pieces and programs. "I wrote out the parts on a big piece of cardboard. I saw the whole thing in my mind just in one night, and I couldn't wait to come to school to make it work." Computer scientists will recognize this "top down" strategy as good programming style. And we all recognize in Jeff someone who conforms to our stereotype of a computer person or an engineer—someone who would be good with machines, good at science, someone organized, who approaches the world of things with confidence and sure intent, with the determination to make it work.

Kevin is a very different sort of child. Where Jeff is precise in all of his actions, Kevin is dreamy and impressionistic. Where Jeff tends to try to impose his ideas on other children, Kevin's warm, easygoing nature and interest in others make him popular. Meetings with Kevin are often interrupted by his being called out to rehearse for a school play. He has been given the role of Prince Charming in *Cinderella*. Kevin comes from a military family; his father and grandfather were both in the Air Force. But Kevin has no intention of following in their footsteps. "I don't want to be an Army man. I don't want to be a fighting man. You can get killed." Kevin doesn't like fighting or competition in general.

Jeff has been playing with machines all his life—Tinkertoys, motors, bikes—but Kevin has never played with machines. He likes to read, he is proud of knowing the names of a "lot of different trees." He is artistic and introspective. When Jeff is asked questions about his activities, about what he thinks is fun, he answers in terms of how to do them right. He talks about video games by describing his strategy breakthroughs on the new version of Space Invaders: "Much harder, much trickier than the first one." By contrast, Kevin talks about the experiences in terms of how they make him feel. Video games make him feel anxious, he says. "The computer is better," he adds. "It's easier. You get more relaxed. You're not being bombarded with stuff all the time."

Kevin too is making a space scene. But the way he goes about it is not at all like Jeff's approach. Jeff doesn't care too much about the detail of the form of his rocketship; what is important is getting a complex system to work. But Kevin cares more about the aesthetics of the graphics. He spends a lot of time on the shape of his rocket. He abandons his original idea ("It didn't look right against the stars") but continues to doodle with the scratchpad shape maker. He works without plan, experimenting, throwing different shapes onto the screen. He frequently stands back to inspect his work, finally settling on a white shape with red fire "at the bottom." He spends a long time making the red fireball, finding ways to give it spikes, and adding detail to the ship. New possibilities emerge—insignias, stripes, windows, and Kevin's most enthusiastic project: "It can have a little seat for the astronaut."

Kevin has lovingly worked on creating the rocket, the flare, and a background of twinkling stars. Now he wants the stars to stay in place and the rocket and the flare to move through them together. But without a master plan he gets confused about the code numbers he has assigned to the different parts of his program, and the flare doesn't stay with the rocket but flies off with the stars. It takes a lot of time to get the flare and the ship back together.

In correcting his error, Kevin explores the system, discovering new special effects as he goes along. He adds a moon, some planets. He tries out different trajectories for the rocketship, different headings, and different speeds. By the end of the week Kevin too has programmed a space scene.

Jeff and Kevin represent cultural extremes. Some children are at home with the manipulation of formal objects, while others develop their ideas more impressionistically, usually with language or visual image, with attention to less formal aspects of the world such as feeling, color, sound, and personal rapport. Scientific and technical fields are usually seen as the natural home for people like Jeff; the arts and humanities seem to belong to Kevin.

In a classroom, we often see each type failing at the other's forte. Watching Kevin and Jeff at the same computer shows us two very different children succeeding at the same thing. Each child developed a distinctive style of mastery—styles that can be called hard and soft mastery.

Hard mastery is the imposition of will over the machine through the implementation of a plan. A program is the instrument of premeditated control. Getting the program to work is more like getting to "say one's piece" than allowing ideas to emerge in the give and take of conversation. The details of the specific program obviously need to be debugged—there has to be room for change, for some degree of flexibility in order to get it right—but the goal is always getting the program to realize the plan.

Soft mastery is more interactive. Kevin is like a painter who stands back between brushstrokes, looks at the canvas, and only from this contemplation decides what to do next. Hard mastery is the mastery of the planner, the engineer. Soft mastery is the mastery of the artist: Try this, wait for a response, try something else, let the overall shape emerge from an interaction with the medium. It is more like a conversation than a monologue.

The sprite, the computational object that is there to command on the screen, stands between the world of physical objects and the world of abstract ideas. Ambivalent in its nature, it is taken up differently by the hard and soft masters, the hard masters treating it more like an abstract entity—a Newtonian particle—the soft masters treating it more as a physical object—a dab of paint, a building block, a cardboard cutout.

In all of this, the computer acts as a Rorschach, allowing the expression of what is already there. But it does more than allow the expression of personality. It is a constructive as well as projective medium. It allows "softs" such as Kevin to operate in a domain of machines and formal systems that has been thought to be the exclusive cultural preserve of the "hards." For the first time Kevin could march into a mathematical world with artistic colors flying full mast.

I have used boys as examples in order to detail hard and soft masters without reference to gender. But now it is time to state what might be anticipated by many readers: Girls tend to be soft masters; the hard masters are overwhelmingly male. At Austen, girls are trying to forge relationships with the computer that bypass objectivity altogether. They see computational objects as sensuous and tactile and relate to the computer's formal system not as a set of unforgiving rules but as a language for communicating with, negotiating with, a behaving, psychological entity.

In the eyes of a true hard programmer like Jeff, his classmate Anne, also nine, is an enigma. On the one hand she hardly seems serious about the computer. Her projects are frivolous, or at least their goals seem to be. She spends days creating shimmering patterns on the screen and writing "dialogue" programs in which she gets the computer to respond to typed-in messages. Her enthusiasm depends on achieving visual or conversational effects, and she doesn't seem to care whether she gets them with what Jeff would classify as "tricks"—uninteresting from the standpoint of the program code. All the same, this doesn't keep her from getting down to serious programming. She has made some technical inventions, and Jeff and the other male hard masters recognize that if they want to keep abreast of the state of the art at Austen, they must pay attention to what Anne is doing. And Anne knows how to take advantage of her achievements. She was heard explaining to a visitor how much she enjoyed seeing versions of her ideas on half a dozen screens. "They didn't copy me exactly, but I can recognize my idea." Jeff's grudging acknowledgment of what he sees as Anne's not quite serious accomplishments seems almost a microcosm of reactions to competent women in society as a whole. There, as at Austen, there is appreciation, incomprehension, and ambivalence.

Anne has become an expert at writing programs to produce visual effects of appearance and disappearance. In one, a flock of birds flies through the sky, disappears at the horizon, and reappears some other place and time. If all the birds are the same color, such as red, the disappearance and appearance could be produced by the commands, "Set color invisible" to get rid of them, and "Set color red" to make them appear. But since Anne wants the birds to have different colors, the problem of the birds reappearing with their original color is more complicated.

There is a classical method for getting this done: Get the program to store away each bird's original color before changing that color to "invisible" and then to recall the color when the birds are to reappear. This method calls for an algebraic style of thinking. You have to think about variables and use a variable for each color, for example, letting A equal the color of the first bird, B the color of the second bird, and so on. Anne will use this method when she has to, but she prefers another, a method of her own invention that has a different feel. She lets the bird keep its color, but she makes her program hide it by placing a screen over it. She designs a sprite that will screen the bird when she doesn't want it seen.

This way of doing things makes Anne feel in direct contact with her material. She likes to feel that she is there among her birds, manipulating them much in the way she can manipulate physical materials. When you want to hide something on a canvas you paint it out, you cover it with something that looks like the background. This is Anne's solution. She covers the birds with a sky-colored screen to make them disappear.

But how does the program "know" where the bird is in order to place the screen on it? Anne attaches the screen to the bird when the bird is created, instead of putting it on later. The screen is on top of the bird at all times and moves with the bird wherever it goes. Thus she has invented a new kind of object, a screened bird. When Anne wants the bird to be seen, the screen is given the "invisible" color, so the bird, whatever its color, shows right through it. The problem of the multiplicity of bird colors is solved. A bird can have any color. But the screens need only two colors, invisible or sky blue. The problem of remembering the color of a particular bird and reassigning it at a particular time has been bypassed.

Anne's program is ingenious, but her programming style is characteristic of many of the girls in her class. Most of the boys seem driven by the pleasure of mastering and manipulating a formal system. For them, the programming instructions are what it is all about. For Anne, pleasure comes from being able to put herself in the space of the birds. Her method of manipulating screens and birds allows her to feel that these objects are close, not distant and untouchable things that need designation by variables.

Children working with computers are a reflection of the larger world of relations between gender and science. Jeff took the sprite as an object apart from him, an object in a world of its own. When he entered the sprite world, it was to command it better. Kevin used the sprite world to fantasize in. Anne does something more. She moves further in the direction of seeing the sprite as sensuous rather than abstract. When Anne puts herself into the sprite world, she imagines herself to be part of the system, playing with the birds and the screens as though they were tactile materials.

Science is usually defined in terms of the hard masters: It is the place for the abstract, the domain for a clear separation between subject and object. The Austen classroom, with its male hard masters, mirrors the male genderization of science. But what about Anne? What about the other girls like her who are exploring and mastering the computer? At Austen we see not only the male model that characterizes official science, but a model of how females, when given a chance, can find another way to think and talk about the mastery not simply of machines but of formal systems. And here the computer may have a special role. It provides an entry to formal systems that is more accessible to women. It can be negotiated with, responded to, it can be psychologized.

Computers affect children's psychological development in many ways. They enter children's perceptions of where they stand in the world of nature and of artifact. In their intimacies and interactions with the machine, children may find new ways to sort out who they are and what they are to become.

## QUESTIONS

1. In what ways, according to Turkle, can computers affect children's development?

2. Does working with computers affect the way you think? If so, how?

3. Can you list some additional impacts that computers are having on culture and society?

*Leonard I. Stein*

# 13. Male and Female: The Doctor-Nurse Game

*Sociology has traditionally focused mainly on the larger structures and processes of society—on institutions such as politics and religion, for example, or on issues of social order and social change. But sociologists have a continuing and lively interest in even the most minute and apparently routine details of the social interaction that occurs as people go about their daily lives.*

*When other social animals interact, their interaction is essentially physical. But human social interaction is different, for we live in a world of socially created meanings. Our interaction, therefore, is symbolic: we respond not just to what other people do or say, but to what we think they mean by their deeds or words. In short, human social interaction is filled with verbal and nonverbal messages and signals—some obvious and some not so obvious. Much of our interaction is so routine, of course, that we scarcely think about what we are doing. Yet the whole edifice of human society rests on the countless interactions of those who participate in it.*

*Sociology teaches us to look at social interaction with special care, seeking the subtle meanings that lie behind the routine behaviors. A favored context for sociological research in this area has been organizational settings, such as schools and hospitals, for it is here that people work within—yet manage to bend—formal rules, regulations, and hierarchies of authority. In this article, Leonard Stein shows how doctors and nurses participate in a "game" of shared niceties, rituals, and even pretenses—all designd to lubricate their professional interaction within the organization of the hospital.*

From *Archives of General Psychiatry*, June 1967. Copyright 1967, American Medical Association.

The relationship between the doctor and the nurse is a very special one. There are few professions where the degree of mutual respect and cooperation between co-workers is as intense as that between the doctor and nurse. Superficially, the stereotype of this relationship has been dramatized in many novels and television serials. When, however, it is observed carefully in an interactional framework, the relationship takes on a new dimension and has a special quality which fits a game model. The underlying attitudes which demand that this game be played are unfortunate. These attitudes create serious obstacles in the path of meaningful communications between physicians and nonmedical professional groups.

The physician traditionally and appropriately has total responsibility for making the decisions regarding the management of his patients' treatment. To guide his decisions he considers data gleaned from several sources. He acquires a complete medical history, performs a thorough physical examination, interprets laboratory findings, and at times, obtains recommendations from physician-consultants. Another important factor in his decision-making is the recommendations he receives from the nurse. The interaction between doctor and nurse through which these recommendations are communicated and received is unique and interesting.

## The Game

One rarely hears a nurse say, "Doctor, I would recommend that you order a retention enema for Mrs. Brown." A physician, upon hearing a recommendation of that nature, would gape in amazement at the effrontery of the nurse. The nurse, upon hearing the statement, would look over her shoulder to see who said it, hardly believing the words actually came from her own mouth. Nevertheless, if one observes closely, nurses make recommendations of more import every hour and physicians willingly and respectfully consider them. If the nurse is to make a suggestion without appearing insolent and the doctor is to seriously consider that suggestion, their interaction must not violate the rules of the game.

### Object of the Game

The object of the game is as follows: the nurse is to be bold, have initiative, and be responsible for making significant recommendations, while at the same time she must appear passive. This must be done in such a manner as to make her recommendations appear to be initiated by the physician.

Both participants must be acutely sensitive to each other's nonverbal and cryptic verbal communications. A slight lowering of the head, a minor shifting of position in the chair, or a seemingly nonrelevant comment concerning an event which occurred eight months ago must be interpreted as a powerful message. The game requires the nimbleness of a high wire acrobat, and if either participant slips the game can be shattered; the penalties for frequent failure are apt to be severe.

### Rules of the Game

The cardinal rule of the game is that open disagreement between the players must be avoided at all costs. Thus, the nurse must communicate her recommendations without appearing to be making a recommendation statement. The physician, in requesting a recommendation from a nurse, must do so without appearing to be asking for it. Utilization of this technique keeps anyone from committing themselves to a position before a sub rosa agreement on that position has already been established. In that way open disagreement is avoided. The greater the significance of the recommendation, the more subtly the game must be played.

To convey a subtle example of the game with all its nuances would require the talents of a literary artist. Lacking these talents, let me give you the following example which is unsubtle, but happens frequently. The medical resident on hospital call is awakened by telephone at 1:00 A.M. because a patient on a ward, not his own, has not been able to fall asleep. Dr. Jones answers the telephone and the dialogue goes like this:

This is Dr. Jones.

(An open and direct communication.)

Dr. Jones, this is Miss Smith on 2W—Mrs. Brown, who learned today of her father's death, is unable to fall asleep.

(This message has two levels. Openly, it describes a set of circumstances, a woman who is unable to sleep and who that morning received word of her father's death. Less openly, but just as directly, it is a diagnostic and recommendation statement; i.e., Mrs. Brown is unable to sleep because of her grief, and she should be given a sedative.

Dr. Jones, accepting the diagnostic statement and replying to the recommendation statement, answers.)

What sleeping medication has been helpful to Mrs. Brown in the past?

(Dr. Jones, not knowing the patient, is asking for a recommendation from the nurse, who does know the patient, about what sleeping medication should be prescribed. Note, however, his question does not appear to be asking her for a recommendation. Miss Smith replies.)

Pentobarbital mg 100 was quite effective night before last.

(A disguised recommendation statement. Dr. Jones replies with a note of authority in his voice.)

Pentobarbital mg 100 before bedtime as needed for sleep; got it?

(Miss Smith ends the conversation with the tone of a grateful supplicant.)

Yes, I have, and thank you very much, doctor.

The above is an example of a successfully played doctor-nurse game. The nurse made appropriate recommendations which were accepted by the physician and were helpful to the patient. The game was successful because the cardinal rule was not violated. The nurse was able to make her recommendation without appearing to, and the physician was able to ask for recommendations without conspicuously asking for them.

### The Scoring System

Inherent in any game are penalties and rewards for the players. In game theory, the doctor-nurse game fits the nonzero sum game model. It is not like chess, where the players compete with each other and whatever one player loses the other wins. Rather, it is the kind of game in which the rewards and punishments are shared by both players. If they play the game successfully they both win rewards, and if they are unskilled and the game is played badly, they both suffer the penalty.

The most obvious reward from the well-played game is a doctor-nurse team that operates efficiently. The physician is able to utilize the nurse as a valuable consultant, and the nurse gains self-esteem and professional satisfaction from her job. The less obvious rewards are no less important. A successful game creates a doctor-nurse alliance; through this alliance the physician gains the respect and admiration of the nursing service. He can be confident that his nursing staff will smooth the path for getting his work done. His charts will be organized and waiting for him when he arrives, the ruffled feathers of patients and relatives will have been smoothed down, his pet routines will be happily followed, and he will be helped in a thousand and one other ways.

The doctor-nurse alliance sheds its light on the nurse as well. She gains a reputation for being a "damn good nurse." She is respected by everyone and appropriately enjoys her position. When physicians discuss the nursing staff it would not be unusual for her name to be mentioned with respect and admiration. Their esteem for a good nurse is no less than their esteem for a good doctor.

The penalties for a game failure, on the other hand, can be severe. The physician who is an unskilled gamesman and fails to recognize the nurses' subtle recommendation messages is tolerated as a "clod." If, however, he interprets these messages as insolence and strongly indicates he does not wish to tolerate suggestions from nurses, he creates a rocky path for his travels. The old truism "If the nurse is your ally you've got it made, and if she has it in for you, be prepared for misery" takes on life-sized proportions. He receives three times as many phone calls after midnight as his colleagues. Nurses will not accept his telephone orders because "telephone orders are against the rules." Somehow, this rule gets suspended for the skilled players. Soon he becomes like Joe Bfstplk in the "Li'l Abner" comic strip. No matter where he goes, a black cloud constantly hovers over his head.

The unskilled gamesman nurse also pays heavily. The nurse who does not view her role as that of consultant, and therefore does not attempt to communicate recommendations, is perceived as a dullard and is mercifully allowed to fade into the woodwork.

The nurse who does see herself as a consultant but refuses to follow the rules of the game in making her recommendations has hell to pay. The outspoken nurse is labeled a "bitch" by the surgeon. The psychiatrist describes her as unconsciously suffering from penis envy and her behavior is the acting out of her hostility towards men. Loosely translated, the psychiatrist is saying she is a bitch. The employment of the unbright outspoken nurse is soon terminated. The outspoken bright nurse whose recommendations are worthwhile remains employed. She is, however, constantly reminded in a hundred ways that she is not loved.

## Genesis of the Game

To understand how the game evolved, we must comprehend the nature of the doctors' and nurses' training which shaped the attitudes necessary for the game.

### Medical Student Training

The medical student in his freshman year studies as if possessed. In the anatomy class he learns every groove and prominence on the bones of the skeleton as if life depended on it. As a matter of fact, he literally believes just that. He not infrequently says, "I've got to learn it exactly; a life may depend on me knowing that." A con-

sequence of this attitude, which is carefully nurtured throughout medical school, is the development of a phobia: the overdetermined fear of making a mistake. The development of his fear is quite understandable. The burden the physician must carry is at times almost unbearable. He feels responsible in a very personal way for the lives of his patients. When a man dies leaving young children and a widow, the doctor carries some of her grief and despair inside himself; and when a child dies, some of him dies too. He sees himself as a warrior against death and disease. When he loses a battle, through no fault of his own, he nevertheless feels pangs of guilt, and he relentlessly searches himself to see if there might have been a way to alter the outcome. For the physician a mistake leading to a serious consequence is intolerable, and any mistake reminds him of his vulnerability. There is little wonder that he becomes phobic. The classical way in which phobias are managed is to avoid the source of the fear. Since it is impossible to avoid making some mistakes in an active practice of medicine, a substitute defensive maneuver is employed. The physician develops the belief that he is omnipotent and omniscient, and therefore incapable of making mistakes. This belief allows the phobic physician to actively engage in his practice rather than avoid it. The fear of committing an error in a critical field like medicine is unavoidable and appropriately realistic. The physician, however, must learn to live with the fear rather than handle it defensively through a posture of omnipotence. This defense markedly interferes with his interpersonal professional relationships.

Physicians, of course, deny feelings of omnipotence. The evidence, however, renders their denials to whispers in the wind. The slightest mistake inflicts a large narcissistic wound. Depending on his underlying personality structure the physician may be obsessed for days about it, quickly rationalize it away, or deny it. The guilt produced is unusually exaggerated and the incident is handled defensively. The ways in which physicians enhance and support each other's defenses when an error is made could be the topic of another paper. The feeling of omnipotence becomes generalized to other areas of his life. A report of the Federal Aviation Agency (FAA), as quoted in *Time* magazine (August 5, 1966), states that in 1964 and 1965 physicians had a fatal-accident rate four times as high as the average for all other private pilots. Major causes of the high death rate were risk-taking attitudes and judgments. Almost all of the accidents occurred on pleasure trips, and were therefore not necessary risks to get to a patient needing emergency care. The trouble, suggested an FAA official, is that too many doctors fly with "the feeling that they are omnipotent." Thus, the extremes to which the physician may go in preserving his self-concept of omnipotence may threaten his own life. This overdetermined preservation of omnipotence is indicative of its brittleness and its underlying foundation of fear of failure.

The physician finds himself trapped in a paradox. He fervently wants to give his patients the best possible medical care, and being open to the nurses' recommendations helps him accomplish this. On the other hand, accepting advice from nonphysicians is highly threatening to his omnipotence. The solution for the paradox is to receive sub rosa recommendations and make them appear to be initiated by himself. In short, he must learn to play the doctor-nurse game.

Some physicians never learn to play the game. Most learn in their internship, and a perceptive few learn during their clerkships in medical school. Medical students frequently complain that the nursing staff treats them as if they had just completed a junior Red Cross first-aid class instead of two years of intensive medical training. Interviewing nurses in a training hospital sheds considerable light on this phenomenon. In their words they said,

> A few students just seem to be with it, they are able to understand what you are trying to tell them, and they are a pleasure to work with; most, however, pretend to know everything and refuse to listen to anything we have to say and I guess we do give them a rough time.

In essence, they are saying that those students who quickly learn the game are rewarded, and those that do not are punished.

Most physicians learn to play the game after they have weathered a few experiences like the one described below. On the first day of his internship, the physician and nurse were making rounds. They stopped at the bed of a fifty-two-year-old woman who, after complimenting the young doctor on his appearance, complained to him of her problem with constipation. After several minutes of listening to her detailed description of peculiar diets, family home remedies, and special exercises that have helped her constipation in the past, the nurse politely interrupted the patient. She told her the doctor would take care of the problem and that he had to move on because there were other patients waiting to see him. The young doctor gave the nurse a stern look, turned toward the patient, and kindly told her he would order an enema for her that very afternoon. As they left the bedside, the nurse told him the patient has had a normal bowel movement every day for the past week and that in the twenty-three days the patient has been in the hospital she has never once passed up an opportunity to complain of her constipation. She quickly added that *if* the doctor wanted to order an enema, the patient would certainly receive one. After hearing this report the intern's mouth fell open and the wheels began turning in his head. He remembered the nurse's comment to the patient that "the doctor had to move on," and it occurred to him that perhaps she was really giving him a message. This experience and a few more like it, and the young doctor learns to listen for the subtle recommendations the nurses make.

### Nursing Student Training

Unlike the medical student who usually learns to play the game after he finishes medical school, the nursing student begins to learn it early in her training. Throughout her education she is trained to play the doctor-nurse game.

Student nurses are taught how to relate to physicians. They are told he has infinitely more knowledge than they, and thus he should be shown the utmost respect. In addition, it was not many years ago when nurses were instructed to stand whenever a physician entered a room. When he would come in for a conference the nurse was expected to offer him her chair, and when both entered a room the nurse would open the door for him and allow him to enter first. Although these practices are no longer rigidly adhered to, the premise upon which they were based is still promulgated. One nurse described that premise as, "He's God almighty and your job is to wait on him."

To inculcate subservience and inhibit deviancy, nursing schools, for the most part, are tightly run, disciplined institutions. Certainly there is great variation among nursing schools, and there is little question that the trend is toward giving students more autonomy. However, in too many schools this trend has not gone far enough, and the climate remains restrictive. The student's schedule is firmly controlled and there is very little free time. Classroom hours, study hours, mealtime, and bedtime with lights out are rigidly enforced. In some schools meaningless chores are assigned, such as cleaning bedsprings with cotton applicators. The relationship between student and instructor continues this military flavor. Often their relationship is more like that between recruit and drill sergeant than between student and teacher. Open dialogue is inhibited by attitudes of strict black and white, with few, if any, shades of gray. Straying from the rigidly outlined path is sure to result in disciplinary action.

The inevitable result of these practices is to instill in the student nurse a fear of independent action. This inhibition of independent action is most marked when relating to physicians. One of the student's greatest fears is making a blunder while assisting a physician and being publicly ridiculed by him. This is really more a reflection of the nature of their training than the prevalence of abusive physicians. The fear of being humiliated for a blunder while assisting in a procedure is generalized to the fear of humiliation for making any independent act in relating to a physician, especially the act of making a direct recommendation. Every nurse interviewed felt that making a suggestion to a physician was equivalent to insulting and belittling him. It was tantamount to questioning his medical knowledge and insinuating he did not know his business. In light of her image of the physician as an omniscient and punitive figure, the questioning of his knowledge would be unthinkable.

The student, however, is also given messages quite contrary to the ones described above. She is continually told that she is an invaluable aid to the physician in the treatment of the patient. She is told that she must help him in every way possible, and she is imbued with a strong sense of responsibility for the care of her patient. Thus she, like the physician, is caught in a paradox. The first set of messages implies that the physician is omniscient and that any recommendation she might make would be insulting to him and leave her open to ridicule. The second set of messages implies that she is an important asset to him, has much to contribute, and is duty-bound to make those contributions. Thus, when her good sense tells her a recommendation would be helpful to him she is not allowed to communicate it directly, nor is she allowed not to communicate it. The way out of the bind is to use the doctor-nurse game and communicate the recommendation without appearing to do so.

## Forces Preserving the Game

Upon observing the indirect interactional system which is the heart of the doctor-nurse game, one must ask the question, "Why does this inefficient mode of communication continue to exist?" The forces mitigating against change are powerful.

### Rewards and Punishments

The doctor-nurse game has a powerful innate self-perpetuating force—its system of rewards and punishments. One potent method of shaping behavior is to reward one set of behavioral patterns and to punish patterns which deviate from it. As described earlier, the rewards given for a well-played game and the punishments meted out to unskilled players are impressive. This system alone would be sufficient to keep the game flourishing. The game, however, has additional forces.

### The Strength of the Set

It is well recognized that sets are hard to break. A powerful attitudinal set is the nurse's perception that making a suggestion to a physician is equivalent to insulting and belittling him. An example of where attempts are regularly made to break this set is seen on psychiatric treatment wards operating on a therapeutic community model. This model requires open and direct communication between members of the team. Psychiatrists working in these settings expend a great deal of energy in urging for and rewarding openness before direct patterns of communication become established. The rigidity of the resistance to break this set is impressive. If the physician himself is a prisoner of a set and therefore does not actively try to destroy it, change is near impossible.

### The Need for Leadership

Lack of leadership and structure in any organization produces anxiety in its members. As the importance of the organization's mission increases, the demand by its members for leadership commensurately increases. In our culture human life is near the top of our hierarchy of values, and organizations which deal with human lives, such as law and medicine, are very rigidly structured. Certainly some of this is necessary for the systematic management of the task. The excessive degree of rigidity, however, is demanded by its members for their own psychic comfort rather than for its utility in efficiently carrying out its mission. The game lends support to this thesis. Indirect communication is an inefficient mode of transmitting information. However, it effectively supports and protects a rigid organizational structure with the physician in clear authority. Maintaining an omnipotent leader provides the other members with a great sense of security.

### Sexual Roles

Another influence perpetuating the doctor-nurse game is the sexual identity of the players. Doctors are predominately men and nurses are almost exclusively women. There are elements of the game which reinforce the stereotyped roles of male dominance and female passivity. Some nursing instructors explicitly tell their students that their femininity is an important asset to be used when relating to physicians.

## The Community

The doctor and nurse have a shared history and thus have been able to work out their game so that it operates more efficiently than one would expect in an indirect system. Major difficulty arises, however, when the physician works closely with other disciplines which are not normally considered part of the medical sphere. With expanding medical horizons encompassing cooperation with sociologists, engineers, anthropologists, computer analysts, etc., continued expectation of a doctor-nurse-like interaction by the physician is disastrous. The sociologist, for example, is not willing to play that kind of game. When his direct communications are rebuffed the relationship breaks down.

The major disadvantage of a doctor-nurselike game is its inhibitory effect on open dialogue which is stifling and anti-intellectual. The game is basically a transactional neurosis, and both professions would enhance themselves by taking steps to change the attitudes which breed the game. . . .

## QUESTIONS

1. Why does Stein call the interaction between doctor and nurse a "game"?

2. How is the relationship between doctors and nurses influenced by society's gender roles?

3. What unspoken signals are used by doctors and nurses to indicate and maintain their relative statuses? Can you think of parallel examples relating to teachers and students?

*Edward T. Hall*
*Mildred Reed Hall*

# 14. The Sounds of Silence

*The human capacity for communication is without parallel in the animal world. Apart from our unique gift for language, we have a remarkable repertoire of nonverbal signals, consisting mostly of messages that are sent and received unconsciously. An encounter between two people, however simple it may appear on the surface, actually includes the mutual transmission and receipt of countless cues and signals.*

*In recent years, social scientists have carefully studied the many ways that messages can be communicated nonverbally. These include facial expressions such as eye contact or smiles; "body language" such as yawning or fidgeting, and the manipulation of time or space—for example, by keeping someone waiting, or by keeping someone at a distance.*

*In this article, Edward T. Hall and Mildred Reed Hall describe some forms of nonverbal communication—and draw attention to some problems that can occur when different cultures place different meanings on the same signal or behavior.*

Excerpted from "The Sounds of Silence" by Edward T. Hall and Mildred Reed Hall. Originally appeared in *Playboy* Magazine. Copyright © 1971 by Edward T. Hall and Mildred Reed Hall. Reprinted with permission of the authors.

Bob leaves his apartment at 8:15 A.M. and stops at the corner drugstore for breakfast. Before he can speak, the counterman says, "The usual?" Bob nods yes. While he savors his Danish, a fat man pushes onto the adjoining stool and overflows into his space. Bob scowls and the man pulls himself in as much as he can. Bob has sent two messages without speaking a syllable.

Henry has an appointment to meet Arthur at 11 o'clock; he arrives at 11:30. Their conversation is friendly, but Arthur retains a lingering hostility. Henry has unconsciously communicated that he doesn't think the appointment is very important or that Arthur is a person who needs to be treated with respect.

George is talking to Charley's wife at a party. Their conversation is entirely trivial, yet Charley glares at them suspiciously. Their physical proximity and the movements of their eyes reveal that they are powerfully attracted to each other.

José Ybarra and Sir Edmund Jones are at the same party, and it is important for them to establish a cordial relationship for business reasons. Each is trying to be warm and friendly, yet they will part with mutual distrust and their business transaction will probably fall through. José, in Latin fashion, moved closer and closer to Sir Edmund as they spoke, and this movement was miscommunicated as pushiness to Sir Edmund, who kept backing away from this intimacy, and this was miscommunicated to José as coldness. The silent languages of Latin and English cultures are more difficult to learn than their spoken languages.

In each of these cases, we see the subtle power of nonverbal communication. The only language used throughout most of the history of humanity (in evolutionary terms, vocal communication is relatively recent), it is the first form of communication you learn. You use this preverbal language, consciously and unconsciously, every day to tell other people how you feel about yourself and them. This language includes your posture, gestures, facial expressions, costume, the way you walk, even your treatment of time and space and material things. All people communicate on several different levels at the same time but are usually aware of only the verbal dialog and don't realize that they respond to nonverbal messages. But when a person says one thing and really believes something else, the discrepancy between the two can usually be sensed. Nonverbal-communication systems are much less subject to the conscious deception that often occurs in verbal systems. When we find ourselves thinking, "I don't know what it is about him, but he doesn't seem sincere," it's usually this lack of congruity between a person's words and his behavior that makes us anxious and uncomfortable.

Few of us realize how much we all depend on body movement in our conversation or are aware of the hidden rules that govern listening behavior. But we know instantly whether or not the person we're talking to is "tuned in" and we're very sensitive to any breach in listening etiquette. In white middle-class American culture, when someone wants to show he is listening to someone else, he looks either at the other person's face or, specifically, at his eyes, shifting his gaze from one eye to the other.

If you observe a person conversing, you'll notice that he indicates he's listening by nodding his head. He also makes little "Hmm" noises. If he agrees with what's being said, he may give a vigorous nod. To show pleasure or affirmation, he smiles; if he has some reservations, he looks skeptical by raising an eyebrow or pulling down the corners of his mouth. If a participant wants to terminate the conversation, he may start shifting his body position, stretching his legs, crossing or uncrossing them, bobbing his foot or diverting his gaze from the speaker. The more he fidgets, the more the speaker becomes aware that he has lost his audience. As a last measure, the listener may look at his watch to indicate the imminent end of the conversation.

Talking and listening are so intricately intertwined that a person cannot do one without the other. Even when one is alone and talking to oneself, there is part of the brain that speaks while another part listens. In all conversations, the listener is positively or negatively reinforcing the speaker all the time. He may even guide the conversation without knowing it, by laughing or frowning or dismissing the argument with a wave of his hand.

The language of the eyes—another age-old way of exchanging feelings—is both subtle and complex. Not only do men and women use their eyes differently but there are class, generation, regional, ethnic and national cultural differences. Americans often complain about the way foreigners stare at people or hold a glance too long. Most Americans look away from someone who is using his eyes in an unfamiliar way because it makes them self-conscious. If a man looks at another man's wife in a certain way, he's asking for trouble, as indicated earlier. But he might not be ill-mannered or seeking to challenge the husband. He might be a European in this country who hasn't learned our visual mores. Many American women visiting France or Italy are acutely embarrassed because, for the first time in their lives, men really look at them—their eyes, hair, nose, lips, breasts, hips, legs, thighs, knees, ankles, feet, clothes, hairdo, even their walk. These same women, once they have become used to being looked at, often return to the United States and are overcome with the feeling that "No one ever really looks at me anymore."

Analyzing the mass of data on the eyes, it is possible to sort out at least three ways in which the eyes are used to communicate: dominance versus submission, involvement versus detachment and positive versus negative attitude. In addition, there are three levels of consciousness and control, which can be categorized as follows: (1) conscious use of the eyes to communicate, such as the flirting blink and the intimate nose-wrinkling squint; (2) the very extensive category of unconscious but learned behavior governing where the eyes are directed and when (this unwritten set of rules dictates how and under what circumstances the sexes, as well as people of all status categories, look at each other); and (3) the response of the eye itself, which is completely outside both awareness and control—changes in the cast (the sparkle) of the eye and the pupillary reflex.

The eye is unlike any other organ of the body, for it is an extension of the brain. The unconscious pupillary reflex and the cast of the eye have been known by people of Middle Eastern origin for years—although most are unaware of their knowledge. Depending on the context, Arabs and others look either directly at the eyes or deeply *into* the eyes of their interlocutor. We became aware of this in the Middle East several years ago while looking at jewelry. The merchant suddenly started to push a particular bracelet at a customer and said, "You buy this one." What interested us was that the bracelet was not the one that had been consciously selected by the purchaser. But the merchant, watching the pupils of the eyes, knew what the purchaser really wanted to buy. Whether he specifically knew *how* he knew is debatable.

A psychologist at the University of Chicago, Eckhard Hess, was the first to conduct systematic studies of the pupillary reflex. His wife remarked one evening, while watching him reading in bed, that he must be very interested in the text because his pupils were dilated. Following up on this, Hess slipped some pictures of nudes into a stack of photographs that he gave to his male assistant. Not looking at the photographs but watching his assistant's pupils, Hess was able to tell precisely when the assistant came to the nudes. In further experiments, Hess retouched the eyes in a photograph of a woman. In one print, he made the pupils small, in another, large; nothing else was changed. Subjects who were given the photographs found the woman with the dilated pupils much more attractive. Any man who has had the experience of seeing a woman look at him as her pupils widen with reflex speed knows that she's flashing him a message.

The eye-sparkle phenomenon frequently turns up in our interviews of couples in love. It's apparently one of the first reliable clues in the other person that love is genuine. To date, there is no scientific data to explain eye sparkle; no investigation of the pupil, the cornea or even the white sclera of the eye shows how the sparkle originates. Yet we all know it when we see it.

One common situation for most people involves the use of the eyes in the street and in public. Although eye behavior follows a definite set of rules, the rules vary according to the place, the needs and feelings of the people, and their ethnic background. For urban whites, once they're within definite recognition distance (16–32 feet for people with average eyesight), there is mutual avoidance of eye contact—unless they want something specific: a pickup, a handout or information of some kind. In the West and in small towns generally, however, people are much more likely to look at and greet one another, even if they're strangers.

It's permissible to look at people if they're beyond recognition distance; but once inside this sacred zone, you can only steal a glance at strangers. You *must* greet friends, however; to fail to do so is insulting. Yet, to stare too fixedly even at them is considered rude and hostile. Of course, all of these rules are variable.

A great many blacks, for example, greet each other in public even if they don't know each other. To blacks, most eye behavior of whites has the effect of giving the impression that they aren't there, but this is due to white avoidance of eye contact with *anyone* in the street.

Another very basic difference between people of different ethnic backgrounds is their sense of territoriality and how they handle space. This is the silent communication, or miscommunication, that caused friction between Mr. Ybarra and Sir Edmund Jones in our earlier example. We know from research that everyone has around himself an invisible bubble of space that contracts and expands depending on several factors: his emotional state, the activity he's performing at the time and his cultural background. This bubble is a kind of mobile territory that he will defend against intrusion. If he is accustomed to close personal distance between himself and others, his bubble will be smaller than that of someone who's accustomed to greater personal distance. People of North European heritage—English, Scandinavian, Swiss and German—tend to avoid contact.

Those whose heritage is Italian, French, Spanish, Russian, Latin American or Middle Eastern like close personal contact.

People are very sensitive to any intrusion into their spatial bubble. If someone stands too close to you, your first instinct is to back up. If that's not possible, you lean away and pull yourself in, tensing your muscles. If the intruder doesn't respond to these body signals, you may then try to protect yourself, using a briefcase, umbrella or raincoat. Women—especially when traveling alone— often plant their pocketbook in such a way that no one can get very close to them. As a last resort, you may move to another spot and position yourself behind a desk or a chair that provides screening. Everyone tries to adjust the space around himself in a way that's comfortable for him; most often, he does this unconsciously.

Emotions also have a direct effect on the size of a person's territory. When you're angry or under stress, your bubble expands and you require more space. New York psychiatrist Augustus Kinzel found a difference in what he calls Body-Buffer Zones between violent and nonviolent prison inmates. Dr. Kinzel conducted experiments in which each prisoner was placed in the center of a small room and then Dr. Kinzel slowly walked toward him. Nonviolent prisoners allowed him to come quite close, while prisoners with a history of violent behavior couldn't tolerate his proximity and reacted with some vehemence.

Apparently, people under stress experience other people as looming larger and closer than they actually are. Studies of schizophrenic patients have indicated that they sometimes have a distorted perception of space, and several psychiatrists have reported patients who experience their body boundaries as filling up an entire room. For these patients, anyone who comes into the room is actually inside their body, and such an intrusion may trigger a violent outburst.

Unfortunately, there is little detailed information about normal people who live in highly congested urban areas. We do know, of course, that the noise, pollution, dirt, crowding and confusion of our cities induce feelings of stress in most of us, and stress leads to a need for greater space. The man who's packed into a subway, jostled in the street, crowded into an elevator and forced to work all day in a bull pen or in a small office without auditory or visual privacy is going to be very stressed at the end of his day. He needs places that provide relief from constant overstimulation of his nervous system. Stress from overcrowding is cumulative and people can tolerate more crowding early in the day than later; note the increased bad temper during the evening rush hour as compared with the morning melee. Certainly one factor in people's desire to commute by car is the need for privacy and relief from crowding (except, often, from other cars); it may be the only time of the day when nobody can intrude.

In crowded public places, we tense our muscles and hold ourselves stiff, and thereby communicate to others our desire not to intrude on their space and, above all, not to touch them. We also avoid eye contact and the total effect is that of someone who has "tuned out." Walking along the street, our bubble expands slightly as we move in a stream of strangers, taking care not to bump into them. In the office, at meetings, in restaurants, our bubble keeps changing as it adjusts to the activity at hand.

Most white middle-class Americans use four main distances in their business and social relations: intimate, personal, social and public. Each of these distances has a near and a far phase and is accompanied by changes in the volume of the voice. Intimate distance varies from direct physical contact with another person to a distance of six to eighteen inches and is used for our most private activities—caressing another person or making love. At this distance, you are overwhelmed by sensory inputs from the other person—heat from the body, tactile stimulation from the skin, the fragrance of perfume, even the sound of breathing—all of which literally envelop you. Even at the far phase, you're still within easy touching distance. In general, the use of intimate distance in public between adults is frowned on. It's also much too close for strangers, except under conditions of extreme crowding.

In the second zone—personal distance—the close phase is one and a half to two and a half feet; it's at this distance that wives usually stand from their husbands in public. If another woman moves into this zone, the wife will most likely be disturbed. The far phase—two and a half to four feet—is the distance used to "keep someone at arm's length" and is the most common spacing used by people in conversation.

The third zone—social distance—is employed during business transactions or exchanges with a clerk or repairman. People who work together tend to use close social distance—four to seven feet. This is also the distance for conversation at social gatherings. To stand at this distance from someone who is seated has a dominating effect (for example, teacher to pupil, boss to secretary). The far phase of the third zone—seven to twelve feet—is where people stand when someone says, "Stand back so I can look at you." This distance lends a formal tone to business or social discourse. In an executive office, the desk serves to keep people at this distance.

The fourth zone—public distance—is used by teachers in classrooms or speakers at public gatherings. At its farthest phase—25 feet and beyond—it is used for important public figures. Violations of this distance can lead to serious complications. During his 1970 U.S. visit, the president of France, Georges Pompidou, was harassed by pickets in Chicago, who were permitted to get within touching distance. Since pickets in France are kept behind barricades a block or more away, the president was outraged by this insult to his person, and President Nixon was obliged to communicate his concern as well as offer his personal apologies.

It is interesting to note how American pitchmen and panhandlers exploit the unwritten, unspoken conventions of eye and distance. Both take advantage of the fact that once explicit eye contact is established, it is rude to look away, because to do so means to brusquely dismiss the other person and his needs. Once having caught the eye of his mark, the panhandler then locks on, not letting go until he moves through the public zone, the social zone, the personal zone, and finally, into the intimate sphere, where people are most vulnerable.

Touch also is an important part of the constant stream of communication that takes place between people. A light touch, a firm touch, a blow, a caress are all communications. In an effort to break down barriers among people, there's been a recent upsurge in group-encounter activities, in which strangers are encouraged to touch one another. In special situations such as these, the rules for not touching are broken with group approval and people gradually lose some of their inhibitions.

Although most people don't realize it, space is perceived and distances are set not by vision alone but with all the senses. Auditory space is perceived with the ears, thermal space with the skin, kinesthetic space with the muscles of the body and olfactory space with the nose. And, once again, it's one's culture that determines how his senses are programmed—which sensory information ranks highest and lowest. The important thing to remember is that culture is very persistent. In this country, we've noted the existence of culture patterns that determine distance between people in the third and fourth generations of some families, despite their prolonged contact with people of very different cultural heritages.

Whenever there is great cultural distance between two people, there are bound to be problems arising from differences in behavior and expectations. An example is the American couple who consulted a psychiatrist about their marital problems. The husband was from New England and had been brought up by reserved parents who taught him to control his emotions and to respect the need for privacy. His wife was from an Italian family and had been brought up in close contact with all the members of her large family, who were extremely warm, volatile and demonstrative.

When the husband came home after a hard day at the office, dragging his feet and longing for peace and quiet, his wife would rush to him and smother him. Clasping his hands, rubbing his brow, crooning over his weary head, she never left him alone. But when the wife was upset or anxious about her day, the husband's response was to withdraw completely and leave her alone. No comforting, no affectionate embrace, no attention—just solitude. The woman became convinced her husband didn't love her and, in desperation, she consulted a psychiatrist. Their problem wasn't basically psychological but cultural.

Why has man developed all these different ways of communicating messages without words? One reason is that people don't like to spell out certain kinds of messages. We prefer to find other ways of showing our feelings. This is especially true in relationships as sensitive as courtship. Men don't like to be rejected and most women don't want to turn a man down bluntly. Instead, we work out subtle ways of encouraging or discouraging each other that save face and avoid confrontations.

How a person handles space in dating others is an obvious and very sensitive indicator of how he or she feels about the other person. On a first date, if a woman sits or stands so close to a man that he is acutely conscious of her physical presence—inside the intimate-distance zone—the man usually construes it to mean that she is encouraging him. However, before the man starts moving in on the woman, he should be sure what message she's really sending; otherwise, he risks bruising his ego. What is close to someone of North European background may be neutral or distant to someone of Italian heritage. Also, women sometimes use space as a way of misleading a man and there are few things that put men off more than women who communicate contradictory messages—such as women who cuddle up and then act insulted when a man takes the next step.

How does a woman communicate interest in a man? In addition to such familiar gambits as smiling at him, she may glance shyly at him, blush and then look away. Or she may give him a real come-on look and move in very close when he approaches. She may touch his arm and ask for a light. As she leans forward to light her cigarette, she may brush him lightly, enveloping him in her perfume. She'll probably continue to smile at him and she may use what ethologists call preening gestures—touching the back of her hair, thrusting her breasts forward, tilting her hips as she stands or crossing her legs if she's seated, perhaps even exposing one thigh or putting a hand on her thigh and stroking it. She may also stroke her wrists as she converses or show the palm of her hand as a way of gaining his attention. Her skin may be unusually flushed or quite pale, her eyes brighter, the pupils larger.

If a man sees a woman whom he wants to attract, he tries to present himself by his posture and stance as someone who is self-assured. He moves briskly and confidently. When he catches the eye of the woman, he may hold her glance a little longer than normal. If he gets an encouraging smile, he'll move in close and engage her in small talk. As they converse, his glance shifts over her face and body. He, too, may make preening gestures—straightening his tie, smoothing his hair or shooting his cuffs.

How do people learn body language? The same way they learn spoken language—by observing and imitating people around them as they're growing up. Little girls imitate their mothers or an older female. Little boys imitate their fathers or a respected uncle or a character on television. In this way, they learn the gender signals appropriate for their sex. Regional, class and ethnic patterns of body behavior are also learned in childhood and persist throughout life.

Such patterns of masculine and feminine body behavior vary widely from one culture to another. In America, for example, women stand with their thighs together. Many walk with their pelvis tipped slightly forward and their upper arms close to their body. When they sit, they cross their legs at the knee or cross their ankles. American men hold their arms away from their body, often swinging them as they walk. They stand with their legs apart (an extreme example is the cowboy, with legs apart and thumbs tucked into his belt). When they sit, they put their feet on the floor with legs apart and, in some parts of the country, they cross their legs by putting one ankle on the other knee.

Leg behavior indicates sex, status, and personality. It also indicates whether or not one is at ease or is showing respect or disrespect for the other person. Young Latin American males avoid crossing their legs. In their world of *machismo*, the preferred position for young males when with one another (if there is no older dominant male present to whom they must show respect) is to sit on the base of their spine with their leg muscles relaxed and their feet wide apart. Their respect position is like our military equivalent: spine straight, heels and ankles together—almost identical to that displayed by properly brought up young women in New England in the early part of this century.

American women who sit with their legs spread apart in the presence of males are *not* normally signaling a come-on—they are simply (and often unconsciously) sitting like men. Middle-class women in the presence of other women to whom they are very close may on occasion throw themselves down on a soft chair or sofa and let themselves go. This is a signal that nothing serious will be taken up. Males, on the other hand, lean back and prop their legs up on the nearest object.

The way we walk, similarly, indicates status, respect, mood and ethnic or cultural affiliation. The many variants of the female walk are too well known to go into here, except to say that a man would have to be blind not to be turned on by the way some women walk—a fact that made Mae West rich before scientists ever studied these matters. To white Americans, some French middle-class males walk in a way that is both humorous and suspect. There is a bounce and looseness to the French walk, as though the parts of the body were somehow unrelated. Jacques Tati, the French movie actor, walks this way: so does the great mime, Marcel Marceau.

Blacks and whites in America—with the exception of middle- and upper-middle-class professionals of both groups—move and walk very differently from each other. To the blacks, whites often seem incredibly stiff, almost mechanical in their movements. Black males, on the other hand, have a looseness and coordination that frequently makes whites a little uneasy; it's too different, too integrated, too alive, too male. Norman Mailer has said that squares walk from the shoulders, like bears, but blacks and hippies walk from the hips, like cats.

All over the world, people walk not only in their own characteristic way but have walks that communicate the nature of their involvement with whatever it is they're doing. The purposeful walk of North Europeans is an important component of proper behavior on the job. Any male who has been in the military knows how essential it is to walk properly (which makes for a continuing source of tension between blacks and whites in the Service). The quick shuffle of servants in the Far East in the old days was a show of respect. On the island of Truk, when we last visited, the inhabitants even had a name for the respectful walk that one used when in the presence of a chief or when walking past a chief's house. The term was *sufan*, which meant to be humble and respectful.

The notion that people communicate volumes by their gestures, facial expressions, posture and walk is not new; actors, dancers, writers and psychiatrists have long been aware of it. Only in recent years, however, have scientists begun to make systematic observations of body motions. Ray L. Birdwhistell of the University of Pennsylvania is one of the pioneers in body-motion research and coined the term *kinesics* to describe this field. He developed an elaborate notation system to record both facial and body movement, using an approach similar to that of the linguist, who studies the basic elements of speech. Birdwhistell and other kinesicists such as Albert Shellen, Adam Kendon and William Condon take movies of people interacting. They run the film over and over again, often at reduced speed for frame-by-frame analysis, so that they can observe even the slightest body movements not perceptible at normal interaction speeds. These movements are then recorded in notebooks for later analysis.

To appreciate the importance of nonverbal-communication systems, consider the unskilled inner-city black looking for a job. His handling of time and space alone is sufficiently different from the white middle-class pattern to create great misunderstandings on both sides. The black is told to appear for a job interview at a certain time. He arrives late. The white interviewer concludes from his tardy arrival that the black is irresponsible and not really interested in the job. What the interviewer doesn't know is that the black time system (often referred to by blacks as C.P.T.—colored people's time) isn't the same as that of whites. In the words of a black student who had been told to make an appointment to see his professor: "Man, you *must* be putting me on. I never had an appointment in my life."

The black job applicant, having arrived late for his interview, may further antagonize the white interviewer by his posture and his eye behavior. Perhaps he slouches and avoids looking at the interviewer: to him, this is playing it cool. To the interviewer, however, he may well look shifty and sound uninterested. The interviewer has failed to notice the actual signs of interest and eagerness in the black's behavior, such as subtle shift in the quality of the voice—a gentle and tentative excitement—an almost imperceptible change in the cast of the eyes and a relaxing of the jaw muscles.

Moreover, correct reading of black-white behavior is continually complicated by the fact that both groups are comprised of individuals—some of whom try to accommodate and some of whom make it a point of pride *not* to accommodate. At present, this means that many Americans, when thrown into contact with one another, are in the precarious position of not knowing which pattern applies. Once identified and analyzed, nonverbal-communication systems can be taught, like a foreign language. Without this training, we respond to nonverbal communications in terms of our own culture; we read everyone's behavior as if it were our own, and thus we often misunderstand it.

Several years ago in New York City, there was a program for sending children from predominantly black and Puerto Rican low-income neighborhoods to summer school in a white upper-class neighborhood on the East Side. One morning, a group of young black and Puerto Rican boys raced down the street, shouting and screaming and overturning garbage cans on their way to school. A doorman from an apartment building nearby chased them and cornered one of them inside a building. The boy drew a knife and attacked the doorman. This tragedy would not have occurred if the doorman had been familiar with the behavior of boys from low-income neighborhoods, where such antics are routine and socially acceptable and where pursuit would be expected to invite a violent response.

The language of behavior is extremely complex. Most of us are lucky to have under control one subcultural system—the one that reflects our sex, class, generation and geographic region within the United States. Because of its complexity, efforts to isolate bits of nonverbal communication and generalize from them are in vain; you don't become an instant expert on people's behavior by watching them at cocktail parties. Body language isn't something that's independent of the person, something that can be donned and doffed like a suit of clothes.

Our research and that of our colleagues has shown that, far from being a superficial form of communication that can be consciously manipulated, nonverbal-communication systems are interwoven into the fabric of the personality and, as sociologist Erving Goffman has demonstrated, into society itself. They are the warp and woof of daily interactions with others, and they influence how one expresses oneself, how one experiences oneself as a man or a woman.

Nonverbal communications signal to members of your own group what kind of person you are, how you feel about others, how you'll fit into and work in a group, whether you're assured or anxious, the degree to which you feel comfortable with the standards of your own culture, as well as deeply significant feelings about the self, including the state of your own psyche. For most of us, it's difficult to accept the reality of another's behavioral system. And, of course, none of us will ever become fully knowledgeable of the importance of every non-verbal signal. But as long as each of us realizes the power of these signals, this society's diversity can be a source of great strength rather than a further—and subtly powerful—source of division.

## QUESTIONS

1. What are some of the ways that people use to communicate without words?

2. How can cultural differences in nonverbal communication lead to misunderstandings between people from different groups or societies?

3. What would happen if you stared directly at a stranger in an elevator? How would you feel about conducting an informal series of such experiments yourself?

*Robert Levine*
*Ellen Wolff*

# 15. Social Time: The Heartbeat of Culture

*What is time? We are inclined to take time for granted, but if we think about it, the concept proves to be very problematic. Investigators of all kinds—philosophers, physicists, and even science-fiction writers—have wrestled with the elusive nature of time and its passing.*

*Sociologists point out that our understandings of time are socially constructed. In other words, each society creates a shared agreement about what time is, how it should be measured, how important punctuality is, and so on. Some societies, for example, see time as a series of repetitive cycles, like the rising and setting of the sun; others—including our own—see time in a linear way, as a straight line traveling at constant speed from the past to the future. Similarly, some societies measure time in relatively long and imprecise intervals, and the members may be quite casual about punctuality; other societies measure time in brief, precise intervals, and see punctuality as a civic virtue.*

*In this article, Robert Levine and Ellen Wolff draw attention to differences in social time among several different societies.*

*"If a man does not keep pace with his companions, perhaps it is because he hears a different drummer."* This thought by Thoreau strikes a chord in so many people that it has become part of our language. We use the phrase "the beat of a different drummer" to explain any pace of life unlike our own. Such colorful vagueness reveals how informal our rules of time really are. The world over, children simply "pick up" their society's time concepts as they mature. No dictionary clearly defines the meaning of "early" or "late" for them or for strangers who stumble over the maddening incongruities between the time sense they bring with them and the one they face in a new land.

I learned this firsthand, a few years ago, and the resulting culture shock led me halfway around the world to find answers. It seemed clear that time "talks." But what is it telling us?

My journey started shortly after I accepted an appointment as visiting professor of psychology at the federal university in Niteroi, Brazil, a midsized city across the bay from Rio de Janeiro. As I left home for my first day of class, I asked someone the time. It was 9:05 a.m., which allowed me time to relax and look around the campus before my 10 o'clock lecture. After what I judged to be half an hour, I glanced at a clock I was passing. It said 10:20! In panic, I broke for the classroom, followed by gentle calls of "Hola, professor" and "Tudo bem, professor?" from unhurried students, many of whom, I later realized, were my own. I arrived breathless to find an empty room.

Frantically, I asked a passerby the time. "Nine forty-five" was the answer. No, that couldn't be. I asked someone else. "Nine fifty-five." Another said: "Exactly 9:43." The clock in a nearby office read 3:15. I had learned my first lesson about Brazilians: Their timepieces are consistently inaccurate. And nobody minds.

My class was scheduled from 10 until noon. Many students came late, some very late. Several arrived after 10:30. A few showed up closer to 11. Two came after that. All of the latecomers wore the relaxed smiles that I came, later, to enjoy. Each one said hello, and although a few apologized briefly, none seemed terribly concerned about lateness. They assumed that I understood.

The idea of Brazilians arriving late was not a great shock. I had heard about "mānha," the Portuguese equivalent of "mañana" in Spanish. This term, meaning "tomorrow" or "the morning," stereotypes the Brazilian who puts off the business of today until tomorrow. The real surprise came at noon that first day, when the end of class arrived.

Back home in California, I never need to look at a clock to know when the class hour is ending. The shuffling of books is accompanied by strained expressions that say plaintively, "I'm starving. . . . I've got to go to the bathroom. . . . I'm going to suffocate if you keep us one more second." (The pain usually becomes unbearable at two minutes to the hour in undergraduate classes and five minutes before the close of graduate classes.)

When noon arrived in my first Brazilian class, only a few students left immediately. Others slowly drifted out during the next 15 minutes, and some continued asking me questions long after that. When several remaining students kicked off their shoes at 12:30, I went into my own "starving/bathroom/suffocation" routine.

I could not, in all honesty, attribute their lingering to my superb teaching style. I had just spent two hours lecturing on statistics in halting Portuguese. Apparently, for many of my students, staying late was simply of no more importance than arriving late in the first place. As I observed this casual approach in infinite variations during the year, I learned that the "mānha" stereotype oversimplified the real Anglo/Brazilian differences in conceptions of time. Research revealed a more complex picture.

With the assistance of colleagues Laurie West and Harry Reis, I compared the time sense of 91 male and female students in Niteroi with that of 107 similar students at California State University in Fresno. The universities are similar in academic quality and size, and the cities are both secondary metropolitan centers with populations of about 350,000.

We asked students about their perceptions of time in several situations, such as what they would consider late or early for a hypothetical lunch appointment with a friend. The average Brazilian student defined lateness for lunch as 33½ minutes after the scheduled time, compared to only 19 minutes for the Fresno students. But Brazilians also allowed an average of about 54 minutes before they'd consider someone early, while the Fresno students drew the line at 24.

Are Brazilians simply more flexible in their concepts of time and punctuality? And how does this relate to the stereotype of the apathetic, fatalistic and irresponsible

Latin temperament? When we asked students to give typical reasons for lateness, the Brazilians were less likely to attribute it to a lack of caring than the North Americans were. Instead, they pointed to unforeseen circumstances that the person couldn't control. Because they seemed less inclined to feel personally responsible for being late, they also expressed less regret for their own lateness and blamed others less when they were late.

We found similar differences in how students from the two countries characterized people who were late for appointments. Unlike their North American counterparts, the Brazilian students believed that a person who is consistently late is probably more successful than one who is consistently on time. They seemed to accept the idea that someone of status is expected to arrive late. Lack of punctuality is a badge of success.

Even within our own country, of course, ideas of time and punctuality vary considerably from place to place. Different regions and even cities have their own distinct rhythms and rules. Seemingly simple words like "now," snapped out by an impatient New Yorker, and "later," said by a relaxed Californian, suggest a world of difference. Despite our familiarity with these homegrown differences in tempo, problems with time present a major stumbling block to Americans abroad. Peace Corps volunteers told researchers James Spradley of Macalester College and Mark Phillips of the University of Washington that their greatest difficulties with other people, after language problems, were the general pace of life and the punctuality of others. Formal "clock time" may be a standard on which the world agrees, but "social time," the heartbeat of society, is something else again.

How a country paces its social life is a mystery to most outsiders, one that we're just beginning to unravel. Twenty-six years ago, anthropologist Edward Hall noted in *The Silent Language* that informal patterns of time "are seldom, if ever, made explicit. They exist in the air around us. They are either familiar and comfortable, or unfamiliar and wrong." When we realize we are out of step, we often blame the people around us to make ourselves feel better.

Appreciating cultural differences in time sense becomes increasingly important as modern communications put more and more people in daily contact. If we are to avoid misreading issues that involve time perceptions, we need to understand better our own cultural biases and those of others.

When people of different cultures interact, the potential for misunderstanding exists on many levels. For example, members of Arab and Latin cultures usually stand much closer when they are speaking to people than we usually do in the United States, a fact we frequently misinterpret as aggression or disrespect. Similarly, we assign personality traits to groups with a pace of life that is markedly faster or slower than our own. We build ideas of national character, for example, around the traditional Swiss and German ability to "make the trains run on time." Westerners like ourselves define punctuality using precise measures of time: 5 minutes, 15 minutes, an hour. But according to Hall, in many Mediterranean Arab cultures there are only three sets of time: no time at all, now (which is of varying duration) and forever (too long). Because of this, Americans often find difficulty in getting Arabs to distinguish between waiting a long time and a very long time.

According to historian Will Durant, "No man in a hurry is quite civilized." What do our time judgments say about our attitude toward life? How can a North American, coming from a land of digital precision, relate to a North African who may consider a clock "the devil's mill"?

Each language has a vocabulary of time that does not always survive translation. When we translated our questionnaires into Portuguese for my Brazilian students, we found that English distinctions of time were not readily articulated in their language. Several of our questions concerned how long the respondent would wait for someone to arrive, as compared with when they hoped for arrival or actually expected the person would come. In Portuguese, the verbs "to wait for," "to hope for" and "to expect" are all translated as "esperar." We had to add further words of explanation to make the distinction clear to the Brazilian students.

To avoid these language problems, my Fresno colleague Kathy Bartlett and I decided to clock the pace of life in other countries by using as little language as possible. We looked directly at three basic indicators of time: the accuracy of a country's bank clocks, the speed at which pedestrians walked and the average time it took a postal clerk to sell us a single stamp. In six countries on three continents, we made observations in both the nation's largest urban area and a medium-sized city: Japan (Tokyo and Sendai), Taiwan (Taipei and Tainan), Indonesia (Jakarta and Solo), Italy (Rome and Florence), England (London and Bristol) and the United States (New York City and Rochester).

What we wanted to know was: Can we speak of a unitary concept called "pace of life"? What we've learned suggests that we can. There appears to be a very strong relationship (see chart on the next page) between the accuracy of clock time, walking speed and postal efficiency across the countries we studied.

We checked 15 clocks in each city, selecting them at random in downtown banks and comparing the time they showed with that reported by the local telephone company. In Japan, which leads the way in accuracy, the clocks averaged just over half a minute early or late. Indonesian clocks, the least accurate, were more than three minutes off the mark.

I will be interested to see how the digital-information age will affect our perceptions of time. In the United States today, we are reminded of the exact hour of the day more than ever, through little symphonies of beeps emanating from people's digital watches. As they become the norm, I fear our sense of precision may take an absurd twist. The other day, when I asked for the time, a student looked at his watch and replied, "Three twelve and eighteen seconds."

*" 'Will you walk a little faster?' said a whiting to a snail. 'There's a porpoise close behind us, and he's treading on my tail.' "*

So goes the rhyme from *Alice in Wonderland,* which also gave us that famous symbol of haste, the White Rabbit. He came to mind often as we measured the walking speeds in our experimental cities. We clocked how long it took pedestrians to walk 100 feet along a main downtown street during business hours on clear days. To eliminate the effects of socializing, we observed only people walking alone, timing at least 100 in each city. We found, once again, that the Japanese led the way, averaging just 20.7 seconds to cover the distance. The English nosed out the Americans for second place—21.6 to 22.5 seconds—and the Indonesians again trailed the pack, sauntering along at 27.2 seconds. As you might guess, speed was greater in the larger city of each nation than in its smaller one.

Our final measurement, the average time it took postal clerks to sell one stamp, turned out to be less straightforward than we expected. In each city, including those in the United States, we presented clerks with a note in the native language requesting a common-priced stamp—a 20-center in the United States, for example. They were also handed paper money, the equivalent of a $5 bill. In Indonesia, this procedure led to more than we bargained for.

At the large central post office in Jakarta, I asked for the line to buy stamps and was directed to a group of private vendors sitting outside. Each of them hustled for my business: "Hey, good stamps, mister!" "Best stamps here!" In the smaller city of Solo, I found a volleyball game in progress when I arrived at the main post office on Friday afternoon. Business hours, I was told, were over. When I finally did get there during business hours, the clerk was more interested in discussing relatives in America. Would I like to meet his uncle in Cincinnati? Which did I like better: California or the United States? Five people behind me in line waited patiently. Instead of complaining, they began paying attention to our conversation.

When it came to efficiency of service, however, the Indonesians were not the slowest, although they did place far behind the Japanese postal clerks, who averaged 25 seconds. That distinction went to the Italians, whose infamous postal service took 47 seconds on the average.

*"A man who wastes one hour of time has not discovered the meaning of life. . . ."*

That was Charles Darwin's belief, and many share it, perhaps at the cost of their health. My colleagues and I have recently begun studying the relationship between pace of life and well-being. Other researchers have demonstrated that a chronic sense of urgency is a basic component of the Type A, coronary-prone personality. We expect that future research will demonstrate that pace of life is related to rate of heart disease, hypertension, ulcers, suicide, alcoholism, divorce and other indicators of general psychological and physical well-being.

As you envision tomorrow's international society, do you wonder who will set the pace? Americans eye Japan carefully, because the Japanese are obviously "ahead of us" in measurable ways. In both countries, speed is frequently confused with progress. Perhaps looking carefully at the different paces of life around the world will help us distinguish more accurately between the two qualities. Clues are everywhere but sometimes hard to distinguish. You have to listen carefully to hear the beat of even your own drummer.

### The Pace of Life in Six Countries

|  | *Accuracy of Bank Clocks* | *Walking Speed* | *Post Office Speed* |
|---|---|---|---|
| **Japan** | 1 | 1 | 1 |
| **United States** | 2 | 3 | 2 |
| **England** | 4 | 2 | 3 |
| **Italy** | 5 | 4 | 6 |
| **Taiwan** | 3 | 5 | 4 |
| **Indonesia** | 6 | 6 | 5 |

Numbers (1 is the top value) indicate the comparative rankings of each country for each indicator of time sense.

### QUESTIONS

1. What is meant by "social time" and how does it differ from one culture to another?

2. What is your reaction to the description of "social time" in the Brazilian university described by the authors? How do you think the Brazilian students might react to "social time" in an American college?

3. It is often said in North America that "time is money." What are some implications of this attitude?

*Vivian Gornick*

# 16.  On the Jury

*The group, rather than the individual, is the primary
focus of sociology, for it is only in the group—even in
one as small as two people—that social processes can
be observed. In groups we see cooperation and conflict,
conformity and deviance, authority and obedience, and
a variety of other forms of social interaction.*

*Sociologists have been particularly interested in the
decision-making process in small groups. In the past,
much sociological study of groups has taken place in
experimental settings, in which groups are created,
given a problem to solve, and then observed by
researchers. These investigations have yielded a great
deal of information, but they lack the "real life" vitality
of group processes in less artificial settings.*

*One interesting group setting is a jury—which, after
all, is a small group charged with solving a significant,
real-life problem. In this article, Vivian Gornick
recounts her experience as a jury member. Her
description touches on many of the factors that
influence the decision-making process, such as the
prejudices of the participants, the impact of individual
personalities, and the pressure for conformity to the
group.*

The case before the court was a criminal one: illegal
possession of a loaded gun. The elements in the case
were the testimony of two undercover policemen, the
testimony of the accused, and the presence of a gun on
the prosecutor's table. The policemen—both white, in
their middle thirties—said the defendant had the gun in
his hand when they arrested him. The defendant—black,
eighteen—said it was all a lie, he'd never seen the gun
until the moment the cops were pushing him up against
a wall and handcuffing him. The gun—silver-plated, .32
caliber—lay there mute, an indifferent prop to be seized
upon alternately by the prosecuting and the defending
lawyers.

It took a day and a half for all the principals in the
case to say what they had to say. At the end of that time,
the judge turned to the jury box. He reminded the jurors,
twelve good and true, that the burden of proof lay with
the People; that unless, in their judgment, the People had
proved beyond a reasonable doubt the guilt of the accused, it was incumbent upon them to bring in a verdict
of not guilty. He enjoined the jurors to reason out of the
evidence. He further enjoined them to search and make
up their own minds, but at the same time to be open to
the thought and feeling of their fellows, as the essence
of deliberation was the interaction of open minds.

The judge spoke these profound words easily and
carefully, yet mechanically and rhetorically: somewhat
like a stewardess on a plane rehearsing her passengers
in the lifesaving steps they were to take in case of an
emergency whose potential reality no one believed in.

The policemen (whom I will call Galella and Kowalski) told substantially the same story: At approximately 7:30 P.M. one night last July, while on a regular
tour of duty (wearing street clothes, driving an unmarked
car), they spotted two boys, one of whom was the defendant, sitting at the edge of an alley on West 37th Street,
a few feet in from 10th Avenue. As this was a neighborhood that Galella and Kowalski knew well—densely
commercial during the day, equally dense with prostitution after dark—they automatically registered the pres-

ence of strangers. They drove on by and continued their tour. An hour later they heard over their car radio a report that someone had been seen with a gun in or around those same streets. They drove back and found a marked patrol car parked at the corner of 10th and 37th. The uniformed police said they too had had the gun report and had seen two boys they thought suspicious, had questioned and searched them, found nothing, and sent them on their way. The uniformed police described the two boys Galella and Kowalski had seen earlier. The four policemen parted and went back to their respective cars.

Galella and Kowalski drove up 10th Avenue, turning east on 38th Street. Halfway to 9th Avenue, they spotted the two boys in question walking back toward 10th Avenue. Why, they wondered, when the boys had been told to leave the neighborhood? They decided to swing through a bus lot in the middle of the block and return to 37th Street. They parked their car a third of the way up the block, beside a parking lot enclosed by a chain-link fence. In a few minutes they saw the boys standing on the corner, looking around. Then, the cops said, the boys walked into 37th Street, one of them ducked for a moment in and out of the alley, and they continued at a quick pace, half walking, half loping up the street toward Galella and Kowalski. When the two boys were within thirty feet or so of the unmarked car, both Galella and Kowalski said, they saw a gun in the left hand of one of the two. They leaped from their car, their own guns drawn, and said to the two: "Don't move. Police." The boys froze in their tracks. Kowalski said, "Drop the gun." The boy with the gun stood motionless. A second time Kowalski said, "Drop the gun." Then, Kowalski said, in one swift motion the boy raised his arm and threw the gun back and up over the chain-link fence. The cops pushed the boys up against the building beside the fence, their faces turned toward the wall. Galella stood watch over them. Kowalski climbed the fence, retrieved the gun (with four bullets in it), and arrested the two. The one with the gun was the defendant.

The defendant (whom I will call David Moore) told an entirely different story. He said he and a friend from his neighborhood in Queens had decided to go that evening to a disco at 39th Street and 9th Avenue. They took the train into Manhattan, arriving at Times Square at 8:30 P.M. When they got to the disco, it was just opening for the evening. They decided to take a walk and return later, when their friends would have arrived. They walked down 9th Avenue, looking for a place to buy a beer. Couldn't find one. Walked over to 10th Avenue. Found a grocery store, bought the beers, and, returning along 10th, found the alley on 37th Street with steel drums in front of it. They sat down on the drums and began to drink their beers. Suddenly, a police car appeared at the corner. One of the cops came over and began questioning

them: Who were they? What were they doing here? Did they have any weapons? They told them who they were, said no, they didn't have any weapons. The cop looked around, pushed his feet through the trash around the steel drums, frisked them, then told them to get going.

The boys got up and began walking up 37th Street toward 9th. As they walked, David Moore's friend said to him: "Come on. They're gonna be back. They ain't gonna leave us alone." And they began to walk quickly. Halfway up the block, as they came alongside a chain-link fence, two men with guns in their hands appeared from out of nowhere. They said they were police, and they wanted to know where the gun was. "We know you got a gun," they said. "Where is it?" The boys said: "We got no gun." The police pushed them up against the wall, made them kneel facing the wall. David Moore said: "We asked them, 'Why you doin' this?' One of them began to climb the fence. The other one said, 'It's all right. If he don't find a gun, we'll let you go.' And then the other one, he came back with a gun."

We were six women, six men, five blacks, seven whites on that jury. Our occupations were postal worker, nurse's aide, clerk-typist, school secretary, community center worker, engineer, actor, writer, carpenter, investment analyst, housewife. It was impossible, sitting on the jury box during the trial, to know much more about any one of us, so well concealed did the people behind these surface identifications remain during the voir dire (jury selection process).

I had become irritated with the questions about possible police prejudice, and had said I thought these questions were designed to elicit stereotypic responses rather than to encourage thinking about individuals; after all, a policeman was only one human being, not the entire police force. Afterward, the postal worker (a bull-necked black man with steady eyes behind thick glasses, who had been chosen as a juror during the same round in which I was chosen) shook his head at me and said, "Didn't think you'd make it. Nosir. Not after all that lip you give 'em."

I looked around at the ten people then occupying jurors' seats: Mary Davis, the clerk-typist; Loren Levine, the investment analyst; Todd Graham, the engineer; Shirley Silvers and Laura O'Connell, the housewives; Oscar Williams, the community center worker; Anna James, the nurse's aide; David Barnes, the postal worker; Claire Moran, the school secretary; Richard Garcia, the carpenter. I thought back to the moment when the judge and the lawyers had asked each of us to assure them that we could and would be impartial listeners, that we would reason out of the evidence given, that a policeman's testimony would "give us no trouble" (what a euphemism!). Each of us had without hesitation simply said yes or no, and I remember thinking then, We lie. Every last one of us.

But we were all surprised when Gerald Anderson, the actor, was chosen as the last juror. The judge asked him if he was married and Anderson replied, "I live in sin, judge, but no children." All heads in the courtroom jerked in his direction, but Anderson's face bore an unflappable expression, and his smile of resignation said plainly: "I've seen it all; nothing you can say or do would unbalance me; being off balance is my natural condition." Then, when Anderson revealed that one of his many odd jobs as an often unemployed actor had been that of a worker in the New York courts, Richard Garcia laughed merrily and poked Claire Moran in an open, friendly manner, saying, "that's it."

Suddenly, we all knew why Anderson was accepted as the twelfth juror: it was six o'clock in the evening; we had been jury-picking for a full day and a half; if Anderson was rejected, the court would have to call for a fresh batch of prospective jurors. Neither lawyer was willing to sustain such a delay on "a simple gun possession case."

The jury room was a gray-green, institutional rectangle: coat hooks on the wall, two small bathrooms off to one side, a long, scarred table surrounded by wooden armchairs, wastebaskets, and a floor superficially clean, deeply filthy. We entered this room on a Friday at noon, most of us expecting to be gone from it by four or five that same day. We did not see the last of it until a full twelve hours had elapsed, by which time the grimy oppressiveness of the place had become, for me at least, inextricably bound up with psychological defeat.

We ate the sandwiches brought up from the coffee shop, drank the atrocious coffee, carefully put the wrappings and the remains of our lunches into a large paper carton, wiped off the table. Then the guard took out the garbage, locked us into the room, and we began with a vote around the table. It took exactly two minutes for each of those voices to be heard pronouncing the words *guilty, not guilty*. The vote was eight *not guilty*, four *guilty*. I was one of the four who voted guilty; the other three were Loren Levine, Gerald Anderson, and Shirley Silvers.

A wave of surprise. Most of the jurors voting *not guilty* had seemed vigorously conservative as they sat in the box, the ones voting *guilty*, predictably liberal. Then—perhaps appropriately—the *guilty*s had been spoken in hesitant, musing, this-is-open-for-discussion voices, while the *not guilty*s had been announced in flat, closed, nothing-to-discuss voices.

"Well," said I, the novice juror, to myself, "it's just like the movies. Now we begin. Now we will talk, we *will* listen to one another, we will see how we have arrived at these opinions. Because that, surely, is all they are now: opinions, not settled convictions."

But I was wrong. The twelve hours that followed would in no essential alter the attitudes made clear during those first two minutes. What did happen, though, is that, one by one, all four *guilty*s were "persuaded" to change their votes to *not guilty*. That persuasion came about not through the irresistible uses of reason but through the disintegrating power of emotional cave-in.

Nearly everyone seemed to speak at once: over, under, and through each other. No one heard anything anyone else said, and no one actually *said* anything new, just repeated, in ever louder tones, *guilty, not guilty*. Richard Garcia said: "I just *feel* he's innocent. Don't ask me why, I just feel it." Anna James—whose voice bore an uncanny resemblance to that of Butterfly McQueen—said, "I can't be-*lieve* that boy ain't innocent." Claire Moran and Laura O'Connell stated flatly: "I don't believe the cops." Todd Graham, a solid man whose rimless glasses made his large afro look conservative, simply smiled and shook his head repeatedly, "No way, no way." Mary Davis, a large black woman endowed with a maternal appearance, compressed her lips, crossed her arms on her huge bosom, and shook her head, *loudly*. Shirley Silvers, middle-aged, well-dressed, brimming with nervous sweetness, turned agitatedly from one to another, chattering: "I don't know, maybe I'm wrong, I *think* he's guilty, I don't know."

In the midst of all this, a sudden flare-up between Richard Garcia and Loren Levine: yelling, foot-stamping, slamming of bathroom doors, Garcia's voice shrill, crying, "Let me talk! Dammit, *will* you let me talk?" Levine retorting hotly, "That's all you've *been* doing. And not saying a single thing of substance. If we let *you* go on, we'll be here for a week!"

What was this? Levine—thin, remote, with a voice trapped between nasal drip and lockjaw, always reading the *Times* when the others were talking, and polishing his glasses, thoughtfully—why was he standing there with a faceful of twitching irritation as though he were exploding inside? And Garcia—black-haired, wide-faced, mustachioed, manner expansive, above all jolly—why was he on his feet, his voice screeching, his hands on his hips, as though to say, "I can't take this another minute"? Were we going to have juror "revelations" so soon? We had only just begun.

Order. Order. Let's have some order here. Now—*calmly*—let each one of us tell the others exactly why we think *guilty, not guilty*.

We went around the table again. Richard Garcia, Mary Davis, and Anna James repeated that they couldn't believe that boy wasn't innocent.

Loren Levine, under tight control again, said quietly that he felt the police story hung together; it was logical in all its parts and it made sense to him.

Todd Graham said that he felt the police story *didn't* hang together; why, he couldn't or wouldn't say.

Laura O'Connell—born, raised, married, and still living in the same working-class neighborhood—said in an uninflected, tenement-pitched voice: "I don't believe the cops. I know cops. Some of my best friends are cops. I know what they do. I just don't believe them."

Claire Moran, a small, thin, birdlike woman in her forties, nodded her head and said, "That's right. I can't help feeling the same. I just don't believe that police story."

It was my turn. I said, "In order for me to vote *not guilty*, I would have to believe that these two policemen deliberately framed this boy. I would have to believe they planted that gun on him. I find that almost impossible to believe."

"Oh, for God's sake," said Mary Davis.

"They do it all the time," protested Todd Graham.

"Everybody knows *that*," cried Laura O'Connell.

"That's true, you know," said Claire Moran.

"Yes," said Gerald Anderson, speaking for the first time, "they *do* do it all the time. But only for a reason. In this case there was no reason." Everyone turned to Gerald, the street-smart actor who proved to be the best juror in the room, the man who most loved reason, and the only one to return again and again to the question of the evidence before us.

"I probably know more about cops than anyone else in this room," Gerald said, "and I certainly know they are capable of planting a weapon on somebody. But, in my experience, it's almost always because they know or they think they know a person they're after is guilty of a crime they can't prove. Usually it's narcotics. Sometimes it's some hard-nosed kid in a neighborhood they've worked in who's given them trouble, they hate the kid, they want to put him away. But to plant a gun on a perfectly strange kid? Just to bring a charge of gun possession? When there are a thousand such arrests a day in New York, all perfectly legit? That doesn't make any sense to me at all."

"Besides, where would the gun have come from?" asked Shirley Silvers.

"Oh, cops have two guns on them quite often," said Todd Graham. "The one you see, and the one you don't."

"Oh, for Chrissake," said Gerald Anderson. "Do you realize what you're saying? You know if a cop walks out of the station house with a gun secreted on his person, and he's discovered, it's his job? Right then and there. He's finished. You think a cop does a thing like that so lightly?"

Todd Graham shrugged his shoulders, closed his mouth, and looked down at the table. Clearly, Gerald's words had only silenced him.

"Well, that may be true, Mr. Anderson," said David Barnes softly, his voice all self-conscious dignity, "although we only have your word for it, you'll pardon my pointing out, and some of us here may have had experiences that contradict that statement, but I don't believe the police story either. I can't exactly say why. It just don't sit right with me. And if it don't sit right, I gotta vote *not guilty*."

Six people turned to the right and to the left and mouthed, "That's right. That's the way *I* see it, too. If you don't believe the cops . . ."

Oscar Williams, the community center worker—tall, thin, middle-aged, very black-skinned, a face and manner suffused with a quiet that passed for calm—had not said one word during this entire time. I turned to him: "Mr. Williams, what do *you* think?" He looked at me for a long moment before he spoke. There was silence in the room. And then, in a low, steady voice, making extraordinary use of the rhetorical device of dividing a sentence into its phrases, Oscar Williams said: "I cannot believe. That boy raised his arm. With a gun in it. When a policeman had told him to freeze. And that boy ain't a dead boy. I simply cannot believe that."

One instant of utter stillness, and then a jam of voices in the already thickening air: "Amen!" "That's right, that's right." "I'm with *him*." "I can't believe that either." "Nosir. I don't believe that either."

Gerald Anderson and I stared at each other. We were shaken by Williams's eloquence and its effect on the room. "But *still*," I could almost see me and Gerald thinking at the same moment.

"Mr. Williams, does that mean you think the cops framed the boy?" I asked.

"I didn't say that." He closed his eyes and spread the fingers of his thin, fine hand in the air. "I don't know whether they framed the boy or not. And I'm not sayin' they *did*. I'm only sayin' I cannot *see* that thing happening."

Williams took off his glasses; the skin just below his eyes and on the bridge of his nose glistened. He wiped his face with a soft white handkerchief. He carefully lifted one pressed pants leg over the other. Then he said: "I'm no social worker. I'm no bleeding heart. I know how rotten kids are. They *stink*. And there is absolutely nothing worse than a teenager with a gun in his hand. Don't you think I *know* that? But," his voice dropped one husky octave, "I cannot see that thing happening. And I keep thinking: If I blow this, if I give that kid a record . . . well, I just wouldn't be able to live with myself."

Mary Davis removed her arms from across her capacious chest and said, "Well, as far as I'm concerned, the man just said it all. Now we either all vote *not guilty* or we go in and tell the judge we are stuck." She was sitting directly opposite me. She leaned across the table toward me and said, "Sweetheart, cops, they shoot first, ask questions later. All of 'em."

"You said in the courtroom you weren't prejudiced against the police," I said faintly.

"I *ain't* prejudiced!" she replied angrily. "I'm just telling you what they *do*."

"It doesn't matter what *they* do," I said. "You've got to look at what *these* two did. Or what you *think* they did. And *why* you think they did it."

"Oh, there's no talking to this girl," Mary Davis said, twisting her face and body into a tortured profile position. (She really was a very large woman.)

"Yes," said Gerald Anderson drily. "Well, I *do* think the question of whether we think the police framed the boy is the crucial one, and it isn't enough to say you can't or won't think about that one. Now, no one's experience here is sacred. It carries no more authority than anyone else's. Our experience is all supposed to be in the service of the evidence before us. Not the other way around."

Everyone nodded, but Gerald's words meant nothing. On and on it went. For hours. It was not merely that the same words and phrases were repeated endlessly; it was that our "positions" seemed to have become congealed; minds and eyes glazed over; we didn't even hear ourselves speaking after a while.

Two curiosities emerged during these hours. One was that Anna James—the nurse's aide who just couldn't believe that boy wasn't innocent—proved to be a near mental incompetent. She could not keep in her mind the details of the story told by the police and the one told by the boy. At one point she mused out loud, "How that boy get over from Lexington Avenue so quick? They must be crazy to think we swallow that." We all stared at her. Lexington Avenue? What on earth was she talking about? Worse yet, what had been transpiring in her mind all this time?

I discovered afterward that Anna James was the most professional juror among us. She had over the years been chosen to serve in innumerable criminal and civil cases; and before my own term as juror was over, I saw her chosen to serve on a complex case of embezzlement. I knew why, too. Her manner was one of middle-class reserve, indicating (to one who asked no vital questions) a quiet but firm capacity to think, slowly but responsibly. During the twelve hours I was locked up with her, I discovered that that manner masked a slow-witted stubbornness functioning in the service of two profound disabilities: she was at all times oblivious to evidence, and she hated the cops. Hated them.

The second curiosity was that each of the others who had voted *not guilty* also hated the police. Hated, distrusted, disbelieved, did not want to think about anything said or done by anyone who was a policeman. "Cops shoot first, ask questions later." Young, old, black, white, blue-collar, white-collar: they all drew a pugnacious blank on police testimony.

At six o'clock, Gerald Anderson, who had been staring morosely at a diagrammatic chart of the streets in which "the incident" had taken place, said, "Hey, wait a minute. I just realized something." Everyone perked up. Anything

to break this deadly boring tension. "The kid may or may not be innocent," Gerald went on, "but one thing is certain. He lied on that stand. Look, everyone agrees that four policemen questioned him. I mean, the cops said that, and he said that, too. There's no argument there. Now, *he* says he was questioned at the corner by the uniformed police. And then questioned again *halfway down the block* by the undercover cops. If that's true, then the undercover cops must have been sitting in their car when he was questioned by the uniformed police. Because it only takes half a minute to get down the block. They'd have *seen* it. Why would they have grabbed the kids a minute later if they'd just seen them questioned and searched? That certainly doesn't make sense. He *must* be lying about that."

Excitement generated quickly. Confused, disturbed, everyone was glad to have something new to think about. Eager attention was turned to Gerald's "discovery." None but one thought of where this attention could lead. Oscar Williams sat still and silent, hands folded on knobby knees, glasses glistening in the dull yellow light. He looked up into the noise and very softly said, "Just because he's lyin' don' mean he's guilty as charged." It was as though a schoolmaster had rapped the children for rowdiness. Todd Graham said very soberly, "Yeah, that's right." So did Mary Davis. So did Claire Moran. So did Richard Garcia.

Shortly after this we were taken to dinner, herded together at two or three tables in a chop house, given a selective menu that did not permit so much as a glass of beer, watched over by the guards. It was a depressed and depressing meal.

No sooner had we returned to the jury room, hung up our coats, and taken our seats, than David Barnes stood up, approached the diagram, cleared his throat, and said, "I've been thinking." We all looked at him, supposing him about to carry Gerald's point further. Barnes then, after a fashion, repeated the original point as though he were introducing it for the first time, and then proceeded to garble the details so that the point was utterly lost and the exercise at the diagram without meaning.

It seemed impossible that everyone in the room would not instantly see that Barnes had just caricatured not only the point but the point of the point. But no. Garcia said, "Now there's an idea." Claire Moran said, "Would you mind going over that again, Mr. Barnes?" Laura O'Connell, straining nearsightedly at the diagram, said, "I kinda see what you're getting at." Todd Graham looked down at the sheet of doodle drawings under his right hand. Oscar Williams inspected his fingernails. Loren Levine nearly took out the *Times*.

I swung in my seat to look at Gerald. He was staring into space. I thought I saw something close over his eyes, some invisible shutter come down, and I think in that moment his switched vote was being born. As I looked at his face I knew we were lost. I remembered a moment a few hours earlier when Williams had said something, and Gerald had replied curtly: "You *know* you're putting pressure on us," and Williams had demurred, and I had thought: "No, the pressure is being applied from within."

I did not know if my conviction that the police did not frame David Moore constituted evidence any more than Oscar Williams's conviction that the boy could not have raised his arm with a gun in it and not be shot dead constituted a reasonable doubt. And I did not really care if the boy was guilty or not guilty, if he was punished or set free, if the police were supported or attacked. But the abdication of thought frightened me. That *did* matter. In fact it seemed to be the only thing that mattered, and it mattered that it was we—Gerald and I and all the rest—who wouldn't do the thinking.

I realized that I had become strangely attached to the people in the room. In these hours together, unwilling and most peculiar bonds had been forged. It was not that we had revealed ourselves to each other, although to some extent we had. It was certainly not that we were sealed by shared understandings of the mind or heart. No, it was rather, I began to see, that we had been locked up here randomly, thrown together willy-nilly like a family, and like a family had inflicted our emotional prejudices on each other. This act cast long shadows. Certainly it touched something in me, made me responsive to mysterious claims I could not at that moment identify. The situation began to seem metaphoric. Civilization seemed to hang on the willingness here in this room to think. In the emotional grandiosity of that moment was born *my* switched vote.

For an instant I saw things clearly. "Hang the jury," I said to myself, "there is no way out of this." But the next moment I said to myself, "No. They must see. I must *make* them see." And from that moment on I was, essentially, pleading with everyone "to see" what was happening here. I knew I should hang the jury but I simply could not do what I knew should be done. It was then a given that I would let myself be overcome. Clearly, I needed them more than they needed me.

At nine o'clock Shirley Silvers cried out, "I change my vote! I vote *not guilty*." Half an hour later, Gerald Anderson, still staring into space, looking absolutely bleak, said, "I vote *not guilty*." Directly afterward, Loren Levine, who had retreated into near total silence since his altercation with Richard Garcia, said crisply "Me, too. *Not guilty*." Why had none of them hung the jury? What personal mystery struggled up in each of them? To what were they "attached" that they had caved in, one by one?

I was the last holdout. All around me pressed voices, faces, shadows, that said, "Explain yourself. Justify yourself. We know who *we* are. Can you say as much? What is all this nonsense about? Never mind the others. What are *you* doing here?"

I looked at Oscar Williams now sitting silent, watching me. I begged him with my eyes to understand and support me. He looked at me. His face said, "I do understand, but you're in this alone." The memory of his voice saying, "That boy would be a dead boy" entered into me, made me quail somewhere inside myself. Conveniently, I lost my nerve against that haughty pain of his; conveniently, couldn't hold on to what I knew, began to get fogged up, didn't quite know anymore what was evidence, what a reasonable doubt . . .

"For God's sake," I cried as though I were going under. "What *reason* would these two cops have had for framing this kid? Cynically, recklessly, cold-bloodedly, framing a boy they'd never seen before? Now you know goddamn well it's not these two people whose testimony you've been listening to. It's *cops*. All cops. So what have we got here? Where does that leave us? With two stereotypes: on the one hand" (I raised my left arm at the elbow, hand palm out), "we have 'the cops.' On the other hand" (I raised my right arm), "we have 'a young black boy' . . ."

The word black was a match struck to a can of gasoline: conflagration blazed in less than thirty seconds.

"Color, color, who said anything about color?" David Barnes thundered. "What chu bringing in color for? I don't like that. Nosiree, I don't like that one bit."

"I *knew* she had that in her mind all the time!" Anna James shrieked, "I knew it."

"I don' wanna hear a word about black or white," Mary Davis boomed. "Now you hear me? That boy's mama raised him up just like everybody else's. Didn't do it no different from yours."

Shirley Silvers got hysterical and began to scream: "She didn't mean it. She didn't mean it."

Todd Graham smiled mockingly at me and said, "I know. You're not prejudiced."

Oscar Williams's eyes met mine in amazement for a single second. Then he buried his face in his hands.

Gerald Anderson and Loren Levine stared, open-mouthed, but remained silent.

It was just easier for everyone to let happen what was happening.

As for me, I felt relief. The charge of racism—painful and frightening at first—was, in fact, a smokescreen behind which everyone, myself included, was only too glad to hide. "You win," I said. "*Not guilty*." Everyone looked down, or away.

At midnight the verdict was announced in the courtroom. The jurors fell all over themselves fleeing the building. Claire Moran turned in the doorway and said, "Please don't misunderstand this, but I hope I never see any of you again!"

Only Gerald Anderson and I stayed behind. Ours was the sick feeling of cowards that compels hanging around. The lawyers, both of whom were young and eager for details as to what had happened in the jury room, also hung around. We talked a long while together.

We told them many things, and then we told them how persuasive had been Oscar Williams's assertion that he couldn't imagine the boy making a motion with a gun in his hand while facing a cop and not being shot, and how Williams had agonized that this was the boy's first arrest and Williams would be ruining his life with a conviction. The young assistant district attorney listened silently, nodding his head forlornly at every word I spoke as though he knew *this* litany by heart. I looked at him, puzzled.

"It *was* Moore's first arrest, wasn't it?" I asked.

"No," he shook his head. "He was arrested in 1974 at the age of fourteen."

"What was the charge?" asked Gerald.

"Pointing a loaded .22 caliber gun at a policeman."

---

## QUESTIONS

1. Would you say that the jury is a primary group or a secondary group?

2. Would you say that the jury's verdict was based mainly on the evidence, or mainly on group processes within the jury? Explain.

3. Most juries eventually give unanimous verdicts. Why do you think that is the case?

Rosabeth Moss Kanter

# 17. How the Top Is Different

*One of the outstanding features of modern societies is the growth of large formal organizations, mostly in the form of corporations or government departments. Although secondary groups of this kind are virtually unknown in preindustrial societies, they dominate political and economic life in the modern world. Most American workers, in fact, are employed by large formal organizations, and the chances are good that you will spend at least part of your own working life in such an environment.*

*Every formal organization has a hierarchical authority structure: the official lines of responsibility, from the top of the organization to its lowest reaches, can be diagrammed on a chart. But sociologists are well aware that the theory and the practice of organizational structure often diverge from one another, for the behavior of officials is partly shaped by personal relationships and other circumstances that the organizational chart could never anticipate. For example, power over the day-to-day affairs of an organization often rests with middle-level managers rather than the supposed decision makers at the top, who are often isolated from, and ignorant of, much of what is taking place.*

*In this article, Rosabeth Moss Kanter draws on her case study of a large corporation to provide insights into that part of an organization whose inner workings are often least accessible to outsiders—the leadership.*

Excerpted from *Men and Women of the Corporation*, by Rosabeth Moss Kanter, © 1977 by Rosabeth Moss Kanter, Basic Books, Inc., Publishers, New York, pp. 34–36, 48–49, 52–54, 68, 75, 118–22, and additions.

Corporate headquarters of the company I have called Indsco, occupied many floors in a glass and steel office building in a large city. The surroundings were luxurious. At ground level was a changing art exhibit in glass cases with displays of awards to Indsco executives for meritorious public service or newspaper clippings about the corporation. There might be piles of company newspapers on a nearby table or special publications like the report by foreign students who spent the summer with Indsco families. Such public displays almost always stressed Indsco's contributions to the welfare of the larger community. Across from gleaming chrome elevators and a watchman's post were doors leading into the employees' dining room. In the morning a long table with coffee, sweet rolls, and bagels for sale was set up outside the dining room; during the day coffee carts were available on each floor. Inside, the dining room was divided into two parts: a large cafeteria for everyone and a small area with already set tables, hostess seating, menus, and waitress service. Those tables were usually occupied by groups of men; the largely female clerical work force tended to eat in the cafeteria. Special luncheon meetings arranged by managers were held in the individual executive dining rooms and conference areas on the top floor; to use these rooms, reservations had to be made well in advance by someone with executive status.

Indsco executives were also likely to go out for lunch, especially if they were entertaining an outside visitor, to any of the numerous posh restaurants in the neighborhood. At these lunches a drink was a must; at one time it was two extra-dry martinis, but more recently it became a few glasses of wine. However, despite the fact that moderate social drinking was common, heavy drinking was frowned upon. A person's career could be ruined by the casual comment that he or she had alcoholic tendencies. Stories told about men who cavorted and caroused in bars, staying up all night, were told with the attitude that "that was really crazy."

The office floors were quietly elegant, dominated by

modern design, white walls, and beige tones. At one end, just off the elevators, sat a receptionist who calls on a company telephone line to announce visitors. A secretary would then appear to escort a visitor to his or her appointment. Offices with windows were for higher-status managers, and their secretaries were often proud of having drapes. Corner offices were reserved for the top. They were likely to be larger in size, with room for coffee tables and couches, and reached through a reception area where a private secretary sat. Inside offices went to assistants and other lower-status salaried personnel; conference rooms were also found along the inside rim. Secretaries and other hourly workers occupied rows of desks with banks of cabinets and files in the public spaces between. There were few signs of personal occupancy of space, except around the secretaries' desks. Managers might put up a painting or poster on the wall, and they usually had a small set of photographs of their families somewhere on or near their desk. Rarely would more than a few books or reports be visible, and the overall impression was one of tidiness, order, and uniformity from office to office. In fact, it was often true that the higher the status of an executive, the less cluttered was his desk. Office furnishings themselves reflected status rather than personality. There was a clear system of stratification. As status increased, desks went from a wood top with steel frame through solid wood to the culmination in a marble-top desk. Type of ashtray was also determined by the status system; and a former executive secretary, promoted into a management position herself, reported that her former peers were upset that she took her stainless steel file trays with her because a secretary working for her would not be entitled to such luxurious equipment. The rational distribution of furniture and supplies was thought to make the system more equitable and to avoid competition for symbols of status....

The secretary also contributed in minor ways to the boss's status. Some people have argued that secretaries function as "status symbol" for executives, holding that the traditional secretarial role is developed and preserved because of its impact on managerial egos, not its contribution to organizational efficiency. Robert Townsend, iconoclastic former president of Avis, claimed in *Up the Organization* that the existence of private secretaries was organizationally inefficient, as proven by his experience in gaining half a day's time by giving up what he called "standard executive equipment." One writer was quite explicit about the meaning of a secretary: "In many companies a secretary outside your door is the most visible sign that you have become an executive; a secretary is automatically assigned to each executive, whether or not his work load requires one.... When you reach the vice-president level, your secretary may have

an office of her own, with her name on the door. At the top, the president may have two secretaries...." A woman professional at Indsco agreed with the idea that secretaries were doled out as rewards rather than in response to job needs, as she talked about her own problems in getting enough secretarial help.

At Indsco, the secretary's function as a status symbol increased up the ranks as she became more and more bound to a specific boss. "It's his image, his status, sitting out in front," a personnel administrator said. "She's the sign of how important he is."...

Physical height corresponded to social height at Indsco, like other major corporations. Corporate officers resided at the very top on the forty-fifth floor, which was characterized by many people in Indsco as "a hospital ward." The silence was deafening. The offices were huge. According to one young executive who had served as an assistant to an officer, "One or two guys are sitting there; there's not much going on. It's the brain center, but there is no activity. It's like an old folks' home. You can see the cobwebs growing. A secretary every quarter mile. It's very sterile." An executive secretary told the story of her officer boss's first reaction to moving onto the forty-fifth floor. "He was the one human being," she said, "who was uncomfortable with the trappings of status. When he moved up, he had to pick an office." She wouldn't let him take anything but a corner—it was the secretary who had to tell him that. Finally he agreed for the sake of the corporate image, but he was rarely there, and he set up the office so that everything was in one corner and the rest was useless space.

Some people felt that the physical insulation of top executives also had its counterpart in social insulation. Said a former officer's assistant, "There are courtiers around the top guys, telling them what they want to hear, flattering them. For example, there was a luncheon with some board members. The vice-chairman mentioned that he was looking for a car for his daughter. A courtier thought, 'We'll take care of it.' He went down the line, and someone in purchasing had to spend half a day doing this. The guy who had to do it resented it, so he became antagonistic to the top. The vice-chairman had no idea this was going on, and if he had known, he would probably have stopped it; but you can't say anything at the top without having it be seen as an order. Even ambiguous remarks may get translated into action. At the top you have to figure out the impact of all of your words in advance because an innocent expression can have a major effect. A division president says, 'It might be a good idea to _____.' He's just ruminating, but that gets sent down to the organization as an ultimatum, and everyone scrambles around to make sure it gets done. He looks down and says, 'What the hell is happening?'"

At the same time, officers could also be frustrated by

their distance from any real action. One remarked, "You get into a position like mine, and you think you can get anything done, but I shout down an order, and I have to wait years for any action. The guy in the plant turns a valve and sees the reaction, or the salesman offers a price, but I may never live to see the impact of my decisions." For this reason, it was known that once in a while officers could be expected to leave their protected environment and try to get involved in routine company activities. Some would go down and try to do something on the shop floor. Once in a while one would make a sales call at a very high level or make an appearance at a customer golf outing. It was also a legend that an early president had his own private laboratory outside of his office—his own tinkering room. As a manager put it, "He would close the door and go play. It was almost as though he was babied. He was given a playroom." . . .

## Conformity Pressures at the Top: Uncertainty and the Growth of Inner Circles

Leaders who already have power seek as new recruits those they can rely upon and trust. They demand that the newcomers to top positions be loyal, that they accept authority, and that they conform to a prescribed pattern of behavior.

Unlike a more communal environment, where eccentrics can be lovingly tolerated because trust is based on mutual commitments and deep personal knowledge, those who run the bureaucratic corporation often rely on outward manifestations to determine who is the "right sort of person." Managers tend to carefully guard power and privilege for those who fit in, for those they see as "their kind." Wilbert Moore was commenting on their phenomenon when he used the metaphor of a "bureaucratic kinship system" to describe the corporation—but a kinship system based on homosocial reproduction in which men reproduce themselves in their own image. The metaphor is apt. Because of the *situation* in which managers function, because of the position of managers in the corporate structure, social similarity tends to become extremely important to them. The structure sets in motion forces leading to the replication of managers as the same kind of social individuals. And people at the top reproduce themselves in kind.

Conformity pressures and the development of exclusive management circles closed to "outsiders" stem from the degree of uncertainty surrounding managerial positions. Bureaucracies are social inventions that supposedly reduce the uncertain to the predictable and routine. Yet much uncertainty remains—many situations in which individual people rather than impersonal procedures must be trusted. "Uncertainty," James Thompson wrote in a recent major statement on organizations,

"appears as the fundamental problem for complex organizations, and coping with uncertainty as the essence of the administrative process." Thompson identified three sources of uncertainty in even the most perfect of machine-like bureaucracies: a lack of cause-effect understanding in the culture at large (limiting the possibility for advance planning); contigencies caused by the fact that the bureaucracy is not alone, so that outcomes of organizational action are in part determined by action of other elements in the environment; and the interdependence of parts, the human interconnections inside the organization itself, which can never fully be reduced to predictable action. The requirements for a perfectly technically "rational" bureaucracy that never has to rely on the personal discretion of a single individual can never be met: complete knowledge of all cause-effect relationships plus control over all of the relevant variables. Thus, sources of uncertainty that are inherent in human institutions mean that some degree of reliance on individual persons must always be present.

It is ironic that in those most impersonal of institutions the essential communal problem of trust remains. For wherever there is uncertainty, *someone* (or some group) must decide, and thus, there must be persoanl discretion. And discretion raises not technical but human, social, and even communal questions: trust, and its origins in loyalty, commitment, and mutual understanding based on the sharing of values. It is the uncertainty quotient in managerial work, as it has come to be defined in the large modern corporation, that causes management to become so socially restricting: to develop tight inner circles excluding social strangers; to keep control in the hands of socially homogeneous peers; to stress conformity and insist upon a diffuse, unbounded loyalty; and to prefer ease of communication and thus social certainty over the strains of dealing with people who are "different."

If conditions of uncertainty mean that people have to be relied on, then people fall back on social bases for trust. The greater the uncertainty, the greater the pressures for those who have to trust each other to form a homogeneous group. At different times in an organization's history, and at different places in its structure, a higher degree of uncertainty brings with it more drive for social similarity. . . .

Uncertainty can stem from either the time-span of decisions and the amount of information that must be collected, or from the frequency with which non-routine events occur and must be handled. The impossibility of specifying contingencies in advance, operating procedures for all possible events, leaves an organization to rely on personal discretion. (It is also this pressure that partly accounts for the desire to centralize responsibility in a few people who can be held accountable for discretionary decisions.) Commented a sales manager at Indsco, "The need for flexibility is primary in my job. The situation changes from minute to minute. One minute it's a tank truck that collapsed. Another it's a guy whose wife just had a hysterectomy and is going to die. . . . I'm dealing with such different problems all the time."

The importance of discretion increases with closeness to the top of a hierarchical organization. Despite the institutionalization and routinization of much of the work of large organizations and despite the proliferation of management experts, uncertainty remains a generic condition, increasing with rank. Jobs are relatively unstructured, tasks are non-routine, and decisions must be made about a variety of unknown elements. Issues such as "direction" and "purpose" cannot be reduced to rational formulae. Organizational improvement, or even maintenance, is not a simple matter that can be summarized in statements about "the ten functions of managers" or techniques of operation. If the "big picture" can be viewed from the top, it also looks bigger and fuzzier. Computers have not necessarily reduced the uncertainty of decisions at the top; in some cases, they have merely increased the amount of information that decision-makers must take into account. A major executive of Indsco confessed in a meeting that "we don't know how to manage these giant structures; and I suspect no one does. They are like dinosaurs, lumbering on of their own accord, even if they are no longer functional."

Criteria for "good decisions" or good management performance also get less certain closer to the top. The connection between an upper management decision and a factor such as production efficiency several layers below or gross sales is indirect, if it is even apparent. (An Indsco division president said, "In the 1960s we thought we were really terrific. We patted ourselves on the back a lot because every decision was so successful. Business kept on expanding. Then came the recession, and we couldn't do anything to stop it. We had been lucky before. Everything turned to gold in the 1960s. But it became clear that we don't know the first thing about how to make this enterprise work.")

Financial measures of performance are sometimes even artifactual because of the juggling of figures; for example, when and how a loss is recorded. There are also a variety of dilemmas in trying to evaluate the success of managers: qualitative versus quantitative measures, short-run versus long-run outcomes. Decisions that look good in the short-term might be long-term disasters, but by that time the failure can be blamed on other factors, and those responsible for the decisions might be so entrenched in power that they now call the shots anyway. A former public relations manager at DuPont formulated what he called the Law of Inverse Certainty: "The more important the management decision, the less precise the

tools to deal with it . . . and the longer it will take before anyone knows it was right." One example was a rigid cost cutter who helped increase profits by eliminating certain functions; by the time the company began to feel the loss of those functions, he had been promoted and was part of the inner power group. Someone else picked up the pieces.

The uncertainty up the ranks, like the uncertainty of beginnings, also puts trust and homogeneity at a premium. The personal loyalty normally demanded of subordinates by officials is most intense at the highest levels of organizations, as others have also noted. The lack of structure in top jobs makes it very important for decision-makers to work together closely in at least the harmony of shared understanding and a degree of mutual trust. Since for an organization to function at all requires that, to some extent, people will pull together around decisions, the solidarity that can be mustered through common membership in social networks, and the social control this provides, is a helpful supplement for decision-makers. Indeed, homogeneity of class and ethnic background and prior social experiences is one important "commitment mechanism" found to build a feeling of communion among members of viable utopian communities. Situational pressures, then, place a great emphasis on personal relations and social homogeneity as functional elements in the carrying out of managerial tasks. And privilege is also kept within a small circle.

The social homogeneity of big business leaders from the early-to-middle twentieth century has been noted frequently by critics such as C. Wright Mills as well as business historians. Their class background and social characteristics tended to be similar: largely white, Protestant men from elite schools. Much attention has also been paid to the homogeneity of type within any particular company. In one industrial organization, managers who moved ahead needed to be members of the Masonic Order and the local yacht club; not Roman Catholic; Anglo-Saxon or Germanic in origin; and Republican.

At Indsco, until ten years ago, top executives in the corporation were traceable to the founders of the company or its subsidiaries—people who held stock or were married to people who did. There was a difference between who did well in the divisions, where performance tended to account for more, and who got into top positions in the corporation itself. To get ahead in the corporation, social connections were known to be very important. Indeed, corporate staff positions became a place to put people who were nonmovers, whose performance was not outstanding, but were part of the "family." The social homogeneity of corporate executives was duly noted by other managers. One asked a consultant, "Do all companies have an ethnic flavor? Our top men all seem to be Scotch-Irish." (But as management has become more rationalized, and the corporation has involved itself more heavily in divisional operations, there has also been a trend, over the past five years, toward more "objective" criteria for high-level corporate positions.)

We expect a direct correlation, then, between the degree of uncertainty in a position—the extent to which organizations must rely on personal discretion—and a reliance on "trust" through "homosocial reproduction"—selection of incumbents on the basis of social similarity. . . .

Management becomes a closed circle in the absence of better, less exclusionary responses to uncertainty and communication pressures. Forces stemming from organizational situations help foster social homogeneity as a selection criterion for managers and promote social conformity as a standard for conduct. Concerned about giving up control and broadening discretion in the organization, managers choose others that can be "trusted." And thus they reproduce themselves in kind. Women are occasionally included in the inner circle when they are part of an organization's ruling family, but more usually this system leaves women out, along with a range of other people with discrepant social characteristics. Forces insisting that trust means total dedication and non-diffuse loyalty also serve to exclude those, like women, who are seen as incapable of such a single-minded attachment.

There is a self-fulfilling prophecy buried in all of this. The more closed the circle, the more difficult it is for "outsiders" to break in. Their very difficulty in entering may be taken as a sign of incompetence, a sign that the insiders were right to close their ranks. The more closed the circle, the more difficult it is to share power when the time comes, as it inevitably must, that others challenge the control by just one kind. And the greater the tendency for a group of people to try to reproduce themselves, the more constraining becomes the emphasis on conformity. It would seem a shame, indeed, if the only way out of such binds lay in increasing bureaucratization—that is, in a growth in routinization and rationalization of areas of uncertainty and a concomitant decline in personal discretion. But somehow corporations must grapple with the problem of how to reduce pressures for social conformity in their top jobs. . . .

## Conformity Reaches Home

It is one of the prevailing ironies of modern corporate life that the closer to the top of the organization, the more traditional and non-"modern" does the system look. As Max Weber noted, at this point more charismatic, symbolic, and "non-rational" elements come into play. At the

top—and especially in interaction with its environment—the organization is most likely to show strong elements of a personal, familistic system imbued with ritual, drawing on traditional behavior modes, and overlaid with symbolism. The irony stems from the fact that it is the top level that prescribes routine and impersonality—the absence of particularism and familism—for the rest of the organization. The modern organization formally excludes the family from participation in organizational life and excludes family ties as a basis for organizational position, even to the extent of anti-nepotism rules. Yet, at the top the wife may come into the picture as a visible member of the husband's "team"; she may be given a position and functions (and, in some cases, may even jump over qualified employees in taking on official, paid, executive position). The wife who is excluded below may be included at the top, as part of the diplomatic apparatus of the corporation. And she has little freedom to refuse participation.

The dilemma that can confront people at this level is the issue of publicness/privateness. Both husband and wife can be made into public figures, with no area of life remaining untinged with responsibilities for the company. Here, as Wilbert Moore said, "The man, and his wife, simply cannot divest themselves of corporate identification. Their every activity with persons outside the immediate family is likely to be tinged with recognition of the man's position. He represents the company willy-nilly. His area of privacy, and that of his wife, is very narrowly restricted." One rising young Indsco executive felt that the following had to be considered the "modern risks" of corporate vice-presidential and presidential jobs: traveling 80 percent of the time, getting shot at or kidnapped by radicals, prostituting yourself to customers, and opening your private life to scrutiny.

The higher executive's work spills over far beyond the limits of a working day. There may be no distinction between work and leisure. Activities well out of the purview of the organization's goals and defined as pleasure for other people (golf club memberships, symphony attendance, party-giving) are allowable as business expenses on income tax returns because the definition of what is "business" becomes so broad and nonspecific. People entertain one another on yachts or over long, lavish lunches—all in an attempt to mutually obligate, to create personal relations that will give someone an inside track when it comes to more formal negotiations. Whenever "selling" is a part of the organization's relations with its environment and sufficient sums of money rest on each deal, those who sell tend to offer gifts (tickets to a sports event, dinners at fancy restaurants, expensive pen and pencil sets) to those who buy, trying to bind the others beyond the limits of a rational contractual relationship. Entertaining in the home with the wife as hostess is especially binding, since it appears to be a more personal offering not given to all, sets up a social obligation, implicates others, and also calls on ancient and traditional feelings about the need to reward hospitality.

Fusion of business and private life also occurs around longer-term relationships. At the top, all friendships may have business meaning. Business relations can be made because of social connections. (One unlikely merger between two companies in very different fields was officially said to result from one company's need for a stock exchange listing held by the other, but off the record it was known to have been brought about by the friendship of the two presidents and their wives.) Charitable and community service activities, where the wife's role is especially pivotal, may generate useful business and political connections. Wives may meet each other through volunteer work and bring their husbands into contact, with useful business results. Stratification of the volunteer world paralleling class and ethnic differentiation in the society ensures that husbands and wives can pinpoint the population with which they desire connections by an appropriate choice of activity. As one chief executive wife wrote, "Any public relations man worth his salt will recognize the corporate wife as an instrument of communication with the community far more sincere and believable than all the booze poured down the press to gain their favor."

The importance of the wife stems not only from her own skills and activities (which could be, and are, performed by paid employees) but also from the testimony her behavior provides, its clue to the character and personal side of her husband. The usefulness of this testimony, in turn, is derived from unique aspects of top leadership. Image, appearance, background, and likability are all commodities traded at the top of the system, where actors are visible and where they put pressure on one another to demonstrate trustworthiness. . . . Farther down a hierarchy, jobs can be broken down into component skills and decisions about people and jobs made on the basis of ability to demonstrate those skills. At the top, decisions about people are not so easy or mechanical; they rest on personal factors to a degree perhaps much greater than systems themselves officially admit. The situations that a corporation president or a president of a country face are not routine and predictable; indeed, constituents are less interested in their handling of routine matters than in their capacities for the unexpected. So there is no test except a vague one: Is this person trustworthy? Even questions about philosophy and intelligence are proxies for trust.

Furthermore, the capacities of an organization itself are unknown and cannot be reduced precisely either to

history or to a set of facts and figures. Thus, the character of its leaders can become a critical guide to making a decision about a future relationship with it: whether to invest, to donate funds, to allow it into the community, to provide some leeway in the regulation of its activities. Indsco was always concerned about character in its managers. Company newspapers from field locations routinely stressed church leadership in articles about individual managers, and "integrity" and "acceptance of accountability" appeared on the list of eleven traits that must be possessed by candidates for officer level jobs. Disclosures of corrupt practices by other companies in the mid-1970s enhanced Indsco's concerns about public respectability. Whereas, at lower levels of the organization, there was a tendency to formalize demands, to create routinized job descriptions, to ensure continuity of functioning by seeing to it that the occupant did not make over the job in his own image, and to exclude as much as possible of the personal and emotional life of the worker, close to the top, opposite pressure prevailed. Those with whom leaders entered into relationships looked for the private person behind the role and for the qualities and capacities that could not be encompassed by a job description but on which they must bet when deciding to trust the leader or the organization. Here's where the wives are important.

One way leaders can offer glimpses of their private beings is by bringing along their wives, by inviting others into their homes, and by making sure that their wives confirm the impression of themselves they are trying to give. By meeting in social circumstances, by throwing open pieces of private life for inspection, leaders try to convey their taste and their humanity. Wives, especially, are the carriers of this humanity and the shapers of the image of the private person. Of course, to the extent that social events and "informal" occasions are known to communicate an image for the purposes of making appropriate relationships, they may come to be as carefully managed and rationally calculated as any production task within the organization. The public relations department might even stage-manage the performance of the leader and his wife; when Dollie Ann Cole, wife of a General Motors president, wrote that p.r. departments no longer tell the wife what to wear and what to say, she made it explicit that they once did: ". . . a new day has dawned. Corporate wives no longer ask the public relations office what charity they should work with or whether they can debate for a cause on a local or national radio or television show—or even who is coming for dinner."

The wife is thus faced with an added task at the boundary of the public and the private: to make an event seem personal that is instead highly ritualized and contrived. She must recognize also the meanings conveyed by small acts (who sits next to whom, how much time she and her husband spend with each person, the taste implied by objects in the home, how much she drinks, who seem to be the family friends) and manage even small gestures with extreme self-consciousness, as one high-level wife at Indsco recalled she did at managers' meetings: "I had to be very careful to be invariably cordial, friendly, to remember everyone's names—and then to stay away. If I was too involved with someone, it would look like I was playing favorites; that would set up waves in highly inappropriate ways. Some of the young wives were terrified, but there was only so much I could do because I had other things to worry about."

Private life thus becomes penetrable and not very private at the top. Wives face the demand to suppress private beliefs and self-knowledge in the interest of public appearance. As an instrument of diplomacy and a critical part of her husband's image, the corporate wife must often hide her own opinions in order to preserve a united front, play down her own abilities to keep him looking like the winner and the star. The women's intelligence and superior education—assets when the men looked for wives—give way to other, more social traits, such as gregariousness, adaptability, attractiveness, discretion, listening ability, and social graces.

Thus, unless serving as a surrogate for the husband, voicing opinions was not easily allowed of corporate wives at Indsco, like those political wives who must beware of outshining their husbands. An aide to Eleanor McGovern spoke of the contradictory pressures on a candidate's wife: to be able to give the speech when he can't make it but to shut her mouth and listen adoringly when he is there. Indeed, Eleanor was told to stop looking so good when she started getting better press notices than George. Abigail McCarthy recalled the anxiety she felt about how words would affect her husband's prospects: "After every interview, I lay awake in a black nightmare of anxiety, fearful that I had said something which would do Gene irreparable harm." Betty Ford became an object of controversy (and of admiration) precisely because she violated these rules of the game and refused to distort her private life. Yet, wives of upper management at Indsco felt they did not have that luxury, even though they characterized the pressure to suppress independent opinions as "nonsense" and "frustrating." Not everyone complained. One wife reported that she was proud of never having unburdened herself, even to a confidante, and never having forgotten her public role throughout her husband's career.

Stresses, choices, and dilemmas in the top leadership phase, then, center around the tension between the public and the private. If men and their wives at the top gained public recognition, they also lost private freedoms. The emotional pressure this entailed was too much for some wives, as literature in the corporate-wives-as-victims tradition made clear; but it should be pointed out, too, that emotional breakdowns and secret deviances could also reflect defiant independence, unobtainable in any other way under constraining role definitions. The wishes expressed by wives in this position were of two kinds. Some women said that if they were going to be used by the company anyway, they would like the opportunity to do a real job, exercise real skills—by which they meant take on official areas of responsibility. Others wanted merely to be able to carve out more areas of privacy and independence in an otherwise public existence.

## Power and Its Prices

The top leadership of an organization has all of the privileges of office: the signs of status, the benefits and perquisites, the material advantages their position is seen to warrant. They play ball in a large field, and the scope of their decisions is vast and far-reaching. They have, on occasion, gigantic power which does not even have to be used; a mere wish on their part is translated into action, with full cooperation and without the show of force.

But such power exists in a vise of checks and constraints; it comes out of a system, and the system, in turn, exacts its price. What if a top leader tries to exercise power that violates the expectations of other top leaders and organization members—if he or she steps out of line, out of character, or out of role? Would obedience be so easily forthcoming? Power at the top is contingent on conformity. Pressures to "fit in" also mean restraints on the unbridled exercise of power.

Furthermore, power which in some respects is contingent on trust for its effective exercise also, ironically, breeds suspicion: Can people at the top trust what they hear? Can they trust each other? What beyond social appearance can they use as keys to trust? Sometimes cut off from the "real action," they are seen by the organization's rank and file as remote from the daily events which truly constitute the organization—as once potent actors who now make whimsical decisions with little real understanding of organizational operations. And, as the final price of power, top leaders have to acknowledge the organization's ownership of that ultimate piece of property, their own private lives and beings. Life at the top is life in a goldfish bowl, an existence in which all the boundaries can be rendered transparent at the twitch of the public's curiosity.

The room at the top is all windows.

## QUESTIONS

1. What are the differences between the picture of the corporation we might get from its organizational chart and the picture we get from this sociological case study?

2. Despite their formal authority, the leaders of the organization experience restraints on the exercise of their power. What are these restraints?

3. Many college students hope one day to be senior executives of corporations such as that described by Kanter. On the basis of her findings, would you expect to feel comfortable in such an environment?

*Saul V. Levine*

# 18. Radical Departures

*Deviance is behavior that violates significant social norms and is disapproved by large numbers of people as a result. Some forms of deviance, such as robbery, are so socially destructive that they are considered crimes. Other forms of deviance, such as membership in religious cults, seem less socially damaging and therefore do not attract the same degree of social hostility. Even so, a certain amount of stigma attaches to people who join groups whose beliefs are radically different from those of the religious mainstream.*

*The objection to these groups appears to be twofold. First, from the viewpoint of the dominant Judeo-Christian tradition their beliefs appear to be somewhat bizarre. Second, the joiners are widely regarded as the victims of "brainwashing"—in other words, as persons whose thought processes and freedom of choice have been crippled by intense, systematic psychological pressure, often applied within closed communities. Some parents and other family members actually try to win the converts back from the groups, sometimes by means that include kidnapping and forcible "deprogramming" by self-styled experts.*

*In this article, Saul V. Levine throws light on the motives young people have for joining cults and similar groups, and indicates the likely outcome of their deviant behavior.*

From *Psychology Today*, August 1984, pp. 20–27. Copyright © 1984 by Saul V. Levine (Harcourt Brace Jovanovich, 1984). Reprinted by permission of The Balkin Agency.

June 27, 1983, was a cloudy, breezy day in the San Francisco Bay area. Around a breakfast table in the Thomas home in an affluent suburb, good-humored conversation was interrupted by the honk of a horn. Mark got up from the table and made for the door to join his friends waiting in the car.

His father stopped him. Pressing a $20 bill into Mark's hand, he rested his arm on his son's shoulder for a moment and made an embarrassed joke about the money. "Just in case you get in trouble in the big city," he winked. He could afford to make such jokes. Mark, as clean-cut a blond as any middle-class family could hope for, had never been in trouble in his life. He was willing and reliable, the kind of boy who had been given responsibilities since elementary school.

After kissing his mother good-bye, Mark strode out the door to the waiting car. It was the Monday after high school graduation, and Mark and his friends were on their way to celebrate for a day in San Francisco. When the group returned that evening, Mark wasn't with them. His friends had last seen him late that afternoon in Golden Gate Park, where they had gone to share a six-pack of beer and watch the sun go down. The Thomases weren't worried. He had probably missed his train; he would call them from the station shortly.

But Mark didn't call his parents that night, nor the next night. After 72 hours, the Thomases finally heard from Mark. They weren't to worry, he told them during the collect call from Oregon. He said he was fine. Mark had joined the followers of Bhagwan Shree Rajneesh. He had made a "radical departure."

Every year thousands of young people abruptly turn their backs on family, friends and future to join one or another of an estimated 2,500 communal groups in North America whose values, dress and behavior seem totally alien to everything the joiner has stood for. Practitioners of Rajneeshism wear clothes in the "sunrise colors." Around their necks hang pendants bearing a portrait of their enlightened Master. When the Thomases next saw their son, he was on a street corner in Portland chanting in a circle dance, robed in red. He refused to acknowledge his father's greeting; indeed he showed no sign of recognizing his parents.

Mark Thomas is a composite of several young men among the hundreds I have studied since the late 1960s (see the "Questions and Answers" box). In my book, *Radical Departures,* I follow nine such young men and women through their journeys into and out of communal groups.

Radical departures are a fact of life, a cultural phenomenon that has inspired more fear, agony, anger, disgust—and misinterpretation—than almost any other. When I started my studies, most people agreed that the groups were hostile to the fundamental standards of middle-class conduct, but beyond that judgment there was a lot of confusion. Were the joiners troubled, academic failures; loners from embattled homes; drug addicts? Certainly there was a subpopulation of such dropouts, and mental-health professionals were quick to indict all radical departures as a manifestation of pathology. The most charitable judgment was that kids who joined charismatic fringe groups were gullible innocents who had been brainwashed.

Given this widespread sentiment, I was surprised to find, as my research got under way, that these young people, massed in urban communes or converted to a variety of intensely ideological groups, came right off the cover of *The Saturday Evening Post.* There were no more signs of pathology among them than among any group of youngsters. They came from warm, concerned families that had given them every material, social and intellectual benefit. They were, in short, Mark Thomases— good kids with everything to look forward to.

Those who followed press reports on these "cults," as they were invariably called, were treated to a first impression much like what I at first perceived. Such groups were controlled by a charismatic leader who used his power to enrich himself unconscionably. The beliefs he perpetrated were counterfeit, and those who followed him had been duped into serving against their will. They might be held captive by force, deprived of financial means to escape and prevented from communicating with their families.

The details varied from group to group, but the press reports were uniformly negative. One cult censored incoming and outgoing mail and prevented privacy through an intrusive "buddy system." It used the words of the Bible, "For I am come to set a man at variance against his father, and the daughter against her mother," to turn children against their parents. Young girls were encouraged to be "happy hookers in Christ"—that is, to seduce new members sexually.

Another group practiced "heavenly deception," begging donations in public places by selling flowers to benefit a fictional home for the retarded or some other nonexistent cause. Their tactic was to bar the way of hurried travelers with smiling entreaty, making it clear that it would be easier to reach for some change than to brush them off.

Other cults practiced extreme asceticism, foisting inadequate nutrition, clothing and housing on their converts. A zealous leader of one group considered five hours of sleep a night sufficient for members, some of them still growing children.

As I gradually became involved in the study of communal groups, first in the United States, and later in Europe, Israel and my native Canada, I found that the reality of the ones I dealt with simply did not accord with press sensationalism. I have seen bad things, but in the hundreds of groups I know of firsthand, I have never seen excesses worthy of the pejorative label of "cult." Furthermore, not all of these intense groups are religious; some are political, therapeutic or social in nature.

Because these groups don't easily lend themselves to existing terminology, I have chosen the rather inexact term "radical" to describe both the groups and the joining that makes them possible. It is a relative term: To the families of joiners, their children's beliefs and behavior seem radically opposed to the families' own intellectual, spiritual and social standards.

Although there is an underlying structure that makes these groups similar—the fantasized omniscience of leaders, rigid belief systems opposed to the outside world and a studied strangeness—the earmark of a radical departure is less the specific characteristics of the group than the rapid, total transformation of the joiner. Mark Thomas could not say when, if ever, he would return. His previous plans for college no longer meant a thing to him. Similarly, voracious readers stop reading; musicians abandon their instruments; athletes stop exercising. There is an ominous narrowing of horizons, and their absolute commitment is, they believe, for the rest of their lives.

I have worked among radical departers and their families since 1969, thoroughly studying more than 400 subjects in 15 groups. In no case was the sudden leave-taking expected by those who knew them best. These departures are called "out of character" by people who can make no sense of them; the radical departers appear to have taken leave of their senses.

I have come to realize how much sense radical departures make, despite their appearance of irrationality, as desperate attempts to grow up in a society that places obstacles in the way of normal youthful yearnings. The strangeness that unnerves, the hostility that enrages and even the euphoria that puzzles are expressions of belief and belonging that adolescents use as catalysts in growing up.

To understand what this means, we must consider the entire history of a radical departure, beginning with the months just prior to it, then the moment of first approach, the screening process the groups employ and on through life in the group during the peak period of commitment. This history helps us understand the remarkable endings to radical departures: More than 90 percent end in a return home within two years, and virtually all joiners eventually abandon their groups. Most important, they resume their previous lives and find gratification in the middle-class world they had totally abjured. In short, they use their radical departures to grow up.

Radical departers share certain characteristics. While there are exceptions, the majority are between 18 and 26 years of age, unmarried, affluent, well-educated, white and from intact families. But only a few such adolescents make radical departures; to understand what makes them different, one must examine what normally happens during these years.

The school years up to about age 12 are ordinarily a time of smooth progress. By each birthday, a child has grown taller, reads at a grade level higher and acts with measurably greater sophistication. But in the following six years, adolescents' bodies change so radically and rapidly that they must constantly look in the mirror to see who they are and how they like it. Nature dumps on adolescents the makings of adulthood but doesn't tell them what to make of it.

In our middle-class culture, we strongly believe that during these years, children must separate from their families and establish their individuality both practically and psychologically. No radical departer I have known has been able to separate gradually to everyone's satisfaction. All of them are still so closely tied to their parents that I tend to refer to joiners as children despite their true age.

Normally, as children become teenagers, parents begin to diminish control. They no longer try to supervise homework or to act as constant chaperones. Even if they wish to, they can no longer control their children's aggressiveness and sexual impulses, so adolescents are forced to a degree of independence. At the same time, parents also make it clear to high school students that adult responsibilities loom ahead. They are asked to think about college and to make tentative career choices; most are expected to leave home. These challenges, unlike most challenges of childhood, smack of permanence.

At the same time that parents withdraw control, their children withdraw the unconditional love and faith that typify childhood. But because they cannot proceed into adulthood without love and without faith, they seek intimacy with friends and lovers.

That is the normal course. But of the radical departers I have studied, few have been involved in relationships that were more than exploitive or tentative. None felt committed to a value system at the time of joining.

Joiners look to belief as a way to avoid their personal dilemma. Feeling so little self-esteem, they can't shoulder the responsibility of perhaps making a wrong moral choice and thereby feeling even more worthless. They are looking for ideology that will bolster whatever is admirable in them and purge whatever is bad.

Everyone must experience self-doubt, disillusion and loneliness on the way to adulthood. Radical departers are notable not only for the degree of their pain, but for the fact that everything seems to hit them at once. Too much has been put off, and the confluence of unfaced dilemmas causes a developmental logjam. They open the dam of their own development by the abrupt and violent breaking away that is a radical departure.

The final ingredient is often an accident. At just this critical period in their lives, they are offered what seems a magical solution: separation without accompanying pain. It is very common to make a radical departure while away from home, sometimes for the first time. These children wish to be back at home, safe from the frightening freedom of travel, but then how can they be separate? Separate, they feel empty—a word frequently used by radical departers—as if there is not enough to fill them. The departure is a compromise solution to this conflict.

Despite the public perception that teenagers are somehow tricked into joining radical groups, the initial encounter is actually only the beginning of a screening process that will sort out those who do belong from those who might be alien to the group. The process varies from group to group, but it often involves three basic steps.

The first step is for a member of the group to approach a youth of about the same age and background as the members themselves. Anyone may be the target of propaganda or solicitation, but approaches are made only to those who appear interested, who ask questions or linger longer than most passersby. Friendly conversation leads quite naturally to an invitation to spend an evening with the group.

Only about 5 of every 100 approached in this way feel so attracted to these new friends that they consent to the first visit. Direct proselytizing is rare, but members and candidate are indirectly checking one another's values for a match. Those who are not screened out by the group or themselves are invited for a two- or three-day retreat.

The retreat is usually held in a secluded, rural and often strikingly beautiful spot away from the busy city that surrounds most groups' central meeting place. There is ordinarily no television, radio or telephone. It is as though there were no outside—no appointments, no hassles to endure, no criticism to answer, no worldly chores, schedules, deadlines or expectations.

Joiners have told me that during the retreat, the group's ideology, which seemed mere background noise before, suddenly makes immense sense. They feel a new clarity to their thoughts; the words they hear seem rich with significance and truth. Meaning dawns: This is the way that they and the world are to be seen. Interestingly, as gripping as the euphoria is, fewer than 10 percent of those who attend the first retreat decide to stay within the group. Indeed, the screening process is so accurate that, while only 1 in 500 of those originally approached chooses to join, those who do usually stay at least six months.

I have spent hundreds of hours reading the voluminous works of all the many ideological groups I've studied in an effort to understand what their beliefs are and why radical departers should be so moved by them. The vocabulary is theological, political or therapeutic, depending on the avowed nature of the group, but they all sound the same. They are replete with tautologies ("Being here as a group brings us together") and truisms ("Life can be difficult"). Mostly the beliefs are incomprehensible to outsiders and, I suspect, to most members as well. But in a curious way, it doesn't matter. There is even relief in not understanding, comfort in knowing that there are those at the top who do understand.

One common characteristic of these various belief systems is that they closely match the ideals of the joiner's family. One young woman who joined the Children of God could just as well have joined two other sects whose teachings echoed perfectly the Sunday School lessons of her childhood. Beneath the verbiage there inevitably lie the goals all mankind has always wished for, but the rationale for achieving this peace and unity is lost in anti-intellectualism. To me, this smacks of the innocence of early childhood when, in union with one's parents who need not be understood to be trusted utterly, prayers are answered and endings are always happy.

Belonging is the heart of radical departure. They are a unity, all doing the same things, believing the same beliefs, speaking the same stock phrases, eating the same food, wearing the same clothes and working for the same cause. For the period of their commitment, they give up the usual adolescent struggle to form an independent self and instead participate with relief in a flawless group self.

But this is by no means a complete retreat from growing up. The departers have taken a giant step. Because the group self is vehemently not bound up with that of the parents, psychological separation from them has begun. For these children, however, separation can be accomplished only within the safety of joining. Or perhaps rejoining is more accurate, because these groups are built along the lines of an exaggerated and idealized family. Careful attention is given to serving good, nutritious food, for example, an emphasis that closely echoes a mother's care in assuring that her children have a wholesome diet. Health in general is high on the list of most groups' concerns, and in fact my studies revealed a bunch of unusually healthy youngsters, who are free from stress, anxiety and depression.

I don't believe, however, that these radical departers are happy in the way that happiness is generally understood. As much as I have looked at beatific faces and witnessed gushes of joy, something has always prevented me from being swept up. Again and again, with hundreds of committed group members, I have felt that theirs is a performance, a case of bad acting in which the actor is himself carried away by the ringing truth of his role yet fails to convince the audience.

It is this spurious air, I think, that leads parents to the mistaken conclusion that their children have been brainwashed and to the public perception that joiners were weird to begin with. They are not brainwashed or weird, but neither are they quite whole. The happy face that joiners wear is uncontagious precisely because it does not accurately represent their inner dynamics. Conflict, fear and resentment may have the weight of bad baggage, but these feelings cannot be dumped so easily outside the mind. They can, however, be put temporarily in the unconscious while the radical departer goes through the psychological adjustment necessary for dealing with those feelings.

One of the most fascinating findings about radical departures, given the impenetrable commitment of group members, is that nine out of ten members leave their group within two years. After a period of some months, subtle but unmistakable changes begin. Dogmatic attitudes relax; there are fewer unequivocal opinions and less inflexible faith. This is quickly followed by a siege of doubt about the perfection of the group and its leader, an upwelling of longing for the family and, finally, a return to the world.

Some joiners are able to identify the specific event that triggered or crystallized their doubts. Others describe instead a gradual creeping of ambiguity into a faith that had been absolute. During this period of doubt, criticism of the group by the family and society that previously had been ignored is suddenly reheard. In many ways this echoes the joiners' period of self-doubt just prior to their radical departures. The leader of the group, once perceived to be as perfect as a child supposes his parents to be, is revealed as flawed. Beliefs, once accepted with childlike faith and lack of understanding, begin to seem less significant, then hypocritical, finally nonsensical. Formerly committed members now entertain rebellious thoughts and contemplate another departure, with an important difference: This time they know what they are doing and feel the conflict of impending separation.

What has happened to create this difference? I'm convinced that a radical departure is a rehearsal for separation, practice for the real task of growing up. While the departers appear to be passively frozen into their narrow mold of commitment, they are actively rehearsing for their coming out. The new perceptions that intrude upon them during this second period of doubt mark the reentry into their conscious minds of the unwanted feelings that were cast out during the time of commitment. They are now psychologically fortified to deal with conflict.

The fact that the original departure is never accompanied by conflict gives away its play-like nature. Now the young people are ready to come out of rehearsal and try the painful thrust to adulthood for real. All the fears and failures that had prevented them from taking a more direct path earlier now come back to trouble them.

The most overwhelming feeling the returnees have to deal with is guilt, not about making the departure but about how they treated family and friends. They sometimes say that if they had it to do over again they would handle departures differently—less suddenly and with more careful explanations—but they rarely feel that joining was a mistake. Former members seldom vilify the group to which they once belonged or look back on the experience with shock and distaste. I have found quite the opposite: Former members almost always extract from their experience permanent values which they integrate into their present lives.

To understand this, it is important to appreciate the voluntary nature of both the radical departure and the return. Going back to the very beginning, we have seen that the percentage of potential joiners who drop out at each escalation of group pressure also escalates; of every 500 youngsters who are approached, only one actually joins. If recruitment techniques are so sinister, why do they so rarely work? The answer is that very few children are looking for what radical groups have to offer. They don't buy it because they don't want it. Those who do usually get what they want.

This doesn't mean that raidcal groups don't use group-pressure techniques to assure conformity. They do. But so do corporations intent on whipping up the enthusiasm of the sales force, preachers who seek generous donations from their congregation and football coaches eager for a winning season. The short-term outcome of a young person's recruitment into a group is not likable, and some mental-health professionals even consider the characteristic "symptoms," from tunnel vision to uncontagious bliss, to be pathological. But such judgments are inaccurate. Mourning takes extreme forms in many societies, but it would be inaccurate to label such

a crucial period of psychological reorganization pathological. Radical departure, like mourning, is in the end therapeutic, although excesses can occur in both.

Just as the original departure is voluntary, so must the return be. In my experience, if there is no voluntary homecoming, physical or emotional, the joiner who has left a group is merely "between jobs" and has not set for himself the task of resolution. Some radical departers stay with a group not because they are able to use it in a true resolution of their problems, but because any resolution at all has been cut off by the brutality of the parents' response.

One dramatic, and rare, kind of brainwashing I have come upon during 15 years of research is that practiced by deprogrammers. Frustrated by their children's departure, thousands of parents have resorted to kidnapping and deprogamming, practices that are expensive, illegal and developmentally harmful. Designed to whip away the group member's defenses with duplicity and duress, the method does just that; and whether it "works" or fails, it can cause permanent psychological damage.

More often, deprogramming does not work. Or, more accurately, it works against the possibility that the joiners will resolve their conflicts, leave the group and rejoin their families in the kind of mature relationship that cements generations. Deprogramming interferes with the natural rhythm of a radical departure, and it can drive young people back into their group, or into a pattern of cult-hopping, for years. The grotesque experience of young adults suing their parents for unlawful acts of deprogramming has been played out too often.

When deprogramming works—brings the joiner back to the family—the loss is even greater. Halted before they have been able to utilize the group self in their own behalf, former members are thrown back upon their psychological dependency on parents. The more clearly they perceive their "mistake," the less trust former members have in their own ability to make wise choices and the more dangerous freedom seems to them.

Like other reformed "sinners," successfully deprogrammed group members feel great hostility toward the group they once found congenial and now preach against it with the same fervor with which they once proselytized for it. They exhibit exactly the alarming traits of intolerance, rigidity and closed-minded hostility that society finds unsettling in the groups themselves.

This can be avoided only by letting radical departures run their course. Although many returning group members experience severe emotional upheaval in the first few months, my experience indicates that a reassuring majority have not been damaged. To be certain, there is a cost: Families suffer extreme pain, some relationships suffer irrevocably and time lost from school and other goals may be irretrievable. To say that nine out of ten children who make radical departures return within a few years to pick up the threads of their lives successfully is not to wish a radical departure on anyone. It is a desperate move.

But by understanding what it is that joiners seek, why they find commitment gratifying and—most important—how the experience is of genuine psychological use to them, we are in a better position to judge what we as a society should do. While most radical groups disappear within a few years, new groups spring up to supplant them. This cultural phenomenon may be telling us what we can and should be doing as a society to enable our youth to emancipate themselves and find meaning in their lives.

## QUESTIONS

1. Would you regard sect and cult members as deviants? Explain.

2. What is the meaning of a "radical departure" (and often, a return) for the socialization of the individual concerned?

3. People who join communities of sect and cult members are sometimes said to be "brainwashed." Do you think this view is justified? Can the same be said of people who join convents or monasteries?

*Steven Phillips*

# 19.  Justice for Whom?

*It is common knowledge that the U.S. criminal justice system is close to breaking down, particularly in the nation's largest cities. Many crimes are never reported, partly because the victims feel it would be a waste of time. Many reported crimes go uninvestigated through lack of police resources, and a majority of crimes (except for homicide) go unsolved. Yet even so, the number of people arrested each year on criminal charges threatens to clog the court system.*

*Largely as a response to the pressures of time on the courts, the police, and the public prosecutors, the American courts have developed a curious informal system, virtually unknown in most other countries, called plea bargaining. Under this behind-the-scenes system, the prosecuting and defense attorneys, with the connivance of the judge, privately negotiate the exchange of a guilty plea for a reduced charge. Thus, a person accused of attempted murder and facing a possible fifteen-year prison sentence may, through plea bargaining, end up pleading guilty to a lesser charge of aggravated assault in return for the prosecutor's promise to ask for no more than eighteen months' imprisonment. The actual courtroom proceeding takes a few minutes, rather than the hours, days, or even weeks that a full criminal trial might occupy. The overwhelming majority of cases, in fact, are now settled by plea bargaining.*

*In this even-handed article, Steven Phillips looks at the merits and demerits of plea bargaining from various perspectives, using as his point of departure an actual case study of a homicide prosecution.*

He was on his way home from a schoolyard pickup basketball game, dribbling his ball down Arthur Avenue in the Bronx, when a white teenager walked up and stabbed him once in the abdomen. The black boy was dead before he hit the ground. The assailant turned and fled, leaving his victim sprawled face upward on the sidewalk. From start to finish, the killing took no more than five seconds.

It took the detective almost a month before he broke the case. At first it was a total mystery, with no apparent motive for the killing and no decent leads to work on. In fact, several days passed before the detective even learned the victim's identity.

When they undressed the boy at the morgue, all the detective found were a set of keys and a dollar and a half in change. There was no wallet and no identification cards. He fingerprinted the corpse and ran the prints through the computer, but drew a blank. The dead boy had never been arrested. Finally, the detective took photographs of the victim's face, and distributed copies to the desk officers and detective squads of all the neighboring precincts. He hoped someone reporting a missing person would identify the photo. As it happened, the boy's parents had reported him missing on the day of his death. Four days had passed, however, before anyone remembered to show them a copy of the morgue photo. He was 17 when he was killed, a senior in high school.

For two weeks the detective got nowhere. The boy had no enemies, he had not been robbed, and no clues had been found at the scene of the crime. A canvass of the scene had produced only one eyewitness, a middle-aged black gas-station attendant who had seen the killing from about half a block away. He described the assailant as a white teenager of about average height and weight, with dark hair. He did not remember what the youth was wearing, or anything else about him.

The detective interviewed students at the dead boy's high school, where he had been an honor student. He also questioned members of the local youth gangs. But he made no progress. As the investigation stretched into its third fruitless week, the detective's squad commander began to talk about pulling him off the case. Summer was approaching, the homicide rate was climbing as fast as the temperature, and vacation schedules were cutting into available police manpower. The commander figured it made no sense to waste a good man on what appeared to be a hopeless task. They talked it over and decided to give the case one more week.

## A Lead on the Killer

On the final day of that third week a lead finally developed. The gas-station attendant called and told the detective that a kid driving an old souped-up Thunderbird had been around the gas station several times asking what he knew about the homicide. The attendant decided these questions were suspicious. Although the driver did not resemble the killer, he took down the license-plate number and passed it along to the detective.

It took the detective a day and a half to track down the driver of the Thunderbird. He was the kind of street tough who had been in and out of minor trouble since he was 13. The youngster denied all knowledge of the killing. In a whining, plaintive voice he asked why he had been brought in. The detective then took his cigar out of his mouth, put his face close to the boy's and grabbed him by the shirt front with both hands. Like the Marine noncom he had once been, he told the boy the facts of life. "Now you listen to me, you punk. This isn't an auto larceny or a burglary I'm investigating, its a goddamn murder. And I know that one of your punk friends did it! You're going to tell me who did it, 'cause if you don't I'm gonna lock your ass up for hindering prosecution! And you'd better believe I'm gonna make it stick! I'm gonna send you upstate for sure. You understand?"

The detective left the boy alone in the squadroom to think that over. Within an hour, he told the detective everything he knew. He had not been an eyewitness to the killing, and his knowledge was second-hand. The killer was an 18-year-old who worked as a delivery boy for a local pastry shop. The detective also learned the names of a number of youngsters who had actually witnessed the stabbing.

There was no need to run right out to arrest the suspect. The detective knew from long experience that if the boy had not already vanished after three weeks, he was not about to. Instead, the detective rounded up all the eyewitnesses (an easy task, since they were all attending local high schools), and brought them back to the station house. He kept them separated, and spoke to each one individually. A half hour later he had six signed eyewitness statements identifying the killer. The time had come to make the arrest.

The suspect lived with his aged parents in a two-bedroom apartment over a shoemaker's shop, not four blocks from the scene of the killing. The apartment was immaculate, and had a warm, old-world immigrant flavor the detective knew all too well. He had grown up in such a home himself. In the entrance hallway were framed pictures of Pope John, John Kennedy, and the Virgin Mary.

## "I Didn't Mean to Do It"

The boy's father answered the door. He was a frail but intense white-haired man in his 60s, and he spoke with a heavy Italian accent. Asked what he wanted, the detective said he had to speak to the boy about a crime that had been committed. As he stood there, the detective was embarrassed by the old man. He could see that the boy's father did not have the slightest inkling of what this was all about, and the detective had little stomach for what he knew was about to happen. Grimly he pushed on.

"Where is the boy?"

"He's in his bedroom, studying," the father replied. "I'll call him, but first you tell me what crime this is you want to talk to him about."

"It's a murder. A black kid was killed up on Arthur Avenue three weeks ago. I've got to talk to him about it."

"Are you here to arrest my boy?"

"Yes, I am," the detective said softly.

The old man looked hard at the detective, and began to shake. His eyes widened, and he began to look a little wild. But then, just as suddenly, he seemed to regain control of himself. He called out the boy's name.

The boy emerged from his bedroom and walked up to his father and the detective. He was short and slender, almost fragile in build, dressed in blue jeans and a white T-shirt. He was smooth-cheeked, and the detective was struck by the boy's eyes. They were large and dark and liquid, the sort of eyes you would expect to see on a beautiful woman. The boy looked straight at the detective and then lowered his eyes. He knew what this was all about.

The old man spoke first.

"This may says you killed a black kid up on Arthur Avenue three weeks ago."

The boy hung his head and began to cry. "Papa, I did it. I didn't mean to do it, and I wanted to tell you, but I couldn't. It just happened, and I'm sorry." The old man was in a state of shock. The three of them stood silently, and then the old man too began to cry. The detective waited a minute and then put the boy in handcuffs and led him away.

It was almost 24 hours from the time of arrest until the boy was arraigned. They spent it waiting for transportation, waiting for the Correction Department red tape at Central Booking, and finally, waiting for the court. The boy and the detective chatted to kill the time. The detective found that he liked his prisoner, and it bothered him. As he reflected upon what was in store for the boy in prison he felt sick. For the first time in his career he found himself wishing he had not broken a case.

By the time the boy was arraigned, his father had spoken to his neighbors, and a delegation of them went with him to the Bronx Criminal Court Building on Washington Avenue and 161st Street. When his case was called, they all stepped forward to vouch for the boy, his character, and his family. Impressed by this unusual show of neighborhood solidarity, and by the impeccable character of the local merchants who spoke up for the boy, the judge set bail at the modest sum (for a murder) of $15,000. It was raised within the hour. The boy walked out of the court after spending only one night in jail, and the case was referred to the grand jury.

There were over 400 homicides in Bronx County that year. Almost 350 were solved by the police, leading to arrests that were turned over for prosecution to the 12 of us in the Homicide Bureau of the District Attorney's office. The death of the black boy on Arthur Avenue was only one of these homicides.

## An Airtight Case

It was bound to be a low-priority case, with the defendant out on bail at a time when we had prisoners who had been languishing in jail for up to two years awaiting trial. This case had to be put on a back burner. Besides, with six eye-witnesses, an oral confession, and a vicious, senseless crime to work with, any trial of the case was bound to result in a murder conviction and a mandatory life sentence.

From the very beginning, when I was first assigned the case, I knew no defense attorney would risk taking it to trial. It was foreordained to result in a plea bargain. The grand-jury presentation took a little less than 15 minutes. Two of the eyewitnesses and the detective testified, and I read from the medical examiner's report. The grand jury deliberated about 30 seconds before handing up a murder indictment.

It was two months or so before I heard from the boy's defense attorney, a man I had dealt with before and respected. Late one afternoon, several days later, we met in my office. Although I was eager to avoid a trial, there wasn't much I could offer the boy as a plea bargain and I said so. I had close to an airtight case, one that was bound to lead to a murder conviction. The crime itself was both shocking and senseless, and the defendant, then 18 years old, would be treated as an adult . . . I saw no reason why I should not take a very hard position.

The defense attorney listened, and then asked me what I would offer the boy. I thought for a minute, and told him I would agree to a plea to manslaughter in the

first degree. I added that at the time of sentence I would ask the judge to impose a very lengthy jail term with a fixed minimum to guarantee that substantial time would actually be served.

The defense attorney was candid in his response. He acknowledged right away that his client was guilty and admitted he didn't dare take the case to trial. He had to plead his client guilty, and did not care what particular crime he pleaded to so long as it was not murder, which carried with it a mandatory life sentence. What he did care about was the sentence his client would receive, and in this regard he had two requests. Before discussing the question of sentencing he asked me to read a report on his client prepared at his family's request by a forensic psychiatrist. Then he asked me to meet the boy myself and size him up. I agreed.

## Killer on the Couch

The psychiatrist's report read, in part, as follows:

*. . . Although I am unable to state that [this young man] was unaware of the nature and consequences of his actions, or that he was unaware of the fact that his conduct was morally wrong, I do believe that there are circumstances that should weigh heavily in determining the disposition of his case.*

*. . . [he] is the only son of immigrant parents and was born at a time when his parents were already on the brink of middle age. Since early childhood he has been overprotected and overindulged by his mother who had made him the central focus of her life. His father, a stern disciplinarian, has always attempted to instill in [this young man] his own rather rigid set of values. Needless to say, this interparental conflict over the nature and style of his rearing, has left [the boy] with an ambivalent and deeply troubled attitude toward his parents.*

*This ambivalence was exacerbated by a phenomenon that is rather common in the first general offspring of newly arrived immigrants. [The boy], whose English is, of course, fluent and unaccented, and who is very much a product of this society, is ashamed of his parents' heavy accents, and what he described as their "foreign ways." He is reluctant to bring friends into the house for fear that his parents might embarrass him, and is equally reluctant to share his "American" school or "street" life with his parents, for fear that they would misunderstand or disapprove of things he has come to cherish as he struggles to find his own identity. On the other hand, [the boy] loves his parents deeply, and has great difficulty coping with this shame over their "old fashionedness."*

*. . . [He] has also had serious trouble in coping with peer-group pressure which is, of course, a particularly intense force in late adolescence. The young people in [his] neighborhood place great emphasis upon a young man's*

having "machismo," e.g., on being both sexually and physically powerful. These values directly conflict with the overprotected and unyielding values the boy has learned at home. In addition, [the boy] has gone through a relatively late puberty, and to this day is relatively small and frail for his age. He does not yet need to shave frequently, and his boyish appearance makes him the butt of a considerable amount of peer-group teasing. He has had considerable difficulty dealing with these pressures both in school and at play in the streets. In view of this it is quite remarkable that he has done as well as he has in his studies. He is a B student, a fact that reinforces my own impression that he is both a sensitive and an intelligent young man.

... There is no gainsaying the fact that he has committed a most horrible crime, and it is not my purpose to in any way diminish or make light of his offense. Nevertheless, it must be understood that [the boy] acted as he did out of a kind of neurotic desperation, from a terrible need to win acceptance from his peers, and to rebel against the strict morality of his parents. In [his] mind, the grotesque action of taking a baking knife and stabbing a strange black boy in the presence of his friends became a means of showing them, and himself, that he could outdo any of them in both violence, and at least symbolically in sexuality. The use of the knife as a chosen weapon is significant, for it's a phallic substitute, and was used to assuage doubts that he had developed about his own masculinity. I am not suggesting that [he] did not know that what he was doing was wrong. What I do find though, was that [his] actions were not wholly voluntary, but were precipitated by conflicts between intense psychological forces over which he ultimately lost control.

... I have been seeing [him] for two months now on an intensive basis, and even in this short time there has been extraordinary progress. He has begun to discuss his feelings and has begun to face directly the ambivalences that have so deeply disturbed him. His parents, who are deeply concerned, have cooperated fully in his therapy, and my sessions with them and the boy have been particularly fruitful.

While no one can ever pretend to predict these things with certainty, it is my strong feeling and my professional judgment that with continued care [this young man] will become a well-adjusted and valuable member of society. I view with horror the prospect of his going to prison. Such an eventuality would hopelessly undermine all hopes of effective treatment, would exacerbate his problems, and would most likely destroy him as an individual. Sending this young man to prison in his present psychological state would be a tragedy ...

As I read the report, I realized it was a partisan document prepared at the defendant's expense. Nevertheless, I could not completely discount what it contained.

The psychiatrist's comments seemed both thoughtful and sincere.

## "A Pretty Good Kid"

Two weeks later the lawyer brought the boy and his parents to my office. They were dressed in their Sunday best and obviously ill at ease. Their discomfort made me feel uncomfortable too. The defense attorney's purpose in arranging this meeting was not hard to divine. He wanted me to meet his client so that I might develop some sympathy for him and his family. He knew his only real hope for obtaining lenient treatment for the boy lay in winning my acquiescence.

I did find myself feeling sorry for the boy. He looked so terribly frail, young and insecure, completely unlike what I had expected. He was polite, and had soft, almost effeminate features that could not be squared with the conventional image of the vicious killer. In talking to him, I came to understand what the detective had meant when he had told me the boy was "a pretty good kid, who shouldn't get hit too hard."

The boy asked me for permission to go see the parents of the boy he had killed. He wanted to seek their forgiveness, to tell them how terribly sorry he was for what he had done. It was a pathetic request. The whole thing was pathetic. But I believed he was sincere. I kept reminding myself that I was talking to a vicious killer who had taken a human life for no reason at all and then calmly gone about his business for three weeks. He had come very close to getting away with murder. I knew it was possible that he was trying to con me into feeling sorry for him, but somehow I just did not believe it. The boy was not putting on an act.

I talked to the boy's parents briefly. They were restrained and subdued, and seemed to be good people. I could see that the prospect of losing their only child to prison was taking a terrible toll on them, and it was impossible not to sympathize with their plight. I thought about the boy's request, and then told them that it would be unwise for him to try to see the dead boy's family.

That afternoon I spoke to the dead boy's father on the telephone, and arranged for him to come to my office the following day. When I arrived that morning at 9:00 I found him already waiting for me. He was a darkskinned, hefty man with a receding hairline. We shook hands firmly and he met my gaze with unwavering eyes. I ushered him into my office, and he sat down in the same chair where 24 hours earlier the other boy's father had sat.

I offered my condolences, and then, before asking him the questions that were on my mind, I tried to make my position clear. I was not his lawyer. I worked for the State of New York and my responsibility was to the people of the state and not to any particular individual. I wanted to talk to him about his son's death and I wanted his opinion about the treatment his son's killer should receive. But in the end, he had to understand that whatever he might feel and whatever he might think, I had to be the one to decide how the case was handled. When I asked him if he understood, he continued to look levelly at me, and answered, "Yes, I do."

I went on to outline in some detail the results of the detective's investigation. He learned that I had a powerful case, and that a trial was almost certain to result in a murder conviction with a mandatory life sentence for his son's killer. I also told him what I had learned from the psychiatrist's report and described the interview in my office the preceding day. I described my problem to him. In about a week the case was scheduled to come up on the court calendar, and I would be obliged to make a recommendation to a judge on the question of plea and sentence. The judge would most likely follow my recommendation. The defense would have no choice but to go along with my offer, and in the final analysis I would bear a heavy responsibility for what would happen. I asked the man for his help in reaching a decision. He sat silently, pondering what I had said.

When he spoke, it was with great force. There was a lot bottled up inside him and he had come to my office to get it off his chest. He was blunt. He said he was not about to make things easy for me by telling me not to go hard on the white boy. As far as he was concerned "that white boy" had to go to jail for a long time and the longer the better. He told me his wife had planned to come with him to my office, but at the last moment she had broken down and couldn't come. Their son's death had just about killed his wife. The death had made her old before her time and he knew she would never be the same again.

And then there was their younger son. He had been doing really well in school, almost as well as his dead brother had been doing. But ever since the murder, the knowledge that his brother's killer was free had been eating at him. The parents did not know what to say to him. He was turning bitter, neglecting his studies, and for the first time had begun to get into trouble with the law. Was it right that their only remaining child be condemned to grow up with such hatred?

Then there was the question of race. He asked me whether a black kid who had senselessly killed a white honor student would be out on bail receiving such gentle treatment. It was a rhetorical question, and he supplied his own answer. He knew damn well that if the tables were turned his son, or any black boy, would be rotting in jail facing a certain life sentence. I listened quietly and didn't argue. I let the man talk himself out and then thanked him for coming to see me and for speaking so candidly. Then we parted.

The case got some minor press coverage, especially in the local newspapers serving the black community. We had received some mail on the case and there was one editorial highly critical of the way the criminal justice system was handling it. Here was an extraordinary young black senselessly cut down by a youthful white racist, and nobody was doing anything about it. There were letters calling for the defendant's head, and many of them were rational and forceful. It was reasoned that the failure to punish the white killer severely was a clear signal to other white youths with similar inclinations that black life was cheap and could be taken with impunity. Similarly, it told someone in the black community that there was no justice in the courts, and that recourse to justice in the streets was a wiser alternative. The newspaper clippings, the editorial, and the letters all found their way into the file. I read them, and found that I could not ignore the message they contained.

By the time the case came up for a pretrial conference I had decided unheroically to pass the buck. The judge, I thought to myself, was elected by the people, and is paid about three times as much as I am to make these tough sentencing decisions. I decided to recommend a plea to manslaughter one and take no position on the question of sentence. This would give the judge latitude to choose anything from a 25-year sentence down to no sentence at all. Let him read the presentence report, talk to both sets of parents, and decide what to do with the boy. That's his job really, not mine.

It did not work out that way, and deep down I had known it wouldn't. The judge listened courteously enough while the defense attorney and I outlined the facts of the case. Then I proposed the open plea to manslaughter in the first degree with the question of sentence left entirely in the judge's hands. The proposal was turned down on the spot.

"What, are you out of your mind?" the judge asked. "You want me to stick my neck out all alone on a case like this? No way! Here's what I'll do. I'll adjourn the case for one week. If, at that time, the district attorney's office is prepared to make a recommendation on sentence, I will accept the plea and follow that recommendation. If not, I will set the case down for trial."

As we were leaving the courtroom the defense attorney called me inside. He was angry and spoke harshly. Again I was asked rhetorical questions. Didn't I know what was going to happen to the boy in jail? A soft, good-looking kid like that would certainly be gang-raped by homosexuals in prison. He would almost certainly end up becoming a homosexual himself, and probably would become the "wife" of some stronger inmate just to obtain protection. Hadn't I read the psychiatrist's report? Didn't I know what the prisons were like?

I did not reply to the defense attorney's outburst. There was nothing I could say. I did know what the prisons were like and I had read the psychiatrist's report. I didn't need the defense attorney to remind me of these realities. They had been nagging at me all along. The defense attorney paused a minute waiting for an answer. When I said nothing, he went on. Didn't I know that 80 percent of the prison population was black or Hispanic? Once they find out what the boy is in jail for they would probably cut his throat. He said his client would never survive a lengthy jail term.

I did not argue with the defense attorney as he said this. I too had considered this possibility, and frankly, I just did not know whether he was right or wrong. I heard him out, and then excused myself. It was a bad week for me. The case would not leave my mind, and the more I thought about it, the more impossible it seemed to reach a sentencing decision. I would have liked to have had more information about the boy before making a decision. But with our crushing caseloads, neither I nor the detective could possibly devote more time to this particular case.

I turned to my colleagues for advice, but as I expected, they showed no inclination to make the decision for me. This was only one case among many, and only I had any knowledge of its complexity. The advice I got was both wise and useless. "Do the right thing, and don't worry," I was told.

The trouble, of course, was that I did not know what the right thing was, and I could not stop worrying. I wanted to reach a just result, but justice, I quickly came to realize, was a relative thing. It all depended upon your perspective. Justice for an emotionally disturbed boy, gripped by psychological forces partially beyond his control, or for his aged parents, faced with the loss of their only son? Justice for the dead boy, senselessly cut down in his youth, or for his family, grief-stricken and embittered by their loss, and by the seeming indifference of the judicial process? Society needed justice too. But what kind? Stern justice to clearly show that racial violence would not be tolerated? Or a more humane justice that sought to heal and rehabilitate rather than punish?

There was no end to the conflicting values at stake, and the conflicts, such as they were, would not resolve themselves in my mind. I had no difficulty articulating the arguments to justify either harsh or lenient treatment. But in the end, I came to realize that the arguments were pointless. Each one was based upon a different assumption about the purpose of punishment; and in effect, in making the argument, the unspoken assumption would dictate the conclusion reached. For example, if the purpose of punishment was retribution, then the very seriousness of the boy's offense, independent of all other considerations, required harsh punishment. But if the idea was rehabilitation rather than retribution, then I had a boy who most probably could be transformed

through sympathetic and therapeutic, i.e., lenient, treatment into a valuable member of society.

If, on the other hand, punishment was designed to be exemplary, if it was to teach and to deter, then harsh treatment was necessary to demonstrate that racial violence would not be tolerated.

Retribution, rehabilitation, and deterrence, they all have a certain validity, and I could not easily choose between them. Besides, I was haunted by the images of the two families, and concerned about the impact of my decision upon all of these decent and innocent people.

I tried to take a pragmatic approach and asked myself what was to be gained by sending the boy to prison. It wasn't going to bring the dead boy back, and it wasn't really going to end racial violence or make the streets of the Bronx any safer. In one way or another, prison would probably destroy the boy, and in the final analysis, wasn't it more important to save this life, than to bow to the imagined dictates of abstract social justice? The boy was so young, and in a sense he was the victim of powerful social and psychological forces that were beyond his control. Was it right to make him pay as an individual for a crime that found its origins, at least in part, in peer-group pressure and the collective racial attitudes of society in general? I toyed with all these arguments, but I could not escape the idea that the boy, however young, bore an individual responsibility for his actions, and had to answer for that responsibility.

A decision had to be made, and one week later I made a sentencing recommendation. Later, at the time of sentence, the judge followed it. Whether or not I did the right thing I shall never know. No doubt reasonable people will differ about the rightness of my decision and what ought to have been done.

The boy is currently serving a 15-year term in state prison. He will be eligible for parole in three years. Two months after sentence, the white youth's father suffered a stroke. He is now an invalid. The dead boy's brother is now under indictment, charged with armed robbery. There has been no noticeable decrease in the amount of crime or racial violence in the Bronx.

## QUESTIONS

1. What are the advantages of plea bargaining? What are the disadvantages?

2. Would you agree that the right decision was made in the case discussed? Do you think it likely that the same decision would have been made if the races of the offender and the victim were reversed?

3. Only a tiny handful of criminals end up in jail. Is this the result of random chance, or is their fate the result of a process of social selection? Explain.

*D. L. Rosenhan*

# 20. On Being Sane in Insane Places

*According to the labeling theory of deviance, people become deviant through a process in which significant others "label" them—perhaps as addicts, whores, drunks, crooks, nuts, and the like—with the result that they are generally perceived, and come to perceive themselves, in such terms. Their subsequent behavior tends to live up to the expectations aroused by the label, and their deviance eventually becomes a confirmed habit.*

*One of the most troubling forms of deviance is mental disorder, which involves a violation of social norms concerning sane behavior. Social scientists are convinced that many forms of mental disorder are in fact learned behaviors that are unconsciously adopted by the individual as a means of escaping from intolerable social or psychological pressures. Once a person is labeled "mentally disordered," after all, he or she can take on a "sick role" that offers exemption from the normal obligations and responsibilities of daily life.*

*In the study described in this article, David Rosenhan tried to find out what would happen if perfectly sane people presented themselves for admission at mental hospitals. The answer, as you will see, is that these "pseudopatients" were quickly classified as schizophrenics and admitted. Although they behaved quite normally inside the hospitals, their conduct was constantly interpreted in the light of the false label, and taken as further evidence of their mental disorder. Rosenhan's study raises disturbing questions not only about the power of labeling but also about the validity of much psychiatric diagnosis.*

From *Science*, 179, pp. 250–258, 19 January 1973. Copyright 1973 by the American Association for the Advancement of Science.

If sanity and insanity exist, how shall we know them?

The question is neither capricious nor itself insane. However much we may be personally convinced that we can tell the normal from the abnormal, the evidence is simply not compelling. It is commonplace, for example, to read about murder trials wherein eminent psychiatrists for the defense are contradicted by equally eminent psychiatrists for the prosecution on the matter of the defendant's sanity. More generally, there are a great deal of conflicting data on the reliability, utility, and meaning of such terms as "sanity," "insanity," "mental illness," and "schizophrenia."[1] Finally, as early as 1934, Benedict suggested that normality and abnormality are not universal.[2] What is viewed as normal in one culture may be seen as quite aberrant in another. Thus, notions of normality and abnormality may not be quite as accurate as people believe they are.

To raise questions regarding normality and abnormality is in no way to question the fact that some behaviors are deviant or odd. Murder is deviant. So, too, are hallucinations. Nor does raising such questions deny the existence of the personal anguish that is often associated with "mental illness." Anxiety and depression exist. Psychological suffering exists. But normality and abnormality, sanity and insanity, and the diagnoses that flow from them may be less substantive than many believe them to be.

At its heart, the question of whether the sane can be distinguished from the insane (and whether degrees of insanity can be distinguished from each other) is a simple matter: do the salient characteristics that lead to diagnoses reside in the patients themselves or in the environments and contexts in which observers find them? From Bleuler, through Kretchmer, through the formulators of the recently revised *Diagnostic and Statistical Manual* of the American Psychiatric Association, the belief has been strong that patients present symptoms, that those symptoms can be categorized, and, implicitly, that the sane are distinguishable from the insane. More recently, however, this belief has been questioned. Based in part on theoretical and anthropological considerations, but also on philosophical, legal, and therapeutic ones, the view has grown that psychological categorization of mental illness is useless at best and downright harmful, misleading, and pejorative at worst. Psychiatric diagnoses, in this view, are in the minds of the observers and are not valid summaries of characteristics displayed by the observed.[3,4,5]

Gains can be made in deciding which of these is more nearly accurate by getting normal people (that is, people who do not have, and have never suffered, symptoms or serious psychiatric disorders) admitted to psychiatric hospitals and then determining whether they were discovered to be sane and, if so, how. If the sanity of such pseudopatients were always detected, there would be prima facie evidence that a sane individual can be distinguished from the insane context in which he is found. Normality (and presumably abnormality) is distinct enough that it can be recognized wherever it occurs, for it is carried within the person. If on the other hand, the sanity of the pseudopatients were never discovered, serious difficulties would arise for those who support traditional modes of psychiatric diagnosis. Given that the hospital staff was not incompetent, that the pseudopatient had been behaving as sanely as he had been outside of the hospital, and that it had never been previously suggested that he belonged in a psychiatric hospital, such an unlikely outcome would support the view that psychiatric diagnosis betrays little about the patient but much about the environment in which an observer finds him.

This article describes such an experiment. Eight sane people gained secret admission to 12 different hospitals.[6] Their diagnostic experiences constitute the data of the first part of this article; the remainder is devoted to a description of their experiences in psychiatric institutions. Too few psychiatrists and psychologists, even those who have worked in such hospitals, know what the experience is like. They rarely talk about it with former patients, perhaps because they distrust information coming from the previously insane. Those who have worked in psychiatric hospitals are likely to have adapted so thoroughly to the settings that they are insensitive to the impact of that experience. And while there have been occasional reports of researchers who submitted themselves to psychiatric hospitalization,[7] these researchers have commonly remained in the hospitals for short periods of time, often with the knowledge of the hospital staff. It is difficult to know the extent to which they were treated like patients or like research colleagues. Nevertheless, their reports about the inside of the psychiatric hospital have been valuable. This article extends those efforts.

## Pseudopatients and Their Settings

The eight pseudopatients were a varied group. One was a psychology graduate student in his 20's. The remaining seven were older and "established." Among them were three psychologists, a pediatrician, a psychiatrist, a painter, and a housewife. Three pseudopatients were women, five were men. All of them employed pseudonyms, lest their alleged diagnoses embarrass them later. Those who were in mental health professions alleged another occupation in order to avoid the special attentions that might be accorded by staff, as a matter of courtesy or caution, to ailing colleagues.[8] With the exception of myself (I was the first pseudopatient and my presence was known to the hospital administrator and chief psychologist and, so far as I can tell, to them alone), the presence of pseudopatients and the nature of the research program was not known to the hospital staff.[9]

The settings were similarly varied. In order to generalize the findings, admission into a variety of hospitals was sought. The 12 hospitals in the sample were located in five different states on the East and West coasts. Some were old and shabby, some were quite new. Some were research-oriented, others not. Some had good staff-patient ratios, others were quite understaffed. Only one was a strictly private hospital. All of the others were supported by state or federal funds or, in one instance, by university funds.

After calling the hospital for an appointment, the pseudopatient arrived at the admissions office complaining that he had been hearing voices. Asked what the voices said, he replied that they were often unclear, but as far as he could tell they said "empty," "hollow," and "thud." The voices were unfamiliar and were of the same sex as the pseudopatient. The choice of these symptoms was occasioned by their apparent similarity to existential symptoms. Such symptoms are alleged to arise from painful concerns about the perceived meaninglessness of one's life. It is as if the hallucinating person were saying, "My life is empty and hollow." The choice of these symptoms was also determined by the *absence* of a single report of existential psychoses in the literature.

Beyond alleging the symptoms and falsifying name, vocation, and employment, no further alterations of person, history, or circumstances were made. The significant events of the pseudopatient's life history were presented as they had actually occurred. Relationships with parents and siblings, with spouse and children, with people at work and in school, consistent with the aforementioned exceptions, were described as they were or had been. Frustrations and upsets were described along with joys and satisfactions. These facts are important to remember. If anything, they strongly biased the subsequent results in favor of detecting sanity, since none of their histories or current behaviors were seriously pathological in any way.

Immediately upon admission to the psychiatric ward, the pseudopatient ceased simulating *any* symptoms of abnormality. In some cases, there was a brief period of mild nervousness and anxiety, since none of the pseudopatients really believed that they would be admitted so easily. Indeed, their shared fear was that they would be immediately exposed as frauds and greatly embarrassed. Moreover, many of them had never visited a psychiatric ward; even those who had nevertheless had some genuine fears about what might happen to them. Their nervousness, then, was quite appropriate to the novelty of the hospital setting, and it abated rapidly.

Apart from that short-lived nervousness, the pseudopatient behaved on the ward as he "normally" behaved. The pseudopatient spoke to patients and staff as he might ordinarily. Because there is uncommonly little to do on a psychiatric ward, he attempted to engage others in conversation. When asked by staff how he was feeling, he indicated that he was fine, that he no longer experienced symptoms. He responded to instructions from attendants, to calls for medication (which was not swallowed), and to dining-hall instructions. Beyond such activities as were available to him on the admissions ward, he spent his time writing down his observations about the ward, its patients, and the staff. Initially these notes were written "secretly," but as it soon became clear that no one much cared, they were subsequently written on standard tablets of paper in such public places as the dayroom. No secret was made of these activities.

The pseudopatient, very much as a true psychiatric patient, entered a hospital with no foreknowledge of when he would be discharged. Each was told that he would have to get out by his own devices, essentially by convincing the staff that he was sane. The psychological stresses associated with hospitalization were considerable, and all but one of the pseudopatients desired to be discharged almost immediately after being admitted. They were, therefore, motivated not only to behave sanely, but to be paragons of cooperation. That their behavior was in no way disruptive is confirmed by nursing reports, which have been obtained on most of the patients. These reports uniformly indicate that the patients were "friendly," "cooperative," and "exhibited no abnormal indications."

## The Normal Are Not Detectably Sane

Despite their public "show" of sanity, the pseudopatients were never detected. Admitted, except in one case, with a diagnosis of schizophrenia,[10] each was discharged with a diagnosis of schizophrenia "in remission." The label

"in remission" should in no way be dismissed as a formality, for at no time during any hospitalization had any question been raised about any pseudopatient's simulation. Nor are there any indications in the hospital records that the pseudopatient's status was suspect. Rather, the evidence is strong that, once labeled schizophrenic, the pseudopatient was stuck with that label. If the pseudopatient was to be discharged, he must naturally be "in remission"; but he was not sane, nor, in the institution's view, had he ever been sane.

The uniform failure to recognize sanity cannot be attributed to the quality of the hospitals, for, although there were considerable variations among them, several are considered excellent. Nor can it be alleged that there was simply not enough time to observe the pseudopatients. Length of hospitalization ranged from 7 to 52 days, with an average of 19 days. The pseudopatients were not, in fact, carefully observed, but this failure clearly speaks more to traditions within psychiatric hospitals than to lack of opportunity.

Finally, it cannot be said that the failure to recognize the pseudopatients' sanity was due to the fact that they were not behaving sanely. While there was clearly some tension present in all of them, their daily visitors could detect no serious behavioral consequences—nor, indeed, could other patients. It was quite common for the patients to "detect" the pseudopatients' sanity. During the first three hospitalizations, when accurate counts were kept, 35 of a total of 118 patients on the admissions ward voiced their suspicions, some vigorously. "You're not crazy. You're a journalist, or a professor [referring to the continual note-taking]. You're checking up on the hospital." While most of the patients were reassured by the pseudopatient's insistence that he had been sick before he came in but was fine now, some continued to believe that the pseudopatient was sane throughout his hospitalization.[11] The fact that the patients often recognized normality when staff did not raises important questions.

Failure to detect sanity during the course of hospitalization may be due to the fact that physicians operate with a strong bias toward what statisticians call the type 2 error.[5] This is to say that physicians are more inclined to call a healthy person sick (a false positive, type 2) than a sick person healthy (a false negative, type 1). The reasons for this are not hard to find: it is clearly more dangerous to misdiagnose illness than health. Better to err on the side of caution, to suspect illness even among the healthy.

But what holds for medicine does not hold equally well for psychiatry. Medical illnesses, while unfortunate, are not commonly pejorative. Psychiatric diagnoses, on the contrary, carry with them personal, legal, and social stigmas.[12] It was therefore important to see whether the tendency toward diagnosing the sane insane could be reversed. The following experiment was arranged at a research and teaching hospital whose staff had heard these findings but doubted that such an error could occur in their hospital. The staff was informed that at some time during the following 3 months, one or more pseudopatients would attempt to be admitted into the psychiatric hospital. Each staff member was asked to rate each patient who presented himself at admission or on the ward according to the likelihood that the patient was a pseudopatient. A 10-point scale was used, with a 1 and 2 reflecting high confidence that the patient was a pseudopatient.

Judgments were obtained on 193 patients who were admitted for psychiatric treatment. All staff who had had sustained contact with or primary responsibility for the patient—attendants, nurses, psychiatrists, physicians, and psychologists—were asked to make judgments. Forty-one patients were alleged, with high confidence, to be pseudopatients by at least one member of the staff. Twenty-three were considered suspect by at least one psychiatrist. Nineteen were suspected by one psychiatrist *and* one other staff member. Actually, no genuine pseudopatient (at least from my group) presented himself during this period.

The experiment is instructive. It indicates that the tendency to designate sane people as insane can be reversed when the stakes (in this case, prestige and diagnostic acumen) are high. But what can be said of the 19 people who were suspected of being "sane" by one psychiatrist and another staff member? Were these people truly "sane," or was it rather the case that in the course of avoiding the type 2 error the staff tended to make more errors of the first sort—calling the crazy "sane"? There is no way of knowing. But one thing is certain: any diagnostic process that lends itself so readily to massive errors of this sort cannot be a very reliable one.

## The Stickiness of Psychodiagnostic Labels

Beyond the tendency to call the healthy sick—a tendency that accounts better for diagnostic behavior or admission than it does for such behavior after a lengthy period of exposure—the data speak to the massive role of labeling in psychiatric assessment. Having once been labeled schizophrenic, there is nothing the pseudopatient can do to overcome the tag. The tag profoundly colors others' perceptions of him and his behavior.

From one viewpoint, these data are hardly surprising, for it has long been known that elements are given meaning by the context in which they occur. Gestalt psychology made this point vigorously, and Asch[13] demonstrated that there are "central" personality traits (such as "warm" versus "cold") which are so powerful that

they markedly color the meaning of other information in forming an impression of a given personality.[14] "Insane," "schizophrenic," "manic-depressive," and "crazy" are probably among the most powerful of such central traits. Once a person is designated abnormal, all of his other behaviors and characteristics are colored by that label. Indeed, that label is so powerful that many of the pseudopatients' normal behaviors were overlooked entirely or profoundly misinterpreted. Some examples may clarify this issue.

Earlier I indicated that there were no changes in the pseudopatient's personal history and current status beyond those of name, employment, and, where necessary, vocation. Otherwise, a veridical description of personal history and circumstances was offered. Those circumstances were not psychotic. How were they made consonant with the diagnosis of psychosis? Or were those diagnoses modified in such a way as to bring them into accord with the circumstances of the pseudopatient's life, as described by him?

As far as I can determine, diagnoses were in no way affected by the relative health of the circumstances of a pseudopatient's life. Rather, the reverse occurred: the perception of his circumstances was shaped entirely by the diagnosis. A clear example of such translation is found in the case of a pseudopatient who had had a close relationship with his mother but was rather remote from his father during his early childhood. During adolescence and beyond, however, his father became a close friend, while his relationship with his mother cooled. His present relationship with his wife was characteristically close and warm. Apart from occasional angry exchanges, friction was minimal. The children had rarely been spanked. Surely there is nothing especially pathological about such a history. Indeed, many readers may see a similar pattern in their own experiences, with no markedly deleterious consequences. Observe, however, how such a history was translated in the psychopathological context, this from the case summary prepared after the patient was discharged.

> This white 39-year-old male . . . manifests a long history of considerable ambivalence in close relationships, which begins in early childhood. A warm relationship with his mother cools during his adolescence. A distant relationship to his father is described as becoming very intense. Affective stability is absent. His attempts to control emotionality with his wife and children are punctuated by angry outbursts and, in the case of the children, spankings. And while he says that he has several good friends, one senses considerable ambivalence embedded in those relationships also. . . .

The facts of the case were unintentionally distorted by the staff to achieve consistency with a popular theory of the dynamics of a schizophrenic reaction.[15] Nothing of an ambivalent nature had been described in relations with parents, spouse, or friends. To the extent that ambivalence could be inferred, it was probably not greater than is found in all human relationships. It is true the pseudopatient's relationships with his parents changed over time, but in the ordinary context that would hardly be remarkable—indeed, it might very well be expected. Clearly, the meaning ascribed to his verbalizations (that is, ambivalence, affective instability) was determined by the diagnosis: schizophrenia. An entirely different meaning would have been ascribed if it were known that the man was "normal."

All pseudopatients took extensive notes publicly. Under ordinary circumstances, such behavior would have raised questions in the minds of observers, as, in fact, it did among patients. Indeed, it seemed so certain that the notes would elicit suspicion that elaborate precautions were taken to remove them from the ward each day. But the precautions proved needless. The closest any staff member came to questioning these notes occurred when one pseudopatient asked his physician what kind of medication he was receiving and began to write down the response. "You needn't write it," he was told gently. "If you have trouble remembering, just ask me again."

If no questions were asked of the pseudopatients, how was their writing interpreted? Nursing records for three patients indicate that the writing was seen as an aspect of their pathological behavior. "Patient engages in writing behavior" was the daily nursing comment on one of the pseudopatients who was never questioned about his writing. Given that the patient is in the hospital, he must be psychologically disturbed. And given that he is disturbed, continuous writing must be a behavioral manifestation of that disturbance, perhaps a subset of the compulsive behaviors that are sometimes correlated with schizophrenia.

One tacit characteristic of psychiatric diagnosis is that it locates the sources of aberration within the individual and only rarely within the complex of stimuli that surrounds him. Consequently, behaviors that are stimulated by the environment are commonly misattributed to the patient's disorder. For example, one kindly nurse found a pseudopatient pacing the long hospital corridors. "Nervous, Mr. X?" she asked. "No, bored," he said.

The notes kept by pseudopatients are full of patient behaviors that were misinterpreted by well-intentioned staff. Often enough, a patient would go "berserk" because he had, wittingly or unwittingly, been mistreated by, say, an attendant. A nurse coming upon the scene would rarely inquire even cursorily into the environmental stimuli of the patient's behavior. Rather, she assumed that his upset derived from his pathology, not from his present interactions with other staff members.

Occasionally, the staff might assume that the patient's family (especially when they had recently visited) or other patients had stimulated the outburst. But never were the staff found to assume that one of themselves or the structure of the hospital had anything to do with a patient's behavior. One psychiatrist pointed to a group of patients who were sitting outside the cafeteria entrance half an hour before lunchtime. To a group of young residents he indicated that such behavior was characteristic of the oral-acquisitive nature of the syndrome. It seemed not to occur to him that there were very few things to anticipate in a psychiatric hospital besides eating.

A psychiatric label has a life and an influence of its own. Once the impression has been formed that the patient is schizophrenic, the expectation is that he will continue to be schizophrenic. When a sufficient amount of time has passed, during which the patient has done nothing bizarre, he is considered to be in remission and available for discharge. But the label endures beyond discharge, with the unconfirmed expectation that he will behave as a schizophrenic again. Such labels, conferred by mental health professionals, are as influential on the patient as they are on his relatives and friends, and it should not surprise anyone that the diagnosis acts on all of them as a self-fulfilling prophecy. Eventually, the patient himself accepts the diagnosis, with all of its surplus meanings and expectations, and behaves accordingly.[5]

The inferences to be made from these matters are quite simple. Much as Zigler and Phillips have demonstrated that there is enormous overlap in the symptoms presented by patients who have been variously diagnosed,[16] so there is enormous overlap in the behaviors of the sane and the insane. The sane are not "sane" all of the time. We lose our tempers "for no good reason." We are occasionally depressed or anxious, again for no good reason. And we may find it difficult to get along with one or another person—again for no reason that we can specify. Similarly, the insane are not always insane. Indeed, it was the impression of the pseudopatients while living with them that they were sane for long periods of time—that the bizarre behaviors upon which their diagnoses were allegedly predicated constituted only a small fraction of their total behavior. If it makes no sense to label ourselves permanently depressed on the basis of an occasional depression, then it takes better evidence than is presently available to label all patients insane or schizophrenic on the basis of bizarre behaviors or cognitions. It seems more useful, as Mischel[17] has pointed out, to limit our discussion to *behaviors*, the stimuli that provoke them, and their correlates.

It is not known why powerful impressions of personality traits, such as "crazy" or "insane," arise. Conceivably, when the origins of and stimuli that give rise to a behavior are remote or unknown, or when the behavior strikes us as immutable, trait labels regarding the *behaver* arise. When, on the other hand, the origins and stimuli are known and available, discourse is limited to the behavior itself. Thus, I may hallucinate because I am sleeping, or I may hallucinate because I have ingested a peculiar drug. These are termed sleep-induced hallucinations, or dreams, and drug-induced hallucinations, respectively.

But when the stimuli to my hallucinations are unknown, that is called craziness, or schizophrenia—as if that inference were somehow as illuminating as the others.

## The Experience of Psychiatric Hospitalization

The term "mental illness" is of recent origin. It was coined by people who were humane in their inclinations and who wanted very much to raise the station of (and the public's sympathies toward) the psychologically disturbed from that of witches and "crazies" to one that was akin to the physically ill. And they were at least partially successful, for the treatment of the mentally ill *has* improved considerably over the years. But while treatment has improved, it is doubtful that people really regard the mentally ill in the same way that they view the physically ill. A broken leg is something one recovers from, but mental illness allegedly endures forever.[18] A broken leg does not threaten the observer, but a crazy schizophrenic? There is by now a host of evidence that attitudes toward the mentally ill are characterized by fear, hostility, aloofness, suspicion, and dread.[19] The mentally ill are society's lepers.

That such attitudes infect the general population is perhaps not surprising, only upsetting. But that they affect the professionals—attendants, nurses, physicians, psychologists, and social workers—who treat and deal with the mentally ill is more disconcerting, both because such attitudes are self-evidently pernicious and because they are unwitting. Most mental health professionals would insist that they are sympathetic toward the mentally ill, that they are neither avoidant nor hostile. But it is more likely that an exquisite ambivalence characterizes their relations with psychiatric patients, such that their avowed impulses are only part of their entire attitude. Negative attitudes are there too and can easily be detected. Such attitudes should not surprise us. They are the natural offspring of the labels patients wear and the places in which they are found.

Consider the structure of the typical psychiatric hospital. Staff and patients are strictly segregated. Staff have their own living space, including their dining facilities, bathrooms, and assembly places. The glassed quarters that contain the professional staff, which the pseudopatients came to call "the cage," sit out on every day-room. The staff emerge primarily for caretaking purposes—to give medication, to conduct a therapy or group meeting, to instruct or reprimand a patient. Otherwise, staff keep to themselves, almost as if the disorder that afflicts their charges is somehow catching.

So much is patient-staff segregation the rule that, for four public hospitals in which an attempt was made to measure the degree to which staff and patients mingle, it was necessary to use "time out of the staff cage" as the operational measure. While it was not the case that all time spent out of the cage was spent mingling with patients (attendants, for example, would occasionally emerge to watch television in the day-room), it was the only way in which one could gather reliable data on time for measuring.

The average amount of time spent by attendants outside of the cage was 11.3 percent (range, 3 to 52 percent).

This figure does not represent only time spent mingling with patients, but also includes time spent on such chores as folding laundry, supervising patients while they shave, directing ward cleanup, and sending patients to off-ward activities. It was the relatively rare attendant who spent time talking with patients or playing games with them. It proved impossible to obtain a "percent mingling time" for nurses, since the amount of time they spent out of the cage was too brief. Rather, we counted instances of emergence from the cage. On the average, daytime nurses emerged from the cage 11.5 times per shift, including instances when they left the ward entirely (range, 4 to 39 times). Late afternoon and night nurses were even less available, emerging on the average 9.4 times per shift (range, 4 to 41 times). Data on early morning nurses, who arrived usually after midnight and departed at 8 a.m., are not available because patients were asleep during most of this period.

Physicians, especially psychiatrists, were even less available. They were rarely seen on the wards. Quite commonly, they would be seen only when they arrived and departed, with the remaining time being spent in their offices or in the cage. On the average, physicians emerged on the ward 6.7 times per day (range, 1 to 17 times). It proved difficult to make an accurate estimate in his regard, since physicians often maintained hours that allowed them to come and go at different times.

The hierarchical organization of the psychiatric hospital has been commented on before,[20] but the latent meaning of that kind of organization is worth noting again. Those with the most power have least to do with patients, and those with the least power are most involved with them. Recall, however, that the acquisition of role-appropriate behaviors occurs mainly through the observation of others, with the most powerful having the most influence. Consequently, it is understandable that attendants not only spend more time with patients than do any other members of the staff—that is required by their station in the hierarchy—but also, insofar as they learn from their superiors' behavior, spend as little time with patients as they can. Attendants are seen mainly in the cage, which is where the models, the action, and the power are.

I turn now to a different set of studies, these dealing with staff response to patient-initiated contact. It has long been known that the amount of time a person spends with you can be an index of your significance to him. If he initiates and maintains eye contact, there is reason to believe that he is considering your requests and needs. If he pauses to chat or actually stops and talks, there is added reason to infer that he is individuating you. In four hospitals, the pseudopatient approached the staff member with a request which took the following form: "Pardon me, Mr. [or Dr. or Mrs.] X, could you tell me when I will be eligible for grounds privileges?" (or " . . . when I will be presented at the staff meeting?" or " . . . when I am likely to be discharged?"). While the content of the question varied according to the appropriateness of the target and the pseudopatient's (apparent) current needs the form was always a courteous and relevant request for information. Care was taken never to approach a particular member of the staff more than once a day, lest the staff member become suspicious or irritated. . . . Remember that the behavior of the pseudopatients was neither bizarre nor disruptive. One could indeed engage in good conversation with them.

. . . Minor differences between these four institutions were overwhelmed by the degree to which staff avoided continuing contacts that patients had initiated. By far, their most common response consisted of either a brief response to the question, offered while they were "on the move" and with head averted, or no response at all.

The encounter frequently took the following bizarre form: (pseudopatient) "Pardon me, Dr. X. Could you tell me when I am eligible for grounds privileges?" (physician) "Good morning, Dave. How are you today?" (Moves off without waiting for a response.)

. . .

## Powerlessness and Depersonalization

Eye contact and verbal contact reflect concern and individuation; their absence, avoidance and depersonalization. The data I have presented do not do justice to the rich daily encounters that grew up around matters of depersonalization and avoidance. I have records of patients who were beaten by staff for the sin of having initiated verbal contact. During my own experience, for example, one patient was beaten in the presence of other patients for having approached an attendant and told him, "I like you." Occasionally, punishment meted out to patients for misdemeanors seemed so excessive that it could not be justified by the most radical interpretations of psychiatric canon. Nevertheless, they appeared to go unquestioned. Tempers were often short. A patient who had not heard a call for medication would be roundly excoriated, and morning attendants would often wake patients with, "Come on, you m———f———s, out of bed!"

Neither anecdotal nor "hard" data can convey the overwhelming sense of powerlessness which invades the individual as he is continually exposed to the depersonalization of the psychiatric hospital. It hardly matters *which* psychiatric hospital—the excellent public ones and the very plush private hospital were better than the rural and shabby ones in this regard, but, again, the features that psychiatric hospitals had in common overwhelmed by far their apparent differences.

Powerlessness was evident everywhere. The patient is deprived of many of his legal rights by dint of his psychiatric commitment.[21] He is shorn of credibility by virtue of his psychiatric label. His freedom of movement is restricted. He cannot initiate contact with the staff, but may only respond to such overtures as they make. Personal privacy is minimal. Patient quarters and possessions can be entered and examined by any staff member, for whatever reason. His personal history and anguish are available to any staff member (often including the "grey lady" and "candy striper" volunteer) who chooses to read his folder, regardless of their therapeutic relationship to him. His personal hygiene and waste evacuation are often monitored. The water closets may have no doors.

At times depersonalization reached such proportions that pseudopatients had the sense that they were invisible, or at least unworthy of account. Upon being admitted, I and other pseudopatients took the initial physical examinations in a semipublic room, where staff members went about their own business as if we were not there.

On the ward, attendants delivered verbal and occasionally serious physical abuse to patients in the presence of other observing patients, some of whom (the pseudopatients) were writing it all down. Abusive behavior, on the other hand, terminated quite abruptly when other staff members were known to be coming. Staff are credible witnesses. Patients are not.

A nurse unbuttoned her uniform to adjust her brassiere in the presence of an entire ward of viewing men. One did not have the sense that she was being seductive. Rather, she didn't notice us. A group of staff persons might point to a patient in the day-room and discuss him animatedly, as if he were not there.

One illuminating instance of depersonalization and invisibility occurred with regard to medications. All told, the pseudopatients were administered nearly 2100 pills, including Elavil, Stelazine, Compazine, and Thorazine, to name but a few. (That such a variety of medications should have been administered to patients presenting identical symptoms is itself worthy of note.) Only two were swallowed. The rest were either pocketed or deposited in the toilet. The pseudopatients were not alone in this. Although I have no precise records on how many patients rejected their medications, the pseudopatients frequently found the medications of other patients in the toilet before they deposited their own. As long as they were cooperative, their behavior and the pseudopatients' own in this matter, as in other important matters, went unnoticed throughout.

Reactions to such depersonalization among pseudopatients were intense. Although they had come to the hospital as participant observers and were fully aware that they did not "belong," they nevertheless found themselves caught up in and fighting the process of depersonalization. Some examples: a graduate student in psychology asked his wife to bring his textbooks to the hospital so he could "catch up on his homework"—this despite the elaborate precautions taken to conceal his professional association. The same student, who had trained for quite some time to get into the hospital, and who had looked forward to the experience, "remembered" some drag races that he had wanted to see on the weekend and insisted that he be discharged by that time. Another pseudopatient attempted a romance with a nurse. Subsequently, he informed the staff that he was applying for admission to graduate school in psychology and was very likely to be admitted, since a graduate professor was one of his regular hospital visitors. The same person began to engage in psychotherapy with other patients—all of this as a way of becoming a person in an impersonal environment.

## The Sources of Depersonalization

What are the origins of depersonalization? I have already mentioned two. First are attitudes held by all of us toward the mentally ill—including those who treat them—attitudes characterized by fear, distrust, and horrible expectations on the one hand, and benevolent intentions on the other. Our ambivalence leads, in this instance as in others, to avoidance.

Second, and not entirely separate, the hierarchical structure of the psychiatric hospital facilitates depersonalization. Those who are at the top have least to do with patients, and their behavior inspires the rest of the staff. Average daily contact with psychiatrists, psychologists, residents, and physicians combined ranged from 3.9 to 25.1 minutes, with an overall mean of 6.8 (six pseudopatients over a total of 129 days of hospitalization). Included in this average are time spent in the admissions interview, ward meetings in the presence of a senior staff

member, group and individual psychotherapy contacts, case presentation conferences, and discharge meetings. Clearly, patients do not spend much time in interpersonal contact with doctoral staff. And doctoral staff serve as models for nurses and attendants.

Psychiatric installations are presently in serious financial straits. Staff shortages are pervasive, staff time at a premium. Something has to give, and that something is patient contact. Yet, while financial stresses are realities, too much can be made of them. I have the impression that the psychological forces that result in depersonalization are much stronger than the fiscal ones and that the addition of more staff would not correspondingly improve patient care in this regard. The incidence of staff meetings and the enormous amount of record-keeping on patients, for example, have not been as substantially reduced as has patient contact. Priorities exist, even during hard times. Patient contact is not a significant priority in the traditional psychiatric hospital, and fiscal pressures do not account for this. Avoidance and depersonalization may.

Heavy reliance upon psychotropic medication tacitly contributes to depersonalization by convincing staff that treatment is indeed being conducted and that further patient contact may not be necessary. Even here, however, caution needs to be exercised in understanding the role of psychotropic drugs. If patients were powerful rather than powerless, if they were viewed as interesting individuals rather than diagnostic entities, if they were socially significant rather than social lepers, if their anguish truly and wholly compelled our sympathies and concerns, would we not *seek* contact with them, despite the availability of medications? Perhaps for the pleasure of it all?

## The Consequences of Labeling and Depersonalization

Whenever the ratio of what is known to what needs to be known approaches zero, we tend to invent "knowledge" and assume that we understand more than we actually do. We seem unable to acknowledge that we simply don't know. The needs for diagnosis and remediation of behavioral and emotional problems are enormous. But rather than acknowledge that we are just embarking on understanding, we continue to label patients "schizophrenic," "manic-depressive," and "insane," as if in those words we had captured the essence of understanding. The facts of the matter are that we have known for a long time that diagnoses are often not useful or reliable, but we have nevertheless continued to use them. We now know that we cannot distinguish insanity from sanity. It is depressing to consider how that information will be used.

Not merely depressing, but frightening. How many people, one wonders, are sane but not recognized as such in our psychiatric institutions? How many have been needlessly stripped of their privileges of citizenship, from the right to vote and drive to that of handling their own accounts? How many have feigned insanity in order to avoid the criminal consequences of their behavior, and, conversely, how many would rather stand trial than live interminably in a psychiatric hospital—but are wrongly thought to be mentally ill? How many have been stigmatized by well-intentioned, but nevertheless erroneous, diagnoses? On the last point, recall again that a "type 2 error" in psychiatric diagnosis does not have the same consequences it does in medical diagnosis. A diagnosis of cancer that has been found to be in error is cause for celebration. But psychiatric diagnoses are rarely found to be in error. The label sticks, a mark of inadequacy forever.

Finally, how many patients might be "sane" outside the psychiatric hospital but seem insane in it—not because craziness resides in them, as it were, but because they are responding to a bizarre setting, one that may be unique to institutions which harbor nether people? Goffman[4] calls the process of socialization to such institutions "mortification"—an apt metaphor that includes the processes of depersonalization that have been described here. And while it is impossible to know whether the pseudopatients' responses to these processes are characteristic of all inmates—they were, after all, not real patients—it is difficult to believe that these processes of socialization to a psychiatric hospital provide useful attitudes or habits of response for living in the "real world."

## Summary and Conclusions

It is clear that we cannot distinguish the sane from the insane in psychiatric hospitals. The hospital itself imposes a special environment in which the meanings of behavior can easily be misunderstood. The consequences to patients hospitalized in such an environment—the powerlessness, depersonalization, segregation, mortification, and self-labeling—seem undoubtedly countertherapeutic.

I do not, even now, understand this problem well enough to perceive solutions. But two matters seem to have some promise. The first concerns the proliferation of community mental health facilities, of crisis intervention centers, of the human potential movement, and of behavior therapies that, for all of their own problems, tend to avoid psychiatric labels, to focus on specific problems and behaviors, and to retain the individual in a relatively nonpejorative environment. Clearly, to the extent that we refrain from sending the distressed to insane places, our impressions of them are less likely to be distorted. (The risk of distorted perceptions, it seems to me, is always present, since we are much more sensitive to an individual's behaviors and verbalizations than we are to the subtle contextual stimuli that often promote them. At issue here is a matter of magnitude. And, as I have shown, the magnitude of distortion is exceedingly high in the extreme context that is a psychiatric hospital.)

The second matter that might prove promising speaks to the need to increase the sensitivity of mental health workers and researchers to the *Catch 22* position of psychiatric patients. Simply reading materials in this area will be of help to some such workers and researchers. For others, directly experiencing the impact of psychiatric hospitalization will be of enormous use. Clearly, further research into the social psychology of such total institutions will both facilitate treatment and deepen understanding.

I and the other pseudopatients in the psychiatric setting had distinctly negative reactions. We do not pretend to describe the subjective experiences of true patients. Theirs may be different from ours, particularly with the passage of time and the necessary process of adaptation to one's environment. But we can and do speak to the relatively more objective indices of treatment within the hospital. It could be a mistake, and a very unfortunate one, to consider that what happened to us derived from malice or stupidity on the part of the staff. Quite the contrary, our overwhelming impression of them was of people who really cared, who were committed and who were uncommonly intelligent. Where they failed, as they sometimes did painfully, it would be more accurate to attribute those failures to the environment in which they, too, found themselves than to personal callousness. Their perceptions and behavior were controlled by the situation, rather than being motivated by a malicious disposition. In a more benign environment, one that was less attached to global diagnosis, their behaviors and judgments might have been more benign and effective.

## QUESTIONS

1. What are the implications of Rosenhan's study for labeling theory?

2. Many critics have contended that psychiatry is a pseudoscience, in which diagnostic labels and other jargon are used to obscure the fact that psychiatrists really understand very little about mental disorder. How much support does the study give to this view?

3. Was Rosenhan's study a fair one? Could he have reasonably expected the pseudopatients to be detected, given that hospital personnel had no expectation that any sane person would attempt to gain admittance?

# REFERENCES AND NOTES

1. P. Ash, *J. Abnorm. Soc. Psychol.* **44**, 272 (1949); A. T. Beck, *Amer. J. Psychiat.* **119**, 210 (1962); A. T. Boisen, *Psychiatry* **2**, 233 (1938); N. Kreitman, *J. Ment. Sci.* **107**, 876 (1961); N. Kreitman, P. Sainsbury, J. Morrisey, J. Towers, J. Scrivener, *ibid.*, p. 887; H. O. Schmitt and C. P. Fonda, *J. Abnorm. Soc. Psychol.* **52**, 262 (1956); W. Seeman, *J. Nerv. Ment. Dis.* **118**, 541 (1953). For an analysis of these artifacts and summaries of the disputes, see J. Zubin, *Annu. Rev. Psychol.* **18**, 373 (1967); L. Phillips and J. G. Draguns, *ibid.* **22**, 447 (1971).

2. R. Benedict, *J. Gen. Psychol.* **10**, 59 (1934).

3. See in this regard H. Becker, *Outsiders: Studies in the Sociology of Deviance* (Free Press, New York, 1963); B. M. Braginsky, D. D. Braginsky, K. Ring, *Methods of Madness: The Mental Hospital as a Last Resort* (Holt, Rinehart & Winston, New York, 1969); G. M. Crocetti and P. V. Lemkau, *Amer. Sociol. Rev.* **30**, 577 (1965); E. Goffman, *Behavior in Public Places* (Free Press, New York, 1964); R. D. Laing, *The Divided Self: A Study of Sanity and Madness* (Quadrangle, Chicago, 1960); D. L. Phillips. *Amer. Sociol. Rev.* **28**, 963 (1963); T. R. Sarbin, *Psychol. Today* **6**, 18 (1972); E. Schur, *Amer. J. Sociol.* **75**, 309 (1969); T. Szasz, *Law, Liberty and Psychiatry* (Macmillan, New York, 1963); *The Myth of Mental Illness: Foundations of a Theory of Mental Illness* (Hoeber-Harper, New York, 1963). For a critique of some of these views, see W. R. Gove, *Amer. Sociol. Rev.* **35**, 873 (1970).

4. E. Goffman, *Asylums* (Doubleday, Garden City, N.Y., 1961).

5. T. J. Scheff, *Being Mentally Ill: A Sociological Theory* (Aldine, Chicago, 1966).

6. Data from a ninth pseudopatient are not incorporated in this report because, although his sanity went undetected, he falsified aspects of his personal history, including his marital status and parental relationships. His experimental behaviors therefore were not identical to those of the other pseudopatients.

7. A. Barry, *Bellevue Is a State of Mind* (Harcourt Brace Jovanovich, New York, 1971); I. Belknap, *Human Problems of a State Mental Hospital* (McGraw-Hill, New York, 1956); W. Caudill, F. C. Redlich, H. R. Gilmore, E. B. Brody, *Amer. J. Orthopsychiat.* **22**, 314 (1952); A. R. Goldman, R. H. Bohr, T. A. Steinberg, *Prof. Psychol.* **1**, 427 (1970); unauthored, *Roche Report* **1** (No. 13), 8 (1971).

8. Beyond the personal difficulties that the pseudopatient is likely to experience in the hospital, there are legal and social ones that, combined, require considerable attention before entry. For example, once admitted to a psychiatric institution, it is difficult, if not impossible, to be discharged on short notice, state law to the contrary notwithstanding. I was not sensitive to these difficulties at the outset of the project, nor to the personal and situational emergencies that can arise, but later a writ of habeas corpus was prepared for each of the entering pseudopatients and an attorney was kept "on call" during every hospitalization. I am grateful to John Kaplan and Robert Bartels for legal advice and assistance in these matters.

9. However distasteful such concealment is, it was a necessary first step to examining these questions. Without concealment, there would have been no way to know how valid these experiences were; nor was there any way of knowing whether whatever detections occurred were a tribute to the diagnostic acumen of the staff or to the hospital's rumor network. Obviously, since my concerns are general ones that cut across individual hospitals and staffs, I have respected their anonymity and have eliminated clues that might lead to their identification.

10. Interestingly, of the 12 admissions, 11 were diagnosed as schizophrenic and one, with the identical symptomatology, as manic-depressive psychosis. This diagnosis has a more favorable prognosis, and it was given by the only private hospital in our sample. On the relations between social class and psychiatric diagnosis, see A. deB. Hollingshead and F. C. Redlich, *Social Class and Mental Illness: A Community Study* (Wiley, New York, 1958).

11. It is possible, of course, that patients have quite broad latitudes in diagnosis and therefore are inclined to call many people sane, even those whose behavior is patently aberrant. However, although we have no hard data on this matter, it was our distinct impression that this was not the case. In many instances, patients not only singled us out for attention, but came to imitate our behaviors and styles.

12. J. Cumming and E. Cumming. *Community Ment. Health* **1**, 135 (1965); A. Farina and K. Ring, *J. Abnorm. Psychol.* **70**, 47 (1965); H. E. Freeman and O. G. Simmons, *The Mental Patient Comes Home* (Wiley, New York, 1963); W. J. Johannsen, *Ment. Hygiene* **53**, 218 (1969); A. S. Linsky, *Soc. Psychiat.* **5**, 166 (1970).

13. S. E. Asch, *J. Abnorm. Soc. Psychol.* **41**, 258 (1946); *Social Psychology* (Prentice-Hall, New York, 1952).

14. See also I. N. Mensh and J. Wishner, *J. Personality* **16**, 188 (1947); J. Wishner, *Psychol. Rev.* **67**, 96 (1960); J. S. Bruner and R. Tagiuri, in *Handbook of Social Psychology*, G. Lindzey, Ed. (Addison-Wesley, Cambridge, Mass., 1954), vol. 2, pp. 634–654; J. S. Bruner, D. Shapiro, R. Tagiuri, in *Person Perception and Interpersonal Behavior*, R. Tagiuri and L. Petrullo, Eds. (Stanford Univ. Press, Stanford, Calif., 1958), pp. 277–288.

15. For an example of similar self-fulfilling prophecy, in this instance dealing with the "central" trait of intelligence, see R. Rosenthal and L. Jacobson, *Pygmalion in the Classroom* (Holt, Rinehart & Winston, New York, 1968).

16. E. Zigler and L. Phillips, *J. Abnorm. Soc. Psychol.* **63**, 69 (1961). See also R. K. Freudenberg and J. P. Robertson, *A.M.A. Arch. Neurol. Psychiatr.* **76**, 14 (1956).

17. W. Mischel, *Personality and Assessment* (Wiley, New York, 1968).

18. The most recent and unfortunate instance of this tenet is that of Senator Thomas Eagleton.

19. T. R. Sarbin and J. C. Mancuso, *J. Clin. Consult. Psychol.* **35**, 159 (1970); T. R. Sarbin, *ibid.* **31**, 447 (1967); J. C. Nunnally, Jr., *Popular Conceptions of Mental Health* (Holt, Rinehart & Winston, New York, 1961).

20. A. H. Stanton and M. S. Schwartz, *The Mental Hospital: A Study of Institutional Participation in Psychiatric Illness and Treatment* (Basic, New York, 1954).

21. D. B. Wexler and S. E. Scoville, *Ariz. Law Rev.* **13**, 1 (1971).

22. I thank W. Mischel, E. Orne, and M. S. Rosenhan for comments on an earlier draft of this manuscript.

E. E. LeMaster

# 21.  The Sexual Way of Life

*There is almost infinite variety in the ways that men and women relate to one another. We often think of this variety as being an individual matter, linked to the personalities of the people concerned. There is certainly much truth to that view, but it is also the case that our sexual attitudes and relationships are strongly influenced by social factors—such as our membership in a specific society, social class, or subculture. In some human groups, for example, women are expected to be demure and submissive; in others, provocative or flirtatious. Similarly, some groups expect men to treat women with courtesy and respect; others encourage a more brash and aggressive approach.*

*In North America, as anywhere else in the world, social life is suffused with overt and covert sexual signals and interactions. Despite individual variations, two themes influence these relationships. First, the sexes are in many respects unequal, with men taking the dominant role in most interactions. Second, many men tend to regard women in general as sex objects, valuing them for their physical charms to the exclusion of their other attributes. These themes are sometimes expressed in apparently harmless ways, but they can take much more extreme forms—such as sexual harassment, abusive pornography, and even rape.*

*In this article, which is based on a participant-observation study, E. E. LeMaster describes the sexual attitudes that he heard expressed among "blue-collar aristocrats"—relatively highly paid artisans—in a working-class tavern called The Oasis.*

## Virginity Is a State of Affairs to Be Ended as Soon as Possible

The writer has never heard chastity defended *for either sex* at The Oasis, except for children. And even then, "If a girl is big enough, she's old enough, and if she's old enough, then she's big enough."

A man at The Oasis once described in considerable detail how he began his sex life at thirteen having intercourse with a young married woman. This account met with approval (if not envy) from the other men present. A white-collar man who was at the bar on this occasion said that he had not "had a woman" until he was nineteen. The blue-collar men present were surprised at the late date. In the Kinsey research of the 1940s and 1950s it was concluded that boys from blue-collar backgrounds tend to begin their heterosexual activities earlier than boys from middle-class families (Kinsey et al., 1946). This seems to be true for the men at The Oasis. My data indicate that the average man at The Oasis had his first heterosexual affair by the age of sixteen, with a range from thirteen to eighteen years. In this group a boy who had not "had a woman" by the end of high school is considered to be retarded in his sexual development.

There are humorous "defloration" stories told in this group which describe how a certain boy "lost his cherry." "We fixed Joe up with this widow who was putting out around town and she taught him the facts of life. When he came back from the date he was white as a sheet. He had to buy all the beer that night!"

It is considered unhealthy for a boy to be eighteen or over without some heterosexual outlet. "Something" might happen to him. It is never very clear what this "something" refers to, but it appears to have reference to the possibility of homosexuality.

If a girl is a virgin, a man should try to seduce her.[1]

From E. E. LeMaster, *Blue-Collar Aristocrats* (Madison, Wis.: University of Wisconsin Press, 1975), pp. 93–105. Reprinted by permission.

[1]They, of course, exclude young children from this discussion.

"If you don't, some other guy will—and then you'll be sorry you didn't."

Implicit in this attitude is a belief that no woman in our society can remain a virgin very long once she starts going out with men. And since her virginity is sure to be taken by some man sooner or later, it might as well be you.

If a boy is a virgin he should try to remedy the situation as soon as possible. By no means should he get married without previous sexual experience; this might make it difficult for him to know how to "satisfy" his wife.

### Men Do Not Marry Virgins

I have never heard a man at The Oasis argue that a girl should be a virgin when she gets married. In fact it is difficult to imagine any of these men dating a girl seriously for any length of time who was unwilling to have sexual relations—this would reflect on the man's virility. It would also put the girl in a dominant power position that she might try to perpetuate after the marriage.

Another problem about marrying a virgin is that she might not be very passionate: a girl who can retain her virginity once she is "in love" with a boy is probably not "very hot. . . ."

### A Girl Should Not Be a Virgin but at the Same Time She Should Not Be Promiscuous

. . . Blue-collar aristocrats divide women into two types: good (or nice) women and "bad" (promiscuous) women. But the "nice" girls need not be virgins; they merely have to choose their sexual partner (or partners) with some care.

The "bad" women are sexually promiscuous; they sleep with almost any man who propositions them. As a rule these women are to be avoided because (*a*) no status in the male peer group is achieved by "making" them, and (*b*) they are not capable of being loyal to a man—they will "cheat" on you. And a man loses status in this group if his woman goes to bed with somebody else.

. . . The blue-collar aristocrats do not really differentiate between "sluts" (bad women) and prostitutes—to them, a promiscuous woman is a "whore," whether she charges for her sexual favors or not. To some extent this attitude reflects the thin line that currently exists in our society between the promiscuous amateur woman and the prostitute; both are using their sexual favors to get what they need out of men and are viewed in that context.

### Sex Has Very Little (*If Anything*) to Do with Love

The expression "making love" is not used by the men at The Oasis when referring to sexual intercourse. They have a colorful assortment of terms which do refer to this behavior but none of them include the word "love." One can only conclude that for these men sex is sex: it refers to a physical (or organic) experience between a man and a woman. If affection accompanies the sexual act, this is a bonus, but the main ingredient is passion (sexual desire).

To these men, sex is a physical need, and sexual satisfaction refers to physical relief, not psychological fulfillment.

### A Normal Man Needs Sexual Relief to Remain Healthy

Except for elderly men, this principle is taken for granted. Any man in the prime years of life who disputed this point would open himself to the charge of being "abnormal."

### A Double Standard of Sexual Morality Is Assumed to Be the Normal State of Affairs

This principle is related to the above; a man *has* to have regular sex to remain healthy, whereas this is not necessary for women. This means that a man is justified in taking sex where he can find it if his wife (or his girl friend) is not providing sexual relief.

This belief in the sexual needs of men versus those of women leads to a justification of adultery on the part of husbands while this right is denied wives. In other words, a woman who seeks extramarital sexual partners is a "slut," where a man who engages in the same behavior is "starved" for sexual relief by his wife.

It is recognized that some husbands are sexually inadequate, and the wives of such men may be justified in seeking other sexual partners. But this is regarded as unusual, not common.

### Prostitution Is a Necessary Evil

A man is not honored for going to a prostitute; this means that he was unable to seduce an "amateur." As one man put it: "I sure as hell will never pay a woman to go to bed—hell, I think they should pay *me*!"

It is recognized, however, that a man in the armed forces, or under some other unusual circumstances, might have to resort to prostitutes, but this carries no prestige in the group.

It follows from the above that most of these men believe in legalized prostitution; they think it meets the sexual needs of a certain category of men in our society.

### Masturbation Is Also a Necessary Evil

It is better, of course, if a man "can find a woman" (almost any woman) to satisfy his sexual needs, but if this is impossible, then masturbation is "better than no sex at all" (as one man put it).

### There Is No Justification for Homosexuality

The writer has heard almost every type of sexual behavior defended at The Oasis except homosexuality. Adultery, prostitution, and even incest are accepted within limits, but nobody speaks a word in behalf of the homosexual—male or female. This strikes one as remarkable in a group that seems to be "emancipated" in its attitudes toward human sexuality.

### Married Women Are a Special Prize in Seduction

In this group special satisfaction is obtained by the seduction of a married woman. Since there is always some hazard in adultery, only the more daring members of the group pursue this sport. If they are not caught, their achievement (if known to others) carries prestige in the group.

It also seems to be true ... that the seduction of a married woman of a higher social class carries special satisfaction and special recognition. One could develop a point system for scoring seductions in this male subculture. The scale would look something like this:

| Type of Seduction | Points |
| --- | --- |
| **Married women** | |
| Higher social class | 15 |
| Same social class | 10 |
| Lower social class | 0 |
| **Divorced or widowed women** | 0 |
| **Single women** | |
| Virgin | 15 |
| Nonvirgin | 5 |

### The Cardinal Rule in Sex Is Not to Be Stupid

While it is recognized that sex is a wonderful way of life, it is also recognized that sex (as well as liquor) can ruin your life. Thus a married man whose wife catches him having an affair is not immoral—he is "stupid."

A man who gets a girl pregnant that he does not intend to marry is also "stupid." 'The dumb bastard," one man said of this predicament, "didn't he ever hear of rubbers? A man's pecker can get him into a helluva mess if he isn't careful."

The most "stupid" man of all, however, is a man who marries a promiscuous woman cund then doesn't realize she is "running around' with other men. In one

famous situation of this nature at The Oasis the following comments were heard: "What in the hell did he think would happen when he took that job out of town? Did he expect her to screw herself? You know damn well that babe will get her screwing somewhere."

Another man made the following observation: "That dumb bastard hardly got out of town before she was down here sitting at the bar—all dressed up. I hear she hits a different tavern every night."

### Some Types of Rape Are To Be Defended

These men have an ambivalent attitude toward rape. While they do not approve of males using force to obtain sexual favors from a female, at the same time they believe that many forcible rape charges are fictitious—that the woman "had it coming to her."

"By God," one man said, "if I were on a jury the woman would have to prove her case. A lot of women lead a man on until he can't control himself and then they yell *rape*. Bullshit, I say."

Another man said: "Did you ever try to screw a woman that didn't want to screw? It ain't easy, I can tell you. They can put up a hell of a fight. Take my word for it.

"Of course," he added, "if a man uses a knife or gun that's a different story. Then the sonafabitch deserves a good stretch in the state prison."

One man remarked, humorously, that he had been raped several times by women. "I can't help myself," he said. "When they threaten to make me walk home or beat me up I just give in. You might say that I rape very easy."

The men at The Oasis are also skeptical about statutory rape. Many of them feel that the age of consent for girls is too high—eighteen in this particular state.

"Jesus Christ!" one man said. "I picked up a broad in Denver once when I was in the air force and later on I found out she was only fifteen. She was in an adult bar when I met her—how in the hell was I to know she wasn't old enough to screw?"

"They should tattoo their birth date on the girl's belly at birth," a plumber said. "Then a man would know whether they're old enough or not."

"Why don't they issue the girls ID cards like they do for bars?" another man said. "The card could say 'I am old enough to screw' or 'Don't screw me—I'm not old enough.'"

"That's a good idea," the bartender said, "but some guys in here don't read too good, especially when they're loaded."

"You could make the cards different colors," the other man said. "Red for the young ones and green for the old ones."

"Some guys are color blind," the bartender pointed out.

Kinsey claimed that statutory rape was a common experience for the American male. It is easy to believe listening to these men (Kinsey, 1946).

The men do not, of course, approve of adults who molest children sexually; their argument is that some girls (and boys) mature sexually at a very early age, and they feel that the courts should take this into account in statutory rape cases.

## Divorced Men and Women

The men and women at The Oasis take it for granted that divorced or widowed persons "going steady" are having sex relations (Hunt, 1966). This causes no comment at the tavern. In fact, comment would result if such a couple were *not* having an affair. A divorced man said: "If I had three dates with a divorced woman and couldn't go to bed with her I'd feel impotent."

The basic attitude seems to be that divorced adults of both sexes need sexual relations and are entitled to them whether remarried or not. It would seem that fornication statutes, which prohibit heterosexual relations between unmarried adults, have no support in this group.

Camping trips and vacation trips by divorced couples who are not married produce no comment at The Oasis. It is assumed that such persons are testing their compatibility for marriage.

Divorced or widowed persons at The Oasis may also live together without comment if their behavior otherwise is "respectable"—that is, if they are employed, do not drink excessively, take care of their children (if any), and are not promiscuous in their sexual relations.

As Morton Hunt has demonstrated, the world of the divorced adult is a strange new world; the norms for single youth do not apply, nor do those of married couples (Hunt, 1966). A moral code is, however, apparent for such couples at The Oasis. It is flexible but it exists.

## The Women Look at Sex

One evening at The Oasis a man of fifty or so announced that he was going home to watch television, "after which I intend to make a pass at my wife." All the men present seemed to think this was the way to spend "a perfect evening" (as one man put it), but a married woman at the bar took exception. She had had a few drinks and her tongue was a bit loose. "You guys are nuts," she said to the man who had announced his plans for the evening. "All you think about is sex. Here you are, fifty years old, and you talk about going home and making a pass at your wife. Christ, you ought to be over that by now."

Most of the men at the bar groaned at this point. One

man became belligerent. "That's the trouble with you goddamn women!" he shouted. "Soon as a man gets to be forty or fifty you want to shut it off, to make a damn priest out of him. No wonder the guys run around looking for a piece all the time. You women make me sick."

It was clear that most (if not all) of the men present supported the male customer in this argument. The other women at the bar maintained silence.

In the years of this study three or four "promiscuous" women have been observed at the tavern—women who are known to be sexually available to almost any male who might make advances to them. These women are not regular patrons of The Oasis; they show up from time to time with some man who is usually not a regular customer of the tavern either.

. . . The men at The Oasis have no respect for these promiscuous women. Neither do the women. The regular women patrons can't imagine how the average man could even touch such a woman, to say nothing of going to bed with her.

In contrast, most of the men at The Oasis are potentially promiscuous sexually in that they would seldom refuse a sexual opportunity that is not too repulsive or too dangerous. They certainly do not view with disfavor men who are sexually promiscuous—in fact they tend to admire such a man if his taste in sexual partners is good and if he doesn't get into any trouble.

"You know that——who comes in here?" one man said. I nodded.

"Well that son-of-a-gun gets more tail than all the rest of us put together in here. Good-looking women, too. I don't see how he does it."

Notice that the speaker here doesn't ask *why* the other man is sexually promiscuous; he wonders *how* the man can manage it. In contrast, a woman who is sexually promiscuous may be thought of as being "sick"; they wonder *why* she engages in such behavior.

The promiscuous man referred to above is popular with the other men at The Oasis. The reason they admire him is that he has been able to sustain a good marriage with an attractive wife while engaging in numerous extramarital affairs. If such a man "got into trouble" by his sexual activity the other men would no longer admire him. By "trouble" they mean that (1) his wife divorced him, or (2) some man caught him out with the man's wife, or (3) he lost his job as the result of some sexual escapade.

In contrast, it appears that the married women at The Oasis do not admire women who "cheat" on their husbands—unless the husband "had it coming to him." This means that the man was neglecting his wife and/ or going out with other women, so "he got what he deserved."

Why do the men at The Oasis seem to be obsessed

with sex? One hypothesis would be that high sexual interest carries prestige for men in tavern society; it is a bad thing to be uninterested in sex or "over the hill" sexually. Another hypothesis would be that taverns (and bars in general) tend to attract men who are highly motivated sexually. A third hypothesis would be that American men in general are frustrated sexually and that this frustration is readily apparent in a tavern study (Cauan, 1966).

It seems that the basic difference between male and female attitudes toward sex at The Oasis results from the different priority assigned sex: the younger men rank it first, and "way ahead of whatever is in second place," while the younger women place sex among the top three or four items in their life. For the women, children, a good marriage, and a nice home are just as important as a good sex life.

Whatever the factors may be that produce the differences, it seems that the men and women at The Oasis have substantial disagreements over the part that sex should play in human society.

## A Liberated Woman

Promiscuous women who come into The Oasis are ostracized by the regular female customers. In 1970, when the women's liberation movement was making headlines, a young woman of twenty-seven or so began to frequent the tavern. In a conversation with me she revealed that she was divorced and that her child was being reared by her parents.

"I should never have gotten married," she said. "I was pregnant and wanted to have an abortion but my parents talked me out of it. They kept yelling at me about motherhood being sacred and all of that bullshit." She paused to light a cigarette and order another beer.

"I started screwing in high school and just loved it— I still do. Not just one man but different men. My husband was good in bed but it got to be monotonous sleeping with the same guy every night."

"Are you attracted by men's bodies the way men are to women's bodies?"

"Yes, I am. When a guy walks in that door I look him over. Some of them appeal to me and some of them don't but I don't know why. One guy I'm sleeping with now is fifty years old and homely as hell but he does something to me. I don't know what it is."

"You sound like the men in here."

"Sure I do. I'm always wondering how some guy sitting at the bar would be in bed. Do you think I'm terrible?"

"Well, I don't think the local PTA will ever honor you as Mother of the Year."

"You can say that again."

This young woman insisted that she had the same sexual rights as men. She also felt that fathers had as much responsibility as mothers for young children. After a few exciting months this liberated women disappeared from The Oasis. One had the impression that both the husbands and wives were relieved—they felt safer now.

## Conversations About Sex

Sex is a favorite topic of conversation among these men (perhaps all men in our society). I would estimate the four most commonly discussed subjects to be jobs, people, sports, and sex—not necessarily in that order. The men tell a great many "bar stories" with either an implicit or explicit sexual content: "Did you hear the one about the new young parish priest and the nun? Well it seems . . ."

These men "kid" each other about alleged sexual prowess or impotence—"he can't cut the mustard any more." An older man made this remark when he left the bar to urinate: "Well, I'll go back and shake hands with the unemployed." Since he was heading for the men's room I didn't get the significance of this statement for a minute or so; it was, of course, a reference to sexual inactivity.

There is quite a bit of "joshing" among these men about their sexual ability: the younger men tend to brag while the older men often comment on their declining sexual capacity. Sometimes the older men will reminisce about how great their sexual capacity was in their younger days. I have never heard any man in the tavern admit that he was sexually inadequate as a *young* man; this sort of remark can only be made by or about older men, sixty or over.

References to the size of the penis are not rare, in particular the implication that some member of the group is better endowed than others, or that somebody has an unusually small penis. In the latter case the usual reply is: "It's not what God gave you but what you can do with it that counts."

These men often tell humorous stories about their sexual ineptitude when they were young and inexperienced—for example, how "dumb" they were in not having taken advantage of some earlier sexual opportunity. These stories always carry the same point: the teller is not that "stupid" any more.

These workers are mostly veterans of the armed forces, and they talk a great deal about their sexual experiences while in military service: World War II, Korea, the Japanese and German occupation periods. Most of these anecdotes imply that foreign women are easier "to make" than are American women. One has the impression that every living American veteran had at least one exciting sexual affair while in the armed forces.

Stories about how a man lost his virginity are common at the tavern. Quite often it appears that the young man was more of less "seduced" by an older woman. Here is the story of the man mentioned above who was seduced in his early teens:

"I was 13 years old when I got my first piece of ass. I was plowing a field in the hot sun and the dust was flying all over hell. There was a young married couple living in a house next to this field and as I came down by the fence on the tractor this woman waved for me to stop. She wanted to know if I was thirsty and said she had some lemonade in the kitchen.

"Well, I was thirsty as hell and over that fence I went.

"When we got into the kitchen she kept talking about her husband working out of town and how lonely it was living out in the country.

"When she brought the lemonade over to me she sort of brushed herself against me and that did it—my peter jumped right up and before I knew what happened we were in the bedroom.

"After that I screwed her every night until her husband came back to town. Then they moved away and I never saw her again."

Stories like this seem to cast a magic spell over the men as each one recalls his youth and how he lost his virginity.

Stories about passionate women are popular: women who bite, or scratch, or moan, or cry while having sexual intercourse, or women whose sexual desires are insatiable. "This gal I had out in Frisco during the war was really something. We would knock off a piece when we went to bed—and by God about twenty minutes later she would start fooling around to see if I was ready to go again.

"She would wake me up two or three times a night to see if I was ready. Christ, I had to go back to the base to get some sleep."

Then he added: "Sure as hell wish she lived around here."

At this the other men laughed:

"Like hell you do," one man said, "A woman like that would put you in the grave inside of two weeks!"

The original speaker just smiled.

"What a way to go," he said.

A great many stories with sexual themes are told at The Oasis. The following is typical except that it is "cleaner" than some of the others.

"Do you know why prostitutes are now putting zip codes on their stomachs?"

"No."

"Because it makes the male come faster."

End of joke.

## REFERENCES

Barzini, L. *The Italians.* New York: Atheneum Press, 1964.

Cauan, S. *Liquor license: An ethnography of bar behavior.* Chicago: Aldine, 1966.

Hunt, M. *The world of the formerly married.* New York: McGraw-Hill, 1966.

Kinsey, A. C. et al. *Sexual behavior in the human male.* Philadelphia: W. B. Saunders, 1946.

## QUESTIONS

1. How would you characterize the men's attitudes toward women? Are these attitudes unusual, or are they found—perhaps expressed in a more genteel manner—throughout the society?

2. What is the relationship between the attitudes reported here and the fact of economic and social inequality between the sexes?

3. Why do these men talk about sex so much? Are college men similar or different?

# UNIT 3

# Social Inequality

123
123

Alison Lurie

# 22. Fashion and Status

*Most societies are marked by significant social inequality—the unequal distribution of such rewards as wealth, power, and prestige. Historically, the members of the elite in stratified societies have used a variety of ways of ensuring public recognition of their high status. In the Indian caste system, for example, people of higher status kept themselves physically separate from those of lower status, whom they regarded as "untouchable." A more common means of signaling status in stratified societies was through elaborate rules concerning the type or color of clothing that people of different statuses could wear. Thus, in ancient Rome only members of the imperial family were allowed to wear purple.*

*Although the modern United States is a stratified society, distinctions of class are much more blurred than in most of the stratified societies of the past, and Americans can wear whatever clothes they like and can afford. In practice, people often use fashions as a way of demonstrating their status (or pretended status) to others. More than half a century ago, the social scientist Thorstein Veblen observed that Americans were fond of what he called "conspicuous consumption"—the public use or display of expensive goods and services. The person who can obviously afford what others cannot is thereby able to demonstrate some appearance of superiority.*

*In this article, Alison Lurie shows how people use fashions to indicate their status to other people, and thus to gain some prestige in an unequal society.*

*Man from the earliest times has worn clothes to overcome his feelings of inferiority and to achieve a conviction of his superiority to the rest of creation, including members of his own family and tribe, and to win admiration and to assure himself that he "belongs."*

—Lawrence Langner

Clothing designed to show the social position of its wearer has a long history. Just as the oldest languages are full of elaborate titles and forms of address, so for thousands of years certain modes have indicated high or royal rank. Many societies passed decrees known as sumptuary laws to prescribe or forbid the wearing of specific styles by specific classes of persons. In ancient Egypt only those in high position could wear sandals; the Greeks and Romans controlled the type, color and number of garments worn and the sorts of embroidery with which they could be trimmed. During the Middle Ages almost every aspect of dress was regulated at some place or time—though not always with much success. The common features of all sumptuary laws—like that of edicts against the use of certain words—seem to be that they are difficult to enforce for very long.

Laws about what could be worn by whom continued to be passed in Europe until about 1700. But as class barriers weakened and wealth could be more easily and rapidly converted into gentility, the system by which color and shape indicated social status began to break down. What came to designate high rank instead was the evident cost of a costume: rich materials, superfluous trimmings and difficult-to-care-for styles; or, as Thorstein Veblen later put it, Conspicuous Consumption, Conspicuous Waste and Conspicuous Leisure. As a result, it was assumed that the people you met would be dressed as lavishly as their income permitted. In Fielding's *Tom Jones*, for instance, everyone judges strangers by their clothing and treats them accordingly; this is presented as natural. It is a world in which rank is very exactly indicated by costume, from the rags of Molly the gamekeeper's daughter to Sophia Western's riding habit "which was so very richly laced" that "Partridge and the post-boy instantly started from their chairs, and my landlady fell to her curtsies, and her ladyships, with great eagerness." The elaborate wigs characteristic of this period conferred status partly because they were both expensive to buy and expensive to maintain.

By the early eighteenth century the social advantages of conspicuous dress were such that even those who could not afford it often spent their money on finery. This development was naturally deplored by supporters of the status quo. In Colonial America the Massachusetts General Court declared its "utter detestation and dislike, that men or women of mean condition, should take upon them the garb of Gentlemen, by wearing Gold or Silver lace, or Buttons, or Points at their knees, or to walk in great Boots; or Women of the same rank to wear Silk or Tiffiny hoods, or Scarfes . . ." What "men or women of mean condition"—farmers or artisans—were supposed to wear were coarse linen or wool, leather aprons, deerskin jackets, flannel petticoats and the like.

To dress above one's station was considered not only foolishly extravagant, but deliberately deceptive. In 1878 an American etiquette book complained,

> It is . . . unfortunately the fact that, in the United States, but too much attention is paid to dress by those who have neither the excuse of ample means nor of social claims. . . . We Americans are lavish, generous, and ostentatious. The wives of our wealthy men are glorious in garb as are princesses and queens. They have a right so to be. But when those who can ill afford to wear alpaca persist in arraying themselves in silk . . . the matter is a sad one.

## Contemporary Status: Fine Feathers and Tattered Souls

Today simple ostentation in dress, like gold or silver lace, is less common than it used to be; but clothes are as much a sign of status as ever. The wives of our wealthy men are no longer praised for being glorious in garb; indeed, they constantly declare in interviews that they choose their clothes for ease, comfort, convenience and practicality. But, as Tom Wolfe has remarked, these comfortable, practical clothes always turn out to have been bought very recently from the most expensive shops; moreover, they always follow the current rules of Conspicuous Consumption, Waste and Leisure.

At the same time, as high-status clothes have become superficially less gorgeous they have increasingly tended to take on an aura of moral virtue. A 1924 guide to good manners clearly suggests this:

> An honest heart may beat beneath the ragged coat, a brilliant intellect may rise above the bright checked suit and the yellow tie, the man in the shabby suit may be a famous writer, the girl in the untidy blouse may be an artist of great promise, but as a general rule, the chances are against it and such people are dull, flat, stale, and unprofitable both to themselves and to other people.

The implication is that an ill-dressed person is also probably dishonest, stupid and without talent. Today this idea is so well established that one of our foremost historians of costume, Anne Hollander, has refused to admit that true virtue can shine through ugly or ragged clothes, as in the tale of Cinderella:

> In real life . . . rags obviously cannot be "seen through" to something lovely underneath because they themselves express and also create a tattered condition of soul. The habit of fine clothes, however, can actually produce a true personal grace.

In a society that believes this, it is no wonder that many of those who can ill afford to wear alpaca—or its modern equivalent, polyester—are doing their best to array themselves in silk. Popular writers no longer complain that those of modest means wear clothes above their rank; instead they explain how best to do so: how to, as the title of one such book puts it, *Dress for Success*. At the moment there are so many such guidebooks it may seem surprising that their advice is not followed by more people. However, as my friend the lady executive remarks, "wardrobe engineering won't do much for you if your work is lousy . . . or if you're one of an army of aspirants in impeccable skirted suits all competing for the same spot. As with investment advice, once everyone agrees that it's the thing to do, it's time to look for value somewhere else."

There are other problems with dressing to advance your status professionally. First and most obviously, it is very expensive. The young executive who buys a high-priced suit instead of a stereo system or a week's vacation in Portugal or the Caribbean is giving up certain present pleasure for possible future success in a society that regards hedonistic self-fulfillment as a right. Second, there are one's colleagues to consider. For many people, agreeable working conditions and well-disposed birds are worth more than a possible promotion in the bush. The clerk who dresses like his boss is apt to be regarded by other clerks as a cold fish or an ass-kisser; the secretary in her severe skirted suit is seen as snotty and pretentious: Who does she think she is, in that getup? Moreover, somebody who is distrusted and disliked by his or her equals is very unlikely ever to become their superior. It is also a rare boss who wants to have employees who dress exactly as he or she does—especially since they are usually younger and may already have the edge in appearance. Fortunately for the manufacturers, however, there are more ways than one of advertising high status. Today, "simple," "easy-care" and "active" may be the bywords of fashion copy; but fashionable luxury, waste and inconvenience continue to flourish in new forms.

## Conspicuous Addition: Eating and Layering

The most primitive form of Conspicuous Consumption is simply to consume so much food that one becomes conspicuous by one's bulk, a walking proof of having dined often and well. Fatness, frequently a sign of high status in primitive tribes, has also been admired in more civilized societies. In late nineteenth-century Europe and America it was common among well-to-do men, who often, as Robert Brain has remarked, "were as proud of their girth as a Bangwa chief, the big belly being a sign of imposing male power. It was a culture trait among German men, for whom fatness reflected wealth and status." The late-Victorian woman, too, was often as handsomely solid and well-upholstered as her furniture.

In general, the fashionable size seems to vary accordingly to real or imagined scarcity of food. When a large proportion of the population is known to be actually going hungry, it is chic to be well-padded and to dine lavishly. When (as in England and America in the 1960s) there seems to be at least enough starchy food to go around, it becomes chic to be thin, thus demonstrating that one is existing on an expensive protein diet rather than on proletarian bread, potatoes, franks and beans. Today, when food prices are rising astronomically and the facts of world hunger have come to the attention even of café society, it is again no longer necessary to be very thin in order to be chic.

Another simple and time-honored way of consuming conspicuously is to wear more clothes than other people do. "More" of course is relative: when most people went naked, the mere wearing of garments conferred prestige. In ancient Egypt, for instance, slaves and servants often wore nothing, or at most a brief loincloth; aristocrats put on clothes not out of modesty or for warmth, but to indicate rank. Even in colder climates and more Puritanical societies it has generally been true that the more clothes someone has on, the higher his or her status. This principle can be observed in medieval and Renaissance art, where peasants wear relatively few garments, while kings and queens (including the King and Queen of Heaven) are burdened with layers of gowns and robes and mantles, even in indoor scenes. The recent fashion for "layered" clothes may be related, as is sometimes claimed, to the energy shortage; it is also a fine way of displaying a large wardrobe.

In any contemporary gathering, no matter what its occasion, the well-to-do can be observed to have on more clothes. The men are more likely to wear vests; the women are more apt to wear panty hose, superfluous scarves and useless little wraps. Even in hot weather the difference is plain. At an outdoor restaurant on a summer day the customers who have more money and have had it longer will be the ones in jackets and/or long-sleeved shirts and dresses. If it gets frightfully hot they may roll up their sleeves, but in such a way that there is no doubt about their actual length. On the beach, though the rich may splash into the waves in suits as skimpy as anyone else's, the moment they emerge they will make a dash for the conspicuous raw-silk beach kimono, terry swim dress or linen shirt that matches their bathing suit and restores the status quo.

## Conspicuous Division

It is also possible to advertise one's rank by wearing more clothes consecutively rather than simultaneously. Traditionally, the more different outfits one can display, the higher one's status; high society in the past has made this sort of display possible by the division of daily life into many different types of activity, each of which demands a special costume. As a 1924 book on etiquette puts it:

> In the world of good society, dress plays an important part in the expression of culture. There is proper dress for afternoon wear, and another for evening functions. There are certain costumes for the wedding, and others for the garden fête. The gentleman wears one suit to business, and another to dinner. Where civilization has reached its highest point, there has dress and fashion reached its finest and most exquisite development.

The contemporary man does not need to have a morning coat, a frock coat, a dress coat and a dinner jacket (and the appropriate trousers, shirts and shoes) as he did in the 1900s. Nor must the contemporary woman possess morning costumes, walking costumes, afternoon costumes, tea gowns, motoring outfits and evening dresses—all of which it would have been considered extremely improper and embarrassing to wear at the wrong time or place. Today, the conspicuous multiplication of clothing continues to thrive, but now the emphasis is on sports rather than on social life. The truly fashionable person will have separate getups for tennis, jogging, hiking (winter and summer), bicycling, swimming, skiing, golf and that anonymous and disagreeable sport known simply as "exercise." If he or she also goes in for team sports or dancing (ballet, modern, tap, folk or disco) yet more costumes must be acquired, each one unique. From a utilitarian point of view there is no reason not to play golf in jogging clothes, or ride your bike in a bathing suit on a hot day—except of course that it would cause a drastic loss of prestige.

In order to maintain (or better yet to advance) status, it is not merely necessary to have separate costumes for each sporting activity; one must also have costumes—and where relevant, equipment—of properly high prestige. Just any jogging shoes, tennis racket or leotards will not do; they must bear the currently correct brand and model names, which tend to change so fast that if I were to list them here they would be out of date by the time this book appears.

## Conspicuous Multiplication

Wearing a great many clothes at once is a burdensome and often unpleasantly hot form of Conspicuous Consumption; changing into different outfits for different activities is a nuisance. An alternative or supplementary way of demonstrating high status is to own many similar garments, so that you almost never wear exactly the same costume. The extreme case of this is the person who—like Marie Antoinette—never wears the same thing twice. Today such extravagance is rare and felt to be excessive, but the possession of a very large wardrobe is still considered charming by those who follow what Veblen called "pecuniary canons of taste." F. Scott Fitzgerald, in a famous scene, describes the effect of Jay Gatsby's extensive collection of shirts on Daisy Buchanan:

> He took out a pile of shirts and began throwing them, one by one, before us, shirts of sheer linen and thick silk and fine flannel, which lost their folds as they fell and covered the table in many-colored disarray. While we admired, he brought more and the soft rich heap mounted higher—shirts with stripes and scrolls and plaids in coral and apple-green and lavender and faint orange, with monograms of Indian blue. Suddenly, with a strained sound, Daisy bent her head into the shirts and began to cry stormily. "They're such beautiful shirts," she sobbed, her voice muffled in the thick folds. "It makes me sad because I've never seen such—such beautiful shirts before."

The particular type of Conspicuous Consumption that consists in the multiplication of similar garments is most common among women. In men it is more rare, and usually associated either with dandyism or with great and rapidly acquired wealth, as in the case of the bootlegger Gatsby. A man who gets a raise or a windfall usually buys better clothes rather than more of them, and he has no need to wear a different outfit each day. Indeed, if he were seen to vary his costume as often as his female colleagues do he would be thought vain and capricious—perhaps even unstable. Monotony of dress is only a minor fault, though a man who wore the same tie to the office every day for a week would probably be considered a dull fellow.

For a woman, on the other hand, variety in dress is essential, and the demand for it starts very early. In America many girls in secondary school or even younger feel acute embarrassment about wearing the same outfit twice in the same week—let alone on consecutive days. Even if they own relatively few garments they will go to great lengths to combine them differently and to alter the total effect with accessories. So strong is this compulsion that quantity is usually preferred to quality, and shoddy new garments to well-made old ones. In terms of the struggle for status, this may be the right decision: young girls may not be able to recognize good clothes, but they can certainly count.

This female sense of the shamefulness of repetition persists into adult life. One of the most double-edged compliments one woman can give another is "Oh, you're wearing that pretty dress *again!*" (Men, who know no better, are forgiven such remarks.) Often the compulsion continues into old age: my mother, when nearly ninety, still liked to appear in a different outfit each day "so as not to be boring." But it seems to be strongest among women in offices, for whom the fact that a colleague arrives at work on Tuesday in the same costume she was wearing on Monday is positive proof that she spent the intervening night unexpectedly at somebody else's apartment.

The constant wearing of new and different garments is most effective when those you wish to impress see you constantly—ideally, every day. It is also more effective if these people are relative strangers. If you live and work in an isolated country village, most of the people you meet will already have a pretty good idea of your rank and income, and they will not be much impressed if you keep changing your clothes. If you live in or near a city and work in a large organization, however, you will be seen often by the same peole, but most of them will know little about you. Having a large and up-to-date sartorial vocabulary then becomes a matter of the first importance, especially if you have not yet established yourself socially or professionally. For this reason, it's not surprising that the most active supporters of the fashion industry today are young women in places like London and New York.

What is surprising, though, is the lengths to which this support can go. Many young working women now seem to take it for granted that they will spend most of their income on dress. "It's awfully important to look right," a secretary in a London advertising agency explained to me. "If a girl lives at home it'll be her main expense. If she's living in town, even sharing a flat, it's much harder. I'm always in debt for clothes; when I want something I just put it on my credit card. I know things cost more that way. But, well, take these boots. They were eighty-nine pounds, but they were so beautiful, I just had to have them, and they make me feel fantastic, like a deb or a film star. All my friends are the same."

## Conspicuous Labeling

Not long ago, expensive materials could be identified on sight, and fashionable men and women recognized Savile Row tailoring or a Paris designer dress at a glance. In the twentieth century, however, synthetics began to counterfeit wool, silk, linen, leather, fur, gold and precious stones more and more successfully. At the same time, manufacturing processes became more efficient, so that a new and fashionable style could be copied in a few months and sold at a fraction of its original price. Moreover, the economic ability to consume conspicuously had been extended to millions of people who were ignorant of the subtleties of dress, who could not tell wool from Orlon or Schiaparelli from Sears Roebuck. As a result there was a world crisis in Conspicuous Consumption. For a while it seemed as if it might actually become impossible for most of us to distinguish the very rich from the moderately rich or the merely well-off by looking at what they were wearing.

This awful possibility was averted by a bold and ingenious move. It was realized that a high-status garment need not be recognizably of better quality or more difficult to produce than other garments; it need only be recognizably more expensive. What was necessary was somehow to incorporate the price of each garment into the design. This was accomplished very simply: by moving the maker's name from its former modest inward retirement to a place of outward prominence. Ordinary shoes, shirts, dresses, pants and scarves were clearly and indelibly marked with the names, monograms or insignia of their manufacturers. The names or trademarks were then exhaustively publicized—a sort of saturation bombing technique was used—so that they might become household words and serve as an instant guide to the price of the clothes they adorned. These prices were very high, not because the clothes were made of superior materials or constructed more carefully, but because advertising budgets were so immense.

When this system was first tried, certain critics scoffed, averring that nobody in their right mind would pay sixty dollars for a pair of jeans labeled Gloria Vanderbilt when a more or less identical pair labeled Montgomery Ward could be purchased for twelve. Others claimed that consumers who wanted a monogram on their shirts and bags would want it to be their own monogram and not that of some industrialist they had never met. As everyone now knows, they were wrong. Indeed, it soon became apparent that even obviously inferior merchandise, if clearly labeled and known to be extravagantly priced, would be enthusiastically purchased. There was, for instance, a great boom in the sale of very ugly brown plastic handbags, which, because they were boldly stamped with the letters "LV," were known to cost far more than similar but less ugly brown leather handbags. Cotton T-shirts that faded or shrank out of shape after a few washings but had the word Dior printed on them were preferred to better-behaved but anonymous T-shirts. Those who wore them said (or were claimed in advertisements to say) that they felt "secure." After all, even if the shirt was blotchy and tight, everyone knew it had cost a lost of money, and if it got too bad you could always buy another of the same kind. Thus Conspicuous Consumption, as it so often does, merged into Veblen's second type of sartorial status.

## Conspicuous Waste: Superfluous Drapery

Historically speaking, Conspicuous Waste has most often involved the use of obviously unnecessary material and trimmings in the construction of clothing. The classical toga portrayed in Greek and Roman sculpture, for instance, used much more fabric than was really needed to cover the body, the excess being artistically if inconveniently draped over one arm.

Anne Hollander has written most perceptively about the use of superfluous draped cloth in medieval, Renaissance and Baroque art. In preindustrial Europe, as she points out, cloth was the most important manufactured commodity, "the primary worldly good." Beautiful material was as admirable as gold or blown glass, and occupied far more space. The ownership of elaborate and expensive clothing was an important proof of social dominance. A single aristocrat sitting for his portrait, however, could only wear one luxurious outfit at a time. The display of many yards of velvet or satin behind him would suggest that he owned more such stuff and was able, in modern terms, to fling it around. Even after immensely full and trailing garments ceased to be worn, at least by men, excess drapery survived in art: it is notable for example in the paintings of Hals and Van Dyck and the sculptures of Bernini. The Frick Collection portrait of the Earl of Derby and his family "shows the family out of doors, standing on bare earth with shrubbery in the foreground and trees behind. But on the right side of the painting, behind the earl, next to a column that might conceivably be part of a house, fifty yards of dark red stuff cascade to the ground from nowhere. So skillfully does Van Dyck fling down these folds that their ludicrous inconsequence is unnoticeable . . ."

Traditionally, as Ms. Hollander remarks, superfluous drapery has been a sign not only of wealth and high rank but of moral worth: angels, saints, martyrs and Biblical characters in medieval and Renaissance art often wear yards and yards of extra silk and velvet. Drapery derived additional prestige from its association with classical art, and thus with nobility, dignity and the ideal. Marble columns and togalike folds (occasionally, actual togas) were felt to transform the political hack into a national statesman and the grabby businessman into a Captain of Industry. As Ms. Hollander notes, Westminster Abbey and the Capitol in Washington, D.C., are full of such attempted metamorphoses, frozen into soapy marble.

Excess drapery survives today in middlebrow portrait painting, causing over-the-hill industrialists, mayors and society women to appear against stage backgrounds of draped velvet or brocade, the moral and economic prestige of which is somehow felt to transfer itself to them. Successful academics, I have noticed, are often painted in this manner: posed before velvet curtains, with their gowns and hoods and mortarboards treated in a way that recalls the idealized drapery and stiffened halos of Renaissance saints. (Appropriately, the halos of professors and college presidents are square rather than round.)

The use of superfluous fabric in costume never died out completely. During most of the period between 1600 and 1900, for instance, respectable middle-class and upper-class women wore a minimum of three petticoats; fewer than this was thought pathetic, and indicated negligence or poverty. Skirts were inflated with hoops or bustles to provide a framework on which to display great quantities of cloth, while overskirts, panniers, flounces and trains demanded additional superfluous fabric. A fashionable dress might easily require twenty or thirty yards of material. Elaborate trimmings of bows, ribbons, lace, braid and artificial flowers permitted yet more prestigious waste of goods. Men's clothing during the same period used relatively little excess fabric except in outerwear, where long, full coats and heavy capes employed yards of unnecessary cloth, adding greatly to their cost and the apparent bulk of their wearers.

A glance through any current fashion magazine will show that the use of superfluous fabric today, though on a much more modest scale, is by no means outmoded. Expensive clothes are often cut more generously, and fashion photography tends to make the most of whatever extra material the designer provides, spreading it over prop sofas or blowing it about in the air. Even the most miserly excess of cloth may now be touted as a sign of prestige: a recent advertisement in *The New York Times* boasts of an extra inch in the back yoke of Hathaway shirts which, the manufacturer sobs, costs them $52,000 a year.

Wastage of material in the form of trimming, though less striking than it was in the past, still persists. Today, however, it is often thinly distinguished as practical. A prestigious shirt, for instance, has a breast pocket into which nothing must ever be put; the habit of filling it with pens and pencils is a lower-middle-class indicator, and also suggests a fussy personality. A related ploy, es-

pecially popular between the two World Wars, was the custom of embroidering everything with the owner's initials. This may in some cases have had a practical function, as in the separation of laundry, but—and more importantly—it also added conspicuously to the cost of the garment.

## Superfluous Personalities

Changing styles, of course, are another and very effective form of Conspicuous Waste. Although I do not believe that fashions alter at the whim of designers and manufacturers—otherwise they would do so far more often— it is certainly true that when social and cultural changes prompt a shift in the way we look the fashion industry is quick to take advantage of it, and to hint in advertising copy that last year's dress will do our reputation no good. When new styles do not catch on other ploys are tried. A recent one is to announce with disingenuous enthusiasm that fashion is dead; that instead of the tyranny of "this year's look" we now have a range of "individual" looks—which are given such names as Classic, Feminine, Sporty, Sophisticate and Ingénue. The task of the well-dressed liberated woman, the ads suggest, is to choose the look—or, much better and more liberated, *looks*—that suit her "life style." She is encouraged, for instance, to be sleek and refined on the job, glowingly energetic on holiday, sweetly domestic at home with her children and irresistibly sexy in the presence of what one department at my university has taken to calling her "spouse-equivalent." Thus, most ingeniously, life itself has been turned into a series of fashionable games, each of which, like jogging or scuba-diving or tennis, demands a different costume—or, in this case, a different set of costumes (winter/summer, day/night, formal/informal). The more different looks a woman can assume, the more fascinating she is supposed to be: personality itself has become an adjunct of Conspicuous Waste.

Men traditionally are not supposed to have more than one personality, one real self. Lately, however, they have been encouraged by self-styled "wardrobe engineers" to diversify their outward appearance for practical reasons. According to these experts, the successful businessman needs different sets of clothes in order to "inspire confidence in" (or deceive) other businessmen who inhabit different regions of the United States. This idea is not new, nor has it been limited to the mercantile professions. A former journalist has reported that as a young man he consciously varied his costume to suit his assignment. When sent to interview rich and powerful Easterners, he wore clothes to suggest that he was one of them: a dark-grey flannel Savile Row suit, a shirt from André Oliver or Turnbull & Asser, a Cartier watch of a sort never available at Bloomingdale's and John Lobb shoes. "What you have to convey to rich people any-where," he explained, "is that you don't have to try; so what you're wearing shouldn't ever be brand-new." New clothes, on the other hand, were appropriate when in-terviewing the *nouveau riche;* and since they might not recognize understated wealth, he (somewhat reluctantly, but a job is a job) would also put on a monogrammed shirt and Italian shoes with tassels.

When assigned to official Washington, this particular journalist took care to be three or four years behind cur-rent New York modes. "Washington hates fashion, es-pecially New York fashion. The message should be, I am not attempting style; I am a man of the people, a regular fellow." He would therefore wear a somewhat rumpled pin-striped suit, a white shirt and a nondescript tie. Be-fore leaving Manhattan he would get his hair cut shorter than usual. On the other hand, if he were sent to Cali-fornia, or were interviewing a writer, artist or musician anywhere in the country, he would try to let his hair grow or rumple it up a bit. He would wear slacks and a good tweed jacket over a turtleneck shirt; if the interviewee were financially successful he would add an expensive watch or pair of shoes to this costume. Still other getups were appropriate—and available—for the Midwest, Texas, the South, Continental Europe and Britain.

When this system works it is no longer Waste; nor, since the clothes are deliberately chosen to blend into their surroundings, can they be called Conspicuous. But as the journalist himself remarked, clothes alone cannot disguise anyone, and the traveling salesman or sales-woman who engineers his or her wardrobe but not his or her voice, vocabulary or manners may simply be prac-ticing Conspicuous Waste without its usual reward of enhanced status—let alone a rise in sales figures.

## Conspicuous Leisure: Discomfort and Helplessness

Once upon a time leisure was far more conspicuous than it usually is today. The history of European costume is rich in styles in which it was literally impossible to per-form any useful activity: sleeves that trailed on the floor, curled and powdered wigs the size, color and texture of a large white poodle, skirts six feet in diameter or with six-foot dragging trains, clanking ceremonial swords, starched wimples and ruffs and cravats that prevented their wearers from turning their heads or looking at any-

thing below waist level, high-heeled pointed shoes that made walking agony and corsets so tight that it was im-possible to bend at the waist or take a normal breath. Such clothes proclaimed, indeed demanded, an unpro-ductive life and the constant assistance of servants.

These conspicuously uncomfortable and leisurely styles reached an extreme in the late eighteenth century at the court of Versailles. The political and sartorial rev-olution that followed freed both sexes temporarily, and men permanently, from the need to advertise their aris-tocratic helplessness. Men's clothes became, and have remained ever since, at least moderately comfortable. Women's fashions on the other hand, after barely ten years of ease and simplicity, rapidly became burdensome again and continued so for the next hundred years.

Urban middle-class clothing today, though it does not usually cause pain, makes anything more than lim-ited activity awkward. It is hard to run or climb in busi-ness suit and slick-soled shoes; and the easily soiled white or pale-colored shirt that signifies freedom from manual labor is in constant danger of embarrassing its wearer with grimy cuffs or ring-around-the-collar. Ur-ban women's dress is equally inconvenient. It should be pointed out, however, that inconvenience may be an ad-vantage in some situations. A friend who often does his-torical research in libraries tells me that she always gets dressed up for it. If she is obviously handicapped by high heels, a pale, elegant suit and ruffled white blouse, the librarians will search the stacks for the heavy volumes of documents and old newspapers she needs and carry them to her, dusting them on the way. If she wears a sweater, casual slacks and sensible shoes, they will let her do it herself. The same ploy would probably work for a man if he were middle-aged or older.

---

## QUESTIONS

1. What are some of the ways in which people in-dicate their status through the use of fashions?

2. What is meant by conspicuous consumption? How important a part do you think it plays in American so-ciety?

3. To what extent are your own material ambitions influenced by a desire to signal your status and achieve-ments to others?

Daniel Yankelovich

# 23. Who Gets Ahead in America?

*One of the most cherished of all American beliefs is that everyone has the same chance to "make it" up the economic and social ladder—or, to put it in more sociological terms, that there is equality of opportunity for social mobility. The successful maintenance of the class system requires, of course, that such a belief be widespread. So long as the poor believe they have as good a chance as the next person to become rich, and that they have only themselves to blame if they do not, they will tend to accept the system.*

*But actually the poor, like most Americans, are deceived by the myth. Decades of sociological research have produced overwhelming evidence that many of the factors that influence social mobility are beyond personal control. In general, the offspring of the advantaged accrue more advantages, and the offspring of the disadvantaged remain relatively disadvantaged; but the picture is complicated by a variety of other factors, such as sex, race, and education.*

*Exactly who, then, is likely to achieve social mobility? Christopher Jencks surveyed the sociological literature to find the answer to this question for his book* Who Gets Ahead? *(1979). In this article, Daniel Yankelovich summarizes some of Jencks's main findings.*

Seven years ago, Christopher Jencks unsettled many believers in traditional American values with his book, *Inequality: A Reassessment of the Effect of Family and Schooling in America.* What Jencks and several colleagues found, by examining the body of research material then available, was that neither family background nor education could account for all the variations in income and status among Americans. Economic success, he concluded, was explained not as much by birth, or striving, or "competence" as by a number of other unmeasured variables, which he described collectively as "luck."

Even though it discounted the importance of family advantage, Jencks's analysis upset liberals by downplaying the value of education and special compensatory programs—which educational reformers and antipoverty warriors believed would eventually narrow the income gap between the rich and the poor. As Jencks saw it, the only real way to achieve economic equality in America was some form of income redistribution that would remove inequities through the tax system or through government subsidies.

Now, Jencks and 11 colleagues at the Harvard Center for Educational Policy Research have published a new report that analyzes a broader range of studies covering a number of new variables. In *Who Gets Ahead?—The Determinants of Economic Success in America,* Jencks abandons the conclusion that "luck" is the most critical factor in economic success. He and his colleagues report a host of other findings that appear, on the surface, to be less controversial, but may turn out to be more so.

The investigators examined the five large-scale national surveys of men, covering a 12-year span, along with six special-purpose surveys, four of which had never been previously analyzed. They worked during a five-year period, with research costs estimated at $400,000 (most of it from the U.S. Department of Health, Education, and Welfare and from private foundations).

The portrait drawn by Jencks and his colleagues is of a classridden America in which being born into the "right" family looms large. It is a rigid America, in which a man's academic test scores in the sixth grade shape his own expectations and those of others toward him. The men who were studied (none of the 11 surveys included women, a serious drawback) seem to be divided at an early stage of their lives into two fixed groups: those with promise and those without. Those with promise finish college, the gateway to success.

*Who Gets Ahead?* also depicts a superficial America, in which surface characteristics, such as college credentials or the color of a man's skin, count so heavily that what he is really worth as a person, his moral character, what he knows, what he can do, how hard he tries, hardly seem to count at all. Finally, although Jencks's group would acknowledge it was concerned with just one important set of values—economic success—their report furthers the impression of a unidimensional America, in which only making money and achieving occupational success seem to count in life. I recognize Jencks's America as one might recognize a friend whose features suddenly appear abstract, contorted, remote. I know the image from my own surveys—yet something is amiss.

Jencks's report contains many important findings, but we cannot draw valid prescriptions for action from them unless we see the work in a broader social context. For several powerful reasons, we must exercise extreme caution in accepting its messages at face value.

Probably to avoid the controversy stimulated by *Inequality,* Jencks's team has gone out of its way to avoid discussing the policy implications of its findings. The conclusions are largely descriptive, leaving the task of drawing inferences to the reader.

. . .

## What Really Counts? Possible Interpretations

Inevitably, academic readers, for whom the book is primarily intended, will draw one kind of inference, policy analysts another, and journalists still another. The public itself will draw no direct inferences at all, because not many people will be able to read the book. But the determined journalist, on whom the public ultimately depends, might reasonably uncover the following logical but misleading messages in *Who Gets Ahead?*:

• If you are black and have been persuaded to stay in high school because "finishing high school will help you find a better job later on," forget what you've been told. Even for whites, the economic advantages of finishing high school without going on to college are marginal at best; for blacks, they count for almost nothing.

• If you are black and in college and suspect that finishing college is not going to help you economically, you are wrong. Buckle down, hang in, and finish—at all costs. If it's money and a good job you are after, stay in college and graduate, no matter

how you do it. Take gut courses, if necessary. Go to some second- or third-rate college, if you must. Economically, it doesn't matter what you study, how much you learn, or where you go to college—as long as you finish.

• If you are white, the same holds true. It is the degree that really counts; that credential is worth more than almost anything else—including what you may have learned.

• Be careful to be born into the "right" family. The right family is one in which your father occupies a high-status position in a field like law, medicine, or business. He earns an excellent income. He and your mother received good educations, have used birth control so you are part of a small family, and have had the foresight to be white. If you come from a family like that, measured by income and status, is one of the top one-fifth in the country, your earnings are likely to be 150 to 186 percent of the national average. If you come from a family in the bottom one-fifth, your earnings are likely to be only 56 to 67 percent of the national average. Your occupational status will be affected by "family foresight" even more sharply than your income will be.

• If you have not exercised much foresight, do not despair—as long as you had good test scores in the sixth grade. If your academic test scores are high (about 15 points or more above average), you may still get ahead—poor family background notwithstanding. That is because you are likely to be encouraged to go to college. There is, however, some cash value to being academically "test smart." Among those who have the same family background and the same level of educational attainment, the ones that test well earn about 11 to 14 percent more than their less intelligent cohorts. But, lest you rejoice prematurely, it should be pointed out that 11 to 14 percent is not very much, once you realize that the difference between the lowest-paying and the highest-paying jobs in America lies on a 600-percent spectrum!

• If you have not done well on academic tests in the sixth grade, perhaps you should think of giving up. Your test grades are not likely to improve, because people are not going to encourage you much after that point, and you are not likely to motivate yourself to do better. You will probably not go to college.

• If you have high academic test scores but decide to forgo college, the chances are that your superior intelligence will not do you much good economically, unless it enables you to capitalize on unexpected opportunities.

• If you have leadership ability—and clearly exhibit it from the sixth to 10th grades—this gift of personality is worth as much to you as your cognitive skills are (especially if you finish college).

• If you are sociable in high school and date heavily, you are likely to end up in a lower-status position than some of your less sociable friends who are more attentive to their studies. But there is one consolation: apparently your sociability will gain you extra earnings, within the limits of your lower occupational status.

• If you come from the right kind of family, and are academically gifted, you may develop highly cultural interests. If so, you are likely to wind up with lots of education, but your refined tastes will be of little extra economic value to you.

• If you are Jewish, WASP, or German Catholic, you have a small economic edge over other ethnic groups; if you are Italian, French Catholic, or Irish Protestant, you are at a small but not decisive disadvantage. If you were born in the South and choose to stay there, you are likely to earn less money than if you chose to leave the South. (The same holds true for being born on a farm and choosing to stay there.)

• If you are determined not to succeed economically, you must be careful to do all the following: fail to finish college; choose the wrong family background; express low aspirations about your future; undervalue your leadership abilities and under no circumstances display them for others to see. If you follow that prescription, you will not make out very well—statistically— even if you are smarter than the other boys and perform well on academic tests.

All these generalizations could be extracted from the patchwork of 11 surveys analyzed by Jencks and his colleagues that covered men from the ages of 25 to 64 in a period from the early 1960s to the early 1970s. To bring this massive study into sharper focus, it is necessary to take a closer look at the sources of the information and the analysis to which the data was subjected.

Among the national studies were a survey of "productive Americans" conducted by the University of Michigan's Survey Research Center in 1965, and the U.S. Current Population Survey of 1962. The special-purpose surveys included a study of veterans under the age of 35 done in 1964, and another of brothers who were given questionnaires twice, once in 1960, when they were in the 11th and 12th grades, and again [in 1971–1972.]

The two measures of success the researchers used were earned income, determined in several ways, and occupational status, as reflected on the Duncan scale, a well-established measure that ranks occupations according to the number of years of education they require and how much people in them earn.

The Jencks team tried to determine the degree to which four sets of factors studied in the surveys were associated with success. They were: family background; cognitive ability, as reflected in scores on academic tests in primary and secondary school; personality traits and behavior in high school, as described by the subjects themselves and their teachers; and number of years of school completed.

Through statistical analysis, an effort was made to isolate how much of the variation in men's later economic success was attributable to each of those variables when considered independently of the others. Since the four sets of factors interact with one another in complex fashion, pulling them apart to assess the contribution of each was not easy. It involved some deft statistical footwork, especially since complete data for all four sets of factors were not available for any of the respondents.

The breakdown shows that some factors contributed more to occupational status than to earnings. If all other factors were ignored, for example, the years of schooling men completed would have accounted for 45 to 55 percent of the variations in occupational status, but only 15 to 20 percent of variations in earnings. Family background was reckoned to account for 45 to 50 percent of the variation in occupational status, but apparently for only about 15 to 35 percent of variations in men's incomes.

Of the 13 demographic specifics that came under the heading of "family background," not all have equal weight. One of the 13, "father's occupation" by itself accounts for about one-third of the influence attributed to family background; another third is accounted for by a cluster of variables that included father's and mother's education, parental income, family size, and race.

Another group of variables appears to have a weight equal to each of the others. That is the group of "unmeasured variables," which were part of what Jencks in his first study referred to as "luck," and which deserve special attention.

How could the researchers attribute so much weight to variables their sources of data had failed to identify? One ingenious feature of the research design permitted them to do so: an analysis of the occupational parallels between large numbers of pairs of brothers. Suppose, for example, we select a sample of doctors. On the Duncan scale, doctors would stand well above the national average for all occupations. If one looks at the occupational status of their brothers, one finds that *their* occupations are also well above the national average. The similarity between the brothers can be accounted for partly by the occupational status of the father, and partly by various demographic factors, race and size of family, for example. That leaves roughly one-third of the resemblance unexplained. The authors conclude: "The remaining third is presumably due to unmeasured social, psychological, or genetic factors, that vary within demograpic groups."

One difficulty in discerning relative influences on economic success stems from the fact that everything seems to be related to everything else. If you come from the right family background, you are more likely to finish college, to have high academic test scores, and to have the personality traits associated with economic success. But the correlations are far from perfect. In fact, 52 percent of the variations in occupational status come from factors other than family background.

The most important of those is educational attainment: the number of years of schooling completed. One of the most interesting findings shows how important the last year of college is, relative to other years. What counts is *finishing* college and getting credentials, rather than what one might learn in the last year, or any year. Besides family background, the single most important factor contributing to a man's economic success is finishing college. Of course, academic promise, motivation, and other personality characteristics may help a man graduate. But if you don't translate promising academic ability into college credentials, you gain precious little economic advantage.

For men coming from the same types of homes and having similar test scores, the earnings advantage of completing only high school is not great, especially for non-whites. Completing college, on the other hand, brings considerable economic advantage. Completing high school gives whites a 15 to 25 percent future earnings advantage over those not completing high school (the figure is smaller for blacks). But completing college gives whites a whopping 49 percent advantage over those who do not—the percentage is even larger for blacks. This income advantage derives primarily from the fact that those who finish college have won the credential needed for entering higher-status occupations. "Unless high school attendance is followed by a college education," the researchers conclude, "its economic value appears quite modest"—especially for blacks.

The results of academic tests in the sixth grade can predict future success, as can scores on tests taken in later years. The ability to predict from early performance is attributed to the presence of stable motivational attitudes in the person being tested. The researchers point out that this pattern has remained fairly constant since the turn of the century. They underscore the point, frequently made, that those with academic ability succeed because they are selectively encouraged to have higher aspirations and to attend school for longer periods. The researchers emphasize that the mere ability to remain in school is more important than the results of academic test scores. "A man's ability in the sixth to 11th grade has important effects on his later occupational status," they say, "but 60 to 80 percent of the effect is explained by *the amount of schooling he gets*" (italics added).

The contribution of personality characteristics to success is more elusive. Indeed, the chapter on personality in *Who Gets Ahead?* is meager, reflecting the paucity of survey data on such characteristics. The material covered by Jencks and his team included only self-descriptions of personality traits by 10th-graders, followed up by a mail questionnaire that large numbers of respondents failed to return; 10th grade teachers' observations of "executive ability" and other characteristics in their pupils, and descriptions by the students themselves, in self-administered questionnaires, of their goals, aspirations, study habits, and participation as leaders in various activities.

The authors admit, "All our conclusions about . . . noncognitive traits have been general and tentative." Among their tentative findings is that "leadership, assessed both by the individual himself or his teacher, or expressed through behavior, has an appreciable positive effect on earnings." However, such personality attributes as being "vigorous, calm, and tidy" produce no economic advantage. Men who rated themselves high in sociability (including such activity as frequent dating) were destined to end up in lower-status jobs than those who claimed to have good study habits.

The data on racial factors in success are more clearcut. Given the same test scores and years of schooling, blacks have fewer opportunities to get ahead than whites do. The researchers state: "A strong prima facie case can be made for assuming . . . that despite affirmative action, nonwhites suffer from discrimination." Discrimination appears to operate less for those who graduate from college than for those who attain lower levels of education, the investigators conclude.

. . .

## Some Crucial Reservations

If we are not to be misled by literal interpretations of the analysis—such as those I sketched earlier—we must keep in mind the limited scope of the data. Jencks's report excludes women. Several of the studies it examines focus solely on a man's characteristics when he *first* enters the labor market and how those match up with both initial and subsequent earnings; none takes into account changes in skill, competence, and emotional growth after he is launched on his career, and how those factors affect earnings. (I have no quarrel with the conclusion that traits measured in the sixth and 10th grades may have an important bearing on eventual occupational success or failure. I have more difficulty in believing that changes occurring in those factors during a man's career have *no* bearing on subsequent earnings and status.) And, perhaps most seriously of all, there is virtually no data later than 1973. Jencks and his associates are forthcoming in acknowledging the limitations in the scope of their study, but they do not tell us how to adjust for them.

The time gap is particularly serious. If the six-to-17-year lag between the data and the analysis had occurred in any earlier period, it would pose a difficulty, but not a grave one. However, the period from 1973 to the present has brought changes in the country's economic position and in the public's outlook that substantially affect the interpretation of prior research findings on issues of economic success.

Not only was the nation shaken by the Arab oil embargo in 1973, but since that time we have become familiar with the phenomenon of stagflation—high inflation combined with high unemployment. In the past, our political stability has depended heavily on economic growth, high rates of productivity, and material abundance. In the years since 1973, overall economic growth has slowed down and the rate of increase in productivity has been cut in half. At the same time, women have flooded the work force, filling jobs that policymakers had assumed would go to blacks, and once again widening the gap between white and nonwhite incomes—after a trend toward closing the gap in earlier years. In the period since 1973, we have entered an age of shrinking expectations: we have begun to realize that we must accustom ourselves to limits, shortages, and inflation as disagreeable facts of life. Those changes are of such a magnitude that, while they do not invalidate Jencks's findings, they oblige us to interpret them in a different light.

I worry, too, about the "unmeasured variables" in the study, because I interpret this category more broadly than the Harvard team does. Jencks and his associates assume that most of the unmeasured variables are clustered under the heading of family background. But some of them must surely enter in disguised form in the category they call noncognitive factors. They have gone further in identifying and acknowledging such factors in their models than have many previous researchers. While conceding that that part of their analysis is thin, they are pleased that their study attributes greater importance to individual personality characteristics than previous research does. Nevertheless, the measures of noncognitive factors they are forced to use are quite narrow and insubstantial. Indeed, most of the noncognitive factors discovered to be important by social scientists in the past 150 years have been excluded from consideration.

The researchers have no really sensitive measures of cultural influence beyond those subsumed under family background. Parents, friends, teachers, ministers, and others in the larger culture convey to children the norms, rules, meanings, and behaviors that are critical to their eventual success or failure. But few questions are raised about possible differences in the values, authority, and impact of those adult figures that may contribute to success or failure.

The Harvard researchers take up the question of genetic influences on success, but push it aside like a hot potato; they say the existing data cannot measure the impact of heredity adequately. In addition, there are almost no measures in the study of how attitudes and values may correlate with income and status. Apart from some assessments by young boys of their own qualities, the all-important category of ego strength and characteristics associated with it that seem important to success, such as self-esteem and assertiveness, are absent. Finally, and most important of all, there is virtually no discussion of "character" or "judgment," which blend cognitive and noncognitive skills.

Even if Jencks's model had taken into account all the important variables, I would still have trouble accepting the rather deterministic picture it draws of mobility in America. In the history of humankind, needless suffering has often been rationalized as "fate." Slaves, on occasion, were taught that their condition was dictated by divine providence, which was not to be questioned. For centuries, poverty was assumed to be the inevitable lot of the majority. In the 19th and early 20th centuries, the Social Darwinists saw fate in the evolutionary principle of "survival of the fittest," which enabled the successful to assert their inherent superiority. And Freud saw anatomy as destiny.

The newest and most devious version of this ancient form of tyranny is that of statistical norms. Mere averages are reified into the national norms against which many individuals measure themselves. Properly understood, these averages constitute useful bits of information, but their meaning for any individual calls for exquisite qualification.

It would be tragic, for example, if Jencks's findings were interpreted to mean that blacks should drop out of high school, that people with low scores in the sixth grade should give up trying, that people who don't finish college should assume they cannot achieve the kind of success they seek, that lack of leadership ability in school closes the door to future economic success, and that credentials count more heavily than skill, character, knowledge, or judgment.

It would be tragic and yet, almost inevitably, that is what will happen. Few people will give research studies such as this the kind of attention required to understand the true meaning of the findings. Decades of research and five years of analysis will be mined for the few obvious "messages" that lie closest to the surface.

Another caveat: In the light of some of my recent research, the Harvard group's preoccupation with economic success rings a faintly old-fashioned and archaic note. American values have been changing in far-reaching ways over the past decade. To be sure, economic success and mobility continue to play an important role in our lives. People still want money; they still want to be successful. But, in complex and subtle ways, many Americans also want to give less of themselves to what they've come to regard as a nose-to-the-grindstone way of life. Jencks's analysis presupposes a homogeneity in American values centering on the idea of getting ahead. It fails to take even passing note of the pluralism in values that has developed in recent years.

For millions of Americans, new questions are appearing. Instead of just asking, "Will I be able to make a good living?" "Will I be successful?" "Will I raise happy, healthy, successful children?"—the typical questions of the 1950s and 1960s—Americans today are pondering more introspective matters. "How can I find self-fulfillment?" they are now asking. "What kinds of commitments should I be making?" "What is worth sacrificing for?" "How can I grow?"

Fifty-eight percent of the respondents in one of our recent studies indicated that they no longer believe it is the responsibility of a man with a family to take the job that pays the most, rather than one that may be more satisfying but pays less. Although predictably larger proportions of high- and middle-income Americans who can afford that sentiment subscribe to it, fully half of those in the sample with family incomes under $10,000 agreed that self-fulfillment is an important part of the definition of success—suggesting that the shift in values is not confined to the upper and middle classes.

## Science, Intuition, and Policy

Jencks and his colleagues have taken long strides in developing techniques to study the enigma of economic success in America. But even after this excellent and thorough study, we must assume that the present state of the investigative art does not yet tell us why some people achieve success while others do not. We may know more now than we did before, but not enough to allow us to build public policy on the results with any confidence.

Eventually, effective bridges may be built between scientific study and public policy. But they have not yet been built, and, in the end, studies such as this one will always be haunted by philosophical questions that have not yet been resolved: Can we ever understand complex human behavior by preselecting all the relevant variables and measures (thereby excluding other, perhaps more elusive, influences)? Will this approach ever bring us deeper knowledge of human behavior than more direct, insightful approaches? In its present form, social science forces us to choose between, on the one hand, *a priori* statistical models of human behavior and, on the other, understanding based on intuition, experience, insight, judgment, and observation—all of which pose serious difficulties of their own. Until the two paths of study are integrated and understood, as many uneasy questions must be raised about computer-based models as about intuitive judgment. Calling one "science" and the other "intuition" does not prove the superiority or inadequacy of either method.

The effort put forth in *Who Gets Ahead?* is a little like that of someone who has put on blinders to show what a wonderful job he can do finding his way with a cane. The virtuoso performance is impressive, but the practical person cannot resist asking, "Why not open your eyes and look?" When the next large-scale study of success in America is done, I hope it will rely on fewer equations and contain more sensitive interpretation of factors that may affect success but do not lend themselves to statistical analysis.

Even with all its drawbacks, the Jencks report, properly understood, can be of considerable value. One of the most provocative suggestions in the book, for instance, is that the nature of racial prejudice in America may be changing in significant ways. I believe that it is. In earlier years, racial discrimination was due more to the kinds of gross disenfranchisement that could be combated by legal action and legislative mandate. More recently, it seems to be based mainly on stereotype and "image" factors, some of which operate subliminally.

These stereotypes serve, in much the same way as the presence or absence of academic credentials do, to close the door to minority groups, whose cultural styles and mannerisms are different from those of the white majority. They are quick, mindless methods of communicating information about people, much of which may not be germane to questions of competence or employability.

Many blacks mistrust survey findings that show a lessening of prejudice, believing they are meaningless when evidence shows that the economic situation of blacks has, in fact, grown worse in recent years. This is a complex and distressing situation, and I believe Jencks's findings suggest a number of constructive approaches to the problem.

The psychological aspects of the problem, though intangible, may be even more important for individual blacks. To blacks, there may be little difference between being blocked from advancement by a "real prejudice" and being blocked by a "negative stereotype." Such fine distinctions may seem like hair-splitting—evidence of obtuseness or bad faith. Perhaps the fault lies in our language.

Deeply rooted racial prejudice is difficult to extirpate. To do so requires all the authority, even the coerciveness, of the law. But the kind of stereotypes that appear to exist today may be easier to get around. For example, the Jencks findings show that where a negative black stereotype is upheld (the black-as-high-school-dropout, for instance), blacks fare worse economically than comparable white high school dropouts. But when the black stereotype is broken (the black-as-college-graduate), blacks do *better* than white counterparts when other variables are controlled. The black who finishes college makes two significant breakthroughs: he measurably improves his occupational and employment position, and he breaks the stereotype for himself and for others. If social and economic stereotypes can be broken by education, then they are not totally racial (based on skin color alone), but at least partly a matter of social-class prejudice and mental laziness.

Equal rights leaders, it seems to me, must unceasingly monitor the sources of negative stereotypes in the media. They should be especially careful to avoid the inadvertent effects of some of their own strategies. By stressing the accumulated failures of vocational and educational programs targeted for blacks, they may reinforce negative stereotypes. Television producer Norman Lear's recent withdrawal of a new series that reinforced such existing stereotypes about blacks was an act of statesmanship for which the country should be grateful. Techniques exist in abundance for conveying, both in the media and educational institutions, stereotype-breaking aspects of black experience, black competence, and black success that whites may not encounter in their daily experience.

Also, public policy should probably focus sharply on developing cognitive skills normally associated with high school training through actual work experience. When people who do not intend to go to college realize that a high school degree has lost much of its economic value, some will be reluctant to go through with what they may view as an empty ritual. Under present conditions, they have little choice. But federal (CETA) monies and other programs have just begun to lay the groundwork for job training that combines high school level skills with actual experience in the workplace. Those programs can be upgraded and improved if we give the matter real thought.

If *Who Gets Ahead?* provides clues on how to undermine the social damage done by racism, prejudice, and excessive credentialism, then that alone makes it a major contribution to American society. But if implications for educational, governmental, and familial behavior are plucked prematurely and indelicately from the study's regression equations, the good work done by Jencks and his colleagues will become part of the problem rather than part of the solution.

## QUESTIONS

1. Will those who work hard in the United States get ahead? Is there equal opportunity in this country?

2. What social, rather than individual, factors can affect a person's social mobility?

3. To what extent are the poor responsible for their poverty?

*Herbert J. Gans*

# 24. The Uses of Poverty: The Poor Pay All

*The United States is, by many measures, the richest society on earth. It could well afford to eliminate poverty by providing an income "floor" for the poorest members of society, at a cost that would be almost negligible in the context of total governmental expenditures. Moreover, Americans are agreed that poverty is undesirable, that it breeds ignorance, ill health, crime, and many other forms of human misery. Why, then, does poverty persist?*

*Perhaps a little tongue-in-cheek, Herbert Gans suggests that poverty remains an enduring feature of the society because it is functional: in other words, it is a feature of society—like religion, the family, the courts, the schools, and so on—that helps to maintain the stability of the entire social system. In his provocative article, Gans maintains that poverty is so useful to the society, or at least to that part of society that benefits from it, that its persistence is hardly surprising.*

*The underlying message of Gans's argument is that an act of political will would be required to redistribute wealth and income from the rich to the poor. And since the rich, not the poor, have political power, poverty will remain a feature of the society, with only token efforts made to redress its effects. If the privileged benefit from the plight of the underprivileged, change is unlikely unless the power relationship between the two groups changes also.*

Reprinted from *Social Policy*, July–August 1971, pp. 20–24, published by Social Policy Corporation, New York, New York 10010. Copyright 1971 by Social Policy Corporation.

Some twenty years ago Robert K. Merton applied the notion of functional analysis to explain the continuing though maligned existence of the urban political machine: if it continued to exist, perhaps it fulfilled latent—unintended or unrecognized—positive functions. Clearly it did. Merton pointed out how the political machine provided central authority to get things done when a decentralized local government could not act, humanized the services of the impersonal bureaucracy for fearful citizens, offered concrete help (rather than abstract law or justice) to the poor, and otherwise performed services needed or demanded by many people but considered unconventional or even illegal by formal public agencies.

Today, poverty is more maligned than the political machine ever was; yet it, too, is a persistent social phenomenon. Consequently, there may be some merit in applying functional analysis to poverty, in asking whether it also has positive functions that explain its persistence.

Merton defined functions as "those observed consequences [of a phenomenon] which make for the adaptation or adjustment of a given [social] system." I shall use a slightly different definition; instead of identifying functions for an entire social system, I shall identify them for the interest groups, socioeconomic classes, and other population aggregates with shared values that "inhabit" a social system. I suspect that in a modern heterogeneous society, few phenomena are functional or dysfunctional for the society as a whole, and that most result in benefits to some groups and costs to others. Nor are any phenomena indispensable; in most instances, one can suggest what Merton calls "functional alternatives" or equivalents for them, i.e., other social patterns or policies that achieve the same positive functions but avoid the dysfunctions.

Associating poverty with positive functions seems at first glance to be unimaginable. Of course, the slumlord and the loan shark are commonly known to profit from the existence of poverty, but they are viewed as evil men, so their activities are classified among the dysfunctions of poverty. However, what is less often recognized, at least by the conventional wisdom, is that poverty also makes possible the existence or expansion of respectable professions and occupations, for example, penology, criminology, social work, and public health. More recently, the poor have provided jobs for professional and para-professional "poverty warriors," and for journalists and social scientists, this author included, who have supplied the information demanded by the revival of public interest in poverty.

Clearly, then, poverty and the poor may well satisfy a number of positive functions for many nonpoor groups in American society. I shall describe thirteen such functions—economic, social, and political—that seem to me most significant.

## The Functions of Poverty

*First,* the existence of poverty ensures that society's "dirty work" will be done. Every society has such work: physically dirty or dangerous, temporary, dead-end and underpaid, undignified and menial jobs. Society can fill these jobs by paying higher wages than for "clean" work, or it can force people who have no other choice to do the dirty work—and at low wages. In America, poverty functions to provide a low-wage labor pool that is willing—or, rather, unable to be *un*willing—to perform dirty work at low cost. Indeed, this function of the poor is so important that in some Southern states, welfare payments have been cut off during the summer months when the poor are needed to work in the fields. Moreover, much of the debate about the Negative Income Tax and the Family Assistance Plan has concerned their impact on the work incentive, by which is actually meant the incentive of the poor to do the needed dirty work if the wages therefrom are no larger than the income grant. Many economic activities that involve dirty work depend on the poor for their existence: restaurants, hospitals, parts of the garment industry, and "truck farming," among others, could not persist in their present form without the poor.

*Second,* because the poor are required to work at low wages, they subsidize a variety of economic activities that benefit the affluent. For example, domestics subsidize the upper middle and upper classes, making life easier for their employers and freeing affluent women for a variety of professional, cultural, civic, and partying activities. Similarly, because the poor pay a higher proportion of their income in property and sales taxes, among others, they subsidize many state and local governmental services that benefit more affluent groups. In addition, the poor support innovation in medical practice as patients in teaching and research hospitals and as guinea pigs in medical experiments.

*Third,* poverty creates jobs for a number of occupations and professions that serve or "service" the poor, or protect the rest of society from them. As already noted, penology would be minuscule without the poor, as would the police. Other activities and groups that flourish because of the existence of poverty are the numbers game, the sale of heroin and cheap wines and liquors, pentecostal ministers, faith healers, prostitutes, pawn shops, and the peacetime army, which recruits its enlisted men mainly from among the poor.

*Fourth,* the poor buy goods others do not want and thus prolong the economic usefulness of such goods—day-old bread, fruit and vegetables that would otherwise have to be thrown out, second-hand clothes, and deteriorating automobiles and buildings. They also provide incomes for doctors, lawyers, teachers, and others who are too old, poorly trained, or incompetent to attract more affluent clients.

In addition to economic functions, the poor perform a number of social functions.

*Fifth,* the poor can be identified and punished as alleged or real deviants in order to uphold the legitimacy of conventional norms. To justify the desirability of hard work, thrift, honesty, and monogamy, for example, the defenders of these norms must be able to find people who can be accused of being lazy, spendthrift, dishonest, and promiscuous. Although there is some evidence that the poor are about as moral and law-abiding as anyone else, they are more likely than middle-class transgressors to be caught and punished when they participate in deviant acts. Moreover, they lack the political and cultural power to correct the stereotypes that other people hold of them and thus continue to be thought of as lazy, spendthrift, etc., by those who need living proof that moral deviance does not pay.

*Sixth,* and conversely, the poor offer vicarious participation to the rest of the population in the uninhibited sexual, alcoholic, and narcotic behavior in which they are alleged to participate and which, being freed from the constraints of affluence, they are often thought to enjoy more than the middle classes. Thus many people, some social scientists included, believe that the poor not only are more given to uninhibited behavior (which may be true, although it is often motivated by despair more than by lack of inhibition) but derive more pleasure from it than affluent people (which research by Lee Rainwater, Walter Miller, and others shows to be patently untrue). However, whether the poor actually have more sex and enjoy it more is irrelevant; so long as middle-class people believe this to be true, they can participate in it vicariously when instances are reported in factual or fictional form.

*Seventh,* the poor also serve a direct cultural function when culture created by or for them is adopted by the more affluent. The rich often collect artifacts from extinct folk cultures of poor people; and almost all Americans listen to the blues, Negro spirituals, and country music, which originated among the Southern poor. Recently they have enjoyed the rock styles that were born, like the Beatles, in the slums; and in the last year, poetry written by ghetto children has become popular in literary circles. The poor also serve as culture heroes, particularly, of course, to the left; but the hobo, the cowboy, the hipster, and the mythical prostitute with a heart of gold have performed this function for a variety of groups.

*Eighth,* poverty helps to guarantee the status of those who are not poor. In every hierarchical society someone has to be at the bottom; but in American society, in which social mobility is an important goal for many and people need to know where they stand, the poor function as a reliable and relatively permanent measuring rod for status comparisons. This is particularly true for the working class, whose politics is influenced by the need to maintain status distinctions between themselves and the poor, much as the aristocracy must find ways of distinguishing itself from the *nouveaux riches.*

*Ninth,* the poor also aid the upward mobility of groups just above them in the class hierarchy. Thus a goodly number of Americans have entered the middle class through the profits earned from the provision of goods and services in the slums, including illegal or nonrespectable ones that upper-class and upper-middle-class businessmen shun because of their low prestige. As a result, members of almost every immigrant group have financed their upward mobility by providing slum housing, entertainment, gambling, narcotics, etc., to later arrivals—most recently to blacks and Puerto Ricans.

*Tenth,* the poor help to keep the aristocracy busy, thus justifying its continued existence. "Society" uses the poor as clients of settlement houses and beneficiaries of charity affairs; indeed, the aristocracy must have the poor to demonstrate its superiority over other elites who devote themselves to earning money.

*Eleventh,* the poor, being powerless, can be made to absorb the costs of change and growth in American society. During the nineteenth century, they did the backbreaking work that built the cities; today, they are pushed out of their neighborhoods to make room for "progress." Urban renewal projects to hold middle-class taxpayers in the city and expressways to enable suburbanites to commute downtown have typically been located in poor neighborhoods, since no other group will allow itself to be displaced. For the same reason, universities, hospitals, and civic centers also expand into land occupied by the poor. The major costs of the industrialization of agriculture have been borne by the poor, who are pushed off the land without recompense; and they have paid a large share of the human cost of the growth of American

power overseas, for they have provided many of the foot soldiers for Vietnam and other wars.

*Twelfth,* the poor facilitate and stabilize the American political process. Because they vote and participate in politics less than other groups, the political system is often free to ignore them. Moreover, since they can rarely support Republicans, they often provide the Democrats with a captive constituency that has no other place to go. As a result, the Democrats can count on their votes, and be more responsive to voters—for example, the white working class—who might otherwise switch to the Republicans.

*Thirteenth,* the role of the poor in upholding conventional norms (see the *fifth* point, above) also has a significant political function. An economy based on the ideology of laissez faire requires a deprived population that is allegedly unwilling to work or that can be considered inferior because it must accept charity or welfare in order to survive. Not only does the alleged moral deviancy of the poor reduce the moral pressure on the present political economy to eliminate poverty but socialist alternatives can be made to look quite unattractive if those who will benefit most from them can be described as lazy, spendthrift, dishonest, and promiscuous.

## The Alternatives

I have described thirteen of the more important functions poverty and the poor satisfy in American society, enough to support the functionalist thesis that poverty, like any other social phenomenon, survives in part because it is useful to society or some of its parts. This analysis is not intended to suggest that because it is often functional, poverty *should* exist, or that it *must* exist. For one thing, poverty has many more dysfunctions than functions; for another, it is possible to suggest functional alternatives.

For example, society's dirty work could be done without poverty, either by automation or by paying "dirty workers" decent wages. Nor is it necessary for the poor to subsidize the many activities they support through their low-wage jobs. This would, however, drive up the costs of these activities, which would result in higher prices to their customers and clients. Similarly, many of the professionals who flourish because of the poor could be given other roles. Social workers could provide counseling to the affluent, as they prefer to do anyway; and the police could devote themselves to traffic and organized crime. Other roles would have to be found for badly trained or incompetent professionals now relegated to serving the poor, and someone else would have to pay their salaries. Fewer penologists would be employable, however. And pentecostal religion could probably not survive without the poor—nor would parts of the second- and third-hand-goods market. And in many cities, "used" housing that no one else wants would then have to be torn down at public expense.

Alternatives for the cultural functions of the poor could be found more easily and cheaply. Indeed, entertainers, hippies, and adolescents are already serving as the deviants needed to uphold traditional morality and as devotees of orgies to "staff" the fantasies of vicarious participation.

The status functions of the poor are another matter. In a hierarchical society, some people must be defined as inferior to everyone else with respect to a variety of attributes, but they need not be poor in the absolute sense. One could conceive of a society in which the "lower class," though last in the pecking order, received 75 percent of the median income, rather than 15–40 percent, as is now the case. Needless to say, this would require considerable income redistribution.

The contribution the poor make to the upward mobility of the groups that provide them with goods and services could also be maintained without the poor's having such low incomes. However, it is true that if the poor were more affluent, they would have access to enough capital to take over the provider role, thus competing with, and perhaps rejecting, the "outsiders." (Indeed, owing in part to antipoverty programs, this is already happening in a number of ghettos, where white storeowners are being replaced by blacks.) Similarly, if the poor were more affluent, they would make less willing clients for upper-class philanthropy, although some would still use settlement houses to achieve upward mobility, as they do now. Thus "Society" could continue to run its philanthropic activities.

The political functions of the poor would be more difficult to replace. With increased affluence the poor would probably obtain more political power and be more active politically. With higher incomes and more political power, the poor would be likely to resist paying the costs of growth and change. Of course, it is possible to imagine urban renewal and highway projects that properly reimbursed the displaced people, but such projects would then become considerably more expensive, and many

might never be built. This, in turn, would reduce the comfort and convenience of those who now benefit from urban renewal and expressways. Finally, hippies could serve also as more deviants to justify the existing political economy—as they already do. Presumably, however, if poverty were eliminated, there would be fewer attacks on that economy.

In sum, then, many of the functions served by the poor could be replaced if poverty were eliminated, but almost always at higher costs to others, particularly more affluent others. Consequently, a functional analysis must conclude that poverty persists not only because it fulfills a number of positive functions but also because many of the functional alternatives to poverty would be quite dysfunctional for the affluent members of society. A functional analysis thus ultimately arrives at much the same conclusion as radical sociology, except that radical thinkers treat as manifest what I describe as latent: that social phenomena that are functional for affluent or powerful groups and dysfunctional for poor or powerless ones persist; that when the elimination of such phenomena through functional alternatives would generate dysfunctions for the affluent or powerful, they will continue to persist; and that phenomena like poverty can be eliminated only when they become dysfunctional for the affluent or powerful, or when the powerless can obtain enough power to change society.

## QUESTIONS

1. Gans lists only the functions of poverty. Can you list some dysfunctions that poverty might have for American society?

2. Who do you think Americans would tend to regard more highly: an idle millionaire whose wealth was inherited or an unemployed person on welfare in an inner-city area of high unemployment? Why?

3. Discuss some of the ways in which economic power can be translated into political power.

*Allan M. Brandt*

# 25. Racism and Research: The Case of the Tuskegee Syphilis Study

*The Tuskegee study of untreated syphilis was one of the most sordid episodes in American race relations—and American medicine—in this century. For a period of forty years, until 1972, doctors and public officials held a deathwatch over some 400 syphilitic black sharecroppers in Alabama, in a "scientific" experiment that was riddled with invalid methods and in any case could produce no new useful information about syphilis.*

*The subjects of the study were never told they were participating in an "experiment"; treatment that could easily have cured them was deliberately withheld; and they were systematically deceived about the purpose of this "health program." As a result, scores of people died of the disease; others became permanently blind or insane; and the children of several were born with congenital syphilis.*

*How could this extraordinary episode, requiring the collaboration of doctors, county and state health departments, draft boards, and the U.S. Public Health Service, ever have occurred? As Allan Brandt suggests, the Tuskegee study can be understood only in terms of racism. It had its roots in pseudoscientific theories about race and about black sexuality. The study's willingness to treat people as less than human merely reflected the deep, irrational prejudice that permeated the rest of American life.*

From *Hastings Center Magazine*, December 1978. Reprinted with permission of The Hastings Center. © Institute of Society, Ethics and the Life Sciences, 360 Broadway, Hastings-on-Hudson, N.Y. 10706.

In 1932 the U.S. Public Health Service (USPHS) initiated an experiment in Macon County, Alabama, to determine the natural course of untreated, latent syphilis in black males. The test comprised 400 syphilitic men, as well as 200 uninfected men who served as controls. The first published report of the study appeared in 1936 with subsequent papers issued every four to six years, through the 1960s. When penicillin became widely available by the early 1950s as the preferred treatment for syphilis, the men did not receive therapy. In fact, on several occasions, the USPHS actually sought to prevent treatment. Moreover, a committee at the federally operated Center for Disease Control decided in 1969 that the study should be continued. Only in 1972, when accounts of the study first appeared in the national press, did the Department of Health, Education and Welfare halt the experiment. At that time seventy-four of the test subjects were still alive; at least twenty-eight, but perhaps more than 100, had died directly from advanced syphilitic lesions.[1] In August 1972, HEW appointed an investigatory panel which issued a report the following year. The panel found the study to have been "ethically unjustified," and argued that penicillin should have been provided to the men.[2]

This article attempts to place the Tuskegee Study in a historical context and to assess its ethical implications. Despite the media attention which the study received, the HEW *Final Report*, and the criticism expressed by several professional organizations, the experiment has been largely misunderstood. The most basic questions of *how* the study was undertaken in the first place and *why* it continued for forty years were never addressed by the HEW investigation. Moreover, the panel misconstrued the nature of the experiment, failing to consult important documents available at the National Archives which bear significantly on its ethical assessment. Only by examining the specific ways in which values are engaged in scientific research can the study be understood.

## Racism and Medical Opinion

A brief review of the prevailing scientific thought regarding race and heredity in the early twentieth century is fundamental for an understanding of the Tuskegee Study. By the turn of the century, Darwinism had provided a new rationale for American racism.[3] Essentially primitive peoples, it was argued, could not be assimilated into a complex, white civilization. Scientists speculated that in the struggle for survival the Negro in America was doomed. Particularly prone to disease, vice, and crime, black Americans could not be helped by education or philanthropy. Social Darwinists analyzed census data to predict the virtual extinction of the Negro in the twentieth century, for they believed the Negro race in America was in the throes of a degenerative evolutionary process.[4]

The medical profession supported these findings of late nineteenth- and early twentieth-century anthropologists, ethnologists, and biologists. Physicians studying the effects of emancipation on health concluded almost universally that freedom had caused the mental, moral, and physical deterioration of the black population.[5] They substantiated this argument by citing examples in the comparative anatomy of the black and white races. As Dr. W. T. English wrote: "A careful inspection reveals the body of the negro a mass of minor defects and imperfections from the crown of the head to the soles of the feet . . ."[6] Cranial structures, wide nasal apertures, receding chins, projecting jaws, all typed the Negro as the lowest species in the Darwinian hierarchy.[7]

Interest in racial differences centered on the sexual nature of blacks. The Negro, doctors explained, possessed an excessive sexual desire, which threatened the very foundations of white society. As one physician noted in the *Journal of the American Medical Association,* "The negro springs from a southern race, and as such his sexual appetite is strong; all of his environments stimulate this appetite, and as a general rule his emotional type of religion certainly does not decrease it."[8] Doctors reported a complete lack of morality on the part of the blacks.

> Virtue in the negro race is like angels' visits—few and far between. In a practice of sixteen years I have never examined a virgin negro over fourteen years of age.[9]

A particularly ominous feature of this overzealous sexuality, doctors argued, was the black males' desire for white women. "A perversion from which most races are exempt," wrote Dr. English, "prompts the negro's inclination toward white women . . ."[10] Though English estimated the "gray matter of the negro brain" to be at least a thousand years behind that of the white races, his genital organs were overdeveloped. As Dr. William Lee Howard noted:

> The attacks on defenseless white women are evidences of racial instincts that are about as amenable to ethical culture as is the inherent odor of the race. . . . When education will reduce the size of the negro's penis as well as bring about the sensitiveness of the terminal fibers which exist in the Caucasian, then will it also be able to prevent the African's birthright to sexual madness and excess.[11]

One southern medical journal proposed "Castration Instead of Lynching," as retribution for black sexual crimes. "An impressive trial by a ghost-like kuklux klan [sic] and a 'ghost' physician or surgeon to perform the operation would make it an event the 'patient' would never forget," noted the editorial.[12]

According to these physicians, lust and immorality, unstable families, and reversion to barbaric tendencies made blacks especially prone to venereal diseases. One doctor estimated that over 50 percent of all Negroes over the age of twenty-five were syphilitic.[13] Virtually free of disease as slaves, they were now overwhelmed by it, according to informed medical opinion. Moreover, doctors believed that treatment for venereal disease among blacks was impossible, particularly because in its latent stage the symptoms of syphilis become quiescent. As Dr. Thomas W. Murrell wrote:

> They come for treatment at the beginning and at the end. When there are visible manifestations or when harried by pain, they readily come, for as a race they are not averse to physic; but tell them not, though they look well and feel well, that they are still diseased. Here ignorance rates science a fool. . . .[14]

Even the best educated black, according to Murrell, could not be convinced to seek treatment for syphilis.[15] Venereal disease, according to some doctors, threatened the future of the race. The medical profession attributed the low birth rate among blacks to the high prevalence of venereal disease which caused stillbirths and miscarriages. Moreover, the high rates of syphilis were thought to lead to increased insanity and crime. One doctor writing at the turn of the century estimated that the number of insane Negroes had increased thirteen-fold since the end of the Civil War.[16] Dr. Murrell's conclusion echoed the most informed anthropological and ethnological data:

> So the scourge sweeps among them. Those that are treated are only half cured, and the effort to assimilate a complex civilization drives their diseased minds until the results are criminal records. Perhaps here, in conjunction with tuberculosis, will be the end of the negro problem. Disease will accomplish what man cannot do.[17]

This particular configuration of ideas formed the core of medical opinion concerning blacks, sex, and disease in the early twentieth century. Doctors generally discounted socioeconomic explanations of the state of black health, arguing that better medical care could not alter the evolutionary scheme.[18] These assumptions provide the backdrop for examining the Tuskegee Syphilis Study.

## The Origins of the Experiment

In 1929, under a grant from the Julius Rosenwald Fund, the USPHS conducted studies in the rural South to determine the prevalence of syphilis among blacks and explore the possibilities for mass treatment. The USPHS found Macon County, Alabama, in which the town of Tuskegee is located, to have the highest syphilis rate of the six counties surveyed. The Rosenwald Study concluded that mass treatment could be successfully implemented among rural blacks.[19] Although it is doubtful that the necessary funds would have been allocated even in the best economic conditions, after the economy collapsed in 1929, the findings were ignored. It is, however, ironic that the Tuskegee Study came to be based on findings of the Rosenwald Study that demonstrated the possibilities of mass treatment.

Three years later, in 1932, Dr. Taliaferro Clark, Chief of the USPHS Venereal Disease Division and author of the Rosenwald Study report, decided that conditions in Macon County merited renewed attention. Clark believed the high prevalence of syphilis offered an "unusual opportunity" for observation. From its inception, the USPHS regarded the Tuskegee Study as a classic "study in nature," rather than an experiment.[20] As long as syphilis was so prevalent in Macon and most of the blacks went untreated throughout life, it seemed only natural to Clark that it would be valuable to observe the consequences. He described it as a "ready-made situation."[21] Surgeon General H. S. Cumming wrote to R. R. Moton, Director of the Tuskegee Institute:

> The recent syphilis control demonstration carried out in Macon County, with the financial assistance of the Julius Rosenwald Fund, revealed the presence of an unusually high rate in this county and, what is more remarkable, the fact that 99 per cent of this group was entirely without previous treatment. This combination, together with the expected cooperation of your hospital, offers an unparalleled opportunity for carrying on this piece of scientific research which probably cannot be duplicated anywhere else in the world.[22]

Although no formal protocol appears to have been written, several letters of Clark and Cumming suggest what the USPHS hoped to find. Clark indicated that it would be important to see how disease affected the daily lives of the men:

> The results of these studies of case records suggest the desirability of making a further study of the effect of un-

treated syphilis on the human economy among people now living and engaged in their daily pursuits.[23]

It also seems that the USPHS believed the experiment might demonstrate that antisyphilitic treatment was unnecessary. As Cumming noted: "It is expected the results of this study may have a marked bearing on the treatment, or conversely the non-necessity of treatment, of cases of latent syphilis."[24]

The immediate source of Cumming's hypothesis appears to have been the famous Oslo Study of untreated syphilis. Between 1890 and 1910, Professor C. Boeck, the chief of the Oslo Venereal Clinic, withheld treatment from almost two thousand patients infected with syphilis. He was convinced that therapies then available, primarily mercurial ointment, were of no value. When arsenic therapy became widely available by 1910, after Paul Ehrlich's historic discovery of "606," the study was abandoned. E. Bruusgaard, Boeck's successor, conducted a follow-up study of 473 of the untreated patients from 1925 to 1927. He found that 27.9 percent of these patients had undergone a "spontaneous cure," and now manifested no symptoms of the disease. Moreover, he estimated that as many as 70 percent of all syphilitics went through life without inconvenience from the disease.[25] His study, however, clearly acknowledged the dangers of untreated syphilis for the remaining 30 percent.

Thus every major textbook of syphilis at the time of the Tuskegee Study's inception strongly advocated treating syphilis even in its latent stages, which follow the initial inflammatory reaction. In discussing the Oslo Study, Dr. J. E. Moore, one of the nation's leading venereologists wrote, "This summary of Bruusgaard's study is by no means intended to suggest that syphilis be allowed to pass untreated."[26] If a complete cure could not be effected, at least the most devastating effects of the disease could be avoided. Although the standard therapies of the time, arsenical compounds and bismuth injection, involved certain dangers because of their toxicity, the alternatives were much worse. As the Oslo Study had shown, untreated syphilis could lead to cardiovascular disease, insanity, and premature death.[27] Moore wrote in his 1933 textbook:

> Though it imposes a slight though measurable risk of its own, treatment markedly diminishes the risk from syphilis. In latent syphilis, as I shall show, the probability of progression, relapse, or death is reduced from a probable 25–30 percent without treatment to about 5 percent with it; and the gravity of the relapse if it occurs, is markedly diminished.[28]

"Another compelling reason for treatment," noted Moore, "exists in the fact that every patient with latent syphilis may be, and perhaps is, infectious, for others."[29] In 1932, the year in which the Tuskegee Study began, the USPHS sponsored and published a paper by Moore and six other syphilis experts that strongly argued for treating latent syphilis.[30]

The Oslo Study, therefore, could not have provided justification for the USPHS to undertake a study that did not entail treatment. Rather, the suppositions that conditions in Tuskegee existed "naturally" and that men would not be treated anyway provided the experiment's rationale. In turn, these two assumptions rested on the prevailing medical attitudes concerning blacks, sex, and disease. For example, Clark explained the prevalance of venereal disease in Macon County by emphasizing promiscuity among blacks:

> This state of affairs is due to the paucity of doctors, rather low intelligence of the Negro population in this section, depressed economic conditions, and the very common promiscuous sex relations of this population group which not only contribute to the spread of syphilis but also contribute to the prevailing indifference with regard to treatment.[31]

In fact, Moore, who had written so persuasively in favor of treating latent syphilis, suggested that existing knowledge did not apply to Negroes. Although he had called the Oslo Study "a never-to-be-repeated human experiment,"[32] he served as an expert consultant to the Tuskegee Study:

> I think that such a study as you have contemplated would be of immense value. It will be necessary of course in the consideration of the results to evaluate the special factors introduced by a selection of the material from negro males. Syphilis in the negro is in many respects almost a different disease from syphilis in the white.[33]

Dr. O. C. Wenger, chief of the federally operated venereal disease clinic at Hot Springs, Arkansas, praised Moore's judgment, adding, "This study will emphasize those differences."[34] On another occasion he advised Clark, "We must remember we are dealing with a group of people who are illiterate, have no conception of time, and whose personal history is always indefinite."[35]

The doctors who devised and directed the Tuskegee Study accepted the mainstream assumptions regarding blacks and venereal disease. The premise that blacks, promiscuous and lustful, would not seek or continue treatment, shaped the study. A test of untreated syphilis seemed "natural" because the USPHS presumed the men would never be treated; the Tuskegee Study made that a self-fulfilling prophecy.

## Selecting the Subjects

Clark sent Dr. Raymond Vonderlehr to Tuskegee in September 1932 to assemble a sample of men with latent syphilis for the experiment. The basic design of the study called for the selection of syphilitic black males between the ages of twenty-five and sixty, a thorough physical examination including x-rays, and finally, a spinal tap to determine the incidence of neuro-syphilis.[36] They had no intention of providing any treatment for the infected men.[37] The USPHS originally scheduled the whole experiment to last six months; it seemed to be both a simple and inexpensive project.

The task of collecting the sample, however, proved to be more difficult than the USPHS had supposed. Vonderlehr canvassed the largely illiterate, poverty-stricken population of sharecroppers and tenant farmers in search of test subjects. If his circulars requested only men over twenty-five to attend his clinics, none would appear, suspecting he was conducting draft physicals. Therefore, he was forced to test large numbers of women and men who did not fit the experiment's specifications. This involved considerable expense since the USPHS had promised Macon County Board of Health that it would treat those who were infected, but not included in the study.[38] Clark wrote to Vonderlehr about the situation: "It never once occurred to me that we would be called upon to treat a large part of the county as return for the privilege of making this study ... I am anxious to keep the expenditures for treatment down to the lowest possible point because it is the one item of expenditure in connection with the study most difficult to defend despite our knowledge of the need therefor."[39] Vonderlehr responded: "If we could find from 100 to 200 cases ... we would not have to do another Wassermann on useless individuals ..."[40]

Significantly, the attempt to develop the sample contradicted the prediction the USPHS had made initially regarding the prevalence of the disease in Macon County. Overall rates of syphilis fell well below expectations; as opposed to the USPHS projection of 35 percent, 20 percent of those tested were actually diseased.[41] Moreover, those who had sought and received previous treatment far exceeded the expectations of the USPHS. Clark noted in a letter to Vonderlehr:

> I find your report of March 6th quite interesting but regret the necessity for Wassermanning [sic] ... such a large number of individuals in order to uncover this relatively limited number of untreated cases.[42]

Further difficulties arose in enlisting the subjects to participate in the experiment, to be "Wassermanned," and to return for a subsequent series of examinations. Vonderlehr found that only the offer of treatment elicited the cooperation of the men. They were told they were ill and were promised free care. Offered therapy, they became willing subjects.[43] The USPHS did not tell the men that they were participants in an experiment; on the contrary, the subjects believed they were being treated for "bad blood"—the rural South's colloquialism for syphilis. They thought they were participating in a public health demonstration similar to the one that had been conducted by the Julius Rosenwald Fund in Tuskegee several years earlier. In the end, the men were so eager for medical care that the number of defaulters in the experiment proved to be insignificant.[44]

To preserve the subjects' interest, Vonderlehr gave most of the men mercurial ointment, a noneffective drug, while some of the younger men apparently received inadequate dosages of neoarsphenamine.[45] This required Vonderlehr to write frequently to Clark requesting supplies. He feared the experiment would fail if the men were not offered treatment.

> It is desirable and essential if the study is to be a success to maintain the interest of each of the cases examined by me through to the time when the spinal puncture can be completed. Expenditure of several hundred dollars for drugs for these men would be well worth while if their interest and cooperation would be maintained in so doing. . . . It is my desire to keep the main purpose of the work from the negroes in the county and continue their interest in treatment. That is what the vast majority wants and the examination seems relatively unimportant to them in comparison. It would probably cause the entire experiment to collapse if the clinics were stopped before the work is completed.[46]

On another occasion he explained:

> Dozens of patients have been sent away without treatment during the past two weeks and it would have been impossible to continue without the free distribution of drugs because of the unfavorable impression made on the negro.[47]

The readiness of the test subjects to participate of course contradicted the notion that blacks would not seek or continue therapy.

The final procedure of the experiment was to be a spinal tap to test for evidence of neuro-syphilis. The USPHS presented this purely diagnostic exam, which often entails considerable pain and complications, to the men as a "special treatment." Clark explained to Moore:

> We have not yet commenced the spinal punctures. This operation will be deferred to the last in order not to unduly disturb our field work by any adverse reports by the patients subjected to spinal puncture because of some disagreeable sensations following this procedure. These negroes are very ignorant and easily influenced by things that would be of minor significance in a more intelligent group.[48]

The letter to the subjects announcing the spinal tap read:

> Some time ago you were given a thorough examination and since that time we hope you have gotten a great deal of treatment for bad blood. You will now be given your last

chance to get a second examination. This examination is a very special one and after it is finished you will be given a special treatment if it is believed you are in a condition to stand it . . .

> REMEMBER THIS IS YOUR LAST CHANCE FOR SPECIAL FREE TREATMENT. BE SURE TO MEET THE NURSE.[49]

The HEW investigation did not uncover this crucial fact: the men participated in the study under the guise of treatment.

Despite the fact that their assumption regarding prevalence and black attitudes toward treatment had proved wrong, the USPHS decided in the summer of 1933 to continue the study. Once again, it seemed only "natural" to pursue the research since the sample already existed, and with a depressed economy, the cost of treatment appeared prohibitive—although there is no indication it was ever considered. Vonderlehr first suggested extending the study in letters to Clark and Wenger:

> At the end of this project we shall have a considerable number of cases presenting various complications of syphilis, who have received only mercury and may still be considered untreated in the modern sense of therapy. Should these cases be followed over a period of from five to ten years many interesting facts could be learned regarding the course and complications of untreated syphilis.[50]

"As I see it," responded Wenger, "we have no further interest in these patients *until they die.*"[51] Apparently, the physicians engaged in the experiment believed that only autopsies could scientifically confirm the findings of the study. Surgeon General Cumming explained this in a letter to R. R. Moton, requesting the continued cooperation of the Tuskegee Institute Hospital:

> This study which was predominantly clinical in character points to the frequent occurrence of severe complications involving the various vital organs of the body and indicates that syphilis as a disease does a great deal of damage. Since clinical observations are not considered final in the medical world, it is our desire to continue observation on the cases selected for the recent study and if possible to bring a percentage of these cases to autopsy so that pathological confirmation may be made of the disease processes.[52]

Bringing the men to autopsy required the USPHS to devise a further series of deceptions and inducements. Wenger warned Vonderlehr that the men must not realize that they would be autopsied:

> There is one danger in the latter plan and that is if the colored population become aware that accepting free hospital care means a post-mortem every darkey will leave Macon County and it will hurt [Dr. Eugene] Dibble's hospital.[53]

"Naturally," responded Vonderlehr, "it is not my intention to let it be generally known that the main object of the present activities is the bringing of the men to necropsy."[54] The subjects' trust in the USPHS made the plan viable. The USPHS gave Dr. Dibble, the Director of the Tuskegee Institute Hospital, an interim appointment to the Public Health Service. As Wenger noted:

> One thing is certain. The only way we are going to get post-mortems is to have the demise take place in Dibble's hospital and when these colored folks are told that Doctor Dibble is now a Government doctor too they will have more confidence.[55]

After the USPHS approved the continuation of the experiment in 1933, Vonderlehr decided that it would be necessary to select a group of healthy, uninfected men to serve as controls. Vonderlehr, who had succeeded Clark as Chief of the Venereal Disease Division, sent Dr. J. R. Heller to Tuskegee to gather the control group. Heller distributed drugs (noneffective) to these men, which suggests that they also believed they were undergoing treatment.[56] Control subjects who became syphilitic were simply transfered to the test group—a strikingly inept violation of standard research procedure.[57]

The USPHS offered several inducements to maintain contact and to procure the continued cooperation of the men. Eunice Rivers, a black nurse, was hired to follow their health and to secure approval for autopsies. She gave the men noneffective medicines—"spring tonic" and aspirin—as well as transportation and hot meals on the days of their examinations.[58] More important, Nurse Rivers provided continuity to the project over the entire forty-year period. By supplying "medicinals," the USPHS was able to continue to deceive the participants, who believed that they were receiving therapy from the government doctors. Deceit was integral to the study. When the test subjects complained about spinal taps one doctor wrote:

> They simply do not like spinal punctures. A few of those who were tapped are enthusiastic over the results but to most, the suggestion causes violent shaking of the head; others claim they were robbed of their procreative powers (regardless of the fact that I claim It stimulates them).[59]

Letters to the subjects announcing an impending USPHS visit to Tuskegee explained: "[The doctor] wants to make a special examination to find out how you have been feeling and whether the treatment has improved your health."[60] In fact, after the first six months of the study, the USPHS had furnished no treatment whatsoever.

Finally, because it proved difficult to persuade the men to come to the hospital when they became severely ill, the USPHS promised to cover their burial expenses. The Milbank Memorial Fund provided approximately $50 per man for this purpose beginning in 1935. This was a particularly strong inducement as funeral rites consti-

tuted an important component of the cultural life of rural blacks.[61] One report of the study concluded, "Without this suasion it would, we believe, have been impossible to secure the cooperation of the group and their families."[62]

Reports of the study's findings, which appeared regularly in the medical press beginning in 1936, consistently cited the ravages of untreated syphilis. The first paper, read at the 1936 American Medical Association annual meeting, found "that syphilis in this period [latency] tends to greatly increase the frequency of manifestations of cardiovascular disease."[63] Only 16 percent of the subjects gave no sign of morbidity as opposed to 61 percent of the controls. Ten years later, a report noted coldly, "The fact that nearly twice as large a proportion of the syphilitic individuals as of the control group has died is a very striking one." Life expectancy, concluded the doctors, is reduced by about 20 percent.[64]

A 1955 article found that slightly more than 30 percent of the test group autopsied had died *directly* from advanced syphilitic lesions of either the cardiovascular or the central nervous system.[65] Another published account stated, "Review of those still living reveals that an appreciable number have late complications of syphilis which probably will result, for some at least, in contributing materially to the ultimate cause of death."[66] In 1950, Dr. Wenger had concluded, "We now know, where we could only surmise before, that we have contributed to their ailments and shortened their lives."[67] As black physician Vernal Cave, a member of the HEW panel, later wrote, "They proved a point, then proved a point, then proved a point."[68]

During the forty years of the experiment the USPHS had sought on several occasions to ensure that the subjects did not receive treatment from other sources. To this end, Vonderlehr met with groups of local black doctors in 1934, to ask their cooperation in not treating the men. Lists of subjects were distributed to Macon County physicians along with letters requesting them to refer these men back to the USPHS if they sought care.[69] The USPHS warned the Alabama Health Department not to treat the test subjects when they took a mobile VD unit into Tuskegee in the early 1940s.[70] In 1941, the Army drafted several subjects and told them to begin antisyphilitic treatment immediately. The USPHS supplied the draft board with a list of 256 names they desired to have excluded from treatment, and the board complied.[71]

In spite of these efforts, by the early 1950s many of the men had secured some treatment on their own. By 1952, almost 30 percent of the test subjects had received some penicillin, although only 7.5 percent had received what could be considered adequate doses.[72] Vonderlehr wrote to one of the participating physicians, "I hope that the availability of antibiotics has not interfered too much with this project."[73] A report published in 1955 considered whether the treatment that some of the men had obtained had "defeated" the study. The article attempted to explain the relatively low exposure to penicillin in an age of antibiotics, suggesting as a reason: "the stoicism of these men as a group; they still regard hospitals and medicines with suspicion and prefer an occasional dose of time-honored herbs or tonics to modern drugs."[74] The authors failed to note that the men believed they already were under the care of the government doctors and thus saw no need to seek treatment elsewhere. Any treatment which the men might have received, concluded the report, had been insufficient to compromise the experiment.

When the USPHS evaluated the status of the study in the 1960s they continued to rationalize the racial aspects of the experiment. For example, the minutes of a 1965 meeting at the Center for Disease Control recorded:

> Racial issue was mentioned briefly. Will not affect the study. Any questions can be handled by saying these people were at the point that therapy would no longer help them. They are getting better medical care than they would under any other circumstances.[75]

A group of physicians met again at the CDC in 1969 to decide whether or not to terminate the study. Although one doctor argued that the study should be stopped and the men treated, the consensus was to continue. Dr. J. Lawton Smith remarked, "You will never have another study like this; take advantage of it."[76] A memo prepared by Dr. James B. Lucas, Assistant Chief of the Venereal Disease Branch, stated: "Nothing learned will prevent, find, or cure a single case of infectious syphilis or bring us closer to our basic mission of controlling venereal disease in the United States."[77] He concluded, however, that the study should be continued "along its present lines." When the first accounts of the experiment appeared in the national press in July 1972, data were still being collected and autopsies performed.[78]

## The HEW Final Report

HEW finally formed the Tuskegee Syphilis Study Ad Hoc Advisory Panel on August 28, 1972, in response to criticism that the press descriptions of the experiment had triggered. The panel, composed of nine members, five of them black, concentrated on two issues. First, was the study justified in 1932 and had the men given their informed consent? Second, should penicillin have been provided when it became available in the early 1950s? The panel was also charged with determining if the study should be terminated and assessing current policies regarding experimentation with human subjects.[79] The group issued their report in June 1973.

By focusing on the issues of penicillin therapy and informed consent, the *Final Report* and the investigation betrayed a basic misunderstanding of the experiment's purposes and design. The HEW report implied that the failure to provide penicillin constituted the study's major ethical misjudgment; implicit was the assumption that no adequate therapy existed prior to penicillin. Nonetheless medical authorities firmly believed in the efficacy of arsenotherapy for treating syphilis at the time of the experiment's inception in 1932. The panel further failed to recognize that the entire study had been predicated on nontreatment. Provision of effective medication would have violated the rationale of the experiment—to study the natural course of the disease until death. On several occasions, in fact, the USPHS had prevented the men from receiving proper treatment. Indeed, there is no evidence that the USPHS ever considered providing penicillin.

The other focus of the *Final Report*—informed consent—also served to obscure the historical facts of the experiment. In light of the deceptions and exploitations which the experiment perpetrated, it is an understatement to declare, as the *Report* did, that the experiment was "ethically unjustified," because it failed to obtain informed consent from the subjects. The *Final Report*'s statement, "Submitting voluntarily is not informed consent," indicated that the panel believed that the men had volunteered *for the experiment*.[80] The records in the National Archives make clear that the men did not submit voluntarily to an experiment; they were told and they believed that they were getting free treatment from expert government doctors for a serious disease. The failure of the HEW *Final Report* to expose this critical fact—that the USPHS lied to the subjects—calls into question the thoroughness and credibility of their investigation.

Failure to place the study in a historical context also made it impossible for the investigation to deal with the essentially racist nature of the experiment. The panel treated the study as an aberration, well-intentioned but misguided.[81] Moreover, concern that the *Final Report* might be viewed as a critique of human experimentation in general seems to have severely limited the scope of the inquiry. The *Final Report* is quick to remind the reader on two occasions: "The position of the Panel must not be construed to be a general repudiation of scientific research with human subjects."[82] The *Report* assures us that a better designed experiment could have been justified:

> It is possible that a scientific study in 1932 of untreated syphilis, properly conceived with a clear protocol and conducted with suitable subjects who fully understood the implications of their involvement, might have been justified in the pre-penicillin era. This is especially true when one considers the uncertain nature of the results of treatment of late latent syphilis and the highly toxic nature of therapeutic agents then available.[83]

32. **Joseph Earle Moore,** "Latent Syphilis," unpublishd type-script (n.d.), p. 7. American Social Hygiene Association Papers, Social Welfare History Archives Center, University of Minnesota, Minneapolis, Minnesota.

33. Moore to Clark, September 28, 1932, NA-WNRC. Moore had written in his textbook, "In late syphilis the negro is particularly prone to the development of bone or cardiovascular lesions." See Moore, *The Modern Treatment of Syphilis,* p. 35.

34. O. C. Wenger to Clark, October 3, 1932, NA-WNRC.

35. Wenger to Clark, September 29, 1932. NA-WNRC.

36. Clark Memorandum, September 26, 1932, NA-WNRC. See also, Clark to Davis, October 29, 1932, NA-WNRC.

37. As Clark wrote: "You will observe that our plan has nothing to do with treatment. It is purely a diagnostic procedure carried out to determine what has happened to the syphilitic Negro who has had no treatment." Clark to Paul A. O'Leary, September 27, 1932, NA-WNRC.

38. D. G. Gill to O. C. Wenger, October 10, 1932, NA-WNRC.

39. Clark to Vonderlehr, January 25, 1933, NA-WNRC.

40. Vonderlehr to Clark, February 28, 1933, NA-WNRC.

41. Vonderlehr to Clark, November 2, 1932, NA-WNRC. Also, Vonderlehr to Clark, February 6, 1933, NA-WNRC.

42. Clark to Vonderlehr, March 9, 1933, NA-WNRC.

43. Vonderlehr later explained: "The reason treatment was given to many of these men was twofold: First, when the study was started in the fall of 1932, no plans had been made for its con-tinuation and a few of the patients were treated before we fully realized the need for continuing the project on a permanent basis. Second it was difficult to hold the interest of the group of Negroes in Macon County unless some treatment was given." Vonderlehr to Austin V. Diebert, December 5, 1938, Tuskegee Syphilis Study Ad Hoc Advisory Panel Papers, Box 1, National Library of Medicine, Bethesda, Maryland. (Hereafter, TSS-NLM.) This collection contains the materials assembled by the HEW investigation in 1972.

44. Vonderlehr to Clark, February 6, 1933, NA-WNRC.

45. H. S. Cumming to J. N. Baker, August 5, 1933, NA-WNRC.

46. January 22, 1933; January 12, 1933, NA-WNRC.

47. Vonderlehr to Clark, January 28, 1933, NA-WNRC.

48. Clark to Moore, March 25, 1933, NA-WNRC.

49. Macon County Health Department, "Letter to Subjects," n.d., NA-WNRC.

50. Vonderlehr to Clark, April 8, 1933, NA-WNRC. See also, Von-derlehr to Wenger, July 18, 1933, NA-WNRC.

51. Wenger to Vonderlehr, July 21, 1933, NA-WNRC. The italics are Wenger's.

52. Cumming to Moton, July 27, 1933, NA-WNRC.

53. Wenger to Vonderlehr, July 21, 1933, NA-WNRC.

54. Vonderlehr to Murray Smith, July 27, 1933, NA-WNRC.

55. Wenger to Vonderlehr, August 5, 1933, NA-WNRC. (The de-gree of black cooperation in conducting the study remains un-clear and would be impossible to properly assess in an article of this length. It seems certain that some members of the Tus-kegee Institute staff such as R. R. Moton and Eugene Dibble understood the nature of the experiment and gave their support to it. There is, however, evidence that some blacks who assisted the USPHS physicians were not aware of the deceptive nature of the experiment. Dr. Joshua Williams, an intern at the John A. Andrew Memorial Hospital [Tuskegee Institute] in 1932, as-sisted Vonderlehr in taking blood samples of the test subjects. In 1973 he told the HEW panel: "I know we thought it was merely a service group organized to help the people in the area. We didn't know it was a research project at all at the time." [See, "Transcript of Proceedings," Tuskegee Syphilis Study Ad Hoc Advisory Panel, February 23, 1973, Unpublished typescript. National Library of Medicine, Bethesda, Maryland.] It is also apparent that Eunice Rivers, the black nurse who had primary responsibility for maintaining contact with the men over the forty years, did not fully understand the dangers of the exper-iment. In any event, black involvement in the study in no way mitigates the racial assumptions of the experiment, but rather demonstrates their power.)

56. Vonderlehr to Wenger, October 24, 1933, NA-WNRC. Con-trols were given salicylates.

57. **Austin V. Diebert and Martha C. Bruyere,** "Untreated Sy-philis in the Male Negro, III," *Venereal Disease Information* 27 (December 1946), 301–14.

58. **Eunice Rivers, Stanley Schuman, Lloyd Simpson, Sidney Olansky,** "Twenty-Years of Followup Experience In a Long-Range Medical Study," *Public Health Reports* 68 (April 1953), 391–95. In this article Nurse Rivers explains her role in the experiment. She wrote: "Because of the low educational status of the majority of the patients, it was impossible to appeal to them from a purely scientific approach. Therefore, various methods were used to maintain their interest. Free medicines, burial assistance or insurance (the project being referred to as 'Miss Rivers' Lodge'), free hot meals on the days of examination, transportation to and from the hospital, and an opportunity to stop in town on the return trip to shop or visit with their friends on the streets all helped. In spite of these attractions, there were some who refused their examinations because they were not sick and did not see that they were being benefitted." (p. 393).

59. Austin V. Diebert to Raymond Vonderlehr, March 20, 1939, TSS-NLM, Box 1.

60. Murray Smith to Subjects (1938), TSS-NLM, Box 1. See also, Sidney Olansky to John C. Cutler, November 6, 1951, TSS-NLM, Box 2.

61. The USPHS originally requested that the Julius Rosenwald Fund meet this expense. See Cumming to Davis, October 4, 1934, NA-WNRC. This money was usually divided between the un-dertaker, pathologist, and hospital. Lloyd Isaacs to Raymond Vonderlehr, April 23, 1940, TSS-NLM, Box 1.

62. **Stanley H. Schuman, Sidney Olansky, Eunice Rivers, C. A. Smith, Dorothy S. Rambo,** "Untreated Syphilis in the Male Negro: Background and Current Status of Patients in the Tus-kegee Study," *Journal of Chronic Diseases* 2 (November 1955), 555.

63. **R. A. Vonderlehr and Taliaferro Clark,** "Untreated Syphilis in the Male Negro," *Venereal Disease Information* 17 (September 1936), 262.

64. **J. R. Heller and P. T. Bruyere,** "Untreated Syphilis in the Male Negro: II. Mortality During 12 Years of Observation," *Ve-nereal Disease Information* 27 (February 1946), 34–38.

65. **Jesse J. Peters, James H. Peers, Sidney Olansky, John C. Cutler, and Geraldine Gleeson,** "Untreated Syphilis in the Male Negro: Pathologic Findings in Syphilitic and Non-Syphilitic Pa-tients," *Journal of Chronic Diseases* 1 (February 1955), 127–48.

66. **Sidney Olansky, Stanley H. Schuman, Jesse J. Peters,**

C. A. Smith, and Dorothy S. Rambo, "Untreated Syphilis in the Male Negro, X. Twenty Years of Clinical Observation of Untreated Syphilitic and Presumably Nonsyphilitic Groups," *Journal of Chronic Diseases* 4 (August 1956), 184.

67. O. C. Wenger, "Untreated Syphilis in Male Negro," unpublished typescript, 1950, p. 3. Tuskegee Files, Center for Disease Control, Atlanta, Georgia. (Hereafter TF-CDC.)

68. Vernal G. Cave, "Proper Uses and Abuses of the Health Care Delivery System for Minorities with Special Reference to the Tuskegee Syphilis Study," *Journal of the National Medical Association* 67 (January 1975), 83.

69. See for example, Vonderlehr to B. W. Booth, April 18, 1934; Vonderlehr to E. R. Lett, November 20, 1933, NA-WNRC.

70. "Transcript of Proceedings—Tuskegee Syphilis Ad Hoc Advisory Panel," February 23, 1973, unpublished typescript, TSS-NLM, Box 1.

71. Raymond Vonderlehr to Murray Smith, April 30, 1942; and Smith to Vonderlehr, June 8, 1942, TSS-NLM, Box 1.

72. Stanley H. Schuman, Sidney Olansky, Eunice Rivers, C. A. Smith, and Dorothy S. Rambo, "Untreated Syphilis in the Male Negro: Background and Current Status of Patients in the Tuskegee Study," *Journal of Chronic Diseases* 2 (November 1955), 550–53.

73. Raymond Vonderlehr to Stanley H. Schuman, February 5, 1952, TSS-NLM, Box 2.

74. Schuman et al. p. 550.

75. "Minutes, April 5, 1965," unpublished typescript, TSS-NLM, Box 1.

76. "Tuskegee Ad Hoc Committee Meeting—Minutes, February 6, 1969," TF-CDC.

77. James B. Lucas to William J. Brown, September 10, 1970, TF-CDC.

78. Elizabeth M. Kennebrew to Arnold C. Schroeter, February 24, 1971, TSS-NLM, Box 1.

79. See *Medical Tribune* (September 13, 1972), pp. 1, 20; and "Report on HEW's Tuskegee Report," *Medical World News,* (September 14, 1973), pp. 57–58.

80. HEW *Final Report,* p. 7.

81. The notable exception is Jay Katz's eloquent "Reservations About the Panel Report on Charge 1," HEW *Final Report,* pp. 14–15.

82. HEW *Final Report,* pp. 8, 12.

83. HEW *Final Report,* pp. 8, 12.

84. See R. H. Kampmeier, "The Tuskegee Study of Untreated Syphilis," *Southern Medical Journal* 65 (October 1972), 1247–51; and "Final Report on the 'Tuskegee Syphilis Study,'" *Southern Medical Journal* 67 (November 1974), 1349–53.

85. Leonard J. Goldwater, "The Tuskegee Study in Historical Perspective," unpublished typescript, TSS-NLM; see also, "Treponemes and Tuskegee," *Lancet* (June 3, 1973), p. 1438; and Louis Lasagna, *The VD Epidemic* (Philadelphia: Temple University Press, 1975), pp. 64–66.

86. Quoted in "Debate Revives on the PHS Study," *Medical World News* (April 19, 1974), p. 37.

87. Heller to Vonderlehr, November 28, 1933, NA-WNRC; quoted in *Medical Tribune* (August 23, 1972), p. 14.

88. Although it is now known that syphilis is rarely infectious after its early phase, at the time of the study's inception latent syphilis was thought to be communicable. The fact that members of the control group were placed in the test group when they became syphilitic proves that at least some infectious men were denied treatment.

89. When the subjects are drawn from minority groups, espcially those with which the researcher cannot identify, basic human rights may be compromised. Hans Jonas has clearly explicated the problem in his "Philosophical Reflections on Experimentation," *Daedalus* 98 (Spring, 1969), 234–37. As Jonas writes: "If the properties we adduced as the particular qualifications of the members of the scientific fraternity itself are taken as general criteria of selection, then one should look for additional subjects where a maximum of identification, understanding, and spontaneity can be expected—that is, among the most highly motivated, the most highly educated, and the least 'captive' members of the community."

*William J. Wilson*

# 26. The Black Underclass

*Black Americans have a historical experience that is
utterly different from that of other racial and ethnic
groups in the United States. Unlike all other immigrant
groups, black Americans were forcibly imported to the
United States as slaves and were subject to legalized
discrimination right up to the 1960s. But since that time,
there have been significant changes in the status of this
minority. Congress has made segregation and other
forms of discrimination illegal, and has enacted various
measures to improve equality of opportunity in
education, housing, and employment. Over the past two
decades, there has been significant progress on many
fronts, and an unprecedented number of blacks—
perhaps a third—have now entered the American
middle class.*

*Yet this visible progress has tended to obscure the
fact that a black "underclass" has been left behind.
Living in impoverished rural areas and decaying inner-
city ghettos, this underclass is a powder keg in
America's future. This significant minority of the black
population is trapped in a cycle of unemployment, poor
education, high crime rates, drug abuse, illegitimate
births, and welfare dependency. A new controversy has
developed over the causes of this predicament. Some
analysts claim that the underlying factor is continued
racism and informal discrimination. Others advance a
more novel argument: that while racism may have been
an underlying factor, the plight of the underclass is now
primarily a matter of class, not race. Because they are
concentrated in areas of high unemployment and
limited opportunity, significant numbers of blacks have
come to occupy the lowest rung in the American class
system.*

*In this article, William J. Wilson argues that race is
of declining significance in explaining the plight of the
underclass, and that we must look instead to economic
factors that are perpetuating the underclass from one
generation to the next.*

From *The Wilson Quarterly*, Spring 1984, pp. 88–89. Copyright 1984, by
The Woodrow Wilson International Center for Scholars.

It is no secret that the social problems of urban life in
the United States are, in great measure, associated with
race.

While rising rates of crime, drug addiction, out-of-
wedlock births, female-headed families, and welfare dependency have afflicted American society generally in
recent years, the increases have been most dramatic
among what has become a large and seemingly permanent black underclass inhabiting the cores of the nation's major cities.

And yet, liberal journalists, social scientists, policymakers, and civil-rights leaders have for almost two decades been reluctant to face this fact. Often, analysts of
such issues as violent crime or teenage pregnancy deliberately make no reference to race at all, unless perhaps to emphasize the deleterious consequences of
racial discrimination or the institutionalized inequality
of American society.

Some scholars, in an effort to avoid the appearance
of "blaming the victim," or to protect their work from
charges of racism, simply ignore patterns of behavior
that might be construed as stigmatizing to particular racial minorities.

Such neglect is a relatively recent phenomenon.
Twenty years ago, during the mid-1960s, social scientists
such as Kenneth B. Clark (*Dark Ghetto*, 1965), Daniel
Patrick Moynihan (*The Negro Family*, 1965), and Lee
Rainwater (*Behind Ghetto Walls*, 1970) forthrightly examined the cumulative effects on inner-city blacks of
racial isolation and class subordination. They vividly described aspects of ghetto life that, as Rainwater observed,
"are usually forgotten or ignored in polite discussions."
All of these studies attempted to show the connection
between the economic and social environment into
which many blacks are born and the creation of patterns
of behavior that, in Clark's words, frequently amounted
to a "self-perpetuating pathology."

Why have scholars lately shied away from this line
of research? One reason has to do with the vitriolic attacks by many black leaders against Moynihan upon
publication of his report in 1965—denunciations that

generally focused on the author's unflattering depiction of the black family in the urban ghetto rather than on his proposed remedies or his historical analysis of the black family's special plight. The harsh reception accorded to *The Negro Family* undoubtedly dissuaded many social scientists from following in Moynihan's footsteps.

The "black solidarity" movement was also emerging during the mid-1960s. A new emphasis by young black scholars and intellectuals on the positive aspects of the black experience tended to crowd out older concerns. Indeed, certain forms of ghetto behavior labeled pathological in the studies of Clark et al. were redefined by some during the early 1970s as "functional" because, it was argued, blacks were displaying the ability to survive and in some cases flourish in an economically depressed environment. Scholars such as Andrew Billingsley (*Black Families in White America,* 1968), Joyce Ladner (*Tomorrow's Tomorrow,* 1971), and Robert Hill (*The Strengths of Black Families,* 1971) described the ghetto family as resilient and capable of adapting creatively to an oppressive, racist society.

In the end, the promising efforts of the early 1960s—to distinguish the black community, and to identify the structural problems of the U.S. economy that affected minorities—were cut short by calls for "reparations" or for "black control of institutions serving the black community." In his 1977 book, *Ethnic Chauvinism,* sociologist Orlando Patterson lamented that black ethnicity had become "a form of mystification, diverting attention from the correct kinds of solutions to the terrible economic condition of the group."

Meanwhile, throughout the 1970s, ghetto life across the nation continued to deteriorate. The situation is best seen against the backdrop of the family.

In 1965, when Moynihan pointed with alarm to the relative instability of the black family, one-quarter of all such families were headed by women; 15 years later, the figure was a staggering 42 percent. (By contrast, only 12 percent of white families and 22 percent of Hispanic families in 1980 were maintained by women.) Not surprisingly, the proportion of black children living with both their father and their mother declined from nearly two-thirds in 1970 to fewer than half in 1978.

In the inner city, the trend is more pronounced. For example, of the 27,178 families with children living in Chicago Housing Authority projects in 1980, only 2,982, or 11 percent, were husband-and-wife families.

## Teenage Mothers

These figures are important because even if a woman is employed full-time, she almost always is paid less than a man. If she is not employed, or employed only part-time, and has children to support, the household's situation may be desperate. In 1980, the median income of families headed by black women ($7,425) was only 40 percent of that of black families with both parents present ($18,593). Today, roughly five out of 10 black children under the age of 18 live below the poverty level; the vast majority of these kids have only a mother to come home to.

The rise in the number of female-headed black families reflects, among other things, the increasing incidence of illegitimate births. Only 15 percent of all births to black women in 1959 were out of wedlock; the proportion today is well over one-half. In the cities, the figure is invariably higher: 67 percent in Chicago in 1978, for example. Black women today bear children out of wedlock at a rate nine times that for whites. In 1982, the number of black babies born out of wedlock (328,879) nearly matched the number of illegitimate white babies (337,050). White or black, the women bearing these children are not always mature adults. Almost half of all illegitimate children born to blacks today will have a teenager for a mother.

The effect on the welfare rolls is not hard to imagine. A 1976 study by Kristin Moore and Steven B. Cardwell of Washington's Urban Institute estimated that, nationwide, about 60 percent of the children who are born outside of marriage and are not adopted receive welfare; furthermore, "more than half of all AFDC [Aid to Families with Dependent Children] assistance in 1975 was paid to women who were or had been teenage mothers." A 1979 study by the Department of City Planning in New York found that 75 percent of all children born out of wedlock in that city during the previous 18 years were recipients of AFDC.

## Why No Progress?

I have concentrated on young, female-headed families and out-of-wedlock births among blacks because these indices have become inextricably connected with poverty and welfare dependency, as well as with other forms of social dislocation (including joblessness and crime).

As James Q. Wilson observed in *Thinking About Crime* (1975), these problems are also associated with a "critical mass" of young people, often poorly supervised. When that mass is reached, or is increased suddenly and substantially, "a self-sustaining chain reaction is set off that creates an explosive increase in the amount of crime, addiction, and welfare dependency." The effect is magnified in densely populated ghetto neighborhoods, and further magnified in the massive public housing projects.

Consider Robert Taylor Homes, the largest such project in Chicago. In 1980, almost 20,000 people, all black, were officially registered there, but according to one report "there are an additional 5,000 to 7,000 who are not registered with the Housing Authority." Minors made up 72 percent of the population and the mother alone was present in 90 percent of the families with children. The unemployment rate was estimated at 47 percent in 1980, and some 70 percent of the project's 4,200 official households received AFDC. Although less than one-half of one percent of Chicago's population lived in Robert Taylor Homes, 11 percent of all the city's murders, nine percent of its rapes, and 10 percent of its aggravated assaults were committed in the project in 1980.

Why have the social conditions of the black underclass deteriorated so rapidly?

Racial discrimination is the most frequently invoked explanation, and it is undeniable that discrimination continues to aggravate the social and economic problems of poor blacks. But is discrimination really greater today than it was in 1948, when black unemployment was less than half of what it is now, and when the gap between black and white jobless rates was narrower?

As for the black family, it apparently began to fall apart not before but after the mid-20th century. Until publication in 1976 of Herbert Gutman's *The Black Family in Slavery and Freedom,* most scholars had believed otherwise. "Stimulated by the bitter public and academic controversy over the Moynihan report," Gutman produced data demonstrating that the black family was not significantly disrupted during slavery or even during the early years of the first migration to the urban North, beginning after the turn of the century. The problems of the modern black family, he implied, were a product of modern forces.

Those who cite racial discrimination as the root cause of poverty often fail to make a distinction between the effects of *historic* discrimination (that is, discrimination prior to the mid-20th century) and the effects of *contemporary* discrimination. That is why they find it so hard to explain why the economic position of the black underclass started to worsen soon after Congress enacted, and the White House began to enforce, the most sweeping civil-rights legislation since Reconstruction.

## Making Comparisons

My own view is that historic discrimination is far more important than contemporary discrimination in understanding the plight of the urban underclass; that, in any event, there is more to the story than discrimination (of whichever kind).

Historic discrimination certainly helped to create an impoverished urban black community in the first place. In his recent *A Piece of the Pie: Black and White Immigrants since 1880* (1980), Stanley Lieberson shows how,

in many areas of life, including the labor market, black newcomers from the rural South were far more severely discriminated against in Northern cities than were the new white immigrants from southern, central, and eastern Europe. Skin color was part of the problem, but it was not all of it.

The disadvantage of skin color—the fact that the dominant whites preferred whites over nonwhites—is one that blacks shared with Japanese, Chinese, and others. Yet the experience of the Asians, whose treatment by whites "was of the same violent and savage character in areas where they were concentrated," but who went on to prosper in their adopted land, suggests that skin color per se was not an "insurmountable obstacle." Indeed, Lieberson argues that the greater success enjoyed by Asians may well be explained largely by the different context of their contact with whites. Because changes in immigration policy cut off Asian migration to America in the late 19th century, the Japanese and Chinese populations did not reach large numbers and therefore did not pose as great a threat as did blacks.

Furthermore, the discontinuation of large-scale immigration from Japan and China enabled Chinese and Japanese to solidify networks of ethnic contacts and to occupy particular occupational niches in small, relatively stable communities. For blacks, the situation was different. The 1970 census recorded 22,580,000 blacks in the United States but only 435,000 Chinese and 591,000 Japanese. "Imagine," Lieberson exclaims, "22 million Japanese Americans trying to carve out initial niches through truck farming."

## The Youth Explosion

If different population sizes accounted for a good deal of the difference in the economic success of blacks and Asians, they also helped determine the dissimilar rates of progress of urban blacks and the new *European* arrivals. European immigration was curtailed during the 1920s, but black migration to the urban North continued through the 1960s. With each passing decade, Lieberson writes, there were many more blacks who were recent migrants to the North, whereas the immigrant component of the new Europeans dropped off over time. Eventually, other whites muffled their dislike of the Poles and Italians and Jews and saved their antagonism for blacks. As Lieberson notes, "The presence of blacks made it harder to discriminate against the new Europeans because the alternative was viewed less favorably."

The black migration to New York, Philadelphia, Chicago, and other Northern cities—the continual replenishment of black populations there by poor newcomers—predictably skewed the age profile of the urban black community and kept it relatively young. The number of central-city black youths aged 16–19 increased by almost 75 percent from 1960 to 1969. Young black adults (ages 20–24) increased in number by two-thirds during the same period, three times the increase for young white adults. In the nation's inner cities in 1977, the median age for whites was 30.3 for blacks 23.9. The importance of this jump in the number of young minorities in the ghetto, many of them lacking one or more parent, cannot be overemphasized.

Age correlates with many things. For example, the higher the median age of a group, the higher its income; the lower the median age, the higher the unemployment rate and the higher the crime rate. (More than half of those arrested in 1980 for violent and property crimes in American cities were under 21.) The younger a woman is, the more likely she is to bear a child out of wedlock, head up a new household, and depend on welfare. In short, much of what has gone awry in the ghetto is due in part to the sheer increase in the number of black youths. As James Q. Wilson has argued, an abrupt rise in the proportion of young people in *any* community will have an "exponential effect on the rate of certain social problems."

The population explosion among minority youths occurred at a time when changes in the economy were beginning to pose serious problems for unskilled workers. Urban minorities have been particularly vulnerable to the structural economic changes of the past two decades: the shift from goods-producing to service-providing industries, the increasing polarization of the labor market into low-wage and high-wage sectors, technological innovations, and the relocation of manufacturing industries out of the central cities. During the 1970s, Chicago lost more than 200,000 jobs, mostly in manufacturing, where many inner-city blacks had traditionally found employment. New York City lost 600,000 jobs during the same period, even though the number of white-collar professional, managerial, and clerical jobs increased in Manhattan. Today, as John D. Kasarda has noted, the nation's cities are being transformed into "centers of administration, information exchange, and service provision." Finding work now requires more than a willing spirit and a strong back.

## Beyond Race

Roughly 60 percent of the unemployed blacks in the United States reside within the central cities. Their situation, already more difficult than that of any other major ethnic group in the country, continues to worsen. Not only are there more blacks without jobs every year; many, especially young males, are dropping out of the labor force entirely. The percentage of blacks who were

in the labor force fell from 45.6 in 1960 to 30.8 in 1977 for those aged 16–17 and from 90.4 to 78.2 for those aged 20–24. (During the same period, the proportion of white teenagers in the labor force actually *increased*.)

More and more black youths, including many who are no longer in school, are obtaining no job experience at all. The proportion of black teenage males who have *never* held a job increased from 32.7 to 52.8 percent between 1966 and 1977; for black males under 24, the percentage grew from 9.9 to 23.3. Research shows, not surprisingly, that joblessness during youth has a harmful impact on one's future success in the job market.

There have been recent signs, though not many, that some of the inner city's ills may have begun to abate. For one, black migration to urban areas has been minimal in recent years; many cities have experienced net migration of blacks *to* the suburbs. For the first time in the 20th century, a heavy influx from the countryside no longer swells the ranks of blacks in the cities. Increases in the urban black population during the 1970s, as demographer Philip Hauser has pointed out, were mainly due to births. This means that one of the major obstacles to black advancement in the cities has been removed. Just as the Asian and European immigrants benefited from a cessation of migration, so too should the economic prospects of urban blacks improve now that the great migration from the rural South is over.

Even more significant is the slowing growth in the number of *young* blacks inhabiting the central cities. In metropolitan areas generally, there were six percent fewer blacks aged 13 or under in 1977 than there were in 1970; in the inner city, the figure was 13 percent. As the average age of the urban black community begins to rise, lawlessness, illegitimacy, and unemployment should begin to decline.

Even so, the problems of the urban black underclass will remain crippling for years to come. And I suspect that any significant reduction of joblessness, crime, welfare dependency, single-parent homes, and out-of-wedlock pregnancies would require far more comprehensive social and economic change than Americans have generally deemed appropriate or desirable. It would require a radicalism that neither the Republican nor the Democratic Party has been bold enough to espouse.

The existence of a black underclass, as I have suggested, is due far more to historic discrimination and to broad demographic and economic trends than it is to racial discrimination in the present day. For that reason, the underclass has not benefited significantly from "race specific" antidiscrimination policies, such as affirmative action, that have aided so many trained and educated blacks. If inner-city blacks are to be helped, they will be helped not by policies addressed primarily to inner-city minorities but by policies designed to benefit all of the nation's poor.

I am reminded in this connection of Bayard Rustin's plea during the early 1960s that blacks recognize the importance of *fundamental* economic reform (including a system of national economic planning along with new education, manpower, and public works programs to help achieve full employment) and the need for a broad-based coalition to achieve it. Politicians and civil-rights leaders should, of course, continue to fight for an end to racial discrimination. But they must also recognize that poor minorities are profoundly affected by problems that affect other people in America as well, and that go beyond racial considerations. Unless those problems are addressed, the underclass will remain a reality of urban life.

## QUESTIONS

1. Do you think that the persistence of poverty in the black community is better explained through economic factors or through racism?

2. To what extent would you say that the United States is still a racist society?

3. In some cases, affirmative-action programs give preference in employment to minority-group members. Are such programs justified?

*Howell Raines*

# 27. Struggling for Power and Identity

*When white settlers and the indigenous inhabitants of North America fought a series of bitter conflicts over possession of land and natural resources, the victory went to the side with superior military technology. The vanquished were banished to reserves, relegated to second-class citizenship and wretched material conditions, and absurdly stereotyped (notably in Western movies) as warlike savages who had cruelly and without provocation gone to war, and thus brought retribution upon themselves.*

*In recent years, history has been gradually revised, and most Americans are now aware of the injustices visited on Indians in the past. If anything, there is something of a collective guilt among whites on the issue, a sense that some recompense is due the Indians. As it happens, militant Indian organizations have successfully demanded recompense in many ways—for example, by claiming title to lands illegally seized from them, or by asserting their controversial rights over the rivers that flow through their reserves and the rich mineral resources that lie below them.*

*Inevitably, however, the rising militancy of the Indians threatens to generate new tension between them and the whites, for once again the two groups face the prospect of conflict over access to scarce resources. In this article, Howell Raines examines the changing attitude of the Indians and the potential difficulties that they face as they demand a larger slice of the American pie.*

American Indians gave up beads-and-blanket capitalism on Jan. 31, 1975, in Billings, Mont. That day, at a meeting in a small college planted on a frigid escarpment of the Rockies, a group of tribal leaders got a look at the generous contracts under which American energy companies now do business with oil-rich third-world nations. For the Indians, it was an instant education in the real value of their "worthless" reservations. They learned that, unlike the canny oil merchants of the Middle East, their tribes were still being ripped off with Colonial-era prices for the vast mineral wealth that lies under the feet of this nation's most impoverished minority. Prophetically, the meeting in Billings was entitled "Indian Tribes as Emerging Nations."

In the ensuing years, more and more Indians have come to think of their reservations as tiny sovereign nations within the United States. If a new generation of Indian leaders has its way, they are going to be rich little nations, too. For the 50 million acres of despised and for the most part barren lands pawned off on the Indians in the last century contain about one-third of the American West's strippable coal and half of the nation's uranium, not to mention enough oil to bedazzle the eyes of Texas. At today's prices, the 70 billion tons of coal under Indian land is worth over $1,000 billion, or $1 trillion.

Swiftly, the drive for economic power has become the main thrust of Indian activism throughout the nation—in the Rocky Mountain coal fields, along the salmon rivers of the Northwest and on vast Eastern tracts where, after almost 200 years of silence, Indians stunned and infuriated whites by claiming "aboriginal title." "We are trying to prove," said LaDonna Harris, the Comanche activist whose Americans for Indian Opportunity organized the Billings conference, "that you don't have to be poor to be an Indian."

But development-minded Indians face formidable obstacles, including proposals to take over their energy reserves by abolishing the reservations. Indeed, white sympathy and guilt over the treatment of Indians seem to be fading before a new mood of fiscal austerity. The first Americans are facing a white backlash that, spreading east from Seattle in ever-widening circles of outrage, may be felt all the way from oil-company board rooms to the United States Supreme Court. Last summer's 3,000 mile, cross-country trek to the nation's capital, the Longest Walk, was an attempt to combat this problem, but because of deep and historic divisions in their own ranks, Indians have so far been unable to meet the backlash with an effective, united front.

There is, for instance, the cultural gap between the 650,000 Indians living on or near reservations and the 350,000 urban Indians in the red ghettos of Minneapolis, Chicago, Los Angeles and other cities. Also, the tribal tradition means that many native Americans think of themselves as, say, Kiowas first and Indians second. Within most major tribes, government is so radically democratic that it is virtually impossible to find a native American who expects to see the emergence of a red Martin Luther King Jr. who can speak for Indian America. Beyond that, conservative Indians view with suspicion those tribal leaders who want to rip open Mother Earth. To them, the cancer outbreak among Navajo uranium miners symbolizes the deadly dangers of bringing white commerce to Indian Country.

The term Indian Country first came into the language as a name for the seemingly limitless territories beyond the westernmost white settlements. As used by today's Indians, it refers to both their scattered pockets of land and to a state of mind. What should white Americans think about both the territory and the mentality that is Indian Country? Can even a rough justice be now imposed on the despair-filled history of the nation's oldest social conflict? Does history, in fact, demand a justice that penalizes 200 million people for the good of a minority that has willfully resisted the assimilative process that has brought prosperity to other impoverished minorities? The answers, such as they are, are as diverse as the terrain and people of an Indian Country that stretches from the beige corridors of the Bureau of Indian Affairs in Washington, D.C., to the red grit hills of Arizona and New Mexico.

## Coal-Smoke Signal

In her tarpaper shack on a windy hilltop in Fruitland, N.M., Emma Yazzie dreams of an enchanted ancestral past. But she is living, literally and quite unwillingly, on the ramparts of the Indian future. "I want it to be as though I was living a long time ago," said the 72-year-old Navajo sheepherder, speaking carefully in English, her second language. "It used to be such a beautiful place. We had all kinds of colored grass."

Today, the grass that feeds Emma Yazzie's 19 sheep is uniformly brown. For this, she blames pollution from the nearby Four Corners Power Plant, the huge, coal-fired electrical generator whose plume of smoke is visible for miles across the desert.

That plant towers over Emma Yazzie's tiny farmstead on the northern rim of the 14-million-acre Navajo Reservation. To the west, where the one-room hogans of her relatives once dotted the mesas, lies the 31,000-acre strip mine leased from her tribe to provide the Four Corners plant with cheap Navajo coal. To the south, along the San Juan River where the Yazzie clan once held idyllic summer encampments, the pumps of the generating plant suck at the stream beside which Miss Yazzie was born.

Emma Yazzie has lost much and gained nothing. Gone are the landscapes and pellucid skies she loved. Yet, the pumps bring her no water, and the humming power lines bypass her lightless shack. So, of course, does the money. Utah International Mining Company, a subsidiary of General Electric, pays a royalty of only 15 cents per ton to the Navajo tribe for the coal used at Four Corners. Yet, on today's market, a white landowner would receive a royalty of $1.50 per ton. Utah International and General Electric owe this windfall to the Bureau of Indian Affairs: For years, the B.I.A. negotiated all reservation coal leases for the Indians to assure that the tribal leaders wouldn't make any naive or stupid deals.

But Emma Yazzie and the other American Indians who own 4 perent of the nation's land want to make their own decisions about how their lands are used. "Self-determination" and "sovereignty" are the Indians' new catchwords. Like the black movement that started in the South in the 50's, the Indian movement gained its momentum from Federal court decisions that have upset many whites. In 1975, for example, the courts upheld tribal claims to the northern two-thirds of Maine, and that case signaled Easterners that the "Indian problem" was not restricted to the Far West. Last October, the Maine case was finally settled when the Passamaquoddy and Penobscot tribes gave up their claim to 12.5 million acres in return for a relatively modest payment of $37 million and the right to expand their reservations by 100,000 acres. But the settlement left standing the ruling that Indians have an aboriginal title to lands occupied by whites who never obtained the Congressional approval required by the long-ignored Indian Non-Intercourse Act of 1790.

Comparisons between the black movement and the Indian movement can be pushed too far. Indians lack the numbers and unity of the black minority, and, while blacks sought assimilation into the American mainstream, Indians face the far more complicated question of whether to preserve separate Indian culture. Moreover, the key issue to the blacks was social justice, and, to many Indian leaders, at least, it is economic power. They want to take advantage of the world's new competition for scarce land and dwindling resources. So, Emma Yazzie notwithstanding, the leaders want to use the new leverage gained from the mineral wealth of their reservations as a substitute for the marching feet that carried black demands to national attention.

Emma Yazzie has been educated by history to view all developers, white and Indian alike, with contempt and despair. "They want to stick their noses in the ground like a pig," she says. Clasping rough hands around her chipped turquoise brooch, the old woman gazes toward the plant. "They kill the grass," she continues. "They kill a lot of Navajo, too. That smoke smells bad and it goes into our hearts. The horse is not strong anymore. It's weak. And the sheep come up blind."

## Indian OPEC

Eighty miles from Emma Yazzie and her dreams of the past, lives the man who has offered himself as the hope of the Indian future. He drives a Lincoln Continental, favors pin-striped suits and when indicted for embezzlement in 1977 hired F. Lee Bailey to plead his case, which ended in a hung jury. The most important icon in his office in Window Rock, Ariz., is not a tribal artifact, but a softball-sized lump of coal on a brass stand.

Peter MacDonald, the 50-year-old chairman of the Navajo Nation, is organizer and chairman of the Council of Energy Resources Tribes (CERT), which he described in a letter to President Carter as "the native American OPEC." Mr. MacDonald intends for CERT to serve much the same function for the Indian tribes, whose reservations he views as "dependent, yet sovereign," nations within the United States.

"We used the same trick that John Wayne would use," Mr. MacDonald said of the impulse that led to the founding of CERT. "We circled the wagons. We circled the tribes and said, 'By golly, if you're going to get the coal, you're not going to deal with just the Crow or just with the Navajo or just with the Cheyenne. You've got to deal with the rest of us.'"

The CERT wagons are circled over the richest unexploited fossil fuel and mineral deposits on the continent. Mr. MacDonald created a public-relations crisis for the organization in 1977 when, snubbed in his request for a White House meeting, he announced he had contacted OPEC's Arab oil experts for advice on how to develop the reservations most profitably. Rather quickly, $200,000 and then $2 million in Federal grants showered on CERT—presumably to divert the Indians from striking an alliance with the Arab organization. Despite this Federal largesse, Mr. MacDonald, a Marine veteran of World War II, is still furious about accusations that he was unpatriotic to consult OPEC. "It sounded like I'm a traitor, that CERT tribes are enemies of the United States," he said. "It's all because I'm trying to cling to what little is left to us."

It is simply a matter, noted Mr. MacDonald, an electrical engineer who once worked in missile development for Hughest Aircraft, of Indians learning to play by the white man's rules. After all, the reservation system was structured to confine Indians to land that the Government experts of 100 years ago believed forever worthless. "We have now decided," he said with obvious delight at the irony, "to use the very structure devised by whites for their protection to assert what we describe as Indian self-determination, meaning that this is our reservation, that we have a certain sovereignty and we're going to exercise it."

As defined by CERT, self-determination and sovereignty mean, for one thing, that tribal governments rather than the Bureau of Indian Affairs ought to negotiate energy contracts. The argument heard all over Indian Country is that Indians couldn't possibly do any worse than the B.I.A. The bureau, for instance, neglected to put escalation or termination clauses in leases negotiated when coal was selling for $6 a ton. As a result, the Navajos are saddled with the 15-cents- to 37.5-cents-per-ton royalties even though the retail price of coal has soared to $15 to $20 per ton and standard royalties are up to $1.50 and more. The CERT tribes are, indeed, doing better. For one thing, the tribes are insisting on joint-venture contracts rather than the B.I.A.-approved leases under which the Indians signed over most of their powers as landowners to the mining companies. The Navajo tribal council recently received $6 million in front money in a proposed joint venture with Exxon to develop the uranium deposits on the nation's largest reservation. (Its 14 million acres in Utah, New Mexico and Arizona make the Navajo Nation the equal in size of West Virginia.) Unhappy with the 17.5-cents-per-ton royalty negotiated for them by the B.I.A., the Crow tribe of Montana is suing to overturn strip-mining contracts with Shell and AMAX, and is now shopping for a better deal. Mr. MacDonald and his tribe's Wall Street-trained attorney, George Vlassis of Phoenix, plan to challenge every company that enjoys a cheap lease, incuding the coal suppliers at the Four Corners Power Plant. "The next one on the hit list," Mr. Vlassis says bluntly, "is Utah International."

Mr. MacDonald's critics question whether his government can, and will, use the increased income to give the reservation the self-sufficient, business economy he envisions. With its $200 million a year in Federal subsidies, the reservation has, by tradition, a welfare-state economy in which the tribal government, with 7,000 workers, is the largest employer. Also, in the past few years, a number of other tribal officials have been charged with embezzlement, sparking demonstrations in which dissidents accused the "Mac-Dollar" government of ripping off tribal income. (Mr. MacDonald said his own indictment, in which he was accused of getting about $7,900 by submitting false travel vouchers to an Arizona utility, was part of a conspiracy to discredit him as an Indian spokesman.) . . .

Such controversies aside, Mr. MacDonald and leaders of other tribes may face political obstacles to their plans to use mining income for economic development. So far, only a handful of Indians have benefited personally from the coal boom. For example, the 160 Navajos at a Gulf Oil subsidiary's strip mine near Window Rock make $9 to $12 per hour. But per capita income on the reservation remains only about $1,000 per year—one-seventh of the national average. In many cases, grandparents, parents and children live on dirt floors of one-room hogans with no plumbing and no privacy. And there is always the possibility that these impoverished reservation residents might vote against investment programs for their energy income and demand "per caps"—lump-sum, per capita payments that have a disastrous history of winding up in the pockets of a few white merchants and Indian hustlers.

"In a generation, the resource will be played out and you'll have a few native American sheiks and an impoverished mass," predicted John Redhouse, a Navajo activist who has organized traditionalist Indians to fight a coal-gasification plant proposed for Burnham, N.M., in the Four Corners area of the reservation. The Government and energy companies are simply using CERT, he says, to legitimize their plans to turn the Western reservations into "national-sacrifice areas." He called the plans "spiritual and physical genocide." Even Indians sympathetic to Mr. MacDonald's general goal of economic development fear that his tactics will contribute to the backlash. "My notion is that it's harmful to Indians," says Sam Deloria, the Standing Rock Sioux who heads the American Indian Law Center at the University of New Mexico, "to communicate the idea that Indians are going to get rich off other Americans' heating bills."

. . .

## The Red and The White

If the prospect of unaccustomed prosperity looms before the Western reservations, a familiar despair still lurks in the bars of the red ghetto along East Franklin Avenue in Minneapolis. "The State Alcohol and Drug Commission says 43 to 45 percent of the Indian population are directly involved in alcoholism," says Dennis Hisgun, a 35-year-old Sioux. "And 80 to 85 percent are indirectly involved; that is, they belong to the family of a drinker. I can't prove those figures, but I think they're pretty accurate. We're now seeing our chronic age dropping to the late 20's and early 30's. It used to be in the 40's. So that means alcoholism is epidemic. We have three counselors. We're hardly making a dent."

Mr. Hisgun is social-services director of the Minneapolis Native American Center, and a former alcoholic who has discovered the Catch-22 of many Government programs for Indians. "Indian alcoholism is getting worse. Traditional treatment modalities don't work. Yet we're forced to use them to get funding. For instance, when I sobered up, I did it by turning to a group of Indian people attempting to stay sober. All we had was a house—a place to help one another get up off the ground. They were very unorthodox and that's not acceptable to funding agencies."

The nation's red ghettos are, like the alcohol therapies described by Mr. Hisgun, showcases for Federal policies and programs that don't work. The Eisenhower Administration's termination policy—so named because it sought to end the Government's legal relationship with the tribes—encouraged the relocation of Indians to the cities. Today, an estimated 8,000 to 15,000 Chippewas, Sioux and Oneidas live in what Mr. Hisgun describes as a chronically frustrated community that combines the worst of the reservation and urban worlds.

"One of the detrimental things of reservation life is it's a welfare state—homes, everything, on a hand-out basis—and they bring a lot of that to the city," Mr. Hisgun says. "But I think everybody who comes to the city has a dream—a dream of making it, a dream about improving their lives. But then prejudice slaps them right in the face and they're worse off. Call it culture shock. When your bubble is burst, there's nothing left but to go back home and start dreaming again. They get into that cycle. There's a high mobility between reservations and cities."

In the cities, Indians are not moving in any substantial way into the middle class, and they suffer disproportionately from the social, economic and health problems that go along with urban poverty. Half the Indian families in Minneapolis are on welfare; in more than half there is only one parent. At the American Indian Health Center, one of several agencies funded in response to the burst of activism that spawned the American Indian Movement (AIM) in 1968, the staff considers a patient over 50 "an old Indian." Infant mortality is three times the rate for whites, and doctors see a disproportionately high rate of mental-health problems.

One response to that panoply of problems has been a rebirth of faith in apocalyptic Indian prophecies about the doom of the white world. Clyde Bellecourt, the militant founder and president of AIM, has turned from confrontation politics to running the Heart of the Earth Survival School. It is one of several "bilingual, bicultural" schools around the country that, according to Mr. Bellecourt, are the only institutions that can save Indians from sharing the white man's fate.

"For our children to survive," he says, "they have to be able to hunt, fish, put up a tepee and go into a sacred sweat to purify themselves." A tall man who wears his hair in long braids, he fiddles with a butane cigarette lighter. "When the energy crisis closes the Safeway store, our children will be able to survive."

Such doomsday prophecies have been a powerful force in Indian Country since 1889, when the Ghost Dance cult sprang from a medicine man's vision that predicted the disappearance of the white man and the return of the buffalo. Last July's Longest Walk to Washington was inspired by the vision of a Sioux holy man, Eagle Feather. The protest, which was intended to remind Congress to respect Indian treaty rights, had little impact, and perhaps one reason is that many of its participants, including Mr. Bellecourt, now have less faith in the political process than in the Old Prophecy that the end for the white man must be near.

. . .

## Taos Tug-of-War

The Taos have never been a craft people. They were an agricultural people. Just in the last five years they've started making crafts. "There's no reason not to accommodate the tourist traffic." As he speaks, the proprietor of Tony Reyna's Indian Shop in Taos, N.M., leans on a showcase full of turquoise jewelry and contemplates the paradox of his "traditionalist" tribe adapting itself to the marketplace. "It's a money age we live in," he concludes rather sadly. "Now we don't have time to raise our own crops. It's a deterioration of our heritage and culture. But let's face it. We're not pure."

The cultural tug-of-war he describes has been going on for almost 500 years, and remains the most heated debate in Indian Country. Even in the cities, Indian leaders give lip service to the slogan of the Red Power activists who proclaimed during the 1969 occupation of Alcatraz Island that "we must keep the old ways." But as the Pueblos of Taos and the Reyna family have learned, keeping the old ways is not so easy.

Mr. Reyna's shop—"Indian-owned since 1950"—is halfway between the Anglo town of Taos, where D. H. Lawrence and Mabel Dodge Luhan established a famed artists' colony, and the Pueblo village of Taos, where 1,700 Indians still live in the adobe high-rises that have stood on this red earth for more than 900 years. With one eye on the past and one on the future, Mr. Reyna built his shop in the old way, shaping the adobe bricks by hand. He stocked only genuine Indian goods made in the traditional patterns. As a member of the tribal council, he worked for return to tribal ownership of the sacred Blue Lake, from which, according to the tribe's religion, the Taos people first emerged. Mr. Reyna supported the ordinance passed by the council that prohibited electric lights and modern plumbing within 50 yards of the village walls.

Thus, every morning, as in centuries past, the Taos women fill water buckets at the clear creek that tumbles down to the village from the Blue Lake in the Sangre de Cristo Mountains. Alas, many mornings bring angry exchanges, too, between the villagers and the camera-toting tourists who are at once the village's curse and its indispensable economic resource. At Mrs. Luhan's suggestion, the Taos tribe long ago began charging admission at the village gate. Today, "photographers' fees" and "artists' fees" range from $2 for a still camera to $25 for the right to make a finished painting. The daily flow of out-of-state cars into the Taos Pueblo parking lot—at a $1.50 each—aggravates that deep sense of anger that Indians feel at being regarded as tourist attractions for the master race. Yet, as J. Vince Lujan, the tribal secretary explains, "a bulk of the tribal government is financed from tourist fees."

Equally paradoxical is the village rule against electricity. The ambiance it creates attracts tourists but the inconvenience works against the goal of cultural preservation by creating a village of the elderly. "Most of our young people are giving way to Western culture," says Mr. Lujan. "They're moving out and finding dwellings in the countryside."

The same shift that is taking place in the Taos Pueblo is taking place in Tony Renya's gift shop. Philip Reyna, 19, helps his father in the shop and is extremely knowledgeable about Indian jewelry and art. Philip does not credit the talk that the Indian economic movement will spark a Pan-Indian cultural renaissance among people his age. "It would be nice, but it's not going to happen," he says. "Indians have always been fighting among themselves—the Navajos were always attacking the Pueblos—and it hasn't changed. Then you have urbanized Indians in Los Angeles and elsewhere, and they have a completely different point of view. Their only contact with their culture is the powwows, and that's not real. Look at the costumes—polyester and artificial dyes. No uprising will ever occur because, as times go by, the culture will go down."

Philip himself is studying to become a sound engineer in a rock-and-roll recording studio.

## Fishing Rights, Civil Rights

"We've been called the niggers of Washington," says Ramona Bennett, a small woman with a fine-boned face and a fierce manner. Her outrage fairly fills her office in the Puyallup headquarters at Tacoma, Wash., as she speaks of the court's guaranteeing "our rights that we can't get enforced because our skins are the wrong color."

"I was shot at last November when I was seven months pregnant," says Mrs. Bennett, former chairman of the tribal council, to which she still belongs as an elected member. She suspects it was white fishermen who "tried to blow my head off—our fishermen have been facing this harassment for 90 years."

And as so often happened with the black movement in the South, a gritty and lonely Federal judge stands at the epicenter of this controversy. George H. Boldt, now 74 and in frail health, was nearing the end of his career in 1974 when the fishing-rights case came before him. Then, like his fellow Eisenhower appointees to the Federal bench—Judges Frank Johnson and Richard Rives in Montgomery, Ala., and Elbert Tuttle in Atlanta—Judge Boldt found himself compelled by his reading of the law to render a civil-rights decision that made him a social and political outcast in the eyes of many whites who expected conservative rulings from a judge appointed by a conservative President.

In a rare interview, Judge Boldt recalls how he summoned his law clerk to his office in the Tacoma Post Office building and instructed him "to put on that table every single case from the beginning of the country that pertains in any way to the rights of Indians. The two of us went through every single one—an enormous task. We came down on Sundays."

Treaties enacted with Washington's Indians more than 100 years ago guaranteed the Indians the right to fish "at all usual and accustomed grounds . . . in common with all citizens of the territory." After studying 19th-century legal dictionaries, Judge Boldt decided that the term "in common with" meant, at the time the treaties were drafted, that the Indians had a right to the opportunity to take 50 percent of the fish in an annual salmon catch now worth $200 million a year.

White reaction was intense. When state fishery officials refused to enforce the judge's ruling, he took over regulation of the fishery, Washington's fifth-largest industry, in much the same way that other Federal judges have taken over school districts that refused to desegregate. His critics claimed to have raised $100,000 to finance an impeachment campaign. He was accused of having an Indian mistress. The Interstate Congress for Equal Rights and Responsibilities, which was formed to combat the decision and is now a political presence in 23 states, investigated the "background" of the judge and his wife. Bumper stickers read: "Let's Give 50 Percent of Judge Boldt to the Indians." A bomb was exploded in the Federal building at Tacoma. When Judge Boldt had heart surgery in February, he was confined to an isolated, heavily guarded wing of the hospital.

"I was burned in effigy and they still do that," Judge Boldt says. "The [non-Indian] fishermen have a champion and he maligns me continually and steadily, and he's spurred on by the Attorney General here. He's got to be with the fishermen, don't you see? You can't just be honest in this state and get anywhere because of the enormous amount of condemnation heaped on me since I wrote that decision that day."

. . .

Sid Mills, with the music of the Nisqually roaring in his ears, sings the heart song of Indian Country. Two Seattle writers, Roberto Maestas and Bruce Johansen, have discovered that faith in white greed is so deeply ingrained in Indian culture that when the first white miners swept into the Black Hills gold fields, the Lakota didn't even bother to identify the invaders by skin color. They simply called them *Wasi-chu*—a campfire term that means "greedy person" or "he who takes the fat."

Who is to take the fat of the Indians' land is, of course, the issue to be decided. On some reservations, the militant young and old Indians who weep with nostalgia at the sight of a buffalo are banding together to stop the bulldozers. Others like LaDonna Harris, the wife of former Senator Fred Harris of Oklahoma, believe that, in an energy-hungry nation grumpily facing leaner times, development is inevitable. The only choice before the Indians, she said, is whether they get a good price or simply more beads and blankets.

The Indians who are ready to do business believe money from the earth can provide a defense against a threat to Indian survival that could prove as devastating as the Indian wars that ended in 1890 with the slaying of 200 Sioux at Wounded Knee, S.D. This new threat is the toughening mood of an American majority disenchanted with a doctrine of white guilt. As expressed in lawsuits challenging special treatment for minorities and in the spread of organizations such as the Interstate Congress for Equal Rights and Responsibilities, this view holds that there are no due bills to be collected from history. "I get sick and tired of these tribal leaders saying you took our land away," says Howard Gray, the dapper, 72-year-old Seattle public-relations man who founded the I.C.E.R.R. "There's not a soul living today that had anything to do with the injustice done to the Indians. I say discount the past. We're living in the present."

To Indians who cannot so easily forget the past, those words are as frightening as the rattle and thunder of approaching cavalry.

---

## QUESTIONS

1. It has long been federal policy to treat reservation Indians as a separate group, rather than to encourage their integration into society. Comment on this policy.

2. Indians suffer today because of wrongs perpetrated generations ago. But do whites today still have a moral obligation to make amends for past injustices?

3. What was the stereotype of Indians in Western movies until a few years ago? How and why is this stereotype changing? What is the current stereotype, and how accurate do you think it might be?

*Myra Sadker*
*David Sadker*

# 28. Sexism in the Schoolroom of the '80s

*It is easy to forget that a mere quarter-century ago, American women were generally paid much less than men for doing the identical job, and that women were frequently unable to get credit or sign contracts without the co-signature of a husband or father. But since the 1960s, thanks largely to the campaigns of the women's movement, many overt forms of sexist prejudice and discrimination have now been eliminated. Even so, there is still significant sexual inequality—as reflected, for example, in the relative earnings of men and women, or in the low proportion of women in high-status positions in public and private life.*

*As sociologists point out, the inequality of the sexes is a form of social stratification, similar in many respects to inequalities of class, caste, race, or age. As with other forms of structured social inequality, the relationship between the sexes is not maintained primarily by force. Rather, it rests on the power of cultural traditions and assumptions, which help ensure that people are socialized to accept their respective statuses in society. Subtle sexism thus becomes institutionalized in the society—built into the very fabric of the social structure in ways that easily escape attention.*

*Since the 1960s, reformers have focused a great deal of attention on education—for example, they have urged the elimination of sexist language in textbooks and sexist stereotypes in career counseling. A good deal of progress has been made, but, as Myra and David Sadker point out in this article, more subtle forms of sexism still persist in the schools.*

If a boy calls out in class, he gets teacher attention, especially intellectual attention. If a girl calls out in class, she is told to raise her hand before speaking. Teachers praise boys more than girls, give boys more academic help and are more likely to accept boys' comments during classroom discussions. These are only a few examples of how teachers favor boys. Through this advantage boys increase their chances for better education and possibly higher pay and quicker promotions. Although many believe that classroom sexism disappeared in the early '70s, it hasn't.

Education is not a spectator sport. Numerous researchers, most recently John Goodlad, former dean of education at the University of California at Los Angeles and author of *A Place Called School*, have shown that when students participate in classroom discussion they hold more positive attitudes toward school, and that positive attitudes enhance learning. It is no coincidence that girls are more passive in the classroom and score lower than boys on SAT's.

Most teachers claim that girls participate and are called on in class as often as boys. But a three-year study we recently completed found that this is not true; vocally, boys clearly dominate the classroom. When we showed teachers and administrators a film of a classroom discussion and asked who was talking more, the teachers overwhelmingly said the girls were. But in reality, the boys in the film were outtalking the girls at a ratio of three to one. Even educators who are active in feminist issues were unable to spot the sex bias until they counted and coded who was talking and who was just watching. Stereotypes of garrulous and gossipy women are so strong that teachers fail to see this communications gender gap even when it is right before their eyes.

Field researchers in our study observed students in more than a hundred fourth-, sixth- and eighth-grade classes in four states and the District of Columbia. The teachers and students were male and female, black and white, from urban, suburban and rural communities. Half of the classrooms covered language arts and English—subjects in which girls traditionally have excelled; the other half covered math and science—traditionally male domains.

We found that at all grade levels, in all communities and in all subject areas, boys dominated classroom communication. They participated in more interactions than girls did and their participation became greater as the year went on.

Our research contradicted the traditional assumption that girls dominate classroom discussion in reading while boys are dominant in math. We found that whether the subject was language arts and English or math and science, boys got more than their fair share of teacher attention.

Some critics claim that if teachers talk more to male students, it is simply because boys are more assertive in grabbing their attention—a classic case of the squeaky wheel getting the educational oil. In fact, our research shows that boys are more assertive in the classroom. While girls sit patiently with their hands raised, boys literally grab teacher attention. They are eight times more likely than girls to call out answers. However, male assertiveness is not the whole answer.

Teachers behave differently, depending on whether boys or girls call out answers during discussions. When boys call out comments without raising their hands, teachers accept their answers. However, when girls call out, teachers reprimand this "inappropriate" behavior with messages such as, "In this class we don't shout out answers, we raise our hands." The message is subtle but powerful: Boys should be academically assertive and grab teacher attention; girls should act like ladies and keep quiet.

Teachers in our study revealed an interaction pattern that we called a "mind sex." After calling on a student, they tended to keep calling on students of the same sex. While this pattern applied to both sexes, it was far more pronounced among boys and allowed them more than their fair share of airtime.

It may be that when teachers call on someone, they continue thinking of that sex. Another explanation may be found in the seating patterns of elementary, secondary and even postsecondary classrooms. In approximately half of the classrooms in our study, male and female students sat in separate parts of the room. Sometimes the teacher created this segregation, but more often, the students segregated themselves. A teacher's tendency to interact with same-sex students may be a simple matter of where each sex sits. For example, a teacher calls on a female student, looks around the same area and then continues questioning the students around this girl, all of whom are female. When the teacher refocuses to a section of the classroom where boys are seated, boys receive the series of questions. And because boys are more assertive, the teacher may interact with their section longer.

Girls are often shortchanged in quality as well as in quantity of teacher attention. In 1975 psychologists Lisa Serbin and K. Daniel O'Leary, then at the State University of New York at Stony Brook, studied classroom interaction at the preschool level and found that teachers gave boys more attention, praised them more often and were at least twice as likely to have extended conversations with them. Serbin and O'Leary also found that teachers were twice as likely to give male students detailed instructions on how to do things for themselves. With female students, teachers were more likely to do it for them instead. The result was that boys learned to become independent, girls learned to become dependent.

Instructors at the other end of the educational spectrum also exhibit this same "let me do it for you" behavior toward female students. Constantina Safilios-Rothschild, a sociologist with the Population Council in New York, studied sex desegregation at the Coast Guard Academy and found that the instructors were giving detailed instructions on how to accomplish tasks to male students, but were doing the jobs and operating the equipment for the female students.

Years of experience have shown that the best way to learn something is to do it yourself; classroom chivalry is not only misplaced, it is detrimental. It is also important to give students specific and direct feedback about the quality of their work and answers. During classroom discussion, teachers in our study reacted to boys' answers with dynamic, precise and effective responses, while they often gave girls bland and diffuse reactions.

Teachers' reactions were classified in four categories: praise ("Good answer"); criticism ("That answer is wrong"); help and remediation ("Try again—but check your long division"); or acceptance without any evaluation or assistance ("OK." "Uh huh").

Despite caricatures of school as a harsh and punitive place, fewer than 5 percent of the teachers' reactions were criticisms, even of the mildest sort. But praise didn't happen often either; it made up slightly more than 10 percent of teachers' reactions. More than 50 percent of teachers' responses fell into the "OK" category.

Teachers distributed these four reactions differently among boys than among girls. Here are some of the typical patterns.

Teacher: "What's the capital of Maryland? Joel?"
Joel: "Baltimore."
Teacher: "What's the largest city in Maryland, Joel?"
Joel: "Baltimore."
Teacher: "That's good. But Baltimore isn't the capital. The capital is also the location of the U.S. Naval Academy. Joel, do you want to try again?"
Joel: "Annapolis."

Teacher: "Excellent. Anne, what's the capital of Maine?"

Anne: "Portland."

Teacher: "Judy, do you want to try?"

Judy: "Augusta."

Teacher: "OK."

In this snapshot of a classroom discussion, Joel was told when his answer was wrong (criticism); was helped to discover the correct answer (remediation); and was praised when he offered the correct response. When Anne was wrong, the teacher, rather than staying with her, moved to Judy, who received only simple acceptance for her correct answer. Joel received the more specific teacher reaction and benefited from a longer, more precise and intense educational interaction.

Too often, girls remain in the dark about the quality of their answers. Teachers rarely tell them if their answers are excellent, need to be improved or are just plain wrong. Unfortunately, acceptance, the imprecise response packing the least educational punch, gets the most equitable sex distribution in classrooms. Active students receiving precise feedback are more likely to achieve academically. And they are more likely to be boys. Consider the following:

Although girls start school ahead of boys in reading and basic computation, by the time they graduate from high school, boys have higher SAT scores in both areas.

By high school, some girls become less committed to careers, although their grades and achievement-test scores may be as good as boys'. Many girls' interests turn to marriage or stereotypically female jobs. Part of the reason may be that some women feel that men disapprove of their using their intelligence.

Girls are less likely to take math and science courses and to participate in special or gifted programs in these subjects, even if they have a talent for them. They are also more likely to believe that they are incapable of pursuing math and science in college and to avoid the subjects.

Girls are more likely to attribute failure to internal factors, such as ability, rather than to external factors, such as luck.

The sexist communication game is played at work, as well as at school. As reported in numerous studies it goes like this:

Men speak more often and frequently interrupt women.

Listeners recall more from male speakers than from female speakers, even when both use a similar speaking style and cover identical content.

Women participate less actively in conversation. They do more smiling and gazing; they are more often the passive bystanders in professional and social conversations among peers.

Women often transform declarative statements into tentative comments. This is accomplished by using qualifers ("kind of" or "I guess") and by adding tag questions ("This is a good movie, isn't it?"). These tentative patterns weaken impact and signal a lack of power and influence.

Sexist treatment in the classroom encourages formation of patterns such as these, which give men more dominance and power than women in the working world. But there is a light at the end of the educational tunnel. Classroom biases are not etched in stone, and training can eliminate these patterns. Sixty teachers in our study received four days of training to establish equity in classroom interactions. These trained teachers succeeded in eliminating classroom bias. Although our training focused on equality, it improved overall teaching effectiveness as well. Classes taught by these trained teachers had a higher level of intellectual discussion and contained more effective and precise teacher responses for all students.

There is an urgent need to remove sexism from the classroom and give women the same educational encouragement and support that men receive. When women are treated equally in the classroom, they will be more likely to achieve equality in the workplace.

---

## QUESTIONS

1. Do the interaction patterns described in the article occur in other social settings as well? How do you think they shape the content of gender roles?

2. Do you think that men are made uncomfortable by intelligent women? Do the men and women in your class have similar opinions on this question?

3. What are the similarities and differences between sexual and other forms of social stratification?

*Elizabeth W. Fernea*
*Robert A. Fernea*

# 29. A Look Behind the Veil

*Because men are the dominant sex in all societies, it is they who basically determine what the ideal woman should look like, how she should behave, and how she should dress. In some societies, notably some African tribes, the ideal woman is fat, so many women overeat; in others, notably the contemporary United States, the ideal woman is slim, so many women diet. Male expectations have similarly shaped women's social behavior. A century ago, for example, women in polite society would withdraw from men's company after dinner, to allow the men to discuss "serious" matters alone; and earlier in this century, women were not expected to want a college education or a vote. In contrast, women have never had quite the same prerogative over the appearance, dress, and behavior of men.*

*The most striking contemporary examples of women's apparent submission to the wishes of men probably occur in fundamentalist Islamic societies, such as Saudi Arabia and Iran. Westerners find the status of women in these societies perplexing and disturbing. Among many other restrictions, these women are barred from visible participation in public life. This means not only that they cannot hold high political or economic office, but even that they may be prohibited from driving cars in public, working in the same office as men, or mixing with males socially in such contexts as college cafeterias. Perhaps most strikingly, women typically wear a veil in public, so that their faces as well as their bodies are permanently concealed from the view of anyone except members and guests of their households.*

*In this article, Elizabeth and Robert Fernea examine the practice of veiling in Islamic societies and its meaning for the men and women concerned.*

What objects do we notice in societies other than our own? Ishi, the last of a "lost" tribe of North American Indians who stumbled into 20th Century California in 1911, is reported to have said that the truly interesting objects in the white man's culture were pockets and matches. Rifa'ah Tahtawi, one of the first young Eygptians to be sent to Europe to study in 1826, wrote an account of French society in which he noted that Parisians used many unusual articles of dress, among them something called a belt. Women wore belts, he said, apparently to keep their bosoms erect, and to show off the slimness of their waists and the fullness of their hips. Europeans are still fascinated by the Stetson hats worn by American cowboys; an elderly Dutch lady of our acquaintance recently carried six enormous Stetsons back to The Hague as presents for the male members of her family.

Many objects signify values in society and become charged with meaning, a meaning that may be different for members of the society and for observers of that society. The veil is one object used in Middle Eastern societies that stirs strong emotions in the West. "The feminine veil has become a symbol: that of the slavery of one portion of humanity," wrote French ethnologist Germaine Tillion in 1966. A hundred years earlier, Sir Richard Burton, British traveler, explorer, and translator of the *Arabian Nights*, recorded a different view. "Europeans inveigh against this article [the face veil] ... for its hideousness and jealous concealment of charms made to be admired," he wrote in 1855. "It is, on the contrary, the most coquettish article of woman's attire ... it conceals coarse skins, fleshy noses, wide mouths and vanishing chins, whilst it sets off to best advantage what in these lands is most lustrous and liquid—the eye. Who has not remarked this at a masquerade ball?"

In the present generation, the veil and purdah, or seclusion, have become a focus of attention for Western writers, both popular and academic, who take a measure of Burton's irony and Tillion's anger to equate modernization of the Middle East with the discarding of the veil. "Iranian women return to veil in a resurgence of spirituality," headlines one newspaper; another writes, "Iran's 16 million women have come a long way since their floor-length cotton veil officially was abolished in 1935." The thousands of words written about the appearance and disappearance of the veil and of purdah do little to help us understand the Middle East or the cultures that grew out of the same Judeo-Christian roots as our own. The veil and the all-enveloping garments that inevitably accompany it (the *milayah* in Eygpt, the *abbayah* in Iraq, the *chadoor* in Iran, the *yashmak* in Turkey, the *burga'* in Afghanistan, and the *djellabah* and the *haik* in North Africa) are only the outward manifestations of a cultural pattern and idea that is rooted deep in Mediterranean society.

"Purdah" is a Persian word meaning curtain or barrier. The Arabic word for veiling and secluding comes from the root *hajaba*. A *hijab* is an amulet worn to keep away the evil eye; it also means a diaphragm used to prevent conception. The gatekeeper or doorkeeper who guards the entrance to a government minister's office is a *hajib*, and in casual conversation a person might say, "I want to be more informal with my friend so-and-so, but she always puts a *hijab* (barrier) between us."

In Islam, the Koranic verse that sanctions the barrier between men and women is called the Sura of the *hijab* (curtain): "Prophet, enjoin your wives, your daughters and the wives of true believers to draw their veils close round them. That is more proper, so that they may be recognized and not molested. Allah is forgiving and merciful."

Certainly seclusion and some forms of veiling had been practiced before the time of Muhammad, at least among the upper classes, but it was his followers who apparently felt that his women should be placed in a special category. According to history, the *hijab* was established after a number of occasions on which Muhammad's wives were insulted by people who were coming to the mosque in search of the prophet. When chided for their behavior, they said they had mistaken Muhammad's wives for slaves. The *hijab* was established, and in the words of the historian Nabia Abbott, "Muhammad's women found themselves, on the one hand, deprived of personal liberty, and on the other hand, raised to a position of honor and dignity."

The veil bears many messages and tells us many things about men and women in Middle Eastern society; but as an object in and of itself it is far less important to members of the society than the values it represents. Nouha al Hejailan, wife of the Saudi Arabian ambassador to London, told Sally Quinn of *The Washington Post*, "If I wanted to take it all off (her *abbayah* and veil), I would

have long ago. It wouldn't mean as much to me as it does to you." Early Middle Eastern feminists felt differently. Huda Sh'arawi, an early Eygptian activist who formed the first Women's Union, made a dramatic gesture of removing her veil in public to demonstrate her dislike of society's attitudes toward women and her defiance of the system. But Basima Bezirgan, a contemporary Iraqi feminist, says, "Compared to the real issues that are involved between men and women in the Middle East today, the veil is unimportant." A Moroccan linguist who buys her clothes in Paris laughs when asked about the veil. "My mother wears a *djellabah* and a veil. I have never worn them. But so what? I still cannot get divorced as easily as a man, and I am still a member of my family group and responsible to them for everything I do. What is the veil? A piece of cloth."

"The seclusion of women has many purposes," states Egyptian anthropologist Nadia Abu Zahra. "It expresses men's status, power, wealth, and manliness. It also helps preserve men's image of virility and masculinity, but men do not admit this; on the contrary they claim that one of the purposes of the veil is to guard women's honor." The veil and purdah are symbols of restriction, to men as well as to women. A respectable woman wearing a veil on a public street is signaling, "Hands off. Don't touch me or you'll be sorry." Cowboy Jim Sayre of Deadwood, South Dakota, says, "If you deform a cowboy's hat, he'll likely deform you." In the same way, a man who approaches a veiled woman is asking for trouble; not only the woman but also her family is shamed, and serious problems may result. "It is clear," says Egyptian anthropologist Ahmed Abou Zeid, "that honor and shame which are usually attributed to a certain individual or a certain kinship group have in fact a bearing on the total social structure, since most acts involving honor or shame are likely to affect the existing social equilibrium."

Veiling and seclusion almost always can be related to the maintenance of social status. Historically, only the very rich could afford to seclude their women, and the extreme example of this practice was found among the sultans of prerevolutionary Turkey. Stories of these secluded women, kept in harems and guarded by eunuchs, formed the basis for much of the Western folklore concerning the nature of male-female relationships in Middle Eastern society. The stereotype is of course contradictory; Western writers have never found it necessary to reconcile the erotic fantasies of the seragiio with the sexual puritanism attributed to the same society.

Poor men could not always afford to seclude or veil their women, because the women were needed as productive members of the family economic unit, to work in the fields and in cottage industries. Delta village women in Egypt have never been veiled, nor have the Berber women of North Africa. But this lack of veiling placed poor women in ambiguous situations in relation to strange men.

"In the village, no one veils, because everyone is considered a member of the same large family," explained Aisha bint Mohammed, a working-class wife of Marrakech. "But in the city, veiling is *sunnah*, required by our religion." Veiling is generally found in towns and cities, among all classes, where families feel that it is necessary to distinguish themselves from other strangers in the city.

Veiling and purdah not only indicate status and wealth, they also have some religious sanction and protect women from the world outside the home. Purdah delincates private space, distinguishes between the public and private sectors of society, as does the traditional architecture of the area. Older Middle Eastern houses do not have picture windows facing the street, nor walks leading invitingly to front doors. Family life is hidden from strangers; behind blank walls may lie courtyards and gardens, refuges from the heat, the cold, the bustle of the outside world, the world of non-kin that is not to be trusted. Outsiders are pointedly excluded.

Even within the household, among her close relatives, a traditional Muslim woman veils before those kinsmen whom she could legally marry. If her maternal or paternal male cousins, her brothers-in-law, or sons-in-law come to call, she covers her head, or perhaps her whole face. To do otherwise would be shameless.

The veil does more than protect its wearers from known and unknown intruders; it can also be used to conceal identity. Behind the anonymity of the veil, women can go about a city unrecognized and uncriticized. Nadia Abu Zahra reports anecdotes of men donning women's veils in order to visit their lovers undetected; women may do the same. The veil is such an effective disguise that Nouri Al-Said, the late prime minister of Iraq, attempted to escape death by wearing the *abbayah* and veil of a woman; only his shoes gave him away.

Political dissidents in many countries have used the veil for their own ends. The women who marched, veiled, through Cairo during the Nationalist demonstrations against the British after World War I were counting on the strength of Western respect for the veil to protect them against British gunfire. At first they were right. Algerian women also used the protection of the veil to carry bombs through French army checkpoints during the Algerian revolution. But when the French discovered the ruse, Algerian women discarded the veil and dressed like Europeans to move about freely.

The multiple meanings and uses of purdah and the veil do not explain how the pattern came to be so deeply embedded in Mediterranean society. Its origins lie somewhere in the basic Muslim attitudes about men's roles and women's roles. Women, according to Fatima Mernissi, a Moroccan sociologist, are seen by men in Islamic societies as in need of protection because they are unable to control their sexuality, are tempting to men, and hence are a danger to the social order. In other words, they need to be restrained and controlled so that society may function in an orderly way.

The notion that women present a danger to the social order is scarcely limited to Muslim society. Anthropologist Julian Pitt-Rivers has pointed out that the supervision and seclusion of women is also to be found in Christian Europe, even though veiling was not usually practiced there. "The idea that women not subjected to male authority are a danger is a fundamental one in the writings of the moralists from the Archpriest of Talavera to Padre Haro, and it is echoed in the modern Andalusian *pueblo*. It is bound up with the fear of ungoverned female sexuality which had been an integral element of European folklore ever since prudent Odysseus lashed himself to the mast to escape the sirens."

Pitt-Rivers is writing about Mediterranean society, which, like all Middle Eastern societies, is greatly concerned with honor and shame rather than with individual guilt. The honor of the Middle Eastern extended family, its ancestors and its descendants, is the highest social value. The misdeeds of the grandparents are indeed visited on the children. Men and women always remain members of their natal families. Marriage is a legal contract but a fragile one that is often broken; the ties between brother and sister, mother and child, father and child are lifelong and enduring. The larger family is the group to which the individual belongs and to which the individual owes responsibility in exchange for the social and economic security that the family group provides. It is the group, not the individual, that is socially shamed or socially honored.

Male honor and female honor are both involved in the honor of the family, but each is expressed differently. The honor of a man, *sharaf*, is a public matter, involving bravery, hospitality, piety. It may be lost, but it may also be regained. The honor of a woman, *'ard*, is a private matter involving only one thing, her sexual chastity. Once lost, it cannot be regained. If the loss of female honor remains only privately known, a rebuke—and perhaps a reveiling—may be all that takes place. But if the loss of female honor becomes public knowledge, the other members of the family may feel bound to cleanse the family name. In extreme cases, the cleansing may require the death of the offending female member. Although such killings are now criminal offenses in the

Middle East, suspended sentences are often given, and the newspapers in Cairo and Baghdad frequently carry sad stories of runaway sisters "gone bad" in the city and revenge taken upon them in the name of family honor by their brothers or cousins.

This emphasis on female chastity, many say, originated in the patrilineal society's concern with the paternity of the child and the inheritance that follows the male line. How does a man know that the child in his wife's womb is his own, and not that of another man? Obviously he cannot know unless his wife is a virgin at marriage. From this consideration may have developed the protective institutions called variously purdah, seclusion, or veiling.

Middle Eastern women also look upon seclusion as practical protection. In the Iraqi village where we lived from 1956 to 1958, one of us (Elizabeth) wore the *abbayah* and found that it provided a great sense of protection from prying eyes, dust, heat, flies. Parisian ladies visiting Istanbul in the 16th Century were so impressed by the ability of the all-enveloping garment to keep dresses clean of mud and manure and to keep women from being attacked by importuning men that they tried to introduce it into French fashion.

Perhaps of greater importance for many women reared in traditional cultures is the degree to which their sense of personal identity is tied to the use of the veil. Many women have told us that they felt self-conscious, vulnerable, and even naked when they first walked on a public street without the veil and *abbayah*—as if they were making a display of themselves.

The resurgence of the veil in countries like Morocco, Libya, and Algeria, which have recently established their independence from colonial dominance, is seen by some Middle Eastern and Western scholars as an attempt by men to reassert their Muslim identity and to reestablish their roles as heads of families. The presence of the veil is a sign that the males of the household are once more able to assume the responsibilities that were disturbed or unsurped by foreign colonial powers.

But a veiled woman is seldom seen in Egypt or in many parts of Lebanon, Syria, Iran, Tunisia, Turkey, or the Sudan. And as respectable housewives have abandoned the veil, in some of these Middle Eastern countries prostitutes have put it on. They indicate their availability by manipulating the veil in flirtatious ways, but as Burton pointed out more than a century ago, prostitutes are not the first to discover the veil's seductiveness. Like women's garments in the West, the veil can be sturdy, utilitarian, and forbidding—or it can be filmy and decorative, hinting at the charms beneath it.

The veil is the outward sign of a complex reality. Observers are often deceived by the absence of that sign, and fail to see that in most Middle Eastern societies (and

in many parts of Europe) basic attitudes are unchanged. Women who have taken off the veil continue to play the old roles within the family, and their chastity remains crucial. A woman's behavior is still the key to the honor and the reputation of her family.

In Middle Eastern societies, feminine and masculine continue to be strong polarities of identification. This is in marked contrast to Western society, where for more than a generation social critics have been striving to blur distinctions in dress, in status, and in type of labor. Almost all Middle Eastern reformers (most of whom are middle and upper class) are still arguing from the assumption of a fundamental difference between men and women. They do not demand an end to the veil (which is passing out of use anyway) but an end to the old principles, which the veil symbolizes, that govern patrilineal society. Middle Eastern reformers are calling for equal access to divorce, child custody, and inheritance; equal opportunities for education and employment; abolition of female circumcision and "crimes of honor"; and a law regulating the age of marriage.

An English woman film director, after several months in Morocco, said in an interview, "This business about the veil is nonsense. We all have our veils, between ourselves and other people. That's not what the Middle East is about. The question is what veils are used for, and by whom." The veil triggers Western reactions simply because it is the dramatic, visible sign of vexing questions, questions that are still being debated, problems that have still not been solved, in the Middle East or in Western societies.

Given the biological differences between men and women, how are the sexes to be treated equitably? Men and women are supposed to share the labor of society and yet provide for the reproduction and nurture of the next generation. If male fear and awe of woman's sexuality provokes them to control and seclude women, can they be assuaged? Rebecca West said long ago that "the difference between men and women is the rock on which civilization will split before it can reach any goal that could justify its expenditure of effort." Until human beings come to terms with this basic issue, purdah and the veil, in some form, will continue to exist in both the East and the West.

## QUESTIONS

1. What is the meaning of the veil in fundamentalist Islamic societies? Would you say the practice of veiling enhances or diminishes the status of women?

2. In the United States, are there any links between women's dress and the relationships of the sexes?

3. Why do you think that women in fundamentalist

Islamic societies have not developed strong women's movements that demand economic and political equality with men?

---

## REFERENCES

**Abou-Zeid, Ahmed,** "Honor and Shame among the Bedouins of Egypt," *Honor and Shame: The Values of Mediterranean Society,* ed. by J. G. Peristiany, University of Chicago Press, 1966.

**Fernea, Elizabeth Warnock,** *Guests of the Sheik: An Ethnology of an Iraqi Village,* Doubleday/Anchor, 1969.

**Fernea, Elizabeth Warnock,** and **Basima Qattan Bezirgan,** eds., *Middle Eastern Muslim Women Speak,* University of Texas Press, 1977.

**Levy, Reuben,** *The Social Structure of Islam,* Cambridge University Press, 1965.

**Mernissi, Fatima,** *Beyond the Veil: Male-Female Dynamics in a Modern Muslim Society,* Schenkman Publishing Company, 1975.

**Pitt-Rivers, Julian,** *The Fate of Schechem: or The Politics of Sex,* Cambridge University Press, 1977.

*Arnold Arluke*
*Jack Levin*

# 30. Another Stereotype: Old Age as a Second Childhood

*Throughout much of this century, the elderly (those aged sixty-five or over) have had a particularly low status in American society. In recent decades this situation has begun to change. For example, the poverty rate among the aged has declined from 35 percent at the end of the 1950s to about 12 percent today. Even so, the elderly still tend to be excluded by informal prejudice from much of American life, for their juniors are apt to downplay their abilities and potential contributions.*

*A recurrent feature of prejudiced thought is the use of a stereotype—a rigid mental image that summarizes whatever is believed to be typical about a group. If we use a stereotype about another race, social class, or age group, we assume that their members all share the same basic characteristics; we thus ignore people's individuality as human beings. Many stereotyped views of the aged abound—that they are infirm, senile, sexless, conservative, bedridden, and the like. Actually, these images are particularly unfair, because as people grow older they become not more similar but actually more unalike in their experiences, personalities, and abilities.*

*In this article, Arnold Arluke and Jack Levin point out that the elderly are often assumed to share personality characteristics with another age stratum that has low social status—children.*

From *Aging*, August 1984, pp. 7-11. U.S. Department of Health, Education & Welfare.

Stereotypes are more than privately held "pictures in our heads." They are more often culturally shared and institutionalized negative images which are used to justify unequal treatment, or discrimination, directed against minority groups, ranging from perpetrating petty indignities in everyday life to slavery and genocide.

One common and particularly damaging stereotype, "infantilization," reduces minority group members to the status of children, ranging from infants to adolescents, who lack moral, intellectual, or physical maturity. According to this image, they are typically depicted as "irresponsible," "impulsive," "fun-loving," and "immature." In sum, they are seen as dependent on the "more mature" dominant group for guidance to accomplish the tasks to which they are assigned or even to survive.

The antebellum South provides an appropriate example. The "Little Black Sambo" image was extensively applied to sell the ideology of a "white man's burden," whereby slaves would actually perish if denied the paternalistic "protection" of their masters who administered corporal punishment and withheld rewards to assure that tasks were accomplished. To this day, the epithet "boy" remains as a vestige of the infantilization of the slave (Blassingame, 1972). In the same manner, women before the liberation movement of the 1960's were often called "baby," "girl," "honey," and "sweety." Their fashions were made to reflect the fashions of children, frequently imitating the clothing worn by infants or teenages of a previous generation (Lurie, 1982).

Similarly, many stereotypes currently portray old age as a time of second childhood. This dim view of the elderly suggests that they are losing, or have lost, the very things a growing child gains. It implies a backward movment to earlier developmental stages, with no recognition of the lifetime of experience that unquestionably separates the elderly from children (Gresham, 1973).

The image of old people as childlike has been with us for a long time. Tuckman and Lorge (1953) asked graduate students in psychology to indicate their agreement or disagreement with a number of statements about old people. Despite the fact that the students were well acquainted with psychology and enrolled in a course involving the aging process, there was a high level of agreement that old people are unproductive, have to go to bed early, need a nap every day, are in the "happiest" period of their lives, cannot manage their own affairs, and are in their second childhood.

More recent research indicates that stereotyping continues to be an integral part of public images of the aged, and that one of the major stereotypes still perpetuates the second childhood image. McTavish (1971) found considerable acceptance for an image of old people that is distinctly reminiscent of the view of toddlers during the stage known as "the terrible two's." Many of his subjects felt that old people are likely to be annoying, obstinate, and unreasonable. In 1975, the National Council on the Aging reported the results of a survey of 4,254 adult Americans (Harris, 1975). Old people were generally thought of as useless and inactive by participants in the survey. They viewed the elderly as spending most of their time watching television or "doing nothing," in the true spirit of directionless adolescence.

## Viewing the Old as Childlike

The ubiquitousness of the "second childhood" stereotype becomes apparent when we examine its common forms.

First, old people are given the personality and moods of children. It is common, for example, in prescription drug ads to describe senility in terms normally associated with children. An ad for a tranquilizer "for the agitated geriatric" shows an elderly man angrily waving his fist. "TANTRUMS" is printed large across the page. Other tranquilizer ads use terms such as "nuisance," "disruptive," and "obstreperous" to describe the actions of elders. Even in a recent children's book, which was written to acquaint children with old age, the elderly woman who is explaining to a young girl what it is like to be old describes herself as sometimes "cranky," a word usually reserved for children. Television shows and movies characterize the personality of older people as childlike whether it is "Mother Jefferson's" cantankerousness, the silliness of Johnny Carson's "Aunt Blabby," or the impulsiveness and recklessness of Ruth Gordon in the film *Harold and Maude.*

Second, old people are given the dress and appearance of children. On the cover of one birthday card is a blackboard with "You're only young once!" chalked on it along with various doodles. Inside, an overweight, unshaven elderly man smoking a cigar is wearing a summer camp tee shirt, shorts, sneakers and cap and is playing with a yo-yo and a baseball bat. Above his grinning face the card says "Happy Birthday Playboy." In addition to its other connotations, the card suggests that when you get old, you are at liberty to play like a child again. One of the worst examples of attributing childlike qualities to the elderly is the appearance of an older man—dressed in pajamas and a birthday hat and blowing a noisemaker—in an advertisement for a "geriatric highchair." On the chair's tray is a birthday cake.

Third, old people are given the physical problems of children. One ad for catheters, which appears in a geriatric nursing journal, shows the forearms and hands of a baby as its model instead of an elder. A prescription drug ad for a stool-softener features a smiling bifocaled older woman. The text reads: "Minnie moved her bowels today. The day started right for Minnie. That young doctor feller gave her a stool softener to take last night. And it worked! . . . Minnie figures she's got the smartest doctor in town." It is not too farfetched to imagine that Minnie's smile not only expresses her physical relief but also her pride at being told she moved her bowels.

Fourth, old people are given parties in the spirit of children's parties. In a suburban smalltown newspaper, a recent article reported that the patients at a local nursing home "held their very own Christmas party." The article went on to indicate that patients "planned the party, made the invitations, decorated the cookies made by the chef, and took part in the entertainment, which included a group singing of Christmas Carols." The article thanked a local drugstore for supplying "Santa's gifts." The intentions were admirable, but the message rang loud and clear: Old people are like big children.

Posters in a popular chain of fast-food restaurants urge customers to "Have a Senior Birthday Party." For the "birthday kid" who is "young at heart," the fast food chain offers to provide the cake, hats, and party favors. Also consider a telephone company ad for custom phones which can be given as gifts to "celebrate any occasion." One such occasion is "Gertrude's" retirement party, complete with colorful ribbons and balloons. In honor of her retirement, Gertrude is shown receiving her own Snoopy phone from her co-workers. A similar ad shows an elder receiving a Mickey Mouse phone at a party.

Fifth, old people are encouraged to pursue the activities of children. In an article called "The Fun Life for Young and Old," a major city newspaper provided "a guide to August activities for senior citizens and children." Pictures were shown of a puppet show and a magic act. Even the "Kiddies' Menu" of a popular Massachusetts ice cream parlor portrays an older man walking hand-in-hand with a young boy. As clearly stated on the face of the menu, "for all kids under 10 and over 65," the bill of fare consists of a "hot doggie," "kiddie burger," and "peanut butter and jelly samwhich."

Advice books for the elderly often treat them as children by advising them to reduce the work-related activities associated with adulthood (Arluke et al., 1984). Programs in nursing homes and hospitals intended to make life more interesting for elderly patients also become infantilizing at times (Levin et al., 1983). One handbook of activities and recreational programs for nursing homes recommends discussing such topics as "growing things," "boys," "sunshine," "stones," and "favorite story."

Sixth, old people are given the playthings of children. A department store ad in *TV Guide* shows an elderly man riding a child's three wheeler. The caption reads: "Wish they had Hot Cycles when I was a kid . . . Yep, kids sure are lucky today. Hey, maybe when no one's around . . ."

A prescription drug used to treat symptoms associated with organic brain syndrome claims in an ad that it "usually leaves the disturbed elderly patient in the nursing home more alert, more responsive." In the ad, the photograph of an elderly woman shows her smiling limply and holding a large red and white checked cloth flower. Above her is the caption: "I made a flower today." A similar arts-and-crafts portrayal of the aged appears in an ad for a drug used to improve circulation. Three elders who are "deficient in peripheral circulation" but "proficient in the 'home'" are shown hard at work making ceramics—which is evidently considered to be a higher level activity in the nursing home. A major newspaper recently ran an article entitled "Latest Trends from Toyland," in which the reporter suggests that dolls can be a "companion to the elderly as they are to children."

## Implications

"Infantilization" justifies the paternalistic treatment of minority group members with the consequence that they may be "kept in their place" as dependent inferiors. Forms of discrimination supported by infantilization include slavery, forcing women to stay at home and various forms of institutionalization.

Casting old people as children has detrimental effects on old and young alike. The "second childhood" stereotype tends to make young people feel distant from their elders. Having just graduated from childhood, what adolescent wants to endure it again by associating with the old? The stereotype may well also encourage gerontophobia, the neurotic fear of old age. How many adults want to be thought of one day as a six-year-old who isn't toilet trained?

For old people, the second-childhood stereotype creates a self-fulfilling prophecy. Many elderly people come to accept the second-childhood stereotype and play the role with enthusiasm. But is that because they fail to see any alternative? Our society has traditionally offered certain rewards to those elderly citizens who are willing to "stay in their place." Riding on a special bus for senior citizens, or dancing with other seniors to the tune of "Yankee Doodle," may isolate elderly people. But it may be preferable to watching re-runs of "Marcus Welby."

Acting like children has three negative consequences for old people. First, such behavior lowers their social status because their individual responsibility has been diminished, while their dependency has increased. Secondly, the perception of infantile behavior in the elderly may allow certain things to be done to them that would otherwise not be considered: the prescription of psychoactive medications, institutionalization, and declaration of legal incompetency. Thirdly, infantilization robs the "gray power" movement of adults who might otherwise work for political change and social betterment.

Not all old people buy the second-childhood stereotype. A large number of elderly Americans are thoroughly offended by infantilization and seek to avoid the consequences of the stereotype. For many, this means making efforts to "pass" for middle-aged by dyeing hair, lying about their age, and using youth-oriented cosmetics. A positive form of avoidance is reengagement, whereby old people seek to become either re-employed or remarried after the loss of a job or spouse.

On the damaging side, an unknown number of cases of apparent senility may actually represent a refusal to accept the second-childhood syndrome. Rather than comply, some elders may retreat into a more comfortable, more secure psychological state which ironically has the appearance of infantile behavior. So, for example, we might see lack of sexual interest, giddiness, forgetfulness, inability to maintain a stable relationship, and lack of control over bodily functions.

## A Warning

In contemporary America, stereotyped images of the elderly may one day include less emphasis on infantilization and more emphasis on dehumanization. There is a tendency to view some aged people as mere "vegetables"—totally beyond the age of productivity and usefulness. They are viewed as no longer alive in the sense that we understand what it means to be human and therefore not worthy of the medical and social services available to those who are younger—such as expensive dialysis or lengthy rehabiliation for fractures, stroke, and other problems.

Another aspect of this dehumanization of the elderly may be "to color them all gray" and see them as a group that presents a threat. In periods of economic retrenchment, a large and growing elderly population may to an increasing extent be regarded as a major threat to the economic well-being of younger Americans. Those Americans who feel especially frustrated may look for a justification to reduce the power of their older competitors. Substantial reductions in social security and health benefit payments might be a first step.

Stereotypical or dehumanizing views of the elderly (or any age group) damage the social fabric of our nation even though they may not be held by all Americans. Much is being done currently to counter these views through education and advocacy in the public and private sectors. As the examples in this article illustrate, however, much remains to be done.

## QUESTIONS

1. What is the role of stereotypes in prejudiced thinking? What other groups in society are the victims of negative, stereotyped thinking that denies their individuality and differences?

2. What stereotypes do you think middle-aged people have of college students?

3. Which are the "best years of life," and why? Would you have answered the question differently a few years ago? Do you think you might answer it differently in the future?

## REFERENCES

**Arluke, A., Levin, J.,** and **Suchwalko, J.** "Sexuality and Romance in Advice Books for the Elderly." *Gerontologist* 24, 1984.

**Blassingame, J.** *The Slave Community.* New York: Oxford University Press, 1972.

**Gresham, M.** "The Infantilization of the Elderly." *Nursing Forum* 15, 1976, pp. 196-209.

**Harris, L.,** and Associates. *The Myth and Reality of Aging in America.* New York: National Council on Aging, 1975.

**Helmreich, W.** *The Things They Say Behind Your Back.* New York: Doubleday, 1982.

**Levin, J.,** and **Arluke, A.** "Our Elderly's Fate?" *New York Times,* September 29, 1983, p. A31.

**Levin, J., Arluke, A.,** and **Cheren, C.** "The Challenge of Ageism." *American Health Care Association Journal* 9, March 1983, pp. 47-50.

**Lurie, A.** *The Language of Clothes.* New York: Random House, 1981.

**McTavish, D.** "Perceptions of Old People: A Review of Research Methodologies and Findings." *Gerontologist* 11 (4, Part 2), 1971, pp. 90-101.

**Tuckman, J.** and **Lorge, I.** "Attitudes Toward Old People." *Journal of Social Psychology* 37, 1953, pp. 249-260.

Lee Smith

# 31. The War Between the Generations

*In any society, there is a strong tendency for one age category to have higher status than the others. In most traditional societies the old have the highest status, largely because they own the land (which is the main source of wealth) and have accumulated more knowledge than those younger than themselves. In modern industrialized societies, on the other hand, the middle-aged are dominant because they control the new means of production (such as corporate industry), and they are better educated than the old. In these societies, the young and the old generally have lower wealth, power, and prestige than the middle-aged.*

*But conditions can alter, and they are gradually changing in the United States. The American population is becoming steadily older as a result of several demographic factors—an increase in life expectancy, the post–World War II baby boom, and unusually low birth rates over the past two decades. Around the turn of the century, the society will start to become top-heavy with the elderly, and the sheer weight of their numbers will give them increasing political influence. This large stratum of old people will be demanding increased retirement, medical, and other benefits—which will mostly have to be paid for by taxes on the working population. As Lee Smith points out in this article, the shrinking ratio of dependents to workers may set the stage for conflict between the aged and the working generations that succeed them.*

From *Fortune*, July 20, 1987. Copyright © 1987 by Time Inc. Reprinted by permission.

A pig in a python is what demographers whimsically call the baby boom, that troublesome lump of 75 million Americans born between 1946 and 1964. Almost one-third of the population today, the boomers have distended American society at every stage of their lives, bursting schoolroom walls in the 1950s and upending the nation's tastes and values in the 1960s and 1970s. The worst is yet to come. As the boomers start to retire, they could trigger a bitter war between the generations.

Boomers are likely to demand the same levels of retirement benefits that they pay their parents today through mandatory "contributions" to Social Security. When it comes to Medicare, the hospital insurance and medical benefits available to most people over 65, the boomers will probably ask even more, because they are going to live longer, a blessing mixed with expensive health problems. The younger, much less populous generation that is supposed to pay for these goodies—call them the baby-busters—probably will refuse to shoulder the burden. If they balk, says Ken Dychtwald, 37, a San Francisco gerontologist, the graying boomers "could be sent on a five-day camping trip with two days worth of food." The two generations, enraged by mutual feelings of being cheated, will go for each other's throats.

To avoid this civil war the support system for the elderly ought to be reformed, and the time to start is now, before the battle begins in earnest and while the Social Security trust funds still are flush. Boomers, busters, and the 23 million currently retired all must abandon the traditional view of Social Security. "The assumption that each working generation will take care of the one that preceded it is finished," says Senator David F. Durenberger, 52, a Minnesota Republican and founder of Americans for Generational Equity, or AGE. The old will have to rely increasingly on themselves.

At the moment the traditional system is working well enough to mask the coming conflict. The leading edge of the baby boom recently entered its 40s; almost everyone at the trailing edge has left school and joined the labor force. Under FICA—the Federal Insurance Contributions Act—workers chip in 14.3% of the first $43,800 of their wages to Social Security (15.02% beginning next year), half of it withheld and half paid directly by their employers. In 1986 those contributions raised $194 billion for monthly Social Security stipends to the retired, the survivors of deceased wage earners, and the disabled, as well as $50 billion for hospital bills covered under Medicare. From income taxes unrelated to the FICA payroll tax, the federal government paid out another $18 billion in Medicare benefits for visits to the doctor, and the elderly contributed $5 billion in Medicare premiums. In all, the government lavished 27% of its 1986 budget on Social Security and Medicare, almost exactly the same as its spending for defense.

The biggest part of Social Security is purring along as smoothly as a Rolls-Royce. FICA contributions have so exceeded outlays for the old age, survivors, and disability insurance programs, or OASDI, that the OASDI trust funds, where excess contributions are stored, have burgeoned to $47 billion. As the boomers move into their peak earning years and the number of retired remains relatively small, the funds should keep swelling, to some $1.3 trillion by the year 2000.

But another part of the program is rattling like a jalopy. By 1994, according to the projections of government actuaries, the runaway inflation in health care costs will start eating into the $103-billion trust fund that backs up the hospital insurance portion of Medicare. The fund will run out by 2002. To keep making hospital payments, Congress could try raising payroll taxes yet again. But it probably will take the easy way out and shift billions from the robust OASDI trust funds into the decrepit hospital fund.

Even without that jolt, the entire Social Security system is headed off a cliff. In 1965 the number of births dropped below four million a year, signaling the beginning of the baby bust. Today 3.3 workers toil to support a single beneficiary. By 2010, when the first wave of boomers nears 65, only 2.9 workers will be around to do the job. Ten years later, workers' contributions won't cover outlays, and the Social Security trust funds will have to make up the difference. The funds will start shrinking drastically after 2030, when the support ratio withers to 1.9 workers per beneficiary. As AGE expressed it in a brochure that some senior citizen groups branded as bigotry, the working American family will become "indentured servants."

An immediate way to slow the headlong plunge is to manage the surpluses of the next ten years wisely. As the trust funds grow fatter, Congress will be tempted to use them not just to subsidize existing medical benefits but to expand all payments to retired folk, who vote in proportionately greater numbers than the citizens who support them. Some critics see the thin edge of the wedge

in pending legislation to insure the elderly against the costs of catastrophic illness. Though retirees are supposed to pay for the insurance, some Congressmen are already trying to double the size of the program, from $3 billion to about $6 billion. If it keeps mushrooming, the elderly will not be able to afford it, and Congress may dip into Social Security's surpluses.

That would be squandering. The nation must husband surpluses for the boomers' big retirement party or see the Social Security system go broke for sure. True, the system has been close to bankruptcy before and yet has been saved. In 1983 the National Commission on Social Security Reform, chaired by Alan Greenspan, nominee for the job of Federal Reserve chairman, helped keep the system solvent by delaying a cost-of-living allowance and increasing payroll taxes. A stronger economy with minuscule inflation completed the rescue.

But no rescue is in sight for the long run. Even if Congress keeps its hands off the surpluses, allowing them to compound, the demands of the boomers will throw Social Security into deficit. The level of initial retirement benefits is tied to wages, which are likely to keep compounding at 5.4% a year, as they have since 1947. To give retired boomers the same percentages of their pre-retirement income that today's elderly receive, and similar medical care, workers of the future will have to turn over as much as 40% of their paychecks.

It is impossible to believe they will be so generous, especially because the two generations will be separated by racial differences as well. The aged population will be largely white. In states like California and Texas, though, much of the work force will be nonwhite, mainly Hispanic. They are sure to resent paying ever more dollars to grandparents who do not look like their grandparents. "The elderly will be seen as an Anglo problem, pediatric health as a Mexican problem," says David Hayes-Bautista, a professor of medicine at the University of California at Los Angeles.

Solutions that avoid forcing the old to pay more are politically tempting, but they seem unworkable in practice. Philip Longman, 31, author of *Born to Pay,* a study of the boomers' dilemma, suggests that the government swell the size of the future labor force by encouraging families to have more children. People without children, for example, could be taxed to finance day care centers; it will be other people's children, after all, who will take care of childless retirees. But low birth rates seem an inexorable product of affluent societies. France, which has demographic problems similar to those of the U.S., has for years used tax incentives to encourage big families but so far with little success.

Another tactic for beefing up the number of Social Security contributors is to raise immigration quotas. The U.S. could easily boost its labor force by, say, tripling the number of immigrants it admits every year, from 550,000 or so, to 1.7 million. But a flood of immigrants is exactly what organized labor thought it had stemmed with the immigration law that went into effect last May. Congress would be loath to undo its handiwork by radically raising quotas.

Since the supply of contributors is not likely to rise, the demand for Social Security benefits must fall. That will not necessarily lead to hardships that violate the American sense of social justice. The key is a four-point program that would redefine what old is, encourage people to pay more for their own retirement, spread the burden of support among the elderly, and avoid inflating health care costs even more.

### Workers Should Stay on the Job Until 70

Better health care and working conditions are keeping people younger. Most employers are forbidden to impose a mandatory retirement age. Yet the country still is stuck with 65 as the official beginning of old age, the time at which a worker can retire on full Social Security pay and qualify for Medicare.

Despite their fitness for the workplace, Americans are quitting young. Nearly half of all men between 61 and 64 are retired. Corporations encourage early leave-taking these days because they want to trim their payrolls. The Social Security system gives companies and employees an incentive to part company. By retiring at 62 a worker can collect monthly benefits equal to 80% of those he would have received if he had waited until 65. With that kind of deal, most people have little reason for continuing to work.

Thanks to the Social Security reform commission, the age at which a worker can qualify for full retirement benefits will inch up in the next century. Someone who turns 25 this year cannot get full benefits until he is 67. That's the right idea, but the pace is too slow. The scheduled rises in the qualifying age mean that the officially old will constitute 18% of the population in 2030, vs. 12% today.

The government should make 70 the eligibility age for the first of the boomers, today's 41-year-olds. That way only 15% of the population would qualify for full benefits in 2030, easing the burden on working stiffs. Eliminating early retirement, shrinking early retirement benefits, or raising the early retirement age also would help.

### Workers Should Get Bigger Tax Breaks for Funding Their Own Retirement

A typical worker who retired last year at 65 will, by one measure, strike a bonanza. By collecting $583 a month

he will in four years recover everything he paid out. But the young worker starting out may be lucky just to get his money back.

Republican presidential hopeful Pierre "Pete" du Pont is pushing an intricate plan to supplement retirement income. For every $1 a worker pays in FICA tax, he would be able to put another $1, up to a total of $2,500 a year, into a financial security account and earn a tax credit for his investment. FSA trustees would invest in corporate securities, government bonds, and such. Assuming a 4% rate of return, the FSA account would provide nearly four times the retirement income Social Security offers. "All other solutions are just tinkering," says du Pont. "We're going to the core of the problem."

But he's boring too deep. The credits would cost the Treasury $20 billion or more a year by du Pont's estimate, an intolerable loss in an era of towering deficits. A more modest scheme would be to restore tax deductions for all workers who put money into individual retirement accounts. The Tax Reform Act of 1986 took the country half a step in the wrong direction. Workers who earn more than $35,000 a year and are covered by corporate pension plans are no longer allowed to deduct IRA contributions. Congress should reverse itself. Doing so would cost the Treasury about $5 billion a year. To boost IRA saving, the government must also confess the truth: It will pay today's workers much leaner retirement benefits than today's elderly get.

### Rich Retirees Should Subsidize Poor Ones

"People like me don't deserve Social Security," insists Donald MacNaughton, 70, who as a former chairman of Prudential Insurance Co. receives a pension of $180,000 a year. A selfless thought, to be sure, but dropping the wealthy from the rolls would be a dud on Capitol Hill. The protectors of Social Security maintain that the only way to ensure broad support for the program is to give the mighty as well as the humble a stake in it.

The solution is to let rich and poor alike collect Social Security but tax benefits as fully as wage and investment income. At present many of the 2.2 million or so elderly with incomes above $25,000 pay taxes on up to half their Social Security benefits. Alan Greenspan suggests taxing the full amount of benefits like any other income.

The catastrophic illness insurance Congress is fashioning also calls for the elderly rich to help the elderly poor. The fatter cats, with income of $75,000 or more a year, will get the same benefits as the impoverished but will probably pay around $44 a month. Old people with annual incomes below $15,000 are likely to pay little or nothing. With a deductible of $1,000 or $2,000, depending on which version of the bill is enacted, the new insurance will pay for hospital stays that last beyond the 59 days that Medicare covers in full.

### Don't Pay for Nursing Home Care With More Payroll Taxes

Medicare pays nothing for nursing home treatment, which costs $22,000 a year on average. Many retired people in nursing homes are forced to empty their pockets and sell their assets until they are down to several thousand dollars and a house, which qualifies them to apply for Medicaid, the program that helps the poor of all ages. It's a cruel solution to a problem that will only grow with the longer lives and greater numbers of the retired.

Lobbyists for senior citizens hope to use the 1988 elections to push through federal insurance for nursing home care. Alice Rivlin and Joshua Wiener, senior fellows at the Brookings Institution, say it would take an horrendous FICA tax of 2.8% to underwrite a first-rate nursing home payment system.

That indeed is the wrong way to do it. Subsidies that do not require the beneficiaries to pay at least some of the cost inflate demand for care. And a new FICA tax would add to the burden of the baby-boomers, who should be socking the money away for their own golden years.

One option is private insurance. Most insurers have been skittish, but this summer Prudential will begin offering members of the American Association of Retired Persons a policy that will pay them, after 90 days of care, $50 a day for a nursing home stay of up to three years and $25 a day for care at home. Premiums would range from $30.50 to $115.75 a month. Rivlin and Wiener predict that private insurance for nursing home care will boom in the next few years and eventually cover a third of the elderly.

The other two-thirds face a tougher choice. If they want to avoid selling their assets while they are alive, they and their heirs may have to go along with broader, higher inheritance taxes. The net worth of those over 65 amounts to about $2 trillion, according to a 1984 Census Bureau survey, and 5% or so is passed on to heirs every year. Representative Jim Moody, 51, a Democrat from Milwaukee and co-chairman of AGE, sees those assets as a logical way to pay for nursing home care: "It's not fair to spend society's money to preserve assets for someone's children."

None of these steps will ease the pain of dealing with the last big bulge that the baby-boomers make. Today the U.S. spends 11% of GNP on health, more than most other industrial nations. That share will come to 15% by 2000, thanks to the rising cost of high-tech medical care. The biggest jump will come after 2026, when the first boomers reach 80. At that age, they become the "old old," who require the most intensive treatment.

Should society pay without question for costly medical machines and procedures to keep the old old alive? "Taking care of the elderly is an endless open frontier," says Daniel Callahan, director of the Hastings Center in Briarcliff Manor, New York, which studies medical ethics. "Maybe we shouldn't spend any more on health. Our roads are in terrible shape, and so are our secondary schools." Callahan and others argue that society should ration its spending among the generations, which would mean spending less to prolong the lives of the elderly.

The issues that divide the generations are literally matters of life and death. The hard choices must be made eventually. The question is, which generation will make them.

## QUESTIONS

1. In what ways might a markedly older population affect social life in the United States, in such fields as politics, economics, education, sports, and media?

2. What factors contribute to conflict between generations? Is this conflict inevitable?

3. In what ways can inequalities between age categories be considered a form of social stratification? Can valid comparisons be made with other forms of stratification?

# UNIT 4

# Social Institutions

Charles Lindholm
Cherry Lindholm

# 32.  What Price Freedom?

*Human societies display a remarkable variety of norms
relating to sex, marriage, and family. For example,
some societies are permissive, some restrictive; some
allow individual choice of marital partners, some insist
on arranged marriages; some regard sex between
particular kinds of relatives as incestuous, others
regard such a relationship as an obligation. But
whatever the practices of a society are, and however
strange they may seem to outsiders, they "work" in the
culture where they are found. To understand norms of
sex, marriage, and family, we must see them in their
own context.*

*The Lepcha, a traditional people living in the
Himalayan mountains of north India, are a people
whose family system could hardly be more different
from our own. Their elaborate incest rules, for example,
even forbid adult brothers and sisters to touch one
another, and also make it taboo for a son to sleep with
a woman his father has had sex with. The Lepcha think
it normal for a grown man to force a little girl to
perform sexual acts; they know little or no sexual
jealousy and are largely indifferent to adultery; and
they generally do not link sex and emotion. These and
other cultural traits would be considered immoral or
nonsensical in American culture—just as American
traits might seem to the Lepcha.*

*In this article, Charles and Cherry Lindholm
describe the family system of the Lepcha, placing it in
the full context of their social and cultural life.*

First published in *Science Digest,* November/December 1980. Reprinted
with permission from Charles Lindholm and Cherry Lindholm.

The two-day marriage ceremony is almost over. The oxen
have been sacrificed, the Buddhist priests have said their
prayers, the guests have presented their gifts of cloth and
money and have been given proportionate amounts of
meat in return. The bride and her relatives, who have
come from a far-distant village, are sitting against the
left wall of her new family's house, facing the groom and
his family in customary fashion. The girl, though only
14, is slightly older than her young husband and is considered quite mature to be a new bride. She covers her
face with her headcloth to hide her expression as the
ritual discussion of her qualities begins between the families.

"We are giving you," announces her uncle, address-
ing the groom's family, "the yolk of this egg that we have
peeled for you."

One of the groom's party replies, "Thank you very
much. It is very kind of you. But it seems to us as if this
egg has been nibbled at! And we would not be surprised
if her pubic hair were not as long as that of a female
devil or in appearance rather like a field of fresh corn."

"We assure you," retorts the bride's uncle, "that the
egg has been freshly peeled to make it easy for you to
eat."

"Well, it seems to us that the shell has been off for
a very considerable time!"

"And what does it matter if her pubic hair is like a
tangled bush? A clever goat can find its way through any
bramble!"

This sexual joking during a solemn ritual occurs
among the Lepcha people of Sikkim, a small Himalayan
kingdom north of India. Since 1974, it has been an "associate state" of India, and the power of the *chogyal,* or
king, is purely nominal. The Lepchas live primarily on
a royal preserve set aside for them by ancestors of today's
*chogyal.* There, the Lepchas are relatively free to pursue
their ancient culture. The preserve, Jongu, is located in
the precipitous valleys of the high Himalayas. Towering
over all else is snow-capped, 28,208-foot Kanchenjunga,
which ironically enough is worshipped as a war god by
the peace-loving Lepchas.

There is probably not a 100-foot-square piece of flatland in the whole region, and cultivation often takes place at a 60-degree angle. The Lepchas find it impossible to use even mules for porterage and are obliged to carry all baggage on their own backs. But in spite of their harsh environment, the industrious Lepchas manage to grow rice, wheat, millet and maize, as well as a variety of fruits, vegetables and spices, including the spice cardamom, their only cash crop.

The climate is extremely wet, with occasional ruinous hailstorms. Famine is greatly feared, and most of the Lepchas' religious rituals are designed to ward off hunger and disease.

They were first studied in 1876 by Colonel G. G. Mainwaring, a British officer. He was so impressed by their gentleness that he thought they were the original sinless children of Eve. Halfdan Siiger, who visited them in 1949, wrote that "they are by nature extremely kind, and when they lose their immediate fear of a stranger and gain confidence in him, they meet him with a lovely smile and an open mind, and above all with friendliness." The major anthropological work—*Himalayan Village*—was written by Geoffrey Gorer, who visited them in 1937 and was struck not only by their shyness and peaceful ways but also by their humorous verbal preoccupation with sex.

Indeed, to the Lepchas sex is continually and inexhaustibly funny. During village feasts, they spend their time eating, drinking *chi* (the very formidable local millet beer), and laughing heartily at the never-ending flow of sexual jokes and innuendos. In addition to the feasts given at births, marriages, deaths, and when visiting relatives arrive from distant villages, there are the monthly Lamaist festivals and large bimonthly monastery feasts. At such a feast, 80 or 90 people may be present and the merrymaking may even continue into the next day, with people catnapping intermittently. A dozen or so lamas (Buddhist priests) will be sitting in the main prayer room of the monastery, while the smaller prayer room will be occupied by six or seven nuns and a great number of other women, old men and young children. In the monastery yard, the wives of the feast-givers and anyone else who wishes will be busy with the large cook pots, preparing the vegetables, cereal, meat and *chi*.

The younger men and women and the older boys sit about on the grass and stones outside, chatting, joking, and occasionally fetching water or firewood for the cooking. The younger boys may hang about with them and listen to the conversations, but more often they either sit quietly on the grass or else play on the hill outside the monastery grounds, chasing hens or imitating birdcalls. The girls generally tag along with their parents or an older sister and will often be carrying a younger sibling. Small groups of toddlers sit some distance from the grownups, clustering silently around pots of *chi*, which they drink through bamboo straws; after a time, they become quite tipsy and noticeably less quiet; they stagger around for a while and then fall asleep. No one pays them any attention.

As the night wears on, people become more and more mellow, voices become louder, gestures more expansive, and there is much laughter at the obscene remarks that fly back and forth among the guests. Full of food and drink, some guests happily doze, while others occupy themselves with braiding one another's hair. Couples may wander off into the forest or to a nearby shed from time to time. Occasionally, there will be some lighthearted sexual byplay as a young man, or sometimes a young woman, grabs at another young man's penis, to the delight of the onlookers. Or an old man, having become quite drunk, will expose himself to the laughing throng. But for the most part, the sexual joking is verbal, and the ability to talk well and tell good stories is much admired among the Lepcha people.

It is generally thought that such sexual joking is the result of sexual frustration and inhibition, but among the Lepchas this is certainly not the case. Their sex lives are notoriously active. Impotence is unheard of and sexual activity continues until quite late in life for both men and women. There is no language of seduction or foreplay employed, since the Lepchas consider that anticipation alone guarantees sufficient stimulation; one simply makes a straightforward proposition, which is usually accepted. As Gorer notes, "Sexual activity is practically divorced from emotion; it is a pleasant and amusing experience, and as much a necessity as food and drink; and like food and drink it does not matter from whom you receive it, as long as you get it, though you are naturally grateful to the people who provide you with either item regularly."

Sexual jealousy is not considered a normal emotion and there is no word for jealousy in the language. In fact, certain relatives have an absolute right to sleep with one's wife, and as Chudo, a Lepcha man, told Gorer, "If I caught my elder brother's son sleeping with my wife, I shouldn't be cross at all; on the contrary, I should be very pleased, for she would be teaching him how to do it properly, and I would know that he had a good teacher."

Aside from nephews, a man's younger brothers also have free access to his wife, and boys are usually initiated into sex by an uncle's or brother's wife. Other men are also permitted to sleep with her, providing that they are not too blatant about it and do not have sex with her in the house unless the husband is away and unlikely to come home and witness the act.

## Incest Taboos

This is not to say that Lepcha society is totally promiscuous. In fact, the range of partners prohibited by incest taboos is extremely wide; sex is forbidden with a partner related back at least seven generations on the father's side and at least four on the mother's. Ideally, the prohibitions should reach back nine generations on both sides, but this would render marriage almost impossible. It is also forbidden to sleep with a woman one's father has had sex with; this is considered incestuous, and fathers instruct their young sons early as to their permitted and prohibited sexual partners. The choices are limited by the rules of exogamy (marriage outside a group of lineal relatives), the wide range of incest prohibitions, and the fact that the Lepchas are mainly patrilocal (the wife moving in with the husband's family). Hence, sex with most girls who have grown up in the village is forbidden. (A large village consists of 50 to 60 houses.) Marriage and sex partners must come from some distance away. Siiger notes that "real ingenuity has to be exercised in order to find a suitable partner for one's son or daughter," and perhaps this is the reason for allowing the sharing of women within the village. Indeed, the fact that most people at any gathering will be sexually taboo might account for the extraordinary amount of sexual joking.

Girls usually have their first sexual encounters before puberty, as it is believed that a virgin girl will not normally grow breasts or begin menstruating but must have sexual intercourse in order for these transformations to occur. There is no stigma attached to a grown man forcing a little girl of 9 or 10 to have sex with him; such an occurrence, in fact, is considered quite amusing and is a subject for joking and laughter. If a girl starts menstruating while still a virgin—as does happen occasionally—it is thought that she has been visited by a supernatural, and this is considered an extremely lucky sign. Dreams of copulating with a supernatural being are supposed to come to a woman during every menstrual period; if, one month, she fails to have this dream, it signifies that she is shortly to die. This is the only sexual dream that the Lepchas admit to having.

Since most men in the home village are prohibited, women often have their first sexual experience with a visitor, and unrelated guests can therefore be quite popular. Gorer reports that his difficulty in obtaining information about sex from the women was not due to the jealousy of the husbands, as might be the case in many societies, but to "the fact that almost every woman from eight to eighty interpreted any sort of special attention as an attempt at seduction, an attempt which—no matter what their youth or age—they had no intention of repelling."

Marriages are not arranged by the parents but by the village headman. The partners must be the correct genealogical distance and have complementary horoscopes. Girls are usually engaged around the age of 9 and boys around the age of 12. No attention is paid to

the desires of the young couple, and girls especially will often resist marriage, no doubt largely because it means leaving their home village. After the pair is engaged and the bride-price given, the boy and girl are expected to copulate under the watchful eyes of their uncles; this is thought to ensure the stability of the marriage. The period of greatest sexual adventuring for the Lepcha boy and girl occurs during the engagement, especially if the couple do not particularly like each other or if their villages are far apart.

After the engagement, the boy must perform bride-service during visits to his in-laws' house, where he is treated as a servant and subjected to a great deal of sexual teasing. He is not allowed to retaliate in kind, and if he is provoked into doing so, he will be humiliated by his fiancee's family. The relationship with in-laws is one of the utmost respect; one should not direct obscene jokes toward them nor make such jokes in their presence, though when the engagement period is over this latter proscription is often ignored. Ideally, one should also behave with similar decorum toward one's parents and siblings of the opposite sex, but in Jongu the Lepchas are rather lax on this point of etiquette. The major prohibition is one that disallows adult brothers and sisters from touching one another, except during times of illness, and the brother-sister incest taboo is the most stringent of all. (Interestingly enough, the Lepchas' creation myth claims that the original mother and father of the Lepcha people were brother and sister.) The breaking of an incest taboo has extremely serious consequences: it is believed to result in a year of disaster, not only for the man and woman involved but for the entire community in which they live.

This belief illustrates the structure of Lepcha society, for the Lepcha life-style is communal. People find their identity in their *ptso* (patriline) and village membership, and the ideal of cooperation, unselfishness and sharing comes close to being a reality. The Lepchas redistribute their resources to alleviate poverty, and sharing with the poor is considered a very good custom because, as one village headman explained, "It makes everybody realize that they are part of one group and the happiness of one is the happiness of all." Both children and adults are extraordinarily unselfish and always share things. Children are taught to help others, so that others in their turn will help them, and they are told that no one will help a thief. They are instructed to receive a gift in cupped hands and always to give a small gift in return. Gift-giving, which is a continuing motif in Lepcha life, is always an exchange, never simply one-sided receiving.

Among the Lepchas, relations are based on exact reciprocity and mutual obligations, and the individual who fulfills those obligations is automatically a good person and will be well liked. People express their liking for others. "I care for my parents because they gave me food," said one man. Another explained that "When I go out to work and come back tired, my wife has a good meal ready for me and looks after me; then I think 'This is my wife, and I am pleased in my belly.' " It is interesting to note that the stomach, not the heart, is considered to be the center of the emotions, and that past events are often remembered in terms of menus.

Life takes place within the range of the extended family. A man hopes to get responsibility for his family in his mid-thirties and to give up responsibility when he reaches 60. Children are therefore greatly desired, and adoption by childless couples is common. It is expected that the child will help his parents in their old age. Boys and girls, like men and women, are considered alike in their basic natures. The same rules of behavior apply to both sexes. Male and female work roles are not greatly differentiated; both sexes work in the fields, and men will take over the cooking if necessary. Although the society is patrilineal, with women unable to inherit land, the only real difference the Lepchas see between men and women is in the genitals, which are considered to have a sort of independent life very much of their own.

## No Authority Figures

The Lepchas dislike anyone who tries to show authority. They work together in gangs, but no one tells another what to do and the headman leads by suggestion and example. Deviants are those who are aggressive, domineering and violent, and people who attempt to dominate will be excluded from the communal feasting cycle. However, such individuals, and even those who commit sodomy (which is thought to be like incest), are not considered personally responsible. Their behavior is thought to be a result of malevolent action by devils of the Lepcha religion.

The picture given so far of Lepcha life is idyllic. However, there is a darker side to this picture. The suicide rate of the Lepchas is extremely high. Women commit suicide by drowning, men by taking poison, and nearly all suicides occur directly after a public reproof for such transgressions as being lazy and neglecting one's work or failing to carry out properly one's obligations toward another. The Lepchas possess an overly sensitive sense of shame, and it is very easy to shame someone. While the rules of the society are somewhat flexible, antisocial behavior leads to exclusion, and a public shaming can often result in suicide, even when a person is wrongly accused. Not having a strongly developed sense of self, such as prevails in other cultures, a Lepcha cannot withstand the disapproval of the community. His feelings of aggression in this situation find their expression in self-destruction, just as in lesser cases a Lepcha who is angry will destroy his or her own possessions.

Communal life among the Lepchas ignores individual differences and stresses obligation rather than affect, or feeling. People exist only as a part of a larger whole. They are liked and accepted according to their fulfillment of obligations, not according to their individual personalities, which are not really recognized among the Lepchas. This lack of individuality is reflected in the fact that individual names are of almost no consequence in Lepcha culture; people are called by kinship terms, and it is even possible for a man to forget the actual name of his own wife. Arranged marriages are thought to work out well since they are merely a relation of mutual obligation such as might be set up between any two people. Providing both parties fulfill these obligations, they will automatically grow to like each other.

This underdeveloped sense of individuality is accompanied by a lack of creativity. There are no local arts and crafts except storytelling, and it is forbidden to invent new stories to enlarge the traditional stock. Individual inventiveness is seen mainly in the Lepchas' sexual joking. A general sense of lack of affect is apparent in the society, since all strong emotions are suppressed as threatening to the cooperative structure of the community. Relationships tend to be cut-and-dried, without much personal content. The basic cultural stance is one of indifference, and the most commonly heard phrase is *ket manin,* "it doesn't matter." The Lepchas are easily taken advantage of by unscrupulous Hindu merchants, who place them deeply in debt. Their culture requires specific protection by the state, for it soon disappears among Lepchas who leave the preserve. The concreteness and absolute quality of all relationships make the Lepchas extremely weak at working with abstract concepts, and the stress on smooth personal relationships eliminates the tension required for creative effort.

Children are raised to be dependent, passive and conformist. They are breast-fed until the next child comes along, an average of four years, but a youngest or only child may be given the breast until puberty. Though breast-fed by the mother only, infants are handled by everyone in the extended family and given a great deal of diffuse attention, being picked up as soon as they cry. Gorer was impressed by the lack of crying and the general passivity of the children and thought that the passionless quality of adult relationships was due to the diffuseness of childhood relationships. There does not seem to be a very strong emotional tie with the parents, and children tend to relate more to their older siblings.

Though children begin participating in adult labor at a very early age, no specific tasks, such as herding cattle, are assigned them, and Gorer attributes the young men's extreme boyishness, inability to stand alone and lack of self-reliance to their general lack of individual responsibility within the family. The developmental pattern for men is slow and even, with no great life-crisis events. Women seem more mature, perhaps because they must adjust early on in life to the trauma of leaving the home village and friends when they marry.

## Bedeviled Childhood

Family life is not particularly warm. Though infants are given much attention, that attention is rather impersonal, and the older child, though desired for his labor, is treated with a sort of impersonal neglect. Despite the lack of violence in the society, children are often beaten for getting in the way or interfering with adults, though the beatings are given without anger. Children are offered violence or succor with equal impersonality. They are trained by fear, and the most common way to gain obedience is to threaten a child with the vengeance of a devil. A child who still wants the breast after a new infant has been born will be told that the infant is a devil. Children who die are thought to become devils and are considered dangerous; hence, the adults' attitude toward children is ambiguous from the start. For the child, the world is a place of pervasive anxiety, and adults remember their childhoods as times of fear, hurt and obscurity. Children are, quite simply, miniature and relatively incompetent adults who do not even have the recompense of receiving respect for their work in the household.

Anxiety does not vanish with adulthood. The world is not beautiful, it is frightening, and the Lepcha pays no attention to the mountains that rise in splendor all around him but walks instead with his eyes on the ground. The religion of the Lepchas is primarily a religion of fear. Spirits of nature and of the dead are terrifying, and the aim of ritual is to keep them at bay. It may seem contradictory that such a peaceful people should have a religion with such violent and frightening iconography, but the human emotional makeup demands a balance. What cannot be expressed within society finds its expression in ritual, and the aggression the Lepchas deny in their daily lives is encountered in the threatening gods and devils of their religion.

## Unneurotic Adults

Gorer ascribed the Lepcha character to the infants' toilet training, which is out of phase with psychosexual development, combined with diffuse and impersonal attention from many adults. Such a pattern will tend to produce "a society in which the great majority of adults will be unneurotic, unaggressive, generous, with undisturbed sexual potency. . . . They will also be uninventive, with no high art and little development of the crafts; no complexity will be meaningful. There will be little intensity in adult relations, and little passion in either life or art."

This picture may be oversimplifying the factors behind the development of the Lepcha personality. It must also be remembered that the Lepchas have a long history of oppression and have been enslaved several times in the past few hundred years by their more warlike neighbors of Nepalese extraction. The word *Lepcha*, in fact, indicates the people's low status, since it is a derogatory Nepalese term meaning "nonsense speakers." The Lepchas call themselves the Rong. Furthermore, their entire relation with their ecology has totally changed from the freedom of hunting and gathering to the restrictions of intensive agriculture.

The Lepchas—there are perhaps 20,000 of them in Sikkim at this time—are a dying culture. One authority notes that the decade 1961–71 "reveals the dismal fact that the Lepchas have a negative growth rate." They have a low birthrate and a high incidence of sterility, suicide, disease and out-migration. Struggling to protect their cultural integrity, the Lepchas have evolved a complex and inwardly turned social order in which the aggressions of the outer world are countered by cooperation and sharing within the community.

## QUESTIONS

1. List some significant differences between the family pattern of the Lepchas and our own.

2. How would you respond to someone who asserts that the sex life of the Lepchas is immoral?

3. When Europeans colonized much of the undeveloped Third World, Christian missionaries immediately attempted to change whatever sexual and family patterns they found, so that they would conform to the Western, middle-class model. What effects do you think this had on the local culture and social structure?

*Lillian B. Rubin*

# 33. Changing Expectations: New Sources of Strain

*If you study the relationship between husband and wife revealed in such old TV shows as "I Love Lucy," you will see how dramatically American sex roles have changed since the early campaigns of the women's movement some twenty years ago. But although these changes have been generally welcomed, they have inevitably caused some disruption to the traditional American family system—a system, after all, which a majority of Americans were socialized to participate in.*

*There is little question that changing sex-role expectations have been one of the factors that have placed a new stress on American marriages, particularly among the working class, where allegiance to the old sex roles is most firmly entrenched. Traditional roles called for the husband to be the breadwinner, the rational, emotionally aloof, undisputed family head, and for the wife to be the homemaker, the source of emotional support for her husband and children, and the subservient partner in all matters of consequence. But today the family these roles were designed for scarcely exists: most wives work, and most husbands are no longer the sole breadwinner. Women are taking on new and challenging roles outside the home, and are increasingly expecting to be treated as equal partners within the marriage.*

*In this article, Lillian Rubin interweaves quotations from her studies of working-class husbands and wives with an analysis of how changing expectations have placed new strain on working-class marriages.*

I give her a nice home, a nice car, all those fancy appliances. I don't cheat on her. We got three nice kids—nobody could ask for better kids. And with all that, she's not happy. I worry about it, but I can't figure out what's the matter, so how can I know what to do? I just don't know what she wants. [*Twenty-nine-year-old truck driver, married nine years*]

"I just don't know what she wants"—that's the plaintive and uncomprehending cry of most working-class men, the cry that bedevils most marriages. Sadly, she often also doesn't know what she wants. She knows only that the dream is not being fulfilled—that she's married but feels lonely:

> It sounds silly, I know, but here I am in a house with three kids and my husband, and lots of time I feel like I might just as well be living alone.

. . . that life feels curiously empty:

> You wake up one day and you say to yourself, "My God, is this all there is? Is it really possible that this is what life is all about?"

. . . that she's often filled with an incomprehensible anger:

> I feel like I go crazy-angry sometimes. It makes me say and do things to Randy or the kids that I hate myself for. I keep wondering what makes me do those things when one part of me knows I don't really mean it.

. . . and that guilt and anxiety are her steady companions:

> I don't know what's the matter with me that I don't appreciate what I've got. I feel guilty all the time, and I worry about it a lot. Other women, they seem to be happy with being married and having a house and kids. What's the matter with me?

"What's the matter" with her is that, even apart from the financial burdens incurred in buying all those goods, they add little to the emotional satisfactions of life. The advertisers' promises of instant happiness prove to be a lie—good for the gross national product but not for the human soul.

Sure, it's great to show those goodies off to friends and neighbors. After all those years of poverty, it makes you feel good finally to have something and let people see it. Besides, they make life easier, more comfortable. Now there's time for things other than household drudgery. But what things? Companionship? Intimacy? Sharing? What are those things? And how does one find them?

She has a vague idea. Television shows, the women's magazines—they all talk about something called communication. Marriage partners have to communicate, they say; they have to talk, to tell each other how they feel. So she talks. And he tries to listen. But somehow, it doesn't work. He listens, but he cannot hear. Sometimes sooner, sometimes later, he withdraws in silence, feeling attacked:

> When she comes after me like that, yapping like that, she might as well be hitting me with a bat.

. . . vulnerable:

> It makes me feel like I'm doing something wrong, like I'm not a very good husband or somethng.

. . . and helpless:

> No matter what I say, it's no good. If I try to tell her she's excited over nothing, that only makes it worse. I try to keep my cool and be logical, but nothing works.

This is the dilemma of modern marriage—experienced at all class levels, but with particular acuteness among the working-class families I met. For once marriage is conceived of as more than an economic arrangement—that is, as one in which the emotional needs of the individual are attended to and met—the role segregation and the consequent widely divergent socialization patterns for women and men become clearly dysfunctional. And it is among the working class that such segregation has been most profound, where there has been least incentive to change.

Thus, they talk *at* each other, *past* each other, or *through* each other—rarely *with* or *to* each other. He blames her: "She's too emotional." She blames him: "He's always so rational." In truth, neither is blameworthy. The problem lies in the fact that they do not have a language with which to communicate, with which to understand each other. They are products of a process that trains them to relate to only one side of themselves—she, to the passive, tender, intuitive, verbal, emotional side; he, to the active, tough, logical, nonverbal, unemotional one. From infancy, each has been programmed to be split off from the other side; by adulthood, it is distant from consciousness, indeed.

They are products of a disjunction between thought and feeling, between emotionality and rationality that lies deep in Western culture. Even though she complains, both honestly believe what the culture has taught them.

To be rational is the more desired state; it is good, sane, strong, adult. To be emotional is the less desired state; it is bad, weak, childlike. She:

> I know I'm too emotional and I can't really be trusted to be sensible a lot of the time. I need him; he's the one in the family you can always count on to think about things right, not mixed up, like me.

He:

> She's like a kid sometimes, so emotional. I'm always having to reason with her, to explain things to her. If it weren't for me, nothing would happen very rational around here.

This equation of emotional with nonrational, this inability to apprehend the logic of emotions lies at the root of much of the discontent between the sexes, and helps to make marriage the most difficult of all relationships.

Her lifetime training prepares her to handle the affective, expressive side in human affairs; his, to handle the nonaffective, instrumental side. Tears, he has been taught, are for sissies; feelings, for women. A *real* man is the strong, silent type of the folklore—a guy who needs nothing from anyone, who ignores feelings and pain, who can take it on the chin without a whimper. For a lifetime, much of his energy has gone into molding himself in that image—into denying his feelings, refusing to admit they exist. Without warning or preparation, he finds himself facing a wife who pleads, "Tell me your feelings." He responds with bewilderment. "What is there to tell?"

When they try to talk, she relies on the only tools she has, the mode with which she is most familiar; she becomes progressively more emotional and expressive. He falls back on the only tools he has; he gets progressively more rational—determinedly reasonable. She cries for him to attend to her feelings, her pain. He tells her it's silly to feel that way; she's just being emotional. That clenched-teeth reasonableness invalidates her feelings, leaving her sometimes frightened:

> I get scared that maybe I'm crazy. He's always so logical and reasonable that I begin to feel, "What's the matter with me that I'm so emotional?"

. . . sometimes angry:

> When he just sits there telling me I'm too emotional, I get so mad, I go up the wall. Sometimes I get so mad I wish I could hit him. I did once, but he hit me back, and he can hurt me more than I can hurt him.

. . . almost always tearful and despairing:

> I wind up crying and feeling terrible. I get so sad because we can't really talk to each other a lot of times. He looks at me like I'm crazy, like he just doesn't understand a word I'm saying.

Repeatedly, the experience is the same, the outcome

of the interaction, predictable. Yet, each has such a limited repertoire that they are consigned to playing out the same theme over and over again—he, the rational man; she, the hysterical woman.

It hardly need be said that such relationships between men and women are not given to the working class alone. Without doubt, the description I have been rendering represents the most common interactional pattern in American marriage. These are the behavioral consequences of the dominant sex-role socialization patterns in the culture and of the existing structure of family relations within which boys and girls internalize an appropriate identity—patterns which generate the role stereotypes that women and men bring to marriage and which effectively circumscribe their emotional negotiations.

Still, it is also true that the norms of middle-class marriage for much longer have called for more companionate relationships—for more sharing, for more exploration of feelings, and for more exchange of them. Thus, middle-class women and men have more practice and experience in trying to overcome the stereotypes. And, perhaps more important, they have more models around them for how to do so. This is not to suggest that they have done it so well, as a casual glance at the divorce rate will show; only that the demands on the marriage partners for different behaviors have been around for much longer, that there is a language that gives those demands legitimacy, and that there has been more experimentation in modifying the stereotypes.

Among working-class couples, the demand for communication, for sharing, is newer. Earlier descriptions of working-class family life present a portrait of wives and husbands whose lives were distinctly separate, both inside and outside the home—the wife attending to her household role, the husband to his provider role. He came home at night tired and taciturn; she kept herself and the children out of his way. For generations, it was enough that each did their job adequately—he, to bring home the bacon; she, to cook it. Intimacy, companionship, sharing—these were not part of the dream.

But dreams change—sometimes before the people who must live them are ready. Suddenly, new dreams are stirring. *Intimacy, companionship, sharing*—these are now the words working-class women speak to their men, words that turn *both* their worlds upside down. For while it is the women who are the discontented, who are pushing for change, they, no less than their men, are confused about what they are asking:

> I'm not sure what I want. I keep talking to him about communication, and he says, "Okay, so we're talking; now what do you want?" And I don't know what to say then, but I know it's not what I mean.

... and frightened and unsure about the consequences:

> I sometimes get worried because I think maybe I want too much. He's a good husband; he works hard; he takes care of me and the kids. He could go out and find another woman who would be very happy to have a man like that, and who wouldn't be all the time complaining at him because he doesn't feel things and get close.

The men are even worse off. Since it's not *their* dream, they are less likely still to have any notion of what is being asked of them. They only know that, without notice, the rules of the game have been changed; what worked for their fathers, no longer works for them. They only know that there are a whole new set of expectations—in the kitchen, in the parlor, in the bedroom—that leave them feeling bewildered and threatened. She says:

> I keep telling him that the reason people get divorced isn't *only* financial but because they can't communicate. But I can't make him understand.

He says:

> I swear, I don't know what she wants. She keeps saying we have to talk, and then when we do, it always turns out I'm saying the wrong thing.

> I get scared sometimes. I always thought I had to think things to myself; you know, not tell her about it. Now she says that's not good. But it's hard. You know, I think it comes down to that I like things the way they are, and I'm afraid I'll say or do something that'll really shake things up. So I get worried about it, and I don't say anything.

For both women and men, the fears and uncertainties are compounded by the fact that there are no models in their lives for the newly required and desired behaviors. Television shows them people whose lives seem unreal—outside the realm of personal experience or knowledge. The daytime soap operas, watched almost exclusively by women, *do* picture men who may be more open and more available for intimacy. But the men on the soaps don't work at ordinary jobs, doing ordinary things, for eight, ten, twelve hours a day. They're engaged either in some heroic, life-saving, glamour job to which working-class viewers can't relate or, worse yet, work seems to be one long coffee break during which they talk about their problems. Nighttime fare, when the men are home, is different, but no less unreal, featuring the stoic private eye, the brave cop, the tight-lipped cowboy.

The argument about the impact of the mass media on blue-collar workers is complex, contradictory, and largely unsatisfactory. Some observers insist that the mass media represent the most powerful current by which blue-collar workers are swept into conformity with middle-class values and aspirations; others that blue-collar men especially resist exposure to middle-class manners and mores as they are presented on television—minimizing that exposure by exercising great discrimination in program choices; still others that the idealized and romanticized figures on television are so unreal to the average blue-collar viewer that they have little impact on their lives and little effect on their behavior.

Perhaps all three of these seemingly irreconcilable perspectives are true. The issue may not be *whether* television or other mass media affect people's lives and perceptions. Of course they do. The question we must ask more precisely is: In what ways are Americans of any class touched and affected by their exposure to television? For the professional middle class, it may well be an affirming experience; for the working class, a disconfirming one since there are no programs that deal with their problems, their prospects, and their values in sympathetic and respectful ways.

If their own lives in the present provide no models and the media offer little that seems relevant, what about the past? Unfortunately for young working-class couples, family backgrounds provide few examples of openness, companionship, or communication between husbands and wives:

> I don't think we ever had a good concept of what marriage was about. His family was the opposite of mine. They didn't drink like mine did, and they were more stable. Yet he feels they didn't give him a good concept either. There wasn't any drinking and fighting and carrying on, but there wasn't any caring either.

Even those few who recall their parents' marriages as good ones don't remember them talking much to one another and have no sense at all that they might have shared their inner lives:

> *Would you describe a typical evening in the family when you were growing up?*

A twenty-five-year-old manicurist, mother of two, married seven years, replies:

> Let me think. I don't really know what happened; nothing much, I guess. My father came home at four-thirty, and we ate right away. Nobody talked much at the table; it was kind of a quiet affair.

> *What about your parents' relationship? Do you remember how they behaved with each other; whether they talked to each other?*

> Gee, I don't know. It's hard to think about them as being *with* each other. I don't think they talked a lot; at least, I never saw them talking. I can't imagine them sitting down to talk over problems or something like that, if that's what you mean.

Yes, that *is* what I mean. But that was the last generation; what about this one?

> *Would you describe a typical evening in your own family now?*

For some, less than half, it's better—a level of companionship, caring, and sharing that, while not all they dream of, is surely better than they knew in their past. Fathers attend more to children; husbands at least try to "hear" their wives; couples struggle around ... emotional issues ... For most, however, nothing much has changed since the last generation. Despite the yearning for more, relations between husband and wife are benumbed, filled with silence; life seems empty and meaningless; laughter, humor, fun is not a part of the daily ration. Listen to this couple married seven years. The wife:

> Frank comes home from work; now it's about five because he's been working overtime every night. We eat right away, right after he comes home. Then, I don't know. The kids play a while before bed, watch TV, you know, stuff like that. Then, I don't know; we don't do anything except maybe watch more TV or something like that. I don't know what else—nothing, I guess. We just sit, that's all.

> *That's it? Nothing else?*

> Yeah, that's right, that's all. [*A short silence, then angrily.*] Oh yeah, I forgot. Sometimes he's got one of his projects he works on. Like now, he's putting that new door in the kitchen. It's still nothing. When he finishes doing it, we just sit.

Her husband describes the same scene:

> I come home at five and we eat supper right away. Then, I sit down with coffee and a beer and watch TV. After that, if I'm working on a project, I do that for a little while. If not, I just watch.

> Life is very predictable. Nothing much happens; we don't do much. Everyone sits in the same place all the time and does the same thing every night. It's satisfying to me, but maybe it's not for her, I don't know. Maybe she wants to go to a show or something once in a while, I don't know. She doesn't tell me.

> *Don't you ask her?*

> No. I suppose I should, but it's really hard to think about getting out. We'd need someone to stay with the kids and all that. Besides, I'm tired. I've been out all day, seeing different people and stuff. I don't feel like going out after supper again.

> *Is there some time that you two have for yourselves, to talk things over and find out how you feel about things?*

The wife:

> There's plenty of time; we just don't do it. He doesn't ever think there's anything to talk about. I'm the one who has to nag him to talk always, and then I get disgusted.

He'd be content just living, you know, just nothing but living for the rest of his life. It don't make no difference to him where he lives or how people around him are feeling. I don't know how anybody can be like that.

A lot of times I get frustrated. I just wish I could talk to him about things and he could understand. If he had more feelings himself, maybe he'd understand more. Don't you think so?

Her husband agrees that he has problems handling both his feelings and hers:

I'm pretty tight-lipped about most things most of the time, especially personal things. I don't express what I think or feel. She keeps trying to get me to, but, you know, it's hard. Sometimes I'm not even sure what she wants me to be telling her. And when she gets all upset and emotional, I don't know what to say or what to do.

Sometimes she gets to nagging me about what I'm thinking or feeling, and I tell her, "Nothing," and she gets mad. But I swear, it's true; I'm not thinking about anything.

Difficult for her to believe, perhaps, but it *is* true. After a lifetime of repressing his feelings, he often *is* a blank, unaware that he's thinking or feeling anyting. Moreover, when emotions have been stored for that long, they tend to be feared as especially threatening or explosive. He continues:

Maybe it sounds a little crazy, but I'm afraid once I let go, I might get past the point where I know what I'm doing. If I let myself go, I'm afraid I could be dangerous. She keeps telling me that if you keep things pent up inside you like that, something's going to bust one day.

I think a lot of the problem is that our personalities are just very different. I'm the quiet type. If I have something I have to think about, I have to get by myself and do it. Elly, she just wants to talk about it, always talking about her feelings.

Yakketty-yakkers, that's what girls are. Well, I don't know; guys talk, too. But, you know, there's a difference, isn't there? Guys talk about things and girls talk about feelings.

Indeed that *is* the difference, precisely the difference I have been pointing to—"Guys talk about things and girls talk about feelings"—a difference that plagues marriage partners as they struggle to find ways to live with each other.

Again, the question presents itself: Is this just a phenomenon of working-class life? Clearly, it is not, for the social and psychological processes that account for the discrepant and often incompatible development of women and men apply across class and throughout the culture. Still, there are important class differences in the way these broad socio-cultural mandates are interpreted and translated into behavior—differences that are rooted in class situation and experience. Thus, there are dif-

ferences in the early childhood and family experiences of children who grow up in working-class homes and those who live in professional middle-class homes, differences in the range of experiences through their adolescence and young adulthood, and differences in the kinds of problems and preoccupations they face in their adult lives—on the job and in the family.

Whether boys or girls, children in the homes of the professional middle class have more training in exploring the socio-emotional realm and more avenues for such exploration. It's true that for the girls, this usually is the *focus* of their lives, while for the boys, it is not. Nevertheless, compared to childrearing patterns in working-class families, professional middle-class families make fewer and less rigid sex-role distinctions in early childhood. As small children, therefore, boys in such middle-class homes more often get the message that it's all right to cry, to be nurturant as well as nurtured, to be reflective and introspective, even at times to be passive—in essence, in some small measure, to relate to their expressive side.

Not once in a professional middle-class home did I see a young boy shake his father's hand in a well-taught "manly" gesture as he bid him good night. Not once did I hear a middle-class parent scornfully—or even sympathetically—call a crying a boy a sissy or in any way reprimand him for his tears. Yet, these were not uncommon observations in the working-class homes I visited. Indeed, I was impressed with the fact that, even as young as six or seven, the working-class boys seemed more emotionally controlled—more like miniature men—than those in the middle-class families.

These differences in childrearing practices are expressed as well in the different demands the parents of each class make upon the schools—differences that reflect the fact that working-class boys are expected to be even less emotional, more controlled than their middle-class counterparts. For the working-class parent, school is a place where teachers are expected to be tough disciplinarians; where children are expected to behave respectfully and to be punished if they do not; and where one mark of that respect is that they are sent to school neatly dressed in their "good" clothes and expected to stay that way through the day. None of these values is highly prized in the professional middle class. For them, schools are expected to be relatively loose, free, and fun; to encourage initiative, innovativeness, creativity, and spontaneity; and to provide a place where children—boys as well as girls—will learn social and interpersonal skills. The children of these middle-class families are sent to nursery school early—often as young as two and a half—not just because their mothers want the free time, but because the social-skill training provided there is considered a crucial part of their education.

These differences come as no surprise if we understand both the past experience and the future expectations of both sets of parents. Most highly educated parents have little fear that their children won't learn to read, write, and do their sums. Why should they? They learned them, and learned them well. Their children have every advantage that they had and plenty more: books, games, toys—all designed to excite curiosity and to stimulate imagination—and parents who are skillful in aiding in their use.

Working-class parents, however, have no such easy assurances about their children's educational prospects. Few can look back on their own school years without discomfort—discomfort born of painful reminders of all they didn't learn, of the many times they felt deficient and inadequate. Further, when they look at the schools their children attend now, they see the same pattern repeating itself. For, in truth, the socio-economic status of the children in a school is the best indicator of school-wide achievement test scores—that is, the lower the socio-economic status, the lower the scores.

Observing this phenomenon, many analysts and educators argue that these low achievement records in poor and working-class schools are a consequence of the family background—the lack of culture and educational motivation in the home—an explanation that tends to blame the victim for the failure of our social institutions. Elsewhere, I have entered the debate about *who* is to blame for these failures on the side of the victims. Here, the major point is simply that, regardless of where we think responsibility lies, working-class parents quite rightly fear that their children may not learn to read very well; that they may not be able to do even the simple arithmetic required to be an intelligent consumer. Feeling inadequate and lacking confidence that they can pass on their slim skills to their children, such parents demand that the schools enforce discipline in the belief that only then will their children learn all that they themselves did not.

This, however, is only one part of the explanation of why the sons of the professional middle class are brought up in a less rigidly stereotypic mode than are the sons of the working class—the part that is rooted in past experience. But past experience combines with present reality to create future expectations, because parents, after all, do not raise their children in a vacuum—without some idea of what the future holds for them, some sense of what they will need to survive the adult world for which they are destined. In fact, it is out of just such understandings that parental attitudes and values about child-raising are born. Thus, professional middle-class parents, assuming that their children are destined to do work like theirs—work that calls for innovation, initiative, flexibility, creativity, sensitivity to others, and a well-developed set of interpersonal skills—call for an educational system that fosters those qualities. Working-class parents also assume that their children will work at jobs roughly similar to their own. But in contrast to the requirements of professional or executive work, in most working-class jobs, creativity, innovation, initiative, flexibility are considered by superiors a hindrance. ("You're not getting paid to think!" is an oft-heard remonstrance.) Those who must work at such jobs may need nothing so much as a kind of iron-willed discipline to get them to work every day and to keep them going back year after year. No surprise, then, that such parents look suspiciously at spontaneity whether at home or at school. No surprise, either, that early childhood training tends to focus on respect, orderliness, cleanliness—in a word, discipline—especially for the boys who will hold these jobs, and that schools are called upon to reinforce these qualities.

Finally, men in the professional middle class presently live in an environment that gives some legitimacy to their stirrings and strivings toward connection with their emotional and expressive side. The extraordinary proliferation of the "growth-movement" therapies, which thrive on their appeal to both men and women of the upper middle class, is an important manifestation of that development. Another is the nascent men's movement—a response to the women's movement—with its men's groups, its male authors who write to a male audience encouraging their search for expressiveness. While it may be true that numerically all these developments account for only a small fraction of American men, it is also true that whatever the number, they are almost wholly drawn from the professional middle class.

For working-class men, these movements might as well not exist. Most don't know of them. The few who do, look at their adherents as if they were "kooks," "queers," or otherwise deficient, claiming to see no relevance in them to their own lives. Yet if one listens carefully to what lies beneath the surface of their words, the same stirrings for more connection with other parts of themselves, for more intimate relations with their wives are heard from working-class men as well. Often inchoate and inarticulately expressed, sometimes barely acknowledged, these yearnings, nevertheless, exist. But the struggle for their realization is a much more lonely and isolated one—removed not only from the public movements of our time but from the lives of those immediately around them—a private struggle in which there is no one to talk to, no examples to learn from. They look around them and see neighbors, friends, brothers, and sisters who are no better—sometimes far worse off—than they:

We're the only ones in the two families who have any kind of a marriage. One of my brothers ran out on his wife, the other one got divorced. Her sister and her husband are separated because he kept beating her up; her brother is still married, but he's a drunk. It makes it hard. If you never saw it in your family when you were growing up, then all the kids in both families mess up like that, it's hard to know what a good marriage is like. I guess you could say there hasn't been much of a model of one around us.

Without models, it is indeed hard—hard to know what to expect, hard to know how to act. You can't ask friends because they don't seem to have the same problems, not even the same feelings. One twenty-nine-year-old husband lamented:

I sometimes think I'm selfish. She's the support—the moral support—in the family. But when she needs support, I just don't give it to her. Maybe it's not just selfishness, it's that I don't know what she wants and I don't know how.

The worst thing is, I've got nobody to talk to about how a guy can be different. The guys at work, all they ever talk about is their cars or their trucks. Oh, they talk about women, but it's only to brag about how they're making it with this chick or that one. And my brother, it's no use talking to him; he don't know where anything's at. He runs around every night, comes home drunk, beats up his wife.

I know Joanie's not so happy, and I worry about what to do about it. But the guys I know, they don't worry about things like that.

Don't they? He doesn't really know because he dare not ask.

*How do you know they don't worry about such things? Have you asked them?*

He looks up, puzzled, as if wondering how anybody could even think of such a thing, and answers quickly:

Ask them? No! Why would I do that? They'd think I was nuts or something. People don't talk about those things; you just *know* where those guys are; you don't have to ask them.

In fact, many of those men are suffering the same conflicts and concerns—wondering, as he does, what happened to the old familiar world; fearful, as he is, that their masculine image will be impaired if they talk about the things that trouble them. But if they can't talk to brothers, friends, work mates, where do they turn?

*Maybe you could talk to Joan about what you could do to make things better in your marriage?*

Dejectedly, he replies:

What good would that do? She's only a girl. How would she know how a guy is supposed to act?

The women generally also suffer alone. Despite all the publicity generated by the women's movement about the dissatisfactions women experience in marriage, most working-class women continue to believe that their feel-

ings are uniquely theirs. Few have any contact with the movement or the people in it; few feel any support for their struggle from that quarter:

They put you down if you want to be married and raise kids, like there's something the matter with you.

Nor do they want it. For the movement is still a fearsome thing among working-class wives, and their responses to it are largely ambivalent, largely dominated by the negative stereotypes of the media. "Bra-burners," "man-haters"—these labels still are often heard.

Most believe in equal pay for equal work, but even that generally is not unequivocal:

Yes, I believe women should be paid the same as men if they're doing the same job. I mean, most of the time, I believe it. But if a man has a family to support and she doesn't, then it's different.

Few believe that women should compete equally in the job market with men:

If a man with a wife and kids needs a job, no woman ought to be able to take it away from him.

Neither response a surprise, given their history of economic deprivation and concern. Neither response to be heard among the wives of professional men. Also no surprise given their lifetime of greater financial security and the fact that they "take for granted" that their husbands will provide adequately for the family.

Beyond these two issues, one after the other the working-class women responded impatiently and with almost identical words to questions about what they know about the movement:

I don't know anything about it, and I don't care to know either.

*You sound angry at the women's movement.*

That's right, I am. I don't like women who want to be men. Those libbers, they want men and women to be just alike, and I don't want that to happen. I think men should be men and women should be women. They're crazy not to appreciate what men do for women. I like my husband to open the car door for me and to light my cigarettes. It makes me feel like a lady.

As if reciting a litany, several women spoke the same words over and over—"I like a man to open the car door and light my cigarettes." Perplexed at the repetition, at the assertion of value of these two particular behaviors, I finally asked:

*When was the last time your husband opened a car door for you or lit your cigarette?*

Startled, the open face of the woman who sat before me

became suffused with color; she threw her head back and laughed. Finally recovering, she said:

> I've gotta admit, I don't know why I said that. I don't even smoke.

Of course, she doesn't know why. To know would mean she'd have to face her fears and anxieties more squarely, to recognize that in some important ways the movement speaks to the issues that plague and pain her in her marriage. If, instead, she can reach for the stereotypes, she need not deal with the reality that these issues have become a part of her own life and aspirations, that their questions are also hers, that her own discontent is an example of what so many women out there are talking about.

For her, a major problem is that it remains "out there." Unlike the experience of the women in professional families, it is not *her* sisters, *her* friends, *her* neighbors who talk of these things, but women she doesn't know, has never met; women who aren't her "kind." So she hides her pain and internalizes her guilt.

> *Do you talk to your friends about some of the things we've been discussing—I mean about your conflicts about your life and your marriage, and about some of the things you dream about and wish for?*

No, we don't talk about those kinds of things. It's kind of embarrassing, too personal, you know. Besides, the people I know don't feel like I do, so it's no point in talking to them about those things.

> *How do you know how they feel if you don't talk about it?*

You just know, that's all. I know. It's why I worry sometimes that maybe there's something the matter with me that I'm not satisfied with what I've got. I get depressed, and then I wonder if I'm normal. I *know* none of my friends feels like that, like maybe they need a psychiatrist or something.

It's all right to complain about money, about a husband who drinks or stays out late, even about one who doesn't help around the house. But to tell someone you're unhappy because your husband doesn't talk to you—who would understand that?

> You don't talk about things like that to friends like I've got. They'd think I was another one of those crazy women's libbers.

Yes, there is concern among these working-class women and men about the quality of life, about its meaning. Yes, there is a deep wish for life to be more than a constant struggle with necessity. The drinking, the violence, the withdrawn silences—these are responses of despair, giving evidence that hope is hard to hold on to. How can it be otherwise when so often life seems like such an ungiving, uncharitable affair—a struggle without end? In the early years, it's unemployment, poverty, crying babies, violent fights. That phase passes, but a whole new set of problems emerge—problems that often seem harder to handle because they have less shape, less definition; harder, too, because they are less understandable, farther outside the realm of anything before experienced. But if there is one remarkable characteristic about life among the working class, it is the ability to engage the struggle and to survive it—a quality highly valued in a world where life has been and often remains so difficult and problematic. With a certain grim satisfaction, a twenty-six-year-old housewife, mother of two, summed it up:

> I guess in order to live, you have to have a very great ability to endure. And I have that—an ability to endure and survive.

---

## QUESTIONS

1. In what ways have sex roles changed during your lifetime? What changes, if any, do you expect in the future?

2. Why does it appear that changing sex-role expectations have placed the most strain on working-class families?

3. How many members of the class are willing to grant *complete* equality to their partners in marriage? Do males and females view the matter differently?

*Andrew Cherlin*
*Frank F. Furstenberg, Jr.*

# 34. The American Family in the Year 2000

*Despite the many forms it takes in cultures all over the world, the family is the most basic of all social institutions. But, fundamental as it is, the family is not immune to change. Like all institutions, family systems are subject to influences that can alter their structure and functions over time. In the preindustrial societies of the past, the norm was often the large extended family, with more than two generations of the same kinship line living together. Such a family system would be cumbersome and inconvenient in modern industrialized societies, so it is typically superseded by the nuclear family, consisting only of parents and their dependent children. But in recent decades, the nuclear family itself has been undergoing profound changes in the United States.*

*Currently, more than a fifth of American adults live alone. A fifth of the births in America are to unmarried mothers (most of them teenagers), and a quarter of the pregnancies end in abortion. People are marrying later in life than ever before, and about half of all marriages are expected to end in divorce. In the last twenty years, the number of unmarried couples has tripled. There is a steadily growing number of "reconstituted" families, consisting of "fragments" from previous families. Perhaps most important, more than a quarter of all American families are headed by only one parent, usually the mother. Some people regard the changes in the "standard" nuclear family with dismay and call for a variety of interventions—political, religious, economic—to reverse the apparent decay. Others see the changes as inevitable responses to altered social and cultural conditions. In a postindustrial society where people expect the freedom to "do their own thing," diversity in family life (as in religion, the economy, or other institutions) is hardly surprising.*

*In this article, Andrew Cherlin and Frank F. Furstenberg look ahead to the American family at the end of the century. They argue that, despite the increasingly diverse forms the family is taking, most Americans are still very much committed to the ideal of marrying and having children within the nuclear unit.*

- At current rates, half of all American marriages begun in the early 1980s will end in divorce.
- The number of unmarried couples living together has more than tripled since 1970.
- One out of four children is not living with both parents.

The list could go on and on. Teenage pregnancies: up. Adolescent suicides: up. The birthrate: down. Over the past decade, popular and scholarly commentators have cited a seemingly endless wave of grim statistics about the shape of the American family. The trends have caused a number of concerned Americans to wonder if the family, as we know it, will survive the twentieth century.

And yet, other observers ask us to consider more positive developments:

- Seventy-eight percent of all adults in a recent national survey said they get "a great deal" of satisfaction from their family lives; only 3% said "a little" or "none."
- Two-thirds of the married adults in the same survey said they were "very happy" with their marriages; only 3% said "not too happy."
- In another recent survey of parents of children in their middle years, 88% said that if they had to do it over, they would choose to have children again.
- The vast majority of the children (71%) characterized their family life as "close and intimate."

Family ties are still important and strong, the optimists argue, and the predictions of the demise of the family are greatly exaggerated.

Neither the dire pessimists who believe that the family is falling apart nor the unbridled optimists who claim that the family has never been in better shape provide

Reprinted from "The TAP Report," Fall 1982, by permission of the American Council of Life Insurance.

an accurate picture of family life in the near future. But these trends indicate that what we have come to view as the "traditional" family will no longer predominate.

## Diverse Family Forms

In the future, we should expect to see a growing amount of diversity in family forms, with fewer Americans spending most of their life in a simple "nuclear" family consisting of husband, wife, and children. By the year 2000, three kinds of families will dominate the personal lives of most Americans: families of first marriages, single-parent families, and families of remarriages.

In first-marriage families, both spouses will be in a first marriage, frequently begun after living alone for a time or following a period of cohabitation. Most of these couples will have one, two, or, less frequently, three children.

A sizable minority, however, will remain childless. Demographer Charles F. Westoff predicts that about one-fourth of all women currently in their childbearing years will never bear children, a greater number of childless women than at any time in U.S. history.

One other important shift: in a large majority of these families, both the husband and the wife will be employed outside the home. In 1940, only about one out of seven married women worked outside the home; today the proportion is one out of two. We expect this proportion to continue to rise, although not as fast as it did in the past decade or two.

## Single-Parent Families

The second major type of family can be formed in two ways. Most are formed by a marital separation, and the rest by births to unmarried women. About half of all marriages will end in divorce at current rates, and we doubt that the rates will fall substantially in the near future.

When the couple is childless, the formerly married partners are likely to set up independent households and resume life as singles. The high rate of divorce is one of the reasons why more men and women are living in single-person households than ever before.

But three-fifths of all divorces involve couples with children living at home. In at least nine out of ten cases, the wife retains custody of the children after a separation.

Although joint custody has received a lot of attention in the press and in legal circles, national data show that it is still uncommon. Moreover, it is likely to remain the exception rather than the rule because most ex-spouses can't get along well enough to manage raising their children together. In fact, a national survey of children aged 11 to 16 conducted by one of the authors demonstrated that fathers have little contact with their children after a divorce. About half of the children whose parents had divorced hadn't seen their father in the last year; only one out of six had managed to see their father an average of once a week. If the current rate of divorce persists, about half of all children will spend some time in a single-parent family before they reach 18.

Much has been written about the psychological effects on children of living with one parent, but the literature has not yet proven that any lasting negative effects occur. One effect, however, does occur with regularity: women who head single-parent families typically experience a sharp decline in their income relative to before their divorce. Husbands usually do not experience a decline. Many divorced women have difficulty reentering the job market after a long absence; others find that their low-paying clerical or service-worker jobs aren't adequate to support a family.

Of course, absent fathers are supposed to make child-support payments, but only a minority do. In a 1979 U.S. Bureau of the Census survey, 43% of all divorced and separated women with children present reported receiving child-support payments during the previous year, and the average annual payment was about $1,900. Thus, the most detrimental effect for children living in a single-parent family is not the lack of a male presence but the lack of a male income.

## Families of Remarriages

The experience of living as a single parent is temporary for many divorced women, especially in the middle class. Three out of four divorced people remarry, and about half of these marriages occur within three years of the divorce.

Remarriage does much to solve the economic problems that many single-parent families face because it typically adds a male income. Remarriage also relieves a single parent of the multiple burdens of running and supporting a household by herself.

But remarriage also frequently involves blending together two families into one, a difficult process that is complicated by the absence of clear-cut ground rules for how to accomplish the merger. Families formed by remarriages can become quite complex, with children from either spouse's previous marriage or from the new marriage and with numerous sets of grandparents, step-grandparents, and other kin and quasi-kin.

The divorce rate for remarriages is modestly higher than for first marriages, but many couples and their children adjust successfully to their remarriage and, when asked, consider their new marriage to be a big improvement over their previous one.

## The Life Course: A Scenario for the Next Two Decades

Because of the recent sharp changes in marriage and family life, the life course of children and young adults today is likely to be far different from what a person growing up earlier in this century experienced. It will not be uncommon, for instance, for children born in the 1980s to follow this sequence of living arrangements: live with both parents for several years, live with their mothers after their parents divorce, live with their mothers and stepfathers, live alone for a time when in their early twenties, live with someone of the opposite sex without marrying, get married, get divorced, live alone again, get remarried, and end up living alone once more following the death of their spouses.

Not everyone will have a family history this complex, but it is likely that a substantial minority of the population will. And many more will have family histories only slightly less complex.

Overall, we estimate that about half of the young children alive today will spend some time in a single-parent family before they reach 18; about nine out of ten will eventually marry; about one out of two will marry and then divorce; and about one out of three will marry, divorce, and then remarry. In contrast, only about one out of six women born in the period 1910 to 1914 married and divorced and only about one in eight married, divorced, and remarried.

Without doubt, Americans today are living in a much larger number of family settings during their lives than was the case a few generations ago.

The life-course changes have been even greater for women than for men because of the far greater likelihood of employment during the childbearing years for middle-class women today compared with their mothers and grandmothers. Moreover, the increase in life expectancy has increased the difference between men's and women's family lives. Women now tend to outlive men by a wide margin, a development that is new in this century. Consequently, many more women face a long period of living without a spouse at the end of their lives, either as a widow or as a divorced person who never remarried.

Long-lived men, in contrast, often find that their position in the marriage market is excellent, and they are much more likely to remain married (or remarried) until they die.

## Convergence and Divergence

The family lives of Americans vary according to such factors as class, ethnicity, religion, and region. But recent evidence suggests a convergence among these groups in many features of family life. The clearest example is in childbearing, where the differences between Catholics and non-Catholics or between Southerners and Northerners are much smaller than they were 20 years ago. We expect this process of convergence to continue, although it will fall far short of eliminating all social class and subcultural differences.

The experiences of blacks and whites also have converged in many respects, such as in fertility and in patterns of premarital sexual behavior, over the past few decades. But with respect to marriage, blacks and whites have diverged markedly since about 1960.

Black families in the United States always have had strong ties to a large network of extended kin. But in addition, blacks, like whites, relied on a relatively stable bond between husbands and wives. But over the past several decades—and especially since 1960—the proportion of black families maintained by a woman has increased sharply; currently, the proportion exceeds four in ten. In addition, more young black women are having children out of wedlock; in the late 1970s, about two out of three black women who gave birth to a first child were unmarried.

These trends mean that we must qualify our previously stated conclusion that marriage will remain central to family life. This conclusion holds for Americans in general. For many low-income blacks, however, marriage is likely to be less important than the continuing ties to a larger network of kin.

Marriage is simply less attractive to a young black woman from a low-income family because of the poor prospects many young black men have for steady employment and because of the availability of alternative sources of support from public-assistance payments and kin. Even though most black women eventually marry, their marriages have a very high probability of ending in separation or divorce. Moreover, they have a lower likelihood of remarrying.

Black single-parent families sometimes have been criticized as being "disorganized" or even "pathological." What the critics fail to note is that black single mothers usually are embedded in stable, functioning kin networks. These networks tend to center around female kin—mothers, grandmothers, aunts—but brothers, fathers, and other male kin also may be active. The members of these networks share and exchange goods and services, thus helping to share the burdens of poverty. The lower-class black extended family, then, is characterized by strong ties among a network of kin but fragile ties between husband and wife. The negative aspects of this family system have been exaggerated greatly; yet it need not be romanticized, either. It can be difficult and risky for individuals to leave the network in order to try to make it on their own; thus, it may be hard for individuals to raise themselves out of poverty until the whole network is raised.

## The Disintegrating Family?

By now, predictions of the demise of the family are familiar to everyone. Yet the family is a resilient institution that still retains more strength than its harshest critics maintain. There is, for example, no evidence of a large-scale rejection of marriage among Americans. To be sure, many young adults are living together outside of marriage, but the evidence we have about cohabitation suggests that it is not a lifelong alternative to marriage; rather, it appears to be either another stage in the process of courtship and marriage or a transition between first and second marriages.

The so-called "alternative lifestyles" that received so much attention in the late 1960s, such as communes and lifelong singlehood, are still very uncommon when we look at the nation as a whole.

Young adults today do marry at a somewhat older age, on average, than their parents did. But the average age at marriage today is very similar to what it was throughout the period from 1890 to 1940.

To be sure, many of these marriages will end in divorce, but three out of four people who divorce eventually remarry. Americans still seem to desire the intimacy and security that a marital relationship provides.

Much of the alarm about the family comes from reactions to the sheer speed at which the institution changed in the last two decades. Between the early 1960s and the mid-1970s, the divorce rate doubled, the marriage rate plunged, the birthrate dropped from a twentieth-century high to an all-time low, premarital sex became accepted, and married women poured into the labor force. But since the mid-1970s, the pace of change has slowed. The divorce rate has risen modestly and the birthrate even has increased a bit. We may have entered a period in which American families can adjust to the sharp changes that occurred in the 1960s and early 1970s. We think that, by and large, accommodations will be made as expectations change and institutions are redesigned to take account of changing family practices.

Despite the recent difficulties, family ties remain a central part of American life. Many of the changes in family life in the 1960s and 1970s were simply a continuation of long-term trends that have been with us for generations.

The birthrate has been declining since the 1820s, the divorce rate has been climbing since at least the Civil War, and over the last half century a growing number of married women have taken paying jobs. Employment outside the home has been gradually eroding the patriarchal system of values that was a part of our early history, replacing it with a more egalitarian set of values.

The only exception occurred during the late 1940s and the 1950s. After World War II, Americans raised during the austerity of depression and war entered adulthood at a time of sustained prosperity. The sudden turnabout in their fortunes led them to marry earlier and have more children than any generation before or since in this century. Because many of us were either parents or children in the baby-boom years following the war, we tend to think that the 1950s typify the way twentieth-century families used to be. But the patterns of marriage and childbearing in the 1950s were an aberration resulting from special historical circumstances; the patterns of the 1960s and 1970s better fit the long-term trends. Barring unforeseen major disruptions, small families, working wives, and impermanent marital ties are likely to remain with us indefinitely.

A range of possible developments could throw our forecasts off the mark. We do not know, for example, how the economy will behave over the next 20 years, or how the family will be affected by technological innovations still at the conception stage. But we do not envision any dramatic changes in family life resulting solely from technological innovations in the next two decades.

Having sketched our view of the most probable future, we will consider three of the most important implications of the kind of future we see.

## Growing Up in Changing Families

Children growing up in the past two decades have faced a maelstrom of social change. As we have pointed out, family life is likely to become even more complex, diverse, unpredictable, and uncertain in the next two decades.

Even children who grow up in stable family environments will probably have to get along with a lot less care from parents (mothers in particular) than children received early in this century. Ever since the 1950s, there has been a marked and continuous increase in the proportion of working mothers whose preschool children are cared for outside the home, rising from 31% in 1958 to 62% in 1977. The upward trend is likely to continue until it becomes standard practice for very young children to receive care either in someone else's home or in a group setting. There has been a distinct drop in the care of children by relatives, as fewer aunts, grandmothers, or adult children are available to supplement the care provided by parents. Increasingly, the government at all levels will be pressured to provide more support for out-of-home daycare.

How are children responding to the shifting circumstances of family life today? Are we raising a generation of young people who, by virtue of their own family experiences, lack the desire and skill to raise the next generation? As we indicated earlier, existing evidence has not demonstrated that marital disruption creates lasting personality damage or instills a distinctly different set of values about family life.

Similarly, a recent review on children of working mothers conducted by the National Research Council of the National Academy of Sciences concludes:

> If there is only one message that emerges from this study, it is that parental employment in and of itself—mothers' employment or fathers' or both parents'—is not necessarily good or bad for children.

The fact that both parents work *per se* does not adversely affect the well-being of children.

Currently, most fathers whose wives are employed do little childcare. Today, most working mothers have two jobs: they work for pay and then come home to do most of the childcare and housework. Pressure from a growing number of harried working wives could prod fathers to watch less television and change more diapers. But this change in fathers' roles is proceeding much more slowly than the recent spate of articles about the "new father" would lead one to expect. The strain that working while raising a family places on working couples, and especially on working mothers, will likely make childcare and a more equitable sharing of housework prominent issues in the 1980s and 1990s.

## Family Obligations

Many of the one out of three Americans who, we estimate, will enter a second marriage will do so after having children in a first marriage. Others may enter into a first marriage with a partner who has a family from a previous marriage. It is not clear in these families what obligations remain after divorce or are created after remarriage. For one thing, no clear set of norms exists specifying how people in remarriages are supposed to act toward each other. Stepfathers don't know how much to discipline their stepchildren; second wives don't know what they're supposed to say when they meet their husbands' first wives; stepchildren don't know what to call their absent father's new wife.

The ambiguity about family relations after divorce and remarriage also extends to economic support. There are no clear-cut guidelines to tell adults how to balance the claims of children from previous marriages versus children from their current marriages. Suppose a divorced man who has been making regular payments to support his two small children from a previous marriage marries a woman with children from her previous marriage. Suppose her husband isn't paying any child support. Suppose further that the remarried couple have a child of their own. Which children should have first claim on the husband's income? Legally, he is obligated to pay child support to his ex-wife, but in practice he is likely to feel that his primary obligation is to his stepchildren, whose father isn't helping, and to his own children from his remarriage.

Our guess, supported by some preliminary evidence from national studies, is that remarriage will tend to further reduce the amount of child support that a man pays, particularly if the man's new family includes children from his new wife's previous marriage or from the current marriage. What appears to be occurring in many cases is a form of "childswapping," with men exchanging an old set of children from a prior marriage for a new set from their new wife's prior marriage and from the remarriage.

Sociologist Lenore J. Weitzman provides a related example in her book *The Marriage Contract.* Suppose, she writes, a 58-year-old corporate vice president with two grown children divorces his wife to marry his young secretary. He agrees to adopt the secretary's two young children. If he dies of a heart attack the following year:

> In most states, a third to half of his estate would go to his new wife, with the remainder divided among the four children (two from his last marriage, and his new wife's two children). His first wife will receive nothing—neither survivors' insurance nor a survivors' pension nor a share of the estate—and both she and his natural children are likely to feel that they have been treated unjustly.

Since the rate of mid-life divorce has been increasing nearly as rapidly as that of divorce at younger ages, this type of financial problem will become increasingly common. It would seem likely that there will be substantial pressure for changes in family law and in income security systems to provide more to the ex-wife and natural children in such circumstances.

## Intergenerational Relations

A similar lack of clarity about who should support whom may affect an increasing number of elderly persons. Let us consider the case of an elderly man who long ago divorced his first wife and, as is fairly typical, retained only sporadic contact with his children. If his health deteriorates in old age and he needs help, will his children provide it? In many cases, the relationship would seem so distant that the children would not be willing to provide major assistance. To be sure, in most instances the elderly man would have remarried, possibly acquiring stepchildren, and it may be these stepchildren who feel the responsibility to provide assistance. Possibly the two sets of children may be called upon to cooperate in lending support, even when they have had little or no contact while growing up. Currently, there are no clear guidelines for assigning kinship responsibilities in this new type of extended family.

Even without considering divorce, the issue of support to the elderly is likely to bring problems that are new and widespread. As is well known, the low fertility in the United States, which we think will continue to be low, means that the population is becoming older. The difficulties that this change in age structure poses for the Social Security system are so well known that we need not discuss them here. Let us merely note that any substantial weakening of the Social Security system would put the elderly at a great disadvantage with regard to their families, for older Americans increasingly rely on Social Security and other pensions and insurance plans to provide support. A collapse of Social Security would result in a large decrease in the standard of living among older Americans and a return to the situation prevailing a few decades ago in which the elderly were disproportionately poor.

The relations between older people and their children and grandchildren are typically close, intimate, and warm. Most people live apart from their children, but they generally live close by one or more of them. Both generations prefer the autonomy that the increased affluence of the older generation has recently made possible. Older people see family members quite often, and they report that family members are their major source of support. A survey by Louis Harris of older Americans revealed that more than half of those with children had seen them in the past day, and close to half had seen a grandchild. We expect close family ties between the elderly and their kin to continue to be widespread. If, however, the economic autonomy of the elderly is weakened, say, by a drop in Social Security, the kind of friendly equality that now characterizes intergenerational relations could be threatened.

One additional comment about the elderly: Almost everyone is aware that the declining birthrate means that the elderly will have fewer children in the future on whom they can rely for support. But although this is true in the long run, it will not be true in the next few decades. In fact, beginning soon, the elderly will have more children, on average, than they do today. The reason is the postwar baby boom of the late 1940s and 1950s. As the parents of these large families begin to reach retirement age near the end of this century, more children will be available to help their elderly parents. Once the next generation—the baby-boom children—begins to reach retirement age after about 2010, the long-term trend toward fewer available children will sharply reassert itself.

Were we to be transported suddenly to the year 2000, the families we would see would look very recognizable. There would be few unfamiliar forms—not many communes or group marriages, and probably not a large proportion of lifelong singles. Instead, families by and large would continue to center around the bonds between husbands and wives and between parents and children. One could say the same about today's families relative to the 1960s: the forms are not new. What is quite different, comparing the 1960s with the 1980s, or the 1980s with a hypothetical 2000, is the distribution of these forms.

In the early 1960s, there were far fewer single-parent families and families formed by remarriages after divorce than is the case today; and in the year 2000 there are likely to be far more single-parent families and families of remarriage than we see now. Moreover, in the early 1960s both spouses were employed in a much smaller percentage of two-parent families; in the year 2000, the percentage with two earners will be greater still. Cohabitation before marriage existed in the 1960s, but it was a frowned-upon, bohemian style of life. Today, it has become widely accepted; it will likely become more common in the future. Yet we have argued that cohabitation is less an alternative to marriage than a precursor to marriage, though we expect to see a modest rise in the number of people who never marry.

---

## QUESTIONS

1. In what ways is the American family changing?

2. What social forces are undermining the traditional American family system?

3. Would you say that the family is in danger of disintegrating, or is it merely changing to new and more diverse forms that are better suited to altered social conditions?

*Eleanor Holmes Norton*

# 35. Restoring the Traditional Black Family

*The sharpest divergence from the "standard" American family is among poorer black people, primarily in the urban ghettos of the northern cities. Today more than half of all black births are to unmarried teenage mothers, who typically drop out of school to raise their children. More than half of all black children now live in homes with a single parent. As a result of these trends, one of every two black children lives below the poverty line. The plight of the family has become perhaps the gravest problem facing the black minority. Strong families make for a stable community; weak families threaten not only the present generation, but the next one as well.*

*The breakdown of the black family occurs in the context of wider patterns of inequalities of race and class. During the course of this century, blacks have been displaced from jobs in the rural South by such factors as the mechanization of agriculture. Many displaced workers migrated to the northern cities— but they arrived there at a time when unskilled manufacturing jobs were also disappearing. Prejudice, discrimination, poverty, and lack of education has made it difficult for many members of the growing ghetto population to enter the new postindustrial jobs in the cities or to move to better employment opportunities in the expanding suburbs. This situation led to the creation of a ghetto "underclass" in which a high proportion of men are chronically unemployed. The result has been a self-perpetuating cycle of despair, poverty, drug abuse, and promiscuity. In this context, many single women become pregnant and dependent on welfare. Families headed by women—especially minority women—are especially vulnerable to poverty, so the cycle threatens to repeat itself yet again.*

*In this article, Eleanor Holmes Norton traces the historical and economic factors that have contributed to the breakdown of the black family, particularly in the urban ghettos, and offers some suggestions for change.*

From *The New York Times Magazine*, June 2, 1985, pp. 43–98. Copyright © 1985 by The New York Times Company. Reprinted by permission.

What would society be like if the family found it difficult to perform its most basic functions? We are beginning to find out. Half of all marriages in this country end in divorce, and half of all children will spend a significant period with only one parent.

Startling and unsettling changes have already occurred in black family life, especially among the poor. Since the 1960's, birth rates among blacks have fallen dramatically, but two out of every three black women having a first child are single, compared to one out of every six white women. Today, well over half of black children in this country are born to single women. Why are female-headed households multiplying now, when there is less discrimination and poverty than a couple of generations ago, when black family life was stronger?

The disruption of the black family today is, in exaggerated microcosm, a reflection of what has happened to American family life in general. Public anxiety has mounted with the near-doubling of the proportion of white children living with one parent (from 9 percent to 17 percent) since 1970. Single parents of all backgrounds are feeling the pressures—the sheer economics of raising children primarily on the depressed income of the mother (a large component of the so-called "feminization of poverty"); the psychological and physical toll when one person, however advantaged, must be both mother and father, and the effects on children.

The stress on American family life was recently addressed by Senator Daniel P. Moynihan, Democrat of New York, on the 20th anniversary of his controversial "Moynihan Report." The original report confined its analysis to the black family. Moynihan, who in April delivered a series of lectures at Harvard on the family, said, "I want to make clear this is not a black issue." Indeed, just last month, the problem of increasing poverty among all the nation's children was underscored in a major report from two Federal agencies.

Yet until recently, many blacks have had an almost visceral reaction to mention of black family problems. Wounds to the family were seen as the most painful effect of American racism. Many blacks and their supporters have regarded talk of black family weaknesses as tantamount to insult and smear. Some conservatives have taken signs of trouble in the black family as proof that the remaining problems of race are internal and have announced the equivalent of "Physician, heal thyself."

At the heart of the crisis lies the self-perpetuating culture of the ghetto. This destructive ethos began to surface 40 years ago with the appearance of permanent joblessness and the devaluation of working-class black men. As this nation's post-World War II economy has helped produce a black middle class, it has also, ironically, been destroying the black working class and its family structure. Today, the process has advanced so far that renewal of the black family goes beyond the indispensable economic ingredients. The family's return to its historic strength will require the overthrow of the complicated, predatory ghetto subculture, a feat demanding not only new Government approaches but active black leadership and community participation and commitment.

While this crisis was building, it received almost no public attention, in part because of the notorious sensitivity of the subject. Yet 20 years ago, Martin Luther King Jr. spoke candidly about the black family, spelling out the "alarming" statistics on "the rate of illegitimacy," the increase in female-headed households and the rise in families on welfare. The black family, King asserted, had become "fragile, deprived and often psychopathic."

King relied in part on the Moynihan report, written when the Senator was an Assistant Secretary of Labor. Many were stunned by what one critic called the report's "salacious 'discovery' "—its discussion of illegitimacy, matriarchy and welfare and its view that black family structure had become, in its own words, a "tangle of pathology" capable of perpetuating itself without assistance from the white world. As a result, the report's concern with remedies, including jobs, and its call for a national family policy were eclipsed.

The delay has been costly to blacks and to the country. When King spoke out, the statistics he characterized as alarming showed that two-and-a-half times as many black families as white ones were headed by women. Today, it is almost three-and-a-half times as many—43 percent of black families compared with 13 percent of white families. Since 1970, out-of-wedlock births have become more prevalent throughout society, almost doubling among whites to 11 percent. But among blacks, births to single women have risen from 38 percent in 1970 to 57 percent in 1982.

While families headed by women have often proved just as effective as two-parent families in raising children, the most critical danger facing female-headed households is poverty. Seventy percent of black children under the age of 18 who live in female-headed families

are being brought up in poverty. In 1983, the median income for such households was $7,999, compared to almost $32,107 for two-parent families of all races, in which both spouses worked. Without the large increase in female-headed households, black family income would have *increased* by 11 percent in the 1970's. Instead, it fell by 5 percent.

As last month's report from the Congressional Research Service and the Congressional Budget Office pointed out, "The average black child can expect to spend more than five years of his childhood in poverty; the average white child, 10 months."

Buried beneath the statistics is a world of complexity originating in the historic atrocity of slavery and linked to modern discrimination and its continuing effects. What has obscured the problem is its delicacy and its uniqueness. The black family has been an issue in search of leadership. Discussion of problems in the black family has been qualitatively different from debates on voting rights or job discrimination. Fear of generating a new racism has foreclosed whatever opportunity there may have been to search for relief, driving the issue from the public agenda and delaying for a generation the search for workable solutions. Today, when nearly half of all black children are being raised in poverty, further delay is unthinkable.

Blacks themselves have been stunned by recent disclosures of the extent of the growth of poor, alienated female-headed households. The phenomenon is outside the personal experience of many black adults. Many have overcome deep poverty and discrimination only because of the protection and care of stable traditional and extended families. As recently as the early 1960's, 75 percent of black households were husband-and-wife families. The figure represents remarkable continuity—it is about the same as those reported in census records from the late 19th century. Indeed, the evidence suggests that most slaves grew up in two-parent families reinforced by ties to large extended families.

The sharp rise in female-headed households involves mostly those with young children and began in the mid-1960's. The phenomenon—while by no means a trend that permeates the entire black community—affects a significant portion of young people today, many of whom are separated economically, culturally and socially from the black mainstream. They have been raised in the worst of the rapidly deteriorating ghettos of the 1960's, 1970's and 1980's, in cities or neighborhoods that lost first the white and then the black middle and working classes. Drugs, crime and pimps took over many of the old communities. Blacks remaining were often trapped and isolated, cut off from the values of the black working poor and middle class—where husbands often work two jobs, wives return to work almost immediately after childbirth and extended families of interdependent kin are still more prevalent than among whites.

A complete explanation of black family disruption does not emerge from a roundup of the usual suspects, including the many factors that make American family life generally less stable these days: the ease and relative acceptance of separation, divorce and childbirth outside of marriage; the decline of religion and other traditional family-reinforcing institutions, and welfare rules that discourage family unity and penalize economic initiative. Anecdotal explanations—the girl-mothers are said to want to love and receive affection from a baby; the boy-fathers reportedly brag about making babies—are also inadequate. Such anecdotes do not explain how the strong presumption in favor of marriage before childbearing has been overcome so often.

The emergence of single women as the primary guardians of the majority of black children is a pronounced departure that began to take shape following World War II. Ironically, the women and children—the most visible manifestations of the change—do not provide the key to the transformation. The breakdown begins with working-class black men, whose loss of function in the post-World War II economy has led directly to their loss of function in the family.

In the booming post-World War I economy, black men with few skills could find work. Even the white South, which denied the black man a place in its wage economy, could not deprive him of an economic role in the farm family. The poorest, most meanly treated sharecropper was at the center of the work it took to produce the annual crop.

As refugees from the South, the generation of World War I migrants differed in crucial respects from the World War II generation. The World War I arrivals were enthusiastic, voluntary migrants, poor in resources but frequently middle class in aspiration. They were at the bottom of a society that denied them the right to move up very far, but they got a foothold in a burgeoning economy.

Family stability was the rule. According to a 1925 study in New York City, five out of six children under the age of six lived with both parents. Nationally, a small middle class emerged, later augmented by the jobs generated by World War II, service in the armed forces and the postwar prosperity that sometimes filtered down to urban blacks.

Today's inner-city blacks were not a part of these historical processes. Some are the victims of the flight of manufacturing jobs. Others were part of the last wave of Southern migrants or their offspring, arriving in the 1950's and 1960's. They often migrated not because of new opportunities but because of the evaporation of old ones. Mechanized farming made their labor superfluous in agriculture, but unlike the blacks of earlier genera-

tions and European immigrants, later black migrants were also superfluous in the postwar cities as manufacturing work for the less-skilled and poorly educated declined. Today's postindustrial society, demanding sophisticated preparation and training, has only exacerbated these problems.

This permanent, generational joblessness is at the core of the meaning of the American ghetto. The resulting, powerful aberration transforms life in poor black communities and forces everything else to adapt to it. The female-headed household is only one consequence. The underground economy, the drug culture, epidemic crime and even a highly unusual disparity between the actual number of men and women—all owe their existence to the cumulative effect of chronic joblessness among men. Over time, deep structural changes have taken hold and created a different ethos.

An entire stratum of black men, many of them young, no longer performs its historic role in supporting a family. Many are unemployed because of the absence of jobs, or unemployable because their ghetto origins leave them unprepared for the job market. Others have adapted to the demands of the ghetto—the hustle, the crime, the drugs. But the skills necessary to survive in the streets are those least acceptable in the outside world.

The macho role cultivated in the ghetto makes it difficult for many black men, unable to earn a respectable living, to form households and assume the roles of husband and father. Generationally entrenched joblessness joined with the predatory underground economy form the bases of a marginal life style. Relationships without the commitments of husband and father result.

This qualitative change in fundamental family relationships could have occurred only under extreme and unrelentingly destructive conditions. Neither poverty nor cyclical unemployment alone could have had this impact. After all, poverty afflicts most of the world's people. If economic and social hardships could in themselves destroy family life, the family could not have survived as the basic human unit throughout the world.

The transformation in poor black communities goes beyond poverty. These deep changes are anchored in a pervasively middle-class society that associates manhood with money. Shocking figures show a long, steep and apparently permanent decline in black men's participation in the labor force, even at peak earning ages. In 1948, before the erosion of unskilled and semiskilled city and rural jobs had become pronounced, black male participation in the labor force was 87 percent, almost a full point higher than that of white males.

In the generation since 1960, however, black men have experienced a dramatic loss of jobs—dropping from an employment rate of 74 percent to 55 percent in 1982, according to the Center for the Study of Social Policy in

Washington. While white male employment slipped in that period, much of the white decline, unlike that of the blacks, is attributed to early retirement. Since 1960, the black male population over the age of 18 has doubled, but the number employed has lagged badly.

These figures tell a story not only of structural unemployment, but of structural changes in low-income black families. The unemployment rates of young blacks have been the most devastating and militate against the establishment of stable marriages. This year, for instance, black teen-agers overall had an unemployment rate of 39 percent, two-and-a-half times that of white teen-agers. The loss of roles as workers has led to the acceptance of other roles for financial gain, many of them antisocial. Aside from the fact that large numbers of young men are imprisoned, disabled by drugs or otherwise marginal or unavailable as marriage partners, there is an unusual disparity between the sheer numbers of black men and black women. Among whites, the ratio of men to women does not change significantly until age 50, when men's shorter life expectancy creates a gap. But among blacks, beginning at age 20, women outnumber men significantly enough to have a major impact upon the possibility of marriage.

Some argue persuasively that the female-headed family is an adaptation that facilitates coping with hardship and demographics. This seems undeniable as an explanation, but unsatisfactory as a response. Are we willing to accept an adaptation that leaves the majority of black children under the age of 6—the crucial foundation years of life—living in poverty? Given a real choice, poor blacks, like everybody else, would hardly choose coping mechanisms over jobs, educational opportunity and family stability.

Yet, the remedy for ghetto conditions is not as simple as providing necessities and opportunities. The ghetto is not simply a place. It has become a way of life. Just as it took a complex of social forces to produce ghetto conditions, it will take a range of remedies to dissolve them. The primary actors unavoidably are the Government and the black community itself.

The Government is deeply implicated in black family problems. Its laws enforced slavery before the Civil War and afterward created and sanctioned pervasive public and private discrimination. The effects on the black family continue to this day. Given the same opportunities as others, blacks would almost certainly have sustained the powerful family traditions they brought with them from Africa, where society itself is organized around family.

Quite apart from its historical role, the Government cannot avoid present responsibility. It can choose, as it now does, to ignore and delay the search for ways to break the hold of the ghetto, such as early intervention with young children and training and education for the

hard-core poor. Although programs capable of penetrating ghetto conditions have proved elusive, the current Government posture of disengagement is folly. With the poor growing at a faster rate than the middle class, the prospect is that succeeding generations will yield more, not fewer, disadvantaged blacks. An American version of a *lumpenproletariat* (the so-called underclass), without work and without hope, existing at the margins of society, could bring down the great cities, sap resources and strength from the entire society and, lacking the usual means to survive, prey upon those who possess them.

Perhaps the greatest gap in corrective strategies has been the failure to focus on prevention. Remedies for deep-rooted problems—from teen-age pregnancy to functional illiteracy—are bound to fail when we leave the water running while we struggle to check the overflow. A primary incubator for ghetto problems is the poor, female-headed household. Stopping its proliferation would prevent a spectrum of often-intractable social and economic problems.

Remedies often focus at opposite ends—either on the provision of income or of services. Neither seems wholly applicable to entrenched ghetto conditions. Public assistance alone, leaving people in the same defeatist environment, may reinforce the status quo. The service orientation has been criticized for using a disproportionate amount of the available resources relative to the results obtained.

More appropriate solutions may lie between income and service strategies. Programs are likely to be more successful if they provide a rigorous progression through a series of steps leading to "graduation." This process, including a period of weaning from public assistance, might prove more successful in achieving personal independence. Such programs would be far more disciplined than services to the poor generally have been. They would concentrate on changing life styles as well as imparting skills and education. The test of their effectiveness would be the recipients' progress in achieving economic self-sufficiency.

To reach boys and men, especially the hard-core unemployed, more work needs to be done to cull the successful aspects of training and job programs. Effective training models need to be systematically replicated. It is untenable to abandon the hard-core unemployed, as the Reagan Administration has done, by moving to a jobs program that focuses on the most, rather than the least, trainable. Ghetto males will not simply go away. As we now see, they will multiply themselves.

The welfare program—a brilliant New Deal invention now stretched to respond to a range of problems never envisioned for it—often deepens dependence and lowers self-esteem. Although welfare enjoys little support anywhere along the political spectrum, it continues for lack of an alternative.

Reconceived, a public-assistance program could reach single mothers and offer them vehicles to self-sufficiency. The counterparts of young women on welfare are working downtown or attending high school or junior college on grants to low-income students. Far from foreclosing such opportunities because a woman has a child, public assistance should be converted from the present model of passive maintenance to a program built around education or work and prospective graduation.

Studies of the hard-core unemployed have shown women on welfare to be the most desirous of, open to and successful with training and work. Some, especially with young children, will remain at home, but most want work or training because it is the only way out of the welfare life. Some promising experiments in work and welfare are underway in such cities as San Diego and Baltimore. But the old "workfare" approach, when administered as another form of welfare with no attempt to break the cycle of dependency, is self-defeating. Gainful employment, even if in public jobs for those unaccommodated by the private sector, would have beneficial effects beyond earning a living. Jobs and training would augment self-esteem by exposing women to the values and discipline associated with work, allowing them to pass on to their children more than their own disadvantages.

The ghetto, more than most circumscribed cultures, seeks to perpetuate itself and is ruthless in its demand for conformity. However, it contains institutions of the larger society—schools, churches, community groups. With minor additional resources, schools, for example, could incorporate more vigorous and focused ways to prevent teen-age pregnancy. If pregnancy occurs, girls could be motivated to remain in school, even after childbirth, thus allowing an existing institution to accomplish what training programs in later life do more expensively and with greater difficulty.

Schools and other community institutions also need to become much more aggressive with boys on the true meaning and responsibilities of manhood, and the link between manhood and family. Otherwise, many boys meet little resistance to the ghetto message that associates manhood with sex but not responsibility.

Most important, nothing can substitute for or have a greater impact than the full-scale involvement of the black community. Respect for the black family tradition compels black initiative. Today, blacks are responding. Many black organizations are already involved, including the National Urban League, the National Association for the Advancement of Colored People, the National Council of Negro Women and the National Urban Coalition. In 1983, the country's major black leaders endorsed a frank statement of the problems of the black family and a call for solutions. The statement, published by the Joint Center for Political Studies, a black research center in Washington, represented the first consensus view by black leadership on the problems of the black family. Significantly, it went beyond a call for Government help, stressing the need for black leadership and community efforts.

With the increase in the number of black public officials, many black mayors, legislators and appointed officials control some of the resources that could help shape change. Although they cannot redesign the welfare system by themselves, for example, some are in a position to experiment with model projects that could lead to more workable programs—such as supplementing welfare grants with training or work opportunities for single mothers; promoting family responsibility and pregnancy prevention for boys and girls through local institutions, and encouraging the completion of school for single teen-aged parents.

The new black middle class, a product of the same period that saw the weakening of the black family, still has roots in the ghetto through relatives and friends. From churches, Girl Scout troops and settlement houses to civil-rights organizations, Boys' Clubs and athletic teams, the work of family reinforcement can be shared widely. The possibilities for creative community intervention are many—from family planning and counseling and various roles as surrogate parents and grandparents, to sex education, community day care and simple, but crucial, consciousness-raising. Most important is passing on the enduring values that form the central content of the black American heritage: hard work, education, respect for family, and, notwithstanding the denial of personal opportunity, achieving a better life for one's children.

## QUESTIONS

1. What historical factors have led to the current predicament of the ghetto family?

2. What is the relationship between unemployment and the predicament of the black family in inner-city areas?

3. What is meant by the "feminization of poverty"? Why do women have higher poverty rates than men?

*Jules Henry*

# 36. Golden Rule Days: American Schoolrooms

*Education is a crucial institution in all modern societies. To function effectively in these societies, people must be introduced to a large and complex body of knowledge, a need that is achieved most efficiently through the use of schools and teachers. Unhappily, however, not everyone can agree on what should be taught in school or how it should be taught, and there is no guarantee that people will learn what is expected of them.*

*As Jules Henry points out in this article, formal schooling must cope with a series of cultural contradictions. For example, the need for education is greatest when cultural knowledge is expanding the fastest—but that is precisely when the schools are most likely to lag behind, teaching yesterday's or today's knowledge to tomorrow's citizens. Similarly, the schools are expected to teach an approved body of knowledge, including cultural norms and values—but the very process of education stimulates independent thought, thus encouraging some people to question and challenge what they have been taught (and their teachers).*

*In his article, Henry draws on extensive observations of actual classroom situations to illustrate these and other paradoxes of schooling.*

## Introduction

School is an institution for drilling children in cultural orientations. Educationists have attempted to free the school from drill, but have failed because they have gotten lost among a multitude of phantasms—always choosing the most obvious "enemy" to attack. Furthermore, with every enemy destroyed, new ones are installed among the old fortifications—the enduring contradictory maze of the culture. Educators think that when they have made arithmetic or spelling into a game; made it unnecessary for children to "sit up straight"; defined the relation between teacher and children as democratic; and introduced plants, fish, and hamsters into schoolrooms, they have settled the problem of drill. They are mistaken.

## Education and the Human Condition

### Learning to Learn

The paradox of the human condition is expressed more in education than elsewhere in human culture, because learning to learn has been and continues to be *Homo sapiens'* most formidable evolutionary task. Although it is true that mammals, as compared to birds and fishes, have to learn so much that it is difficult to say by the time we get to chimpanzees what behavior is inborn and what is learned, the learning task has become so enormous for man that today learning—education—along with survival, constitutes a major preoccupation. In all the fighting over education we are simply saying that we are not yet satisfied—after about a million years of struggling to become human—that we have mastered the fundamental human task, learning. It must also be clear that we will never quite learn how to learn, for since *Homo sapiens* is self-changing, and since the *more* culture changes the *faster* it changes, man's methods and rate of learning will never quite keep pace with his need to learn. This is the heart of the problem of "cultural lag," for each fundamental scientific discovery presents man with an incalculable number of problems which he cannot foresee. Who, for example, would have anticipated that the discoveries of Einstein would have presented us with the social problems of the nuclear age, or that information theory would have produced unemployment and displacement in world markets?

### Fettering and Freeing

Another learning problem inherent in the human condition is the fact that we must conserve culture while changing it; that we must always be *more* sure of surviving than of adapting—*as we see it.* Whenever a new idea appears our first concern as *animals* must be that it does not kill us; then, and only then, can we look at it from other points of view. While it is true that we are often mistaken, either because we become enchanted with certain modes of thought or because we cannot anticipate their consequences, this tendency to look first at survival has resulted in fettering the capacity to learn new things. In general, primitive people solved this problem simply by walling their children off from new possibilities by educational methods that, largely through fear (including ridicule, beating, and mutilation) so narrowed the perceptual sphere that other than traditional ways of viewing the world became unthinkable. Thus throughout history the cultural pattern has been a device for binding the intellect. Today, when we think we wish to free the mind so it will soar, we are still, nevertheless, bound by the ancient paradox, for we must hold our culture together through clinging to old ideas lest, in adopting new ones, we literally cease to exist.

In searching the literature on the educational practices of other civilizations I have found nothing that better expresses the need to teach and to fetter than the following, from an account by a traveler along the Niger River in Africa in the fourteenth century:

> . . . their zeal for learning the Koran by heart [is so great that] they put their children in chains if they show any backwardness in memorizing it, and they are not set free until they have it by heart. I visited the *qadi* in his house on the day of the festival. His children were chained up, so I said to him. "Will you not let them loose?" He replied, "I shall not do so until they learn the Koran by heart."[1]

Perhaps the closest material parallel we have to this from our own cultural tradition is the stocks in which ordinary English upper-class children were forced to stand in the eighteenth century while they pored over their lessons at home. The fettering of the mind while we "set the spirit free" or the fettering of the spirit as we free the mind is an abiding paradox of "civilization" in its more refined dimensions. It is obvious that chimpanzees are incapable of this paradox. It is this capacity to pass from the jungles of the animal world into the jungle of paradox of the human condition that, more than anything else, marks off human from animal learning. It is this jungle that confronts the child in his early days at school, and that seals his destiny—if it has not previously been determined by poverty—as an eager mind or as a faceless learner.

Since education is always against some things and for others, it bears the burden of the cultural obsessions. While the Old Testament extols without cease the glory of the One God, it speaks with equal emphasis against the gods of the Philistines; while the children of the Dakota Indians learned loyalty to their own tribe, they learned to hate the Crow; and while our children are taught to love our American democracy, they are taught contempt for totalitarian regimes. It thus comes about that most educational systems are imbued with anxiety and hostility, that they are against as many things as they are for. Because, therefore, so much anxiety inheres in any human educational system—anxiety that it may free when it should fetter; anxiety that it may fetter when it should free; anxiety that it may teach sympathy when it should teach anger; anxiety that it may disarm where it should arm—our contemporary education system is constantly under attack. When, in anxiety about the present state of our world, we turn upon the schools with even more venom than we turn on our government, we are "right" in the sense that it is in the schools that the basic binding and freeing processes that will "save" us will be established. But being "right" derives not so much from the faults of our schools but from the fact that the schools are the central conserving force of the culture. The Great Fear thus turns our hostility unerringly in the direction of the focus of survival and change, in the direction of education.

### Creativity and Absurdity

The function of education has never been to free the mind and the spirit of man, but to bind them; and to the end that the mind and spirit of his children should never escape, *Homo sapiens* has employed praise, ridicule, admonition, accusation, mutilation, and even torture to chain them to the culture pattern. Throughout most of his historic course *Homo sapiens* has wanted from his children acquiescence, not originality. It is natural that this should be so, for where every man is unique there is no society, and where there is no society there can be no man. Contemporary American educators think they want creative children, yet it is an open question as to what they expect these children to create. And certainly the classrooms—from kindergarten to graduate school—in which they expect it to happen are not crucibles of creative activity and thought. It stands to reason that were young people truly creative the culture would fall apart, for originality, by definition, is different from what is given, and what is given is the culture itself. From the endless, pathetic, "creative hours" of kindergarten to the most abstruse problems in sociology and anthropology, the function of education is to prevent the truly creative intellect from getting out of hand. Only in the exact and the biological sciences do we permit unlimited freedom, for we have (but only since the Renaissance, since Galileo and Bruno underwent the Inquisition) found a way—or *thought* we had found a way—to bind the explosive powers of science in the containing vessel of the social system.

American classrooms, like educational institutions anywhere, express the values, preoccupations, and fears found in the culture as a whole. School has no choice; it must train the children to fit the culture as it is. School can give training in skills; it cannot teach creativity. All the American school can conceivably do is nurture creativity when it appears. And who has the eyes to see it? Since the creativity that is conserved and encouraged will always be that which seems to do the most for culture, which seems at the moment to do the most for the obsessions and the brutal preoccupations and anxieties from which we all suffer, schools nowadays encourage the child with gifts in mathematics and the exact sciences. But the child who has the intellectual strength to see through social shams is of no consequence to the educational system.

Creative intellect is mysterious, devious, and irritating. An intellectually creative child may fail, for example, in social studies, simply because he cannot understand the stupidities he is taught to believe as "fact." He may even end up agreeing with his teachers that he is "stupid" in social studies. Learning social studies is, to no small extent, whether in elementary school or the university, learning to be stupid. Most of us accomplish this task before we enter high school. But the child with a socially creative imagination will not be encouraged to play among new social systems, values, and relationships; nor is there much likelihood of it, if for no other reason than that the social studies teachers will perceive such a child as a poor student. Furthermore, such a child will simply be unable to fathom the absurdities that seem transparent *truth* to the teacher. What idiot believes in the "law of supply and demand," for example? But the children who do tend to *become* idiots, and learning to be an idiot is part of growing up! Or, as Camus put it, learning to be *absurd*. Thus the child who finds it impossible to learn to think the absurd the truth, who finds it difficult to accept absurdity as a way of life, the intellectually creative child whose mind makes him flounder like a poor fish in the net of absurdities flung around him in school, usually comes to think himself stupid.

The schools have therefore never been places for the stimulation of young minds. If all through school the young were provoked to question the Ten Commandments, the sanctity of revealed religion, the foundations of patriotism, the profit motive, the two-party system, monogamy, the laws of incest, and so on, we would have more creativity than we could handle. In teaching our children to accept fundamentals of social relationships and religious beliefs without question we follow the ancient highways of the human race, which extend backward into the dawn of the species, and indefinitely into the future. There must therefore be more of the caveman than of the spaceman about our teachers.

Up to this point I have argued that learning to learn is man's foremost evolutionary task, that the primary aim of education has been to fetter the mind and the spirit of man rather than to free them, and that nowadays we confront this problem in our effort to stimulate thought while preventing the mind of the child from going too far. I have also urged that since education, as the central institution for the training of the young in the ways of the culture, is thus burdened with its obsessive fears and hates, contemporary attacks upon our schools are the reflection of a nervousness inherent in the school as a part of the central obsession. Finally, I argued that creativity is the last thing wanted in any culture because of its potentialities for disruptive thinking; that the primordial dilemma of all education derives from the necessity of training the mighty brain of *Homo sapiens* to be stupid; and that creativity, when it is encouraged (as in science in our culture), occurs only after the creative thrust of an idea has been tamed and directed toward socially approved ends. In this sense, then, creativity can become the most obvious conformity. In this sense we can expect scientists—our cultural maximizers—to be socially no *more* creative than the most humble elementary school teacher, and probably less creative socially than a bright second-grader.

## Communication

Much of what I have to say in the following pages pivots on the inordinate capacity of a human being to learn more than one thing at a time. Although it is true that all the higher orders of animals can learn several things at a time, this capacity for polyphasic learning reaches unparalleled development in man. A child writing the word "August" on the board, for example, is not only learning the word "August" but also how to hold the chalk without making it squeak, how to write clearly, how to keep going even though the class is tittering at his slowness, how to appraise the glances of the children in order to know whether he is doing it right or wrong, et cetera. If the spelling, arithmetic, or music lesson were only what it appeared to be, the education of the American child would be much simpler; but it is all the things the child learns *along with* his subject matter that really constitute the drag on the educational process as it applies to the curriculum.

A classroom can be compared to a communications system, for certainly there is a flow of messages between teacher (transmitter) and pupils (receivers) and among the pupils; contacts are made and broken, messages can be sent at a certain rate of speed only, and so on. But there is also another interesting characteristic of communications systems that is applicable to classrooms, and that is their inherent tendency to generate *noise*. *Noise,* in communications theory, applies to all those random fluctuations of the system that cannot be controlled. They are the sounds that are not part of the message: the peculiar quality communicated to the voice by the composition of the telephone circuit, the static on the radio, and so forth. In a classroom lesson on arithmetic, for example, such *noise* would range all the way from the competitiveness of the students, the quality of the teacher's voice ("I remember exactly how she sounded when she told me to sit down"), to the shuffling of the children's feet. The striking thing about the child is that along with his arithmetic—his "messages about arithmetic"—he learns all the noise in the system also. It is this inability to avoid *learning the noise with the subject matter* that constitutes one of the greatest hazards for an organism so prone to polyphasic learning as man. It is this that brings it about that an objective observer cannot tell which is being learned in any lesson, the *noise* or the formal subject matter. But—and mark this well—it is *not* primarily the message (let us say, the arithmetic or the spelling) that constitutes the most important subject matter to be learned, but the noise! The most significant cultural learnings—primarily the cultural drives—are communicated as *noise.*

Let us take up these points by studying selected incidents in some of the suburban classrooms my students and I studied over a period of six years.

## The Realm of Song

It is March 17 and the children are singing songs from Ireland and her neighbors. The teacher plays on the piano, while the children sing. While some children sing, a number of them hunt in the index, find a song belonging to one of Ireland's neighbors, and raise their hands in order that they may be called on to name the next song. The singing is of that pitchless quality always heard in elementary school classrooms. The teacher sometimes sings through a song first, in her off key, weakishly husky voice.

The usual reason for having this kind of a song period is that the children are broadened, while they learn something about music and singing.

It is true that the children learn something about singing, but what they learn is to sing like everybody else, in the standard, elementary school pitchlessness of the English-speaking world—a phenomenon impressive enough for D. H. Lawrence to have mentioned it in *Lady Chatterly's Lover.* The difficulty in achieving true pitch is so pervasive among us that missionaries carry it with them to distant jungles, teaching the natives to sing hymns off key. Hence on Sundays we would hear our Pilagá Indian friends, all of them excellent musicians in the Pilagá scale, carefully copy the missionaries by singing Anglican hymns, translated in Pilagá, off key exactly as sharp or as flat as the missionaries sang. Thus one of the first things a child with a good ear learns in elementary school is to be musically stupid; he learns to doubt or to scorn his innate musical capacities.

But possibly more important than this is the use to which teacher and pupils put the lesson in ways not related at all to singing or to Ireland and her neighbors. To the teacher this was an opportunity to let the children somehow share the social aspects of the lesson with her, to democratically participate in the selection of the songs. The consequence was distraction from singing as the children hunted in the index and raised their hands to have their song chosen. The net result was to activate the competitive, achievement, and dominance drives of the children, as they strove with one another for the teacher's attention, and through her, to get the class to do what they wanted it to do. In this way the song period on Ireland and her neighbors was scarcely a lesson in singing but rather one in extorting the maximal benefit for the Self from *any* situation. The first lesson a child has to learn when he comes to school is that lessons are not what they seem. He must then forget this and act as if they were. This is the first step toward "school mental health"; it is also the first step in becoming absurd. In the first and second grades teachers constantly scold children because they do not raise their hands enough—the prime symbol of having learned what school is all about. After that, it is no longer necessary; the kids have "tumbled" to the idea.

The second lesson is to put the teachers' and students' criteria in place of his own. He must learn that the proper way to sing is tunelessly and not the way *he* hears the music; that the proper way to paint is the way the teacher says, not the way he sees it; that the proper attitude is not pleasure but competitive horror at the success of his classmates, and so on. And these lessons must be so internalized that he will fight his parents if they object. The early schooling process is not successful unless it has accomplished in the child an acquiescence in its criteria, unless the child *wants* to think the way school has taught him to think. He must have accepted alienation as a rule of life. What we see in the kindergarten and the early years of school is the pathetic surrender of babies. How could it be otherwise?

Now, if children are taught to adopt alienation as a way of life, it follows that they must have feelings of inadequacy, for nothing so saps self-confidence as alienation from the Self. It would follow that school, the chief agent in the process, must try to provide the children with "ego support," for culture tries to remedy the ills it creates.

Hence the effort to give recognition; and hence the conversion of the songfest into an exercise in Self-realization. That anything essential was nurtured in this way is an open question, for the kind of individuality that was recognized as the children picked titles out of the index was mechanical, without a creative dimension, and under the strict control of the teacher. Let us conclude this discussion by saying that *school metamorphoses the child, giving it the kind of Self the school can manage, and then proceeds to minister to the Self it has made.*

Perhaps I have put the matter grossly, appearing to credit the school with too much formative power. So let us say this: let us grant that American children, being American, come to school on the first day with certain potentialities for experiencing success and failure, for enjoying the success of their mates or taking pleasure in their failure, for competitiveness, for cooperation, for driving to achieve or for coasting along, et cetera. But school cannot handle variety, for as an institution dealing with masses of children it can manage only on the assumption of a homogeneous mass. Homogeneity is therefore accomplished by defining the children in a certain way and by handling all situations uniformly. In this way no child is directly coerced. It is simply that the child must react in terms of the institutional definitions or he fails. The first two years of school are spent not so much in learning the rudiments of the three Rs, as in learning definitions.

It would be foolish to imagine that school, as a chief molder of character, could do much more than homogenize the children, but it does do more—it sharpens to a cutting edge the drives the culture needs.

If you bind or prune an organism so it can move only in limited ways, it will move rather excessively in that way. If you lace a man into a strait jacket so he can only wiggle his toes, he will wiggle them *hard*. Since in school children are necessarily constrained to limited human expression, under the direction of the teacher, they will have a natural tendency to do with exaggerated enthusiasm what they are permitted to do. They are like the man in the strait jacket. In class children are usually not permitted to talk much, to walk around much, to put their arms around each other during lessons, to whistle or sing. But they are permitted to raise their hands and go

to the pencil sharpener almost at will. Thus hand-raising, going to the pencil sharpener, or hunting in the back of a song book for a song for the class to sing are not so much activities stemming from the requirements of an immediate situation as expressions of the intensified need of the organism for relief from the five-hour-a-day pruning and confining process. This goes under the pedagogical title of "release of tension"; but in our view the issue is that what the children are at length permitted—and invited—to do, and what they therefore often throw themselves into with the enthusiasm of multiple pent-up feelings, are cultural drive-activities narrowly construed by the school. In that context the next example is not only an expression by the children of a wish to be polite, but an inflated outpouring of contained human capacities, released enthusiastically into an available—because approved—cultural channel.

## On Hanging Up a Coat

The observer is just entering her fifth-grade classroom for the observation period. The teacher says, "Which one of you nice, polite boys would like to take [the observer's] coat and hang it up?" From the waving hands, it would seem that all would like to claim the title. The teacher chooses one child, who takes the observer's coat. The teacher says, "Now, children, who will tell [the observer] what we have been doing?"

The usual forest of hands appears, and a girl is chosen to tell. . . . The teacher conducted the arithmetic lessons mostly by asking, "Who would like to tell the answer to the next problem?" This question was usually followed by the appearance of a large and agitated forest of hands, with apparently much competition to answer.

What strikes us here are the precision with which the teacher was able to mobilize the potentialities in the boys for proper social behavior, and the speed with which they responded. One is impressed also with the fact that although the teacher could have said, "Johnny, will you please hang up [the observer's] coat?" she chose rather to activate all the boys, and thus give *them* an opportunity to activate their Selves, in accordance with the alienated Selfhood objectives of the culture. The children were thus given an opportunity to exhibit a frantic willingness to perform an act of uninvolved solicitude for the visitor; in this way each was given also a chance to communicate to the teacher his eagerness to please her "in front of company."

The mere appearance of the observer in the doorway sets afoot a kind of classroom destiny of self-validation and actualization of pupil-teacher communion, and of activation of the cultural drives. In the observer's simple act of entrance the teacher perceives instantly the possibility of exhibiting her children and herself, and of proving to the visitor, and once again to herself, that the pupils are docile creatures, eager to hurl their "company" Selves into this suburban American tragicomedy of welcome. From behind this scenery of mechanical values, meanwhile, the most self-centered boy might emerge a *papier mâché* Galahad, for what he does is not for the benefit of the visitor but for the gratification of the teacher and of his own culturally molded Self. The large number of waving hands proves that most of the boys have already become absurd; but they have no choice. Suppose they sat there frozen?

From this question we move to the inference that the skilled teacher sets up many situations in such a way that *a negative attitude can be construed only as treason.* The function of questions like, "Which one of you nice polite boys would like to take [the observer's] coat and hang it up?" is to bind the children into absurdity—to compel them to acknowledge that absurdity is existence, to acknowledge that it is better to exist absurd than not to exist at all.

It is only natural, then, that when the teacher next asks, "Now who will tell what we have been doing?" and "Who would like to tell the answer to the next problem?" there should appear "a large and agitated forest of hands," for failure to raise the hand could be interpreted only as an act of aggression. The "arithmetic" lesson, transformed by the teacher, had become an affirmation of her matriarchal charisma as symbol of the system.

The reader will have observed that the next question is not put, "Who *has* the answer to the next problem?" but "Who *would like to tell*" it? Thus, what at one time in our culture was phrased as a challenge to skill in arithmetic, becomes here an invitation to group participation. What is sought is a sense of "groupiness" rather than a distinguishing of individuals. Thus, as in the singing lesson an attempt was made to deny that it was a group activity, in the arithmetic lesson the teacher attempts to deny that it is an individual one. The essential issue is that *nothing is but what it is made to be by the alchemy of the system.*

In a society where competition for the basic cultural goods is a pivot of action, people cannot be taught to love one another, for those who do cannot compete with one another, except in play. It thus becomes necessary for the school, without appearing to do so, to teach children how to hate, for our culture cannot tolerate the idea that babes should hate each other. How does the school accomplish this ambiguity? Obviously through competition itself, for what has greater potential for creating hostility than competition? One might say that this is one of the most "creative" features of school. Let us consider an incident from a fifth-grade arithmetic lesson.

## At the Blackboard

> Boris had trouble reducing "$^{12}/_{16}$" to the lowest terms, and could only get as far as "$^{6}/_{8}$". The teacher asked him quietly if that was as far as he could reduce it. She suggested he "think." Much heaving up and down and waving of hands by the other children, all frantic to correct him. Boris pretty unhappy, probably mentally paralyzed. The teacher, quiet, patient, ignores the others and concentrates with look and voice on Boris. She says, "Is there a bigger number than two you can divide into the two parts of the fraction?" After a minute or two, she becomes more urgent, but there is no response from Boris. She then turns to the class and says, "Well, who can tell Boris what the number is?" A forest of hands appears, and the teacher calls Peggy. Peggy says that four may be divided into the numerator and the denominator.

Thus Boris's failure has made it possible for Peggy to succeed; his depression is the price of her exhilaration; his misery the occasion for her rejoicing. This is the standard condition of the American elementary school, and is why so many of us feel a contraction of the heart even if someone we never knew succeeds merely at garnering plankton in the Thames: because so often somebody's success has been bought at the cost of our failure. To a Zuni, Hopi, or Dakota Indian, Peggy's performance would seem cruel beyond belief, for competition, the wringing of success from somebody's failure, is a form of torture foreign to those noncompetitive redskins. Yet Peggy's action seems natural to us; and so it is. How else would you run our world! And since all but the brightest children have the constant experience that others succeed at their expense they cannot but develop an inherent tendency to hate—to hate the success of others, to hate others who are successful, and to be determined to prevent it. Along with this, naturally, goes the hope that others will fail. This hatred masquerades under the euphemistic name of "envy."

Looked at from Boris's point of view, the nightmare at the blackboard was, perhaps, a lesson in controlling himself so that he would not fly shrieking from the room under the enormous public pressure. Such experiences imprint on the mind of every man in our culture the *Dream of Failure,* so that over and over again, night in, night out, even at the pinnacle of success, a man will dream not of success, but of failure. *The external nightmare is internalized for life.* It is this dream that, above all other things, provides the fierce human energy required by technological drivenness. It was not so much that Boris was learning arithmetic, but that he was learning the *essential nightmare. To be successful in our culture one must learn to dream of failure.*

From the point of view of the other children, of course, they were learning to yap at the heels of a failure. And why not? Have they not dreamed the dream of flight themselves? If the culture does not teach us to fly from failure or to rush in, hungry for success where others have failed, who will try again where others have gone broke? Nowadays, as misguided teachers try to soften the blow of classroom failure, they inadvertently sap the energies of success. The result will be a nation of chickens unwilling to take a chance.

When we say that "culture teaches drives and values" we do not state the case quite precisely. One should say, rather, that culture (and especially the school) provides the occasions in which drives and values are *experienced in events* that strike us with *overwhelming and constant force.* To say that culture "teaches" puts the matter too mildly. Actually culture invades and infests the mind as an obsession. If it does not, culture will not "work," for only an obsession has the power to withstand the impact of critical differences; to fly in the face of contradiction; to engulf the mind so that it will see the world only as the culture decrees that it shall be seen; to compel a person to be absurd. The central emotion in obsession is fear, and the central obsession in education is fear of failure. In order not to fail most students are willing to believe anything and to care not whether what they are told is true or false. Thus one becomes absurd through being afraid; but paradoxically, *only by remaining absurd can one feel free from fear.* Hence the immovableness of the absurd.

In examining education as a process of teaching the culture pattern, I have discussed a singing lesson, an arithmetic lesson, and the hanging up of a coat. Now let us consider a spelling lesson in a fourth-grade class.

## "Spelling Baseball"

The children form a line along the back of the room. They are to play "spelling baseball," and they have lined up to be chosen for the two teams. There is much noise, but the teacher quiets it. She has selected a boy and a girl and sent them to the front of the room as team captains to choose their teams. As the boy and girl pick the children to form their teams, each child chosen takes a seat in orderly succession around the room. Apparently they know the game well. Now Tom, who has not yet been chosen, tries to call attention to himself in order to be chosen. Dick shifts his position to be more in the direct line of vision of the choosers, so that he may not be overlooked. He seems quite anxious. Jane, Tom, Dick, and one girl whose name the observer does not know, are the last to be chosen. The teacher even has to remind the choosers that Dick and Jane have not been chosen....

The teacher now gives out words for the children to spell, and they write them on the board. Each word is a pitched

ball, and each correctly spelled word is a base hit. The children move around the room from base to base as their teammates spell the words correctly. With some of the words the teacher gives a little phrase: "Tongue: watch your tongue; don't let it say things that aren't kind." "Butcher: the butcher is a good friend to have." "Dozen: twelve of many things." "Knee: get down on your knee." "Pocket: keep your hand out of your pocket, and anybody else's." "No talking! Three out!" The children say, "Oh, oh!"

The outs seem to increase in frequency as each side gets near the children chosen last. The children have great difficulty spelling "August." As they make mistakes, those in the seats say, "No!" The teacher says, "Man on third." As a child at the board stops and thinks, the teacher says, "There's a time limit; you can't take too long, honey." At last, after many children fail on "August" one child gets it right and returns, grinning with pleasure, to her seat.... The motivation level in this game seems terrific. All the children seem to watch the board, to know what's right and wrong, and seem quite keyed up. There is no lagging in moving from base to base. The child who is now writing "Thursday" stops to think after the first letter, and the children snicker. He stops after another letter. More snickers. He gets the word wrong. There are frequent signs of joy from the children when their side is right.

Since English is not pronounced as it is spelled, "language skills" are a disaster for educators as well as for students. We start the problem of "spelling baseball" with the fact that the spelling of English is so mixed up and contradictory and makes such enormous demands on the capacity for being absurd that nowadays most people cannot spell. "Spelling baseball" is an effort to take the "weariness, the fever, and the fret" out of spelling by absurdly transforming it into a competitive game. Over and over again it has seemed to our psychologist designers of curriculum scenery that the best way to relieve boredom is to transmute it into competition. Since children are usually good competitors, though they may never become good spellers, and although they may never learn to *spell* "success" (which really should be written sukses), they know what it *is,* how to go after it, and how it feels not to have it. A competitive game is indicated when children are failing, because the drive to succeed in the *game* may carry them to victory over the *subject matter.* At any rate it makes spelling less boring for the teacher and the students, for it provides the former with a drama of excited children, and the latter with a motivation that transports them out of the secular dreariness of classroom routine. "Spelling baseball" is thus a major effort in the direction of making things seem not as they are. But once a spelling lesson is cast in the form of a game of baseball a great variety of *noise* enters the system, because the sounds of *baseball* (the baseball "message") cannot but be *noise* in a system intended to communicate *spelling*. Let us therefore analyze some of the baseball noise that has entered this spelling system from the sand-lots and the bleachers.

We see first that a teacher has set up a choosing-rejecting system directly adopted from kid baseball. I played ball just that way in New York. The two best players took turns picking out teammates from the bunch, coldly selecting the best hitters and fielders first; as we went down the line it did not make much difference who got the chronic muffers (the kids who couldn't catch a ball) and fanners (the kids who couldn't hit a ball). I recall that the kids who were not good players danced around and called out to the captains, "How about me, Slim? How about me?" Or they called attention to themselves with gestures and intense grimaces, as they pointed to their chests. It was pretty noisy. Of course, it didn't make any difference because the captains knew whom they were going to try to get, and there was not much of an issue after the best players had been sorted out to one or the other team. It was an honest jungle and there was nothing in it that did not belong to the high tension of kid baseball. But nobody was ever left out; and even the worst were never permitted to sit on the sidelines.

"Spelling baseball" is thus sandlot baseball dragged into the schoolroom and bent to the uses of spelling. If we reflect that one could not settle a baseball game by converting it into a spelling lesson, we see that baseball is bizarrely *irrelevant* to spelling. If we reflect further that a kid who is a poor speller might yet be a magnificent ballplayer, we are even further impressed that learning spelling through baseball is learning by absurd association. In "spelling baseball" words become detached from their real significance and become assimilated to base-balls. Thus a spelling game that promotes absurd associations provides an indispensable bridge between the larger culture, where doubletalk is supreme, and the primordial meaningfulness of language. It provides also an introduction to those associations of mutually irrelevant ideas so well known to us from advertising—girls and vodka gimlets, people and billiard balls, lipstick and tree-houses, et cetera.

In making spelling into a baseball game one drags into the classroom whatever associations a child may have to the impersonal sorting process of kid baseball, and in this way some of the *noise* from the baseball system enters spelling. But there are differences between the baseball world and the "spelling baseball" world also. Having participated in competitive athletics all through my youth, I seem to remember that we sorted ourselves by skills, and we recognized that some of us were worse than others. In baseball I also seem to remember that if we struck out or muffed a ball we hated ourselves and

turned flips of rage, while our teammates sympathized with our suffering. In "spelling baseball" one experiences the sickening sensation of being left out as others are picked—to such a degree that the teachers even have to remind team captains that some are unchosen. One's failure is paraded before the class minute upon minute, until, when the worst spellers are the only ones left, the conspicuousness of the failures has been enormously increased: Thus the *noise* from baseball is amplified by a *noise* factor specific to the classroom.

It should not be imagined that I "object" to all of this, for in the first place I am aware of the indispensable social functions of the spelling game, and in the second place, I can see that the rendering of failure conspicuous, the forcing of it on the mind of the unchosen child by a process of creeping extrusion from the group, cannot but intensify the quality of the essential nightmare, and thus render an important service to the culture. Without nightmares human culture has never been possible. Without hatred competition cannot take place.

One can see from the description of the game that drive is heightened in a complex competitive interlock: each child competes with every other to get the words right; each child competes with all for status and approval among his peers; each child competes with the other children for the approval of the teacher; and finally, each competes as a member of a team. Here failure will be felt doubly because although in an ordinary spelling lesson one fails alone, in "spelling baseball" one lets down the children on one's team. Thus though in the game the motivation toward spelling is heightened so that success becomes triumph, so does failure become disaster. The greater the excitement the more intense the feeling of success and failure, and the importance of spelling or failing to spell "August" becomes exaggerated. But it is in the nature of an obsession to exaggerate the significance of events.

We come now to the *noise* introduced by the teacher. In order to make the words clear she puts each one in a sentence: "Tongue: watch your tongue; don't let it say things that aren't kind." "Butcher: the butcher is a good friend to have." "Dozen: twelve of many things." "Knee: get down on your knee." "Pocket: keep your hand out of your pocket, and anybody else's." More relevant associations to the words would be, "The leg bends at the knee." "A butcher cuts up meat." "I carry something in my pocket," etc. What the teacher's sentences do is introduce a number of her idiosyncratic cultural preoccupations, without clarifying anything; for there is no *necessary* relation between butcher and friend, between floor and knee, between pocket and improperly intrusive hands, and so on. In her way, therefore, the teacher establishes the same irrelevance between words and associations as the game does between spelling and base-ball. She amplifies the *noise* by introducing ruminations from her own inner communication system.

## Carping Criticism

The unremitting effort by the system to bring the cultural drives to a fierce pitch must ultimately turn the children against one another; and though they cannot punch one another in the nose or pull each other's hair in class, they can vent some of their hostility in carping criticism of one another's work. Carping criticism is so destructive of the early tillerings of those creative impulses we cherish, that it will be good to give the matter further review.

Few teachers are like Miss Smith in this sixth-grade class:

> The Parent-Teachers Association is sponsoring a school frolic, and the children have been asked to write jingles for publicity. For many of the children, the writing of a jingle seems painful. They are restless, bite their pencils, squirm in their seats, speak to their neighbors, and from time to time pop up with questions like, "Does it have to rhyme, Miss Smith?" At last she says, "Alright, let's read some of the jingles now." Child after child says he "couldn't get one," but some have succeeded. One girl has written a very long jingle, obviously the best in the class. However, instead of using "Friday" as the frolic day, she used "Tuesday," and several protests were heard from the children. Miss Smith defended her, saying, "Well, she made a mistake. But you are too prone to criticize. If *you* could only do so well!"

In our six years of work, in hundreds of hours of observation in elementary and high schools, Miss Smith is unique in that she scolded the children for tearing down the work of a classmate. Other teachers support such attacks, sometimes even somewhat against their will.

"For many of the children, the writing of a jingle seems painful" says the record. "They are restless, bite their pencils, squirm in their seats...." What are they afraid of but failure? This is made clear by Miss Smith's angry defense of the outstanding child as she says to her critics, "If only *you* could do so well!"

In a cooperative society carping is less likely to occur. Spiro says of the *kibbutz:*

> ... The emphasis on group criticism can potentially engender competitive, if not hostile feelings among the children. Frequently, for example, the children read their essays aloud, and the others are then asked to comment. Only infrequently could we detect any hostility in the criticisms of the students, and often the evaluations were filled with praise.[2]

But in Miss Smith's class, because the children have failed while one of their number has succeeded, they carp. And why not? However we may admire Miss Smith's defense of the successful child, we must not let our own "inner Borises" befog our thinking. A competitive culture endures by tearing people down. Why blame the children for doing it?

Let us now consider two examples of carping criticism from a fifth-grade class as the children report on their projects and read original stories.

> Bill has given a report on tarantulas. As usual the teacher waits for volunteers to comment on the child's report.
>
> > Mike: The talk was well illustrated and well prepared.
> > Bob: Bill had a *piece of paper* [for his notes] and teacher said he should have them on *cards....*
>
> Bill says he could not get any cards, and the teacher says he should tear the paper the next time he has no cards.
>
> > Bob: He held the paper behind him. If he had had to look at it, it wouldn't have been very nice.
>
> The children are taking turns reading to the class stories they have made up. Charlie's is called *The Unknown Guest.*
>
> "One dark, dreary night, on a hill a house stood. This house was forbidden territory for Bill and Joe, but they were going in anyway. The door creaked, squealed, slammed. A voice warned them to go home. They went upstairs. A stair cracked. They entered a room. A voice said they might as well stay and find out now; and their father came out. He laughed and they laughed, but they never forgot their adventure together."
>
> > Teacher: Are there any words that give you the mood of the story?
> > Lucy: He could have made the sentences a little better....
> > Teacher: Let's come back to Lucy's comment. What about his sentences?
> > Gert: They were too short.
>
> Charlie and Jeanne have a discussion about the position of the word "stood" in the first sentence.
>
> > Teacher: Wait a minute; some people are forgetting their manners....
> > Jeff: About the room: the boys went up the stairs and one "cracked," then they were in the room. Did they fall through the stairs, or what?
>
> The teacher suggests Charlie make that a little clearer....
>
> > Teacher: We still haven't decided about the short sentences. Perhaps they make the story more spooky and mysterious.
> > Gwynne: I wish he had read with more expression instead of all at one time.
> > Rachel: Not enough expression.
> > Teacher: Charlie, they want a little more expression from you. I guess we've given you enough suggestions for one time. [Charlie does not raise his head, which is bent over his desk as if studying a paper.]

Charlie! I guess we've given you enough suggestions for one time, Charlie, haven't we? [Charlie half raises his head, seems to assent grudgingly.]

It stands to reason that a competitive system must do this; and adults, since they are always tearing each other to pieces, should understand that children will be no different. School is indeed a training for later life not because it teaches the 3 Rs (more or less), but because it instills the essential cultural nightmare fear of failure, envy of success, and absurdity.

## QUESTIONS

1. In what sense does education both "fetter" and "free" us?

2. Schools have a "hidden curriculum" consisting of norms and values that are not consciously taught or learned, but which form part of the educational process nonetheless. Give some examples, drawing if possible from your own experience.

3. Do the schools merely reflect the society that exists, or can they also change it?

## NOTES

1. Ibn Battuta, *Travels in Asia and Africa.* London: Broadway House, Carter Lane, 1957, p. 330. (Translated and selected by H. A. R. Gibb, from the original written in 1325–54.)

2. Melford Spiro, *Children of the Kibbutz.* Harvard University Press, 1958, p. 261.

*Peter W. Cookson Jr.*
*Caroline Hodges Persell*

# 37. The Price of Privilege

*Education is not a politically or socially neutral subject. The schools are deeply implicated in social inequality, for in all modern industrialized societies they help to reproduce the class system from one generation to the next. The reason is that schooling is an important influence on social mobility. The better educated a person is, the greater that person's chance of getting a superior job and income. Consequently, members of different groups try to ensure the best education for their own children, hoping to secure a lifetime's advantages for them. In this competitive environment, higher-status groups have the advantage, primarily because the home environment is more favorable to scholarly success.*

*Not only do children of different social classes experience different home environments, they also tend to go to different schools. In Britain, for example, sons of the upper class often attend private boarding schools, whose graduates have a disproportionate influence in political and economic life. In the Soviet Union, high-ranking government bureaucrats are able to get their own children into the handful of elite schools that produce the next generation of senior officials. And in the United States, children of the upper class often go to private schools, while the children of the middle class attend suburban public schools and the children of the working and lower classes, inner-city public schools.*

*In this article, Peter W. Cookson and Caroline Hodges Persell report on their study of private preparatory schools and show how the pupils are prepared for their later roles in life.*

It is a clear New England morning and Chip, who is a student guide at an elite American boarding school, seems to be having a splendid time as he shepherds us from chapel to gymnasium to dormitory. Bright and articulate, the tall, slender, red-headed junior is bubbly in his praise for his school. "This is a great school," he repeats several times. "My father went here; this is a great school." A natural at public relations, Chip knows everything about his school. He rattles off figures with ease; he is particularly proud of the new science wing and the Gothic chapel. "Hey, I'll bet you'd be interested in this," Chip says, pointing to a bluff behind the library.

The path up the bluff is narrow and rocky. As we struggle along, Chip glides ahead; he's been here before. Patiently he waits for us at the top. "Isn't the view incredible," he says, sweeping the horizon with his arms.

The view from the bluff is indeed magnificent. The sloping green hills run to the blue water for miles up and down the Atlantic coast. Sailboats, their colorful spinnakers at full wind, dart among the whitecaps. Chip suddenly becomes quiet, his youthful face less poised and more innocent. His eyes follow the boats for several seconds. "And this," he says simply, "is where I come to cry. Everybody's got to have a place to cry."

Pain and poignancy are not what we normally associate with prep schools. Driving by their beautiful, sequestered campuses, we are more apt to think of privilege and power. They seem worlds apart—educational country clubs for privileged children who go away to learn the social graces and acquire the academic skills that will ensure them a place at a selective and socially prestigious college. Like Eton and Harrow in England, America's most elite boarding schools attempt to instill in their students the classic values of duty, honor and service. Franklin D. Roosevelt, Dean Acheson, Adlai Stevenson and John F. Kennedy were all prep school graduates. Vice President George Bush, Secretary of the Treasury James Baker III and Secretary of Commerce Malcolm Baldrige, all graduates of these selective schools, are prominent in contemporary political life. In addition, prep school graduates are disproportionately influential in business, banking and law. As Michael Useem reported in *The Inner Circle*, 17 percent of the rare group of people who are board members of two or more major corporations graduated from 1 of 13 elite prep schools. And preps abound on the governing boards of philanthropic foundations and arts councils. Their influence on contemporary American culture is widespread.

A prep school diploma is still an important credential for membership in the upper class. At one elite school, 4 out of every 10 graduates had parents who were listed in the *Social Register*. And the popularity of books such as Lisa Birnbach's *The Official Preppy Handbook* leaves the distinct impression that membership involves little more than Lacoste shirts and a pair of topsiders. But, in fact, attending an elite prep school is similar to joining an exclusive club. Not only must the new member accept the rules by which the club operates, but he or she must identify with and be loyal to the other members. As E. Digby Baltzell has emphasized in his studies of the upper class, the relationships and shared values of the upper class are an important element in creating a sense of class solidarity. A voluntary sacrifice of individuality is part of the psychological price of privilege. As one dean of admissions put it, "We don't want selfish learners here."

An important stated purpose of boarding schools has always been to develop "character" in their students, and although most prep schools have relaxed extremely repressive regulations since the 1960s, the fundamental psychological process at work in prepping remains essentially unchanged.

In order to examine just how this process works, we have spent the past several years studying what we call the prep "rite of passage"—the systematic wearing down of individual identities into a single collective identity. Through observations and interviews, we have collected information about nearly every aspect of boarding school life, and what we found was a conspiracy of forces—powerful institutional controls, peer pressures and personal resignation—that together almost guarantee the universal, but seldom acknowledged, psychological goal of prepping.

According to sociologist Erving Goffman, boarding schools are "total institutions," which he defines as having these characteristics: Activities are conducted in the same place under a single authority; daily life is carried out in the immediate company of others; life is tightly scheduled and fixed by a set of formal rules; and all activities are designed to fulfill the official aims of the institution. Goffman describes the "encompassing tendencies" of total institutions that bar their "inmates" from outside influences. At boarding schools, these outside influences include parents. We have found through our interviews that the bond between parent and child is almost always weakened when the child is sent away to school, and indeed this is the intent. The transfer of attachment from parents to school to classmates is a key psychological process if the students are to become part of the larger collective identity.

Compared to the typical adolescent, we have found, the prep school student has very little in the way of personal freedom. Just getting off campus, for example, can be an ordeal. Detailed attention is paid to how, when and with whom a student can leave. The dean of students of one girls' school we visited had a three-inch-thick binder with the various kinds of permissions that were required for leaving school. At another school, students invited somewhere (even their parents' home) for the weekend were required to sign up by the previous Thursday; requests made late were flatly denied. As one student wrote, "Teachers and deans monitor every breath you take."

This, of course, is all part of the sacrifice prep school students are expected to make in preparation for the privileged positions they will eventually occupy in society. In exchange for this loss of freedom, preps earn a right to membership in the group and come to believe that they deserve their privilege because of the high personal costs they have paid. Time and time again the students who completed our questionnaires mentioned this sense of entitlement that they derived from their difficult experience. One called it "present pain for future gain." Another noted, "I have become more confident than my friends who do not go to boarding schools about myself and my future."

In order to forge the prep personality, the schools rely on various techniques, including strict discipline, shared rituals and what we call "deep structure regulation." Despite some regulatory relaxation at some schools in recent years, control is by no means lax; the uniforms may be gone but the uniformity remains. At most of the boarding schools we observed, there are still elaborate rules that regulate the most minute aspects of community and personal life. Naturally there are prohibitions against stealing, cheating and possessing firearms, drugs and alcohol; but there are also more ambiguous prohibitions concerning "inappropriate" sexual behavior, for example, and "compromising the reputation of the school." Aside from worrying about these major infractions, a less-than-vigilant student can easily violate dormitory regulations, dining hall regulations, smoking regulations, bicycle regulations and, at some schools, golf course regulations.

The creation of a collective identity, however, requires more than outward discipline. Individuals must also be submerged in a brief system that guides their behavior and instills in them the "proper" values, and to this end schools have long relied on institutional rituals such as chapel attendance. Indeed, many still do. But more permanent behavioral change requires that students be controlled at a much deeper level. A total institution, with its nearly absolute control over the residents' somatic drives, is ideally organized to provide this kind of deep structure regulation. Controlling an individual's body is a show of great power; the opportunities for socialization are increased dramatically when the subject is dependent on the "trainer" for sustenance.

In one sense social dominance starts with repression of the self, and where better to learn the tactics of self-denial than in a setting where gratification is limited and from which there is no escape. Certainly, one of the rudest shocks the prep school initiate experiences is the loss of a full refrigerator. This may sound like a trivial change, but anyone who has observed adolescents in their natural habitat knows the value they place on food. Most of these students have been accustomed to having their mothers (or in many cases cooks) supply them with their choice of foods, in abundance. The unconscious connection between nourishment and nurturing that contributes importantly to the meaning of home is suddenly severed on the first day of school. In its place is substituted group "feeds," as some students call them, where open access to a full refrigerator is replaced by standing in line, accepting what's given and eating silently in large groups. Students at these elite schools are not kept hungry, to be sure; but the diets tend to be simple, at some schools even spartan.

Schools pay close attention to the socializing effects of the feed. The more traditional still have two or three sit-down meals a day. These can be highly organized affairs with assigned seats, monogrammed table settings and clear rules of etiquette; food is served and consumed within a prescribed period of time. Very often the headmaster or headmistress begins the meal with grace and formal announcements. The implicit assumption behind the highly ritualized group feed is that people who eat alike, act alike, perhaps even think alike.

Rest is also subject to close regulation at most of the schools we've studied. School authorities simply prescribe when students must go to sleep and when they must wake. Privacy as it is commonly thought of does not exist at boarding school. This loss of personal freedom often leads to severe stress, according to the reports we got from both students and teachers. Teachers talk of "corks popping" and "freak-outs." At one school, students told us about "treeing," a form of protest against too much intensity in which the entire student body climbs into trees and screams, refusing to come down until the administration agrees to negotiate small matters of individual liberty. We are not the first to report

such stress reactions. In his study of American private schools, Leonard Baird found that nearly half of the students were bothered very much by pressures of their highly regulated environment.

While we do not know the exact number of prep school students who need or seek counseling to deal with stress, we do know that the schools consider it an important problem, as evidenced by the elaborate counseling systems most have in place. Drug and alcohol counseling are now established services at most schools. As one psychological counselor stated in *The New York Times:* "Once they've learned that all you have to do to cope is swallow, it's awfully hard to circumvent that." The prevalence of drug use undoubtedly varies from campus to campus, but none is spared the problem; and drugs, like everything else in a total institution, become an inescapable fact of everyday life with which every student must deal.

Unhappily, offering counseling is in and of itself not enough for many students. Boys in particular seem to fear the stigma of going for psychological help. As one teacher put it, "These boys need to present themselves as being in control. It goes with the nature of the breed. If a boy shows he's in trouble, what will his faculty or college counselor think? It might screw up his chances for college."

Partly to protect themselves, then, students create their own subculture. Our research has documented what novelists have been describing for years: an intense, even overpowering, underground culture with its own rules and regulations. Those who are not granted full cultural membership by other students often suffer feelings of isolation, rejection and inferiority. Joining a clique is indeed a matter of survival, because without a strong group a student is doubly vulnerable: vulnerable to the impersonal force of the total institution and to the antisocial, even cruel, behavior of the other students. Almost all of the alumni we talked to vividly remember the many seemingly trivial things—balloon fights, "panty raids," scandals and triumphs—that work to solidify the student culture.

One might argue that boarding school students are not much different from other teenagers in their fascination with relationships and friends; after all, teenage culture is invariably centered on dating, cruising and hanging out. But few adolescents attending public schools, or even private day schools for that matter, have to live with their friends day in and day out, and this forced intimacy creates an opportunity for more intense and perhaps lasting relations than can be found elsewhere. The students we interviewed often commented on the differences in the intensity of friendships. "Friends who are boarders," one noted, "hang closer than a boarder and a day student."

The ongoing adolescent dilemma involving the trade-off between individual and group identity is heightened in the prep school environment. Goffman notes that in order to survive, "inmates" in total institutions develop strategies for avoiding the institutional impingements upon the self. He calls this "working the system." Some of the cleverest students in prep schools have learned to work the system and have maintained a strong sense of personal identity despite the constraints of authority. Unfortunately, such cleverness is not always untarnished; a popular way of bucking authority, for example, is to deal in drugs. And many of these students have the financial resources to do it big. One prep student returning from Venezuela was arrested at Kennedy International Airport in New York with almost a pound of cocaine in April 1984. The drugs, with an estimated street value of $300,000, had been bought with a $5,000 investment raised by 14 students. All 14 were subsequently expelled.

Much of the prep socialization occurs outside the view of adults; students, to survive, must be tough and resourceful, especially if they want to stay straight. In the face of these pressures, many adolescents become apathetic, cynical or even self-destructive. Many of the students reported in their questionnaires that they had become more cynical and negative. "You are forced to grow up faster than at day school," one senior noted.

We believe, based on what we have learned about the prep culture, that the most important consequence of going through the prep crucible is a loss of innocence, the recognition that goodness unadorned by power is impotent in the struggle for privilege. Power requires the sacrifice of innocence, and often the cost of leadership is the acceptance of the world the way it is rather than the way it ought to be. There's very little youthful idealism to be found here. As one student wrote, boarding school has "made me realize how many jerks are going to be successful and how I'm going to deal with those people in my own business life."

The psychological price of prepping includes a relinquishing of personal identity, a loss of innocence and a growth of cynicism. Having paid their dues, students who survive the rite of passage obtain membership in an elite group, which they embrace with a strong sense of psychological and social entitlement. Membership and entitlement strengthen the will of some prep school graduates to exercise power, a goal that is epitomized in the motto of one school: "To Serve is To Rule." They emerge from the crucible with a sense of earned authority, legitimating to themselves their privileged position in society. As one student phrased it: "Boarding school has made me quite arrogant. I cannot reasonably believe that I am not better than most people."

The underside of prep school socialization is its constricting, even suffocating, nature. One alumna, not at all atypical, said that when she graduated she felt she "knew everyone she needed to know, either through her family or from boarding school connections." She was simply uninterested in meeting new people. If class position is best defined by shared behavior and repeated encounters, then prep school graduates are in a class by themselves. Compared to public school or even private day school graduates, prep school graduates devote an extraordinary amount of time to "staying in touch," swapping life histories, attending alumni parties and gatherings and writing checks for their schools. Part of the pleasure and pain of prepping is that one joins a club from which it is very difficult to resign. Each graduating class has a class agent or correspondent who tries to keep track of who's where, with whom, doing what job and—of course—who's who.

In short, the structure of boarding school life prepares many students for a life as prisoners of their class. After prep school they will go to the right college, marry right, get the right job, join the right clubs, travel to the right places and grow weary in the right style. Thus the prep rite of passage creates generations and generations of individuals, some of whom are crippled, rather than empowered, by privilege.

## QUESTIONS

1. What are the characteristic features of the prep school environment? What is the purpose of these features, and what is their effect on the students?

2. How similar or different is the prep school experience from your own school experience? How important do you think such socialization experiences are for students' later personalities and roles in life?

3. In what ways do schools help to reproduce the class system?

*Perry Garfinkel*

# 38. The Best "Jewish Mother" in the World

*There has been growing concern in recent years about the quality of American education. Scores on Scholastic Aptitude Tests have declined since the early 1960s. Reading levels have fallen so sharply that many textbooks are written at one or two grade levels below the grade for which they are intended. High schools have graduated many students who have great difficulty in reading or writing, and it is estimated that between 17 and 21 million Americans are functionally illiterate—unable to read simple appliance instructions, fill in an application form, or write a check. Remedial English and math classes are now common even in colleges—a phenomenon that was almost unknown a generation ago. Moreover, American standards of academic achievement appear to be slipping behind those of several other industrialized societies.*

*The public reaction to the "crisis of quality" in American education has been to focus on curricula and teachers. In virtually every state, there is a "back to basics" trend in curriculum planning, with a heavy emphasis on fundamental skills in reading, writing, and mathematics. Additionally, state and local authorities are trying to improve the quality of teaching—by applying stricter standards to teacher evaluation and by raising salaries in order to attract more talented people to the profession. Such measures will doubtless prove helpful, but they neglect a crucial finding of sociological research: that pupil achievement is primarily dependent on family background. Given the identical school environment, children from families that value education tend to do much better, on average, than children whose families fail to provide the appropriate encouragement.*

*Japan is one country in which pupil achievement is consistently higher than in the United States. In this article, Perry Garfinkel reports on the Japanese system, particularly on the role that the mother plays in encouraging scholastic achievement.*

Reprinted from *Psychology Today*, September 1983. Copyright © 1983, Ziff-Davis Publishing Company.

Ten-year-old Seiji Hashimoto is not doing well in school. Despite his family's high expectations, he is about to flunk out. His mother, who is particularly upset with his scholastic performance, falls ill. Seiji blames himself for his mother's sickness and redoubles his efforts at school. His grades improve, and his mother's illness suddenly disappears.

The Naganos' only son does no chores. "Why?" asks a researcher. "Because," Mrs. Nagano replies, "it would break my heart to take him away from his studies."

Except for the names, these anecdotes sound like those told by many Jewish sons and daughters. The doting Jewish mother may have finally met her match. The Japanese mother is, according to researchers in the vanguard of cross-cultural studies of scholastic effectiveness, a key factor in the Japanese education advantage. Says George De Vos, A University of California-Berkeley anthropologist who has been studying Japanese culture for 25 years, "She is the best 'Jewish mother' in the world."

Harvard University psychologist Jerome Kagan concurs with this analogy. "Until her child goes to school," says Kagan, "the Japanese mother devotes herself to the rearing of the child. In verbal and nonverbal ways, she reminds the child of her deep, deep, warm feelings and that the child is the most important thing in the world to her. Then she says, 'After all I've done for you, don't disappoint me.' She's like the Jewish mother who says, 'What do you mean you're not hungry—after I've slaved all day over a hot stove for you.' "

The decline of education in the United States has been front-page news for years and may well develop into a prime political issue in the next Presidential election. To cite just one statistic, Scholastic Aptitude Test scores have fallen 49 points in verbal aptitude and 31 points in math in the past 20 years. But while politicians search for ways to redress this shortcoming and educators argue the merits of traditional versus progressive education, a few researchers are looking to the Orient for an answer, and at least one is alarmed at the East-West gap. "Americans just don't understand that they are truly behind," says Harold Stevenson, a psychologist at the University of Michigan. "You talk about Sputnik," Stevenson says, referring to the 1957 Soviet orbital launch that jolted Americans into a frenzied effort to catch up in the space race. "Well, there's a similar message in the Japanese advantage in education."

Since 1971, Stevenson has made nine trips to the Far East to determine how the Japanese and Chinese cultures have won this advantage and Chinese cultures have won this advantage. The answer is complex, but one factor seems paramount. "The Japanese mother is a very important influence on the education of her children," says De Vos. "She takes it upon herself to be the responsible agent, reinforcing the educational process instituted in the schools."

The most single-minded Japanese "Jewish" mother is known as *kyoiku-mama,* which translates roughly as "education-mama." She approaches the responsibility for her children's education with unrelenting fervor. She pushes her children to excel academically and sends them to ubiquitous after-school classes, known as *juku,* or to private tutors to assure good grades. Mothers are also so highly vocal in the influential Japanese PTA's that some Japanese half-jokingly suggest that the organization be renamed the MTA.

Cross-cultural research conducted by Stevenson and others during the past decade has only begun to document the education gap—particularly in the areas of science and math. For example: First and fifth-graders in the United States scored significantly lower in math achievement than Japanese or Taiwanese: 10 percent of American fifth-graders couldn't divide 42 by 6, 9 percent couldn't divide 24 by 3, and 91 percent failed to compute the perimeter of a four-sided figure. The corresponding percentages for Japanese were 6, 5, and 56; for Taiwanese they were 4, 4, and 67.

In science achievement tests, given by the International Association for the Evaluation of Educational Achievement to children in 15 industrialized countries, 10-year-old Japanese children scored 5 points and 14 year-olds 9 points above the average for all countries combined. American children at these ages achieved scores almost identical to the average.

A study comparing fifth-graders in an American Midwestern city to those in a city several hours north of Tokyo found that not one of the 20 American classrooms did as well in math as any of the Japanese classes. In other words, the average score of the highest-achieving American class was below the worst-performing Japanese class. Only one of the 100 top-scoring fifth-grade math students was American.

Two current hypotheses explaining Japanese supremacy in school math and science achievement can be dispensed with. One is that the Japanese are inherently smarter than Americans. This theory, which appeared in *Nature* (May, 1982), used national samples that were not comparable, says Stevenson, who dismisses the notion that there are any national differences in intellectual functioning. The other explanation, that the Japanese have fewer students per classroom, is inaccurate. All available data indicate that American classes are smaller.

Another factor that may warrant further study is the status of teachers in Japan and the United States. While a society's regard is not easy to quantify, starting salaries for Japanese teachers are higher than for any other government employee. And in Japan the term for teacher, *sensei,* is one of the highest forms of address that can be bestowed on a person.

How much time children spend in school *is* easy to quantify. Stevenson and a group from the Center for Human Growth and Development at the University of Michigan found that Japanese children attend school an average of 240 days a year, compared to 178 for Americans. Actual instruction time is 25 percent greater in Japan. What's more, Japanese students spend more time on their homework. According to estimates Stevenson gathered from parents, Japanese first-graders put in an average of 233 minutes a week on their lesson after school, fifth-graders, 368 minutes. In the United States, the times are 79 minutes and 256 minutes respectively.

Stevenson also asked American and Japanese mothers how much time someone in the family spent helping their first-graders with homework. The Japanese mothers reported an average of 24 minutes a night, the American mothers, 14.

This is only one small indication of how deeply mothers are involved in Japanese education. A more profound influence is the intensely close relationship between mother and child. She carries from generation to generation some of the most pervasive values of Japanese society: the work ethic, selflessness, and group endeavor.

"To a Japanese," points out Hideo Kojima of Nagoya University in Japan, "the training of children is not simply a technical matter but one that involves the deepest mutual and reciprocal relationships between parent and child." It's not surprising, then, that the Japanese mother, as one researcher wrote, "views her baby much more than do Western mothers as an extension of herself, and psychological boundaries between the two of them are blurred."

When it comes to disciplining her child, the Japanese mother is more inclined than the American mother to appeal to feelings as a coercive tool. Where an American mother might demand that a child stop doing something of which she disapproved, the Japanese mother is more likely simply to express displeasure. Kojima cites the "many Japanese writers (on child rearing) who recommend mildness in the direct verbal teaching of children.

They say that children should be admonished in a firm but calm manner, and that adults not use abusive language or show anger and impatience. Such behavior leads children to resent and eventually disobey the urgings of the older authority ... thus ceasing their development of wisdom and abilities."

"The Japanese," De Vos adds, "are extremely conscious in their child-rearing of a need to satisfy the feeling of dependency developed within an intense mother-child relationship in order to maintain compliance and obedience. Goodwill must be maintained so that the child willingly undertakes the increasingly heavy requirements and obligations placed upon him in school and at home."

Using obligation to assure compliancy, the Japanese mother sets a style that is reflected in the interdependent fabric of society as a whole. It is seen most clearly in the strong group orientation of the Japanese. They are trained to agree from a very early age. "Harmonious human relationships," Kojima writes, "may be a basic Japanese value orientation."

One further indication of this difference is that certain key Japanese values lose meaning in translation. For example, the translation of *gaman, ninṭai,* or *shimbo* as perseverance or forbearance fails to convey the positive sense of self-sacrifice and suffering in the words. "There is a strong positive value inherent in these terms," says Harumi Befu, a Stanford University anthropologist of Japanese background. They have the effect of exhorting the Japanese to endure experiences with a Spartan attitude.

One example of how these values are carried into the classroom is Stevenson's observation that Japanese students stay at a task longer than do Americans. In his comparative studies of first- and fifth-graders, American children were away from their desks 25 percent more than Japanese. Similarly, Japanese mothers credit "effort" as the key determinant of a child's achievement in school, says Stevenson, while American mothers name "ability" as the more important factor.

Befu describes this Japanese tendency towards perseverance as "role perfectionism," the desire to meet the precise requirements of a given role. Role perfectionism, says Befu, is one of the prime motivators of Japanese children and mothers.

If the Japanese mother-child relationship could be summarized in a word, that word would be *amae.* Again, it is a term that resists English translation, and attempts to define it get verbose. Hiroshi Azuma, professor of ed-

ucation at the University of Tokyo, defines it as "an attitude toward people characterized by affection, feelings of dependency, and the expectation of an emotionally satisfying response." More succinctly, amae is love combined with a strong sense of reciprocal obligation and dependence.

Amae is at the foundation of Japanese teaching, according to Azuma. It is the bond between mother and child, and, later, child and teacher, that makes the child "more attentive to what others say, think and feel, "more willing to accept the intrusion of significant others into his or her learning, thinking, and feeling; more likely to model after them; better ready to work together; more responsive to recognition from them; and more willing to strive for a common goal."

The Japanese approach to education is not without costs. The stress suffered by students vying for coveted acceptances to universities is one of them. Juku, the after-hours school, is an unwanted by-product of this competition, as is the practice of lavishing gifts on teachers in an attempt to gain special attention for their children. In one city, the gift-giving escalated so sharply that the teachers themselves tried to put a stop to it.

Another drawback is the discouragement of intellectual creativity. De Vos tells of the plight of a Japanese graduate student studying in America. "He could quote everyone," De Vos says, "but when someone asked him what he thought, he went into a depression. He realized he had never asked himself that question."

. . .

Future research should yield more definitive distinctions between American and Japanese approaches to education. For now, it appears that a "Japanese advantage" indeed exists. It may be time to ask ourselves whether the Japanese approach can be transplanted to American soil.

---

## QUESTIONS

1. What cultural factors contribute to the relatively higher levels of academic achievement in Japan?

2. What factors do you think have contributed to declining levels of achievement in American education during recent years?

3. The higher a family's social class, the better, on average its children do in school. How can you explain this?

# 39. The Holy Ghost People

*A hallmark of the emerging postindustrial societies of the world is their individualism and diversity. Unlike more traditional societies, where the bulk of the population works and lives in much the same way, people in postindustrial societies value the freedom to choose distinctive lifestyles. One indication of this tendency is the fact that the United States is the most religiously diverse society in history. Recent counts indicate that there are at least 1,300 distinct denominations, sects, and cults, each offering its own vision, doctrines, or prophecies to the public.*

*Most Americans profess Christianity, but even here there is unprecedented diversity. About 28 percent of Americans are Catholic and about 57 percent Protestant, but the Protestants are fragmented among a large number of denominations and sects. The major Protestant denominations adhere to conventional church teachings and practices, but some groups— particularly sects on the fringes of the fundamentalist movement—interpret the scriptures in exceptionally strict and literal ways. These groups generally attract people of relatively low socioeconomic status—perhaps because their sense of religious exclusivity offers compensation for their lack of earthly rewards.*

*In this article, Michael Watterlond describes the rituals of one highly unusual sect, and looks for reasons for its members' behavior.*

For the Holy Ghost people of Appalachia, it is a fragile fabric that separates this world from the next.

They are serpent handlers.

The take up poisonous snakes in church—timber rattlers, copperheads, even cobras—and they drink strychnine. They handle fire, using coal oil torches or blow torches. And they speak "with new tongues." They lay hands on the sick, trusting that—God willing—the sick shall recover. And when necessary they cast out devils in Jesus' name.

"We live in the world, but we are not of the world," they say repeatedly during their twice-weekly church services, as though this were the statement that most distinctly defines them from us.

That these people are of another plane is unquestionable. They exist wholly in the thin, almost dimensionless region of "hard doctrine," of "getting right with Jesus" and most importantly of what they offhandedly call "this thing" or "this."

"This" is the featureless article of language they use to encompass the fiery, dramatic, even deadly practices that set their religion, their lives, and their select social grouping apart from most of Christian culture.

They belong to a variety of independent, fundamentalist sects called loosely Jesus Only. And they belong specifically to churches that subscribe to a doctrine based on what they call "the signs" or "the signs following."

The basis for these doctrines is a stone-hard reading of the last verses of the Gospel according to Mark and other passages in the New and Old Testaments as presented in the King James version of the Bible, an English translation published in 1611.

In the pertinent section of Mark, Jesus has already risen from the tomb and appeared to several characters, including his disciples. As he is about to ascend, he issues these final pronouncements:

Mark 16:17 "And these signs shall follow them that believe; In my name shall they cast out devils; they shall speak with new tongues;

Mark 16:18 "they shall take up serpents; and if they

drink any deadly thing, it shall not hurt them; they shall lay hands on the sick, and they shall recover."

The Book of Daniel, in which Shadrach, Meshach, and Abednego are cast into the fiery furnace, is the basis for fire handling.

The fundamentalist serpent handlers take these passages as absolute. That these verses in Mark do not appear in the earliest extant texts is of no importance to them at all. Only the King James Bible counts. It acts as a major initiator of personal action, behavior, and decision making in their lives. It defines them.

Mary Lee Daugherty, formerly a professor of religion at the University of Charleston, estimates that there are now about 1,000 members of serpent-handling sects in West Virginia. She says numbers have dwindled recently because high unemployment has forced many members to migrate to urban areas. Since no organization links these congregations, a total member count would be guesswork.

Though there are local laws against handling dangerous animals in public in many states where serpent-handling churches exist, the laws aren't always strictly enforced. There are congregations in most areas of Appalachia, stretching from West Virginia south through Kentucky, Tennessee, the Carolinas, and into Georgia. Migrations from hill country into some of the urban areas of the Midwest have led to serpent-handling churches in nonrural areas such as Columbus, Cleveland, Flint, Indianapolis, and Detroit. The Full Gospel Jesus Church of Columbus, under the leadership of Willie Sizemore, has purchased and renovated a building in one of the city's industrial areas.

George Hensley, who began the practice of snake handling in rural Tennessee around 1909, could not have predicted its spread to urban environments. Hensley, a Holiness circuit preacher, died of a snake bite near Atha, Florida, in 1955. He is not revered by these people and is not considered to have been a prophet of any sort. His death, however, does illustrate a point one frequently hears in Jesus Only congregations: The Bible says to take up serpents; it doesn't say they won't bite.

"Make sure it's God," a deacon warns. He holds the microphone close to his lips like an entertainer. His hefty coal miner's shoulders straighten as he whips the mike cord away from his feet. "Only God can do it. Not me. Not you."

The loud, mechanical-sounding buzz from the white pine serpent box makes his point unmistakable. The box this afternoon contains four timber rattlers and a rosy, velvet-textured copperhead.

"Death is in there," he says. "Don't go in the box unless it's with you."

By "it," the deacon means "the anointing"—the protection and spiritual direction of God that is manifest in what believers report as physical and emotional sensations.

"It's different for everyone," according to Sizemore. "Some people get a cold feeling in their hands or in their stomachs. Some don't."

Investigators in the past have reported that members say the anointing has a different and, for them, recognizably distinct sensation for each sign. The anointing to handle serpents may appear as a tingling, chilled feeling in the hands. An anointing to drink strychnine may appear as a trembling in the gut. The reports vary just as the sensations vary.

The deacon's warning about acting on the signs only if the anointing is present is a typical part of services, and the saints, as the members call each other, enthusiastically applaud. As he turns from the pulpit, the underlying rhythmic drum beat that has throbbed subliminally in the background becomes distinct and powerful. It is joined by electric organ, electric guitar, tambourine, and a room full of the clapping hands, stomping feet, and hearty, frantic voices of 40 saints.

As the service gets underway, the saints stand, clapping with the music, and walk slowly toward the open area between the pulpit and the first row of pews. The movement forward and together is called a "press." There is some feeling that the spiritual power of the group is concentrated by this gathering together. Should a member be bitten by a snake or "get down on strychnine," the gathering of saints around the victim is also called a press. Members refer to this communal praying and support of the stricken person as a "good press."

The services themselves have an informal structure that begins with loud, insistent singing. Most songs are belted out in four-four time, and each lasts as long as 20 to 30 minutes. After a few songs there will be requests for prayers or healings and testament. The prayer requests may be for "sinner children" or for members of the church who are sick or injured. There will be more songs before the sermon. Services last from two to five hours depending on the time of year and work schedules in the mines.

The signs may show themselves at any time during the service but are most apt to be manifest in association with the driving rhythms of the music. The enthusiasm may verge on violence. One woman slumps on the floor, "slain in the spirit," they say. As she trembles in front of the pulpit, other saints close in on her, screaming "JESUS! JESUS! JESUS!" in her ears.

"I saw one man get up and run around the inside of the church more than 50 times," says sociologist Michael Carter of Warner Southern College in Lake Wales, Florida, an experienced observer of the sect.

Members wail and shake and lapse into the unintelligible, ecstatic "new tongues" of glossolalia. Each member has his or her own style of speaking. As one saint sails into a new oration of tongues, another clamps his hands to her head and speaks in tongues himself; the ecstasy spreads like contagion. "He's translating," Carter observes.

There are two camps of psychological explanation and description of such services. Some researchers theorize that the wild activities are attempts to transcend reality, while others believe the point is self-actualization. Possibly both are right. It takes only a brief conversation with participants to learn that their daily life is one ongoing seance. They see God's movement and directives in every action, object, or thought.

Jerking as though his head were being battered by some unseen opponent, one brother moves across the floor toward the canister of coal oil next to the pulpit. He lights it quickly and thrusts his hands into the fire as though he were washing himself in flame. Next to him a young woman has been dervish-like for several minutes. She continues spinning under the tent of her long brown hair for nearly half an hour. In the back, the children play tic-tac-toe, practice spelling exercises, or sleep, unconnected to the proceedings.

Investigation into psychological and sociological aspects of fire and serpent handling has been conducted sporadically since the 1940s. A paper presented last year by Carter and sociologist Kenneth Ambrose of Marshall University in Huntington, West Virginia, at the Fifth Annual Appalachian Studies Conference, attempted to determine the satisfaction church members derive from such activities. They interviewed members of an urban congregation to compare the rewards of church versus non-church activity.

Results of the study indicate that taking part in the signs gives these people personal reward equalled in no other aspect of their lives. Participation in "signs of the spirit" were statistically evaluated by Ambrose and Carter to reveal the highest level of satisfaction for members when they spoke in tongues. Handling serpents and handling fire were also rated highly, while drinking strychnine—clearly the most deadly sign—provided more shallow levels of satisfaction.

"When you drink strychnine," members say, "you're already bit"—your fate has been decided. Strychnine, commonly a white or colorless powder, causes a warm feeling in the gut, tingling sensations, and muscle spasms. In poisonous doses—15 to 30 milligrams for a human—the spasms can be severe enough, as the serpent handlers say, to "snap muscles right off the bone" and stop the heart. However, it is possible to ingest a considerable amount of strychnine and not exhibit the symptoms of poisoning. The drug does not accumulate in the body because it is rapidly oxidized in the liver and excreted in urine. The likelihood of developing a tolerance to it is remote.

While members of serpent-handling churches—as well as most Jesus Only churches—forego worldly diversions such as films, television, and politics, they do hold down jobs. Sizemore, for example, is a factory worker. But they consider mingling with the world on the job part of their earthly burden.

Since most members have had to face stern criticism and even ostracism by friends and relatives—including husbands and wives at times—they are even more strongly pushed into this cluster of supportive friends at church, where they speak of themselves as the chosen people. The social and psychological bonds are reinforced more or less constantly by hugging, touching, kissing. This creates a rich, meaningful world for them—a sense of being special.

Also, the pastor rides herd spiritually on the congregation. During service he will approach a member he suspects (or "discerns," as they would say) is backsliding, or going to other churches. He will preach to that member eye-to-eye, only the microphone between them, and talk in generalities about worldliness, sin, or traipsing around.

"I don't hold with people going from one church to another," says Brother Sizemore.

It is sometimes a strenuous task for the outsider to pry himself loose from all this music and high spirits and remind himself that these people take poisonous reptiles out of the countryside, bring them into their churches and drape them over their bodies, wear them in bundles on their heads. While the churchgoers are enthusiastic and emotional and committed, they do not appear to be disturbed and certainly not suicidal.

"I'm just as afraid of serpents as anybody," one 22-year-old West Virginia man says. He has attended these churches since childhood and has left the church his mother attends in recent years because that congregation has stopped handling serpents. "I'm afraid when I am in the flesh," he explains, "but when it is the spirit, there's nothing. I'm just not afraid."

He pulls up his sleeve to illustrate the critical point he wants to make: that these serpents are real and that their venom is real.

"It bit me here," he says, pointing to his wrist. "And it swelled up so much that the skin just pulled apart up here."

"When Richard died," one member says, "his whole arm split open from the shoulder down to the elbow."

Richard was Richard Williams. He died in 1974 after being viciously bitten by a huge eastern diamondback.

Like most members who suffer bites, Williams refused medical aid and waited for fate to reveal itself.

The people of this church still talk about Richard Williams's anointing and about the serpent-handling feats he performed. Pictures on the walls of the church show him with his face in a mound of snakes; lying with his head resting on them like pillows, stuffing them into his shirt next to his skin. In a photo of Williams and the snake that killed him, it appears as if he is holding the felled limb of a tree rather than a snake.

"What really killed him was that the serpent got his vein when it hit the second time," one member says.

"You just can't tell," Willie Sizemore says, "you just have to make sure you have the anointing."

The folk myth that individuals who suffer repeated snakebites develop an immunity to the venom is viewed skeptically by Sherman A. Minton, Indiana University School of Medicine microbiologist and toxicologist. Minton says that such immunity is developed rarely and only when regular, gradually increased doses of the venom are administered. He points out that many people have allergies to venom, making successive bites more painful and causing greater swelling, asthma, and other symptoms.

As one snake expert puts it, however, the chances of dying by snakebite in the United States are comparable to the probability of being struck by lightning. One 10-year study showed that 8,000 venomous bites occur each year resulting in an average of only 14 deaths.

There are many theories about why snakes strike the saints infrequently. It is possible that given many warm-bodied targets pressing closely around it, a snake lapses into a sort of negative panic, a hysteria that makes it unable to single out one target.

Some observers have reported that church members' hands feel cold to the touch after handling fire or snakes. "I have felt their hands after serpent handling or fire handling," says Ambrose, who has observed these services for 15 years. "Their hands are definitely cold, even after handling fire." This would correspond with research in trance states involved in other religious cultures. It would also account for the vagueness of memory, almost sensory amnesia, that researchers have reported in serpent handlers as well as fire handlers. In his doctoral dissertation at Princeton University in 1974, Steven Kane reported that in North Carolina serpent-handling congregations, young women were known to embrace hot stovepipes without injury or memory of the event. It has also been suggested by some observers that cold hands on the body of the snake would camouflage the touch and prevent it from feeling the handler.

Retired sociologist Nathan Gerrard, formerly of the University of Charleston, observed serpent handlers for seven years in the 1960s. By administering portions of a psychological test to measure deviate personalities, Gerrard concluded that serpent handlers had healthier attitudes about death, suffered less from pessimistic hypochondria, and generally seemed better adjusted in certain ways than "conventional" churchgoers he used as a control group.

However, one of Gerrard's conclusions at the time was also that serpent handling represented a sop to desperation. He called them the "stationary working class" and attributed their stern doctrine to highland ignorance and poverty—a fatalistic creed that offered death and salvation as the only way out of West Virginia. Since that time, however, Jesus Only churches have spread out of Appalachia as economic hardships pushed followers into urban centers perched on the edge of the Midwest.

Also, the members of the Full Gospel Jesus Church of Micco, a creek-bank town about 10 miles from Logan, West Virginia, are distinctly not the archetypal mountain folks. They come to church in well-polished, late-model automobiles and dress like middle-class people in most parts of the country.

While it may be difficult for outsiders to say that it is simply common faith that keep these groups together, that would be the first thing they would say themselves. And this is a self-definition that has been immensely important to Western civilization.

"You can clearly see early Christianity as having very strong sectarian overtones," says Robert Bellah, a sociologist at the University of California, Berkeley. "Without that at the beginning, there would not have been any Christian church."

"Sect religions," Bellah says, "are most apt to occur in relatively low-status groups, relatively low-educated groups where a combination of intense religious experience and rather high group discipline create a kind of separate world in which the people in the sect live.

"They largely reject the surrounding culture," Bellah explains, "rejecting many of the prevailing cultural forms. In other words, the whole round of life tends to be bound up in the sect itself. Social contact is limited by the sect, and the meaning of most things that one does derives from the sect."

Bellah makes the distinction that churches involve a structure which attempts to encompass the whole of society. They include a range of social classes and do not oppose the dominant social power but view themselves as having influence on how that power is exercised.

"The church accepts the culture while working within it," Bellah says. "A sect is exclusive."

It is the current public concern about total-commitment sects that has many people wondering about what have come to be called cults these days.

" 'Cult' is really not a sociological category," Bellah explains. "It is a pejorative, popular term that we use for groups that are unfamiliar to our culture." Generally, the word is used to describe groups that are non-American in origin or are aberrantly individualistic—"in that they have been created by some 'kook,'" Bellah says. "Like Jim Jones."

"We are not a cult," Sizemore says forcefully. "If Jim Jones had been right with Jesus, those people wouldn't have died."

And still, outsiders want to know why anyone handles serpents.

"Because it is written," says Bishop Kelly Williams of the Jesus Only Church of Micco, West Virginia. "The main purpose in our doing this is to obey the Word of God." He points out that it really does not matter that the snakes symbolize Satan.

"Now, we don't think that everyone has to take up serpents," Williams says. "It doesn't say that all signs will follow all believers.

"You," he says to a visitor. "You might only speak in tongues. It depends on how God moves.

"Everyone knows that it is the nature of those serpents to bite you," he nods toward the buzzing pine box of copperheads and rattlers. "But you saw last night that God gave us a victory over those serpents. They were new serpents. They'd never been handled."

In fact, in a quiet evening before, Williams had gone to the box, lifted out a rattler and held it close to his body. He stared down at the serpent in his palms, smiled calmly for about three minutes, and set the snake back down in the box.

"You've seen that there is no one way to handle serpents," he says. "You been around enough to know that. There's no trick."

The styles of serpent handling are as various as the vocabulary of new tongues. On one Sunday afternoon, several men lift up the box, shake it hard and dump a mass of rattlers and copperheads onto the wooden floor without much caution. One man reaches into the tangle of scales and rattles and pulls up a timber rattler about four feet long. The other snakes, as well as a microphone cord, are tangled up with it, so he just shakes the whole mess until the excess snakes drop off. They coil stunned on the floor, as if paralyzed by the bad manners of it all.

The serpents are passed between hands. Loose copperheads wander around the box, uncertain of any particular route of escape. The heavy beat of gospel music picks up and the floor vibrates, the congregation claps and wails and sings.

In the back row of pews a girl about eleven turns back over her shoulder to talk to the visitor. She is playing hairdresser with another girl and holds an unfinished braid in her hands. She smiles half-heartedly and rolls her eyes heavenward as though her patience were limitless and unconditional.

"Boring," she says, "isn't it?"

---

## QUESTIONS

1. Why do you think people would participate in a sect such as the Holy Ghost people?

2. To what extent are a person's religious beliefs shaped by the social environment?

3. By most criteria, the United States is easily the most religious of the modern industrialized societies. Why do you think that is the case?

George J. Gmelch

# 40. Baseball Magic

*Earlier in this century, the anthropologist Bronislaw Malinowski studied the native inhabitants of islands in the southwestern Pacific. He was intrigued by one aspect of the people's behavior when they went fishing. If they were in the calm waters of a lagoon, they treated the event as a routine occurrence of no religious significance. But if they were to fish in the dangerous shark-infested waters beyond the coral reef, they performed various rituals designed to harness magical powers for their safety and protection. What caused the difference? Malinowski concluded that, as a general rule, humans are most likely to appeal to magical or other occult powers whenever they face situations whose outcome is uncertain and beyond their own control.*

*Magic is related to, but slightly different from, religion. Religion is a set of beliefs and practices oriented toward some supernatural realm; magic is the attempt to utilize supernatural forces for human ends. The supernatural forces in religion tend to be worshiped or at least appeased; those in magic are merely put to use. Belief in magic is quite common even in a modern industrial society such as the United States: witness people's reliance on rabbits' feet, St. Christopher medals, lucky numbers, and other items supposed to bring good luck.*

*In this article, George Gmelch discusses some of the magical rituals found in baseball, and uses the evidence to test Malinowski's hypothesis that magic is most likely to be used in unpredictable situations.*

Published by permission of *Transaction,* Inc., from *Transaction,* Vol. 8, no. 8, copyright © 1971 by Transaction, Inc.

We find magic wherever the elements of chance and accident, and the emotional play between hope and fear, have a wide and extensive range. We do not find magic wherever the pursuit is certain, reliable, and well under the control of rational methods. [*Bronislaw Malinowski*]

Professional baseball is a nearly perfect arena in which to test Malinowski's hypothesis about magic. The great anthropologist was not, of course, talking about sleight of hand but of rituals, taboos and fetishes that men resort to when they want to ensure that things go their own way. Baseball is rife with this sort of magic, but, as we shall see, the players use it in some aspects of the game far more than in others.

Everyone knows that there are three essentials of baseball—hitting, pitching and fielding. The point is, however, that the first two, hitting and pitching, involve a high degree of chance. The pitcher is the player least able to control the outcome of his own efforts. His best pitch may be hit for a bloop single while his worst pitch may be hit directly to one of his fielders for an out. He may limit the opposition to a single hit and lose, or he may give up a dozen hits and win. It is not uncommon for pitchers to perform well and lose, and vice versa; one has only to look at the frequency with which pitchers end a season with poor won-lost percentages but low earned run averages (number of runs given up per game). The opposite is equally true: some pitchers play poorly, giving up many runs, yet win many games. In brief, the pitcher, regardless of how well he performs, is dependent upon the proficiency of his teammates, the inefficiency of the opposition and the supernatural (luck).

But luck, as we all know, comes in two forms, and many fans assume that the pitcher's tough losses (close games in which he gave up very few runs) are eventually balanced out by his "lucky" wins. This is untrue, as a comparison of pitchers' lifetime earned run averages to their overall won-lost records shows. If the player could apply a law of averages to individual performance, there would be much less concern about chance and uncertainty in baseball. Unfortunately, he cannot and does not.

Hitting, too, is a chancy affair. Obviously, skill is required in hitting the ball hard and on a line. Once the ball is hit, however, chance plays a large role in determining where it will go, into a waiting glove or whistling past a falling stab.

With respect to fielding, the player has almost complete control over the outcome. The average fielding percentage or success rate of .975, compared to a .245 success rate for hitters (the average batting average), reflects the degree of certainty in fielding. Next to the pitcher or hitter, the fielder has little to worry about when he knows that better than 9.7 times in ten he will execute his task flawlessly.

If Malinowski's hypothesis is correct, we should find magic associated with hitting and pitching, but none with fielding. Let us take the evidence by category—ritual, taboo and fetish.

## Ritual

After each pitch, ex-major leaguer Lou Skeins used to reach into his back pocket to touch a crucifix, straighten his cap and clutch his genitals. Detroit Tiger infielder Tim Maring wore the same clothes and put them on exactly in the same order each day during a batting streak. Baseball rituals are almost infinitely various. After all, the ballplayer can ritualize any activity he considers necessary for a successful performance, from the type of cereal he eats in the morning to the streets he drives home on.

Usually, rituals grow out of exceptionally good performances. When the player does well he cannot really attribute his success to skill alone. He plays with the same amount of skill one night when he gets four hits as the next night when he goes hitless. Through magic, such as ritual, the player seeks greater control over his performance, actually control over the elements of chance. The player, knowing that his ability is fairly constant, attributes the inconsistencies in his performance to some form of behavior or a particular food that he ate. When a player gets four hits in a game, especially "cheap" hits, he often believes that there must have been something he did, in addition to his ability, that shifted luck to his side. If he can attribute his good fortune to the glass of iced tea he drank before the game or the new shirt he wore to the ballpark, then by repeating the same behavior the following day he can hope to achieve similar results. (One expression of this belief is the myth that eating certain foods will give the ball "eyes," that is, a ball that seeks the gaps between fielders.) In hopes of maintaining a batting streak, I once ate fried chicken every day at 4:00 P.M., kept my eyes closed during the national anthem and changed sweat shirts at the end of the fourth

inning each night for seven consecutive nights until the streak ended.

Fred Caviglia, Kansas City minor league pitcher, explained why he eats certain foods before each game: "Everything you do is important to winning. I never forget what I eat the day of a game or what I wear. If I pitch well and win I'll do it all exactly the same the next day I pitch. You'd be crazy not to. You just can't ever tell what's going to make the difference between winning and losing."

Rituals associated with hitting vary considerably in complexity from one player to the next, but they have several components in common. One of the most popular is tagging a particular base when leaving and returning to the dugout each inning. Tagging second base on the way to the outfield is habitual with some players. One informant reported that during a successful month of the season he stepped on third base on his way to the dugout after the third, sixth and ninth innings of each game. Asked if he ever purposely failed to step on the bag he replied, "Never! I wouldn't dare, it would destroy my confidence to hit." It is not uncommon for a hitter who is playing poorly to try different combinations of tagging and not tagging particular bases in an attempt to find a successful combination. Other components of a hitter's ritual may include tapping the plate with his bat a precise number of times or taking a precise number of warm-up swings with the leaded bat.

One informant described a variation of this in which he gambled for a certain hit by tapping the plate a fixed number of times. He touched the plate once with his bat for each base desired: one tap for a single, two for a double and so on. He even built in odds that prevented him from asking for a home run each time. The odds of hitting a single with one tap were one in three, while the chances of hitting a home run with four taps were one in 12.

Clothing is often considered crucial to both hitters and pitchers. They may have several athletic supporters and a number of sweat shirts with ritual significance. Nearly all players wear the same uniform and undergarments each day when playing well, and some even wear the same street clothes. In 1954, the New York Giants, during a 16-game winning streak, wore the same clothes in each game and refused to let them be cleaned for fear that their good fortune might be washed away with the dirt. The route taken to and from the stadium can also have significance; some players drive the same streets to the ballpark during a hitting streak and try different routes during slumps.

Because pitchers only play once every four days, the rituals they practice are often more complex than the hitters', and most of it, such as tugging the cap between pitches, touching the rosin bag after each bad pitch or smoothing the dirt on the mound before each new batter, takes place on the field. Many baseball fans have observed this behavior never realizing that it may be as important to the pitcher as throwing the ball.

Dennis Grossini, former Detroit farmhand, practiced the following ritual on each pitching day for the first three months of a winning season. First, he arose from bed at exactly 10:00 A.M. and not a minute earlier or later. At 1:00 P.M. he went to the nearest restaurant for two glasses of iced tea and a tuna fish sandwich. Although the afternoon was free, he observed a number of taboos such as no movies, no reading, and no candy. In the clubhouse he changed into the sweat shirt and jock he wore during his last winning game, and one hour before the game he chewed a wad of Beechnut chewing tobacco. During the game he touched his letters (the team name on his uniform) after each pitch and straightened his cap after each ball. Before the start of each inning he replaced the pitcher's rosin bag next to the spot where it was the inning before. And after every inning in which he gave up a run he went to the clubhouse to wash his hands. I asked him which part of the ritual was most important. He responded: "You can't really tell what's most important so it all becomes important. I'd be afraid to change anything. As long as I'm winning I do everything the same. Even when I can't wash my hands [this would occur when he must bat] it scares me going back to the mound. . . . I don't feel quite right."

One ritual, unlike those already mentioned, is practiced to improve the power of the baseball bat. It involves sanding the bat until all the varnish is removed, a process requiring several hours of labor, then rubbing rosin into the grain of the bat before finally heating it over a flame. This ritual treatment supposedly increases the distance the ball travels after being struck. Although some North Americans prepare their bats in this fashion it is more popular among Latin Americans. One informant admitted that he was not certain of the effectiveness of the treatment. But, he added, "There may not be a God, but I go to church just the same."

Despite the wide assortment of rituals associated with pitching and hitting, I never observed any ritual related to fielding. In all my 20 interviews only one player, a shortstop with acute fielding problems, reported any ritual even remotely connected to fielding.

## Taboo

Mentioning that a no-hitter is in progress and crossing baseball bats are the two most widely observed taboos. It is believed that if the pitcher hears the words "no-hitter" his spell will be broken and the no-hitter lost. As for the crossing of bats, that is sure to bring bad luck; batters are therefore extremely careful not to drop their

bats on top of another. Some players elaborate this taboo even further. On one occasion a teammate became quite upset when another player tossed a bat from the batting cage and it came to rest on top of his. Later he explained that the top bat would steal hits from the lower one. For him, then, bats contain a finite number of hits, a kind of baseball "image of limited good." Honus Wagner, a member of baseball's Hall of Fame, believed that each bat was good for only 100 hits and no more. Regardless of the quality of the bat he would discard it after its 100th hit.

Besides observing the traditional taboos just mentioned, players also observe certain personal prohibitions. Personal taboos grow out of exceptionally poor performances, which a player often attributes to some particular behavior or food. During my first season of professional baseball I once ate pancakes before a game in which I struck out four times. Several weeks later I had a repeat performance, again after eating pancakes. The result was a pancake taboo in which from that day on I never ate pancakes during the season. Another personal taboo, born out of similar circumstances, was against holding a baseball during the national anthem.

Taboos are also of many kinds. One athlete was careful never to step on the chalk foul lines or the chalk lines of the batter's box. Another would never put on his cap until the game started and would not wear it at all on the days he did not pitch. Another had a movie taboo in which he refused to watch a movie the day of a game. Often certain uniform numbers became taboo. If a player has a poor spring training or a bad year, he may refuse to wear the same uniform number again. I would not wear double numbers, especially 44 and 22. On several occasions, teammates who were playing poorly requested a change of uniform during the middle of the season. Some players consider it so important that they will wear the wrong size uniform just to avoid a certain number or to obtain a good number.

Again, with respect to fielding, I never saw or heard of any taboos being observed, though of course there were some taboos, like the uniform numbers, that were concerned with overall performance and so included fielding.

## Fetishes

These are standard equipment for many baseball players. They include a wide assortment of objects: horsehide covers of old baseballs, coins, bobby pins, protective cups, crucifixes and old bats. Ordinary objects are given this power in a fashion similar to the formation of taboos and rituals. The player during an exceptionally hot batting or pitching streak, especially one in which he has "gotten all the breaks," credits some unusual object, often a new possession, for his good fortune. For example, a player in a slump might find a coin or an odd stone just before he begins a hitting streak. Attributing the improvement in his performance to the new object, it becomes a fetish, embodied with supernatural power. While playing for Spokane, Dodger pitcher Alan Foster forgot his baseball shoes on a road trip and borrowed a pair from a teammate to pitch. That night he pitched a no-hitter and later, needless to say, bought the shoes from his teammate. They became his most prized possession.

Fetishes are taken so seriously by some players that their teammates will not touch them out of fear of offending the owner. I once saw a fight caused by the desecration of a fetish. Before the game, one player stole the fetish, a horsehide baseball cover, out of a teammate's back pocket. The prankster did not return the fetish until after the game, in which the owner of the fetish went hitless, breaking a batting streak. The owner, blaming his inability to hit on the loss of the fetish, lashed out at the thief when the latter tried to return it.

Rube Waddel, an old-time Philadelphia Athletic pitching great, had a hairpin fetish. However, the hairpin he possessed was only powerful as long as he won. Once he lost a game he would look for another hairpin, which had to be found on the street, and he would not pitch until he found another.

The use of fetishes follows the same pattern as ritual and taboo in that they are connected only with hitting or pitching. In nearly all cases the player expressed a specific purpose for carrying a fetish, but never did a player perceive his fetish as having any effect on his fielding.

I have said enough, I think, to show that many of the beliefs and practices of professional baseball players are magical. Any empirical connection between the ritual, taboo and fetishes and the desired event is quite absent.

Indeed, in several instances the relationship between the cause and effect, such as eating tuna fish sandwiches to win a ball game, is even more remote than is characteristic of primitive magic. Note, however, that unlike many forms of primitive magic, baseball magic is usually performed to achieve one's own end and not to block someone else's. Hitters do not tap their bats on the plate to hex the pitcher, but to improve their own performance.

Finally, it should be plain that nearly all the magical practices that I participated in, observed or elicited, support Malinowski's hypothesis that magic appears in situations of chance and uncertainty. The large amount of uncertainty in pitching and hitting best explains the elaborate magical practices used for these activities. Conversely, the high success rate in fielding, .975, involving much less uncertainty, offers the best explanation for the absence of magic in this realm.

## QUESTIONS

1. List some "magical" objects and rituals that are in use in American society. Do the conditions of their use tend to confirm Malinowski's theory?

2. Is the use by Americans of St. Christopher medals, rabbits' feet, numerology, and so forth, any different from the bone-throwing, potion-brewing, and pin-sticking rituals of people in simple, preindustrial societies?

3. How widespread in the class is belief in such quasi-religious phenomena as astrology, good luck, ghosts, superstition, fortune-telling, tarot-card reading, seances, palmistry, and the like? Can any of these beliefs be reconciled with a commitment to the Judeo-Christian religious tradition?

*Mark Zborowski*

# 41. Cultural Components in Responses to Pain

*The way that we respond to illness is strongly influenced by cultural factors. Different cultures offer their members quite different definitions of what constitutes disease and provide different guidelines to people seeking a return to health. In some societies, for example, illness may be interpreted as the result of witchcraft. In such a case, a sick person is likely to seek the help of a shaman or similar healer, who uses various magical rituals to remove the spell. In other societies, the identical symptom may be interpreted as the result of infection by microbes, and the sick person is likely to consult a qualified medical practitioner, who may prescribe appropriate drug treatments.*

*Even within a specific society, there may be a variety of different subcultural responses to symptoms of disease. Thus, although most Americans resort to the services of licensed physicians when they are ill, many others turn to unqualified practitioners, ranging from astrologers to faith healers. In some cases, different responses to illness are linked to social class: for example, high-status people are more likely to seek early, professional treatment than are people of lower social status. Other differences are associated with ethnicity: beyond the medical mainstream, there are thriving traditions of Chinese, Mexican, Indian, and other folk medicines that are used by some members of the relevant ethnic groups.*

*In this article, Mark Zborowski shows that even the physical sensation of pain is often interpreted differently by members of various American ethnic groups, for they tend to respond to their discomfort in terms of the meanings that they have learned in their own subculture.*

This paper reports on one aspect of a larger study: that concerned with discovering the role of cultural patterns in attitudes toward and reactions to pain which is caused by disease and injury—in other words, responses to spontaneous pain.

## Some Basic Distinctions

In human societies biological processes vital for man's survival acquire social and cultural significance. Intake of food, sexual intercourse or elimination—physiological phenomena which are universal for the entire living world—become institutions regulated by cultural and social norms, thus fulfilling not only biological functions but social and cultural ones as well. Metabolic and endocrinal changes in the human organism may provoke hunger and sexual desire, but culture and society dictate to man the kind of food he may eat, the social setting for eating or the adequate partner for mating.

Moreover, the role of cultural and social patterns in human physiological activities is so great that they may in specific situations act against the direct biological needs of the individual, even to the point of endangering his survival. Only a human being may prefer starvation to the breaking of a religious dietary law or may abstain from sexual intercourse because of specific incest regulations. Voluntary fasting and celibacy exist only where food and sex fulfill more than strictly physiological functions.

Thus, the understanding of the significance and role of social and cultural patterns in human physiology is necessary to clarify those aspects of human experience which remain puzzling if studied only within the physiological frame of reference.

. . .

In analyzing pain, it is useful to distinguish between self-inflicted, other-inflicted and spontaneous pain. Self-inflicted pain is defined as deliberately self-inflicted. It is experienced as a result of injuries performed voluntarily upon oneself, e.g., self-mutilation. Usually these

From *Journal of Social Issues*, 8:4, 1952, pp. 16–30.

injuries have a culturally defined purpose, such as achieving a special status in the society. It can be observed not only in primitive cultures but also in contemporary societies on a higher level of civilization. In Germany, for instance, members of certain student or military organizations would cut their faces with a razor in order to acquire scars which would identify them as members of a distinctive social group. By other-inflicted pain is meant pain inflicted upon the individual in the process of culturally accepted and expected activities (regardless of whether approved or disapproved), such as sports, fights, war, etc. To this category belongs also pain inflicted by the physician in the process of medical treatment. Spontaneous pain usually denotes the pain sensation which results from disease or injury. This term also covers pain of psychogenic nature.

Members of different cultures may assume differing attitudes towards these various types of pain. Two of these attitudes may be described as pain expectancy and pain acceptance. Pain expectancy is anticipation of pain as being unavoidable in a given situation, for instance, in childbirth, in sports activities or in battle. Pain acceptance is characterized by a willingness to experience pain. This attitude is manifested mostly as an inevitable component of culturally accepted experiences, for instance, as part of initiation rites or part of medical treatment. The following example will help to clarify the differences between pain expectancy and pain acceptance. Labor pain is expected as part of childbirth, but while in one culture, such as in the United States, it is not accepted and therefore various means are used to alleviate it, in some other cultures, for instance in Poland, it is not only expected but also accepted, and consequently nothing or little is done to relieve it. Similarly, cultures which emphasize military achievements expect and accept battle wounds, while cultures which emphasize pacifistic values may expect them but will not accept them.

In the process of investigating cultural attitudes toward pain it is also important to distinguish between pain apprehension and pain anxiety. Pain apprehension reflects the tendency to avoid the pain sensation as such, regardless of whether the pain is spontaneous or inflicted, whether it is accepted or not. Pain anxiety, on the other hand, is a state of anxiety provoked by the pain experience, focused upon various aspects of the causes of pain, the meaning of pain or its significance for the welfare of the individual.

Moreover, members of various cultures may react differently in terms of their manifest behavior toward various pain experiences, and this behavior is often dictated by the culture which provides specific norms according to the age, sex and social position of the individual.

The fact that other elements as well as cultural factors are involved in the response to a spontaneous pain should be taken into consideration. These other factors are the pathological aspect of pain, the specific physiological characteristics of the pain experience, such as the intensity, the duration and the quality of the pain sensation, and finally, the personality of the individual. Nevertheless, it was felt that in the process of a careful investigation it would be possible to detect the role of the cultural components in the pain experience.

## The Research Setting

. . .

With these aims in mind the project was set up at the Kingsbridge Veterans Hospital, Bronx, New York, where four ethno-cultural groups were selected for an intensive study. These groups included patients of Jewish, Italian, Irish and "Old American" stock. Three groups—Jews, Italian, and Irish—were selected because they were described by medical people as manifesting striking differences in their reaction to pain. Italians and Jews were described as tending to "exaggerate" their pain, while the Irish were often depicted as stoical individuals who were able to take a great deal of pain. The fourth group, the "Old Americans," were chosen because the values and attitudes of this group dominate in this country and are held by many members of the medical profession and by many descendants of the immigrants who, in the process of Americanization, tend to adopt American patterns of behavior. The members of this group can be defined as white, native-born individuals, usually Protestant, whose grandparents, at least, were born in the United States and who do not identify themselves with any foreign group, either nationally, socially or culturally.

The Kingsbridge Veterans Hospital was chosen because its population represents roughly the ethnic composition of New York City, thus offering access to a fair sample of the four selected groups, and also because various age groups were represented among the hospitalized veterans of World War I, World War II and the Korean War. In one major respect this hospital was not adequate, namely, in not offering the opportunity to investigate sex differences in attitude toward pain. This aspect of research will be carried out in a hospital with a large female population.

In setting up this project we were mainly interested in discovering certain regularities in reactions and attitudes toward pain characteristic of the four groups. Therefore, the study has a qualitative character, and the efforts of the researchers were not directed toward a collection of material suitable for quantitative analysis. The main techniques used in the collection of the material were interviews with patients of the selected groups, observation of their behavior when in pain and discussion of the individual case with doctors, nurses and other people directly or indirectly involved in the pain experience of the individual. In addition to the interviews with patients, "healthy" members of the respective groups were interviewed on their attitudes toward pain, because in terms of the original hypothesis those attitudes and reactions which are displayed by the patients of the given cultural groups are held by all members of the group regardless of whether or not they are in pain although in pain these attitudes may come more sharply into focus. In certain cases the researchers have interviewed a member of the patient's immediate family in order to check the report of the patient on his pain experience and in order to find out what are the attitudes and reactions of the family toward the patient's experience.

. . .

The discussion of the material presented in this paper is based on interviews with 103 respondents, including 87 hospital patients in pain and 16 healthy subjects. According to their ethno-cultural background the respondents are distributed as follows: "Old Americans," 26; Italians, 24; Jews, 31; Irish, 11; and others, 11. In addition, there were the collateral interviews and conversations noted above with family members, doctors, nurses and other members of the hospital staff.

. . .

## Pain Among Patients of Jewish and Italian Origin

As already mentioned, the Jews and Italians were selected mainly because interviews with medical experts suggested that they display similar reactions to pain. The investigation of this similarity provided the opportunity to check a rather popular assumption that similar reactions reflect similar attitudes. The differences between the Italian and Jewish culture are great enough to suggest that if the attitudes are related to cultural pattern they will also be different despite the apparent similarity in manifest behavior.

Members of both groups were described as being very emotional in their responses to pain. They were described as tending to exaggerate their pain experience and being very sensitive to pain. Some of the doctors stated that in their opinion Jews and Italians have a lower threshold of pain than members of other ethnic groups, especially members of the so-called Nordic group. This statement seems to indicate a certain confusion as to the concept of the threshold of pain. According to people who have studied the problem of the threshold of pain, for instance Harold Wolff and his associates, the threshold of pain is more or less the same for all human beings regardless of nationality, sex or age.

In the course of the investigation the general impres-

sions of doctors were confirmed to a great extent by the interview material and by the observation of the patients' behavior. However, even a superficial study of the interviews has revealed that though reactions to pain appear to be similar the underlying attitudes toward pain are different in the two groups. While the Italian patients seemed to be mainly concerned with the immediacy of the pain experience and were disturbed by the actual pain sensation which they experienced in a given situation, the concern of patients of Jewish origin was focused mainly upon the symptomatic meaning of pain and upon the significance of pain in relation to their health, welfare, and eventually, for the welfare of the families. The Italian patient expressed in his behavior and in his complaints the discomfort caused by pain as such, and he manifested his emotions with regard to the effects of this pain experience upon his immediate situation in terms of occupation, economic situation and so on; the Jewish patient expressed primarily his worries and anxieties as to the extent to which the pain indicated a threat to his health. In this connection it is worth mentioning that one of the Jewish words to describe strong pain is *yessurim,* a word which is also used to describe worries and anxieties.

Attitudes of Italian and Jewish patients toward pain-relieving drugs can serve as an indication of their attitude toward pain. When in pain the Italian calls for pain relief and is mainly concerned with the analgesic effects of the drugs which are administered to him. Once the pain is relieved the Italian patient easily forgets his sufferings and manifests a happy and joyful disposition. The Jewish patient, however, often is reluctant to accept the drug, and he explains this reluctance in terms of concern about the effects of the drug upon his health in general. He is apprehensive about the habit-forming aspects of the analgesic. Moreover, he feels that the drug relieves his pain only temporarily and does not cure him of the disease which may cause the pain. Nurses and doctors have reported cases in which patients would hide the pill which was given to them to relieve their pain and would prefer to suffer. These reports were confirmed in the interviews with the patients. It was also observed that many Jewish patients after being relieved from pain often continued to display the same depressed and worried behavior because they felt that though the pain was currently absent it may recur as long as the disease was not cured completely. From these observations it appears that when one deals with a Jewish and Italian patient in pain, in the first case it is more important to relieve the anxieties with regard to the sources of pain, while in the second it is more important to relieve the actual pain.

Another indication as to the significance of pain for Jewish and Italian patients is their respective attitudes toward the doctor. The Italian patient seems to display a most confident attitude toward the doctor which is usually reinforced after the doctor has succeeded in relieving pain, whereas the Jewish patient manifests a skeptical attitude, feeling that the fact that the doctor has relieved his pain by some drug does not mean at all that he is skillful enough to take care of the basic illness. Consequently, even when the pain is relieved, he tends to check the diagnosis and the treatment of one doctor against the opinions of other specialists in the field. Summarizing the difference between the Italian and Jewish attitudes, one can say that the Italian attitude is characterized by a present-oriented apprehension with regard to the actual sensation of pain, and the Jew tends to manifest a future-oriented anxiety as to the symptomatic and general meaning of the pain experience.

It has been stated that the Italians and Jews tend to manifest similar behavior in terms of their reactions to pain. As both cultures allow for free expression of feelings and emotions by words, sounds and gestures, both the Italians and Jews feel free to talk about their pain, complain about it and manifest their sufferings by groaning, moaning, crying, etc. They are not ashamed of this expression. They admit willingly that when they are in pain they do complain a great deal, call for help and expect sympathy and assistance from other members of their immediate social environment, especially from members of their family. When in pain they are reluctant to be alone and prefer the presence and attention of other people. This behavior, which is expected, accepted and approved by the Italian and Jewish cultures often conflicts with the patterns of behavior expected from a patient by American or Americanized medical people. Thus they tend to describe the behavior of the Italian and Jewish patient as exaggerated and over-emotional. The material suggests that they do tend to minimize the actual pain experience of the Italian and Jewish patient regardless of whether they have the objective criteria for evaluating the actual amount of pain which the patient experiences. It seems that the uninhibited display of reaction to pain as manifested by the Jewish and Italian patient provokes distrust in American culture instead of provoking sympathy.

Despite the close similarity between the manifest reactions among Jews and Italians, there seem to be differences in emphasis especially with regard to what the patient achieves by these reactions and as to the specific manifestations of these reactions in the various social settings. For instance, they differ in their behavior at home and in the hospital. The Italian husband, who is aware of his role as an adult male, tends to avoid verbal complaining at home, leaving this type of behavior to the women. In the hospital, where he is less concerned with his role as a male, he tends to be more verbal and more emotional. The Jewish patient, on the contrary, seems to be more calm in the hospital than at home. Traditionally the Jewish male does not emphasize his mas-

culinity through such traits as stoicism, and he does not equate verbal complaints with weakness. Moreover, the Jewish culture allows the patient to be demanding and complaining. Therefore, he tends more to use his pain in order to control interpersonal relationships within the family. Though similar use of pain to manipulate the relationships between members of the family may be present also in some other cultures it seems that in the Jewish culture this is not disapproved, while in others it is. In the hospital one can also distinguish variations in the reactive patterns among Jews and Italians. Upon his admission to the hospital and in the presence of the doctor the Jewish patient tends to complain, asks for help, be emotional even to the point of crying. However, as soon as he feels that adequate care is given to him he becomes more restrained. This suggests that the display of pain reaction serves less as an indication of the amount of pain experienced than as a means to create an atmosphere and setting in which the pathological cause of pain will be best taken care of. The Italian patient, on the other hand, seems to be less concerned with setting up a favorable situation for treatment. He takes for granted that adequate care will be given to him, and in the presence of the doctor he seems to be somewhat calmer than the Jewish patient. The mere presence of the doctor reassures the Italian patient, while the skepticism of the Jewish patient limits the reassuring role of the physician.

To summarize the description of the reactive patterns of the Jewish and Italian patients, the material suggests that on a semi-conscious level the Jewish patient tends to provoke worry and concern in his social environment as to the state of his health and the symptomatic character of his pain, while the Italian tends to provoke sympathy toward his suffering. In one case the function of the pain reaction will be the mobilization of the efforts of the family and the doctors toward a complete cure, while in the second case the function of the reaction will be focused upon the mobilization of effort toward relieving the pain sensation.

On the basis of the discussion of the Jewish and Italian material two generalizations can be made: (1) *Similar reactions to pain manifested by members of different ethno-cultural groups do not necessarily reflect similar attitudes to pain.* (2) *Reactive patterns similar in terms of their manifestations may have different functions and serve different purposes in various cultures.*

## Pain Among Patients of "Old American" Origin

There is little emphasis on emotional complaining among "Old American" patients. Their complaints about pain can best be described as reporting on pain. In describing pain, the "Old American" patient tries to find the most appropriate ways of defining the quality of pain, its localization, duration, etc. When examined by the doctor he gives the impression of trying to assume the detached role of an unemotional observer who gives the most efficient description of his state for a correct diagnosis and treatment. The interviewees repeatedly state that there is no point in complaining and groaning and moaning, etc., because "it won't help anybody." However, they readily admit that when pain is unbearable they may react strongly, even to the point of crying, but they tend to do it when they are alone. Withdrawal from society seems to be a frequent reaction to strong pain.

There seem to be different patterns in reacting to pain depending on the situation. One pattern, manifested in the presence of members of the family, friends, etc., consists of attempts to minimize pain, to avoid complaining and provoking pity; when pain becomes too strong there is a tendency to withdraw and express freely such reactions as groaning, moaning, etc. A different pattern is manifested in the presence of people who, on account of their profession, should know the character of the pain experience because they are expected to make the appropriate diagnosis, advise the proper cure and give the adequate help. This tendency to avoid deviation from certain expected patterns of behavior plays an important role in the reaction to pain. This is also controlled by the desire to seek approval on the part of the social environment, especially in the hospital, where the "Old American" patient tries to avoid being a "nuisance" on the ward. He seems to be, more than any other patient, aware of an ideal pattern of behavior which is identified as "American," and he tends to conform to it. This was characteristically expressed by a patient who answered the question how he reacts to pain by saying, "I react like a good American."

An important element in controlling the pain reaction is the wish of the patient to cooperate with those who are expected to take care of him. The situation is often viewed as a team composed of the patient, the doctor, the nurse, the attendant, etc., and in this team everybody has a function and is supposed to do his share in order to achieve the most successful result. Emotionality is seen as a purposeless and hindering factor in a situation which calls for knowledge, skill, training and efficiency. It is important to note that this behavior is also expected by American or Americanized members of the medical or nursing staff, and the patients who do not fall into this pattern are viewed as deviants, hypochondriacs and neurotics.

As in the case of the Jewish patients, the American attitude toward pain can be best defined as a future-oriented anxiety. The "Old American" patient is also concerned with the symptomatic significance of pain which is correlated with a pronounced health-consciousness. It seems that the "Old American" is conscious of various threats to his health which are present in his environment and therefore feels vulnerable and is prone to interpret his pain sensation as a warning signal indicating that something is wrong with his health and therefore must be reported to the physician. With some exceptions, pain is considered bad and unnecessary and therefore must be immediately taken care of. In those situations where pain is expected and accepted, such as in the process of medical treatment or as a result of sports activities, there is less concern with the pain sensation. In general, however, there is a feeling that suffering pain is unnecessary when there are means of relieving it.

Though the attitudes of the Jewish and "Old American" patients can be defined as pain anxiety they differ greatly. The future-oriented anxiety of the Jewish interviewee is characterized by pessimism or, at best, by skepticism, while the "Old American" patient is rather optimistic in his future-orientation. This attitude is fostered by the mechanistic approach to the body and its functions and by the confidence in the skill of the expert which are so frequent in the American, in that the body is often viewed as a machine which has to be well taken care of, be periodically checked for dysfunctioning and eventually, when out of order, be taken to an expert who will "fix" the defect. In the case of pain the expert is the medical man who has the "know-how" because of his training and experience and therefore is entitled to full confidence. An important element in the optimistic outlook is faith in the progress of science. Patients with intractable pain often stated that though at the present moment the doctors do not have the "drug" they will eventually discover it, and they will give the examples of sulfa, penicillin, etc.

The anxieties of a pain-experiencing "Old American" patient are greatly relieved when he feels that something is being done about it in terms of specific activities involved in the treatment. It seems that his security and confidence increase in direct proportion to the number of tests, X-rays, examinations, injections, etc., that are given to him. Accordingly, "Old American" patients seem to have a positive attitude toward hospitalization, because the hospital is the adequate institution which is equipped for the necessary treatment. While a Jewish and an Italian patient seem to be disturbed by the impersonal character of the hospital and by the necessity of being treated there instead of at home, the "Old American" patient, on the contrary, prefers the hospital treatment to the home treatment, and neither he nor his family seems to be disturbed by hospitalization.

To summarize the attitude of the "Old American" toward pain, he is disturbed by the symptomatic aspect of pain and is concerned with its incapacitating aspects, but he tends to view the future in rather optimistic colors, having confidence in the science and skill of the professional people who treat his condition.

## Some Sources of Intra-Group Variation

In the description of the reactive patterns and attitudes toward pain among patients of Jewish and "Old American" origin certain regularities have been observed for each particular group regardless of individual differences and variations. This does not mean that each individual in each group manifests the same reactions and attitudes. Individual variations are often due to specific aspects of pain experience, to the character of the disease which causes the pain or to elements of the personality of the patient. However, there are also other factors that are instrumental in provoking these differences and which can still be traced back to the cultural backgrounds of the individual patients. Such variables as the degree of Americanization of the patient, his socio-economic background, education and religiosity may play an important role in shaping individual variations in the reactive patterns. For instance, it was found that the patterns described are manifested most consistently among immigrants, while their descendants tend to differ in terms of adopting American forms of behavior and American attitudes toward the role of the medical expert, medical institutions and equipment in controlling pain. It is safe to say that the further the individual is from the immigrant generation the more American is his behavior. This is less true for the attitudes toward pain, which seem to persist to a great extent even among members of the third generation and even though the reactive patterns are radically changed. A Jewish or Italian patient born in this country of American-born parents tends to *behave* like an "Old American" but often expresses *attitudes* similar to those which are expressed by the Jewish or Italian people. They try to appear unemotional and efficient in situations where the immigrant would be excited and disturbed. However, in the process of the interview, if a patient is of Jewish origin he is likely to express attitudes of anxiety as to the meaning of his pain, and if he is an Italian he is likely to be rather unconcerned about the significance of his pain for the future.

The occupational factor plays an important role when pain affects a specific area of the body. For instance, manual workers with herniated discs are more disturbed by their pain than are professional or business people with a similar disease because of the immediate significance of this particular pain for their respective abilities to earn a living. It was also observed that headaches cause more concern among intellectuals than among manual workers.

The educational background of the patient also plays an important role in his attitude with regard to the symptomatic meaning of a pain sensation. The more educated patients are more health-conscious and more aware of pain as a possible symptom of a dangerous disease. However, this factor plays a less important role than might be expected. The less educated "Old American" or Jewish patient is still more health-conscious than the more educated Italian. On the other hand, the less educated Jew is as much worried about the significance of pain as the more educated one. The education of the patient seems to be an important factor in fostering specific reactive patterns. The more educated patient, who may have more anxiety with regard to illness, may be more reserved in specific reactions to pain than an unsophisticated individual, who feels free to express his feelings and emotions.

. . .

## QUESTIONS

1. How did cultural factors influence responses to pain among the subjects in the study?

2. Cultural factors affect the way people express their feelings about pain. Can you think of cultural influences on the way people express other emotions, such as grief or anger?

3. In the United States, people of high socioeconomic status tend to enjoy better health and longer lives than people of low socioeconomic status. How can you explain this fact?

*Thomas McKeown*

# 42. Determinants of Health

*Opinion polls about the relative prestige of various occupations have consistently shown that physicians rank higher than the holders of any other job. This fact is indicative of the immense respect that the general population has for modern medicine and its many achievements, which are supposed to include returning us to health when we are ill, and dramatically extending our life expectancies by combating the diseases that once sent so large a part of humanity to an early grave.*

*In this article, Thomas McKeown questions whether modern medicine can really take all the credit for these achievements. While he does not downplay the remarkable and effective advances that have taken place in medical science during this century, he argues that other factors have been more important in extending life expectancy, and can have a greater influence on keeping us well.*

*The high infant mortality rates of the past, he points out, began a sharp decline before, not after, such innovations as vaccinations, and they did so for reasons that were primarily social. Similarly, he argues that our health depends less on the ability of physicians to make us well when we are ill than on the social and environmental factors that make us ill when we should be well.*

Modern medicine is not nearly as effective as most people believe. It has not been effective because medical science and service are misdirected and society's investment in health is misused. At the base of this misdirection is a false assumption about human health. Physicians, biochemists, and the general public assume that the body is a machine that can be protected from disease primarily by physical and chemical intervention. This approach, rooted in 17th Century science, has led to widespread indifference to the influence of the primary determinants of human health—environment and personal behavior—and emphasizes the role of medical treatment, which is actually less important than either of the others. It has also resulted in the neglect of sick people whose ailments are not within the scope of the sort of therapy that interests the medical professions.

An appraisal of influences on health in the past suggests that the contribution of modern medicine to the increase of life expectancy has been much smaller than most people believe. Health improved, not because of steps taken when we are ill, but because we become ill less often. We remain well, less because of specific measures such as vaccination and immunization than because we enjoy a higher standard of nutrition, we live in a healthier environment, and we have fewer children.

For some 300 years an engineering approach has been dominant in biology and medicine and has provided the basis for the treatment of the sick. A mechanistic concept of nature developed in the 17th Century led to the idea that a living organism, like a machine, might be taken apart and reassembled if its structure and function were sufficiently understood. Applied to medicine, this concept meant that understanding the body's response to disease would allow physicians to intervene in the course of disease. The consequences of the engineering approach to medicine are more conspicuous today than they were in the 17th Century, largely because the resources of the physical and chemical sciences are so much greater. Medical education begins with the study of the structure and function of the body, continues with examination of disease processes, and ends with clinical instruction on selected sick people. Medical service is dominated by the image of the hospital for the acutely ill, where technological resources are concentrated. Medical research also reflects the mechanistic approach, concerning itself with problems such as the chemical basis of inheritance and the immunological response to transplanted tissues.

No one disputes the predominance of the engineering approach in medicine, but we must now ask whether it is seriously deficient as a conceptualization of the problems of human health. To answer this question, we must examine the determinants of human health. We must first discover why health improved in the past and then go on to ascertain the important influences on health today, in the light of the change in health problems that has resulted from the decline of infectious diseases.

It is no exaggeration to say that health, especially the health of infants and young children, has been transformed since the 18th Century. For the first time in history, a mother knows it is likely that all her children will live to maturity. Before the 19th Century, only about three out of every 10 newborn infants lived beyond the age of 25. Of the seven who died, two or three never reached their first birthday, and five or six died before they were six. Today, in developed countries fewer than one in 20 children die before they reach adulthood.

The increased life expectancy, most evident for young children, is due predominantly to a reduction of deaths from infectious diseases. Records from England and Wales (the earliest national statistics available) show that this reduction was the reason for the improvement in health before 1900 and it remains the main influence to the present day.

But when we try to account for the decline of infections, significant differences of opinion appear. The conventional view attributes the change to an increased understanding of the nature of infectious disease and to the application of that knowledge through better hygiene, immunization, and treatment. This interpretation places particular emphasis on immunization against diseases like smallpox and polio, and on the use of drugs for the treatment of other diseases, such as tuberculosis, meningitis, and pneumonia. These measures, in fact, contributed relatively little to the total reduction of mortality; the main explanation for the dramatic fall in the number of deaths lies not in medical intervention, but elsewhere.

Deaths from the common infections were declining long before effective medical intervention was possible. By 1900, the total death rate had dropped substantially, and over 90 percent of the reduction was due to a decrease of deaths from infectious diseases. The relative importance of the major influences can be illustrated by reference to tuberculosis. Although respiratory tuberculosis was the single largest cause of death in the mid-19th Century, mortality from the disease declined continuously after 1838, when it was first registered in England and Wales as a cause of death.

Robert Koch identified the tubercle bacillus in 1882, but none of the treatments used in the 19th or early 20th Centuries significantly influenced the course of the disease. The many drugs that were tried were worthless; so, too, was the practice of surgically collapsing an infected lung, a treatment introduced about 1920. Streptomycin, developed in 1947, was the first effective treatment, but by this time mortality from the disease had fallen to a small fraction of its level during 1848 to 1854. Streptomycin lowered the death rate from tuberculosis in England and Wales by about 50 percent, but its contribution to the decrease in the death rate since the early 19th Century was only about 3 percent.

Deaths from bronchitis, pneumonia, and influenza also began to decline before medical science provided an effective treatment for these illnesses. Although the death rate in England and Wales increased in the second half of the 19th Century, it has fallen continuously since the beginning of the 20th. There is still no effective immunization against bronchitis or pneumonia, and influenza vaccines have had no effect on deaths. The first successful treatment for these respiratory diseases was a sulfa drug introduced in 1938, but mortality attributed to the lung infections was declining from the beginning of the 20th Century. There is no reason to doubt that the decline would have continued without effective therapeutic measures, if at a slower rate.

In the United States, the story was similar; Thomas Magill noted that "the rapid decline of pneumonia death rates began in New York State before the turn of the century and many years before the 'miracle drugs' were known." Obviously, drug therapy was not responsible for the total decrease in deaths that occurred since 1938, and it could have had no influence on the substantial reduction that occurred before then.

The histories of most other common infections, such as whooping cough, measles, and scarlet fever, are similar. In each of these diseases, mortality had fallen to a low level before effective immunization or therapy became available.

In some infections, medical intervention *was* valuable before sulfa drugs and antibiotics became available. Immunization protected people against smallpox and tetanus; antitoxin treatment limited deaths from diphtheria; appendicitis, peritonitis, and ear infections responded to surgery; Salvarsan was a long-sought "magic bullet" against syphilis; intravenous therapy saved people with severe diarrheas; and improved obstetric care prevented childbed fever.

But even if such medical measures had been responsible for the whole decline of mortality from these particular conditions after 1900 (and clearly they were not), they would account for only a small part of the decrease in deaths attributed to all infectious diseases before 1935. From that time, powerful drugs came into use and they were supplemented by improved vaccines. But mortality would have continued to fall even without the presence of these agents; and over the whole period since cause of death was first recorded, immunization and treatment have contributed much less than other influences.

The substantial fall in mortality was due in part to reduced contact with microorganisms. In developed countries an individual no longer encounters the cholera bacillus, he is rarely exposed to the typhoid organism, and his contact with the tubercle baccillus is infrequent. The death rate from these infections fell continuously from the second half of the 19th Century when basic hygienic measures were introduced: purification of water; efficient sewage disposal; and improved food hygiene, particularly the pasteurization of milk, the item in the diet most likely to spread disease.

Pasteurization was probably the main reason for the decrease in deaths from gastroenteritis and for the decline in infant mortality from about 1900. In the 20th Century, these essential hygienic measures were supported by improved conditions in the home, the work place, and the general environment. Over the entire period for which records exist, better hygiene accounts for approximately a fifth of the total reduction of mortality.

But the decline of mortality caused by infections began long before the introduction of sanitary measures. It had already begun in England and Wales by 1838, and statistics from Scandinavia suggest that the death rate had been decreasing there since the first half of the 18th Century.

A further explanation for the falling death rate is that an improvement in nutrition led to an increase in resistance to infectious diseases. This is, I believe, the most credible reason for the decline of the infections, at least until the late 19th Century, and also explains why deaths from airborne diseases like scarlet fever and measles have decreased even when exposure to the organisms that cause them remains almost unchanged. The evidence demonstrating the impact of improved nutrition is indirect, but it is still impressive.

Experience in developing countries today leaves no doubt that nutritional state is a critical factor in a person's response to infectious disease, particularly in young children. Malnourished people contract infections more often than those who are well fed and they suffer more when they become infected. According to a recent World Health Organization report on nutrition in developing countries, the best vaccine against common infectious diseases is an adequate diet.

...

In summary: The death rate from infectious diseases fell because an increase in food supplies led to better nutrition. From the second half of the 19th Century this advance was strongly supported by improved hygiene and safer food and water, which reduced exposure to infection. With the exception of smallpox vaccination, which played a small part in the total decline of mortality, medical procedures such as immunization and therapy had little impact on human health until the 20th Century.

One other influence needs to be considered: a change in reproductive behavior, which caused the birth rate to decline. The significance of this change can hardly be exaggerated, for without it the other advances would soon have been overtaken by the increasing population. We can attribute the modern improvement in health to food, hygiene, and medical intervention—in that order of time and importance—but we must recognize that it is to a modification of behavior that we owe the permanence of this improvement.

But it does not follow that these influences have the same relative importance today as in the past. In technologically advanced countries, the decline of infectious diseases was followed by a vast change in health problems, and even in developing countries advances in medical science and technology may have modified the effects of nutrition, sanitation, and contraception. In order to predict the factors likely to affect our health in the future, we need to examine the nature of the problems in health that exist today.

Because today's problems are mainly with noncommunicable diseases, physicians have shifted their approach. In the case of infections, interest centers on the organisms that cause them and on the conditions under which they spread. In noninfective conditions, the engineering approach established in the 17th Century remains predominant and attention is focused on how a disease develops rather than on why it begins. Perhaps the most important question now confronting medicine is whether the commonest health problems—heart disease, cancer, rheumatoid arthritis, cerebrovascular disease—are essentially different from health problems of the past or whether, like infections, they can be prevented by modifying the conditions that lead to them.

To answer this question, we must distinguish between genetic and chromosomal diseases determined at the moment of fertilization and all other diseases, which are attributable in greater or lesser degree to the influence of the environment. Most diseases, including the common noninfectious ones, appear to fall into the second category. Whether these diseases can be prevented is likely to be determined by the practicability of controlling the environmental influences that lead to them.

The change in the character of health problems that followed the decline of infections in developed countries has not invalidated the conclusion that most diseases, both physical and mental, are associated with influences that might be controlled. Among such influences, those which the individual determines by his own behavior (smoking, eating, exercise, and the like) are now more important for his health than those that depend mainly on society's actions (provision of essential food and protection from hazards). And both behavioral and environmental influences are more significant than medical care.

The role of individual medical care in preventing sickness and premature death is secondary to that of other influences; yet society's investment in health care is based on the premise that it is the major determinant. It is assumed that we are ill and are made well, but it is nearer the truth to say that we are well and made ill. Few people think of themselves as having the major responsibility for their own health, and the enormous resources that advanced countries assign to the health field are used mainly to treat disease or, to a lesser extent, to prevent it by personal measures such as immunization.

. . .

The most immediate requirement in the health services is to give sufficient attention to behavioral influences that are now the main determinants of health. The public believes that health depends primarily on intervention by the doctor and that the essential requirement for health is the early discovery of disease. This concept should be replaced by recognition that disease often cannot be treated effectively, and that health is determined predominantly by the way of life individuals choose to follow. Among the important influences on health are the use of tobacco, the misuse of alcohol and drugs, excessive or unbalanced diets, and lack of exercise. With research, the list of significant behavioral influences will undoubtedly increase, particularly in relation to the prevention of mental illness.

Although the influences of personal behavior are the main determinants of health in developed countries, public action can still accomplish a great deal in the environmental field. Internationally, malnutrition probably remains the most important cause of ill health, and even in affluent societies sections of the population are inadequately, as distinct from unwisely, fed. The malnourished vary in proportion and composition from one country to another, but in the developed world they are mainly the younger children of large families and elderly people who live alone. In light of the importance of food for good health, governments might use supplements and subsidies to put essential foods within the reach of everyone, and provide inducements for people to select beneficial in place of harmful foods. Of course these aims cannot exclude other considerations such as international agreements and the solvency of farmers who have been encouraged to produce meat and dairy products

rather than grains. Nevertheless, in future evaluations of agricultural and related economic policies, health implications deserve a primary place.

Perhaps the most sensitive area for consideration is the funding of the health services. Although the contribution of medical intervention to prevention of sickness and premature death can be expected to remain small in relation to behavioral and environmental influences, surgery and drugs are widely regarded as the basis of health and the essence of medical care, and society invests the money it sets aside for health mainly in treatment for acute diseases and particularly in hospitals for the acutely ill. Does it follow from our appraisal that resources should be transferred from acute to chronic care and to preventive measures?

Restricting the discussion to personal medical care, I believe that neglected areas, such as mental illness, mental retardation, and geriatric care need greatly increased attention. But to suggest that this can be achieved merely by direct transfer of resources is an oversimplification. The designation "acute care" comprises a wide range of activities that differ profoundly in their effectiveness and efficiency. Some, like surgery for accidents and the treatment of acute emergencies, are among the most important services that medicine can offer and any reduction of their support would be disastrous. Others, however, like coronary care units and iron treatment of some anemias, are not shown to be effective, while still others—most tonsillectomies and routine check-ups—are quite useless and should be abandoned. A critical appraisal of medical services for acute illnesses would result in more efficient use of available resources and would free some of them for preventive measures.

What health services need in general is an adjustment in the distribution of interest and resources between prevention of disease, care of the sick who require investigation and treatment, and care of the sick who do not need active intervention. Such an adjustment must pay considerable attention to the major determinants of health: to food and the environment, which will be mainly in the hands of specialists, and to personal behavior, which should be the concern of every practicing doctor.

## QUESTIONS

1. What social factors have contributed toward the generally improved conditions of health in the modern industrial societies?

2. Is the high prestige of physicians really justified?

3. What social and environmental factors contribute to illness in modern America?

*Howard S. Becker*
*Blanche Geer*

# 43. The Fate of Idealism in Medical School

*For many centuries, the physicians of the Western world were held in low regard. Generally ignorant of the causes or cures of diseases, they learned their skills on the job, often without any academic training. Physicians often relied on useless or even dangerous procedures to treat patients, such as bleeding them no matter what their symptoms were. Yet, during the course of the past century and a half, the public image of the doctor has been transformed. The status of physicians has risen steadily over the decades, and today they enjoy exceptionally high prestige and income.*

*The current high status of physicians is no accident. One reason is that medical science has now become much more sophisticated than in the past, so that doctors can achieve much appreciated successes in combating disease and injury. However, the high status of physicians is also the result of a deliberate, organized attempt, beginning in the mid-nineteenth century and culminating early in the twentieth century, to professionalize the occupation. The process of converting a mere "job" into a highly regarded "profession" involves a fundamental requirement: membership is restricted to those persons who can meet admission standards that are dictated by the existing members. To become eligible for a license to practice medicine, a person must acquire the necessary academic credentials. These credentials can be earned only through a long and demanding socialization process that is conducted or approved by established physicians. The rigorous nature of this socialization experience serves two purposes: it limits the number of entrants to the profession and thus preserves high incomes; and it ensures that those who do become doctors are well versed in medical knowledge and skills.*

*In this article, Howard S. Becker and Blanche Geer describe one aspect of the arduous socialization process of medical students—the impact that their schooling has on their early idealism about their chosen profession.*

From *American Sociological Review*, 23, 1958, pp. 50–56.

It makes some difference in a man's performance of his work whether he believes wholeheartedly in what he is doing or feels that in important respects it is a fraud, whether he feels convinced that it is a good thing or believes that it is not really of much use after all. The distinction we are making is the one people have in mind when they refer, for example, to their calling as a "noble profession" on the one hand or a "racket" on the other. In the one case they idealistically proclaim that their work is all that it claims on the surface to be; in the other they cynically concede that it is first and foremost a way of making a living and that its surface pretensions are just that and nothing more. Presumably, different modes of behavior are associated with these perspectives when wholeheartedly embraced. The cynic cuts corners with a feeling of inevitability while the idealist goes down fighting. *The Blackboard Jungle* and *Not as a Stranger* are only the most recent in a long tradition of fictional portrayals of the importance of this aspect of a man's adjustment to his work.

Professional schools often receive a major share of the blame for producing this kind of cynicism—and none more than the medical school. The idealistic young freshman changes into a tough, hardened, unfeeling doctor; or so the popular view has it. Teachers of medicine sometimes rephrase the distinction between the clinical and preclinical years into one between the "cynical" and "precynical" years. Psychological research supports this view, presenting attitude surveys which show medical students year by year scoring lower on "idealism" and higher on "cynicism."[1] Typically, this cynicism is seen as developing in response to the shattering of ideals consequent on coming face-to-face with the realities of professional practice.

In this paper, we attempt to describe the kind of idealism that characterizes the medical freshmen and to trace both the development of cynicism and the vicissitudes of that idealism in the course of the four years of medical training. Our main themes are that though they develop cynical feelings in specific situations directly associated with their medical school experience, the medical students never lose their original idealism about the practice of medicine; that the growth of both cynicism and idealism are not simple developments, but are instead complex transformations; and that the very notions "idealism" and "cynicism" need further analysis, and must be seen as situational in their expressions rather than as stable traits possessed by individuals in greater or lesser degree. Finally, we see the greater portion of these feelings as being collective rather than individual phenomena.

Our discussion is based on a study we are now conducting at a state medical school[2] in which we have carried on participant observation with students of all four years in all of the courses and clinical work to which they are exposed. We joined the students in their activities in school and after school and watched them at work in labs, on the hospital wards, and in the clinic. Often spending as much as a month with a small group of from five to fifteen students assigned to a particular activity, we came to know them well and were able to gather information in informal interviews and by overhearing the ordinary daily conversation of the group.[3] In the course of our observation and interviewing we have gathered much information on the subject of idealism. Of necessity, we shall have to present the very briefest statement of our findings with little or no supporting evidence.[4] The problem of idealism is, of course, many-faceted and complex and we have dealt with it in a simplified way, describing only some of its grosser features.[5]

## The Freshmen

The medical students enter school with what we may think of as the idealistic notion, implicit in lay culture, that the practice of medicine is a wonderful thing and that they are going to devote their lives to service to mankind. They believe that medicine is made up of a great body of well-established facts that they will be taught from the first day on and that these facts will be of immediate practical use to them as physicians. They enter school expecting to work industriously and expecting that if they work hard enough they will be able to master this body of fact and thus become good doctors.

In several ways the first year of medical school does not live up to their expectations. They are disillusioned when they find they will not be near patients at all, that the first year will be just like another year of college. In fact, some feel that it is not even as good as college because their work in certain areas is not as thorough as courses in the same fields in undergraduate school. They come to think that their courses (with the exception of anatomy) are not worth much because, in the first place, the faculty (being Ph.D.s) know nothing about the practice of medicine, and, in the second place, the subject matter itself is irrelevant, or as the students say, "ancient

history." The freshmen are further disillusioned when the faculty tells them in a variety of ways that there is more to medicine than they can possibly learn. They realize it may be impossible for them to learn all they need to know in order to practice medicine properly. Their disillusionment becomes more profound when they discover that this statement of the faculty is literally true.[6] Experience in trying to master the details of the anatomy of the extremities convinces them that they cannot do so in the time they have. Their expectation of hard work is not disappointed; they put in an eight-hour day of classes and laboratories, and study four or five hours a night and most of the weekend as well.

Some of the students, the brightest, continue to attempt to learn it all, but succeed only in getting more and more worried about their work. The majority decide that, since they can't learn it all, they must select from among all the facts presented to them those they will attempt to learn. There are two ways of making this selection. On the one hand, the student may decide on the basis of his own uninformed notions about the nature of medical practice that many facts are not important, since they relate to things which seldom come up in the actual practice of medicine; therefore, he reasons, it is useless to learn them. On the other hand, the student can decide that the important thing is to pass his examinations and, therefore, that the important facts are those which are likely to be asked on an examination; he uses this as a basis for selecting both facts to memorize and courses for intensive study. For example, the work in physiology is dismissed on both of these grounds, being considered neither relevant to the facts of medical life nor important in terms of the amount of time the faculty devotes to it and the number of examinations in the subject.

A student may use either or both of these bases of selection at the beginning of the year, before many tests have been given. But after a few tests have been taken, the student makes "what the faculty wants" the chief basis of his selection of what to learn, for he now has a better idea of what this is and also has become aware that it is possible to fail examinations and that he therefore must learn the expectations of the faculty if he wishes to stay in school. The fact that one group of students, that with the highest prestige in the class, took this view early and did well on examinations was decisive in swinging the whole class around to this position. The students were equally influenced to become "test-wise" by the fact that, although they had all been in the upper range in their colleges, the class average on the first examination was frighteningly low.

In becoming test-wise, the students begin to develop systems for discovering the faculty wishes and learning them. These systems are both methods for studying their texts and short-cuts that can be taken in laboratory work. For instance, they begin to select facts for memorization by looking over the files of old examinations maintained in each of the medical fraternity houses. They share tip-offs from the lectures and offhand remarks of the faculty as to what will be on the examinations. In anatomy, they agree not to bother to dissect out subcutaneous nerves, reasoning that it is both difficult and time consuming and the information can be secured from books with less effort. The interaction involved in the development of such systems and short-cuts helps to create a social group of a class which had previously been only an aggregation of smaller and less organized groups.

In this medical school, the students learn in this way to distinguish between the activities of the first year and their original view that everything that happens to them in medical school will be important. Thus, they become cynical about the value of their activities in the first year. They feel that the real thing—learning which will help them to help mankind—has been postponed perhaps until the second year, or perhaps even further, at which time they will be able again to act on idealistic premises. They believe that what they do in their later years in school under supervision will be about the same thing they will do, as physicians, on their own; the first year had disappointed this expectation.

There is one matter, however, about which the students are not disappointed during the first year: the so-called trauma of dealing with the cadaver. But this experience, rather than producing cynicism, reinforces the student's attachment to his idealistic view of medicine by making him feel that he is experiencing at least some of the necessary unpleasantness of the doctor's. Such difficulties, however, do not loom as large for the student as those of solving the problem of just what the faculty wants.

On this and other points, a working consensus develops in the new consolidated group about the interpretation of their experience in medical school and its norms of conduct. This consensus, which we call *student culture*,[7] focuses their attention almost completely on their day-to-day activities in school and obscures or sidetracks their earlier idealistic preoccupations. Cynicism, griping, and minor cheating become endemic, but the cynicism is specific to the educational situation, to the first year, and to only parts of it. Thus the students keep their cynicism separate from their idealistic feelings and by postponement protect their belief that medicine is a wonderful thing, that their school is a fine one, and that they will become good doctors.

## Later Years

The sophomore year does not differ greatly from the freshman year. Both the work load and anxiety over examinations probably increase. Though they begin some medical activities, as in their attendance at autopsies and particularly in their introductory course in physical diagnosis, most of what they do continues to repeat the pattern of the college science curriculum. Their attention still centers on the problem of getting through school by doing well in examinations.

During the third and fourth, or clinical years, teaching takes a new form. In place of lectures and laboratories, the students' work now consists of the study of actual patients admitted to the hospital or seen in the clinic. Each patient who enters the hospital is assigned to a student who interviews him about his illnesses, past and present, and performs a physical examination. He writes this up for the patient's chart, and appends the diagnosis and the treatment that he would use were he allowed actually to treat the patient. During conferences with faculty physicians, often held at the patient's bedside, the student is quizzed about items of his report and called upon to defend them or to explain their significance. Most of the teaching in the clinical years is of this order.

Contact with patients brings a new set of circumstances with which the student must deal. He no longer feels the great pressure created by tests, for he is told by the faculty, and this is confirmed by his daily experience, that examinations are now less important. His problems now become those of coping with a steady stream of patients in a way that will please the staff man under whom he is working, and of handling what is sometimes a tremendous load of clinical work so as to allow himself time for studying diseases and treatments that interest him and for play and family life.

The students earlier have expected that once they reach the clinical years they will be able to realize their idealistic ambitions to help people and to learn those things immediately useful in aiding people who are ill. But they find themselves working to understand cases as medical problems rather than working to help the sick and memorizing the relevant available facts so that these can be produced immediately for a questioning staff man. When they make ward rounds with a faculty member they are likely to be quizzed about any of the seemingly countless facts possibly related to the condition of the patient for whom they are "caring."

Observers speak of the cynicism that overtakes the student and the lack of concern for his patients as human beings. This change does take place, but it is not produced solely by "the anxiety brought about by the presence of death and suffering."[8] The student becomes preoccupied with the technical aspects of the cases with which he deals because the faculty requires him to do so. He is questioned about so many technical details that he must spend most of his time learning them.

The frustrations created by his position in the teaching hospital further divert the student from idealistic concerns. He finds himself low man in a hierarchy based on clinical experience, so that he is allowed very little of the medical responsibility he would like to assume. Because of his lack of experience, he cannot write orders, and he receives permission to perform medical and surgical procedures (if at all) at a rate he considers far too slow. He usually must content himself with "mere" vicarious participation in the drama of danger, life, and death that he sees as the core of medical practice. The student culture accents these difficulties so that events (and especially those involving patients) are interpreted and reacted to as they push him toward or hold him back from further participation in this drama. He does not think in terms the layman might use.

As a result of the increasingly technical emphasis of his thinking the student appears cynical to the nonmedical outsider, though from his own point of view he is simply seeing what is "really important." Instead of reacting with the layman's horror and sympathy for the patient to the sight of a cancerous organ that has been surgically removed, the student is more likely to regret that he was not allowed to close the incision at the completion of the operation, and to rue the hours that he must spend searching in the fatty flesh for the lymph nodes that will reveal how far the disease has spread. As in other lines of work, he drops lay attitudes for those more relevant to the way the event affects someone in his position.

This is not to say that the students lose their original idealism. When issues of idealism are openly raised in a situation they define as appropriate, they respond as they might have when they were freshmen. But the influence of the student culture is such that questions which might bring forth this idealism are not brought up. Students are often assigned patients for examination and follow-up whose conditions might be expected to provoke idealistic crises. Students discuss such patients, however, with reference to the problems they create for the *student*. Patients with terminal diseases who are a long time dying, and patients with chronic diseases who show little change from week to week, are more likely to be viewed as creating extra work without extra compensation in knowledge or the opportunity to practice new skills than as examples of illness which raise questions about euthanasia. Such cases require the student to spend time every day checking on progress which he feels will probably not take place and to write long "progress" notes in the patient's chart although little progress has occurred.

This apparent cynicism is a collective matter. Group activities are built around this kind of workaday perspective, constraining the students in two ways. First, they do not openly express the lay idealistic notions they may hold, for their culture does not sanction such expression; second, they are less likely to have thoughts of this deviant kind when they are engaged in group activity. The collective nature of this "cynicism" is indicated by the fact that students become more openly idealistic whenever they are removed from the influence of student culture—when they are alone with a sociologist as they near the finish of school and sense the approaching end of student life, for example, or when they are isolated from their classmates and therefore are less influenced by this culture.[9]

They still feel, as advanced students, though much less so than before, that school is irrelevant to actual medical practice. Many of their tasks, like running laboratory tests on patients newly admitted to the hospital or examining surgical specimens in the pathology laboratory, seem to them to have nothing to do with their visions of their future activity as doctors. As in their freshman year, they believe that perhaps they must obtain the knowledge they will need in spite of the school. They still conceive of medicine as a huge body of proven facts but no longer believe that they will ever be able to master it all. They now say that they are going to try to apply the solution of the practicing M.D. to their own dilemma: learn a few things that they are interested in very well and know enough about other things to pass examinations while in school and, later on in practice to know to which specialist to send difficult patients.

Their original medical idealism reasserts itself as the end of school approaches. Seniors show more interest than students in earlier years in serious ethical dilemmas of the kind they expect to face in practice. They have become aware of ethical problems laymen often see as crucial for the physician—whether it is right to keep patients with fatal diseases alive as long as possible, or what should be done if an influential patient demands an abortion—and worry about them. As they near graduation and student culture begins to break down as the soon-to-be doctors are about to go their separate ways, these questions are more and more openly discussed.

While in school, they have added to their earlier idealism a new and peculiarly professional idealism. Even though they know that few doctors live up to the standards they have been taught, they intend always to examine their patients thoroughly and to give treatment based on firm diagnosis rather than merely to relieve symptoms. This expansion and transformation of idealism appear most explicitly in their consideration of alternative careers, concerning both specialization and the kind of arrangements to be made for setting up practice. Many of their hypothetical choices aim at making it possible for them to be the kind of doctors their original idealism pictured. Many seniors consider specialty training so that they will be able to work in a limited field in which it will be more nearly possible to know all there is to know, thus avoiding the necessity of dealing in a more ignorant way with the wider range of problems general practice would present. In the same manner, they think of schemes to establish partnerships or other arrangements making it easier to avoid a work load which would prevent them from giving each patient the thorough examination and care they now see as ideal.

In other words, as school comes to an end, the cynicism specific to the school situation also comes to an end and their original and more general idealism about medicine comes to the fore again, though within a framework of more realistic alternatives. Their idealism is now more informed although no less selfless.

## Discussion

We have used the words "idealism" and "cynicism" loosely in our description of the changeable state of mind of the medical student, playing on ambiguities we can now attempt to clear up. Retaining a core of common meaning, the dictionary definition, in our reference to the person's belief in the worth of his activity and the claims made for it, we have seen that this is not a generalized trait of the students we studied but rather an attitude which varies greatly, depending on the particular activity the worth of which is questioned and the situation in which the attitude is expressed.

This variability of the idealistic attitude suggests that in using such an element of personal perspective in sociological analysis one should not treat it as homogeneous but should make a determined search for subtypes which may arise under different conditions and have differing consequences. Such subtypes presumably can be constructed along many dimensions. There might, for instance, be consistent variations in the medical students' idealism through the four years of school that are related to their social backgrounds. We have stressed in this report the subtypes that can be constructed according to variations in the object of the idealistic attitude and variations in the audience the person has in mind when he adopts the attitude. The medical students can be viewed as both idealistic and cynical, depending on whether one has in mind their view of their school activities or the future they envision for themselves as doctors. Further, they might take one or another of these positions depending on whether their implied audience is made up of other students, their instructors, or the lay public.

A final complication arises because cynicism and idealism are not merely attributes of the actor, but are as dependent on the person doing the attributing as they are on the qualities of the individual to whom they are attributed.[10] Though the student may see his own dis-

regard of the unique personal troubles of a particular patient as proper scientific objectivity, the layman may view this objectivity as heartless cynicism.[11]

Having made these analytic distinctions, we can now summarize the transformations of these characteristics as we have seen them occurring among medical students. Some of the students' determined idealism at the outset is reaction against the lay notion, of which they are uncomfortably aware, that doctors are money-hungry cynics; they counter this with an idealism of similar lay origin stressing the doctor's devotion to service. But this idealism soon meets a setback, as students find that it will not be relevant for a while, since medical school has, it seems, little relation to the practice of medicine, as they see it. As it has not been refuted, but only shown to be temporarily beside the point, the students "agree" to set this idealism aside in favor of a realistic approach to the problem of getting through school. This approach, which we have labeled as the cynicism specific to the school experience, serves as protection for the earlier grandiose feelings about medicine by postponing their exposure to reality to a distant future. As that future approaches near the end of the four years and its possible mistreatment of their ideals moves closer, the students again worry about maintaining their integrity, this time in actual medical practice. They use some of the knowledge they have gained to plan careers which, it is hoped, can best bring their ideals to realization.

We can put this in propositional form by saying that when a man's ideals are challenged by outsiders and then further strained by reality, he may salvage them by postponing their application to a future time when conditions are expected to be more propitious.

---

## QUESTIONS

1. In what ways does the socialization of medical students affect their idealism toward the profession?

2. What distinguishes a profession from a mere job? Can you think of some other jobs that have been, or are becoming, professionalized?

3. What are the advantages of professionalization, from the point of view of both the professional and society? Are there any disadvantages?

---

## NOTES

1. Leonard D. Eron, "Effect of Medical Education on Medical Students," *Journal of Medical Education* 10 (October, 1955): 559–566.

2. This study is sponsored by Community Studies, Inc., of Kansas City, Missouri, and is being carried on at the University

of Kansas Medical School, to whose dean, staff, and students we are indebted for their wholehearted cooperation. Professor Everett C. Hughes of the University of Chicago is director of the project.

3. The technique of participant observation has not been fully systematized, but some approaches to this have been made. See, for example, Florence R. Kluckhohn, "The Participant Observer Technique in Small Communities," *American Journal of Sociology,* 45 (November, 1940), pp. 331–343; Arthur Vidich, "Participant Observation and the Collection and Interpretation of Data," *ibid.,* 60 (January, 1955), pp. 354–360; William Foote Whyte, "Observational Field-Work Methods," in Maria Jahoda, Morton Deutsch, and Stuart W. Cook (editors), *Research Methods in the Social Sciences,* New York: Dryden Press, 1951, 11, pp. 393–514; and *Street Corner Society* (Enlarged Edition), Chicago: University of Chicago Press, 1955, pp. 279–358; Rosalie Hankey Wax, "Twelve Years Later: An Analysis of Field Experience," *American Journal of Sociology,* 63 (September, 1957), pp. 133–142; Morris S. Schwartz and Charlotte Green Schwartz, "Problems in Participant Observation," *Ibid.,* 60 (January, 1955), pp. 343–353; and Howard S. Becker and Blanche Geer, "Participant Observation and Interviewing: A Comparison," *Human Organization* (forthcoming). The last item represents the first of a projected series of papers attempting to make explicit the operations involved in this method. For a short description of some techniques used in this study, see Howard S. Becker, "Interviewing Medical Students," *American Journal of Sociology,* 62 (September, 1956), pp. 199–201.

4. A fuller analysis and presentation of evidence will be contained in a volume on this study now being prepared by the authors in collaboration with Everett C. Hughes and Anselm L. Strauss.

5. Renée Fox has shown how complex one aspect of this whole subject is in her analysis of the way medical students at Cornell become aware of and adjust to both their own failure to master all available knowledge and the gaps in current knowledge in many fields. See her "Training for Uncertainty," in Robert K. Merton, George G. Reader, and Patricia L. Kendall, *The Student Physician: Introductory Studies in the Sociology of Medical Education,* Cambridge: Harvard University Press, 1957, pp. 207–241.

6. Compare Fox's description of student reaction to this problem at Cornell.

7. The concept of student culture is analyzed in some detail in Howard S. Becker and Blanche Geer, "Student Culture in Medical School," *Harvard Educational Review* (forthcoming).

8. Dana L. Farnsworth, "Some Observations on The Attitudes and Motivations of the Harvard Medical Student," *Harvard Medical Alumni Bulletin,* January, 1956, p. 34.

9. See the discussion in Howard S. Becker, "Interviewing Medical Students," *op. cit.*

10. See Philip Selznick's related discussion of fanaticism in *TVA and the Grass Roots,* Berkeley: University of California Press, 1953, pp. 205–213.

11. George Orwell gives the layman's side in his essay, "How the Poor Die" in *Shooting an Elephant and Other Essays,* London: Secker and Warburg, 1950, pp. 18–32.

*Evan Thomas*

# 44. Peddling Influence

*The "official" picture of the American political process—as envisioned by the Constitution and as still taught in high school civics and social studies classes—is one of representative democracy. According to this model, the people elect representatives whose votes in Congress reflect the will of the electorate. But the actual political process is far more complex—and perhaps less representative of the will of the ordinary voter.*

*In practice, legislative decisions are strongly influenced by the lobbying activities of a variety of organized special-interest groups. These groups vary widely in their size, power, resources, and objectives. Some, such as labor unions, industrial corporations, or even specific large corporations, are primarily interested in protecting or enhancing their economic interests. Others, such as the National Organization of Women or the National Rifle Association, campaign for what they regard as their members' rights. Still others, such as the Right to Life movement, are concerned with issues of public morality.*

*The interest groups use varied tactics in their lobbying, but all have one purpose in common—to short-cut the process of representative democracy by applying direct pressure on the legislative process to make it serve their own ends. In this article, Evan Thomas examines the way in which lobbyists, often working behind the scenes, try to shape the laws of the land.*

The hallway is known as Gucci Gulch, after the expensive Italian shoes they wear. At tax-writing time, the Washington lobbyists line up by the hundreds in the corridor outside the House Ways and Means Committee room, ever vigilant against the attempts of lawmakers to close their prized loopholes. Over near the House and Senate chambers, Congressmen must run a gauntlet of lobbyists who sometimes express their views on legislation by pointing their thumbs up or down. Not long ago, Senator John Danforth, chairman of the Senate Commerce Committee, could be seen on the Capitol steps trying to wrench his hand from the grip of a lobbyist for the textile industry seeking new protectionist legislation. Though Danforth himself wants help for the shoe, auto and agricultural industries in his native Missouri, the Senator, an ordained Episcopal minister, rolled his eyes heavenward and mumbled, "Save me from these people."

There have been lobbyists in Washington for as long as there have been lobbies. But never before have they been so numerous or quite so brazen. What used to be, back in the days of Bobby Baker, a somewhat shady and disreputable trade has burst into the open with a determined show of respectability. Tempted by the staggering fees lobbyists can command, lawmakers and their aides are quitting in droves to cash in on their connections. For many, public service has become a mere internship for a lucrative career as a hired gun for special interests.

With so many lobbyists pulling strings, they may sometimes seem to cancel one another out. But at the very least, they have the power to obstruct, and their overall effect can be corrosive. At times the halls of power are so glutted with special pleaders that government itself seems to be gagging. As Congress and the Administration begin working this month to apportion the deepest spending cuts in America's history and to sort out the most far-reaching reform of the tax laws since World War II, the interests of the common citizen seem to stand no chance against the onslaught of lobbyists. Indeed, the tax bill that emerged from the House already bears their distinctive Gucci prints, and the budget is still filled with programs they have been able to protect.

Of course, the common citizen often benefits from various "special interest" breaks (for example, a deduction for home mortgages or state and local taxes). One man's loophole is another man's socially useful allowance, and one's man's lobbyist is another man's righteous advocate. Nonetheless, the voices most likely to be heard are often the ones that can afford the best-connected access brokers.

As the legislative year cranks up, the whine of special pleaders resonates throughout the Capitol:

In the Senate Finance Committee, heavy industries like steel and autos, led by Veteran Lobbyist Charles Walker, are working to restore tax breaks for investment in new equipment that were whittled down last fall by the House Ways and Means Committee.

In the House and Senate Armed Services Committees, lobbyists for weapons manufacturers are fanning out to make sure that lawmakers do not trim their pet projects from the defense budget.

In the Senate Commerce Committee, business lobbyists are pressing for legislation to limit liability for defective products. They face fierce opposition from consumer groups and personal-injury lawyers.

Throughout the House and Senate, lobbyists for interests ranging from commercial-waterway users to child-nutrition advocates are laboring to spare their favorite federal subsidies from the exigencies of deficit reduction.

A superlobbyist like Robert Gray, a former minor official in the Eisenhower Administration who parlayed his promotional genius and friendship with the Reagans into a $20 million-a-year p.r. and lobbying outfit, is in the papers more than most congressional committee chairmen. He would have his clients believe that he is at least as powerful. "In the old days, lobbyists never got any publicity," says Veteran Lobbyist Maurice Rosenblatt, who has prowled the halls of Congress for several decades. "Congressmen didn't want to be seen with notorious bagmen. But now, he shrugs, "the so-called best lobbyists get the most publicity."

Influence peddling, says Jack Valenti, head of the Motion Picture Association and no mean practitioner of the craft, "is the biggest growth industry around." The number of registered domestic lobbyists has more than doubled since 1976, from 3,420 to 8,800. That figure is understated, however, since reporting requirements under a toothless 1946 law are notoriously lax. Most experts put the influence-peddling population at about 20,000, or more than 30 for every member of Congress. Registered lobbyists reported expenditures of $50 million last year, twice as much as a decade ago, but the true figure is estimated at upwards of $1.5 billion, including campaign contributions.

What does the money buy? "Everybody needs a Washington representative to protect their hindsides, even foreign governments," says Senator Paul Laxalt. "So the constituency for these people is the entire free-world economy." Joseph Canzeri, a former Reagan aide who calls himself a Washington "facilitator," notes, "It's a competitive business. There are a lot of wolves out there. But there are a lot of caribou in government too."

In the amoral revolving-door world of Washington, it has become just as respectable to lobby as to be lobbied. Ronald Reagan may have come to Washington to pare down the size of the Federal Government, but many of his former top aides have quit to profit off Big Government as influence peddlers. None has been more successful more swiftly than Reagan's former deputy chief of staff Michael Deaver, who may multiply his White House income sixfold in his first year out of government by offering the nebulous blend of access, influence and advice that has become so valued in Washington. Other Reaganauts now prowling Gucci Gulch include ex-Congressional Liaison Kenneth Duberstein and two former White House political directors, Lyn Nofziger and Ed Rollins. "I spent a lot of years doing things for love. Now I'm going to do things for money," Rollins told the Washington *Post* after he left the White House. By representing clients like the Teamsters Union, Rollins, who never earned more than $75,000 a year in government, boasts that he can earn ten times as much.

Former Administration officials are often paid millions of dollars by special interests to oppose policies they once ardently promoted. This is particularly true in the area of foreign trade, as documented by the Washington *Post* a week ago. For example, Reagan has ordered an investigation into the unfair trade practices of South Korea. That country will pay former Reagan Aide Deaver $1.2 million over three years to "protect, manage and expand trade and economic interests" of the nation's industry. Deaver refuses to say exactly what he will do to earn his fee, but he has hired Doral Cooper, a former deputy trade representative in the Reagan Administration, as a lobbyist for his firm. Japanese semiconductor and machine-tool firms are also charged by the Administration with engaging in unfair trade practices. They have hired Stanton Anderson, who had served as director of economic affairs for the Administration's 1980 transition team.

Foreign governments are particularly eager to retain savvy Washington insiders to guide them through the bureaucratic and congressional maze and polish their sometimes unsavory images in the U.S. The Marcos government in the Philippines has retained the well-connected lobbying firm of Black, Manafort & Stone for a reported fee of $900,000. Another Black, Manafort client is Angolan Rebel Jonas Savimbi. Not to be outdone, the

Marxist regime of Angola hired Bob Gray's firm to front for it in Washington. Two years ago, Gray told *Time* that he checks with his "good friend," CIA Director William Casey, before taking on clients who might be inimical to U.S. interests. It is unclear just what Casey could have said this time, since the CIA is currently funneling $15 million in covert aid to Savimbi to help his rebellion against the Angolan regime. Last week outraged Savimbi backers chained themselves to a railing in Gray's posh offices in Georgetown and had to be forcibly removed by local police.

Lobbyists call themselves lawyers, government-affairs specialists, public relations consultants, sometimes even lobbyists. They offer a wide array of increasingly sophisticated services, from drafting legislation to creating slick advertisements and direct-mail campaigns. But what enables the big-time influence peddlers to demand upwards of $400 an hour is their connections. "I'll tell you what we're selling," says Lobbyist Frank Mankiewicz. "The returned phone call."

Old-time fixers such as Tommy ("the Cork") Corcoran and Clark Clifford were not merely practiced lawyers but had some genuine legislative expertise to offer. Lately, however, Washington has seen the rise of a new breed of influence peddler, whose real value is measured by his friends in high places—particularly in the White House. Clifford prospered no matter who was in office; after the Reagans go home to California, it is hard to believe that Deaver or Gray will remain quite such hot commodities.

There is, and has long been, a strong whiff of scam about the influence-peddling business. Its practitioners like to imply that they have more clout than they truly do. In the post-Watergate era, power has been fractionated on Capitol Hill. Where a few powerful committee chairmen once held sway, Congress has become a loose federation of 535 little fiefdoms. This had made a lobbyist's job more difficult, but it hardly means that Congress has been liberated from the thrall of special interests. Well-intentioned congressional reform has been subverted over the years by the proliferation of lobbyists and the spiraling cost of election campaigns, two trends that go together like a hand and a pocket. The result has often been institutional paralysis. The very fact that Congress and the White House felt compelled to enact the Gramm-Rudman measure, requiring automatic spending cuts, is a monument to the inability of weak-willed legislators to say no to the lobbyists who buzz around them.

President Reagan has tried to sell his tax-reform bill as the supreme test of the public interest vs. the special interests. In pitching his campaign to the public, he has accused special interests of "swarming like ants through every nook and cranny of Congress," overlooking, per-

haps, that many of the most prominent ants are his former aides. Few lobbyists, however, seem especially offended by his rhetoric, and certainly their livelihoods are not threatened. Indeed, many lobbyists candidly admit that true tax reform would actually mean more business for them, since they would have a fresh slate upon which to write new loopholes.

The way lobbyists have feasted on the President's tax-reform bill illustrates why the bill is known in the law firms and lobbying shops of K Street as the "Lobbyists' Full Employment Act." The 408-page proposal first drafted by the Treasury Department 16 months ago, known as Treasury I, was called a model of simplicity and fairness. It would have swept the tax code virtually clean of loopholes for the few in order to cut tax rates sharply for the many. But the 1,363-page tax bill sent by the House to the Senate last December is so riddled with exemptions and exceptions that the goal of fairness was seriously compromised, and simplicity abandoned altogether.

The lobbyists wasted no time biting into Treasury I. Insurance executives calculated that such loophole closings as taxing employer-paid life insurance and other fringe benefits would cost the industry about $100 billion over five years. Led by Richard Schweiker, who was President Reagan's Secretary of Health and Human Services before becoming head of the American Council of Life Insurance, the industry launched a $5 million lobbying campaign that can only be described as state of the art.

Even before Treasury had finished drafting its original plan, the insurers were showing 30-second spots on TV that depicted a bird nibbling away at a loaf of bread labeled "employee benefits." An actress in the role of frightened housewife exclaimed, "We shouldn't have to pay taxes for protecting our family!" Life insurance agents around the country were revved up by a twelve-minute film entitled *The Worst Little Horror Story in Taxes.* In the film, Senate Finance Chairman Robert Packwood, a strong advocate of preserving tax breaks for fringe benefits, was shown urging the public to write their Congressmen. The insurers also mounted a direct-mail campaign that inundated Congress last year with 7 million preprinted, postage-paid cards. The campaign was successful: by the time the bill passed the House of Representatives last December, the insurance lobby figured that it had managed to restore about $80 billion of the $100 billion in tax breaks cut out by Treasury I. The insurers hope to win back most of the rest when the bill is reported out by the Senate Finance Committee this spring.

Threats to close a single loophole can bring scores of lobbyists rallying round. The original Treasury proposal sought to eliminate Section 936 of the U.S. Tax Code, which gives tax breaks worth some $600 million to companies that invest in Puerto Rico. Treasury Department officials conceded that the tax break helped create jobs by luring business to the island, but figured that each new job was costing the U.S. Treasury about $22,000. To defend Section 936, a coalition of some 75 U.S. companies with factories on the island formed a million-dollar "Puerto Rico–U.S.A. Foundation" and hired more than a dozen lobbyists, including Deaver. Last fall Section 936 advocates flew some 50 Congressmen and staffers to Puerto Rico on fact-finding trips.

Deaver, meanwhile, coordinated a lobbying campaign aimed at National Security staffers and officials in the State, Commerce and Defense Departments. The stragegy was to cast Section 936 as a way to revive the President's moribund Carribbean Basin Initiative and erect a bulwark against Communism in the region. Some two dozen companies with plants in Puerto Rico promised that if Section 936 was retained, they would reinvest their profits in new factories on other Caribbean islands. During a tense moment in the negotiations with the Administration, Deaver even managed to place a ground-to-air call to Air Force One as it flew to the Geneva Summit last November. He wanted to alert Secretary of State George Shultz to stand fast against the maneuverings of the tax reformers at Treasury. Not surprisingly, the Treasury gnomes were overwhelmed. Later that month the Administration committed itself to preserving Section 936.

The fabled three-martini lunch, threatened by the Treasury Department's proposal to end tax deductions for business entertainment, was preserved as at least a two-martini lunch after heavy lobbying by the hotel and restaurant industry. In the House-passed bill, 80% of the cost of a business lunch can still be deducted. The oil-and-gas lobby managed to restore over half the tax breaks for well drilling removed by the original Treasury bill. Lawyers, doctors and accountants won an exemption from more stringent new accounting rules. The lobbying by lawyers was a bit crude: Congressmen received letters that were supposedly written by partners of different law firms but were all signed by the same hand. No matter. Though congressional etiquette demands that each constituent's letter be answered personally, "We just let our word processors talk to their word processors," shrugged a congressional staffer.

The real deal making was done over so-called transition rules, which postpone or eliminate new taxes for certain individual businesses. The House-passed bill is studded with some 200 transition rules, which have been written to protect pet projects in a Congressman's district or large industries with particular clout on the Hill. Drafted behind closed doors, these rules are written in language designed to make it difficult to identify the real beneficiaries. One transition rule, for instance, waives

the cutbacks on investment tax credits and depreciation for the fiberoptic networks of telecommunications companies that have committed a certain number of dollars for construction by a certain date. It turns out that just two companies profit from the exemption: AT&T and United Telecom.

Not every lobbyist made out in the wheeling and dealing, by any means. Some were a little too greedy. The banking lobby pushed an amendment that would actually *increase* its tax breaks for bad-debt reserves. The lobbyists figured that they were just making an opening bid; their real aim was to protect existing tax breaks. To their surprise, however, the amendment passed in the confusion of an early Ways and Means Committee drafting session. When jubilant banking lobbyists began shouting "We won! We won!" outside the hearing room, some Congressmen became angry. Giving more tax breaks to the already well-sheltered banking industry was no way to sell votes on tax reform. The amendment was repealed.

Despite the predations of lobbyists, a tax-reform bill may be signed into law this year. But it must first survive the Senate, and already the advocates are queuing up to be heard. "I wish there were a secret elevator into the committee room," laments Senator David Pryor of Arkansas, a member of the Finance Committee. "Whenever I go there to vote, I try to walk fast and be reading something."

Some Congressmen may try to avoid lobbyists, but many have come to depend on them. "God love 'em," quips Vermont Senator Patrick Leahy. "Without them we would have to decide how to vote on our own." Sarcasm aside, lobbyists do serve a useful purpose by showing busy legislators the virtues and pitfalls of complex legislation. "There's a need here," says Anne Wexler, a former Carter Administration aide turned lobbyist. "Government officials are not comfortable making these complicated decisions by themselves." Says Lobbyist Van Boyette, a former aide to Senator Russell Long of Louisiana: "We're a two-way street. Congress often legislates on issues without realizing that the marketplace has changed. We tell Congress what business is up to, and the other way around."

Lobbyists and Government officials alike are quick to point out that lobbying is cleaner than in earlier eras, when railroad barons bought Senators as if they were so much rolling stock. "It's an open process now," says Jack Albertine, president of the American Business Conference, a trade association of medium-size, high-growth companies. "All sides are represented, the contributions are reported, and the trade-offs are known to everybody. In the old days you never knew who got what until a waterway project suddenly appeared in someone's district."

In some ways the growth of interest groups is healthy. Capital Hill at times seems like a huge First Amendment jamboree, where Americans of all persuasions clamor to be heard. Movie stars plead on behalf of disease prevention, Catholic clerics inveigh against abortion, farmers in overalls ask for extended credit, Wall Street financiers extol the virtues of lower capital-gains taxes. No single group dominates. When the steel, auto and rubber industries saw the Reagan Administration as an opening to weaken the Clean Air and Clean Water acts, the "Green Lobby," a coalition of environmental groups, was able to stop them.

But not every voter has a lobby in Washington. "Sometimes I think the only people not represented up here are the middle class," says Democratic Congressman Barney Frank of Massachusetts. "The average folks—that's what bothers me." Of course, that is not entirely true; many ordinary citizens are represented by such lobbies as the National Association of Retired Persons and Common Cause.

Lobbyists cannot afford to rely solely on well-reasoned arguments and sober facts and figures to make their case. In the scramble to win a hearing, they have developed all manner of stratagems designed to ingratiate themselves and collect IOUs.

Helping Congressmen get re-elected is an increasingly popular device. Veteran Washington Lobbyist Thomas Hale Boggs Jr. is on no fewer than 50 "steering committees" set up to raise money for congressional election campaigns. By night, Good Ole Boy Boggs can be found shmoozing at Capitol Hill fund raisers, where lobbyists drop off envelopes containing checks from Political Action Committees (PACs) at the door before digging into the hors d'oeuvres. By day, Boggs lobbies Congressmen, often the same ones for whom he has raised money the night before. Lately high-power political consulting firms such as Black, Manafort & Stone have taken not only to raising money for candidates but actually to running their campaigns: planning strategy, buying media, and polling. These firms get paid by the candidates for electioneering services, and then paid by private clients to lobby the Congressmen they have helped elect. In the trade this cozy arrangement is known as double dipping.

Special-interest giving to federal candidates has shot up eightfold since 1974, from $12.5 million to more than $100 million by the 1984 election. Nonetheless, PACs can give no more than $5,000 to a single campaign, and all contributions are publicly filed with the Federal Election Commission. "Elections are so expensive that the idea of a PAC's having inordinate influence is ridiculous," says Boggs.

Some Congressmen are not so sure. "Somewhere there may be a race of humans who will take $1,000 from perfect strangers and be unaffected by it," dryly notes Congressman Frank. Says Congressman Leon Panetta of California: "There's a danger that we're putting ourselves on the auction block every election. It's now tough to hear the voices of the citizens in your district. Sometimes the only things you can hear are the loud voices in three-piece suits carrying a PAC check."

Even the most reputable influence peddlers use their political connections to build leverage. As director of the 1984 G.O.P. Convention, Lobbyist William Timmons, a quietly genial man who represents such blue-chippers as Boeing, Chrysler, ABC and Anheuser-Busch, controlled access to the podium. G.O.P. Senators lobbied *him* for prime-time appearances. A *Wall Street Journal* reporter described Senator Pete Domenici of New Mexico, who was running for re-election in the fall of 1984, thanking Timmons a bit too effusively for allotting time for him to address the convention. "You told me you'd give me a shot," gushed Domenici. "So I appreciate it, brother."

Family ties help open doors. Tommy Boggs' mother Lindy is a Congresswoman from Louisiana; his father, the late Hale Boggs, was House majority leader. Other congressional progeny who as lobbyists have traded on their names for various interests: Speaker Tip O'Neill's son Kip (sugar, beer, cruise ships); Senate Majority Leader Robert Dole's daughter Robin (Century 21 real estate); Senator Paul Laxalt's daughter Michelle (oil, Wall Street, Hollywood); and House Appropriations Committee Chairman Jamie Whitten's son Jamie Jr. (steel, barges, cork).

Then there is so-called soft core (as opposed to hardcore) lobbying. Since the real business of Washington is often conducted by night, a whole cottage industry has grown up around the party-giving business. Michael Deaver's wife Carolyn is one of half a dozen Washington hostesses who can be hired to set up power parties, which bring top Government officials together with private businessmen. "Facilitator" Canzeri puts on charitable events to burnish corporate images, like a celebrity tennis tournament that drew scores of Washington lobbyists and netted $450,000 for Nancy Reagan's antidrug campaign. Lobbyists, not surprisingly, work hard not just at re-electing Congressmen but also at befriending them. Congressman Tony Coelho of California describes the methods of William Cable, a former Carter Administration aide who lobbies for Timmons & Co. "Three out of four times," says Coelho, "he talks to you not about lobbying, but about sports, or tennis—I play a lot of tennis with him—or your family. He's a friend, a sincere friend." Congressman Thomas Luken of Ohio is so chummy with lobbyists that he has been known to wave at them from the dais at committee hearings.

Congressmen often find themselves being lobbied

by their former colleagues. More than 200 ex-Congressmen have stayed on in the capital to represent interest groups, sometimes lobbying on the same legislation they helped draft while serving in office. Former Congressmen are free to go onto the floor of Congress and into the cloakrooms, though they are not supposed to lobby there. "Well, they don't call it lobbying," shrugs Senator Pryor. "They call it visiting. But you know exactly what they're there for."

Congressional staffers also cash in by selling their expertise and connections. Indeed, members of the House Ways and Means Committee were concerned that the President's tax-reform bill would provoke an exodus of staffers into the lobbying ranks. Their fears were not unfounded: the committee's chief counsel, John Salmon, quit to work as a lobbyist for the law firm of Dewey, Ballantine; James Healey, former aide to Committee Chairman Dan Rostenkowski, quit to join Black, Manafort.

As Congressmen became more independent of committee chairmen and party chieftains, they have tended to listen more to the folks back home. Predictably, however, lobbyists have skillfully found ways to manipulate so-called grassroots support. Direct-mail outfits, armed with computer banks that are stocked with targeting groups, can create "instant constituencies" for special-interest bills. To repeal a 1982 provision requiring tax withholding on dividends and interest, the small banks and thrifts hired a mass-mailing firm to launch a letter-writing campaign that flooded congressional offices with some 22 million pieces of mail. The bankers' scare tactics were dubious—they managed to convince their depositors that the withholding provision was a tax hike, when in fact it was set up merely to make people pay taxes that they legally owed. But the onslaught worked. Over the objections of President Reagan and most of the congressional leadership, Congress voted overwhelmingly in 1983 to repeal withholding.

One-time liberal activists who learned grass-roots organizing for such causes as opposition to the Viet Nam War now employ these same techniques on behalf of business clients. Robert Beckel, Walter Mondale's campaign manager in 1984, has set up an organization with the grandiose title of the Alliance to Save the Ocean. Its aim is to stop the burning of toxic wastes at sea. Beckel's fee is being paid by Rollins Environmental Services, a waste-disposal company that burns toxic waste on land.

Grass-roots organizations sometimes collide. Lobbyist Jack Albertine recently established the Coalition to Encourage Privatization. Its public policy purpose: to enable private enterprise to run services now performed by the Government. Its more immediate goal: to persuade Congress to sell Conrail to the Norfolk Southern railroad. In the meantime, Anne Wexler has been building the Coalition for a Competitive Conrail, a farm-dominated group pushing for Morgan Guaranty as the prospective purchaser.

Booze, broads and bribes—what 19th century Congressional Correspondent Edward Winslow Martin called "the levels of lust"—are no longer the tools of the trade. This is not to say, however, that lobbyists have stopped wining and dining Congressman and their staffs. Public records indicate that Ways and Means Chairman Rostenkowski spends about as much time playing golf as the guest of lobbyists at posh resorts as he does holding hearings in Washington.

Though it has become more difficult to slip a special-interest bill through Congress in the dead of night, it is not impossible. In 1981, when a group of commodity traders began lobbying for a tax loophole worth $300 million, then Senate Finance Chairman Dole poked fun at the commodity traders on the Senate floor. "They are great contributors. They haven't missed a fund raiser. If you do not pay any taxes, you can afford to go to all the fund raisers." But then commodity PACs and individual traders increased their contributions to Dole's own political action committee from $11,000 in 1981-1982 to $70,500 in 1983-84. Dole, engaged in a campaign to become Senate majority leader, badly needed the money (his PAC contributed some $300,000 to 47 of the Senate's 53 Republicans). In a late-night tax-writing session in the summer of 1984, Dole quietly dropped his opposition to the tax break for the commodity traders, and it became law.

Such victories inspire other loophole-seeking businessmen to hire guides through the congressional maze, at any price. There is no shortage of hungry lobbyists ready to relieve them of their money. "You get hustlers in Washington who get hooked up with hustlers outside of Washington, and the money moves very quickly," says Peter Teeley, former press aide to Vice President George Bush and now a Washington p.r. man. "Some people are getting ripped off." Says Senator Pryor: "Businessmen are very, very naive. It's amazing what they pay these lobbyists. The businessmen panic. They really don't understand Washington."

As one of the most successful lobbyists in town, Bob Gray naturally has his detractors, and they accuse him of overselling businessmen on his ability to solve all their Washington problems with a few phone calls. "Gray is so overrated it's unbelievable," says one U.S. Senator. "He makes a big splash at parties, but his clients aren't getting a lot for their money." Gray insists that he never promises more than he can deliver. But his own clients sometimes grumble that, for a fat fee, they get little more than a handshake from a Cabinet member at a cocktail party.

When the big lobbying guns line up on opposite sides of an issue, they tend to cancel each other out. Threatened with a takeover by Mobil Oil in 1981, Marathon Oil hired Tommy Boggs' firm to push a congressional bill that would block the merger. The firm managed to get the bill through the House by using a little-known procedure rule at a late-night session. In the Senate, however, Mobil—represented by former Carter Aide Stuart Eizenstat—was able to stop the bill when Senator Howell Heflin of Alabama blocked consideration on the Senate floor. Heflin is a friend of Mobil Chairman Rawleigh Warner.

"We're getting to the point of lobby-lock now," says Lobbyist Carl Nordberg. "There are so many lobbyists here pushing and pulling in so many different directions that, at times, nothing seems to go anywhere." The most pernicious effect of the influence-peddling game may simply be that it consumes so much of a Congressman's working day. Every time a Congressmen takes a PAC check, he is obliged at least to grant the contributor an audience. The IOUs mount up. "Time management is a serious problem," says Frank. "I find myself screening out people who just want to bill their clients for talking to a Congressman." The lobbyists are not unmindful of congressional impatience. Lobbyist Dan Dutko, for instance, has a "five-second rule"—all background documents must be simple enough to be absorbed by a Congressman at the rate of five seconds per page. It is no wonder that Congress rarely takes the time to debate such crucial national security questions as whether the U.S. really needs to build a 600-ship Navy, as the Reagan Administration contends; most Congressmen are too preoccupied listening to lobbyists for defense contractors telling them how many jobs building new ships will create back in the district.

In theory at least, there is a partial cure to the growing power of the influence-peddling pack: further limits on campaign expenditures and public financing of elections. But Congress is not likely to vote for these reforms any time soon, in large part because as incumbents they can almost always raise more money than challengers can. Certainly, most Congressmen have become wearily resigned to living with lobbyists. They are sources of money, political savvy, even friendship. In the jaded culture of Washington, influence peddlers are more envied than disdained. Indeed, to lawmakers on the Hill and policymakers throughout the Executive Branch, the feeling increasingly seems to be: well, if you can't beat 'em, join 'em.

---

## QUESTIONS

1. In theory, power in a democracy is ultimately located in the electorate. Is this the case in the United States?

2. Agree or disagree with the argument that special-interest groups stimulate democracy by (a) providing group members with access to power they would not otherwise have, and (b) providing an organized system of checks and balances that offers legislators different opinions on each issue.

3. In your opinion, who runs America? What is your evidence?

# UNIT 5

# Social Change in the Modern World

Colin Turnbull

# 45. Bali's New Gods

*Throughout history, a major source of social change has been diffusion—the spread of cultural elements from one society to another. These elements can include both material culture (such as gunpowder and computers) and nonmaterial culture (such as religions and musical styles). Diffusion occurs as a result of travel, trade, migration, invasion, the spread of literature, and, more recently, through mass tourism and telecommunications.*

*Cultural diffusion can be an invigorating process for any society. Unfortunately, however, it can also have disruptive and even devastating effects—especially if the diffusion flows from a large, modern industrialized society to a simple, preindustrial one that is unprepared for a flood of novel artifacts and ideas. But in the latter part of the twentieth century, the world is becoming a "global village." Telecommunications can in principle make it possible for distant tribal villages to receive a flood of images from modern industrialized societies. Jet aircraft can carry millions of tourists from industrialized societies to remote parts of the world, giving the local people direct exposure to the norms, values, and behavior of another culture. The result can be an unintended assault on the integrity of the local traditions.*

*In this article, Colin Turnbull describes the impact of tourism on the Indonesian island of Bali, which has long had the reputation of being a mystical and secluded paradise.*

Reprinted from *Natural History*, January 1982, with the permission of the author and the author's agents, Scott Meredith Literary Agency.

To the Balinese their home is known as Pulau Dewata, or "Island of the Gods." But sometimes it seems that in the last few years the gods of Bali have descended in the form of tourists. With swimsuits and cameras as their sacred symbols, they appear to hold the power of both desecration and consecration.

The Balinese have traditionally considered their island to be safe as well as sacred, but tourism has changed that too; from tourism and tourists there is little safety. The government of Indonesia has done its best to contain the damage, both social and environmental, by confining tourists to the southern point of the island. But Bali is not much more than a hundred miles long and since it is both encircled and traversed by motor roads, only the western jungles are effectively free from the pollution that tourism brings. Even there, however, the people are not untouched. On this small and densely populated island (approaching three million people for its two thousand square miles), every village, if not every family, has somehow been affected by the massive influx of tourists, an influx so sudden and rapid, the islanders have had little time to adapt.

It would be easy enough to paint a totally negative picture of the impact of tourism on Bali. The once beautiful sandy beach at Kuta, for instance, is now littered with bodies in various stages of undress, interspersed with pimps, hawkers, and masseurs who move from body to body, plying their services. When I was there last year the beach was patrolled by two well-dressed prostitutes riding on scooters for ready pickup and delivery. Even the water was not entirely safe; to reach it one ran the risk of being run down by tourist youths racing and trick riding on motorcycles. And once in the water there was the danger of being hit by speedboats, towing large rubber dinghies loaded with shrieking tourists who seemed to have come thousands of miles to do what they could have done at home.

Yet the local fishermen, whose beach it used to be, continued to go about their business as though none of these intrusions were going on. And sunset was still a beautiful time of day. Kuta Beach is renowned for its sunsets, but apart from some scattered photographers, few tourists are to be found there in the twilight; after all it is cocktail time, and sunsets look just as good from a comfortable lounge, with drink in hand.

Bali's modernization, urban development, and extraordinary economic growth, with all the corresponding benefits of medical, social, and educational services that had previously not existed, also have their negative aspects. It could be argued that prior to the descent of the tourist gods, for whose benefit the island seems largely to be administered, some of these services were not needed; they are needed now to combat problems brought by tourism itself. The economic benefits touch only a few, and the cost to all is high in terms of damage to the social fabric. How high might be measured by the increase in the rate of teen-age suicide.

Nevertheless, tourism is of major, often paramount, economic and even political importance in many remote parts of the world, and one of the major issues that has to be faced is how to weigh the complex advantages against the equally complex disadvantages. Here my focus is on one small segment of the overall problem of the social change induced by tourism: the interaction between the tourist and what is sacred to the people of the place he is visiting. In a vast subcontinent such as India even the most profane tourists are likely to have little effect on what is sacred to the Indian; on a small island like Bali, it is another matter. The Balinese people's way of life is intimately bound up with their religious belief and practice, and there are some 30,000 temples on the island, so the possibility and danger of desecration are very real. But in looking at the desecration and how it takes place, most often unconsciously at the hands of tourists, we find there is also a kind of consecration taking place.

In line with my ongoing analogy between tourism and pilgrimage, of all tourist meccas surely Bali is one that is truly sacred. The quest of most tourists going there involves an ideal of perfection, of beauty and goodness—which, incidentally, are qualities by which the Balinese religion defines the sacred. Since for the Balinese the land itself is sacred, the very environmental and ecological changes wrought in the name of tourism or by tourists are a form of desecration. And since reciprocity in human relationships is also sacred in their essentially egalitarian traditional way of life, the abuse of money is also a form of desecration. With money they have learned to "purchase" human services for individual gain, without involving any further reciprocal personal obligation. Money all too easily and subtly short-circuits mutual concern and consideration. This effect of tourism is perhaps most insidious and most pervasive in a cultural setting such as Bali. What is a small amount of money for the tourist may be a small fortune to the Balinese. Individual wealth in such measure, together with other material appurtenances of Western civilization brought by tourism, readily lures young men and women, even boys and girls, away from their homes and villages. Too late, they discover they have also been lured away from the security their traditions offered and from the ideals their lives were built around.

At the individual level, desecration by tourists may be conscious or unconscious. On Bali it is most often the latter; vandalism, such as the scarification of sacred monuments by graffiti and pilferage from sacred sites, is not yet as common as elsewhere. But it is curious that the most conscious, blatant, and offensive insults are given at the most sacred places and on the most sacred occasions. Sometimes it is the tourist industry itself, through the initiative of local entrepreneurs, that overtly desecrates what is holiest, but individual tourists do their share of conscious profanation. For instance, even at Pura Besakih (the Mother Temple) on Mount Agung, probably the holiest shrine in Bali, I saw some tourists openly ignore polite requests not to enter certain areas. They swaggered wherever they wished, openly ridiculing the sense of propriety so sacred to the Balinese, making loud and coarse jokes concerning customs of modesty in dress and nonadmission of women during their menstrual period. And down the coast at Goa Lawah, the sacred home of the mythical serpent Basuki is noted by most tourists merely for the quantity of bats that infest the cave. The associated temple, a holy place reserved largely for death ceremonies, is ignored or paid scant courtesy at best. Crowds of tourists press through worshipers to see and photograph the bats or push among mourners to take snapshots of a funerary ritual. I saw three particularly unkempt and scantily dressed youths force their way up the steps, ignoring requests to put on the required ritual waist sash readily available to all foreign visitors and ridiculing the offered wraparound apron that would have concealed the immodesty of their very short shorts. They burst among the mourners with whoops and jeers, and one tried to throw stones into the cave to dislodge the bats. Eventually a little old Balinese priest came up to them and politely asked them to leave. There was something about that tiny man that stopped them in their tracks. They looked at each other in surprise, then with a few more self-conscious gymnastics and coarse comments they bounded down the long flight of steps, laughing as they knocked people aside.

I caught up with them on the nearby beach of volcanic lava. All their bounce and bravado had gone; they were arguing about just why they had listened to that silly little old man. After all, they had come all that way to see the bats and they had as much right to be there as anyone else. But none of them suggested turning around and going back. They had been touched by something—and stopped. The Balinese might say that the youths had been stopped by the gods. It was certainly no threat of physical coercion that had prevented them from "having their fun"; and plainly they had no respect for the "silly little old man" or the religion he professed. But evidently he somehow commanded an air of authority that was just as effective as that of any armed policeman or bouncer. I will not insist that the authority was sacred in the sense that any supernatural force was at work, but whatever the source, it was powerful enough to prevent an act of desecration. It touched the desecraters, too, and for a moment compelled them to acknowledge the existence of something sacred to others.

The abusive and offensive behavior of these three young men also affected the rest of us. It annoyed the photographers and those trying to film the mourning ceremony, particularly when one of the three bearded, bandannaed heads popped into a viewfinder. It caused a few to stop taking photographs. What it did to the Balinese I cannot say; apart from the priest who intervened they seemed to pay no attention. Perhaps it merely heightened their awareness of the sanctity of the place and the worship they were about; perhaps that is what it did for all of us.

For those who are uncomfortable with the word *sacred*, some Balinese whom I talked with about this and similar incidents use the word *respect*. The young manager of a beach resort was very clear and emphatic. He did not object to the behavior itself; Basuki, after all, was perfectly capable of looking after himself and could have struck the youths dead. It was rather the lack of human consideration that offended him. More than this overt act of desecration or, only slightly less overt, the insulting condescension of tourists in his hotel, on the beach, or on the streets, he found their manner of dress objectionable. This from him was true desecration. To attack the gods directly is merely foolhardy and ignorant. But to attack the sanctity of "proper human relationships" is an insult and a threat that is as real as it is mortal. Much of Balinese social structure is built around the concept of propriety, and despite the outward appearances of freedom and relaxation, there is an underlying code, which is specific and rigorous, concerning mutual relationships. That code clearly defines the acceptable limits of behavior, and dress is an important element. Other than when bathing, men in shorts are indecent, and without shorts they offer open insult; the same is true for women. On the beach, the pimps, hawkers, masseurs, and even the two motorized prostitutes were all impeccably dressed, the women with blouses buttoned up to the neck and the men in long trousers and open-neck shirts, fastened as high as they would go. Even the totally naked fishermen somehow gave the appearance of being fully clad, in

respectability at least, as they entered or emerged from the water casually concealing their genitals with the left hand, their neat piles of clothes close to the water's edge.

The hotel manager came from the north coast of Bali and talked longingly and lovingly of "the other side of the island," of its beauty and safety. By "safety" he was not referring to physical safety. His home was only a few hours drive away, but he had never been back and said he could not return there. "Like the rest of us who have left our homes, I am not clean. Look at how I dress." He was considerably better dressed than I was, but in Western style. Yet he was in no way bitter or hostile to tourism. He was grateful for the new horizons it had opened up to him and to the island, and while aware of the damage being done to the traditional way of life, he pointed out that he and others were now more aware that they had something to lose. When I asked him what he had gained, other than this knowledge, his Western clothes and dark glasses, his home without a family, and his scooter (all things that he listed), he gave an odd answer. He said, "Now I know there is even more for me to respect."

At the beginning I referred to tourists as the new gods of Bali, with swimsuits and cameras as their sacred symbols, holding the power of desecration and consecration. This was not entirely flippant. One brochure in front of me describes Bali, not as "Island of the Gods," but as a "Photographer's Paradise." And under "Emergencies" it lists four: police, hospital, ambulance, and finally, camera troubles. Since so many of us take cameras with us when we travel abroad we should be aware of the possible sacral power of this device and the way that we handle it.

One could do an amusing study of the ritual behavior of photographers, but that is not what I have in mind. I have in mind what is very clearly in the minds of Muslims when they prohibit photography of the human form, and what the Jewish scriptures had in mind when they forbade graven images. It is the ancient idea of "quintessence," that fifth and *essential* ingredient that was thought to be latent in all being—the stuff of the stars, some thought, the stuff of sanctity and divinity. No representation of man (or God) that does not show that inner reality can do justice to man or God. Since the quintessence is invisible, any pictorial or graven image is wanting, and failing to do justice to a divinity is a desecration.

I think most of us—even the most profane, the most irreligious—have something that to us is sacred. I doubt if many could put their finger on what the invisible quintessence of that sacredness is, any more than the ancients could when they coined the word. But we are aware of its presence. It is what sometimes motivates us to take photographs, and it is very definitely what sometimes motivates us *not* to take photographs. Probably most of us have had moments when, camera in hand, we have seen something deeply moving, so beautiful that it seemed made for photography, yet somehow we came away with the shutter still cocked, the camera unused. The Balinese would call that an act of "respect." We might say it was because the light was not right, but even that excuse is to say that our mechanical apparatus was, at that moment, incapable of making a perfect image of what we "saw."

Or we might recognize that what we saw with our eyes was not really what we wished to capture, that any photographic rendition without the smell, the touch, the feeling, without that indefinable quintessence, would be a failure. Like most other tourists at Kuta Beach I watched sunsets. I watched *every* sunset, and I watched from the beach, bare feet in the sand. And like others I took photographs. They are probably like those everyone else took, and while they are spectacular, they do not have that essential that made some moments standing on the beach in the warm air, with the smell and sound of the surf, sacred. All the photographs do is to help recall the sunsets that were sacred because they occurred when I deliberately went out to the beach *without* my camera, to be a part of the sunset instead of a detached, objective observer.

So it was at the temples of Bali (and of course elsewhere). The act of photography seems on the one hand to diminish what is being photographed by making it commonplace or to insult it by the futility of trying to capture its invisible essence; on the other hand the photographer is demeaned if he or she doesn't realize that there *is* an invisible essence. I observed Balinese noting with obvious approval or disapproval the manner and mood of the photographer. There were times when a cluck of disapproval was heard as a tourist took a quick snapshot of something particularly sacred, hurrying on with hardly a pause or second glance. Then there were times when the photographer's intense concentration, and rigid requirements for perfect conditions, conveyed a sense of respect and brought a quiet sigh of approval; for respect, whatever its origin, can only serve to heighten rather than diminish what is sacred. The drawback is that the act of taking a photograph too often puts a distance between the photographer and the object being photographed. For the tourist in particular there is often neither the time nor the opportunity to empathize and identify in a way that makes for outstanding photography, which is a true art. The snapshot is literally a "taking" and may serve to remove the tourist even further from the very thing he most wants to approach and share.

The cost of using the lure of photography to attract tourists to Bali can be high. The narrow streets of Kuta are lined with indigenous tourist agencies, car hire firms, and bus operators. Outside their one-room offices are blackboards and posters advertising their "specials." The sacred gets top priority and commands the highest price, but how long can the sacred remain intact when subject to such commercialization? Even death is not immune. The most lurid and colorful posters call tourists to come and enjoy cremations—one advertised a mass cremation. For many Balinese the cost of living has grown so enormously that they can no longer afford to finance a cremation for a single family member, so the dead are pooled, so to speak, and the conflagration is made even more dramatic by the glare of floodlights, the explosion of flashbulbs, and the presence of the new gods.

There was even an "underground" tourist traffic in death, surreptitious visits to a lakeside beach where the bodies of the dead are laid out in the open. I wonder how many have the stomach to show such photographs to their friends, and what they say about the custom. I found I did not have the stomach to go and find out. I confined most of my photography thereafter to the profane; mainly to photographs of other tourists at work with their cameras.

---

## QUESTIONS

1. How has the influx of tourists affected Balinese culture?

2. What is likely to be the long-term impact of telecommunications and travel on the cultural diversity that presently exists in the world?

3. Can you list some features of contemporary American society that were incorporated into the culture as a result of diffusion?

*Lauriston Sharp*

# 46. Steel Axes for Stone-Age Australians

*Human beings are tool-using animals. We invent and use tools in order to improve the conditions of our existence, whether the tools are as simple as a hunting knife or as complex as a nuclear reactor. Together, the stock of techniques and the things that they create constitute a society's technology. Social change and technological change are closely intertwined, for each new technological advance inevitably has some social impact. The more advanced a society's technology, the more rapid the pace of its social change is likely to be. That is one reason why change is generally slow in traditional, preindustrial societies, whose technologies are relatively few and simple, but rapid in the advanced industrialized societies.*

*Unhappily, the impact of a new technology can never be anticipated with certainty. New tools or techniques are introduced in the hope of solving some problem, and they often do so successfully. But a new technology frequently creates other, unexpected problems. For example, the invention of the automobile has eventually created a host of problems that were never fully anticipated, such as a dependence on foreign oil, air pollution, urban congestion, and the social costs of highways and traffic accidents.*

*The potential effects of technology on society are perhaps most clearly seen in the case of a simple society that has limited technological resources to begin with. In this article, Lauriston Sharp traces the far-ranging impact of the introduction of a new technological implement—the steel axe—on a tribe of Australian aborigines.*

Like other Australian aboriginals, the Yir Yoront group, which lives at the mouth of the Coleman River on the west Coast of Cape York Peninsula, originally had no knowledge of metals. Technologically their culture was of the Old Stone Age or Paleolithic type. They supported themselves by hunting and fishing and obtained vegetables and other materials from the bush by simple gathering techniques. Their only domesticated animal was the dog; they had no cultivated plants of any kind. Unlike some other aboriginal groups, however, the Yir Yoront did have polished stone axes hafted in short handles, which were most important in their economy.

Towards the end of the nineteenth century, metal tools and other European artifacts began to filter into the Yir Yoront territory. The flow increased with the gradual expansion of the white frontier outward from southern and eastern Queensland. Of all the items of Western technology thus made available, the hatchet, or short-handled steel axe, was the most acceptable to and the most highly valued by all aboriginals.

In the mid-1930s an American anthropologist lived alone in the bush among the Yir Yoront for 13 months without seeing another white man. The Yir Yoront were thus still relatively isolated and continued to live an essentially independent economic existence, supporting themselves entirely by means of their Old Stone-Age techniques. Yet their polished stone axes were disappearing fast and being replaced by steel axes, which came to them in considerable numbers, directly or indirectly, from various European sources to the south.

What changes in the life of the Yir Yoront still living under aboriginal conditions in the Australian bush could be expected as a result of their increasing possession and use of the steel axe?

Events leading up to the introduction of the steel axe among the Yir Yoront begin with the advent of the second known group of Europeans to reach the shores of the Australian continent. In 1623 a Dutch expedition landed on the coast where the Yir Yoront now live. In 1935 the

Yir Yoront were still using the few cultural items recorded in the Dutch log for the aboriginals they encountered. To this cultural inventory the Dutch added beads and pieces of iron, which they offered in an effort to attract the frightened "Indians." Among these natives metal and beads have disappeared, together with any memory of this first encounter with whites.

The next recorded contact in this area was in 1864. Here there is more positive assurance that the natives concerned were the immediate ancestry of the Yir Yoront community. These aboriginals had the temerity to attack a party of cattlemen who were driving a small herd from southern Queensland through the length of the then unknown Cape York Peninsula to a newly established government station at the northern tip. Known as the Battle of the Mitchell River, this was one of the rare instances in which Australian aboriginals stood up to European gunfire for any length of time. A diary kept by the cattlemen records that

> ten carbines poured volley after volley into them from all directions, killing and wounding with every shot with very little return, nearly all their spears having already been expended.... About 30 being killed, the leader thought it prudent to hold his hand, and let the rest escape. Many more must have been wounded and probably drowned, for 59 rounds were counted as discharged.

The European party was in the Yir Yoront area for three days; they then disappeared over the horizon to the north and never returned. In the almost three-year-long anthropological investigation conducted some 70 years later—in all the material of hundreds of free-association interviews, in texts of hundreds of dreams and myths, in genealogies, and eventually in hundreds of answers to direct and indirect questioning on just this particular matter—there was nothing that could be interpreted as a reference to this shocking contact with Europeans.

The aboriginal accounts of their first remembered contact with whites begin in about 1900 with references to persons known to have had sporadic but lethal encounters with them. From that time on whites continued to remain on the southern periphery of Yir Yoront territory. With the establishment of cattle stations (ranches) to the south, cattlemen made occasional excursions among the "wild black-fellows" in order to inspect the country and abduct natives to be trained as cattleboys and "house girls." At least one such expedition reached the Coleman River where a number of Yir Yoront men and women were shot for no apparent reason.

About this time the government was persuaded to sponsor the establishment of three mission stations along the 700-mile western coast of the peninsula in an attempt to help regulate the treatment of natives. To further this purpose a strip of coastal territory was set aside as an aboriginal reserve and closed to further white settlement.

In 1915, an Anglican mission station was established near the mouth of the Mitchell River, about a three-day march from the heart of the Yir Yoront country. Some Yir Yoront refused to have anything to do with the mission, others visited it occasionally, while only a few eventually settled more or less permanently in one of the three "villages" established at the mission.

Thus the majority of the Yir Yoront continued to live their old self-supporting life in the bush, protected until 1942 by the government reserve and the intervening mission from the cruder realities of the encroaching new order from the south. To the east was poor, uninhabited country. To the north were other bush tribes extending on along the coast to the distant Archer River Presbyterian mission with which the Yir Yoront had no contact. Westward was the shallow Gulf of Carpentaria, on which the natives saw only a mission lugger making its infrequent dry-season trips to the Mitchell River. In this protected environment for over a generation the Yir Yoront were able to recuperate from shocks received at the hands of civilized society. During the 1930s their raiding and fighting, their trading and stealing of women, their evisceration and two- or three-year care of their dead, and their totemic ceremonies continued, apparently uninhibited by Western influence. In 1931 they killed a European who wandered into their territory from the east, but the investigating police never approached the group whose members were responsible for the act.

As a direct result of the work of the Mitchell River mission, all Yir Yoront received a great many more Western artifacts of all kinds than ever before. As part of their plan for raising native living standards, the missionaries made it possible for aboriginals living at the mission to earn some Western goods, many of which were then given or traded to natives still living under bush conditions; they also handed out certain useful articles gratis to both mission and bush aboriginals. They prevented guns, liquor, and damaging narcotics, as well as decimating diseases, from reaching the tribes of this area, while encouraging the introduction of goods they considered "improving." As has been noted, no item of Western technology available, with the possible exception of trade tobacco, was in greater demand among all groups of aboriginals than the short-handled steel axe. The mission always kept a good supply of these axes in stock; at Christmas parties or other mission festivals they were given away to mission or visiting aboriginals indiscriminately and in considerable numbers. In addition, some steel axes as well as other European goods were still traded in to the Yir Yoront by natives in contact with cattle stations in the south. Indeed, steel axes had probably come to the Yir Yoront through established lines of aboriginal trade long before any regular contact with whites had occurred.

## Relevant Factors

If we concentrate our attention on Yir Yoront behavior centering about the original stone axe (rather than on the axe—the object—itself) as a cultural trait or item of cultural equipment, we should get some conception of the role this implement played in aboriginal culture. This, in turn, should enable us to foresee with considerable accuracy some of the results stemming from the displacement of the stone axe by the steel axe.

The production of a stone axe required a number of simple technological skills. With the various details of the axe well in mind, adult men could set about producing it (a task not considered appropriate for women or children). First of all a man had to know the location and properties of several natural resources found in his immediate environment: pliable wood for a handle, which could be doubled or bent over the axe head and bound tightly; bark, which could be rolled into cord for the binding; and gum, to fix the stone head in the haft. These materials had to be correctly gathered, stored, prepared, cut to size and applied or manipulated. They were in plentiful supply and could be taken from anyone's property without special permission. Postponing consideration of the stone head, the axe could be made by any normal man who had a simple knowledge of nature and of the technological skills involved, together with fire (for heating the gum), and a few simple cutting tools—perhaps the sharp shells of plentiful bivalves.

The use of the stone axe as a piece of capital equipment used in producing other goods indicates its very great importance to the subsistence economy of the aboriginal. Anyone—man, woman, or child—could use the axe; indeed, it was used primarily by women, for theirs was the task of obtaining sufficient wood to keep the family campfire burning all day, for cooking or other purposes, and all night against mosquitoes and cold (for in July, winter temperature might drop below 40°). In a normal lifetime a woman would use the axe to cut or knock down literally tons of firewood. The axe was also used to make other tools or weapons, and a variety of material equipment required by the aboriginal in his daily life. The stone axe was essential in the construction of the wet-season, domed huts which keep out some rain and some insects; of platforms which provide dry storage; of shelters which give shade in the dry summer when days are bright and hot. In hunting and fishing and in gathering vegetable or animal food the axe was also a necessary tool, and in this tropical culture, where preservatives or other means of storage are lacking, the natives spend more time obtaining food than in any other occupation—except sleeping. In only two instances was the use of the stone axe strictly limited to adult men: for gathering wild honey, the most prized food known to the Yir Yoront; and for making the secret paraphernalia for ceremonies. From this brief listing of some of the activities involving the use of the axe, it is easy to understand why there was at least one stone axe in every camp, in every hunting or fighting party, and in every group out on a "walkabout" in the bush.

The stone axe was also prominent in interpersonal relations. Yir Yoront men were dependent upon interpersonal relations for their stone axe heads, since the flat, geologically recent, alluvial country over which they range provides no suitable stone for this purpose. The stone they used came from quarries 400 miles to the south, reaching the Yir Yoront through long lines of male trading partners. Some of these chains terminated with the Yir Yoront men, others extended on farther north to other groups, using Yir Yoront men as links. Almost every older adult man had one or more regular trading partners, some to the north and some to the south. He provided his partner or partners in the south with surplus spears, particularly fighting spears tipped with the barbed spines of sting ray, which snap into vicious fragments when they penetrate human flesh. For a dozen such spears, some of which he may have obtained from a partner to the north, he would receive one stone axe head. Studies have shown that the sting-ray-barb spears increased in value as they moved south and farther from the sea. One hundred and fifty miles south of Yir Yoront one such spear may be exchanged for one stone axe head. Although actual investigations could not be made, it was presumed that farther south, nearer the quarries, one sting-ray-barb spear would bring several stone axe heads. Apparently people who acted as links in the middle of the chain and who made neither spears nor axe heads would receive a certain number of each as a middleman's profit.

Thus trading relations, which may extend the individual's personal relationships beyond that of his own group, were associated with spears and axes, two of the most important items in a man's equipment. Finally, most of the exchanges took place during the dry season, at the time of the great aboriginal celebrations centering about initiation rites or other totemic ceremonials which attracted hundreds and were the occasion for much exciting activity in addition to trading.

Returning to the Yir Yoront, we find that adult men kept their axes in camp with their other equipment, or carried them when traveling. Thus a woman or child who wanted to use an axe—as might frequently happen during the day—had to get one from a man, use it promptly, and return it in good condition. While a man might speak of "my axe," a woman or child could not.

This necessary and constant borrowing of axes from

older men by women and children was in accordance with regular patterns of kinship behavior. A woman would expect to use her husband's axe unless he himself was using it; if unmarried, or if her husband was absent, a woman would go first to her older brother or to her father. Only in extraordinary circumstances would she seek a stone axe from other male kin. A girl, a boy, or a young man would look to a father or an older brother to provide an axe for their use. Older men, too, would follow similar rules if they had to borrow an axe.

It will be noted that all of these social relationships in which the stone axe had a place are pair relationships and that the use of the axe helped to define and maintain their character and the roles of the two individual participants. Every active relationship among the Yir Yoront involved a definite and accepted status of superordination or subordination. A person could have no dealings with another on exactly equal terms. The nearest approach to equality was between brothers, although the older was always superordinate to the younger. Since the exchange of goods in a trading relationship involved a mutual reciprocity, trading partners usually stood in a brotherly type of relationship, although one was always classified as older than the other and would have some advantage in case of dispute. It can be seen that repeated and widespread conduct centering around the use of the axe helped to generalize and standardize these sex, age, and kinship roles both in their normal benevolent and exceptional malevolent aspects.

The status of any individual Yir Yoront was determined not only by sex, age, and extended kin relationships, but also by membership in one of two dozen patrilineal totemic clans into which the entire community was divided. Each clan had literally hundreds of totems, from one or two of which the clan derived its name, and the clan members their personal names. These totems included natural species or phenomena such as the sun, stars, and daybreak, as well as cultural "species": imagined ghosts, rainbow serpents, heroic ancestors; such eternal cultural verities as fires, spears, huts; and such human activities, conditions, or attributes as eating, vomiting, swimming, fighting, babies and corpses, milk and blood, lips and loins. While individual members of such totemic classes or species might disappear or be destroyed, the class itself was obviously ever-present and indestructible. The totems, therefore, lent permanence and stability to the clans, to the groupings of human individuals who generation after generation were each associated with a set of totems which distinguished one clan from another.

The stone axe was one of the most important of the many totems of the Sunlit Cloud Iguana clan. The names of many members of this clan referred to the axe itself, to activities in which the axe played a vital part, or to the clan's mythical ancestors with whom the axe was prominently associated. When it was necessary to represent the stone axe in totemic ceremonies, only men of this clan exhibited it or pantomimed its use. In secular life, the axe could be made by any man and used by all; but in the sacred realm of the totems it belonged exclusively to the Sunlit Cloud Iguana people.

Supporting those aspects of cultural behavior which we have called technology and conduct is a third area of culture which includes ideas, sentiments, and values. These are most difficult to deal with, for they are latent and covert, and even unconscious, and must be deduced from overt actions and language or other communicating behavior. In this aspect of the culture lies the significance of the stone axe to the Yir Yoront and to their cultural way of life.

The stone axe was an important symbol of masculinity among the Yir Yoront (just as pants or pipes are to us). By a complicated set of ideas the axe was defined as "belonging" to males, and everyone in the society (except untrained infants) accepted these ideas. Similarly spears, spear throwers, and fire-making sticks were owned only by men and were also symbols of masculinity. But the masculine values represented by the stone axe were constantly being impressed on all members of society by the fact that females borrowed axes but not other masculine artifacts. Thus the axe stood for an important theme in Yir Yoront culture: the superiority and rightful dominance of the male, and the greater value of his concerns and of all things associated with him. As the axe also had to be borrowed by the younger people it represented the prestige of age, another important theme running through Yir Yoront behavior.

To understand the Yir Yoront culture it is necessary to be aware of a system of ideas which may be called their totemic ideology. A fundamental belief of the aboriginal divided time into two great epochs: 1) a distant and sacred period at the beginning of the world when the earth was peopled by mildly marvelous ancestral beings or culture heroes who are in a special sense the forebears of the clans; and 2) a period when the old was succeeded by a new order which includes the present. Originally there was no anticipation of another era supplanting the present. The future would simply be an eternal continuation and reproduction of the present which itself had remained unchanged since the epochal revolution of ancestral times.

The important thing to note is that the aboriginal believed that the present world, as a natural and cultural environment, was and should be simply a detailed reproduction of the world of the ancestors. He believed that the entire universe "is now as it was in the beginning" when it was established and left by the ancestors. The ordinary cultural life of the ancestors became the daily life of the Yir Yoront camps, and the extraordinary life of the ancestors remained extant in the recurring symbolic pantomimes and paraphernalia found only in the most sacred atmosphere of the totemic rites.

Such beliefs, accordingly, opened the way for ideas of what *should be* (because it supposedly *was*) to influence or help determine what actually *is*. A man called Dog-chases-iguana-up-a-tree-and-barks-at-him-all-night had that and other names because he believed his ancestral alter ego had also had them; he was a member of the Sunlit Cloud Iguana clan because his ancestor was; he was associated with particular countries and totems of this same ancestor; during an initiation he played a role of a dog and symbolically attacked and killed certain members of other clans because his ancestor (conveniently either anthropomorphic or kynomorphic) really did the same to the ancestral egos of these men; and he would avoid his mother-in-law, joke with a mother's distant brother, and make spears in a certain way because his and other people's ancestors did these things. His behavior in these specific ways was outlined, and to that extent determined for him, by a set of ideas concerning the past and the relation of the present to the past.

But when we are informed that Dog-chases-etc. had two wives from the Spear Black Duck clan and one from the Native Companion clan, one of them being blind, that he had four children with such and such names, that he had a broken wrist and was left-handed, all because his ancestor had exactly these same attributes, then we know (though he apparently didn't) that the present has influenced the past, that the mythical world has been somewhat adjusted to meet the exigencies and accidents of the inescapably real present.

There was thus in Yir Yoront ideology a nice balance in which the mythical was adjusted in part to the real world, the real world in part to the ideal preexisting mythical world, the adjustments occurring to maintain a fundamental tenet of native faith that the present must be a mirror of the past. Thus the stone axe in all its aspects, uses, and associations was integrated into the context of Yir Yoront technology and conduct because a myth, a set of ideas, had put it there.

## The Outcome

The introduction of the steel axe indiscriminately and in large numbers into the Yir Yoront technology occurred simultaneously with many other changes. It is therefore impossible to separate all the results of this single innovation. Nevertheless, a number of specific effects of the change from stone to steel axes may be noted, and the steel axe may be used as an epitome of the increasing quantity of European goods and implements received by the aboriginals and of their general influence on the native culture. The use of the steel axe to illustrate such influences would seem to be justified. It was one of the first European artifacts to be adopted for regular use by the Yir Yoront, and whether made of stone or steel, the axe was clearly one of the most important items of cultural equipment they possessed.

The shift from stone to steel axes provided no major technological difficulties. While the aboriginals themselves could not manufacture steel axe heads, a steady supply from outside continued; broken wooden handles could easily be replaced from bush timbers with aboriginal tools. Among the Yir Yoront the new axe was never used to the extent it was on mission or cattle stations (for carpentry work, pounding tent pegs, as a hammer, and so on); indeed, it has so few more uses than the stone axe that its practical effect on the native standard of living was negligible. It did some jobs better, and could be used longer without breakage. These factors were sufficient to make it of value to the native. The white man believed that a shift from steel to stone axe on his part would be a definite regression. He was convinced that his axe was much more efficient, that its use would save time, and that it therefore represented technical "progress" towards goals which he had set up for the native. But this assumption was hardly borne out in aboriginal practice. Any leisure time the Yir Yoront might gain by using steel axes or other Western tools was not invested in "improving the conditions of life," nor, certainly, in developing aesthetic activities, but in sleep—an art they had mastered thoroughly.

Previously, a man in need of an axe would acquire a stone axe head through regular trading partners from whom he knew what to expect and was then dependent solely upon a known and adequate natural environment and his own skills or easily acquired techniques. A man wanting a steel axe, however, was in no such self-reliant position. If he attended a mission festival when steel axes were handed out as gifts, he might receive one either by chance or by happening to impress upon the mission staff that he was of the "better" bush aboriginals (the missionaries' definition of "better" being quite different from that of his bush fellows). Or, again almost by pure chance, he might get some brief job in connection with the mission which would enable him to earn a steel axe. In either case, for older men a preference for the steel axe helped change the situation from one of self-reliance to one of dependence, and a shift in behavior from well-structured or defined situations in technology or conduct to ill-defined situations in conduct alone. Among the men, the older ones whose earlier experience or knowledge of the white man's harshness made them suspicious were particularly careful to avoid having relations with the mission, and thus excluded themselves from acquiring steel axes from that source.

In other aspects of conduct or social relations, the steel axe was even more significantly at the root of psychological stress among the Yir Yoront. This was the result of new factors which the missionary considered beneficial: the simple numerical increase in axes per capita as a result of mission distribution, and distribution directly to younger men, women, and even children. By winning the favor of the mission staff, a woman might be given a steel axe which was clearly intended to be hers, thus creating a situation quite different from the previous custom which necessitated her borrowing an axe from a male relative. As a result a woman would refer to the axe as "mine," a possessive form she was never able to use of the stone axe. In the same fashion, young men or even boys also obtained steel axes directly from the mission, with the result that older men no longer had a complete monopoly of all the axes in the bush community. All this led to a revolutionary confusion of sex, age, and kinship roles, with a major gain in independence and loss of subordination on the part of those who now owned steel axes when they had previously been unable to possess stone axes.

The trading-partner relationship was also affected by the new situation. A Yir Yoront might have a trading partner in a tribe to the south whom he defined as a younger brother and over whom he would therefore have some authority. But if the partner were in contact with the mission or had other access to steel axes, his subordination obviously decreased. Among other things, this took some of the excitement away from the dry-season fiestalike tribal gatherings centering around initiations. These had traditionally been the climactic annual occasions for exchanges between trading partners, when a man might seek to acquire a whole year's supply of stone axe heads. Now he might find himself prostituting his wife to almost total strangers in return for steel axes or other white-man's goods. With trading partnerships weakened, there was less reason to attend the ceremonies, and less fun for those who did.

Not only did an increase in steel axes and their distribution to women change the character of the relations between individuals (the paired relationships that have been noted), but a previously rare type of relationship was created in the Yir Yoront's conduct toward whites. In the aboriginal society there were few occasions outside the immediate family when an individual would initiate action to several other people at once. In any average group, in accordance with the kinship system, while a person might be superordinate to several people to whom he would suggest or command action, he was also subordinate to several others with whom such behavior would be tabu. There was thus no overall chieftainship or authoritarian leadership of any kind. Such complicated operations as grass-burning animal drives to totemic ceremonies could be carried out smoothly because each person was aware of his role.

On both mission and cattle stations, however, the whites imposed their conception of leadership roles upon the aboriginals, consisting of one person in a controlling relationship with a subordinate group. Aboriginals called together to receive gifts, including axes, at a mission Christmas party found themselves facing one or two whites who sought to control their behavior for the occasion, who disregarded the age, sex, and kinship variables of which the aboriginals were so conscious, and who considered them all at one subordinate level. The white also sought to impose similar patterns on work parties. (However, if he placed an aboriginal in charge of a mixed group of post-hole diggers, for example, half of the group, those subordinate to the "boss," would work while the other half, who were superordinate to him, would sleep.) For the aboriginal, the steel axe and other European goods came to symbolize this new and uncomfortable form of social organization, the leader-group relationship.

The most disturbing effects of the steel axe, operating in conjunction with other elements also being introduced from the white man's several subcultures, developed in the realm of traditional ideas, sentiments, and values. These were undermined at a rapidly mounting rate, with no new conceptions being defined to replace them. The result was the erection of a mental and moral void which foreshadowed the collapse and destruction of all Yir Yoront culture, if not, indeed the extinction of the biological group itself.

From what has been said it should be clear how changes in overt behavior, in technology and conduct, weakened the values inherent in a reliance on nature, in the prestige of masculinity and of age, and in the various kinship relations. A scene was set in which a wife, or a young son whose initiation may not yet have been completed, need no longer defer to the husband or father who, in turn, became confused and insecure as he was forced to borrow a steel axe from them. For the woman and boy the steel axe helped establish a new degree of freedom which they accepted readily as an escape from the unconscious stress of the old patterns—but they, too, were left confused and insecure. Ownership became less well defined with the result that stealing and trespassing were introduced into technology and conduct. Some of the excitement surrounding the great ceremonies evaporated and they lost their previous gaiety and interest. Indeed, life itself became less interesting, although this did not lead the Yir Yoront to discover suicide, a concept foreign to them.

The whole process may be most specifically illustrated in terms of totemic system, which also illustrates the significant role played by a system of ideas, in this case a totemic ideology, in the breakdown of a culture.

In the first place, under pre-European aboriginal

conditions where the native culture has become adjusted to a relatively stable environment few, if any, unheard of or catastrophic crises can occur. It is clear, therefore, that the totemic system serves very effectively in inhibiting radical cultural changes. The closed system of totemic ideas, explaining and categorizing a well-known universe as it was fixed at the beginning of time, presents a considerable obstacle to the adoption of new or the dropping of old culture traits. The obstacle is not insurmountable and the system allows for the minor variations which occur in the norms of daily life. But the inception of major changes cannot easily take place.

Among the bush Yir Yoront the only means of water transport is a light wood log to which they cling in their constant swimming of rivers, salt creeks, and tidal inlets. These natives know that tribes 45 miles farther north have a bark canoe. They know these northern tribes can thus fish from midstream or out at sea, instead of clinging to the river banks and beaches, that they can cross coastal waters infested with crocodiles, sharks, sting rays, and Portuguese men-of-war without danger. They know the materials of which the canoe is made exist in their own environment. But they also know, as they say, that they do not have canoes because their own mythical ancestors did not have them. They assume that the canoe was part of the ancestral universe of the northern tribes. For them, then, the adoption of the canoe would not be simply a matter of learning a number of new behavioral skills for its manufacture and use. The adoption would require a much more difficult procedure: the acceptance by the entire society of a myth, either locally developed or borrowed, to explain the presence of the canoe, to associate it with some one or more of the several hundred mythical ancestors (and how decide which?) and thus establish it as an accepted totem of one of the clans ready to be used by the whole community. The Yir Yoront have not made this adjustment, and in this case we can only say that, for the time being at least, ideas have won out over very real pressures for technological change. In the elaborateness and explicitness of the totemic ideologies we seem to have one explanation for the notorious stability of Australian cultures under aboriginal conditions, an explanation which gives due weight to the importance of ideas in determining human behavior.

At a later stage of the contact situation, as has been indicated, phenomena unaccounted for by the totemic ideological system begin to appear with regularity and frequency and remain within the range of native experience. Accordingly, they cannot be ignored (as the "Battle of the Mitchell" was apparently ignored), and there is an attempt to assimilate them and account for them along the lines of principles inherent in the idealogy. The bush Yir Yoront of the mid-thirties represent this stage of the acculturation process. Still trying to maintain their

aboriginal definition of the situation, they accept European artifacts and behavior patterns, but fit them into their totemic system, assigning them to various clans on a part with original totems. There is an attempt to have the myth-making process keep up with these cultural changes so that the idea system can continue to support the rest of the culture. But analysis of overt behavior, of dreams, and of some of new myths indicates that this arrangement is not entirely satisfactory, that the native clings to his totemic system with intellectual loyalty (lacking any substitute ideology), but that associated sentiments and values are weakened. His attitudes towards his own and toward European culture are found to be highly ambivalent.

All ghosts are totems of the Head-to-the East Corpse clan, are thought of as white, and are of course closely associated with death. The white man, too, is closely associated with death, and he and all things pertaining to him are naturally assigned to the Corpse clan as totems. The steel axe, as a totem, was thus associated with the Corpse clan. But as an "axe," clearly linked with the stone axe, it is a totem of the Sunlit Cloud Iguana clan. Moreover, the steel axe, like most European goods, has no distinctive origin myth, nor are mythical ancestors associated with it. Can anyone, sitting in the shade of a *ti* tree one afternoon, create a myth to resolve this confusion? No one has, and the horrid suspicion arises as to the authenticity of the origin myths, which failed to take into account this vast new universe of the white man. The steel axe, shifting hopelessly between one clan and the other, is not only replacing the stone axe physically, but is hacking at the supports of the entire cultural system.

The aboriginals to the south of the Yir Yoront have clearly passed beyond this stage. They are engulfed by European culture, either by the mission or cattle station subcultures or, for some natives, by a baffling, paradoxical combination of both incongruent varieties. The totemic ideology can no longer support the inrushing mass of foreign culture traits, and the myth-making process in its native form breaks down completely. Both intellectually and emotionally a saturation point is reached so that the myriad new traits which can neither be ignored nor any longer assimilated simply force the aboriginal to abandon his totemic system. With the collapse of this system of ideas, which is so closely related to so many other aspects of the native culture, there follows an appallingly sudden and complete cultural disintegration, and a demoralization of the individual such as has seldom been recorded elsewhere. Without the support of a system of ideas well devised to provide cultural stability in a stable environment, but admittedly too rigid for the new realities pressing in from outside, native behavior and native sentiments and values are simply dead. Apathy reigns. The aboriginal has passed beyond the realm of any outsider who might wish to do him well or ill.

Returning from the broken natives huddled on cattle stations or on the fringes of frontier towns to the ambivalent but still lively aboriginals settled on the Mitchell River mission, we note one further devious result of the introduction of European artifacts. During a wet-season stay at the mission, the anthropologist discovered that his supply of toothpaste was being depleted at an alarming rate. Investigation showed that it was being taken by old men for use in a new toothpaste cult. Old materials of magic having failed, new materials were being tried out in a malevolent magic directed towards the mission staff and some of the younger aboriginal men. Old males, largely ignored by the missionaries, were seeking to regain some of their lost power and prestige. This mild aggression proved hardly effective, but perhaps only because confidence in any kind of magic on the mission was by this time at a low ebb.

For the Yir Yoront still in the bush, a time could be predicted when personal deprivation and frustration in a confused culture would produce an overload of anxiety.

The mythical past of the totemic ancestors would disappear as a guarantee of a present of which the future was supposed to be stable continuation. Without the past, the present could be meaningless and the future unstructured and uncertain. Insecurities would be inevitable. Reaction to this stress might be some form of symbolic aggression, or withdrawal and apathy, or some more realistic approach. In such a situation the missionary with understanding of the processes going on about him would find his opportunity to introduce his forms of religion and to help create a new cultural universe.

## QUESTIONS

1. What effects did the introduction of the steel axe have on Yir Yaront culture and society?

2. Why is technology such a powerful factor in social change? Does technology determine the direction of change?

3. Why is technological change much faster in the United States than among the Yir Yaront?

Arthur C. Clarke

# 47. Hazards of Prophecy

*What will society be like a hundred or a thousand or ten thousand years from now? We cannot know; we can only make informed speculations and inspired guesses. And if the past is any guide, the chances are good that our prophecies will be hopelessly wrong.*

*History is littered with failed prophecies, ranging from the religious to the social and the scientific. Religious zealots have prophesied the end of the world time and again over the centuries, using the same biblical texts but interpreting them to fit the events and concerns of their own time. Theorists of various kinds have anticipated an endless variety of social scenarios, ranging from placid utopias to the Thousand Year Reich. Scientists have anticipated many innovations that now seem absurd—and, all too often, have declared impossible many advances that subsequently did occur.*

*In this article, Arthur C. Clarke examines the latter phenomenon—the recurrent failures of nerve and imagination that have so often made scientists blind to potential advances in their own fields.*

## The Failure of Nerve

Before one attempts to set up in business as a prophet, it is instructive to see what success others have made of this dangerous occupation—and it is even more instructive to see where they have failed.

With monotonous regularity, apparently competent men have laid down the law about what is technically possible or impossible—and have been proved utterly wrong, sometimes while the ink was scarcely dry from their pens. On careful analysis, it appears that these debacles fall into two classes, which I will call "failures of nerve" and "failures of imagination."

The failure of nerve seems to be the more common; it occurs when *even given all the relevant facts* the would be prophet cannot see that they point to an inescapable conclusion. Some of these failures are so ludicrous as to be almost unbelievable, and would form an interesting subject for psychological analysis. "They said it couldn't be done" is a phrase that occurs throughout the history of invention; I do not know if anyone has ever looked into the reasons *why* "they" said so, often with quite unnecessary vehemence.

It is now impossible for us to recall the mental climate which existed when the first locomotives were being built, and critics gravely asserted that suffocation lay in wait for anyone who reached the awful speed of thirty miles an hour. It is equally difficult to believe that, only eighty years ago, the idea of the domestic electric light was pooh-poohed by all the "experts"—with the exception of a thirty-one-year-old American inventor named Thomas Alva Edison. When gas securities nosedived in 1878 because Edison (already a formidable figure, with the phonograph and the carbon microphone to his credit) announced that he was working on the incandescent lamp, the British Parliament set up a committee to look into the matter. (Westminster can beat Washington hands down at this game.)

The distinguished witnesses reported, to the relief of the gas companies, that Edison's ideas were "good enough for our transatlantic friends . . . but unworthy of the attention of practical or scientific men." And Sir William Preece, engineer-in-chief of the British Post Office, roundly declared that "Subdivision of the electric light is an absolute *ignis fatuus*." One feels that the fatuousness was not in the *ignis*.

The scientific absurdity being pilloried, be it noted, is not some wild-and-woolly dream like perpetual motion, but the humble little electric light bulb, which three generations of men have taken for granted, except when it burns out and leaves them in the dark. Yet although in this matter Edison saw far beyond his contemporaries, he too in later life was guilty of the same shortsightedness that afflicted Preece, for he opposed the introduction of alternating current.

The most famous, and perhaps the most instructive, failures of nerve have occurred in the fields of aero- and astronautics. At the beginning of the twentieth century, scientists were almost unanimous in declaring that heavier-than-air flight was impossible, and that anyone who attempted to build airplanes was a fool. The great American astronomer, Simon Newcomb, wrote a celebrated essay which concluded:

> The demonstration that no possible combination of known substances, known forms of machinery and known forms of force, can be united in a practical machine by which man shall fly long distances through the air, seems to the writer as complete as it is possible for the demonstration of any physical fact to be.

Oddly enough, Newcomb was sufficiently broadminded to admit that some wholly new discovery—he mentioned the neutralization of gravity—might make flight practical. One cannot, therefore, accuse him of lacking imagination; his error was in attempting to marshal the facts of aerodynamics when he did not understand that science. His failure of nerve lay in not realizing that the means of flight were already at hand.

For Newcomb's article received wide publicity at just about the time that the Wright brothers, not having a suitable antigravity device in their bicycle shop, were mounting a gasoline engine on wings. When news of their success reached the astronomer, he was only momentarily taken back. Flying machines *might* be a marginal possibility, he conceded—but they were certainly of no practical importance, for it was quite out of the question that they could carry the extra weight of a passenger as well as that of a pilot.

Such refusal to face facts which now seem obvious has continued throughout the history of aviation. Let me quote another astronomer, William H. Pickering, straightening out the uninformed public a few years *after* the first airplanes had started to fly.

> The popular mind often pictures gigantic flying machines speeding across the Atlantic and carrying innumerable passengers in a way analogous to our modern steamships. . . .

> It seems safe to say that such ideas must be wholly visionary, and even if a machine could get across with one or two passengers the expense would be prohibitive to any but the capitalist who could own his own yacht.

> Another popular fallacy is to expect enormous speed to be obtained. It must be remembered that the resistance of the air increases as the square of the speed and the work as the cube. . . . If with 30 h.p. we can now attain a speed of 40 m.p.h., then in order to reach a speed of 100 m.p.h. we must use a motor capable of 470 h.p. . . . it is clear that with our present devices there is no hope of competing for racing speed with either our locomotives or our automobiles.

It so happens that most of his fellow astronomers considered Pickering far *too imaginative;* he was prone to see vegetation—and even evidence for insect life—on the Moon. I am glad to say that by the time he died in 1938 at the ripe age of eighty, Professor Pickering had seen airplanes traveling at 400 m.p.h. and carrying considerably more than "one or two" passengers.

Closer to the present, the opening of the space age has produced a mass vindication (and refutation) of prophecies on a scale and at a speed never before witnessed. Having taken some part in this myself, and being no more immune than the next man to the pleasures of saying, "I told you so," I would like to recall a few of the statements about space flight that have been made by prominent scientists in the past. It is necessary for *someone* to do this, and to jog the remarkably selective memories of the pessimists. The speed with which those who once declaimed "It's impossible" can switch to "I said it could be done all the time" is really astounding.

As far as the general public is concerned, the idea of space flight as a serious possibility first appeared on the horizon in the 1920's, largely as a result of newspaper reports of the work of the American Robert Goddard and the Rumanian Hermann Oberth. (The much earlier studies of Tsiolkovsky in Russia then being almost unknown outside his own country.) When the ideas of Goddard and Oberth, usually distorted by the press, filtered through to the scientific world, they were received with hoots of derision. For a sample of the kind of criticism the pioneers of astronautics had to face, I present this masterpiece from a paper published by one Professor A. W. Bickerton, in 1926. It should be read carefully, for as an example of the cocksure thinking of the time it would be very hard to beat.

> This foolish idea of shooting at the moon is an example of the absurd length to which vicious specialisation will carry scientists working in thought-tight compartments. Let us critically examine the proposal. For a projectile entirely to escape the gravitation of the earth, it needs a velocity of 7 miles a second. The thermal energy of a gramme at this speed is 15,180 calories. . . . The energy of our most violent explosive— nitro-glycerine—is less than 1,500 calories per

gramme. Consequently, even had the explosive nothing to carry, it has only one-tenth of the energy necessary to escape the earth. ... Hence the proposition appears to be basically impossible. ...

Indignant readers in the Colombo public library pointed angrily to the "Silence" notices when I discovered this little gem. It is worth examining it in some detail to see just where "vicious specialisation," if one may coin a phrase, led the professor so badly astray.

His first error lies in the sentence: "The energy of our most violent explosive—nitro-glycerine ..." One would have thought it obvious that *energy*, not violence, is what we want from a rocket fuel; and as a matter of fact nitroglycerin and similar explosives contain much less energy, weight for weight, than such mixtures as kerosene and liquid oxygen. This had been carefully pointed out by Tsiolkovsky and Goddard years before.

Bickerton's second error is much more culpable. What of it, if nitroglycerin has only a tenth of the energy necessary to escape from the Earth? That merely means that you have to use at least ten pounds of nitroglycerin to launch a single pound of payload.

*For the fuel itself* has not got to escape from Earth; it can all be burned quite close to our planet, and as long as it imparts its energy to the payload, this is all that matters. When Lunik II lifted thirty-three years after Professor Bickerton said it was impossible, most of its several hundred tons of kerosene and liquid oxygen never got very far from Russia—but the half-ton payload reached the Mare Imbrium.

As a comment on the above, I might add that Professor Bickerton, who was an active popularizer of science, numbered among his published books one with the title *Perils of a Pioneer*. Of the perils that all pioneers must face, few are more disheartening than the Bickertons.

Right through the 1930's and 1940's, eminent scientists continued to deride the rocket pioneers—when they bothered to notice them at all. Anyone who has access to a good college library can find, preserved for posterity in the dignified pages of the January 1941 *Philosophical Magazine*, an example that makes a worthy mate to the one I have just quoted.

It is a paper by the distinguished Canadian astronomer Professor J. W. Campbell, of the University of Alberta, entitled "Rocket Flight to the Moon." Opening with a quotation from a 1938 Edmonton paper to the effect that "rocket flight to the Moon now seems less remote than television appeared a hundred years ago," the professor then looks into the subject mathematically. After several pages of analysis, he arrives at the conclusion that it would require *a million tons* of take-off weight to carry *one pound* of payload on the round trip.

The correct figure, for today's primitive fuels and technologies, is very roughly one ton per pound—a depressing ratio, but hardly as bad as that calculated by the professor. Yet his mathematics was impeccable; so what went wrong?

Merely his initial assumptions, which were hopelessly unrealistic. He chose a path for the rocket which was fantastically extravagant in energy, and he assumed the use of an acceleration so low that most of the fuel would be wasted at low altitudes, fighting the Earth's gravitational field. It was as if he had calculated the performance of an automobile—when the brakes were on. No wonder that he concluded: "While it is always dangerous to make a negative prediction, it would appear that the statement that rocket flight to the moon does not seem so remote as television did less than one hundred years ago is overoptimistic." I am sure that when the *Philosophical Magazine* subscribers read those words, back in 1941, many of them thought, "Well, *that* should put those crazy rocket men in their place!"

Yet the correct results had been published by Tsiolkovsky, Oberth and Goddard years before; though the work of the first two would have been very hard to consult at the time, Goddard's paper "A Method of Reaching Extreme Altitudes" was already a classic and had been issued by that scarcely obscure body, the Smithsonian Institution. If Professor Campbell had only consulted it (or indeed *any* competent writer on the subject—there were some, even in 1941) he would not have misled his readers and himself.

The lesson to be learned from these examples is one that can never be repeated too often, and is one that is seldom understood by laymen—who have an almost superstitious awe of mathematics. But mathematics is only a tool, though an immensely powerful one. No equations, however impressive and complex, can arrive at the truth if the initial assumptions are incorrect. It is really quite amazing by what margins competent but conservative scientists and engineers can miss the mark, when they start with the preconceived idea that what they are investigating is impossible. When this happens, the most well-informed men become blinded by their prejudices and are unable to see what lies directly ahead of them. What is even more incredible, they refuse to learn from experience and will continue to make the same mistake over and over again.

Some of my best friends are astronomers, and I am sorry to keep throwing stones at them—but they do seem to have an appalling record as prophets. If you still doubt this, let me tell a story so ironic that you might well accuse me of making it up. But I am not that much of a cynic; the facts are on file for anyone to check.

Back in the dark ages of 1935, the founder of the British Interplanetary Society, P. E. Cleator, was rash enough to write the first book on astronautics published in England. His *Rockets through Space* gave an (incidentally highly entertaining) account of the experiments that had been carried out by the German and American rocket pioneers, and their plans for such commonplaces of today as giant multi-stage boosters and satellites. Rather surprisingly, the staid scientific journal *Nature* reviewed the book in its issue for March 14, 1936, and summed up as follows:

> It must be said at once that the whole procedure sketched in the present volume presents difficulties of so fundamental a nature that we are forced to dismiss the notion as essentially impracticable, in spite of the author's insistent appeal to put aside prejudice and to recollect the supposed impossibility of heavier-than-air flight before it was actually accomplished. An analogy such as this may be misleading, and we believe it to be so in this case....

Well, the whole world now knows just how misleading this analogy was, though the reviewer, identified only by the unusual initials R.v.d.R.W. was of course fully entitled to his opinion.

Just twenty years later—*after* President Eisenhower had announced the United States satellite program—a new Astronomer Royal arrived in England to take up his appointment. The press asked him to give his views on space flight, and after two decades Dr. Richard van der Riet Woolley had seen no reason to change his mind. "Space travel," he snorted, "is utter bilge."

The newspapers did not allow him to forget this, when Sputnik I went up the very next year. And now—irony piled upon irony—Dr. Woolley is, by virtue of his position as Astronomer Royal, a leading member of the committee advising the British government on space research. The feelings of those who have been trying, for a generation, to get the United Kingdom interested in space can well be imagined.

Even those who suggested that rockets might be used for more modest, though much more reprehensible, purposes were overruled by the scientific authorities—except in Germany and Russia.

When the existence of the 200-mile-range V-2 was disclosed to an astonished world, there was considerable speculation about intercontinental missiles. This was firmly squashed by Dr. Vannevar Bush, the civilian general of the United States scientific war effort, in evidence before a Senate committee on December 3, 1945. Listen:

> There has been a great deal said about a 3,000 miles high-angle rocket. In my opinion such a thing is impossible for many years. The people who have been writing these things that annoy me, have been talking about a 3,000 mile high-angle rocket shot from one continent to another, carrying an atomic bomb and so directed as to be a precise weapon which would land exactly on a certain target, such as a city.

> I say, technically, I don't think anyone in the world knows how to do such a thing, and I feel confident that it will not be done for a very long period of time to come.... I think we can leave that out of our thinking. I wish the American public would leave that out of their thinking.

A few months earlier (in May 1945) Prime Minister Churchill's scientific advisor Lord Cherwell had expressed similar views in a House of Lords debate. This was only to be expected, for Cherwell was an extremely conservative and opinionated scientist who had advised the government that the V-2 itself was only a propaganda rumor.

In the May 1945 debate on defense, Lord Cherwell impressed his peers by a dazzling display of mental arithmetic from which he correctly concluded that a very long-range rocket must consist of more then 90 per cent fuel, and thus would have a negligible payload. The conclusion he let his listeners draw from this was that such a device would be wholly impracticable.

That was true enough in the spring of 1945, but it was no longer true in the summer. One astonishing feature of the House of Lords debate is the casual way in which much-too-well-informed peers used the words "atomic bomb," at a time when this was the best-kept secret of the war. (The Alamogordo test was still two months in the future!) Security must have been horrified, and Lord Cherwell—who of course knew all about the Manhattan Project—was quite justified in telling his inquisitive colleagues not to believe everything they heard, even though in this case it happened to be perfectly true.

When Dr. Bush spoke to the Senate committee in December of the same year, the only important secret about the atomic bomb was that it weighed five tons. Anyone could then work out in his head, as Lord Cherwell had done, that a rocket to deliver it across intercontinental ranges would have to weigh about 200 tons—as against the mere 14 tons of the then awe-inspiring V-2.

The outcome was the greatest failure of nerve in all history, which changed the future of the world—indeed, of many worlds. Faced with the same facts and the same calculations, American and Russian technology took two separate roads. The Pentagon—accountable to the taxpayer—virtually abandoned long-range rockets for almost half a decade, until the development of thermonuclear bombs made it possible to build warheads five times lighter yet several hundred times more powerful than the low-powered and now obsolete device that was dropped on Hiroshima.

The Russians had no such inhibitions. Faced with the need for a 200-ton rocket, they went right ahead and built it. By the time it was perfected, it was no longer required for military purposes, for Soviet physicists had bypassed the United States' billion-dollar tritium bomb cul-de-sac and gone straight to the far cheaper lithium bomb. Having backed the wrong horse in rocketry, the Russians then entered it for a much more important event—and won the race into space.

Of the many lessons to be drawn from this slice of recent history, the one that I wish to emphasize is this. Anything that is theoretically possible will be achieved in practice, no matter what the technical difficulties, if it is desired greatly enough. It is no argument against any project to say: "The idea's fantastic!" Most of the things that have happened in the last fifty years have been fantastic, and it is only by assuming that they will continue to be so that we have any hope of anticipating the future.

To do this—to avoid that failure of nerve for which history exacts so merciless a penalty—we must have the courage to follow all technical extrapolations to their logical conclusion. Yet even this is not enough, as I shall now demonstrate. To predict the future we need logic; but we also need faith and imagination which can sometimes defy logic itself.

## The Failure of Imagination

[Until now I have] suggested that many of the negative statements about scientific possibilities, and the gross failures of past prophets to predict what lay immediately ahead of them, could be described as failures of nerve. All the basic facts of aeronautics were available—in the writings of Caylay, Stringfellow, Chanute, and others—when Simon Newcomb "proved" that flight was impossible. He simply lacked the courage to face those facts. All the fundamental equations and principles of space travel had been worked out by Tsiolkovsky, Goddard, and Oberth for years—often decades—when distinguished scientists were making fun of would-be astronauts. Here again, the failure to appreciate the facts was not so much intellectual as moral. The critics did not have the courage that their scientific convictions should have given them; they could not believe the truth even when it had been spelled out before their eyes, in their own language of mathematics. We all know this type of cowardice, because at some time or other we all exhibit it.

The second kind of prophetic failure is less blameworthy, and more interesting. It arises when all the available facts are appreciated *and* marshaled correctly—but when the really vital facts are still undiscovered, and the possibility of their existence is not admitted.

A famous example of this is provided by the philosopher Auguste Comte, who in his *Cours de Philosophie Positive* (1835) attempted to define the limits within which scientific knowledge must lie. In his chapter on

astronomy (Book 2, Chapter 1) he wrote these words concerning the heavenly bodies:

> We see how we may determine their forms, their distances, their bulk, their motions, but we can never know anything of their chemical or mineralogical structure; and much less, that of organised beings living on their surface.... We must keep carefully apart the idea of the solar system and that of the universe, and be always assured that our only true interest is in the former. Within this boundary alone is astronomy the supreme and positive science that we have determined it to be ... the stars serve us scientifically only as providing positions with which we may compare the interior movements of our system.

In other words, Comte decided that the stars could never be more than celestial reference points, of no intrinsic concern to the astronomer. Only in the case of the planets could we hope for any definite knowledge, and even that knowledge would be limited to geometry and dynamics. Comte would probably have decided that such a science as "astrophysics" was *a priori* impossible.

Yet within half a century of his death, almost the whole of astronomy *was* astrophysics, and very few professional astronomers had much interest in the planets. Comte's assertion had been utterly refuted by the invention of the spectroscope, which not only revealed the "chemical structure" of the heavenly bodies but has now told us far more about the distant stars than we know of our planetary neighbors.

Comte cannot be blamed for not imagining the spectroscope; *no one* could have imagined it, or the still more sophisticated instruments that have now joined it in the astronomer's armory. But he provides a warning that should always be borne in mind; even things that are undoubtedly impossible with existing or forseeable techniques may prove to be easy as a result of new scientific breakthroughs. From their very nature, these breakthroughs can never be anticipated; but they have enabled us to bypass so many insuperable obstacles in the past that no picture of the future can hope to be valid if it ignores them.

Another celebrated failure of imagination was that persisted in by Lord Rutherford, who more than any other man laid bare the internal structure of the atom. Rutherford frequently made fun of those sensation mongers who predicted that we would one day be able to harness the energy locked up in matter. Yet only five years after his death in 1937, the first chain reaction was started in Chicago. What Rutherford, for all his wonderful insight, had failed to take into account was that a nuclear reaction might be discovered that would release more energy than that required to start it. To liberate the energy of matter, what was wanted was a nuclear "fire" analogous to chemical combustion, and the fission of uranium provided this. Once that was discovered, the harnessing of atomic energy was inevitable, though without the pressures of war it might well have taken the better part of a century.

. . .

Too much imagination is much rarer than too little; when it occurs, it usually involves its unfortunate possessor in frustration and failure—unless he is sensible enough merely to write about his ideas, and not to attempt their realization. In the first category we find all the science-fiction authors, historians of the future, creators of utopias—and the two Bacons, Roger and Francis.

Friar Roger (c. 1214–1292) imagined optical instruments and mechanically propelled boats and flying machines—devices far beyond the existing or even foreseeable technology of his time. It is hard to believe that these words were written in the thirteenth century:

> Instruments may be made by which the largest ships, with only one man guiding them, will be carried with greater velocity than if they were full of sailors. Chariots may be constructed that will move with incredible rapidity without the help of animals. Instruments of flying may be formed in which a man, sitting at his ease and meditating in any subject, may beat the air with his artificial wings after the manner of birds . . . as also machines which will enable men to walk at the bottom of the seas. . . .

This passage is a triumph of imagination over hard fact. Everything in it has come true, yet at the time it was written it was more an act of faith than of logic. It is probable that all long-range prediction, if it is to be accurate, must be of this nature. The real future is not *logically* foreseeable.

A splendid example of a man whose imagination ran ahead of his age was the English mathematician Charles Babbage (1792–1871). As long ago as 1819, Babbage had worked out the principles underlying automatic computing machines. He realized that all mathematical calculations could be broken down into a series of step-by-step operations that could, in theory, be carried out by a machine. With the aid of a government grant which eventually totaled £17,000—a very substantial sum of money in the 1820's—he started to build his "analytical engine."

Though he devoted the rest of his life, and much of his private fortune, to the project, Babbage was unable to complete the machine. What defeated him was the fact that precision engineering of the standard he needed to build his cogs and gears simply did not exist at the time. By his efforts he helped to create the machine-tool industry—so that in the long run the government got back very much more than its £17,000—and today it

would be a perfectly straightforward matter to complete Babbage's computer, which now stands as one of the most fascinating exhibits in the London Science Museum. In his own lifetime, however, Babbage was only able to demonstrate the operation of a relatively small portion of the complete machine. A dozen years after his death, his biographer wrote: "This extraordinary monument of theoretical genius accordingly remains, and doubtless will forever remain, a theoretical possibility."

There is not much left of that "doubtless" today. At this moment there are thousands of computers working on the principles that Babbage clearly outlined more than a century ago—but with a range and a speed of which he could never have dreamed. For what makes the case of Charles Babbage so interesting, and so pathetic, is that he was not one but *two* technological revolutions ahead of his time. Had the precision-tool industry existed in 1820, he could have built his "analytical engine" and it would have worked, much faster than a human computer, but very slowly by the standards of today. For it would have been geared—literally—to the speed with which cogs and shafts and cams and ratchets can operate.

Automatic calculating machines could not come into their own until electronics made possible speeds of operation thousands and millions of times swifter than could be achieved with purely mechanical devices. This level of technology was reached in the 1940's, and Babbage was then promptly vindicated. His failure was not one of imagination: it lay in being born a hundred years too soon.

One can only prepare for the unpredictable by trying to keep an open and unprejudiced mind—a feat which is extremely difficult to achieve, even with the best will in the world. Indeed, a completely open mind would be an empty one, and freedom from all prejudices and preconceptions is an unattainable ideal. Yet there is one form of mental exercise that can provide good basic training for would-be prophets: Anyone who wishes to cope with the future should travel back in imagination a single lifetime—say to 1900—and ask himself just how much of today's technology would be, not merely incredible, but *incomprehensible* to the keenest scientific brains of that time.

1900 is a good round date to choose because it was just about then that all hell started to break loose in science. As James B. Conant has put it:

> Somewhere about 1900 science took a *totally* unexpected turn. There had previously been several revolutionary theories and more than one epoch making discovery in the history of science, but what occurred between 1900 and, say, 1930 was something different; it was a failure of a

general prediction about what might be confidently expected from experimentation.

P. W. Bridgman has put it even more strongly:

The physicist has passed through an intellectual crisis forced by the discovery of experimental facts of a sort which he had not previously envisaged, and which he would not even have thought possible.

The collapse of "classical" science actually began with Roentgen's discovery of X-rays in 1895; here was the first clear indication, in a form that everyone could appreciate, that the common-sense picture of the universe was not sensible after all. X-rays—the very name reflects the bafflement of scientists and laymen alike—could travel through solid matter, like light through a sheet of glass. No one had ever imagined or predicted such a thing; that one would be able to peer into the interior of the human body—and thereby revolutionize medicine and surgery—was something that the most daring prophet had never suggested.

The discovery of X-rays was the first great breakthrough into the realms where no human mind had ever ventured before. Yet it gave scarcely a hint of still more astonishing developments to come—radioactivity, the internal structure of the atom, relativity, the quantum theory, the uncertainty principle. . . .

As a result of this, the inventions and technical devices of our modern world can be divided into two sharply defined classes. On the one hand there are those machines whose working would have been fully understood by any of the great thinkers of the past; on the other, there are those that would be utterly baffling to the finest minds of antiquity. And not merely of antiquity; there are devices now coming into use that might well have driven Edison or Marconi insane had they tried to fathom their operation.

Let me give some examples to emphasize this point. If you showed a modern diesel engine, an automobile, a steam turbine, or a helicopter to Benjamin Franklin, Galileo, Leonardo da Vinci, and Archimedes—a list spanning two thousand years of time—not one of them would have any difficulty in understanding how these machines worked. Leonardo, in fact, would recognize several from his notebooks. All four men would be astonished at the materials and the workmanship, which would have seemed magical in its precision, but once they had got over that surprise they would feel quite at home—as long as they did not delve too deeply into the auxiliary control and electrical systems.

But now suppose that they were confronted by a television set, an electronic omputer, a nuclear reactor, a radar installation. Quite apart from the complexity of these devices, the individual elements of which they are composed would be incomprehensible to any man born before this century. Whatever his degree of education or intelligence, he would not possess the mental framework that could accommodate electron beams, transistors, atomic fission, wave guides and cathode-ray tubes.

The difficulty, let me repeat, is not one of complexity; some of the simplest modern devices would be the most difficult to explain. A particularly good example is given by the atomic bomb (at least, the early models). What could be simpler than banging two lumps of metal together? Yet how could one explain to Archimedes that the result could be more devastation than that produced by all the wars between the Trojans and the Greeks?

Suppose you went to any scientist up to the late nineteenth century and told him: "Here are two pieces of a substance called uranium 235. If you hold them apart, nothing will happen. But if you bring them together suddenly, you will liberate as much energy as you could obtain from burning ten thousand tons of coal." No matter how farsighted and imaginative he might be, your pre-twentieth century scientist would have said: "What utter nonsense! That's magic, not science. Such things can't happen in the real world." Around 1890, when the foundations of physics and thermodynamics had (it seemed) been securely laid, he could have told you exactly why it was nonsense.

"Energy cannot be created out of nowhere," he might have said. "It has to come from chemical reactions, electrical batteries, coiled springs, compressed gas, spinning flywheels, or some other clearly defined source. All such sources are ruled out in this case—and even if they were not, the energy output you mention is absurd. Why, it is more than a *million* times that available from the most powerful chemical reaction!"

The fascinating thing about this particular example is that, even when the existence of atomic energy was fully appreciated—say right up to 1940—almost all scientists would still have laughed at the idea of liberating it by bringing pieces of metal together. Those who believed that the energy of the nucleus ever could be released almost certainly pictured complicated electrical devices—"atom smashers" and so forth—doing the job. (In the long run, this will probably be the case; it seems that we will need such machines to fuse hydrogen nuclei on the industrial scale. But once again, who knows?)

The wholly unexpected discovery of uranium fission in 1939 made possible such absurdly simple (in principle, if not in practice) devices as the atomic bomb and the nuclear chain reactor. No scientist could ever have predicted them; if he had, all his colleagues would have laughed at him,

It is highly instructive, and stimulating to the imagination, to make a list of the inventions and discoveries that have been anticipated—and those that have not. Here is my attempt to do so.

| The Unexpected | The Expected |
| --- | --- |
| X-rays | automobiles |
| nuclear energy | flying machines |
| radio, TV | steam engines |
| electronics | submarines |
| photography | spaceships |
| sound recording | telephones |
| quantum mechanics | robots |
| relativity | death rays |
| transistors | transmutation |
| masers; lasers | artificial life |
| superconductors; superfluids | immortality |
| atomic clocks; Mössbauer effect | invisibility |
| | levitation |
| determining composition of celestial bodies | teleportation |
| | communication with dead |
| dating the past (Carbon 14, etc.) | observing the past, the future |
| | telepathy |
| detecting invisible planets | |
| the ionosphere; Van Allen Belts | |

All the items on the left have already been achieved or discovered, and all have an element of the unexpected or the downright astonishing about them. To the best of my knowledge, not one was foreseen very much in advance of the moment of revelation.

On the right, however, are concepts that have been around for hundreds or thousands of years. Some have been achieved; others will be achieved; others may be impossible. But which?

The right-hand list is deliberately provocative; it includes sheer fantasy as well as serious scientific speculation. But the only way of discovering the limits of the possible is to venture a little way past them into the impossible. . . . This is exactly what I hope to do; yet I am very much afraid that from time to time I too will exhibit failure of imagination if not failure of nerve. For as I glance down the left-hand column I am aware of a few items which, only ten years ago, I would have thought very impossible. . . .

## QUESTIONS

1. Why have scientists so often been wrong in their prophecies about the future? Given the limitations imposed on them by their social environments, could "nerve" and "imagination" really have helped them be more accurate?

2. Which, if any, of the expected but unachieved concepts on Clarke's list do you think will always be impossible? Can you be sure?

3. What will your grandchildren's world be like?

*Jan Harold Brunvand*

# 48. "The Hook" and Other Teenage Horrors

*All societies have a rich store of legends about the past—for example, about the voyages of Ulysses, or about George Washington's chopping down a cherry tree. Such "historical" legends usually recount the exploits of heroes and in doing so they convey some moral to the listener—for example, about the virtues of hard work or of telling the truth. But there are also contemporary, or "urban" legends—realistic but untrue stories with an ironic twist concerning recent alleged events. The recurrent spreading of these legends is a striking example of collective behavior.*

*Urban legends are passed along by people who genuinely believe that the truth lies one or two informants back along the line of transmission. Generally, the legends have three basic components—a strong narrative appeal, a fairly plausible content, and an implicit lesson. The legends are told in various versions in different places and may continue to crop up for many years. Usually, however, they gain credibility because of references to specific times, nearby places, and "reliable" sources such as "a friend of a friend."*

*In this article, Jan Brunvand, a leading researcher of urban legends, reports on some tales that are particularly common among teenagers.*

From *The Vanishing Hitchhiker: American Urban Legends and Their Meanings,* by Jan Harold Brunvand, W. W. Norton, 1981. Copyright © 1981 by Jan Harold Brunvand. Reprinted by permission.

## Growing Up Scared

People of all ages love a good scare. Early childlore is full of semi-serious spooky stories and ghastly threats, while the more sophisticated black humor of Little Willies, Bloody Marys, Dead Babies, and other cycles of sick jokes enters a bit later. Among the favorite readings at school are Edgar Allan Poe's blood-soaked tales, and favorite stories at summer camp tell of maniacal ax-murderers and deformed giants lurking in the dark forest to ambush unwary Scouts. Halloween spook houses and Hollywood horror films cater to the same wish to push the level of tolerable fright as far as possible.

The ingredients of horror fiction change little through time, but the style of such stories does develop, even in oral tradition. In their early teens young Americans apparently reject the overdramatic and unbelievable juvenile "scaries" and adopt a new lore of more plausible tales with realistic settings. That is, they begin to enjoy urban legends, especially those dealing with "folks" like themselves—dating couples, students, and baby-sitters—who are subjected to grueling ordeals and horrible threats. (We looked at one example, "The Boyfriend's Death," in Chapter I.)

One consistent theme in these teenage horrors is that as the adolescent moves out from home into the larger world, the world's dangers may close in on him or her. Therefore, although the immediate purpose of many of these legends is to produce a good scare, they also serve to deliver a warning: Watch out! This could happen to you! Furthermore, the horror tales often contain thinly-disguised sexual themes which are, perhaps, implicit in the nature of such plot situations as parking in a lovers' lane or baby-sitting (playing house) in a strange home. These sexual elements furnish both a measure of further entertainment and definite cautionary notices about the world's actual dangers. Thus, from the teenagers' own major fears, concerns, and experiences, spring their favorite "true" oral stories.

The chief current example of this genre of urban legend—one that is even older, more popular, and more widespread than "The Boyfriend's Death"—is the one usually called "The Hook."

## "The Hook"

On Tuesday, November 8, 1960, the day when Americans went to the polls to elect John F. Kennedy as their thirty-fifth president, thousands of people must have read the following letter from a teenager in the popular newspaper column written by Abigail Van Buren:

> DEAR ABBY: If you are interested in teenagers, you will print this story. I don't know whether it's true or not, but it doesn't matter because it served its purpose for me:
>
> A fellow and his date pulled into their favorite "lovers' lane" to listen to the radio and do a little necking. The music was interrupted by an announcer who said there was an escaped convict in the area who had served time for rape and robbery. He was described as having a hook instead of a right hand. The couple became frightened and drove away. When the boy took his girl home, he went around to open the car door for her. Then he saw—a hook on the door handle! I don't think I will ever park to make out as long as I live. I hope this does the same for other kids.
>
> JEANETTE

This juicy story seems to have emerged in the late 1950s, sharing some common themes with "The Death Car" and "The Vanishing Hitchhiker" and then, as shown in Chapter 1, influencing "The Boyfriend's Death" as that legend developed in the early 1960s. The story of "The Hook" (or "The Hookman") really needed no national press report to give it life or credibility, because the teenage oral-tradition underground had done the job well enough long before the election day of 1960. Teenagers all over the country knew about "The Hook" by 1959, and like other modern legends the basic plot was elaborated with details and became highly localized.

One of my own students, originally from Kansas, provided this specific account of where the event supposedly occurred:

> Outside of "Mac" [McPherson, Kansas], about seven miles out towards Lindsborg, north on old highway 81 is an old road called "Hookman's Road." It's a curved road, a traditional parking spot for the kids. When I was growing up it [the legend] was popular, and that was back in the '60's, and it was old then.

Another student told a version of the story that she had heard from her baby-sitter in Albuquerque in 1960:

> . . . over the radio came an announcement that a crazed killer with a hook in place of a hand had escaped from the local insane asylum. The girl got scared and begged the

boy to take her home. He got mad and stepped on the gas and roared off. When they got to her house, he got out and went around to the other side of the car to let her out. There on the door handle was a bloody hook.

But these two students were told, after arriving in Salt Lake City, that it had actually occurred *here* in Memory Grove, a well-wooded city park. "Oh, no," a local student in the class insisted, "This couple was parked outside of Salt Lake City *in a mountain canyon* one night and . . ." It turned out that virtually every student in the class knew the story as adapted in some way to their hometowns.

Other folklorists have reported collecting "The Hook" in Maryland, Wisconsin, Indiana, Illinois, Kansas, Texas, Arkansas, Oregon, and Canada. Some of the informants' comments echo Dear Abby's correspondent in testifying to the story's effect (to discourage parking) even when its truth was suspect. The students said, "I believe that it *could* happen, and this makes it seem real," or "I don't really [believe it], but it's pretty scary; I sort of hope it didn't happen."

Part of the great appeal of "The Hook"—one of the most popular adolescent scare stories—must lie in the tidiness of the plot. Everything fits. On the other hand, the lack of loose ends would seem to be excellent testimony to the story's near impossibility. After all, what are the odds that a convicted criminal or crazed maniac would be fitted with a hook for a missing hand, that this same threatening figure would show up precisely when a radio warning had been broadcast of his escape, and that the couple would drive away rapidly just at the instant the hookman put his hook through the door handle? Besides, why wouldn't he try to open the door with his good hand, and how is it that the boy—furious at the interruption of their lovemaking—is still willing to go around politely to open the girl's door when they get home? Too much, too much—but it makes a great story.

In an adolescent novel titled *Dinky Hocker Shoots Smack!*, M. E. Kerr captured the way teenagers often react to such legends—with cool acceptance that it might have happened, and that's good enough:

> She told Tucker this long story about a one-armed man who was hanging around a lovers' lane in Prospect Park [Brooklyn]. There were rumors that he tried to get in the cars and carry off the girls. He banged on the windshields with his hooked wooden arm and frothed at the mouth. He only said two words: *bloody murder;* and his voice was high and hoarse.
>
> Dinky claimed this girl who went to St. Marie's was up in Prospect Park one night with a boyfriend. The girl and her boyfriend began discussing the one-armed man while they were parked. They both got frightened and decided to leave. The boy dropped the girl off at her house, and drove home.

When he got out of his car, he found this hook attached to his door handle.

Dinky said, "They must have driven off just as he was about to open the door."

"I thought you weren't interested in the bizarre, anymore," Tucker said.

"It's a true story."

"It's still bizarre."

A key detail lacking in the *Dinky Hocker* version, however, is the boyfriend's frustrated anger resulting in their leaving the scene in a great hurry. Almost invariably the boy guns the motor and roars away: "... so he revs up the car and he goes torquing out of there." Or, "The boy floored the gas pedal and zoomed away," or "Her boyfriend was annoyed and the car screeched off...." While this behavior is essential to explain the sudden sharp force that tears loose the maniac's hook, it is also a reminder of the original sexual purpose of the parking, at least on the boy's part. While Linda Dégh saw "the natural dread of the handicapped," and "the boy's disappointment and suddenly recognized fear as an adequate explanation for the jump start of the car," folklorist Alan Dundes disagreed, mainly because of the curtailed sex quest in the plot.

Dundes, taking a Freudian line, interpreted the hook itself as a phallic symbol which penetrates the girl's door handle (or bumps seductively against her window) but which is torn off (symbolic of castration) when the car starts abruptly. Girls who tell the story, Dundes suggests, "are not afraid of what a man lacks, but of what he has"; a date who is "all hands" may really want to "get his hooks into her." Only the girl's winding up the window or insisting upon going home at once saves her, and the date has to "pull out fast" before he begins to act like a sex maniac himself. The radio—turned on originally for soft, romantic background music—introduces instead "the consciencelike voice from society," a warning that the girl heeds and the boy usually scorns. Dundes concluded that this popular legend "reflects a very real dating practice, one which produces anxiety ... particularly for girls."

## "The Killer in the Backseat"

A similar urban legend also involves cars and an unseen potential assailant; this time a man threatens a woman who is driving alone at night. The following version of "The Killer in the Backseat" was contributed in 1967 by a University of Utah student who had heard other versions set in Denver and Aurora, Colorado:

A woman living in the city [i.e., Salt Lake City] was visiting some friends in Ogden. When she got into her car in front of this friend's house, she noticed that a car started up right behind her car. It was about 2:00 in the morning, and there weren't any other cars on the road. After she had driven to the highway, she began to think that this car was following her. Some of the time he would drive up real close to her car, but he wouldn't ever pass. She was really scared to death and kept speeding to try to get away from him.

When she got to Salt Lake, she started running stop lights to get away from him, but he would run right through them too. So when she got to her driveway she pulled in really fast, and this guy pulled in right behind her. She just laid on the horn, and her husband came running out. Just then, the guy jumped out of the car, and her husband ran over and said, "What the hell's goin' on here?" So he grabbed the guy, and his wife said, "This man's followed me all the way from Ogden." The man said, "I followed your wife because I was going to work, and as I got into my car, I noticed when I turned my lights on, a man's head bob down in her backseat." So the husband went over to her backseat, opened the door, and pulled this guy from out of the backseat.

This legend first appeared in print in 1968 in another version, also—coincidentally—set in Ogden, Utah, but collected at Indiana University, Bloomington. (This shows how the presence of folklorists in a locality will influence the apparent distribution patterns of folk material.) Twenty further texts have surfaced at Indiana University with, as usual, plenty of variations and localizations. In many instances the pursuing driver keeps flashing his headlights between the high and low beam in order to restrain the assailant who is popping up and threatening to attack the driver. Sometimes the pursuer is a burly truck driver or other tough-looking character, and in several of the stories the supposed would-be attacker (the pursuing rescuer) is specifically said to be a black man. (Both motifs clearly show white middle class fears of minorities or of groups believed to be socially inferior.)

In a more imaginative set of these legends the person who spots the dangerous man in back is a gas station attendant who pretends that a ten dollar bill offered by the woman driver in payment for gas is counterfeit. With this ruse he gets her safely away from her car before calling the police. In another version of the story, a passing motorist sharply warns the woman driver to roll up her window and follow him, driving in exactly the same manner he does. She obeys, speeding and weaving along the highway, until a suspected assailant—usually carrying an ax—is thrown from his perch on the roof of her car.

## "The Baby-sitter and the Man Upstairs"

Just as a lone woman may unwittingly be endangered by a hidden man while she is driving at night, a younger one may face the same hazard in a strange house. The horror legend of "The Baby-sitter and the Man Upstairs," similar in structure to "The Killer in the Backseat," is possibly a later variation of the same story relocated to fit teenagers' other direct experiences. This standard version is from a fourteen-year-old Canadian boy (1973):

> There was this baby-sitter that was in Montreal baby-sitting for three children in a big house. She was watching TV when suddenly the phone rang. The children were all in bed. She picked up the phone and heard this guy on the other end laughing hysterically. She asked him what it was that he wanted, but he wouldn't answer and then hung up. She worried about it for a while, but then thought nothing more of it and went back to watching the movie.
>
> Everything was fine until about fifteen minutes later when the phone rang again. She picked it up and heard the same voice laughing hysterically at her, and then hung up. At this point she became really worried and phoned the operator to tell her what had been happening. The operator told her to calm down and that if he called again to try and keep him on the line as long as possible and she would try to trace the call.
>
> Again about fifteen minutes later the guy called back and laughed hysterically at her. She asked him why he was doing this, but he just kept laughing at her. He hung up and about five seconds later the operator called. She told the girl to get out of the house at once because the person who was calling was calling from the upstairs extension. She slammed down the phone and just as she was turning to leave she saw the man coming down the stairs laughing hysterically with a bloody butcher knife in his hand and meaning to kill her. She ran out onto the street but he didn't follow. She called the police and they came and caught the man, and discovered that he had murdered all the children.

The storyteller added that he had heard the story from a friend whose brother's girlfriend was the baby-sitter involved.

By now it should come as no surprise to learn that the same story had been collected two years earlier (1971) some 1500 miles southwest of Montreal, in Austin, Texas, and also in Bloomington, Indiana, in 1973 in a college dormitory. These three published versions are only samples from the wide distribution of the story in folk tradition. Their similarities and differences provide another classic case of folklore's variation within traditional boundaries. In all three legend texts the hour is late and the baby-sitter is watching television. Two of the callers make threatening statements, while one merely laughs. In all versions the man calls three times at regular intervals before the girl calls the operator, then once more afterwards. In both American texts the operator herself calls the police, and in the Indiana story she commands "Get out of the house immediately; don't go upstairs; don't do anything; just leave the house. When you get out there, there will be policemen outside and they'll take

care of it." (One is reminded of the rescuers' orders not to look back at the car in "The Boyfriend's Death.") The Texas telephone operator in common with the Canadian one gives the situation away by adding, "The phone call traces to the upstairs." The murder of the child or children (one, two, or three of them—no pattern) is specified in the American versions: in Texas they are "chopped into little bitty pieces"; in Indiana, "torn to bits." All of the storytellers played up the spookiness of the situation—details that would be familiar to anyone who has ever baby-sat—a strange house, a television show, an unexpected phone call, frightening sounds or threats, the abrupt orders from the operator, and finally the shocking realization at the end that (as in "The Killer in the Backseat") the caller had been there in the house (or behind her) all the time. The technical problems of calling another telephone from an extension of the same number, or the actual procedures of call-tracing, do not seem to worry the storytellers.

Folklorist Sue Samuelson, who examined hundreds of unpublished "Man Upstairs" stories filed in American folklore archives, concluded that the telephone is the most important and emotionally-loaded item in the plot: the assailant is harassing his victim through the device that is her own favorite means of communication. Baby-sitting, Samuelson points out, is an important socializing experience for young women, allowing them to practice their future roles, imposed on them in a male-dominated society, as homemakers and mothers. Significantly, the threatening male figure is *upstairs*—on top of and in control of the girl—as men have traditionally been in the sexual relationship. In killing the children who were in her care, the man brings on the most catastrophic failure any mother can suffer. Another contributing factor in the story is that the baby-sitter herself is too intent on watching television to realize that the children are being murdered upstairs. Thus, the tale is not just another scary story, but conveys a stern admonition to young women to adhere to society's traditional values.

Occasionally these firmly-believed horror legends are transformed from ghastly mysteries to almost comical adventures. The following Arizona version of "The Baby-sitter and the Man Upstairs," collected in 1976, is a good example:

> It was August 8, 1960. She was going to baby-sit at the Smiths who had two children, ages five and seven. She had just put the children to bed and went back to the living room to watch TV.
>
> The phone began to ring; she went to answer it; the man on the other end said, "I'm upstairs with the children; you'd better come up."
>
> She hung the phone up immediately, scared to death. She decided that it must be a prank phone call; again she went

to watch TV. The phone rang again; she went to answer it, this time more scared than last.

The man said, "I'm upstairs with the children," and described them in detail. So she hung up the phone, not knowing what to do. Should I call the police? Instead she decided, "I'll call the operator. They can trace these phone calls." She called the operator, and the operator said that she would try and do what she could. Approximately ten minutes later the phone rang again; this time she was shaking.

She answered the phone and the man again said, "I'm upstairs with the children; you'd better come quick!" She tried to stay on the phone as long as she could so that the operator could trace the call; this time the man hung up.

She called back, and the operator said, "Run out of the house; the man is on the extension."

She didn't quite know what to do; should she go and get the children? "No," she said, "he's up there; if I go and get the children, I'll be killed too!!"

She ran next door to the neighbor's house and called the police. The sirens came—there must have been at least ten police cars. They went inside the house, ran upstairs, and found not a man, but a seven-year-old child who was sitting next to the phone with a tape recorder. Later they found that a boy down the street had told this young boy to do this next time he had a baby-sitter. You see the boy didn't like his parents going out, and he didn't like having baby-sitters. So he felt this was the only way he could get rid of them. The boys [sic] don't have baby-sitters anymore; now they go to the nursery school.

## "The Roommate's Death"

Another especially popular example of the American adolescent shocker story is the widely-known legend of "The Roommate's Death." It shares several themes with other urban legends. As in "The Killer in the Backseat" and "The Babysitter and the Man Upstairs," it is usually a lone woman in the story who is threatened—or thinks she is—by a strange man. As in "The Hook," and "The Boyfriend's Death," the assailant is often said to be an escaped criminal or a maniac. Finally, as in the latter legend, the actual commission of the crime is never described; only the resulting mutilated corpse is. The scratching sounds outside the girl's place of refuge are an additional element of surprise. Here is a version told by a University of Kansas student in 1965 set in Corbin Hall, a freshman women's dormitory there:

These two girls in Corbin had stayed late over Christmas vacation. One of them had to wait for a later train, and the other wanted to go to a fraternity party given that night of vacation. The dorm assistant was in her room—sacked out. They waited and waited for the intercom, and then they heard this knocking and knocking outside in front of the dorm. So the girl thought it was her date and she went down. But she didn't come back and she didn't come back. So real late that night this other girl heard a scratching and

gasping down the hall. She couldn't lock the door, so she locked herself in the closet. In the morning she let herself out and her roommate had had her throat cut, and if the other girl had opened the door earlier, she [the dead roommate] would have been saved.

At all the campuses where the story is told the reasons for the girls' remaining alone in the dorm vary, but they are always realistic and plausible. The girls' homes may be too far away for them to visit during vacation, such as in Hawaii or a foreign country. In some cases they wanted to avoid a campus meeting or other obligation. What separates the two roommates may be either that one goes out for food, or to answer the door, or to use the rest room. The girl who is left behind may hear the scratching noise either at her room door or at the closet door, if she hides there. Sometimes her hair turns white or grey overnight from the shock of the experience (an old folk motif). The implication in the story is that some maniac is after her (as is suspected about the pursuer in "The Killer in the Backseat"); but the truth is that her own roommate needs help, and she might have supplied it had she only acted more decisively when the noises were first heard. Usually some special emphasis is put on the victim's fingernails, scratched to bloody stumps by her desperate efforts to signal for help.

A story told by a California teenager, remembered from about 1964, seems to combine motifs of "The Babysitter and the Man Upstairs" with "The Roommate's Death." The text is unusually detailed with names and the circumstances of the crime:

Linda accepted a baby-sitting job for a wealthy family who lived in a two-storey home up in the hills for whom she had never baby-sat before. Linda was rather hesitant as the house was rather isolated and so she asked a girlfriend, Sharon, to go along with her, promising Sharon half of the baby-sitting fee she would earn. Sharon accepted Linda's offer and the two girls went up to the big two-storey house.

The night was an especially dark and windy one and rain was threatening. All went well for the girls as they read stories aloud to the three little boys they were sitting for and they had no problem putting the boys to bed in the upstairs part of the house. When this was done, the girls settled down to watching television.

It was not long before the telephone rang. Linda answered the telephone, only to hear the heavy breathing of the caller on the other end. She attempted to elicit a response from the caller but he merely hung up. Thinking little of it and not wanting to panic Sharon, Linda went back to watching her television program, remarking that the caller had dialed a wrong number. Upon receiving the second call at which time the caller first engaged in a bit of heavy breathing and then instructed them to check on the children, the two girls became frightened and decided to call the operator for assistance. The operator instructed the girls to keep the caller on the line as long as possible should he call again so that she might be able to trace the call. The operator would check back with them.

The two girls then decided between themselves that one should stay downstairs to answer the phone. It was Sharon who volunteered to go upstairs. Shortly, the telephone rang again and Linda did as the operator had instructed her. Within a few minutes, the operator called back telling Linda to leave the house immediately with her friend because she had traced the calls to the upstairs phone.

Linda immediately hung up the telephone and proceeded to run to the stairway to call Sharon. She then heard a thumping sound coming from the stairway and when she approached the stairs she saw her friend dragging herself down the stairs by her chin, all of her limbs severed from her body. The three boys also lay dead upstairs in their beds.

Once again, the Indiana University Folklore Archive has provided the best published report on variants of "The Roommate's Death," Linda Dégh's summary of thirty-one texts and several subtypes and related plots collected since 1961. The most significant feature, according to her report, is the frequent appearance of a male rescuer at the end of the story. In one version, for example, two girls are left behind alone in the dorm by their roommate when she goes downstairs for food; they hear noises, and so stay in their room all night without opening the door. Finally the mailman comes around the next morning, and they call him from the window:

> The mailman came in the front door and went up the stairs, and told the girls to stay in their room, that everything was all right but that they were to stay in their rooms [sic]. But the girls didn't listen to him 'cause he had said it was all right, so they came out into the hall. When they opened the door, they saw their girlfriend on the floor with a hatchet in her head.

In other Indiana texts the helpful male is a handyman, a milkman, or the brother of one of the roommates.

According to folklorist Beverly Crane, the male-female characters are only one pair of a series of significant opposites, which also includes home and away, intellectual versus emotional behavior, life and death, and several others. A male is needed to resolve the female's uncertainty—motivated by her emotional fear—about how to act in a new situation. Another male has mutilated and killed her roommate with a blow to her head, "the one part of the body with which women are not supposed to compete." The girls, Crane suggested, are doubly out of place in the beginning, having left the haven of home to engage in intellectual pursuits, and having remained alone in the campus dormitory instead of rejoining the family on a holiday. Ironically, the injured girl must use her fingernails, intended to be long, lovely, feminine adornments, in order to scratch for help. But because her roommate fails to investigate the sound, the victim dies, her once pretty nails now bloody stumps.

Crane concluded this ingenious interpretation with these generalizations:

> The points of value implicit in this narrative are then two-fold. If women wish to depend on traditional attitudes and responses they had best stay in a place where these attitudes and responses are best able to protect them. If, however, women do choose to venture into the realm of equality with men, they must become less dependent, more self-sufficient, more confident in their own abilities, and, above all, more willing to assume responsibility for themselves and others.

One might not expect to find women's liberation messages embedded in the spooky stories told by teen-agers, but Beverly Crane's case is plausible and well argued. Furthermore, it is not at all unusual to find up-to-date social commentary in other modern folklore—witness the many religious and sexual jokes and legends circulated by people who would not openly criticize a church or the traditional social mores. Folklore does not just purvey the old codes of morality and behavior; it can also absorb newer ideas. What needs to be done to analyze this is to collect what Alan Dundes calls "oral-literary criticism," the informants' own comments about their lore. How clearly would the girls who tell these stories perceive—or even accept—the messages extrapolated by scholars? And a related question: Have any stories with clear liberationist themes replaced older ones cautioning young women to stay home, be good, and—next best—be careful, and call a man if they need help?

## "The Pet (or Baby) in the Oven"

The ghastliest believed horror story popular among adolescents (though it is told by older people too) is probably the one involving a living creature put into an oven. An old legend (approximately twenty years), and one that incorporates much older themes, it has recently merged in oral tradition with the baby-sitter stories.

### "HOT DOG!"

Folklorists as much as any scholars love to report a new discovery, so it was with understandable pride and delight that Professor Keith Cunningham of Northern Arizona University, Flagstaff, headlined an article in the Winter, 1979, issue of his quarterly journal *Southwest Folklore* "Hot Dog! Another Urban Belief Tale." He provided a sample of this "new" story (one of "more texts . . . than I can count" from the Arizona Friends of Folklore Archive):

> It seems there was an old lady who had been given a microwave oven by her children. After bathing her dog she

put it in the microwave to dry it off. Naturally, when she opened the door the dog was cooked from the inside out.

Other Arizona versions, Cunningham revealed, "involve not only dogs, but also birds, cats, and one unfortunate turtle." The tales, he said, illustrate that "modern technology has a way of getting out of control and wreaking ill instead of good."

The legend of the cooked dog or cat has enjoyed a good deal of recent circulation, but it is not a *new* tradition, having been around for twenty years or so in the form of a cautionary tale about the fates of unlucky pets that crawl into untended gas ovens or clothes dryers and are not noticed the next time the appliance is used. Around 1976 I began to hear the microwave-oven variants, and I inserted the following summary example from Utah into the second edition (1978) of my textbook *The Study of American Folklore:* "[a] child . . . accidentally sprinkles the cat with a hose and puts it into a microwave oven to dry out, whereupon the cat explodes (p. 111)." The phrase in the Arizona text, of the animal being "cooked from the inside out," more accurately describes the molecule-jiggling effect of microwaves than the account of the pet exploding in my text (the only way I have heard it). I am told, however, that eyes might possibly pop when bombarded with microwaves, just as eggs or potatoes are said to do if inserted into an oven whole. People's notions about what would happen to a living creature caught in a microwave oven are doubtless colored by a vague fear of the new devices and intensified by such things as the warning signs posted on public-access microwave ovens and the news stories about microwaves beamed by the Soviets into our foreign embassy. Whatever those mysterious invisible waves may do to a person—or to a pacemaker, as the posted warnings imply—they certainly would not be healthy for the family pet. The animal would surely cook and die in the oven, so the fear is quite realistic.

In Spring, 1978, Nancy Schlehuber, a student in my folklore class, read about the story in the textbook, then heard a similar version while at home visiting in Wills Point, Texas. Back in Utah again, she decided to survey the available material for her term project. Ms. Schlehuber collected a few examples of "scientific" versions of the story in which technicians who ought to have known better bypassed built-in safety features and operated their laboratory microwave ovens with open doors, thereby cooking their own insides as they stood nearby. The bulk of her findings (eighteen versions), however, were what she called "gross tales"—accounts of ordinary people foolishly putting thirteen pet cats, two wet dogs, and two damp human heads of hair into home microwave ovens to be dried, but instead to be cooked or exploded. (The eighteenth version, volunteered by her

informant after he heard another of the microwave legends, concerned a cat that was put by a precocious toddler into a trash compacter with a faulty key-lock system.) In most of her stories the pet is wet from a rain shower, a bath, or an accidental dousing with a hose; the helpful human is either a child (usually a boy) or an older woman. Informants claimed to have heard the stories from a few months to eight years earlier, and they mentioned news reports, as well as other oral accounts, "like the kid putting his cat in the washing machine and that kind of stuff." Both dog versions collected in Salt Lake City concerned poodles being bathed, one in New York and the other in California. The first text mentioned a transition from older to newer appliances:

> Sherrie . . . from Long Island, New York, told this story when there was lull in the conversation. . . . She heard about a lady who had poodles, and she always dried out her poodles in her [conventional] oven. Then she got a microwave, and so she tried to dry her poodles in the microwave; and, of course, the poodle blew up.

By Spring, 1979, the microwave-oven pet tragedy was becoming extremely well known, as folklorist Betty Jane Belanus found in her research. Her first examples of the story came from acquaintances in Toledo, Ohio, and Washington, D.C., both of whom remembered that a newly-washed poodle had been killed by the dangerous waves. Other midwestern versions assembled by Belanus described a dampened cat as often as a wet poodle being the victim. Again, newspaper reports or occasionally children's science or home economics teachers were the supposed sources for the tradition. Related details that Belanus collected were that a live animal's blood will boil in a microwave oven, that scientists use microwaves to kill laboratory animals, and that radiations from television sets are nearly as dangerous to the human body as microwaves. (Microwaves, it should be noted, actually do pose certain dangers to living creatures.)

## "THE HIPPIE BABY-SITTER"

The warnings in several "Hot Dog!" texts of the dangers to human beings of mishandling microwave ovens is a theme shared by another urban legend of this story cycle: the hippie baby-sitter who cooks alive a child placed in her care. Here we also see the influence of other baby-sitter scare-stories as well as of the numerous traditions discussed in Chapter 4 about unlikely creatures found in unexpected places. Folklorist Lydia Fish of the State University College in Buffalo, New York, took the first official scholarly notice in the United States of "The Hippie Baby-sitter" in 1971 when she inserted a request for versions of the story in a folklore journal. While she never received any folklorists' replies she did collect many examples from her own students. In the usual versions current in Buffalo, a somewhat freaky-looking baby-sitter is hired, often one who is previously unknown to the parents (or else new parents are leaving the baby with a sitter for the first time). The sitter gets high on marijuana (or LSD, or even Scotch) and cooks the "turkey," that is, the baby, in the oven. A typical New York state text:

> This couple with a teenage son and a little baby left the baby with this hippie-type girl who was a friend of the son's. They went to a dinner party or something, and the mother called in the middle of the evening to see if everything was all right.
>
> "Sure," the girl says. "Everything's fine. I just stuffed the turkey and put it in the oven."
>
> Well, the lady couldn't remember having a turkey, so she figured something was wrong. She and her husband went home, and they found that the girl had stuffed the baby and put it in the oven. Now the son used a lot of drugs, and this girl was a friend of his, so I guess they figure she took them too.... This is a true story. We had a meeting at school, and this psychologist told the story. I think he said that it happened to a friend's neighbor.

In Professor Fish's 1971 versions the turkey/baby is usually cooked to death before the parents arrive home, although in a few accounts they come back just in time to save their unlucky infant. In all but one version the sitter is thought or proved to be under the influence of drugs; the exception is a text from Binghamton, New York in which she is simply driven out of her mind by the child's behavior:

> After the parents left, the baby started crying. No matter what the sitter did, the baby would not stop. After a time, the baby's crying drove the sitter mad, and she put the kid in the oven and turned it up as high as it would go.

"The Hippie Baby-sitter" has developed along much the same lines across the country, as well as in Canada, as this Toronto version from 1973 illustrates:

> This story was told to me by a friend who heard it on the news on the radio a year or so ago. It is a factual account.
>
> There was a girl and she was baby-sitting. The parents had gone out to a very big party and had left this infant at home with this sixteen-year-old girl. So she was babysitting and they phoned just to see if everything was all right. She said, "Oh, fine. Everything's great. The turkey's in the oven." The mother went, "Oh, okay, fine," and she hung up. Then she looked at her husband and went, "The turkey's in the oven? We didn't have a turkey!" He said, "What's the matter?" So they decided they had better go home and see what was the matter. Maybe there was something wrong with the baby-sitter.
>
> They excused themselves from the party and went home. So they walked in the house and saw the baby-sitter sitting in the chair freaking out. She had put the little infant in the oven and had thought it was a turkey.

Two versions from the Brigham Young University folklore archive (Provo, Utah) give other details; in one the sitter reports to the parents that "your *roast* is done," and in the other the grim homecoming is described this way:

> When they arrived home, they could smell this awful sickening sweet smell. The mother rushed into the kitchen. There she found the table set for two with her best china and crystal. The lights were out and there were lit candles on the table. In the oven was their baby. The girl had roasted the baby! She said, "Look, I fixed a special dinner for you."

These Brigham Young University versions (1972, 1977) were both, of course, said to be absolutely true. One storyteller commented, however, "If that's true, I'm sick ... but like I said, that was told from a reliable source." (It was a relative of a friend of a friend, as usual.)

Versions of "The Hippie Baby-sitter" have been collected in Europe, particularly in Scandinavia, sometimes citing an American locale. The earlier occurrence of themes of infanticide in Europe probably explains why this particular modern legend has been so readily accepted there. For instance, in 1972 a Bergen, Norway, newspaper reported a "terror-tale" (*skrekkhistorie*) that shared some specific motifs of "The Hippie Baby-sitter." A couple just departing for a long overseas vacation leave their infant strapped into a highchair in readiness for the baby-sitter's expected arrival in a few minutes. But in different versions the sitter either dies suddenly, suffers an accident on the way there, or simply cannot get into the locked house and thinks the couple has taken the child along with them after all. Upon the parents' return, the baby is found still strapped in the chair where she has starved to death many days before. In this story the direct moral lesson, applicable to either parents or baby-sitters, is very clear, and the theme of the abandoned child (also found in Hansel and Gretel, for example) suggests a deeper level of aggression towards the baby.

The same gruesome tale about an untrustworthy baby-sitter has also circulated in a fully-localized form in Africa, as reported in 1979 by my folklore student Atim Eyere of Calabar, Nigeria. In 1976, Mrs. Eyere remembered, this terrible story swept through the government office where she was working:

> A certain lady who was working in the Ministry of Agriculture called her baby-sitter by telephone to see how her baby was doing. When her baby-sitter told her that the baby was still in bed, she asked her to take him out of bed and sit him up. The words in Efik—*men eyen oro k'etem*—could mean two things, either "sit the baby up" or "cook the baby." So the baby-sitter, being a novice, took this baby and put him in the oven and roasted him. When the mother

returned from work, she met the baby-sitter's eyes reddened like the setting sun. The mother said, "Come on, don't be so miserable about nothing. Please bring me my baby."

The baby-sitter, very silent, moved reluctantly to the oven and opened it, and behold the baby was stiff dead in the oven! "Wasn't that what you wanted?" With that she stepped out in a hurry, back to her house, leaving the mother of the baby with wild eyes, crying "My son? Dead?"

Mrs. Eyere was told that the incident happened on Afokang Street, so she asked a friend who lived there about the story. "Oh, no," she answered, "It was along Mayne Avenue." And, Mrs. Eyere told me, "for a few days the news kept traveling until it was all said to have really happened in a neighboring town."

Whether "The Hippie Baby-sitter" has been a direct influence on the "Hot Dog" story or not, the convergence of the two legends occurred recently with the appearance of versions in oral tradition in which the hippie sitter puts the turkey/baby into a microwave oven. Evidently this version has been around for some time too, for a friend of mine who demonstrated microwave ovens when they were first introduced in the United States told me that many people had asked her "What would happen if someone put a cat or a baby into a microwave oven and turned it on?" My friend commented, "I don't know why anyone would think of such a thing, it's so ghoulish." Most likely, they did not think of it themselves at all, but were trying to check on a strange story they had heard or read, about a little boy and his wet cat, an old lady and her poodle, or a freaked-out sitter and her infant charge. These stories answer the question "What would happen if . . ." with the assertion, "Well, this is what *did* happen once. . . ."

Some other cycles of horror stories in American folk tradition, as we have seen, warned against criminal or insane human antagonists. These newer legends reflect fears based on contemporary, often technological, threats while retaining reminders of earlier folkloric themes of child abandonment and infanticide. Given the persistence of such themes, and the current wide acceptance of microwave ovens despite their potential dangers, it seems predictable that such legends as "Hot Dog!" and microwave versions of "The Hippie Baby-sitter" would eventually develop to trouble the dreams of contemporary parents and children.

## QUESTIONS

1. How many of these legends are familiar to you? Did you believe them at the time? Did the details vary from those in the article? Did you pass on the legends to others?

2. What are some of the moral lessons that seem to be implied by the urban legends in the article?

3. Are there any other stories you have heard in the past that you now recognize as urban legends?

Karen Janszen

# 49. Meat of Life

*One common form of collective behavior is the fad, a temporary form of conduct that attracts a body of enthusiastic adherents. Notable fads of recent years have included fascinations with the hula hoop, roller disco, CB radio, streaking, so-called organic foods, and video games.*

*Fads have certain characteristics in common. First, their appeal is short-lived, for it relies largely on novelty. Once "everybody is doing it," the appeal wears off. Second, fads are usually regarded a little scornfully by most of the population, who see the actual participants as blindly following a trend simply because it has "caught on." Third, fads appeal primarily to adolescents and young adults, for they seem to provide a means of asserting personal identity; older people, with more stable and secure personalities, are less inclined to indulge themselves in sudden and novel enthusiasms. But fads are not necessarily of little or no significance, for behavior that starts out as a fad can sometimes have an enduring effect if, directly or indirectly, it becomes permanently incorporated into the culture.*

*In this article, Karen Janszen examines a new fad, found primarily on the West Coast: the practice by parents of eating the afterbirth when their child is born.*

"It was a conceptually mind-blowing and radical thing to do. I approached it in a reverent way because it felt spiritual, like something I wouldn't do lightly."

What this American from Seattle found astounding, not just to witness but to experience, was placentophagia. Like some residents of Los Angeles and Boston, he did not journey far to take part in this unusual practice. In fact, he traveled no farther than his own backyard. "It was a natural cadence to the birth—the whole birth was a wonder."

Placentophagia, the act of eating a newborn baby's placenta, has probably been practiced in the United States for as long as the American home-birth movement has been important—about a decade—and may be growing more commonplace as home births continue to increase in popularity.

By having babies at home, parents wind up holding the placenta. What some hospitals sell for about 50 cents to drug and cosmetic companies, some Americans are planting, dumping in the garbage, flushing down the toilet—or eating.

Americans who eat placenta are individualists who do what they believe is natural and take it seriously. Like most parents who prefer home over hospital as their baby's place of birth, placenta eaters tend to be young, white, middle class and college educated. Some are bookkeepers, college teachers, land surveyors, community counselors, furniture designers and chiropractors. But placenta eaters have more often experimented with alternatives such as food cooperatives and macrobiotic vegetarianism.

Midwives from different regions of the United States, the people most knowledgeable about home-birth practices, estimate that placenta eating now occurs following roughly 1 to 2 percent of home births in East Coast states and after about 5 percent in West Coast states.

While there is no consensus among placenta eaters on what "natural" is—solar heating, meatless spaghetti sauce or giving birth without painkillers—all agree there is nothing more "natural" than eating placenta, and that is why they do it. To them, "natural" is what is assumed to be healthful and fitting to the human species. In short, since they believe many other mammals and members of some human societies eat placenta, they assume it must make good sense nutritionally and medically and that the reason Americans do not normally do so is because we are overcivilized.

## Birth Ritual

If placenta eating is natural in concept, it may be more than natural in practice—it may be a new American birth ritual. The occasion is the celebration of a successful home birth.

A human placenta is a small, soft, beefy disk; it is about eight inches long, one and a half inches thick and weighs approximately a pound. It is expelled during the third stage of labor, 15 to 30 minutes after the birth of a baby. For this reason, it is commonly called the afterbirth. Both the placenta and the embryo are made by the fertilized ovum, though the placenta contains maternal as well as fetal blood.

The spongy, blood-filled organ acts as a fetal lung, intestine and kidney and is almost solely responsible for the intra-uterine welfare of the developing fetus. Substances such as salts, amino acids, simple fats and vitamins are exchanged between maternal and fetal bloodstreams via the placenta and umbilical cord. The placenta itself produces progesterone, estrogen and other steroids as well as protein hormones, all necessary to the maintenance of a pregnancy.

While most hospitals incinerate placentas along with other biological waste, some hospitals sell them to pharmaceutical or cosmetic companies that extract the hormones and proteins for use in manufacturing drugs or beauty products. Hospitals associated with medical schools or research institutions often collect them for use in experimental research. Scientists are still working out the details of what the placenta does and how it does it. They say knowledge of placental actions and functions may assist cancer, organ-aging and birth-control research. A few placenta-based beauty products, such as TiaZolin Placenta, an instant hair-repair treatment, list human placenta extract as an ingredient, but most are made from less expensive bovine placenta bought from slaughterhouses.

Placenta is eaten raw or cooked, depending on the sensitivity of diners' palates and stomachs. When cooking it smells like liver frying and even tastes like liver or kidney but is sweeter and milder. It is tender meat. Cooking preparations range from simple to gourmet, limited only by the imaginations of the chefs—usually the new fathers. Placenta can be boiled in salted water, pan fried in butter and garlic, stir fried in soy sauce with

vegetables, sautéd in wine and spices, or sun dried in strips for jerky. Placenta stew is an old favorite; a recipe can be found in the *Birth Book,* a popular collection of first-person accounts of home birth.

Many American placenta eaters admit they found the thought of placenta eating shocking and unimaginable at first. But in time the skeptical and squeamish not only got used to the idea but began to feel it was a good one. "I used to make jokes about placenta burgers, but it began to sound very natural to me in a primitive way," says a father who ate part of his newborn son's placenta.

Placenta eaters believe that some native American tribeswomen ate their placentas by custom and that other mammals eat their placentas by instinct. Placenta eating is viewed as the natural conclusion to the birth process—nature's way of restoring needed hormones, iron and nutrients to contract the uterus, heal tissues and enrich a mother's blood.

## "Unkilled Meat"

Surprisingly, vegetarians are enthusiastic about eating placenta. Some vegetarians simply do not classify placenta as meat. Others do but feel placenta is not taboo for reasons that depend on why they follow a meatless regime. Vegetarians who avoid meat so as not to be party to the killing of another living being for food believe placenta is the only "unkilled" meat available. They reason, "Nobody had to die to get this meat; it is meat of life, not death."

Vegetarians who do not eat meat because they believe most meat sold for public consumption to be contaminated with chemicals and additives say placenta is of known composition and origin if the mother has eaten unadulterated foods. "The whole idea struck us as so perfect that after the birth you eat that concentrated food—meat is the most concentrated form of food—especially if it's your own body and you know what it is. What has come out, you put back in," says one.

Unlike many other vegetarians, placenta-eating vegetarians do not deny that meat contains essential amino acids and vitamins.

Most terrestrial placental mammals eat the afterbirth. This is true of domesticated animals such as cats and dogs, as well as of wild animals such as antelopes and monkeys. Primatologists claim that all monkey mothers lick the afterbirth and usually eat it, too, if other aspects of the delivery have gone normally.

The placenta is either grasped in the mouth by mammalian females and consumed as it emerges from the vaginal opening, or it is picked up off the ground and eaten along with fetal membranes, amniotic fluid, blood and mucus. The placenta is eaten regardless of normal diet. Even such exclusively herbivorous, or vegetarian, mammals as guinea pigs, deer and giraffes eat the afterbirth.

Why mammals eat the placenta is a matter of conjecture among ethologists. Since the placenta contains lactogenic, or milk-stimulating, hormones, its consumption by the female may help establish lactation. Some herbivores, such as the deerlike impala, may consume the afterbirth to clean up the birth site. By eating the odorous birth products, mothers may prevent their relatively helpless newborn from being detected by predators.

The placenta is a more obvious source of nutrition for carnivorous mammals. Placenta, as animal tissue, may provide enough nourishment to make it unnecessary for a female to leave her young to hunt for food for herself during their first day of life. While childbirth customs and the fate of the placenta have interested few travelers, historians or even ethnographers until recently, human placentophagia is referred to in the Bible and has been reported in several areas of the world.

The concluding verses of chapter 28 of Deuteronomy in the King James Version warn the Israelites of punishments they will incur if their Lord's wishes are not heeded. A man shall be forced to "eat the fruit of thine own body, the flesh of thy sons and of thy daughters," while a woman will look toward "her young one that cometh out from between her feet, and toward her children which she shall bear; for she shall eat them...." According to Dr. William Ober, an obstetrical and gynecological pathologist interested in placentophagia, the phrase "that cometh out from between her feet," written in the Greek text as *chorion* and as *secundinae partes* in the Vulgate, clearly refers to the placenta. Ober believes the passage may refer to "a remote tribal memory, now suppressed, of a period when placentas were eaten, at least in times of famine."

## Secret Eaters

In an obscure book on tribal obstetrics published in 1883, Dr. G. J. Englemann, an American professor of obstetrics from Missouri Medical College, wrote of human placentophagia that some of the women of Brazil, "if it can be done secretly, eat the organ which has been recently expelled in a solitary labor. If observed, they bury or burn it."

Anthropoligists have found that placenta is consumed in small portions in cultures that have faith in its medicinal powers. Dr. Donn Hart of Northern Illinois University reports that in the Philippines a new mother will occasionally be fed a porridge by a midwife, containing, without her knowledge, a minute amount of charred placenta or a few drops of placental blood. This secret addition is thought to help the mother regain her strength and guard against relapse. According to Southeast Asia specialist Dr. Richard Coughlin, there are numerous medical prescriptions in traditional Sino-Vietnamese medicine that call for powdered placenta as an ingredient. Such drugs are thought to cure disorders ranging from sterility to senility.

What some mammalian species seem to do instinctively and what some human societies have learned is that the afterbirth is indeed good food for a new mother who has just lost blood during a delivery. While not advocating human-placenta eating, Dr. Judith Wurtman, a member of the Department of Nutrition and Food Science at Massachusetts Institute of Technology, admits that placenta, like any organ rich in blood, contains a wealth of iron, vitamins and proteins. Because of the iron alone, the Harvard biologist John Kirsch believes eating placenta is a "very good idea" for a mother and not eating it is "truly a waste."

## Great Source of Iron

Several medical doctors agree. "Why waste a solid beefsteak containing a pint of blood," asks endocrinologist Ann Forbes of Massachusetts General Hospital. "It is nutritionally equivalent to a pound of liver or any other raw, bloody meat." Dr. Sanford Rosenberg, a reproductive endocrinologist who teaches at the Medical College of Virginia, says, "Placenta seems to be an extraordinary source of iron because it is a very vascular, rapidly growing tissue with a tremendous amount of blood in it."

Placenta may also contain some unknown beneficial substance, according to some physicians. "There must be something unique in it, since most other mammals eat it," says Dr. Forbes. "Predator concealment is an unlikely reason, because the smell of the afterbirth will probably remain no matter how well it is cleaned up." Other doctors suggest that the placenta's hormones, specifically the prostaglandins, may assist muscle contraction; other hormones such as estrogens and placental lactogen may promote blood clotting and lactation respectively. Dr. Forbes points out that human mothers are unusual among mammalian females in having a two-to-three-day delay in milk production—a delay conceivably related to a failure to eat placenta. There are also those who argue that placentophagia among humans may be neither appropriate, natural nor healthful.

For starters, most mammals eat the placenta immediately after the birth; the mother alone and unaided chews the umbilical cord and licks the newborn clean. Eating the placenta is the final step in a sequence of birth actions taken by the female. Females tend to seclude themselves from males for birthing, and so males rarely if ever assist females with cleaning the newborn or eating the placenta.

Some American placenta eaters are aware of the novelty of male placenta consumption. Says one man, "Eating the placenta was nothing for my wife, but it was from her body. When I watched her eat it, it seemed to me like the appropriate thing for her to do, as it is for a mother cat. Male cats certainly wouldn't. I was eating it just to do it—for the experience. I certainly didn't need the nourishment. It's like the difference between biting your own fingernails and biting someone else's. It's just not appropriate."

In fact, placenta may not be all that welcome in the male body, particularly because of its estrogen content. Estrogen has a feminizing effect on males, promoting breast growth, for example, when consumed in large quantities over extended periods. And cooking, while destroying much of what is physiologically active in placenta, does not inactivate estrogen. "Since there is estrogen in the placenta at the time of birth, a male would consume a certain amount of it when eating placenta," says Dr. Rosenberg. But, he adds, "this estrogen is not likely to be orally effective since it cannot be absorbed by the body from the digestive tract." Most doctors concur that "one dose" of placenta is not dangerous to males but that chronic ingestion may be less safe.

Apes, the animals most closely related to humans and the most similar to the animals from which we evolved, frequently leave the placenta unconsumed. While members of other groups of primates, such as prosimians and monkeys, normally eat the placenta, chimpanzees may consume it only in a third to a half of all births. Dr. Jane Goodall reports that a wild chimpanzee, like a captive one in the London Zoo, did not eat the placenta but carried it around together with her infant until it was flyblown and stinking. Gorillas and orangs, at least in captivity, usually do not eat placenta, but they may nibble and suck on it.

Human placentophagia seems to have been relatively uncommon. According to the Human Relations Area File, which documents past and current customs of hundreds of societies throughout the world, the eating of fresh, whole placenta by humans is rare. Even some reported instances of human placentophagia may be suspect.

However, anthropologists have observed the placenta being burned or buried. In most non-Western human cultures, the placenta is an object treated with great respect and is often the subject of a variety of superstitions as well. Some cultures regard it as the baby's brother, others as a twin, as a blood relative of the same sex or as a guardian spirit. Proper disposal is deemed necessary, for what becomes of the placenta might affect the newborn's health or intelligence or his mother's or father's fertility.

## Superstitions

Hopi Indians traditionally bury the placenta at the village's edge so that no one can walk on it. Stepping on a placenta is thought to cause sore and chapped feet, yellowing of the eyes, and thick urine. The Arikara Indians wrap the afterbirth in a bundle along with tobacco and a wisp of sage and hang it in the branches of a thorny tree. Smoke offerings are made and prayers said to encourage disease to attack the bundle, not the newborn. Among the Caticugans of the Philippines, the father buries the placenta to increase the bonds of affection between himself and his new child.

Among Americans who have home births, many buy berry bushes or young fruit trees and place the placenta in the hole dug for planting. The child grows up along with a special tree. Ravin Lang, co-author of the *Birth Book* and a California midwife, claims many parents will not throw placenta away. She is told, "It's too sacred an organ to put in the garbage and to take to the dump." We bury our dead, so why not bury our placentas?

Friends, even doctors, attending home births where the family does not want the placenta sometimes claim it for their gardens and compost pits. But beware, warns Dr. Kirsch: The placenta's iron content may make it a poor fertilizer.

The relative absence of placenta eating among humans has not gone unnoticed. Although the human species is usually distinguished from other animals, including primates, by the presence of unique features such as upright walking and symbolic language, the animal ecologist G. E. Hutchinson has suggested that the human species be defined by the unique absence of a feature: humans can be defined as the primate that does not normally eat placenta.

Harvard's Erik Trinkaus, an expert on human evolution, speculates that humans may not be placenta eaters by nature because our apelike ancestors probably stopped routinely eating placenta when they began cleaning newborns by washing and wiping rather than by the usual mammalian licking. An anthropologist with the San Diego Zoo, Dr. Donald Lindburg, agrees that the loss of placenta eating occurred during the gradual shift from performing tasks with the mouth to performing them with the hands that charcterized human evolution. Cleaning by licking may be the link in the chain of behaviors between birthing and placenta eating, broken sometime during the last million years or more of our past.

Some researchers argue that if placenta eating were adaptive to humans in any way, such as predator avoidance, nutrition or lactation, it would have survived as a universal human behavior.

Dr. Gary Mitchell, a psychologist at the University of California, suggests that the absence of placenta eating in humans may reflect the diminishing reliance on hormones to trigger behaviors such as maternal care in the more advanced primates. Decreasing reliance on placenta eating is already evident in the great apes. The zoologist R. F. Ewer suggests that the chimpanzee habit of carrying the placenta around until it rots is a transitional behavior. "It seems as though the usual habit of eating the placenta is being abandoned, but no satisfactory alternative method of disposing of it has been evolved."

Ewer posits two ways in which placenta eating may actually be maladaptive to apes. Simian mothers may have tended to eat the placenta too enthusiastically, injuring the newborn in the process. Or possibly, in eating the placenta too quickly, mothers deprived newborns of the placenta blood that could have given them a useful reserve of iron.

## Organic-Food Craze?

Clearly, in America, placenta eating is not strictly "natural" in practice even if it is "natural" in rationale. Americans are taking metaphors from nature and elaborating on them. And for the most part they know this. But, if American placentophagia is more than just functional "natural" behavior, what is it? Is it an unusual organic-food craze rooted in back-to-natural ideas? Or is it perhaps a deeply personal and expressive act that satisfies some psychological need?

Those Americans who eat placenta do not agree on its cultural origins or its personal or social importance. To some, placenta eating is "just a thing," "a neat idea," "a fad," "an immediate experience only," which is not mentioned to one's conservative parents.

Many of these Americans feel that placenta eating is part of the ultimate natural childbirth. Says one, "We share a very strong desire to return to basics, a back-to-nature collection of ideas. We think of placenta eating as a symbol of that."

These placenta eaters, very self-conscious about what is natural, approach placentophagia nonchalantly, for the most part, as a practice totally acceptable in their social circles. "I have never been to a party where the idea is to have a feast with a baby's placenta, but I know plenty of people who have," says one.

At the same time, even at the same party, there may be people who say the act of consuming placenta has more meaning, meaning related to both the novelty of the situation and the presence of friends. The words *ritual, ceremony, spiritual, sacred* and *reverence* are fre-

quently used by such placenta eaters when describing their feelings and actions.

But placenta eaters, if they feel moved, feel moved to different degrees. "I felt that if I ate the stew, I would be acknowledging some kind of special relationship to the baby," one said.

An anthropology graduate student likens her presence at a home-birth party and her consumption of placenta to "one of those field experiences like going into the bush and eating grubs."

If the placenta eaters cannot agree on what placenta eating is all about, neither can the social scientists. Most are surprised to hear of American placentophagia, knowing its rarity among the world's cultures, but they will obligingly speculate about what they think is going on.

The Harvard anthropologist Nur Yalman notes that hospital procedure and paperwork usually authenticate the birth and paternity of a child in our society. "In taking births out of hospitals, you take away the bureaucracy as well. The less the bureaucracy, the more the need for some form of hocus-pocus."

Dr. Irven DeVore, an anthropologist, views placenta eating in the United States as "one of various symbolic ways for bringing about stronger social and psychological investment by fathers and by a community in a child."

DeVore and Yalman both think that the social act of eating together, rather than the food itself, is what is crucial. In contrast, other researchers believe the act of eating placenta is especially significant because placenta is human flesh.

Cooked placenta is human flesh. And eating human flesh is usually considered cannibalism. Yet a placenta eater may feel "no more like a cannibal than a Martian." To them, cannibals are "savages" or starving wagon-train pioneers or airplane-crash survivors.

But placenta eating does count as cannibalism, and its practitioners know this subconsciously if not consciously, according to biologists and social scientists alike. Dr. Kirsch says, "Anyone who doesn't see placenta eating as cannibalism must be performing some sort of mental acrobatics. While the placenta is genetically related to both parents and physically grows in the mother, it is created from embryonic tissues. Thus, eating placenta is eating a piece of the child. No matter how you cut it, it's eating human flesh."

## Pros and Cons

Experts on the subject of cannibalism agree with Kirsch. In his recent book, *The Man-Eating Myth*, anthropologist William Arens argues that socially sanctioned cannibalism has never existed anywhere. He believes placenta eating is not cannibalism in the classic sense of eating someone's flesh but that it falls under the general heading of a term such as blood drinking. "It's a very strange case," he says. "The problem is that it doesn't seem to be part of anyone." The author of *Cannibalism* and self-taught psychoanalytic sociologist, Eli Sagan, declares, "Psychologically, if in no other way, it is cannibalism. Placenta is eaten for the same kinds of reasons."

Cannibalism has been reported in many parts of the world, including Fiji, New Guinea, northwestern America, Nigeria, Zaire and Australia, and evidence of it has been found in a Neanderthal archeological site near Rome. It is a behavior that humans share with gorillas, chimpanzees and several other types of primates, as well as other kinds of animals. In some human societies, people eat, during mourning ceremonies, part of a relative who has died of accidental or natural causes. In other societies, only people outside the group, killed during warfare or head-hunting expeditions, are eaten. Different societies are said to favor different parts of the body. The more meaty arms and legs are usually preferred, but skin, liver, brain, genitalia and bone narrow are also eaten.

Many anthropologists think human flesh is consumed for psychological reasons. The wish to acquire the deceased's courage or other personal qualities may motivate cannibalistic acts. Cannibalism is also viewed as a way of dealing with something that is threatening by consuming it. Eli Sagan believes "affectionate" cannibalism, the eating of dead relatives, satisfies the anger of survivors toward the deceased for abandoning them. "Aggressive" cannibalism, the eating of slain enemies, is thought by Sagan to be the ultimate revenge.

To Sagan, American placenta eating combines the affectionate and aggressive motives. "It is aggressive because it is a way of symbolically killing and eating the infant and affectionate because it is a way of identifying with the child. It is an ambivalent situation, but the net result is affectionate: the child lives."

Social scientists agree that American placentophagia is a "very odd business," a practice that is probably even more repugnant to a majority of Americans than black magic, witchcraft and other unconventional activities. People react to it much as they do to another forbidden act, incest. And placenta eaters know this—it's part of why it is such a mind-boggling experience for them.

Most Americans who have eaten placenta felt fine about it when it happened, but some are slightly embarrassed and a little defensive in retrospect. One mother says, "It seemed like a fine thing to do at the time. The first person I thought I wouldn't tell was my mother. Now I am more embarrassed than I was then."

One placenta eater, though unusual in considering herself a cannibal, recalls that she didn't think of it as a violation of her value system. "I'm not ashamed of it now, and I don't think I did anything morally reprehensible."

The anthropologist Bradd Shore of Sarah Lawrence College observes that "We live in a permissive and narcissistic society, one based on individual freedom and self-indulgence, one that gives people incentive to break what are seen as artificial social rules by glorifying what is natural."

Shore believes that people's curiosity about placenta eating is connected to the attention currently being paid to the once forbidden subjects of incest and cannibalism. "These are behaviors that represent the last frontiers of what supposedly makes us human," says Shore. "The conquering of frontiers has always been a part of the American consciousness. The same license to conquer nature that Americans attribute to humans is often presumed in the popular mind as a license to conquer our own nature. If incest and cannibalism are held up as limits, it is perfectly consistent for these limits also to fall." Shore thinks that placenta eating allows people to "play" with the idea of cannibalism.

## "Some Mothers Crave It"

Whatever is behind it, consumption of the afterbirth will only take hold as a new American birth custom if home births continue to rise in popularity. According to Dr. David Stewart, of the National Association of Parents and Professionals for Safe Alternatives in Childbirth, the number of out-of-hospital births has tripled nationwide since 1973 and now accounts for over 2 percent of all registered American births. In California, Oregon and Washington, the number of out-of-hospital births has been doubling every year and may be as high as 15–20 percent of 1980 California births. At the same time, placenta eating is "slowly catching on," says Ravin Lang. "There is something very powerful about that meat. Some mothers crave it."

Just the same, placentophagia is not for everyone. It may not be natural to human beings in an evolutionary sense, but it is probably at worst harmless to one's health and is even perhaps beneficial to one's social and psychological well-being. All the evidence isn't in yet—and it might be years before a combination of biomedical, social and psychological research gives us the whole story.

---

## QUESTIONS

1. What is your reaction to the idea of eating the afterbirth? Explain your response.

2.  Do you think that eating the afterbirth will prove to have been a fad practiced by the few, or do you think it might become a widely accepted practice in American culture? Justify your answer.

3.  It may come as little surprise that this fad is practiced primarily in California. Why do you think California has its reputation as the origin of so many fads and social trends?

John Gliedman

# 50. The Wheelchair Rebellion

*History does not "just happen." Within the context of
the time and place in which human events occur, people
shape their own destinies, whether they do it consciously
or not. And a deliberate attempt to change society need
not arise only from the political leadership: often, broad
masses of people join together to resist or bring about
social change—sometimes on a small scale, sometimes
with sweeping effects. Social movements are of
particular interest to sociologists precisely because they
represent a collective attempt to actively intervene in the
process of social change.*

*Particularly since the 1960s, the United States has
seen campaigns by a number of social movements,
usually for the protection or enhancement of certain
rights. Prominent among these have been the
movements for civil rights, for women's liberation, for
gay liberation, for the rights of the aged, for the
protection of the environment, for consumer rights,
against nuclear power, and against abortion. More
recently, another social movement has begun to
promote the interests of a neglected group of
Americans—the nearly 20 million people who suffer
social and economic discrimination because of their
handicapped status.*

*In this article, John Gliedman outlines some of the
problems faced by the handicapped and describes the
goals that their social movement hopes to achieve.*

By the early 1970s, many of the nation's black leaders,
political activists, and liberal reformers had been exhausted by a decade of confrontation and violence. Un-
daunted, or perhaps too desperate to care, people with
various kinds of handicaps nevertheless began to organize a civil rights movement of their own. A new generation of groups for the disabled was born, such as the
American Coalition of Citizens with Disabilities and
Mainstream, Inc. Like older and more established
groups, they lobbied for better social services and protested the endless Catch-22 provisions in the welfare laws
that hurt the severely disabled. But they also demanded
something more: they called for significant structural
changes in housing, public buildings, and transportation
that have long posed barriers to their mobility; and they
began working for an end to the prejudice and job discrimination that had proved far more obstructive to an
active life than such handicaps as blindness, deafness,
or paraplegia.

For all its achievements in the rehabilitation and
education laws of the 1970s, what many have called the
"Quiet Revolution" in disability was an incomplete and
one-sided revolution. It was one-sided because the new
image of the handicapped as an oppressed minority group
was held only by some of the disabled themselves, their
relatives, and many professionals who cared for them.
The legislative reforms that the organizers succeeded in
winning in the 70s were not the result of massive grass-
roots pressure from millions of handicapped people and
their able-bodied allies. Moreover, key provisions in the
laws are in jeopardy because of the recent Supreme Court
ruling that held that a college is not required to admit a
deaf person who cannot benefit from the program without substantial modification of its standards.

Even today, the civil rights movement for the disabled is relatively small. The impetus for change comes
from the top. A sympathetic Congress (many of whose
members themselves have disabled relatives), the efforts
of diligent lobbyists, the initiative of legal advocates, and
a federal bureaucracy receptive, at least in principle, to

the idea of treating the disabled as another disadvantaged minority group—all contributed to the relatively unpublicized passage of land-mark legislation in the 1970s. Nevertheless, Frank Bowe, director of the American Coalition, sized up the status of the movement this way: "It is possible to legislate rights, and this has been done. But rights become reality only after political struggle."

Bowe says more than half of all working-age disabled adults who could work are jobless. There is systematic discrimination against those who do work, according to Bowe and others, which keeps them in menial or futureless jobs; across the United States, a network of "sheltered workshops" employs 200,000 handicapped people whose wages average under $1 an hour—far less than the minimum wage. Little energy goes to inventing, producing, or marketing products specially designed for the disabled, and what is marketed generally goes through the medical or social-service system as mediator. Thus are the handicapped barred from behaving as independent producers, consumers, and citizens in the economy.

Along with those tangible disadvantages, the disabled must also cope with a kind of paternalism from their able-bodied allies that has long·been discredited in race relations. Even today, many unprejudiced Americans accept traditional stereotypes about different kinds of handicaps. However, instead of reacting cruelly because of the fears and anxieties aroused by those disabilities, we take a more humane approach. We extend to handicapped people what seems to be an enlightened model of medical tolerance. Rather than blame them for their pitiful condition, we say that their social and mental incompetence is produced by a disease or a diseaselike condition beyond their control to alter. We believe that, in a social sense, they are chronic patients; and that we owe them the same struggle with our fears and prejudices, the same understanding and tolerance, that we owe victims of any serious disease or injury.

The problem with this analysis, from the disabled person's point of view, is that it allows him or her no scope whatsoever for leading an adult social life. As Talcott Parsons first noted, the role of a patient in middle-class society is functionally very similar to that of a child. We expect the patient to be cheerful and accepting, to obey doctors' orders, and, in general, to devote all his energies to getting well. When an able-bodied person falls sick, he ceases to be judged as an adult; in return, he is expected to work actively to get well. The area defined as his to control shifts to the sickbed. But in America a person labeled handicapped is assigned a specially destructive variant of the sick role. Not merely powerless because he is sick, he is defined as doubly powerless because he cannot master the job of "getting

well." Unable to fill that role obligation, he is seen as socially powerless, deprived of a political identity—until he chooses to assert one.

Many members of the civil rights movement for the disabled have told me that the annual cerebral palsy telethon symbolizes for them the deeply humiliating paternalism of society's medical tolerance toward handicapped people. Michael Poachovis, a political organizer on the West Coast, said, "It's absolutely degrading. Watching those telethons you might think that all palsied adults are mentally retarded, pathetically trusting, asexual children." Others find little comfort in the usual image of disabled people presented in the media. Ron Whyte, a writer in New York City, summed up his feelings this way: "You don't learn about Harlem by listening to 'Amos 'n' Andy'." Only rarely are we forced to confront the paternalism that lurks behind our attempts to deal fairly with the handicapped. Witness the discomfort of audiences watching Jon Voight as a demanding, rebellious, and unabashedly erotic crippled veteran in the recent film *Coming Home*.

Over the past five years, I have studied the problems of disability while on the research staff of the Carnegie Council on Children. Handicapped children were the point of departure for my work. But, along with my colleague William Roth, I eventually devoted as much time to adults as to children, since the problems of the different age groups tend to be closely related.

In the 1960s and 1970s, about 20 million people of working age described themselves as disabled. Those estimates might easily be 50 percent too high or too low. They might be too low because they do not include most people whom a psychologist would classify as mildly retarded; most people who have experienced a major mental illness; or those with speech or learning disabilities. The figures might be too high because they are based upon answers to the question, "Do you have any medical condition or other impairment lasting three months or longer that limits the kind or amount of work that you can do?" Answers given to this kind of question are highly unreliable. On the other hand, it is perfectly possible that these contradictory factors cancel out, and that the figure of 20 million is not too far off after all.

Accepting this estimate provisionally, it seems reasonable to assume that disabled people comprise between 5 and 10 percent of the total working-age population. This is a huge number, at least as large as the number of able-bodied hispanics in this age range and quite possibly as large as the number of able-bodied blacks.

Disabilities are, of course, much more common among the elderly. The best guess is that between one-third and one-fourth of all people 65 years or older are currently disabled. But the sociological relationships between disability and old age require further study; it is quite possible that the social experiences of most elderly people in possession of their mental faculties can also be described by the minority-group model of disability, which views the social stigma as attached to the condition of being aged rather than a result of any actual disability.

It is even more difficult to assess the number of children with real disabilities. Many kinds of handicaps that pass unnoticed among adults may be blown up out of proportion by parents, teachers, and a child's peers. A host of clinical findings also suggests that perceptions of the severity of a handicap are exquisitely sensitive to social milieu. What some people in one social stratum treat as a mild or negligible disability may be considered severely disabling in another. For the present, one can only guess that the total number of disabled children and youths lies somewhere between five and 10 million.

Members of an oppressed social group have little in common apart from the fact that society singles them out for systematic oppression. Examples abound: European Jews in the 1920s and 1930s, many of whom did not consider themselves primarily Jewish; and, closer to home, women, homosexuals, the elderly. Similarly, handicapped people are beginning to see themselves as an oppressed minority because society exposes most of them to a common set of pressures that violate their civil rights. Long ago, the social psychologist Kurt Lewin called the defining characteristic of a minority group an "interdependence of fate." Discrimination—much of it in the economic marketplace—constitutes the sociological fate of the disabled. This discrimination imposes a minority-group identity upon a collection of adults and children, each of whom has, in most other respects, as much in common with able-bodied people as with one another.

Two or three decades ago, sociologists often studied the phenomenon of "passing"—the attempt of light-skinned blacks to pass as whites, of Jews to pass as gentiles. That phenomenon helps to clarify the relevance of a minority-group analysis to disabled people. The first group of disabled people who fit the minority-group model are those who can rarely pass as able-bodied. They include the deaf, the blind, the physically disabled, the cosmetically disfigured, the very short, and individuals with chronic diseases whose symptoms are unpleasant and obtrusive. Another group of disabled people encounters many of the same problems as the black who passed as white in the 1930s or 1940s. They can usually come off as able-bodied, but they often pay a high psychological price for their successful strategies of concealment. The passers include many people once institutionalized in mental hospitals or custodial institutions for the mildly retarded; many epileptics; many people

with severe reading disabilities; many with concealable but socially stigmatizing medical conditions or chronic diseases.

For most people with cancer, heart disease, diabetes, and back ailments, the minority-group analysis is probably of secondary importance. Still, even those with such disabilities would benefit greatly from an end to job discrimination against disabled persons, improvement in the quality of the nation's social and health services, and, in many instances, elimination of architectural and transportation barriers to mobility. One other group of disabled adults requires mention—those who are so incapacitated by their mental or emotional limitations that they could not lead normal lives even if society's considerable prejudice against them were to melt away. That group includes the severely (and intractably) psychotic, and somewhere between one-tenth and one-fourth of all mentally retarded people.

Measured against two centuries of neglect, stigma, and degradation, the gains registered by disabled people in the 1970s were impressive indeed. Even as the Equal Rights Amendment for women was stalled, Congress overrode two Nixon vetoes of the first legislation that specifically prohibited discrimination against disabled workers. The legislation, the Rehabilitation Act of 1973, required affirmative-action or nondiscriminatory hiring programs to be instituted in all federal agencies for all federal contractors doing more than $2,500-a-year worth of work for the government, as well as in any public or private organization that receives federal funds.

The section of the Rehabilitation Act dealing with discrimination against the disabled has been regularly challenged and regularly reaffirmed in the courts. But in June, the Supreme Court established limits on its scope when it ruled that Southeastern Community College in North Carolina was within its rights in refusing admission of Frances B. Davis, a hearing-impaired woman, to its nursing program. Mrs. Davis, who relies largely on lip-reading to understand others, is a practical nurse who sought admission to the clinical part of the registered-nurse curriculum that would have brought her into contact with patients. Reversing an appeals court ruling, the justices held that the law does not require a college to compromise its admission standards or make "extensive modifications" of its program to accommodate all handicapped persons; it prohibits only discrimination against those who are "otherwise qualified" in spite of their handicaps.

Leaders of handicapped people's organizations believe that while the decision establishes a potentially harmful precedent, it may apply to only a small number of cases. "It's the kind of case I call a 'blind busdriver' claim," said Leslie Milk, executive director of Mainstream, Inc., implying that it is not unreasonable for an employer to refuse to let a blind man drive a bus. "The court ruled very narrowly, apparently to limit the implications of the decision, and left it to HEW to go on clarifying the situation as it makes regulations. It's a limitation on the law, but one we can live with."

Frank Bowe of the American Coalition also thinks the court's decision makes some sense. Bowe, who is himself deaf, said that most people would agree that hearing impairment could prevent a nurse from responding effectively to a patient in all critical situations. "But most disabled people are like me," Bowe said, "They want to enter fields where their disability doesn't interfere with the job." But both Milk and Bowe fear that the ruling will have a deterrent effect: that it may discourage some handicapped people from applying to professional schools, or encourage some schools to believe that they can avoid compliance with the law in the future.

The ruling does not curtail the great progress made in primary and secondary education. While public interest in the desperate plight of the inner-city school ebbed, a series of class-action suits on behalf of mentally retarded children established the right of every handicapped child to a free and appropriately designed public education. Responding to these legal decisions, Congress passed a law that attempts to end the traditional pattern of segregated public education for handicapped children: it stipulates that every child should be educated in the least-segregated educational setting that does justice to his academic and emotional needs. The law's insistence upon the school's accountability to the child's parents and its requirement that the school provide an individualized program of education to every child represent an even more far-reaching departure from traditional practice in public education.

In making its case to the able-bodied mainstream, the central obstacle confronted by the movement is the widespread acceptance of the medical model. Even when it is invoked out of a genuine desire to help the disadvantaged—for instance, as when homosexuality is defined as a disease—this set of assumptions can be damaging. Regardless of whether the economy is growing or contracting, the disabled have a right to their fair share of jobs, goods, and services. But the moment any group is defined as a collection of ill or defective people, social priorities insensibly change. Questions of stigma and systemic discrimination fade into the background: the first priority goes to *treating* the putative inferiority.

As in the case of other disadvantaged groups, the professionals who work with the disabled are often among the worst offenders. Most workers in the human services still acquire in their training a basically medical view of social problems, what the historian Christopher Lasch has recently called the social-pathology model. The disease metaphor is far more pervasive in care of

the disabled than in most other areas. It influences not only the policymakers and the care-givers, but also the social scientists who are doing the very research that could bring about changes in attitudes.

Most often, such researchers will postulate the presence of a single diseaselike entity that colors the attitudes of the majority of able-bodied people—a maladjustment in relating to disabled people—and then proceed to measure the prevalence of the disease among the groups studied. Even the best of this work suffers from the failing of so much social science: the discovery of striking facts whose exact significance is unclear because the underlying social phenomenon is far more complex than the experimenters' theories admit. Studies of the attitudes of able-bodied people toward the handicapped usually report what they say about the disabled, not how they act toward them. Virtually none of the research sorts out the relative roles of fear, ignorance, inexperience, or prejudice.

Jerome Siller, professor of educational psychology at New York University, has done extensive studies on able-bodied people's expressed attitudes toward different disability groups. Siller asked his subjects what characteristics they attribute to different sorts of disability (for instance, amputees may be seen as more intelligent, aggressive, or kind than people with other handicaps).

He uncovered a hierarchy of acceptability. The most acceptable disabilities were the relatively minor ones, like partial vision or hearing loss, a speech impediment or a heart condition. Amputees were a rung lower on the acceptability hierarchy. The deaf and the blind ranked somewhere in the middle, then came the mentally ill; below them stood people with epilepsy, cerebral palsy, or total paralysis.

When ranking included blacks, they usually ended up in the middle of the hierarchy, near the deaf and the blind. In some studies, such as one of employer attitudes made in the early 1970s by clinical psychologist James A. Colbert and his associates, blacks were preferred above all disability groups. Here, too, the sociological implications of these results are unclear. For instance, many investigators have found that the most negative attitudes of all expressed are about obese people. Yet it is hard to believe that we actually equate the stigma attached to being fat, crushing as it may be, with the kinds of stigma experienced by inner-city blacks, epileptics, or people with cerebral palsy. Some important distinctions among those stigmata are being missed by the research design.

Similar ambiguities cloud the interpretation of what is still the most important finding in the field: Stephen A. Richardson of Albert Einstein College of Medicine discovered that as children age, there are significant changes in their expressed attitude toward physical disabilities. Richardson found that a stable preference-ladder first appeared around age six. Asked their feelings about six pictures of children—all but one of them disabled—six-year-olds tended to rank slight facial disfigurement as most acceptable, second only to normalcy. Eight- to 10-year-olds ranked those with crutches and leg braces as most acceptable after the able-bodied child, followed by a child in a wheelchair, one with an amputated forearm, one with facial disfigurement, and finally, an obese child. By senior year, girls set facial disfigurement as least acceptable while boys ranked it fourth out of six in acceptability. (Male and female adults tend to follow the same pattern.) Again, there was the paradoxical finding that race was less stigmatizing than disability, and obesity often more stigmatizing.

. . .

. . . Medical biases compromise the value of much present-day theory and research in education for the handicapped. A generation ago, educators assessed the academic needs of black children and handicapped children in the same way, by measuring the disadvantaged child's academic behavior against what was assumed to be normal for a white, middle-class, able-bodied child. After determining the ways in which the child deviated from these presumably universal norms, the educator devised special compensatory programs to cure or to lessen the child's academic deviance.

Increasingly, this conception of minority education has come under sharp attack. As Frank Riessman, professor of education at Queens College, notes, "If one analyzes the approaches that have been successful in improving the educational performance of inner-city children, one realizes that they are rooted in the strengths and the cognitive styles of the children rather than in a compensatory emphasis on deficiencies." Sadly, the deviance approach so common in minority education in the 1960s continues to go unchallenged in special education.

By far the greatest abuses of the medical model of disability occur in the technical literature that discusses the economic needs of disabled people. Most of this literature simply assumes that the employment problems of disabled people are caused by their physical limitations, rather than by the interaction of their limitation with job discrimination, environmental obstacles to mobility, and other forms of discrimination. The assumption has the unhappy ring of arguments that the economic problems of black Americans are caused by inherited genes that make them biologically inferior.

For society at large, the "therapeutic state" (to recall Nicholas N. Kittrie's term) is a threat, not a reality. But millions of disabled Americans already live within the invisible walls of a therapeutic society. In this society of the "sick," there is no place for the ordinary hallmarks of a present or future adult identity, no place for choice between competing moralities, no place for politics, no place for work, and no place for sexuality. All political, legal, and ethical issues are transformed into questions of disease and health, deviance and normal adjustment, proper and improper "management" of the disability. To recall political scientist Sheldon S. Wolin's fine phrase, the "sublimation of politics" has proceeded furthest of all with handicapped people. Of all America's oppressed groups, only the handicapped have been so fully disenfranchised in the name of health.

## QUESTIONS

1. Characterize the general social attitude toward the handicapped. How do you think this attitude appears from the viewpoint of a handicapped person?

2. How do you react when passing a handicapped person in the street? How do you react when introduced to a handicapped person in a small group? Analyze your responses.

3. What are the similarities between the situation of the handicapped and that of other minorities that suffer stigma, prejudice, and discrimination? Are there any differences?

Paul R. Ehrlich
Anne H. Ehrlich

# 51. What Happened to the Population Bomb?

*There is a general public awareness that population growth poses a threat of severe social and economic inconvenience within the United States, and of a mass calamity in the less developed nations of the world, where resources of land, food, education, health care, and other essentials simply cannot keep pace with population increase.*

*Much of this awareness dates from the publication of Paul Ehrlich's best-selling* The Population Bomb *(1968), which interpreted demographic projections for the ordinary reader and sounded a warning of the dire consequences that would follow if population growth continued on its predicted course. But demography is an inexact science, and its projections are always subject to correction in the light of subsequent unanticipated events. As Paul and Ann Ehrlich point out in this article, population growth in the United States and in the world as a whole has since proved to be somewhat lower than demographers had predicted. The Ehrlichs discuss the reasons for this trend, and suggest why some less developed countries have had far more success in limiting population growth than others.*

*It should be noted that, despite the slight slowing of the population growth rate, the problems of overpopulation still haunt us. Some are already with us, and the others have not disappeared; they have merely been briefly postponed.*

When *The Population Bomb* [1968] was written, the United States population explosion was alive and well—and projected to get even healthier. Virtually all demographers thought that the early 1970s would be a time of rising birth rates in the United States and that it would take decades, at the very least, for fertility to decline to replacement reproduction (an average family size at which each generation just replaces itself). We agreed with them; their reasoning made sense.

But we were all dead wrong. In the early 1970s the women who had been born in the postwar baby boom were in their early 20s, their prime reproductive years. Because a high proportion of the population were young people at an age when they would be having families, demographers had predicted a surge in the birth rate (conventionally expressed as the number of babies born per 1,000 people in the population per year). But contrary to all expectations, the birth rate plunged dramatically from 18.4 in 1970 to around 15 by 1973, and it has remained there ever since.

Correspondingly, the net reproductive rate in the United States has fallen to just below one and has stayed there. The net reproductive rate is a measure of the relative reproduction of generations. A rate of one is replacement reproduction—technically, each female baby born alive in one generation is replaced by exactly one female baby born alive in the next. A rate of two theoretically indicates a population that roughly doubles each generation; a rate of .5, a population that halves each generation. In the mid 1970s the net reproductive rate in the United States was about .9, a little below replacement. If this level of fertility continued and if there were no immigration, population would decline.

Why were the experts confounded by the people? How could there have been a lowering of desired family size so drastic that it overwhelmed the effect of the increased number of women of childbearing age? In retrospect there may have been several factors involved. One was a tight job market for young people as the expansive 1960s gave way to the economically troubled

1970s. Another was the women's liberation movement, which made it increasingly acceptable for women to seek fulfillment in ways other than by producing numerous offspring. A third was increased public awareness of the problems of further population growth—an awareness generated in part by citizen action groups like Zero Population Growth (ZPG) and by books like *The Population Bomb*. Finally, as reasons for having smaller families became widely discussed, effective means for preventing birth became more accessible. The pill and IUDs became available during the 1960s, family planning services were provided for low-income groups, and between 1967 and 1973 abortion was progressively legalized.

Above all, the demographic surprise of the early 1970s showed that, when conditions are right, social change can occur with astounding rapidity. In our view this is the most cheering event since the end of World War II, because it raises the hope that other social transformations necessary to assure the survival of civilization could occur with equal speed.

Unfortunately, the drop of fertility to below replacement level has been widely misinterpreted as meaning the end of population growth in the United States. Newspaper and television commentators proclaimed that the United States had "reached ZPG," membership in population organizations plummeted, and people in general relaxed because "the population expolsion is over." But when a previously growing human population reaches a net reproductive rate of one, its growth does not halt immediately. It continues to expand because human beings of several generations live simultaneously (a generation spans about 25 years). A growing population has disproportionately more people in the high birth-rate, low death-rate younger generation than in the low birth-rate, high death-rate older generations. This means that for a while, even at a net reproductive rate of one or less, the more numerous young adults who are just replacing themselves will generate more births than the relatively few older people will contribute deaths. And as long as births exceed deaths, a population will increase.

This tendency for a population to grow even after replacement reproduction is reached is often referred to as "the momentum of population growth." In the United States that momentum means that, *if completed family sizes remain about where they are now*—which is slightly below replacement—the population will stop its natural increase in about 50 years with a peak population of about 250 million, about 30 million more than today. After that a slow decline will set in. (These estimates include continued legal immigration at current rates, but do not include illegal immigration, for which no solid information exists.)

The slowing of population growth in the United States over the past decade no doubt has already had significant social and economic effects, some of which have gone largely unrecognized. It has, of course, been blamed in part for the sluggishness of economic growth in the 1970s that has plagued most overdeveloped countries. Some problems, such as higher unemployment rates due to the sudden increase of women in the work force, clearly are traceable to the rapid social change of which lower birth rates are a part.

But if our population had continued to expand at rates like those prevailing in the early 1960s, the increased demand for food, energy, and housing, to name a few important examples, would probably have severely strained the social order. All three have been subject to supply shortages and spiraling prices during the 1970s. Even though political factors have played a part, especially for energy, pressures generated by a large, growing, affluent population must bear a large measure of responsibility. A good case can be made for the proposition that the economic troubles of the 1970s (and those we can expect in the 1980s and beyond) would be considerably worse if the birth rate had not been reduced. Conversely, a further reduction in population growth would result in less pressure by affluent Americans on the world's threatened resource base.

What about the population explosion in the rest of the world? Many other overdeveloped countries have also experienced birth-rate declines in the past decade. Several countries in western Europe that have had relatively low birth rates for one or two generations now have passed their population peaks and begun to decline, notably the two Germanies, Luxembourg, and the United Kingdom. (In the latter, emigration has been an important factor in hastening ZPG.) In these comparatively densely populated countries, already heavily dependent on imports of food, energy, and raw materials to maintain high living standards, the ending of population growth can hardly be considered anything but beneficial. The sooner it can be accomplished for overdeveloped countries that are still growing, the better.

According to the latest projections by the U.S. Census Bureau, population momentum ensures that, if present fertility rates persist, the industrialized world as a whole (including the United States) will expand from 1.13 billion people to about 1.33 billion by the year 2000, and slackening growth will continue into the next century. Population projections for the overdeveloped world may seem less alarming than they did a decade ago, but nonetheless the population explosion of the rich countries is far from over. In view of these countries' greatly disproportionate impact on resources and global ecological systems, *any* growth in their populations must be seen as a future threat.

Turning to the less developed countries, we find even less cause for complacency. There the projected effects of population momentum are far more spectacular than in the overdeveloped countries. In 1970 Harvard demographer Nathan Keyfitz predicted that if a typical less developed country reduced fertility to replacement level by the year 2000 (which is unlikely for most), its population nevertheless would continue to grow for a century, soaring to two and a half times its 1970 size. If India, with a 1970 population of about 600 million, were to achieve a birth-control miracle and reach a net reproductive rate of one by the year 2000, its peak population size would be about 1.5 billion people (assuming no rise in death rates). That is more than the present population of Africa, South America, North America, Oceania, and Europe combined.

The most recent demographic estimates anticipate that the world's population will grow from its current size of slightly over four billion to about 6.2 billion at the end of the century. Momentum is expected to carry the population to an ultimate peak of somewhere between nine and 12 billion in the 22nd Century. Such projections make ecologists wish the population-control movement had caught on 50 years ago. With any humane method of stopping population growth, the "braking distance" is long indeed.

Family planning programs have been established in the majority of less developed countries in the last 15 years. But, except for a handful of small, relatively prosperous, and "advanced" countries (such as Hong Kong, Singapore, Taiwan, South Korea, Costa Rica, and Trinidad and Tobago), hardly a dent has been made in their birth rates. Many of their populations are still growing at 2.5 to 3.5 percent per year (doubling in roughly 20 to 30 years). It was something of a mystery that some countries by 1975 had succeeded in reducing their birth rates to around 25 to 30 per 1,000 (almost approaching the levels that had prevailed in overdeveloped countries a decade or two ago), while other countries, apparently equally well "developed," experienced no significant change, their birth rates remaining at approximately 35 to 45 per 1,000.

Then, in 1972, some light was shed on the mystery. The People's Republic of China joined the United Nations and began to disclose previously secret information about its population and its own activities in "birth planning." While externally blasting Malthusian ideas and the family planning efforts of other nations, China had been carrying on what is probably the world's most vigorous population control program—possibly the most successful. The U.S. Census Bureau estimates that China's 1975 population was about 935 million and that its growth rate is about 1.5 percent and declining. The available demographic information on China is, however, by no means solid. Some demographers estimate that both total size and growth rates are somewhat lower; others believe they are higher.

The secret of success in reducing birth rates now appears not to be a high level of industrial development,

as was previously thought. An essential factor seems simply to be equity. When people are given access to the basics of life—adequate food, shelter, clothing, health care, education (particularly for women), and an opportunity to improve their well-being—they seem to be more willing to limit the size of their families. Viewed in this light, it becomes clear why the family planning efforts of many "relatively advanced" less developed countries seem to get nowhere; often only the highest income groups (perhaps a quarter or less of the population) are benefiting from "development." The poor usually are excluded, and in many countries their condition is even deteriorating. This situation unfortunately prevails in numerous less developed countries, including several of the largest and fastest growing, for instance, Brazil, Mexico, and to some extent India.

Because of population momentum, all less developed countries must look forward to vastly increased populations over the next century and to the array of horrendous problems that such growth entails. Doubling a population in a generation implies that all resources (food, energy, raw materials), services, and facilities must also be doubled in that time. Those less developed countries whose growth has begun to slow may have somewhat brighter prospects (depending in part on their resources and political leadership) than countries where birth rates remain high.

All of the standard demographic projections contain the assumption that death rates can only remain constant or decline; they cannot rise. That this assumption is absurd is made clear by the rises in death rates due to famines that in the 1970s afflicted the Sahel and parts of southern Asia. It is made more absurd by even the briefest consideration of the state of Earth's ecosystems and of our social-political-economic systems.

Most people who try to monitor the functioning of these systems agree that the likeliest source of an unpleasant demographic surprise in the next decade or so is a massive famine. The global agricultural system, in combination with the world's fisheries, must provide almost 2 percent more food each year in order to keep up with population growth. In this decade, on the average, agricultural productivity has barely managed to do that and there have been several rather severe setbacks. This would be serious enough if the world's food were reasonably well distributed. But it is not; the rich, especially in overdeveloped countries, are if anything overfed, while the poor, especially in less developed countries, are chronically underfed. There has been no serious attempt at redistribution. The proportion of humanity that is hungry is usually estimated to be about 15 to 25 percent, and this probably has remained roughly constant over the years.

Considering the constant *proportion* of hungry people, however, tends to conceal a vast tragedy that is exposed by a look at the increasing *numbers* of the under-nourished. One sometimes hears statements of the following sort: "The poor are always with us—the proportion of hungry people is no greater today than in 1850." Perhaps that is true (frankly we doubt it). But if so, it means the absolute number of those who go to bed each night inadequately fed has increased from perhaps 250 million to one billion. And a billion people is just about what the *total* population of the earth was in 1850.

Unfortunately, world fisheries production shows every sign of running up against biological limits. In decades to come it may be necessary for agricultural production not only to hold its place in the race with population growth, but also to take up the slack left by faltering fisheries production. There is good reason to believe that it will not be able to do so. The hoped-for transformations in the economics and sociology of agriculture, so widely discussed at the time of the World Food Conference in 1974, are not materializing. The weather has been generally favorable for the past few years, and famines have largely dropped from the headlines. Partly as a result, pressure to create an institution to hold world grain reserves, to institute other distribution reforms, and to improve agricultural productivity on a long-term basis in less developed countries has died away.

In the absence of a large-scale famine, such urgent tasks as land and tenancy reform in the poor nations continue to be neglected, and in the rich ones ecologically unsound agro-ecosystems and dietary habits are perpetuated. Meanwhile those in power can easily ignore the inequities and hazards of the present world food supply system. Widespread famine could, however, be just around the corner. An extended period of bad weather (which is thought to be quite possible by the most knowledgeable meteorologists), combined with environmental deterioration resulting from inadequate land management and ecologically unsound agricultural practices, could precipitate massive famines. This would provide a tragic "solution" to the population problem through a rapid rise in death rates.

There are other routes to such a "solution," routes we travel in part because of population pressures. One might be a pandemic, leading to a breakdown in the world health system. Crowding and malnutrition—common in poor countries—would be major contributors to such a disaster.

Nuclear war could bring about an even more efficient "solution." This route is made more likely by the spread of nuclear power, which we are told (erroneously) is necessary to keep up with a demand for more energy resources and raw materials. Or a war could be precipitated simply by some nation's perceived need for *Lebensraum.* Some of the stickiest international wickets are made even stickier by unequal rates of population growth between adversaries: The Arabs and Israelis and the Chinese and Russians are outstanding examples.

We must emphasize that the rapidly increasing level of overpopulation on our planet is only one element in the human predicament—albeit a major one. Achieving a birth-rate solution to the population explosion—one that would, we hope, lead to a gradual population decline—will not solve all our problems. We must also have profound transformations in our systems of economics and social justice, transformations that above all will permit Earth's ecosystems to continue to supply their indispensable, but little recognized, services to civilization. Hope that such transformations are possible can be taken from the dramatic and unexpected declines of birth rates in the United States and a number of other overdeveloped countries. However, this hope must be balanced by overall trends that remain gloomy. The staggering projected increase in the number of human beings overhangs all of our other problems, threatening not just the functioning of essential ecological systems but of human institutions as well. The old saying remains truer today than ever before: "Whatever your cause, it's a lost cause without population control."

## QUESTIONS

1. The rich nations are growing richer and their populations are stabilizing; the poor nations are growing poorer and their populations are growing. Can and should the rich nations do anything about it?

2. What factors cause population growth in a society to level off or decline?

3. How would (a) population increase, (b) zero population growth, or (c) population decline affect American society?

Otto Friedrich

# 52.  A Proud Capital's Distress

*Rapid population growth in the twentieth century is inseparable from the growth of cities, for that is where an increasing proportion of the planet's people live. Throughout most of the long history of our species, our ancestors lived in small groups of perhaps a few dozen people. Yet, by the end of this century, more than half of the earth's population will be urban—and more than five hundred cities will have populations exceeding one million people. This congested, anonymous urban environment offers challenges of a type and on a scale that are historically unprecedented.*

*In the industrialized world, we tend to think of cities in terms of those that are most familiar to us— New York, Los Angeles, London, Paris. These cities, for all their problems, have grown in a relatively well-planned and orderly fashion, and their population size is fairly stable. In international terms, however, such cities are far from typical. Most urban growth is taking place in the less developed societies, as impoverished rural migrants pour into the cities in search of greater opportunities and higher living standards. All too often, the facilities of the cities—including such items as utilities, transport, education, medical services, housing, and employment—are overwhelmed. The result is a bleak and worsening picture.*

*In this article, Otto Friedrich describes conditions in Mexico City. Soon to be the largest city on earth, Mexico City offers a glimpse of what urban living will mean for most of humanity in the foreseeable future.*

When the ragged and exhausted Spanish conquistadors first beheld the lake-encircled capital of the Aztecs one November morning in 1519, they were stunned by its grandeur. A shining metropolis of some 300,000 people, far larger than any city in Europe, Tenochtitlán displayed immense stone temples to the gods of rain and war and an even more immense royal palace, where Aztec nobles stood guard in jaguar-head helmets and brightly feathered robes. In the nearby marketplace, vendors offered an abundance of jungle fruits and rare herbs and skillfully wrought creations of silver and gold. "The magnificence, the strange and marvelous things of this great city are so remarkable as not to be believed," Hernando Cortés wrote back to the imperial court of Charles V. "We were seeing things," Bernal Díaz del Castillo recalled in his memoir of the Spanish invasion, "that had never been heard of or seen before, nor even dreamed about."

A newcomer today is more apt to arrive by air, and before he even glimpses the dried-up bed of Lake Texcoco, now edged with miles of slum hovels, the first thing he sees is an almost perpetual blanket of smog that shrouds the entire city. It is an ugly grayish brown. There is something strangely sinister about it—a cloud of poison. The pilot orders the seat belts tightened and announces an imminent descent into the murk and filth.

This is Mexico City, grand, proud, beautiful Mexico City, which already boasted a Spanish cathedral and a university when Washington and Boston were still woodlands. Within the past year or so this ancient metropolis has grown to about 17 million people, and it is in the process of surpassing Tokyo as the largest city of the world.* But that growth, which might once have been a point of pride, is a curse. It consists in large part of jobless peasants streaming in from the countryside at a rate of

---

*According to the U.N., greater Mexico City, which sprawls over about 890 sq. mi., will stand first in 1985 with 18.1 million, followed by the Tokyo-Yokohama complex, 17.2 million; São Paulo, 15.9 million; New York and northeastern New Jersey, 15.3 million.

about 1,000 a day. Novelist Carlos Fuentes has called Mexico City the capital of underdevelopment; it has also become a capital of pollution and a capital of slums.

This is the city builder's dream turned nightmare. It is the supercity, the megalopolis, infected by a kind of social cancer that is metastasizing out of control. Its afflictions—a mixture of overcrowding, poverty, pollution and corruption—are a warning to all the other great cities, particularly those in the Third World, but to New York or Los Angeles as well, that what is happening in Mexico City threatens them too.

The statistics of Mexico City's continuing self-destruction are appalling:

More than 2 million of the city's people have no running water in their homes. Mayor Ramón Aguirre of the governing Institutional Revolutionary Party insists that 95% of the inhabitants have access to water, but for many that means one faucet shared by an entire block.

More than 3 million residents have no sewage facilities. So tons of waste are left in gutters or vacant lots to become part of the city's water and part of its dust. "If fecal matter were fluorescent," one Mexico City newspaper has said, "the city wouldn't need lights."

Mexico City produces about 14,000 tons of garbage every day but processes only 8,000. Of the rest, about half gets dumped in landfill, and half is left to rot in the open. One result: legions of rats.

Three million cars and 7,000 diesel buses, many of them old and out of repair, spew contamination into the air. So do the approximately 130,000 nearby factories that represent more than 50% of all Mexican industry. The daily total of chemical air pollution amounts to 11,000 tons. Just breathing is estimated to be equivalent to smoking two packs of cigarettes a day.

The combination of chemical and biological poisons kills 30,000 children every year through respiratory and gastrointestinal diseases. Overall, pollution may account for the deaths of nearly 100,000 people a year.

These are figures that inspire prophecies of disaster. Says one leading environmentalist: "The question is not whether we will be able to live a pleasant life a few years from now. The question is whether we will be able to survive." Says another, Gabriel Quadri: "If nothing is done to cleanse our home, this desert of steel and concrete will be our tomb."

The prospect of urban apocalypse threatens not only the Mexican megacity but also the U.S. The undefended 2,000-mile frontier between Mexico and the U.S. is the only place in the world where a wealthy industrial nation borders on a poor and overcrowded one. The official total of legal Mexican aliens in the U.S. stood at 596,000 as of 1981. Estimates for illegal immigrants vary from 3 million to 6 million. "Traditionally," says one U.S. expert, "about two-thirds of the Mexican peasants who can't survive on the land go to Mexico's cities and one-third somehow make their way into Texas or California. If those proportions were ever reversed, we'd be in terrible trouble."

Yet Mexico City is not some vast urban junk pile. It is one of the most handsome and stylish cities in the Americas, and one of the most sophisticated. It is a city of broad boulevards and gleaming office buildings, of sparkling fountains and scarlet flower beds, of noble baroque churches that welcome every morning with a resonant litany of bells and chimes. In any given week there are a dozen or more plays being performed, plus the celebrated Ballet Folklórico, a French or Japanese film festival, a first-rate bullfight. Eleven major daily newspapers and six TV channels compete for the eye and the mind. The shops in the Zona Rosa near the Paseo de la Reforma are as glittering as those in Paris or New York City. A suede jacket at Aries or a silver serving spoon from Taxco may cost $200. In the garden at Bellinghausen's, visitors savor a splendid *cabrito,* roasted baby goat wrapped in tortillas with a spicy sauce.

That is the Mexico City of the rich, of course, and of the tourists. But as in any city, there are layers and layers of butchers and bakers and candlestick makers, housewives, secretaries, cops and robbers. To them, the basic fact of life is that inflation, which neared an annual rate of 100% in 1982, still gallops along at more than 60%. The peso, which was worth 25 to the dollar in early 1982, has sunk to 194 to the dollar. That makes Mexico's imported goods extremely expensive—or nonexistent. Pablo Fernández and his wife Pía, both 29, do not live at all badly on a combined income of $800 a month, but the budget pinch keeps getting worse. "Forget about buying books, or getting clothes, or going somewhere for the weekend," says Fernández, a professor of social psychology. "We're living by the day," says his wife, who has an administrative job. "The refrigerator seems half empty most of the time."

Still, those who have jobs may consider themselves among the lucky. Officially, 12% of the city's inhabitants are unemployed, but underemployment runs to nearly 40%. As one U.S. expert puts it, "If a 35-year-old man with a wife and children spends his days hoping to shine shoes, is he employed?" To some, the answer lies in burglary and theft, which have risen 35% in the past year.

Below all the other layers of workers come the *pepenadores,* the rubbish pickers, who swarm like rats through the reeking mountains of garbage in the main city dump, the Santa Fe. There are about 2,500 regulars there, roughly one for each ton of trash dumped daily. By picking through the pile for resalable bits of metal or plastic, they hope to earn enough to survive. Says Pablo Téllez Falcón, 45, the chief of the dump: "They regard us as the shabby people who work in the slime with a bottle of tequila in the back pocket."

Below even the garbage pickers, perhaps, are those who can do nothing but beg. On the Zócalo, the vast central square where the monumental cathedral shoulders the equally monumental presidential palace, a balding man in a frayed black suit plays mournfully on his violin while a haggard woman with a baby in her arms stands next to him and holds out an empty tin can. A block away, at the corner of Avenida Madero, a white-stubbled man with no legs holds up a few packs of Chiclets for sale. Just beyond him in the dusk sits one of those silent Indians, who are known as "Marías," this one a grimy-faced girl of perhaps 15, in a ragged shawl and pigtails, with her baby wheezing in its sleep on the sidewalk beside her. She holds out a thin brown palm, but nobody stops.

The various symptoms of Mexico City's illness all work on and worsen one another. But the one problem that underlies all the others is the extraordinary growth in population. The Aztec capital known as Tenochtitlán, with its lakes and flower gardens (and an efficient sewage system), was depopulated by a smallpox epidemic in 1520, which killed more than 80% of all the Indians who survived the Spanish invasion. Mexico City did not reach the 2 million mark until after World War II. But then a systematic national policy of urban industrialization helped send the figures soaring: to 5 million in 1960, 9 million in 1970. About half this growth came from a high yearly birth rate (31 per 1,000), the other half from the continuous migration of peasants, who regard all the hardships of the overcrowded capital as an improvement on the hopeless poverty of their country villages. At current rates of growth, the U.N. estimates that Mexico City will house 26 million people by the year 2000. Mexico City's own, gloomier estimate projects an almost unimaginable 36 million at the end of the century—just 16 more years.

There must be some natural limit to the number of people who can crowd into a restricted urban area, but it is hard to tell just what that limit is. Sprawling Mexico City is by no means the world's most densely populated place, yet the demand for space inexorably devours the city's natural resources. In the past quarter-century, Mexico City has lost nearly 75% of its woodland, which reduces the water supply even as more water is needed. The city now pumps 1 billion gal. per day from natural wells (and loses 20% through leaking pipes), but that supply is so inadequate that an elaborate system of canals and pipelines is being built. These will theoretically bring in an extra 200 million gal. per day by the end of the century, by when the need will have grown still greater, to an extra 700 million gal. per day.

The pumping of so much water out of the subsoil has caused parts of the city to sink, in some places as much as 30 feet, a process worsened by periodic earth-

quakes. The redoubtable Palace of the Arts, which looks rather like some turn-of-the-century world's fair pavilion made of vanilla ice cream, has sunk nearly 10 ft. since it was completed in 1934. The 16th century church of San Francisco, which has sunk 5 ft., can be approached only by going down a flight of stone stairs. At the shrine of Our Lady of Guadalupe, just north of the city, the original basilica tilts forward and sideways at such an alarming angle that it has had to be closed.

Mexico City has another natural peculiarity that makes it unable to support its millions. At 7,350 ft., it is one of the highest cities in the world, and yet it lies in a 50-mile-wide basin surrounded by mountains rising 3,000 ft. higher, notably the snow-covered volcanoes Popocatépetl and Iztaccíhuatl. ("The two monsters," D. H. Lawrence wrote of them, "watching gigantically and terribly over their lofty, bloody cradle of men . . . murmuring like two watchful lions.") The thin air not only contains 30% less oxygen than at sea level but makes auto engines produce nearly twice as much carbon monoxide and hydrocarbon pollution. Then, when the city's befouled air rises, the mountains trap it in the virtually permanent smog that now blocks the snowy crests from sight. The 14 million new saplings that the city planted on many streets between 1976 and 1982 are already withering and turning yellow. Every once in a while an enterprising reporter tests the air by putting a caged bird in the middle of the Zócalo; the bird customarily collapses and dies within two hours.

Technology, according to the dreams of urban planners, is supposed to solve such problems, but in a swollen megalopolis like Mexico City, solutions keep lagging behind the growing needs. Consider, for example, the question of how to get increasing millions of people to their jobs. Seventeen years ago, the government girded Mexico City with the six-lane Periferico, which is now one long series of traffic jams (on a reasonably typical afternoon, a one-mile stretch contained twelve broken-down cars).

Since more highways attract more cars, the newer urban theories insist on mass transit. Mexico City's 69-mile French-built subway system, started in 1969 and still expanding, is a marvel: clean, fast, comfortable and almost free (a ride costs less than 1¢). But it carries 4 million riders a day, and at rush hours the crush is so intense that the authorities gallantly (or chauvinistically) reserve certain cars for women only.

Technology is supposed to guard people's health against a polluted environment, and, according to government statistics, it is doing exactly that. One major reason for the population increase is that Mexico City's death rate declined from 9.6 to 6.7 per 1,000 during the 1970s. The health ministry operates not only six large hospitals but 217 local health centers, and there are hundreds of private hospitals and clinics. However, some experts doubt the rosy figures. "We calculate that 50% of the Mexico City population has no access to medical treatment," says Luís Sánchez Aguilar, head of the opposition Social Democrats.

David Benítez Mendoza, 29, is one of nine doctors working at a new public clinic in Chimalhuacán, typical of the shanty-town suburbs that ring Mexico City. Most of its 120,000 residents live in shacks of concrete and corrugated steel. The streets are unpaved, and there is virtually no sewage system. "People are eating excrement every day without being aware of it," say Benítez. He estimates that the number infested with parasites is close to 100%. Chronic anemia is common, along with malnutrition and respiratory illness, even tuberculosis. "We're fighting," he says, but his clinic has no beds, no ambulances, little equipment.

At the Santa Rita Pharmacy in the northeastern suburb of Texquesquinahuac, Dr. Gilberto López Sánchez, 30, runs his finger slowly along a glass display case. What it displays is a film of grayish dust that has accumulated just in the past 15 minutes. The dust comes from the stacks of Cementos Anáhuac, Latin America's largest cement plant, about a mile away. "Sixty percent of my patients here suffer from respiratory problems," says López. In the neighboring community of Barrientos, Schoolteacher Marisela Mendieta González, 21, keeps her children indoors on windy days from January to June because of the dust. "On a bad day they get very tired in class and their eyes hurt," she says.

There are laws against pollution, but they are not enforced very strictly. Says Armando Báez, head of the Center of Atmospheric Sciences at the National Autonomous University of Mexico: "There have been many cases in which inspectors found factories that were far in excess of the pollution standards. Then the next day they were found to be in compliance. There is no way they could have installed the necessary equipment in 24 hours."

*La mordida* (the bite) is the Mexican term for the system by which underpaid officials supplement their salaries. Those who actually extort money, by such simple methods as stopping motorists for imaginary traffic violations, are known as *mordelones,* or biters. The system is pervasive—and paralyzing. At a customs warehouse in the Mexico City airport, a clerk who types out forms to release confiscated goods has on his desk a plastic cup marked "tips." What goes into the cup helps him decide how long he will take to fill out a form.

It is customary in Mexico to blame all problems on the previous administration, and so it was only this year that victims of *la mordida* learned how sharp were the teeth of former Mexico City Police Chief Arturo Durazo Morreno. Once a semiliterate bank employee, Durazo

allegedly took a cut not only of all police graft but of the drug trade and arms trade as well. According to officials who raided two of Durazo's palatial homes, he also sold police promotions and looted police uniform and gasoline funds. His total take: $12 million. He was arrested last June by the FBI in Puerto Rico and is now in Los Angeles awaiting extradition.

Such thievery by a chief of police seems excessive, but it appears to be inherent in Mexico's half-century-old political system, in which a new President is elected every six years but the same party remains perpetually in power. Each new administration means a shift in nearly 45,000 jobs, most of them appointive. Says Boston University Professor Susan Eckstein in *The Poverty of Revolution:* "The average minister or director finishes his term with two or three houses, two or three automobiles, a ranch and $100,000 in cash; and about 25 directors and ministers hold posts from which they can leave office with 50 times that amount in cash." Even the trash pickers who rummage around on the city garbage dump have to pay off the head of the scavengers' union.

Tales of corruption spice the offerings of Francisco Huerta, 55, who goes on the radio at 7 every morning and spends two hours letting some of his 1.5 million listeners express their criticisms of life in Mexico City. On one recent morning, Huerta's callers protested that taxi drivers were being forced to pay $150 bribes for new license plates, that railroad agents were selling space aboard trains without giving people tickets, that government officials in a nearby state were selling land reserved for farming to developers, and that anyone who complained was likely to be threatened. "Why should we continue to accept a rotten system?" demanded the last caller.

Huerta answers cautiously, for he was temporarily banned from the air two years ago. Mayor Aguirre has a representative in the control booth, ostensibly to follow up on citizens' complaints, but most of the follow-up is actually done by Huerta and three volunteer assistants. "The bureaucracy here is not used to being questioned," says Huerta. "We're not antigovernment, just trying to make the government more efficient."

That was also one of the goals of Manuel Buendía, 58, whose daily column appeared in the Mexico City *Excélsior* and 200 other newspapers. He made a variety of enemies by writing scathingly about the Durazo scandal, about corruption in the powerful Petroleum Workers Union and also about allegations that the CIA had infiltrated the government. After receiving anonymous death threats, Buendía took to carrying a pistol and said, "They will have to kill me from behind, because if they attack me from the front I'll take some of them with me." One evening last May, someone shot him three times in the back, killing him instantly.

Many like to blame all of Mexico's political and social ills on the ruling Institutional Revolutionary Party (PRI, pronounced Pree). It has won every national election since it was organized in 1929 and has consequently become far more institutional than revolutionary. It is the party of the bosses, the bureaucracy, the spoils sharers, the status quo. President Miguel de la Madrid Hurtado was freely elected in 1982, but he in effect rules Mexico City through the PRI machinery and an appointed *regente,* or mayor. Mayor Aguirre is an accountant by training and does not come from Mexico City, nor has any other recent mayor. There is no elected city council.

"Our mayors are outsiders who are imposed on us," says Lorenzo Meyer, a professor of contemporary history at the Colegio de México. "Those who govern us do not feel accountable to us."

The same holds true for the vast bureaucracy that controls an increasing proportion of Mexican life. Ten years ago, government officials managed about 25% of the economy; today they manage about 75%, ranging from oil production to banking to supermarkets and parking lots. Some 1.5 million bureaucrats now occupy 3,500 Mexico City buildings, and nothing seems to work very well. Four years ago, city officials proclaimed the establishment of block committees to express community needs, but those that exist serve mainly as organs of PRI patronage. About the only system that actually functions is *amiguismo,* roughly "friendshipness." Says Meyer: "When the water stops, our neighbor runs over to the waterworks and tells a friend, who sees to it that somebody turns on the right valve."

While the PRI is much criticized for its inertia and ineptitude, it has largely succeeded in one of its original purposes: to achieve conciliation in a violence-ridden land. Some 2 million had died in more than a decade of civil strife that followed the revolution of 1910, and it was the assassination of ex-President Alvaro Obregón that led to the founding of the PRI as a coalition of compromise. Yet it is emblematic of Mexico City that the severed hand of General Obregón is still on display in a jar installed in a monument at the site of the restaurant where he was assassinated.

For Mexico City, whatever its similarities to other great cities, is also uniquely itself, a special expression of its people and its traditions. "In the valley of Mexico [City] man feels himself suspended between heaven and earth, and he oscillates between contrary powers and forces," the poet Octavio Paz wrote in a study, *The Labyrinth of Solitude.* "Reality ... exists by itself here, has a life of its own, and was not invented by man as it was in the United States ... One of the most notable traits of the Mexican's character is his willingness to contemplate horror: he is even familiar and complacent in his dealings with it. The bloody Christs in our village churches ...

the custom of eating skull-shaped cakes and candies on the Day of the Dead, are habits inherited from the Indians and the Spaniards and are now an inseparable part of our being."

The curse bequeathed to Mexico City by the Aztecs was the curse of human sacrifice. That ritual, in which a priest bent over the recumbent victim and cut out his throbbing heart with an obsidian knife, was central to the Aztecs' religion. The war god Huitzilopochtli required blood as the price of Aztec victory and the rain god Tlaloc required it as the price of the harvest; if these gods remained unpropitiated, the world would end. Exactly how many victims were thus sacrificed (and later eaten) remains uncertain, but it is believed that 20,000 prisoners were offered up on the altar of the Great Temple when it was officially dedicated in 1487.

Bernal Díaz, the chronicler of Cortés' conquest, was horrified on his first visit to the temple. "There were some braziers with incense," he wrote, "and in them they were burning the hearts of the three Indians whom they had sacrificed that day ... All the walls of the oratory were so splashed and encrusted with blood that they were black, the floor was the same and the whole place stank vilely."

The king of the Aztecs, Montezuma misguidedly believed Cortés to be a reincarnation of Quetzalcoatl, the fair-haired, white-skinned god who, according to Aztec legend, had sailed off into the East, vowing that he would some day return and rule. It was only because Montezuma offered no resistance that Cortés and his band of about 400 conquistadors were able to enter the royal palace, seize the Aztec king as a hostage and eventually do him to death.

Cortés destroyed the Aztecs' capital, tore town Montezuma's palace and replaced the rituals of human sacrifice with those of the Spanish Inquisition. In the debris of the ruined city, a Spanish friar found a poem describing the Aztecs' misery:

*Broken spears lie in the roads.*
*We have torn our hair in grief.*
*The houses are roofless now, and their walls*
*Are red with blood ...*

But on the rubble of Tenochtitlán, Cortés built a new city that later developed in the grandiose style of the Spanish Renaissance, the capital of New Spain. It is there to this day in the arcades and verandas along the cobblestone streets that lead off the Zócalo. But in the northeastern corner of that square, just to one side of the Spaniards' Baroque cathedral, some workmen digging a hole for electric cable in 1978 unearthed an 11-ft. stone covered with carving. Archaeologists arrived to explore the site. Today the buried Aztec temple stands open to view once more, blood-soaked altar and all. Just last April a group known as the Aztec Sun Cult gathered around for a ceremonial to mark the beginning of summer.

There are few commemorations for the more than two centuries of Spanish rule. Not a single statue in Mexico City honors Cortés. There are no commemorations of the U.S. invasion of Mexico City in 1847 either ("From the halls of Montezuma . . ."), except for six tall white pillars marking the spot where six young Mexican cadets leaped to their deaths from the heights of Chapultepec rather than surrender to the charging U.S. forces. The Castle of Chapultepec itself is a memorial to the showy reign of the French-sponsored Emperor Maximilian, but that brief empire ended before Benito Juárez's firing squad in 1867.

Mexico City today is still a battlefield for the long and violent struggle between its European and Indian traditions. Officially, the government continually emphasizes the splendors of the Indian heritage. The National Museum of Anthropology, with its lavish display of Aztec and Maya masterpieces, is one of the world's finest. On the walls of public buildings all over the city, the superb murals of Diego Rivera, José Clemente Orozco and David Alfaro Siqueiros insistently portray an idyllic Indian culture overwhelmed by brutal conquistadors and rapacious priests (and, later, by potbellied, top-hatted U.S. plutocrats). Yet social snobbery still sets high value on European features and a light skin. Newspaper ads offering jobs to secretaries are apt to request *aparencia agradable,* or "agreeable appearance," meaning no Indians. And when Jesús Sánchez, the patriarch in Oscar Lewis' celebrated *The Children of Sánchez,* got angry at his wife because she was playing his radio, the worst insult he could fling at her was, "You're such an Indian, such an imbecile."

This state of internal conflict, of old rages unresolved, has strongly impressed many observers, both Mexican and European. "In Mexico City, there is never tragedy but only outrage," wrote Carlos Fuentes. Paz, more stoic, suggested that "we admire fortitude in the face of adversity more than the most brilliant triumph." Outsiders can become exasperated. Kate, the heroine of D. H. Lawrence's *The Plumed Serpent,* "felt that bitter hopelessness that comes over people who know Mexico well. A bitter barren hopelessness."

"Aztec things oppress me," she said. "There is no hope in them."

"Perhaps the Aztecs never asked for hope," the General said.

"Surely it is hope that keeps one going?" she said.

"You, maybe. But not the Aztec, nor the Indian today."

This is a fairly widespread view, but it can be argued that the whole tidal wave of peasant migration into Mexico City is nothing but a tidal wave of hope, irrational,

irrepressible hope. Listen, for a moment, to José Toribio, a young Mixtec Indian from the rugged mountains of Oaxaca state, as he sits in a Mexico City café and shovels pasta soup into his squirming son Pablo, 3. "I came to find work so that they could eat," he says, gesturing toward his wife Logina, who sits breast feeding her one-year-old Benito under a grubby, red acrylic shawl.

"I'm looking for work as a bricklayer," says José. He speaks only broken Spanish, his wife none. In Oaxaca, he was a *jornalero,* a day laborer, and there was little work. He has not found anything here yet, so he and his family spend their nights dozing in shop doorways. But he thinks he has a chance for better things in this great city. "It is a pretty place, but there are a lot of buses," he says. "It is very dangerous."

Not only are there no jobs for migrants like the Toribios; there is no housing either. Overall, 26% of the city's families, each averaging 5.5 people, live in single-room homes. Rents in the downtown slums have been frozen since World War II, which means that some families pay only 25¢ a month. But middle-class apartment construction also lags far behind what is needed, about 800,000 units.

The rural migrants cannot wait. The slums in outlying parts of the city were largely constructed by squatters, who built so hastily (on somebody else's land) that they were known as *paracaidistas,* or parachutists. There was—and still is—a lot of double-dealing by the operators who helped organize such invasions: fraudulent deeds and building permits bought and sold.

When the squatters built shacks on government land, the police often knocked the sheds down. When they invaded private land, the owners hired guards. Many slums still do not legally exist; others have won grudging government acceptance.

"The real problems arise when people begin to demand water and other services," says Alejandro Suárez, an architect who counsels groups of people trying to build their own homes. "Then the political game begins, the constant negotiation. The government tells these people, 'We can't give you what you're asking for. You're illegal.'" At the same time, it expects them to vote for the PRI in exchange for services.

In an ideal world, the problems of Mexico City could be solved: overpopulation could be checked, even if harshly, as is being attempted in China; air pollution could be reduced, as in California; government could be decentralized, as in West Germany. But as T. S. Eliot once wrote, "Between the idea/ And the reality,/ Between the motion/ And the act/ Falls the Shadow." In Mexico City, there is the shadow of ideology, both religious and secular, the shadow of corruption, the shadow of inertia—and always the problems growing faster than the solutions.

Take the birth rate. Almost any plan to raise living

standards would include government support of birth control, but Mexico is torn between its quasi-socialist political traditions and the teachings of the Roman Catholic Church (not to mention the Latin tradition of machismo). More than 90% of Mexicans are nominally Roman Catholic; yet anticlerical laws forbid the church to own property, operate primary schools or comment on public affairs. The result is a series of compromises, and the constitution bows to both sides of the birth-control controversy by decreeing that "each person has the right to decide in a free, responsible and informed manner about the number [of] children."

The U.N. has given Mexico $24 million since 1972 to finance birth control, and the government has willingly spent it on educational family-planning programs. Partly as a consequence, the city's estimated birth rate dropped from 42.6 per 1,000 in 1970 to 31 per 1,000 in 1980 (that was largely offset, however, by a corresponding drop in the death rate). Abortions are still banned, unless the mother's life is endangered or she has been raped, but about 1 million women have them performed illegally every year. About 10,000 of these women die. Says Gynecologist Alejandro Hernández: "The knowledge of contraceptives here is minimal."

Decentralization, similarly, is an idea that wins nods of approval but very little action. The current crowding fills Mexico City with not only 28% of all Mexicans but two-thirds of the nation's students. More than half of the country's industry is concentrated there, and seven out of ten banking transactions occur there. Yet every new plan to spur the transfer of business and government out of the capital is largely a recycling of some previous unfulfilled plan. "There have been about five decentralization programs in the past 20 years, and all of them failed because there was no political will to carry them out," says Social Democrat Sánchez.

Government authorities answer that they now screen all proposals for new factories near the capital and offer tax incentives for moves elsewhere, but that is clearly not enough. No corporation is eager to move to a remote outpost; until some do, there are no jobs to attract workers. That applies to the government too. "Why does Pemex (the national oil monopoly) have headquarters here when not a single barrel of oil is produced in Mexico City?" asks Pablo Emilio Madero, head of the opposition National Action Party. "The same with the Agriculture Ministry. It should be in a farming area, not here."

The government has done a bit more about the capital's pollution problems. The Mexican Senate last December proclaimed factory pollution emission limits for the first time, providing fines of up to $90,000 for first offenders and prison sentences for repeaters. A program called Plan Texcoco is supposed to halt the erosion and dust storms along the old lake bed. Pemex oil officials announced a voluntary reduction in the amount of sulfur in diesel fuel sold in Mexico City. But these are only first steps, and there is little sign of substantial progress. The reason: one of the darkest shadows that falls across Mexico City is that of the foreign debt.

When the oil boom reached its height during the 1976–82 regime of President José López Portillo, the government, the business community and ordinary citizens all succumbed to an economic mentality that made it seem perfectly reasonable to borrow large sums against the prospect of future oil royalties. (Mexico's estimated reserves of 72 billion bbl. are the world's fourth largest.) When that prospect faded as a global oil glut began to develop in 1981, it turned out that Mexico's international debt, most of it owed to U.S. private banks, had soared. From $36.6 billion in 1976, the figure has now reached nearly $90 billion, approximately $1,200 for every man, woman and child in the country. The $9.8 billion annual bill for interest alone devours nearly 50% of all Mexico's earnings from exports; each percentage point by which U.S. interest rates rise adds another $900 million to that burden. In short, it is a debt too great to pay, and while protracted negotiations for new terms continue, Mexico simply cannot afford to do what needs to be done in Mexico City or anywhere else.

This applies not only to the government but to major corporations that have been hit hard by recession and the devaluation of the peso. Imported machinery has become prohibitively expensive, and the interest demanded on borrowed capital is more than 50%. At Cementos Anáhuac, which sprays its dust all over its neighborhood, production is down 60%, and the company lost $272,000 last year. Yet the equipment necessary to solve the factory's pollution problem would cost almost $3 million. Says Operations Manager Salvador Carrillo: "You can't ask us to invest money we don't have."

*Ni modo* is a term often applied to various aspects of life in Mexico City. It means literally "No way" or, more generally, "Nothing can be done." That way lies the breakdown of a great city.

Whether other ways exist or can be found depends a great deal on President De la Madrid. Despite his involvement with the PRI system, he started his regime on a note of high rectitude: "Our problems are so grave that only with a moral renovation will we be able to solve them." Traditional rhetoric? Perhaps, but the beleaguered President can already point to a few improvements in the illnesses that afflict his city and country alike. Corruption is still commonplace, but the government has at least started prosecuting a few high officials of the López Portillo regime, notably Police Chief Durazo and Jorge Díaz Serrano, former head of the Pemex oil monopoly, who is now in prison awaiting trial. And as a cheering sign of the times, Mexico City drivers found this year that they could renew their auto registrations without the traditional $25 "gratuity."

Inflation is still eviscerating ordinary people's salaries, but some officials talk hopefully of reaching a mere 40% by the end of the year. Such a deflationary policy requires real belt tightening. One of the reasons that the authorities can claim that nobody starves in Mexico City is that government subsidies held the price of tortillas, the basic food of the poor, to 3¢ per lb. But seven weeks ago, the subsidies had to be reduced, and the price rose to 4¢. Overall, according to one estimate, real living standards have dropped 15% in the past three years. The Mexican poor are often stoic rather than radical, but stoicism has its limits. "The day people have nothing to put in their stomachs," says a priest in a slum in northwestern Mexico City, "that will be the day of uprising."

Whatever gains De la Madrid has made so far have been token ones, small moves that buy time. How much time can be bought depends a good deal on what financial terms he and the other major Latin American debtors can negotiate with Washington. No one in Mexico is talking openly of default yet, but borrowers throughout the continent badly need some form of extension on the billions of dollars they cannot repay.

When De la Madrid went to Washington in May, he and President Reagan disagreed sharply and openly on U.S. policies in Central America. For such a disagreement to jeopardize Mexican recovery and revival would be folly indeed. Mexico City alone is more than twice as populous as El Salvador and Nicaragua combined; it is afflicted with more than twice as many problems—and it is only about half as far from the Texas border.

There are limits, of course, to what Washington can or should do. It can assist in negotiating an extension of Mexico's debts and a limit on the interest rates charged. It can further encourage U.S. industry to build plants in Mexico, and it can deal sympathetically with Mexican immigrants to the U.S. But such steps are merely help, not a solution. That requires not only economic development and political reform but a greater effort toward population control, and it must come from the Mexicans themselves. Otherwise, *ni modo*.

---

## QUESTIONS

1. What factors cause urban population growth, and what impact does this growth have on cities in the less-developed countries?

2. What are the advantages and disadvantages of life in large cities?

3. How many members of your class hope to live in small towns or rural areas? What are their reasons for their choices? Is there any relationship between their home origins and their future residential intentions?

Murray Melbin

# 53. Night as Frontier

*Sociologists often take an ecological approach to the study of urban development. In other words, they see patterns of city growth as the outcome of a variety of environmental pressures and opportunities. For example, natural features, such as rivers and mountains, affect the shape of cities; economic factors, such as the demand for prime residential or industrial property, influence the location of specific activities; social factors, such as population decline or racial prejudice, affect the distribution of various social groups.*

*In essence, this approach sees human beings as colonizing, adapting to, and changing particular ecological niches in space, whether the space is a densely populated city or a sparsely inhabited frontier. But in his thoughtful article, Murray Melbin suggests that people also colonize a different kind of ecological niche—one that exists in a different dimension, time.*

*Just as population pressure may encourage some urban residents to colonize frontier areas, so it may also encourage urbanites to colonize the night. Melbin shows that nighttime activity is very much on the increase in large cities, and draws a number of fascinating parallels between social conditions in the historic frontier and the contemporary urban night.*

Humans are showing a trend toward more and more wakeful activity at all hours of day and night. The activities are extremely varied. Large numbers of people are involved. And the trend is worldwide. A unifying hypothesis to account for it is that night is a frontier, that expansion into the dark hours is a continuation of the geographic migration across the face of the earth. To support this view, I will document the trend and then offer a premise about the nature of time and its relation to space. Third, I will show that social life in the nighttime has many important characteristics that resemble social life on land frontiers.

## The Course of Expansion

We were once a diurnal species bounded by dawn and dusk in our wakeful activity. Upon mastering fire, early humans used it for cooking and also for sociable assemblies that lasted for a few hours after darkness fell. Some bustle throughout the 24-hour cycle occurred too. Over the centuries there have been fires tended in military encampments, prayer vigils in temples, midnight betrothal ceremonies, sentinels on guard duty at city gates, officer watches on ships, the curing ceremonies of Venezuelan Indians that begin at sundown and end at sunrise, innkeepers serving travelers at all hours. In the first century A.D., Rome was obliged to relieve its congestion by restricting chariot traffic to the night hours (Mumford, 1961: 217).

Yet around-the-clock activity used to be a small part of the whole until the nineteenth century. Then the pace and scope of wakefulness at all hours increased smartly. William Murdock developed a feasible method of coal-gas illumination and, in 1803, arranged for the interior of the Soho works in Birmingham, England, to be lighted that way. Other mills nearby began to use gas lighting. Methods of distributing coal-gas to all buildings and street lamps in a town were introduced soon after. In 1820 Pall Mall in London became the first street to be lit by coal-gas. Artificial lighting gave great stimulus to the night-

From *American Sociological Review*, 43: 3–22, February 1978. Reprinted with permission.

time entertainment industry (Schlesinger, 1933: 105). It also permitted multiple-shift factory operations on a broad scale. Indeed by 1867 Karl Marx (1867: chap. 10, sec. 4) was to declare that night work was a new mode of exploiting human labor.

In the closing decades of the nineteenth century two developments marked the changeover from space to time as the realm of human migration in the United States. In 1890 the Bureau of the Census announced that the land frontier in America had come to an end, for it was no longer possible to draw a continuous line across the map of the West to define the edge of farthest advance settlement. Meanwhile, the search for an optimum material for lantern lights, capable of being repeatedly brought to a white heat, culminated in 1885 in the invention of the Welsbach mantle—a chemically impregnated cotton mesh. The use of the dark hours increased thereafter, and grew further with the introduction of electric lighting.

Here and there one may find documentation of the trend. During the First World War there was selective concern, expressed by Brandeis and Goldmark (1918) in *The Case Against Night Work for Women,* about the impact of off-hours work. A decade later the National Industrial Conference Board (1927) published a comprehensive survey with an account of the characteristics of the off-hours workers.

The most systematic evidence of steadily increasing 24-hour activity in the U.S. is the growth of radio and television broadcasting. Broadcasters authorize surveys to learn about the market that can be reached in order to plan programs and to set advertising rates. The number of stations active at given hours and the spread of those hours around the clock reflects these research estimates of the size of the wakeful population—the potential listeners. Television hours in Boston ended at 11:30 in 1949, and then widened to include the Late Show and then the Late Late Show in the intervening years until 1974. Each medium has moved increasingly to 24-hour programming and mirrors the growth in nighttime activity.

In the present decade, for the first time, the U.S. Bureau of Labor Statistics (1976: Table 1) asked about the times of day that people worked. In 1976, of 75 million in the work force, 12 million reported they were on the job mainly after dark and 2.5 million of those persons worked a full shift beginning about midnight. Since these figures do not include *the clientele* that used such establishments as restaurants, hospital emergency wards, gambling rooms, and public transportation, these numbers are conservative estimates of how many people are up and about at night.

Today more people than ever are active outside their homes at all hours engaged in all sorts of activities. There are all-night supermarkets, bowling alleys, department stores, restaurants, cinemas, auto repair shops, taxi services, bus and airline terminals, radio and television broadcasting, rent-a-car agencies, gasoline stations. There are continuous-process refining plants, and three-shift factories, post offices, newspaper offices, hotels, and hospitals. There is unremitting provision of some utilities—electric supply, staffed turnpike toll booths, police patrolling, and telephone service. There are many emergency and repair services on-call: fire fighters, auto towing, locksmiths, suppliers of clean diapers, ambulances, bail bondsmen, insect exterminators, television repairers, plate glass installers, and funeral homes.

## Space and Time Frontiers and Settlements

Time, like space, is part of the ecological niche occupied by a species. Although every type exists throughout the 24-hour cycle, to reflect the way a species uses its niche we label it by *the timing of its wakeful life.* The terms diurnal and nocturnal refer to the periods the creatures are active. We improve our grasp of the ecology of a region by recognizing the nighttime activity of raccoons, owls and rats, as well as by knowing the spatial dispersion of these and other animals. The same area of a forest or meadow or coral reef is used incessantly, with diurnal and nocturnal creatures taking their active turns. We make geographic references to humans in a similar way. We refer to an island people or a desert people, or the people of arctic lands as a means of pointing out salient features of their habitats.

This similar treatment of time and space rests on the assumption that both of them are containers for living. Consider the dictionary definition of the word *occupy:* "2. To fill up (take time or space): *a lecture that occupied three hours*" (*American Heritage Dictionary,* 1970:908). Geographers study activities rather than physical structures to decide whether and how people occupy space (Buttimer, 1976:286). The mere presence of buildings and related physical structures in places like Machu-Pichu, Petra, and Zimbabwe do not make us believe they are habitations now. The once-boisterous mining centers in the American West that have become ghost towns are settlements no longer. Conversely, we say a farming region in which people are active is inhabited even though buildings are few. The presence of human-built structures is not the criterion for occupying a region, it is people and their activities.

Like rural settlements, the occupation of time need not be dense. For example, London Transport lists 21 all-night bus routes. On many of these routes "all-night" service means no more than once an hour. Yet, even though the bus does not pass during the intervening 59 minutes, the schedule is said to be continuous. If an active moment interacts with quiet moments around it, the entire period is taken as occupied.

Of course, no time has ever been used without also using it in some place. No space has ever been used without also using it some hours of the days. Space and time together form the container of life activity. We forget this in the case of former frontiers because expansion then occurred so dramatically across the land. Less notice was paid to the 16 hours of wakefulness because the daily use of time was rather constant as the surge of geographic expansion kept on over the face of the earth. As time use remained unchanged, it was disregarded in human ecological theory. In different eras, however, expansion may proceed more rapidly in either space or time. Recently expansion is taking place in time. Since people may exploit a niche by distributing themselves and their activities over more hours of the day just as they do by dispersing in space, a frontier could occur in the time dimension too.

A *settlement* is a stable occupation of space and time by people and their activities. A *frontier* is a pattern of sparse settlement in space or time, located between a more densely settled and a practically empty region. Below a certain density of active people, a given space-time region is a wilderness. Above that point and continuing to a higher level of density, the presence of people in activities will make that area a frontier. Above that second cutoff point the further denseness of active people turns the area into a fully inhabited region. In a given historical period the frontier's boundaries may be stable or expanding. When expanding, the frontier takes on the aspect of venturing into the unknown and is often accompanied by novelty and change.

## Similarities Between Land Frontiers and Time Frontiers

Two kinds of evidence would support the hypothesis of night as frontier. One is that the forces for expansion into the dark hours are the same as those resulting in expansion across the land. That is, a single causal explanation should account for the spread of people and their activities, whether in space or in time. I offered such an outline in another essay: it includes enabling factors, demand push, supply pull, and stabilizing feedback (Melbin, 1977). The other line of evidence is that the same important features of social life should be found both in time and in space frontiers. The rapid expansion in after-dark activity has been taking place mostly in urban areas. Therefore the culture of the contemporary urban nighttime should reveal the same patterns and moods found in former land frontiers.

I have chosen to review life in the U.S. West in the middle of the nineteenth century along with the present-day nighttime. Of course there were other land frontiers and the hypothesis should apply to all of them. However, there are good reasons to begin by demonstrating it for the U.S. West. One is that the archives holding information about this westward flow are thorough, well organized, and readily available. Another reason is that the U.S. West has continuity with expansion into the night. The movement westward reached the California coast. California's main cities have since become areas of great activity in the dark hours, as if the flow across the continent swerved into the nighttime rather than spilling into the sea.

Specifically, the land frontier to be discussed is the area west of the Mississippi River during the middle decades of the nineteenth century, about 1830–1880. The urban nighttime will be any major urban area during the stretch from about midnight to 7:30 a.m. during the decades of the 1960s and 1970s. Most of my examples will be findings from a recent study of Boston. There are many aspects in which social life at night is like the social life of other frontiers.

### 1. Advance Is in Stages

There is a succession of steps in colonizing any new region. People ventured into the western outskirts "in a series of waves . . . the hunter and the fur trader who pushed into the Indian country were followed by the cattle raiser and he by the pioneer farmer" (Turner, 1965:59; 1893:12, 19–20). Life styles were distinctive in each stage as well. The hunters and trappers did not dwell like the miners who followed, and they in turn lived differently from the pioneer farmers who came later (Billington, 1949:4–5). Although living conditions were generally crude then, there was a decided increase in comfort for the farmers settled in one place compared with the earlier-day trappers who were usually on the move.

There is also a succession of phases in settling the nighttime. Each stage fills the night more densely than before and uses those hours in a different way. First came isolated wanderers on the streets; then groups involved in production activities, the graveyard-shift workers. Still later those involved in consumption activities arrived, the patrons of all-night restaurants and bars, and the gamblers who now cluster regularly by midnight at the gambling table in resorts.

The rates of advance are unequal in both cases. Population gains and development are not unbroken. In the West economic growth was erratic. Periods of depression, dry seasons and other hardships drove many people to abandon their homesteads and move back east. Similarly, during the oil embargo of 1973–1974 there was some retreat from nighttime activity, as restaurants and auto service stations and other businesses cut back hours of serving the public.

## 2. Population Is Sparse and Also More Homogenous

At first only a few people venture into the new region. The frontier line in the U.S. West was drawn by the Census Bureau through an area of density of two to six inhabitants per square mile. The other side of the line was tabled the "wilderness." The demographic composition of the western frontier was mostly vigorous young males with proportionately fewer females and aged persons than found in the populations of the eastern states (Riegel, 1947:624; Godkin, 1896:13; Dick, 1937:7, 232). This demographic picture fits the night as well. There are fewer people up and about and most of them are young males.

. . .

Estimates of the ages of passersby were also made during field observations. Whereas people of all ages were on the streets during the day, no one over 59 was seen between midnight and 5 a.m.; and from 2 to 5 a.m. no one over 41 was seen.

## 3. There Is Welcome Solitude, Fewer Social Constraints, and Less Persecution

The land frontier offered tranquillity, a place for relief from feelings of being hemmed in. "Fur traders . . . were psychological types who found forest solitudes more acceptable than the company of their fellow men" (Billington, 1949:4). It was appealing to escape into the wilderness, to leave deceit and disturbance, and vexing duties and impositions of the government behind (Robbins, 1960:148). " 'Oh, how sweet,' wrote William Penn from his forest refuge, 'is the quiet of these parts, freed from the troubles and perplexities of woeful Europe' " (Turner, 1893:262). Even later the West was "a refuge . . . from the subordination of youth to age" (Turner, 1932:25). The outer fringes offered escape from persecution too. Mormons and Hutterites both made their ways westward to avoid harassment from others.

In a parallel way, many have enjoyed the experience of walking at night along a street that is ordinarily jammed during the day. Individuals who are up and about then report a feeling of relief from the crush and anonymity of daytime city life. The calm of those hours is especially appealing to young people, who come to feel that they possess the streets. (A test of this proposition must of course control for the fear of criminal assault in the dark; I will discuss this further in items 7 and 8 below.) Also, a portion of the people out at night are those avoiding

social constraints and perhaps persecution. Street people and homosexuals, for example, find more peace in the dark because surveillance declines. Some night owls are urban hermits. Some individuals who are troubled or stigmatized—such as the very ugly or obese—retreat from the daytime to avoid humiliation and challenge. They stay up later, come out when most others are gone, and are more secure as they hobnob with nighttime newsdealers and porters and elevator men. In this way the night affords an outlet. Like the West it serves an insulating function that averts possible tensions from unwanted encounters.

## 4. Settlements Are Isolated

Initially migration beyond the society's active perimeter is scattered. The land frontier settlements were small and apart from one another. There was little communication across districts and much went on in each in a self-sufficient way. People in the East did not think of the relevance of borderland activities for their own existence and the pioneers were indifferent to outside society (Billington, 1949:96, 746).

As the city moves through phases of the day it switches from coordinated actions to unconnected ones. Pockets of wakeful activity are separated from one another, are small scale compared to daytime events, and there is less communication between the pockets. The people of the daytime give little thought to those active in the dark and do not view them as part of the main community.

## 5. Government Is Initially Decentralized

Whatever high-level group may decide the laws and policies for a nation or a community, outside the purview of superiors there are subordinates who make decisions that would otherwise be the domain of the higher-ups or subject to their approval. As the land frontier moved farther from the national center of policy making, the interpretation of the law and judicial decisions were carried out by individuals who were rarely checked on and who rarely consulted with their superiors. Hollon (1973:96) notes that events took place "remote from the courts of authorities . . . [and] the frontiersmen not only enforced their own law, they chose which laws should be enforced and which should be ignored."

Today, although many organizations and cities are continually active, their primary administrations—directors, heads of departments, mayors—are generally on duty only during the daytime. At night they go to sleep and a similar decentralization of power follows. To some extent this is an explicit delegation of authority. But discretion is stretched for other reasons too. Night nurses decide not to wake up the doctor on duty because he gets annoyed at being disturbed for minor problems (Kozak, 1974:59). Shift supervisors choose not to bother the plant manager for similar reasons. Lesser officials make decisions that in the daytime are left for higher-ranking administrators. The style and content of the way the organization or the city is run at night changes accordingly. For example, for the same types of cases, decisions by police officers at night will be based less on professional role criteria and more on personal styles. This results in more extreme instances of being strict and lenient, arbitrary and humane.

## 6. New Behavioral Styles Emerge

Both land and time frontiers show more individualism because they are remote, the environment is unusual (compared with the centers of society), and others subjected to the same conditions are tolerant. Those who traveled to the western borders broke from ordinary society. The casual observance by others, the constituted authority, and the familiar settings and the norms they implied were gone. This left room for unconventional behavior. Easterners thought westerners were unsavory. The president of Yale College said, "The class of pioneers cannot live in regular society. They are too idle, too talkative, too passionate, too prodigal, and too shiftless to acquire either property or character" (cited in Turner, 1893:251). Another traveler in the same period wrote, "It is true there are worthless people here [in settlements hundreds of miles from any court of justice] and the most so, it must be confessed, are from New England" (Flint, 1826:402). He did go on to say that there were also many who were worthy.

Deviance was also *created* out west. Many pioneer wives lived on the plains for extended periods without ordinary social contacts, especially when their husbands left on journeys for days or weeks. These women often became withdrawn and untalkative, so shy and uneasy with strangers that they would run away when one approached (Humphrey, 1931:128). From the evidence at hand, these were normal, happy women in the cities when they were growing up, but they were affected by the frontier environment. On the western boundary people were used to this behavior on the part of lonely, isolated women and accepted it. In the eastern cities the same conduct would have been taken as odd.

There is also a popular image of the night as the haunt of weirdos and strange characters, as revealed in comments like "I don't know where they hide during the day but they sure come out after dark." Moreover, at night one can find people who, having lived normal lives are exposed to unusual circumstances that draw them into unconventional behavior. Becker (1963:79, 97, 98) gives such an account of jazz musicians. They work late

in the evening and then associate with very few daytime types in their recreation after midnight. The milieu harbors a deviant subculture that is tolerated and even expected.

## 7. There Is More Lawlessness and Violence

Both land frontier and the nighttime have reputations as regions of danger and outlawry. Interestingly, both do not live up to the myths about them, for the patterns of aggression are selective and localized.

On the one hand there is clear evidence of lawlessness and violence. Walter P. Webb observed that the West was lawless "because the law that was applied there was not made for the conditions that existed. . . . It did not fit the needs of the country, and could not be obeyed" (cited by Frantz and Choate, 1955:83). There was also a lack of policemen and law enforcement agencies were few (Riegel, 1947:627; Billington, 1949:480). There was violence in the gold fields (Hollon, 1974:211). In the cow towns, mining camps and boom towns in the early days, practically everyone carried guns. Fighting words, the ring of revolvers, and groans of pain were common sounds out there. Some western settlements were renowned for concentrations of gamblers and gougers and bandits, dance-hall girls and honky-tonks and bawdy houses. Horse thieving was widespread. The stage coach was held up many times. There was habitual fear of attack from either Indians or renegades. In the face of this, the people practiced constant watchfulness and banded together for self-protection (Billington, 1954:8; Doddridge, 1912:103). Towns had vigilante groups. The covered wagons that crossed the plains were accompanied by armed convoys.

Yet the violence was concentrated in certain places; otherwise killings and mob law were remarkably infrequent. Such infamous towns as Tombstone and Deadwood, and the states of Texas and California had more than their share of gunfights (Frantz and Choate, 1955:83; Billington, 1949:63; Hollon, 1973:96). But the tumult in the cow towns was seasonal, and took place when the cowboys finally reached Abilene, Ellsworth, and Dodge City after the long drive. And the mayhem was selective. Flint (1826:401) wrote, "Instances of murder, numerous and horrible in their circumstances, have occurred in my vicinity . . . in which the drunkenness, brutality, and violence were mutual. . . . [Yet] quiet and sober men would be in no danger of being involved." W. T. Jackson (1973:79) adds, "Homicides and murders occurred so infrequently that when they did the community was shocked and outraged." Concerning violence, Hollon (1973:97–8) concludes that there was

a natural tendency to exaggerate the truth and emphasize the exception . . . not a single shoot-out took place on main street at Dodge City or any of the other Kansas cow towns in the manner of the face-to-face encounter presented thousands of times on television.

Why, then, did the land frontier have the reputation of a "Wild West"? One reason may be that outlaw killers were drifters, so the same person may have contributed exploits over large areas. Another reason was boredom. The stories of violence persisted and spread because there was little to do or to read about in pioneer homes. The tedium of daily life was countered by exciting stories told and retold around the stove in the general store.

It is plausible that western desperados and nighttime muggers would have similar outlooks. Both believe there is less exposure, which improves their chances for succeeding at the risks they take. One relied on dry-gulching; the other uses the dark to set an ambush. Escape is easy because both could move from the scene of the crime into unpopulated areas and elude pursuers.

The nighttime has been noted also as a place of evil. It is thought of as crime-ridden and outside of ordinary social control. Medieval and Renaissance cities had no public illumination. Assaults by ruffians and thieves were so common after dark that wayfarers took to paying others to precede them through the streets carrying lighted torches. In the seventeenth century this escort-for-hire was called a "link boy" in London, and a "falot" (lantern companion) in Paris. Delivery of black market goods to stores, such as fuel oil to gasoline stations during the oil embargo of 1973–1974, was accomplished under cover of darkness. Lawlessness is possible then because police coverage is sparse (Boston *Globe*, 1977:1). In addition, the officers on duty make themselves unavailable by sleeping in their cars, an old custom in New York City where the practice is called "cooping" (*New York Times*, 1968). The same was informally reported to me about Boston police as well; they are found snoozing in their police cars in the Arboretum by the early morning joggers.

In Boston today, carrying arms is more common at night. For fear of mugging or rape, escort services are provided on many college campuses for women returning to their dorms at night, or for women on the evening shift going from their places of work to the parking lot or subway station. An escort is provided for nurses at Boston City Hospital because of an increase in robberies in that area. And some apartment houses, with their sentries at the door, become vertical stockades to which people in the city retreat at night.

However, like the former West, lawlessness and violence at night are concentrated in certain hours in certain places and are otherwise uncommon. Fights reach their peak about midnight, but are least frequent from 2:30 to 11:00 a.m. The area of Boston in which many

brawls and muggings take place, where prostitution is rampant and bars and lounges feature nude go-go dancers, is called the "combat zone." A large transient population of relatively young males come into the area to patronize the moviehouses featuring X-rated films and become drunk and aggressive in bars and on the streets. Although this description may approximate what was once reported of mining towns in the West, these combat zones do not function so after 2:30 a.m. or during the daytime. In the daytime the areas are parts of business districts. Many people shop at department stores nearby, or otherwise pass through and patronize eating places and businesses there. So the combat zone designation refers to these places only at certain hours and is not true for all the city all night.

## 8. *There Is More Helpfulness and Friendliness*

Hollon (1974:211–2) remarks that "For every act of violence during the frontier period, there were thousands of examples of kindness, generosity, and sacrifice ..." He quotes an English traveler who said, " 'Even the rough western men, the hardy sons of the Indian frontier, accustomed from boyhood to fighting for existence, were hospitable and generous to a degree hard to find in more civilized life.' "

Reports of life on the land frontier are replete with accounts of warmth toward strangers, of community house building and barn raisings, and of help for those in need (Darby, 1818:400; Frantz and Choate, 1955:64; Billington, 1949:96, 167; Riegel, 1947:81). "Neighbors were ready to lend anything they possessed. No man driving along with an empty wagon on a good road would pass another on foot without inviting him to ride" (Dick, 1937:512). Travelers returning from the outskirts said they were treated more kindly than they had been in the cities (Flint, 1826:402–03; Hollon, 1974:212).

At first these stories of openhanded western hospitality may seem inconsistent in the face of the high risks of thievery and violence. But the circumstances are actually related to one another. Dick (1937:510) observed that "As the isolated settlers battled against savage men, ... and loneliness, they were drawn together in a fellowship." Billington (1972:166) added,

> Cooperation is normal within every in-group, but accentuates when the in-group is in conflict with an out-group and group solidarity is strengthened. This was the situation in frontier communities where conflicts with Indians, with raw nature, and with dominating Easteners heightened the spirit of interdependence.

That people want to affiliate under such conditions with

others like themselves was demonstrated experimentally by Schachter (1959). He showed that the greater the risk people thought they were facing, the more anxious they were; and the more anxious they were, the more they wanted to be with others—even strangers—facing the same risk. Schachter (1959) concluded that being with others in the same boat served to reduce anxiety, and also provided an opportunity to appraise one's own feelings and adjust them appropriately to the risk. With less emotional uncertainty and with the knowledge that others share the circumstances, individuals feel better about confronting a stressful situation.

Because the night is a time of more violence and people feel more vulnerable then, those up and about have a similar outlook and behave toward others as pioneers did in the West. At night people are more alert to strangers when they pass on the street. Each tries to judge whether the other is potentially dangerous. Upon deciding that the other is to be trusted, one's mood shifts from vigilance to expansiveness. If not foe, then friend. Aware that they are out together in a dangerous environment, people identify with each other and become more outgoing. The sense of safety that spreads over those together at night in a diner or in a coffee shop promotes camaraderie there.

Also, on both frontiers people may be more hospitable because they have time to devote to strangers. Pioneers had plenty to do; yet often they had nothing to do. They were not closely synchronized in daily tasks as people were in the eastern cities, and the norm of punctuality was not emphasized. One man who grew up in the West

> ... recalled the boredom he could never escape.... [T]he worst time of all was Sunday afternoon, when he had nothing to do. There were no newspapers to read and no books other than the family Bible, there was no one his age to talk with and the nearest store was miles away. (Hollon, 1974:196)

In the city during the day, the mood of pressured schedules takes hold of folk and makes their encounters specific and short. The tempo slows markedly after midnight. The few who are out then hurry less because there are fewer places to rush to. Whereas lack of time inhibits sociability and helpfulness available time clears the way for them.

### 9. Exploitation of the Basic Resource Finally Becomes National Policy

Westward expansion began long before anyone officially recognized the land frontier's possibilities for our society. It took years to realize even that the U.S. West was hab-itable. At one time the land west of the Missouri River was labeled on maps as the Great American Desert. Almost no one thought that some day many people would want to migrate and settle there (Hicks, 1948:508). Nor was the catch phrase "Manifest Destiny" applied to colonizing the West until 1845, centuries after the effort had been under way. In 1837 Horace Greeley introduced the slogan "Go West, Young Man, go forth into the Country." He looked upon such migrations as a means of relief from the poverty and unemployment caused by the Panic of 1837. By 1854 Greeley was urging, "Make the Public Lands free in quarter-sections to Actual Settlers ... and the earth's landless millions will no longer be orphans and mendicants" (cited in Smith, 1950:234–5). In 1862, with the passage of the Homestead Act, it became a deliberate policy of the U.S. government to use the western territory to help relieve the conditions of tenant farmers and hard-pressed city laborers. A member of Congress declared, in support of the Homestead Act, "I sustain this measure ... because its benign operation will postpone for centuries, if it will not forever, all serious conflict between capital and labor in the older free states" (Smith, 1950:239). The policy makers finally saw the exploitation of western space as a means of solving social problems.

Similarly, in the first 150 years after Murdock's coal-gas illumination was introduced, there was no national consciousness in England or the United States about colonizing the nighttime. People went ahead, expanding their activities into the dark hours without declaring that a 24-hour community was being forged. Now in the 1970s policy makers have begun talking about cheap time at night the way they once spoke of cheap western land. V. D. Patrushev (1972:429) of the Soviet Union writes that "Time ... is a particular form of national wealth. Therefore it is imperative to plan the most efficient use of it for all members of a society." Daniel Schydlowsky (1976:5), an economist who specializes in development in Latin America and who recently ended a three-year study there, has concluded that multiple-shift work would produce remarkable gains in reducing unemployment and improve the economies of overpopulated developing cities. His claim for the use of time echoes the attitudes of nineteenth century proponents of the use of western lands as a solution for those who were out of work.

The advocates of westward expansion also saw it as a way to draw off great numbers of people from the cities and forestall crowding there (Smith, 1950:8, 238). Today Dantzig and Saaty (1973:190–3) recommended dispersing activities around the clock as a means of reducing congestion. And Meier (1976:965) writes, "Scarce land and expensive human time can also be conserved by encouraging round-the-clock operation....By such means people can live densely without stepping on each other's toes."

### 10. Interest Groups Emerge

As the U.S. frontier matured, the population became more aware of its own circumstances and organized to promote its own concerns. Turner (1893:207; 1965:54) remarked that the West felt a keen sense of difference from the East. He wrote:

> ... [F]rom the beginning East and West have shown a sectional attitude. The interior of the colonies was disrespectful of the coast, and the coast looked down upon the upland folk.... [The westerners finally] became self-conscious and even rebellious against the rule of the East.... [I]t resented the conception that it was merely an emanation from a rival North and South; that it was the dependency of one or another of the Eastern sections.... It took the attitude of a section itself. (1932:25–30)

Sections are geographically-based interest groups. One hundred years ago the West gave rise to such pressure groups and farm bloc organizations as the Greenback Party, the National Grange, and the Populists. The Granger movement, for example, grew with the westerners' problems with transportation in their region. There were no significant river or canal systems out west and so the settlers were at the mercy of railroads. But the rates in the newer regions of the West were far higher than those in the East, and it was protest against the disparity that aided the movement in the 1870s (Robbins, 1960:271).

The night also isolates a group from the main society. Antagonism may develop as daytimers deprecate the nighttimers and the latter resent the neglect shown by the others. People active after dark find their life style differing from that of daytime society, become aware of having a separate identity, and evolve into interest groups. New alignments in the tradition of sectionalism begin to emerge. This has already happened for two groups usually linked with the nighttime: homosexuals and prostitutes. The Gay Liberation Front is one nationwide organization devoted to the rights of homosexuals. Prostitutes also have a union. Appropriately they adopted the name of a creature renowned in the U.S. West for howling at night—the coyote. COYOTES (Call Off Your Old Tired Ethics) seek legislation to decriminalize their activities and protest courtroom discrimination against women who earn their living by prostitution (Boston *Globe*, 1976a).

An actual day vs. night contest has already been fought in Boston. The city's airport is flanked by residential neighborhoods and its afterdark activity became a nuisance to people wanting an undisturbed night's sleep. In 1976 dwellers in those neighborhoods, as private citizens and through two organized groups—Fair Share, and the Massachusetts Air Pollution and Noise Abatement Committee—made a concerted effort to stop air-

plane flights between 11 p.m. and 7 a.m. It led to counterarguments by the business community stressing the economic benefit of continuing the flights. The pro-nighttime group was a coalition among commercial interests, airline companies, unions, and airport employees holding jobs at night (some of whom lived in those very neighborhoods). This group argued that the curfew would result in the loss of thousands of jobs, millions of dollars in sales, and further would discourage business investment in the New England area. Joined by the governor, the mayor and many legislators, the coalition successfully won a decision from the Massachusetts Port Authority that the nighttime flights should be kept going. (Some proposals for noise reduction during the night accompanied the decision.) A month later, Eastern Airlines announced it was adding an airbus and expanding its staff at the airport "as a direct result of the recent decision ... not to impose a night curfew at Logan [airport]." As one businessman put it, "The curfew decision was regarded as the shootout at the OK Corral" (Boston *Globe*, 1976b; 1976c).

...

### Conclusion

What is the gain in thinking of night as a frontier? A single theoretical idea gives coherence to a wide range of events: the kind of people up and about at those hours, why they differ from daytimers in their behavior, the beginnings of political efforts by night people, the slow realization among leaders that public policy might be applied to the time resource. Even the variety of endeavors becomes understandable—from metal smelting plants to miniature golf courses, to mayor's complaint offices, to eating places, to computerized banking terminals that dispense cash. The niche is being expanded. Bit by bit, all of society migrates there. To treat this as a sequel to the geographic spread of past centuries is to summarize the move within familiar ecological concepts of migration, settlement, and frontier.

Though I have reviewed materials for one period in U.S. history, these conditions are features of all frontiers. They should apply to the Russians crossing the Urals, to the Chinese entering Manchuria during the Ch'ing dynasty, to the Boers settling South Africa, to Australians venturing into the Outback, to present-day Brazilians colonizing the Amazon interior, as well as to Americans migrating into the night. The patterns are confirmed by essays in Wyman and Kroeber's anthology on frontiers.

We should also consider the uniqueness of this new frontier. Each settlement beyond established boundaries has its own qualities. Here are some differences between the West and the night: (1) On the land frontier settlers lived rudely with few services at hand. At night a large portion of the total range of activities is services. (2)

Utilities cost more on the western fringes; at night the fees for telephone calls, electricity, and airplane travel are lower. (3) While western settlements were in remote contact with the East, day and night are joined so that either can be affected quickly by events in the other. Twenty-four hour society is more constantly adjusting, more unstable. (4) Looking westward, pioneers saw no end to the possibilities for growth, but we know that expansion into the night can only go as far as the dawn. (5) The land frontier held promise of unlimited opportunity for individuals who ventured there. Miners and pioneers endured hardships because they lived for the future. They hoped to make their fortunes, or at least a better life. At night there are large numbers of unskilled, menial, and dirty tasks; but charwoman and watchman and hospital aide and porter are dead-end jobs. Many people so employed are immigrants or members of minority groups and this expanding margin of society is a *time ghetto.* The ghetto encloses more than minorities and immigrants, for ultimate control in 24-hour organizations remains with top management in the daytime. Policy making, important decisions, employee hiring, and planning are curtailed during off-hours. Since evening and night staffs are prevented from taking many actions that would lead to the recognition of executive ability, and since their performance is not readily observable by the bosses, all have poorer chance for advancement. (6) The western frontier's natural resources were so extensive that we became wasteful and squandered them. At night there is nothing new to exploit but time itself, so we maximize the use of fixed assets and become more frugal. (7) Migrating westward called for rather significant capital investment—outlays for a covered wagon, mining equipment, cattle, the railroad. There is little extra capital required for a move to the night. Instead, the incessant organization's need for more personnel reflects a swing toward more labor intensive operations. So the night frontier may appeal to developing countries with meager treasuries and teeming populations of unemployed.

This expansion is also unusual because it happens in time rather than in space. We change from a diurnal into an incessant species. We move beyond the environmental cycle—alternating day and night—in which our biological and social life evolved, and thus force novelty on these areas. (8) In the past a single set of minds shut down an enterprise one day and started it up the next. It permitted easy continuity and orderly administration. For coverage around the clock, we introduce shifts of personnel. Several times a day another set of minds takes over the same activity and facilities. (9) A physiological upset is imposed on people who work at night and maintain ordinary recreation and social life on their days off. Each time they switch their active hours they undergo

phase shifts in body rhythms such as heartbeat, temperature, and hormonal production. The several days' malaise that results was known to such workers long before air travel across time zones popularized the phrase "jet fatigue."

Ibsen's (1890: Act II) character, Eilert Löuvborg, describes the two sections of the book he has written, "The first deals with the . . . forces of the future. And here is the second forecasting the probable line of development." We may believe we understand the forces, the conditions under which humans enlarge their niche, but what is the probable line of development? Forecasting is called for despite the difficulties of social prediction. We should consider the possibilities of an era in which unremitting activity is even more commonplace. What is the carrying capacity of the 24-hour day? What will happen when saturation occurs? Time will have extraordinary leverage as it gets used up, for time is a resource without direct substitute. It is unstretchable; we cannot do with it as we did with land by building up toward the sky and digging into the ground. Time is unstorable; we cannot save the unused hours every night for future need.

In his essay, "The Frontier in American History," Frederick Jackson Turner (1893:38) reviewed the impact of the advance into western lands upon our society and remarked, "And now, four centuries from the discovery of America, at the end of a hundred years of life under the constitution, the frontier has gone." But it has not gone. During the era that the settlement of our land frontier was being completed, there began—into the night—a large-scale migration of wakeful activity that continues to spread over the world.

## QUESTIONS

1. What are the "frontier" characteristics of the urban night?

2. Are there any practical obstacles to fully colonizing the night, in such a way that the various activities of the day could be duplicated during those hours?

3. What are the ecological factors (social, economic, demographic, environmental, etc.) that might induce people to colonize a frontier (or the night)?

## REFERENCES

**American Heritage Dictionary of the English Language**
  1970 Boston: Houghton Mifflin.

**Becker, Howard**
  1963 Outsiders: Studies in the Sociology of Deviance. New York: Free Press.

**Billington, Ray Allen**
1949 Westward Expansion. New York: Macmillan.
1954 The American Frontiersman. London: Oxford University Press.
1972 "Frontier democracy: social aspects." pp. 160–84 in G. R. Taylor (ed.), The Turner Thesis: Concerning the Role of the Frontier in American History. 3rd ed. Lexington, Ma.: Heath.

**Boston Globe**
1976a "Prostitutes speak of pride, but they are still victims." June 15:1, 10.
1976b "Dukakis decides to go against Logan curfew." August 12:1, 20.
1976c "Logan anti-noise plan offered." August 13:35.
1977 "Boston police today." April 4:1, 3.

**Brandeis, Louis D. and Josephine Goldmark**
1918 The Case Against Night Work for Women. Rev. ed. New York: National Consumers League.

**Buttimer, Anne**
1976 "Grasping the dynamism of lifeworld." Annals of the Association of American Geographers 66:277–92.

**Dantzig, George B. and Thomas I. Saaty**
1973 Compact city. San Francisco: Freeman.

**Darby, William**
[1818] 1969 "Primitivism in the lower Mississippi valley." Pp. 399–401 in M. Ridge and R. A. Billington (eds.), America's Frontier Story. New York: Holt.

**Dick, Everett**
[1937] 1954 The Sod-House Frontier, 1854–1890. New York: Appleton-Century.

**Doddridge, Joseph**
[1912] 1969 "Life in the old west." Pp. 101–6 in M. Ridge and R. A. Billington (eds.), America's Frontier Story. New York: Holt.

**Flint, Timothy**
[1826] 1969 "Frontier society in the Mississippi valley." Pp. 401–3 in M. Ride and R. A. Billington (eds.), America's Frontier Story. New York: Holt.

**Frantz, J. B. and J. E. Choate**
1955 The American Cowboy: The Myth and Reality. Norman: University of Oklahoma Press.

**Godkin, Edwin L.**
[1896] 1969 "The frontier and the national character." Pp. 13–6 in M. Ride and R. A. Billington (eds.), America's Frontier Story. New York: Holt.

**Hicks, John D.**
1948 The Federal Union. Boston: Houghton Mifflin.

**Hollon, W. Eugene**
1973 "Frontier violence: another look." Pp. 86–100 in R. A. Billington (ed.), People of the Plains and Mountains. Westport, Ct.: Greenwood Press.
1974 Frontier Violence. New York: Oxford University Press.

**Humphrey, Seth K.**
1931 Following the Prairie Frontier. Minneapolis: University of Minnesota Press.

**Ibsen, Henrik**
[1890] 1950 Hedda Gabler. Tr. E. Gosse and W. Archer. Pp. 42–74 in J. Gassner (ed.), A Treasury of the Theatre. New York: Simon and Schuster.

**Jackson, W. Turrentine**
1973 "Pioneer life on the plains and in the mines." Pp. 63–85 in R. A. Billington (ed.), People of the Plains and Mountains. Westport, Ct.: Greenwood Press.

**Kozak, Lola Jean**
1974 "Night people: a study of the social experiences of night workers." Michigan State University, Summation 4:40–61.

**Marx, Karl**
[1867] 1906 Capital. New York: Modern Library.

**Meier, Richard L.**
1976 "A stable urban ecosystem." Science 192:962–8.

**Melbin, Murray**
1977 "The colonization of time." In T. Carlstein, D. Parkes, and N. Thrift (eds.), Timing Space and Spacing Time in Social Organization. London: Arnold.

**Mumford, Lewis**
1961 The City in History. New York: Harcourt Brace.

**National Industrial Conference Board**
1927 Night Work in Industry. New York: National Industrial Conference Board.

**New York Times**
1968 " 'Cooping': an old custom under fire." December 15: Sec. 4, 6E.

**Patrushev, V. D.**
1972 "Aggregate time-balances and their meaning for socio-economic planning." Pp. 429–40 in A. Szalai (ed.), The Use of Time. The Hague: Mouton.

**Riegel, Robert E.**
1947 America Moves West. New York: Holt.

**Robbins, Roy M.**
1960 Our Landed Heritage. Princeton: Princeton University Press.

**Schachter, Stanley**
1959 The Psychology of Affiliation. Stanford: Stanford University Press.

**Schlesinger, Arthur**
1933 The Rise of the City: 1878–1895. New York: Macmillan.

**Schydlowsky, Daniel**
1976 "Multiple shifts would produce 'revolutionary results' for Latin American economy." Boston University, Spectrum 4 (September 9):5.

**Smith, Henry Nash**
[1950] 1957 Virgin Land. New York: Vintage.

**Turner, Frederick Jackson**
[1893] 1920 The Frontier in American History. New York: Holt.
1932 The Significance of Sections in American History. New York: Holt.
[1965] America's Great Frontiers and Sections.
1969 Unpublished essays edited by W. R. Jacobs. Lincoln: Nebraska University Press.

**U.S. Bureau of the Census**
1975 Historical Statistics of the United States, Vol. 1: ser. A195–209. Washington, D.C.: U.S. Government Printing Office.

**U.S. Bureau of Labor Statistics**
1976 Current Population Survey. Unpublished paper. May 12: Table 1. Washington, D.C.

**Wyman, Walker D. and Clifton B. Kroeber (eds.)**
1957 The Frontier in Perspective. Madison: University of Wisconsin Press.

*Harry F. Waters*

# 54. Life According to TV

*A striking feature of the modern age is the prevalence of the mass media—forms of communication that reach a large audience without any contact between the senders and the receivers of messages. Until this century, mass media meant printed works such as books and newspapers, which had to be physically transported from the publishers to the readers. But modern technology has made possible telecommunication, the instantaneous transmission of messages from senders to receivers all over the globe.*

*The most significant form of telecommunication is, of course, television. No other society is as permeated by television as the United States. The country has well over 2,000 television stations, and 98 percent of all households have sets—almost two of them, in fact. A TV set is switched on for seven hours a day in the average American home. One result is that television has become a major agent for the socialization of children. The average American between the ages of three and sixteen spends more time in front of a television set than in school, and is saturated with images offering information, role models, viewpoints, norms, values, news, fiction, and divergent lifestyles.*

*There is constant debate about the influence of television on society in general and on children in particular. In this article, Harry F. Waters discusses some research on the content of television programming and the relationship it bears to the reality of the social world.*

*You people sit there, night after night. You're beginning to believe this illusion we're spinning here. You're beginning to think the tube is reality and your own lives are unreal. This is mass madness!*

—Anchorman Howard Beale
in the film "Network"

*If you can write a nation's stories, you needn't worry about who makes its laws. Today television tells most of the stories to most of the people most of the time.*

—George Gerbner, Ph.D.

The late Paddy Chayefsky, who created Howard Beale, would have loved George Gerbner. In "Network," Chayefsky marshaled a scathing, fictional assault on the values and methods of the people who control the world's most potent communications instrument. In real life, Gerbner, perhaps the nation's foremost authority on the social impact of television, is quietly using the disciplines of behavioral research to construct an equally devastating indictment of the medium's images and messages. More than any spokesman for a pressure group, Gerbner has become the man that television watches. From his cramped, book-lined office at the University of Pennsylvania springs a steady flow of studies that are raising executive blood pressures at the networks' sleek Manhattan command posts.

George Gerbner's work is uniquely important because it transports the scientific examination of television far beyond familiar children-and-violence arguments. Rather than simply studying the link between violence on the tube and crime in the streets, Gerbner is exploring wider and deeper terrain. He has turned his lens on TV's hidden victims—women, the elderly, blacks, blue-collar workers and other groups—to document the ways in which video-entertainment portrayals subliminally condition how we perceive ourselves and how we view those around us. Gerbner's subjects are not merely the impressionable young; they include all the rest of us. And it is his ominous conclusion that heavy watchers of the prime-time mirror are receiving a grossly distorted picture of the real world that they tend to accept more readily than reality itself.

The 63-year-old Gerbner, who is dean of Penn's Annenberg School of Communications, employs a methodology that meshes scholarly observation with mundane legwork. Over the past 15 years, he and a tireless trio of assistants (Larry Gross, Nancy Signorielli and Michael Morgan) videotaped and exhaustively analyzed 1,600 prime-time programs involving more than 15,000 characters. Then they drew up multiple-choice questionnaires that offered correct answers about the world at large along with answers that reflected what Gerbner perceived to be the misrepresentations and biases of the world according to TV. Finally, these questions were posed to large samples of citizens from all socioeconomic strata. In every survey, the Annenberg team discovered that heavy viewers of television (those watching more than four hours a day), who account for more than 30 percent of the population, almost invariably chose the TV-influenced answers, while light viewers (less than two hours a day), selected the answers corresponding more closely to actual life. Some of the dimensions of television's reality warp:

## Sex

Male prime-time characters outnumber females by 3 to 1 and, with a few star-turn exceptions, women are portrayed as weak, passive satellites to powerful, effective men. TV's male population also plays a vast variety of roles, while females generally get typecast as either lovers or mothers. Less than 20 percent of TV's married women with children work outside the home—as compared with more than 50 percent in real life. The tube's distorted depictions of women, concludes Gerbner, reinforce stereotypical attitudes and increase sexism. In one Annenberg survey, heavy viewers were far more likely than light ones to agree with the proposition: "Women should take care of running their homes and leave running the country to men."

## Age

People over 65, too, are grossly underrepresented on television. Correspondingly, heavy-viewing Annenberg respondents believe that the elderly are a vanishing breed, that they make up a smaller proportion of the population today than they did 20 years ago. In fact, they form the nation's most rapidly expanding age group. Heavy viewers also believe that old people are less healthy today than they were two decades ago, when quite the opposite is true. As with women, the portrayals of old people trans-

mit negative impressions. In general, they are cast as silly, stubborn, sexually inactive and eccentric. "They're often shown as feeble grandparents bearing cookies," says Gerbner. "You never see the power that real old people often have. The best and possibly only time to learn about growing old with decency and grace is in youth. And young people are the most susceptible to TV's messages."

## Race

The problem with the medium's treatment of blacks is more one of image than of visibility. Though a tiny percentage of black characters come across as "unrealistically romanticized," reports Gerbner, the overwhelming majority of them are employed in subservient, supporting roles—such as the white hero's comic sidekick. "When a black child looks at prime time," he says, "most of the people he sees doing interesting and important things are white." That imbalance, he goes on, tends to teach young blacks to accept minority status as naturally inevitable and even deserved. To assess the impact of such portrayals on the general audience, the Annenberg survey forms included questions like "Should white people have the right to keep blacks out of their neighborhoods?" and "Should there be laws against marriages between blacks and whites?" The more that viewers watched, the more they answered "Yes" to each question.

## Work

Heavy viewers greatly overestimated the proportion of Americans employed as physicians, lawyers, athletes and entertainers, all of whom inhabit prime-time in hordes. A mere 6 to 10 percent of television characters hold blue-collar or service jobs vs. about 60 percent in the real work force. Gerbner sees two dangers in TV's skewed division of labor. On the one hand, the tube so overrepresents and glamorizes the elite occupations that it sets up unrealistic expectations among those who must deal with them in actuality. At the same time, TV largely neglects portraying the occupations that most youngsters will have to enter. "You almost never see the farmer, the factory worker or the small businessman," he notes. "Thus not only do lawyers and other professionals find they cannot measure up to the image TV projects of them, but children's occupational aspirations are channeled in unrealistic directions." The Gerbner team feels this emphasis on high-powered jobs poses problems for adolescent girls, who are also presented with views of women as homebodies. The two conflicting views, Gerbner says, add to the frustration over choices they have to make as adults.

## Health

Although video characters exist almost entirely on junk food and quaff alcohol 15 times more often than water, they manage to remain slim, healthy and beautiful. Frequent TV watchers, the Annenberg investigators found, eat more, drink more, exercise less and possess an almost mystical faith in the curative powers of medical science. Concludes Gerbner: "Television may well be the single most pervasive source of health information. And its overidealized images of medical people, coupled with its complacency about unhealthy life-styles, leaves both patients and doctors vulnerable to disappointment, frustration and even litigation."

## Crime

On the small screen, crime rages about 10 times more often than in real life. But while other researchers concentrate on the propensity of TV mayhem to incite aggression, the Annenberg team has studied the hidden side of its imprint: fear of victimization. On television, 55 percent of prime-time characters are involved in violent confrontations once a week; in reality, the figure is less than 1 percent. In all demographic groups in every class of neighborhood, heavy viewers overestimated the statistical chance of violence in their own lives and harbored an exaggerated mistrust of strangers—creating what Gerbner calls a "mean-world syndrome." Forty-six percent of heavy viewers who live in cities rated their fear of crime "very serious" as opposed to 26 percent for light viewers. Such paranoia is especially acute among TV entertainment's most common victims: women, the elderly, nonwhites, foreigners and lower-class citizens.

Video violence, proposes Gerbner, is primarily responsible for imparting lessons in social power: it demonstrates who can do what to whom and get away with it. "Television is saying that those at the bottom of the power scale cannot get away with the same things that a white, middle-class American male can," he says. "It potentially conditions people to think of themselves as victims."

At a quick glance, Gerbner's findings seem to contain a cause-and-effect, chicken-or-the-egg question. Does television make heavy viewers view the world the way they do or do heavy viewers come from the poorer, less experienced segment of the populace that regards the world that way to begin with? In other words, does the tube create or simply confirm the unenlightened attitudes of its most loyal audience? Gerbner, however, was savvy enough to construct a methodology largely immune to such criticism. His samples of heavy viewers cut across all ages, incomes, education levels and ethnic backgrounds—and every category displayed the same tube-induced misconceptions of the world outside.

Needless to say, the networks accept all this as enthusiastically as they would a list of news-coverage complaints from the Ayatollah Khomeini. Even so, their responses tend to be tinged with a singular respect for Gerbner's personal and professional credentials. The man is no ivory-tower recluse. During World War II, the Budapest-born Gerbner parachuted into the mountains of Yugoslavia to join the partisans fighting the Germans. After the war, he hunted down and personally arrested scores of high Nazi officials. Nor is Gerbner some videophobic vigilante. A Ph.D. in communications, he readily acknowledges TV's beneficial effects, noting that it has abolished parochialism, reduced isolation and loneliness and provided the poorest members of society with cheap, plug-in exposure to experiences they otherwise would not have. Funding for his research is supplied by such prestigious bodies as the National Institute of Mental Health, the surgeon general's office and the American Medical Association, and he is called to testify before congressional committees nearly as often as David Stockman.

## Mass Entertainment

When challenging Gerbner, network officials focus less on his findings and methods than on what they regard as his own misconceptions of their industry's function. "He's looking at television from the perspective of a social scientist rather than considering what is mass entertainment," says Alfred Schneider, vice president of standards and practices at ABC. "We strive to balance TV's social effects with what will capture an audience's interests. If you showed strong men being victimized as much as women or the elderly, what would comprise the dramatic conflict? If you did a show truly representative of society's total reality, and nobody watched because it wasn't interesting, what have you achieved?"

CBS senior vice president Gene Mater also believes that Gerbner is implicitly asking for the theoretically impossible. "TV is unique in its problems," says Mater. "Everyone wants a piece of the action. Everyone feels that their racial or ethnic group is underrepresented or should be portrayed as they would like the world to perceive them. No popular entertainment form, including this one, can or should be an accurate reflection of society."

On that point, at least, Gerbner is first to agree; he hardly expects television entertainment to serve as a mirror image of absolute truth. But what fascinates him about this communications medium is its marked difference from all others. In other media, customers carefully choose what they want to hear or read: a movie, a magazine, a best seller. In television, notes Gerbner, viewers rarely tune in a for a particular program. Instead, most just habitually turn on the set—and watch by the clock rather than for a specific show. "Television viewing fulfills the criteria of a ritual," he says. "It is the only medium that can bring to people things they otherwise would not select." With such unique power, believes Gerbner, comes unique responsibility: "No other medium reaches into every home or has a comparable, cradle-to-grave influence over what a society learns about itself."

## Match

In Gerbner's view, virtually all of TV's distortions of reality can be attributed to its obsession with demographics. The viewers that prime-time sponsors most want to reach are white, middle-class, female and between 18 and 49—in short, the audience that purchases most of the consumer products advertised on the tube. Accordingly, notes Gerbner, the demographic portrait of TV's fictional characters largely matches that of its prime commercial targets and largely ignores everyone else. "Television," he concludes, "reproduces a world for its own best customers."

Among TV's more candid executives, that theory draws considerable support. Yet by pointing a finger at the power of demographics, Gerbner appears to contradict one of his major findings. If female viewers are so dear to the hearts of sponsors, why are female characters cast in such unflattering light? "In a basically male-oriented power structure," replies Gerbner, "you can't alienate the male viewer. But you can get away with offending women because most women are pretty well brainwashed to accept it." The Annenberg dean has an equally tidy explanation for another curious fact. Since the corporate world provides network television with all of its financial support, one would expect businessmen on TV to be portrayed primarily as good guys. Quite the contrary. As any fan of "Dallas," "Dynasty," or "Falcon Crest" well knows, the image of the company man is usually that of a mendacious, dirty-dealing rapscallion. Why would TV snap at the hand that feeds it? "Credibility is the way to ratings," proposes Gerbner. "This country has a populist tradition of bias against anything big, including big business. So to retain credibility, TV entertainment shows businessmen in relatively derogatory ways."

In the medium's Hollywood-based creative community, the gospel of Gerbner finds some passionate adherents. Rarely have TV's best and brightest talents

viewed their industry with so much frustration and anger. The most sweeping indictment emanates from David Rintels, a two-time Emmy-winning writer and former president of the Writers Guild of America, West. "Gerbner is absolutely correct and it is the people who run the networks who are to blame," says Rintels. "The networks get bombarded with thoughtful, reality-oriented scripts. They simply won't do them. They slam the door on them. They believe that the only way to get ratings is to feed viewers what conforms to their biases or what has limited resemblance to reality. From 8 to 11 o'clock each night, television is one long lie."

Innovative thinkers such as Norman Lear, whose work has been practically driven off the tube, don't fault the networks so much as the climate in which they operate. Says Lear: "All of this country's institutions have become totally fixated on short-term bottom-line thinkings. Everyone grabs for what might succeed today and the hell with tomorrow. Television just catches more of the heat because it's more visible." Perhaps the most perceptive assessment of Gerbner's conclusions is offered by one who has worked both sides of the industry street. Deanne Barkley, a former NBC vice president who now helps run an independent production house, reports that the negative depictions of women on TV have made it "nerve-racking" to function as a woman within TV. "No one takes responsibility for the social impact of their shows," says Barkley. "But then how do you decide where it all begins? Do the networks give viewers what they want? Or are the networks conditioning them to think that way?"

Gerbner himself has no simple answer to that conundrum. Neither a McLuhanesque shaman nor a Naderesque crusader, he hesitates to suggest solutions until pressed. Then out pops a pair of provocative notions. Commercial television will never democratize its treatments of daily life, he believes, until it finds a way to broaden its financial base. Coincidentally, Federal Communications Commission chairman Mark Fowler seems to have arrived at much the same conclusion. In exchange for lifting such government restrictions on TV as the fairness doctrine and the equal-time rule, Fowler would impose a modest levy on station owners called a spectrum-use fee. Funds from the fees would be set aside to finance programs aimed at specialized tastes rather than the mass appetite. Gerbner enthusiastically endorses that proposal: "Let the ratings system dominate most of prime time but not every hour of every day. Let some programs carry advisories that warn: 'This is not for all of you. This is for nonwhites, or for religious people or for the aged and the handicapped. Turn it off unless you'd like to eavesdrop.' That would be a very refreshing thing."

## Role

In addition, Gerbner would like to see viewers given an active role in steering the overall direction of television instead of being obliged to passively accept whatever the networks offer. In Britain, he points out, political candidates debate the problems of TV as routinely as the issue of crime. In this country, proposes Gerbner, "every political campaign should put television on the public agenda. Candidates talk about schools, they talk about jobs, they talk about social welfare. They're going to have to start discussing this all-pervasive force."

There are no outright villains in this docudrama. Even Gerbner recognizes that network potentates don't set out to proselytize a point of view; they are simply businessmen selling a mass-market product. At the same time, their 90 million nightly customers deserve to know the side effects of the ingredients. By the time the typical American child reaches the age of reason, calculates Gerbner, he or she will have absorbed more than 30,000 electronic "stories." These stories, he suggests, have replaced the socializing role of the preindustrial church:

they create a "cultural mythology" that establishes the norms of approved behavior and belief. And all Gerbner's research indicates that this new mythological world, with its warped picture of a sizable portion of society, may soon become the one most of us think we live in.

Who else is telling us that? Howard Beale and his eloquent alarms have faded into off-network reruns. At the very least, it is comforting to know that a real-life Beale is very much with us . . . and *really* watching.

---

## QUESTIONS

1. How "true to life" is TV, and what social factors influence the content of television programming?

2. What are some social benefits of television? Are there any social disadvantages?

3. Would you say that the content of television programming influences social behavior? Can the case be proved?

Jeremy Rifkin
Ted Howard

# 55.  Who Should Play God?

*One of the most distinctive features of Western civilization has been an ability to develop scientific knowledge and to apply that knowledge to technology. Upon that cultural trait has been built the entire edifice of the modern industrial society and the array of material conveniences it offers. But scientific and technological innovations have not been without their critics, for many have charged that science and technology create as many problems as they solve.*

*This argument has new relevance now that scientists have cracked the genetic code and are beginning to apply that knowledge to the technology of genetic engineering. This technology is still very much in its infancy, but its potential uses in the decades ahead are awesome. Scientists can already alter the genetic make-up of laboratory specimens, breeding new generations with characteristics their species never had before; and it seems only a matter of time before this technology is available for humans. Scientists have succeeded in making clones—genetic replicas—of some lower animals. Other scientists are studying cellular processes to find some way of slowing down, or even halting, the aging process. And these are only some of the achievements of the new biology. In other, related fields new technologies are being perfected—for example, to allow the sex of a child to be preselected, or to permit one woman to give birth to a child conceived by another.*

*In this article, Jeremy Rifkin and Ted Howard consider some of the ethical and practical problems posed to society by such innovations.*

From *Who Should Play God? The Artificial Creation of Life and What It Means for the Future of the Human Race* by Ted Howard and Jeremy Rifkin. Copyright © 1977 by Center for Urban Education. Reprinted by permission of Delacorte Press.

On a few momentous occasions in mankind's history, the body of accumulated human knowledge has spawned dramatic new inventions and discoveries which people, in turn, have used to regulate, control, and moderate the external world—the discovery of fire, the invention of the wheel, the formulation of written language, the discovery of the principles of gravity, and the development of the internal combustion engine. The splitting of the atom and the dawn of the nuclear age is the latest development in this long pursuit of means by which to harness nature.

Now a dramatic new scientific discovery has given some of us the power, for the first time, to shift attention from shaping and controlling the external world of matter and energy to shaping and controlling the internal world of life itself. With the discovery of DNA and its workings, scientists have unlocked the very secrets of life. It is only a matter of a handful of years before biologists will be able to change the evolutionary wisdom of billions of years by creating new plants, new animals, and new forms of human and post-human beings.

Today, only a tiny handful of people are privy to the secrets of life and how to manipulate and change it. Most of us are totally unaware of this new-found power. The concept of designing and engineering life, especially human life, is so utterly fantastic that it is difficult even to comprehend its meaning and implications. Yet, even as the public is kept virtually ignorant of this unparalleled new scientific discovery, microbiologists are busy in hundreds of laboratories across the country spending tens of millions of dollars in pursuit of the "mastery of life."

Breakthroughs in genetics research are making genetic engineering feasible for the first time, an in-house memorandum prepared by Cetus, a West Coast corporation, proudly announced in 1975. "This concept is so truly revolutionary," the memo asserted, "that by the year 2000 virtually all the major human diseases will regularly succumb to treatment" by genetic procedures.

The most significant genetic breakthrough of recent

years has been recombinant DNA—a laboratory technique for splicing together genetic material from unrelated organisms to manufacture novel forms of life. While the scientific community has become deeply divided over the health and safety problems presented by recombinant DNA, lay observers are increasingly questioning how this new technology will be used to modify human life as we know it.

The goals of today's genetic engineers range from the sublime to the ridiculous. The most modest among them advocate using genetic engineering to cure some 2,000 "monogenic" diseases—disorders caused by the malfunctioning of a single gene. Others are turning their attention to the artificial production of new strains of plants and "super" grains, while still others focus on redesigning various animal species to equip them to do society's unpopular jobs.

More ominous, however, are the well-credentialed and well-financed researchers who propose the complete restructuring of human life. Name your wildest fantasy (or nightmare) and some authority somewhere is seriously proposing it—from redesigning the human stomach so that people, like cows, will be able to consume cheap hay and grass to hybridizing a cross between man and lower primates. There are even genetic engineers who eagerly await the day when their work will produce the "final solution": the construction of a genetic superrace that will move far beyond *homo sapiens* on the evolutionary ladder.

There was a time when all of this could be dismissed as science fiction. No more. No matter how wild or fantastic the scenarios today's prestigious scientists envision, it is clear that they themselves are in earnest. As a tool of human genetic engineering, recombinant DNA literally offers us the opportunity to move beyond ourselves on the evolutionary scale. Man, the engineer, may soon become man, the engineered.

Until recently, population control programs focused on decreasing the numbers of births. Now, with geneticists and social planners worrying aloud about the deterioration of the human gene pool, there is interest in limiting the types and quality of births as well. Bentley Glass, former president of the American Academy for the Advancement of Science, warns, "In an overpopulated world, it can no longer be affirmed that the right of the woman and man to reproduce as they see fit is inviolate. . . ." Glass contends that the right of parents to procreate must become a secondary consideration to the "right of every child to be born with a sound physical and mental constitution, based on a sound genotype."

Thanks to new processes for manufacturing life, scientists can offer at least eight possible ways of controlling reproduction: artificial insemination of a woman with sperm from her mate; artificial insemination of a woman with sperm from an anonymous donor; transplantation of an ovum (egg) from one woman to another and subsequent artificial insemination with sperm from either a mate or a donor; fertilization of an egg in vitro (glass) followed by implantation into a woman; extra-corporeal gestation ("test-tube" life); parthenogenesis (the development of an unfertilized egg); nuclear transplantation or cloning (the reproduction of a cell which has been given a "foreign" nucleus), and embryo fusion (the joining of two individual embryos to form a human with four biological parents instead of two).

The combination of microbiological manipulation with the new reproductive techniques opens the way to full-scale genetic engineering. Bio-engineering is on the verge of moving from promise to performance. Artificial insemination is already marketable, and its popularity is growing. One million living Americans have been born by this process, and the number is increasing by more than 20,000 each year. The ability to deep-freeze human sperm for virtually any length of time has fueled a budding national industry—the commercial sperm bank. Banks are located in twelve cities, and business has never been better. John Olsen, president of Cryogenic Laboratories in St. Paul, notes, "In the last two years, the number of physicians requesting and using frozen donor sperm has doubled. We're having a difficult time keeping up with the requests coming in." Cryogenic supplies doctors in forty-five cities around the country.

Other methods of controlling reproduction represent a greater degree of sophistication. They are not yet perfected, but extensive experimentation has proceeded on each. The process of removing impregnated eggs from one herd animal and implanting them in the uterus of another animal of the same species is a widely used practice among animal breeders who combine artificial insemination with this embryo "flushing" and implantation to create super-herds of prize cattle.

At the next level of sophistication is the use of deep-frozen embryo banks that permit long-term storage of "superembryos." The first success in this area occurred in 1972, when scientists at the Atomic Energy Commission's Oak Ridge Laboratory thawed and implanted frozen mouse embryos. At about the same time, scientists in England announced the birth of Frosty, a bull calf born from a deep-frozen embryo.

Researchers point out that there are considerable similarities in embryo implantation and development between such lower mammals as mice and rabbits, and humans. So far, a human egg transplant has not been attempted, but several egg depositories exist at universities across the country. Commercial human ova banks are right around the corner.

A related area of experimentation is the fertilization of an egg in the laboratory and its subsequent implantation into a woman, a technique which some scientists feel is likely to be general medical practice within ten to twenty years. This research is making significant contributions in the quest to produce test-tube life.

The ability to keep tissue alive in glass has been recognized since 1907, when frog cells were first grown in petri dishes. A few years later, a scientist removed a piece of tissue from a chicken heart and placed it in a glass container filled with fluid, where it lived for thirty-three years (outliving the scientist by two years). As far back as the 1940s, a scientist succeeded in fertilizing a human egg with sperm in a test tube.

Joseph Fletcher, professor of medical ethics at the University of Virginia School of Medicine, regards test-tube life as finishing the work begun by the contraceptive pill. Because laboratory-created life is "willed, chosen, purposed, and controlled," rather than emotionally or accidentally produced, Fletcher believes "laboratory reproduction is radically human compared to conception by ordinary heterosexual intercourse."

Researchers have succeeded in growing a mouse embryo in vitro through approximately half of its gestation period, and E.S.E. Hafez, chairman of the department of animal sciences at Washington State University, is certain that the day of complete test-tube life is nearer than most of us suspect. To drive home his point, Hafez once posed for a photo which appeared in a national news magazine. There, in full color, was the scientist, a set of test tubes labeled "man," "sheep," and "swine" held in his outstretched hands; the caption read, "the barnyard of the future—complete with farmer."

With our present technology, incubators can keep alive a baby born as many as three months prematurely. The key now is to gain control of the first twenty-four weeks of life. Robert Goodlin of Stanford has been a leader in the search for an artificial womb for more than a decade, and has developed a pressurized steel-and-glass world in which an oxygen-rich saline solution constantly bathes a fetus. Intense pressure—roughly the equivalent of pressure felt under water at a depth of 450 feet—drives oxygen through the skin so that the baby's lungs do not have to work. No fetus has survived in the chamber for more than forty-eight hours, but Goodlin is working on a system to draw off carbon dioxide and waste materials that become deadly unless removed.

No genetic engineering possibility provokes more "sci-fi" thinking than cloning. But cloning, the production of genetically duplicate individuals from the biological information contained in a single body cell, is clearly not science fiction. Within our lifetimes, carbon-copy human beings will walk among us.

Recombinant DNA has become an especially useful tool in cloning experiments. A scientist at Oxford has taken an unfertilized egg cell from an African clawed frog, destroyed the egg nucleus with ultraviolet radiation, and then successfully implanted cells taken from the frog's intestinal wall into the empty egg. The egg cell, equipped with the full chromosomal make-up necessary to become an African clawed frog, was then tricked into "thinking" it had been fertilized. The cell began to divide. A clone was born.

Researchers have yet to clone a mammal in this way, but experts agree that human cloning is on the horizon. The switch to control the reproductive power of the human cell is almost known.

Joshua Lederberg, a Nobel Prize winning biologist, is a leading proponent of human cloning. "If a superior individual—and presumably, genotype—is identified," he argues, "why not copy it directly, rather than suffer all the risks, including those of sex determination, involved in the disruptions of recombination [sexual procreation]? Leave sexual reproduction for experimental purposes."

Most scientists agree that, given enough research money, all these reproduction technologies can be operational within the next ten to thirty years. And many argue that selective breeding, using these technologies, is our only option if we are to survive as a society. Joseph Fletcher maintains that not to initiate such policies would be immoral and irresponsible, since we have a sacred duty to control our heredity, just as we accept the responsibility of controlling our social life and behavior. James Bonner of the California Institute of Technology assures us that selective breeding of children is really just an extension of our age-old practice of domesticating animals and plants, and should, therefore, not be viewed with alarm.

Proponents of genetic engineering assert that decisions to procreate cannot be trusted to the individual. Nobel Prize winner Linus Pauling proposes that a symbol showing one's genotype be tattooed on the forehead of every young person. "If this were done," says Pauling, "two young people carrying the same seriously defective gene . . . would recognize the situation at first sight and would refrain from falling in love with one another." Pauling favors legislation along these lines.

In an article published by the National Aeronautics and Space Administration, James Bonner discussed a plan in which genetic material from each individual would be removed immediately after birth, and the individual would promptly be sterilized: "During the individual's lifetime, records will be kept of accomplishments and characteristics. After the individual's death, a committee decides if the accomplishments are worthy of procreation into other individuals. If so, genetic material would be removed from the depository and stimulated to clone a new individual. If the committee decides the genetic material is unworthy of procreation it is destroyed." Bonner contends, "The question is indeed not a moral one but a temporal one—when do we start?"

As selective breeding begins to eliminate certain genotypes that are deemed undesirable, gene surgery will soon be used to "upgrade" existing individuals. This year scientists in California were successful in turning bacteria into a cellular "factory" that manufactures the genes necessary to produce insulin, a substance required by diabetics. The next step is to "switch on" these genes to begin insulin production. Researchers hope there will soon be cures, not only for diabetes, but also for hemophilia, PKU, and Tay-Sachs disease.

Genetic engineers also talk of using genetic surgery to "adapt" people to existing environments. If certain workers are more susceptible than others to the harmful effects of particular pollutants and carcinogens, for example, adapting workers will be less expensive than eliminating dangerous chemicals.

Gene surgery could not only provide a hedge against disease, proponents of genetic engineering believe, but also improve worker satisfaction by adapting brain functions. As justification for extending genetic surgery to the redirection of human emotion and intellect, many molecular biologists maintain that schizophrenia and other "abnormal" psychological states result from genetic disorders. "There can be no twisted thought without a twisted molecule," a prominent neurophysiologist has stated. Reports supposedly demonstrating that crime, social protest, poverty, and intelligence are also the result of people's genetic make-up—not of institutional injustice—are being published in large numbers.

Gene surgery has a high priority within Government-funded medical research. The National Institute of General Medical Sciences yearly awards more than $117 million for its development. With advances in recombinant DNA, the possibilities of gene surgery are almost limitless, suggests one scientist: "If one considers the purpose of a drug to be to restore the normal function of some particular process in the body, then DNA should be considered to be the ultimate drug."

The goal of perfecting the human race (or portions of it) through biological redesign is, of course, not new. It has spawned some of the most brutal social and political movements of the Twentieth Century. Whenever dramatic new discoveries in genetics have been made, they have soon been translated into political and social programs. And whenever societies have wanted to alter the social, economic, or political life of specific classes, they have encouraged geneticists to experiment with new ways to accomplish such ends.

This symbiotic relationship between genetic engineering and social policy reached its most conspicuously abhorrent level in the genetic policies of Hitler's Third Reich. Long before Hitler's rise to power, however, American geneticists and social ideologues had begun working together to fashion similar policies designed both to eliminate the so-called inferior stock from the human species and, at the same time, to create a master race.

The early genetic engineering movement in this country was called "eugenics." It arose in the wake of the first massive immigration wave, militant union organizing drives, and the mushrooming growth of city slums in the late 1890s. It promised an easy cure for economic inequalities and social ills at a time when social reformers were increasingly disheartened and when science was being heralded as the linchpin of American greatness. Eugenics offered both a scientific explanation for social problems and a scientific approach to their solution.

Eugenics appealed to the country's "best people"—powerful old-line ruling families, and upper-middle-class academics and professionals who turned the ideology into a form of secular evangelism. They preached eugenics in university lecture halls, before professional conventions, and on political platforms from one end of the country to the other. The message was always the same: America's salvation hinged on its resolve to eliminate the biologically inferior types and breed the perfect human race.

The acceptance of eugenics by much of the general public was due, in large part, to the early and enthusiastic support of some of the most prominent scientists of the time. Almost half of the nation's geneticists became involved in the movement, believing they could help reverse what they saw as a decline in society's hereditary quality.

Eugenicists looked to sterilization as a major tool in their campaign to weed out biologically inferior stock from the American population. As a result of their relentless drive, tens of thousands of American citizens were involuntarily sterilized under various laws enacted by thirty states to cure everything from crime to feeble-mindedness. The extent to which sterilization mania was carried is perhaps best reflected in a bill introduced in the Missouri legislature calling for sterilization of those "convicted of murder, rape, highway robbery, chicken stealing, bombing, or theft of automobiles."

One of the most bizarre twists in the eugenics movement was the Fitter Family Contests run by the American Eugenics Society. Blue ribbons were presented at county and state fairs throughout the Midwest to those families who could produce the best family pedigrees. Families were judged on their physical and mental qualities right alongside the breeding contests for pigs and cows.

From its peak in 1924, the eugenics movement steadily declined, eventually collapsing with the stock market crash in 1929. With America's financial elite jumping out of windows and middle-class professionals and academics standing in unemployment lines alongside Italian, Polish, and Jewish immigrants, and blacks, and with responsible scientists exposing the racism of their colleagues, the myth that certain groups were biologically superior was no longer tenable.

The American eugenics movement lay dormant through World War II. But the bomb on Hiroshima sparked a new interest in genetics, as scientists and government officials began to worry about the effects of radiation on the gene pool. And the bomb also triggered a renewed interest in eugenics. Prominent scientists claimed that increased radiation was causing massive mutations in the human gene pool, and that these were spreading with each generation. In addition, they argued, breakthroughs in medical treatment of "genetically defective" individuals were keeping alive biologically unfit people who, in turn, were passing on their "defects" to their offspring.

The new eugenics—today called "sociobiology"—has caught on. And as the tools of genetic modification have acquired new sophistication, so has the genetic engineering rhetoric. Today's arguments are couched in less openly racist terms: Many modern-day eugenicists agree with Bernard Davis, professor of bacterial physiology at Harvard, that we need a eugenics program "aimed primarily at reducing the production of individuals whose genetic endowment would limit their ability to cope with a technologically complex environment."

Such pronouncements become of even greater concern when prominent scientists attempt to convince the public that institutional environmental reforms are useless.

The genetic engineers argue that man, the machine, is not keeping pace with the advances that have been made in a larger environment that is becoming increasingly technologized. "Human culture has grown so rapidly," says Joshua Lederberg, "that the biological evolution of the species during the last hundred generations has only begun to adjust to it." Man is still imperfect, often unpredictable, and prone to subjective miscalculations. These imperfections have a dysfunctional effect on the rest of the techno-system. If we are to prevent the entire system that we have synthesized from collapsing on itself, as it is showing signs of doing, then the only hope, says the biological engineer, is to bring the last major component of the system into line with technical design. That means humanity itself.

Our schools are preparing us for the age of genetic engineering. More than one million school children are being given special drugs to control behavior attributed to "minimal brain dysfunction." Genetic injections are being discussed by scientists and educators alike as a means of improving the general intelligence of the population. Proponents of gene therapy contend that it is merely an internal aid to education—designed to achieve the same ends as calculators, computers, and videotapes.

The consumer market for mood-altering genetic surgery is already so firmly established that even critics doubt it will be possible to forestall its widespread use as soon as it becomes available. Their pessimism is based on the fact that psycho-active drugs have, in just a few years, become the most heavily prescribed medications in the country, and are now used by more than 40 per cent of all women and 22 per cent of all men.

Ciba Geigy advertises that its anti-depressant, Tofranil, will help the individual readjust when "losing a job to the computer may mean frustration, guilt, and loss of esteem." Merck Company's Triavil is for people who are "sad or unhappy about the future. . . . easily tired and who have difficulty in making decisions." The Sandoz Company claims its product Serentil is "for the anxiety that comes from not fitting in. The newcomer in town who can't make friends. The organization man who can't adjust to altered status within his company. The woman who can't get along with her daughter-in-law. The executive who can't accept retirement."

In a society in which millions of people feel increasingly alienated at the hands of the giant bureaucracies that regulate their lives, and powerless to cope with pollution, urban decay, unemployment, inflation, and a host of other problems, psycho-drugs offer the ideal solution. And any consumer who has become habitually addicted to the purchase of psycho-drugs is a ready market for a "genetic fix."

The Cetus Corporation knows this and is prepared. The significance of the power of genetic engineering cannot be exaggerated, Cetus contends in its in-house memo: "A new industry with untold potential is about to appear."

Recognizing this untold potential, Standard Oil of Indiana is spending $5 million to capture controlling interest in Cetus. Cetus shareholders with convertible preferred stock are being offered $330 a share for stock that cost only $100 a share less than five years ago. The giant corporation sees Cetus as a hedge against the world's dwindling oil reserves.

Cetus is only the tip of the iceberg of corporate involvement in genetic engineering. Seven major pharmaceutical companies are also engaged in the race to exploit this new industry, and a dozen more drug, chemical, and agricultural companies are poised to enter the field, which *Fortune* magazine predicts will soon become a "multibillion dollar industry."

Many scientists advocating genetic engineering have a financial stake in these corporations. On the board

of directors and advisers at Cetus are such world renowned scientists as Joshua Lederberg; Stanley Cohen,
associate professor of medicine at Stanford University
Medical School and the acknowledged leader in the new
technology of gene manipulation; Arnold Demain, professor of applied microbiology at MIT; and Donald
Glaser, Nobel laureate and professor of physics and molecular biology at the University of California.

Broad-scale genetic engineering will probably be introduced to Americans gradually, almost imperceptibly.
As each new genetic advance becomes commercially
practical, corporations, aided by scientific expertise and
Government approval, will attempt to exploit a new consumer need, either real or manufactured. Whether the
genetic revolution or the social revolution prevails depends, ultimately, on how we respond. Restructuring the
institutions of society means rejecting the technological

imperative and making an active commitment. Genetic
engineering, to succeed, will require only our passive
acceptance.

## QUESTIONS

1. Ought there to be a system of formal control over
the application of some kinds of scientific knowledge? If
so, who should exercise control—scientists, voters,
courts, government, industry, or some other authority?

2. Some scientists believe they will be able to arrest
the aging process and thus indefinitely postpone death.
What impact might such an innovation have on society?

3. How do you respond to the idea that scientists
might be able to intervene genetically to perfect the human species?

William F. Allman

# 56. Staying Alive in the 20th Century

*Modern technology has changed the nature of social life, often to our great convenience and benefit. It is difficult to imagine a world without telephones and elevators, fertilizers and medicines, aircraft and electricity. But technology has also had negative effects. For example, technological advances have helped to pollute the natural environment, to throw workers out of their jobs, to make existing knowledge or skills obsolete, and to enhance the power of an elite of technical "experts." Additionally, technological change has altered and in some respects increased the risks to health and safety that people face in their daily lives.*

*Of course, life has always been a fairly risky business, and in many respects modern technologies—such as new medical procedures—can help to reduce that risk. But other technological innovations, such as the automobile or the nuclear reactor, pose actual or potential hazards. We are reminded of these hazards whenever there is a major technological mishap, such as a chemical spill or an airplane crash. Yet people are often very inaccurate in their assessments of technological risks. For example, they may fear traveling in a plane more than traveling in a car—even though the auto fatality rate is more than ten times as great, per passenger mile, as the aircraft fatality rate. And technological risks that offer the possibility of a sudden and dramatic impact—such as the risk of a reactor meltdown—may cause more concern than the reality of such risks as the slow, invisible poisoning of ground water through chemical pollutants.*

*In this article, William F. Allman looks at the statistical probabilities of risk from various sources and shows that public attitudes often bear little relationship to the real dangers involved. The experts can tell us what's risky—but most of us take our own chances.*

Crashing an automobile at 30 miles per hour is like diving head first off a three-story building. As the car stops, you slam with about the same force into the windshield, steering wheel, or dashboard—or, if you're lucky, the protective arms of a seat belt. Traffic accidents are the leading cause of death for people between the ages of five and 34; last year nearly 45,000 people died in auto collisions, the equivalent of a fully loaded passenger jet crashing with no survivors every day. If everybody wore seat belts, more than half of these deaths could have been avoided.

Chances are, you've heard all this before. Chances are, you still don't wear a seat belt.

Despite millions of dollars spent on advertisements urging people to "buckle up for safety" and "make it click," only about one out of seven American drivers puts on a seat belt before driving away.

Paul Slovic, a psychologist and former president of the Society for Risk Analysis, thought he might be able to convince people to take better care of themselves.

According to Slovic and his colleagues Sarah Lichtenstein and Baruch Fischhoff at Decision Research in Eugene, Oregon, a cursory look at the probabilities of death by car can be misleading. The chance of being killed in any single automobile trip is about one in four million—less than the chance of being killed in a year of mowing the lawn. But the long view yields a different story. "We make about 50,000 automobile trips in a lifetime," says Slovic, "and the probabilities add up to a risk that is not trivial." About one out of every 140 people dies in a car accident; one out of three is injured seriously enough to be disabled for at least a day. If motorists would think in terms of a lifetime of driving rather than single trips, says Slovic, then perhaps they would decide once and for all to buckle up.

Slovic and coworker Norman Schwalm produced new seat belt messages emphasizing the lifetime risks of automobiles. Several hundred volunteers watched the ads and answered questionnaires about which ads they found most effective. Though the results seemed to indicate that the approach showed promise, one thing did not: Slovic and his colleagues, surreptitiously watching their volunteers drive away from the parking lot, noted with dismay that there was no increase in seat belt use. The advertising effort, says Slovic, added "one more flop to an impressive list of failures." He now supports laws, recently passed in New York and several other states, that make wearing seat belts mandatory.

If you think the apparent irrationality of Slovic's subjects frustrated him, imagine how people in the nuclear power business must feel. Slovic's subjects were, after all, drawn from the general public, the same general public whose concern for the safety of nuclear reactors—which have claimed a total of three lives in accidents in the last 30 years—brought the industry to a virtual standstill. It's the same general public that smokes billions of cigarettes a year while banning artificial sweetener because of a one-in-a million chance it will cause cancer, eats meals full of fat, flocks to cities prone to earthquakes, and goes hang gliding while it frets about pesticides in foods, avoids the ocean for fear of sharks, and breaks into a cold sweat on airline flights.

In short, we the general public are irrational, uninformed, superstitious, even stupid. We don't understand probability, are biased by the news media, and have a fear of some technologies that borders on the primeval.

And we have no business, say many professional risk assessors, trying to force our unscientific worries into policy decisions about the hazards of modern living. Many hazards involve sophisticated technologies, statistics, and economic and political considerations. Assessing how such hazards threaten society is a task many believe is better left to experts. Why should the public have a say about the risk of a technology like nuclear power—which some experts believe poses a lesser threat than bicycles—when we don't have enough sense to put on a seat belt?

The experts have a point: When it comes to numbers, news, and neutrons, we're numskulls. But a few scientists are beginning to ask if technical savvy is the only qualification needed to be a legitimate worrier. They are finding that, while our behavior often appears irrational and confused, perhaps we're not so dumb after all. We may be lousy with mortality statistics, but our fears may tell us a lot about how a risk affects society as a whole.

One problem with the way we deal with risk is that our decisions can be influenced by the way a situation is presented. Suppose someone made you a simple, no-risk offer: flip a coin—if it's heads, you get $1,000; tails, you get nothing. Suppose further that you have the option of foregoing the coin flip in exchange for sure money. What's the least amount of money you would take? If you flipped the coin hundreds of times your average reward would be $500, so in a utilitarian sense the offer is worth $500, and the rational choice would be to accept no less than $500. According to one study, however, most people would settle for around $350.

Now suppose someone gave you $1,000 but with two options: you can flip a coin to determine if you have to give it all back—or you can simply return a portion of the money. How much would you be willing to give up to avoid flipping? Again, the rational choice would be $500. But if you were content to accept $350 in the first game, it would seem logical that you should be willing to give up $650 rather than risk flipping for the entire $1,000. Most people, however, would not give back more than $350.

The outcomes of the games are identical: in each there is a 50-50 chance of winning $1,000. But the presentations of the two games are not identical. In the first, the choices are between two gains; in the second, the choices appear to be between two losses.

According to Amos Tversky and Daniel Kahneman, that makes all the difference. The two psychologists discovered one of the fundamentals of our flip-flops about risks: "When it comes to taking risks for gains, people are conservative. They will take a sure gain over a probable gain," says Stanford University's Tversky. "But we are also finding that when people are faced with a choice between a small, certain loss and a large, probable loss, they will gamble."

And people are willing to gamble on more than money. Tversky and Kahneman, at the University of British Columbia, presented two groups of physicians with a hypothetical problem concerning an imminent outbreak of a rare Asian disease. The disease, if left unchecked, was expected to kill 600 people. One group of physicians was given a choice between two programs designed to counter the disease. If program A were adopted, 200 victims would be saved. If program B were used, there was a one-third probability that everyone would be saved, but a two-thirds probability that no one would be saved. The majority of physicians preferred not to gamble and chose program A.

Another group of doctors was asked to choose between two other programs. Program C would result in the deaths of 400 people. In program D, there was a two-thirds chance that 600 people would die, but there was a one-third chance that no one would die. Faced with the sure death of 400 people, these physicians chose to gamble with program D.

Programs A and C, of course, are the same program, as are programs B and D. The only difference is that in the first instance they are described in terms of lives saved; in the second, lives lost. Because losses loom larger than gains, we are more willing to gamble to avoid them. That is why, perhaps, we often seem more willing to spend money to rescue a trapped miner than to increase the overall safety of mining.

An essential part of worrying is knowing what the chances are that something will happen. But just a little knowledge of probability theory can be a dangerous thing. Everyone knows that when the odds of something occurring are, for example, 50-50, then half the time, on average, the event will happen. But fewer realize that the average usually nears 50 percent only after a large number of events. With a very small number, wide variations can occur.

Because the overall outcome usually gets closer to the average as the number of events increases, some of us conclude, incorrectly, that chance is self-correcting—a deviation in one direction promotes a deviation in the other to compensate for it. This is the infamous gambler's fallacy, where, say, roulette players think that the ball is more likely to land on red after three blacks in a row. This fallacy is a serious problem in assessing risks outside casinos as well. In one study, victims of a recent flood thought that the chances were remote that another would happen again.

Our inability to cope with probabilities, says Tversky, makes certainty appealing. In one study people who were asked to play a simple game of chance were given the opportunity to pay to increase their chances of winning. The researchers found that people were willing to pay more to increase their chances from 90 to 100 percent than they would pay for a 10-percent increase from 60 to 70 percent. This desire for absolutes goes beyond games. Former Food and Drug Administration commissioner Alexander Schmidt, looking forward to an upcoming scientific evaluation of cyclamates, said, "I'm looking for a clean bill of health, not a wishy-washy, iffy answer." When asked about the health effects of pollution, Edmund Muskie responded by asking for a "one-armed" scientist who does not say, "On the one hand, the evidence is so, but on the other hand. . . ."

Our desire for absolute certainty makes a high probability, such as 85 percent, seem insufficient. Likewise the desire for impossibility sometimes makes a five percent probability seem like a lot. The result is that low probabilities seem greater than they are and high probabilities seem less. This is perhaps the reason some of us feel comfortable buying a lottery ticket—even though there is an extremely low chance of winning—at the same time that we purchase a pack of cigarettes and dismiss the health risks as improbable.

If we can't be certain about the risks we face, we at least want to have some control over the technologies and activities that produce them. It has long been known, much to the frustration of some risk experts, that we may

be much more willing to accept higher risks in activities over which we have control, such as smoking, drinking, driving, or skiing, than things over which we have little control, such as industrial pollution, food additives, and commercial airlines.

In many cases, however, the feeling of control provides false comfort. In one study, tickets to a lottery were sold for a dollar to people in an office. Participants in one group were simply handed their tickets; in another group, the participants were allowed to choose their own. Just before the drawing, ticket holders were asked if they were willing to resell their tickets. The average resale price asked by those who had been handed tickets was $1.96. Those who had chosen their own tickets asked an average of $8.67. Being in control of the selection process apparently made people think they had a better chance of winning.

A feeling of control can actually make a risky technology even more dangerous. That's because we often have inflated opinions of ourselves. Most of us consider ourselves above-average drivers, safer than most when using appliances and power tools, and less likely to suffer medical problems such as heart attacks. "Such overconfidence is dangerous," says Slovic. "It indicates that we often do not realize how little we know and how much additional information we need about the risks we face."

Unfortunately, when we want additional information, we often turn to the news media, and the media are more chroniclers of the extraordinary than a bank of information. Slovic and his colleague Barbara Combs at Decision Research examined how two newspapers, one from New Bedford, Massachusetts, and the other from Eugene, Oregon, reported deaths from various causes. They found the coverage seldom reflected the actual frequency of death in the population. Diseases such as diabetes, cancer, and heart disease take about 16 times the number of lives as accidents, yet there were more than six times as many articles about accidental deaths in the newspapers. There were also about three times as many stories about homicides, though disease claims 1,000 times more lives.

This media emphasis on the sensational may be responsible for some of our skewed worries about the world. Slovic and his colleagues asked people to estimate the frequency of various causes of death such as tornadoes, heart disease, and homicides. Most people overestimated the numbers of deaths from causes that were sensational and underestimated more common causes of death that were less dramatic. Homicides, for example, were incorrectly estimated to take more lives annually than diabetes, stomach cancer, and strokes. Strokes actually take 10 times as many lives as homicides. Deaths from botulism, pregnancy, and floods were also overestimated. Botulism was thought to cause nearly 200 deaths—it usually kills fewer than 10. Most people judged that tornadoes and asthma each kill about 500 people annually; tornadoes usually kill about 100; asthma, about 3,000.

Because things that recently occurred or are easy to imagine tend to stick in our minds, we can be difficult to educate about risks. A nuclear engineer, for example, talking of the many low-probability events that must happen in succession to cause a nuclear waste site to leak, may actually alarm someone into thinking, "I didn't realize there were so many things that could go wrong."

Which is not to say that we don't want to know more about the risks we face, especially if they concern medicine. Surveys show that most of us want as much information as possible when making a decision to have surgery or to take a certain drug. But according to one study, confusion can arise when doctors try to inform us about medical risks. Physician Barbara McNeil at Harvard University and her colleagues asked a group of radiologists, graduate students, and patients to imagine that they had lung cancer and to choose between surgery or radiation treatment. The researchers presented actual statistics, telling one group that 10 out of 100 people die during surgery, and 66 out of 100 die within five years. With radiation no one dies during treatment, but 78 out of 100 die within five years. Fifty-six percent of the group chose surgery. The group was then told there was a new study of the risks. The number of deaths during surgery remained the same, but the study showed the life expectancy of surgery survivors is 6.8 years, while the life expectancy of those treated with radiation is 4.7 years. While in fact, the statistics are based on the same death and survival data as in the first example, the number of people choosing surgery rose to 75 percent.

"There are no neutral ways to present information," says psychologist Fischoff. Perhaps the best way to inform people about risks, he says, is to give them the information in several different ways.

In the summer of 1969, Lester Maddox, then the governor of Georgia, was speaking at a news conference about inmate conditions in the state's prisons. He was asked if there were any way of improving the correctional institutions. "What we need," Maddox replied, "is a better class of prisoner."

Many risk assessors share Maddox's feelings about the people entrusted to their care. After all, they have honed their models of technical failure, designed sensitive tests for screening new drugs and chemicals, and held countless symposia on how to save the lives of the people who, by and large, pay their salaries. But we— the American public—often seem intent on making a mess of their work. We ignore their advice, killing ourselves by the thousands because we find seat belts uncomfortable. We disregard their scientific findings,

preferring to risk cancer rather than give up cigarettes.

What's worse, say sociologists Mary Douglas and Aaron Wildavsky, authors of *Risk and Culture*, is that often our fears seem unrelated to a particular technology's potential to kill. Instead, they say, our concerns are aroused by an elite group of people who are often more worried about what is perceived as overly centralized power or too much technological growth.

But in a world in which there are limited resources and needless deaths, say many risk assessors, the bottom line is drawn by the Grim Reaper. "In the case of policy towards public safety," says Ernest Siddall, a risk expert at Atomic Energy of Canada, "the objective can be clearly stated: it is to reduce the total rate of mortality in the society."

Because death rates are sometimes ignored by the public, says physicist Bernard Cohen of the University of Pittsburgh, a technology may be replaced by one that is actually riskier. Some experts, for example, estimate that coal-generated electricity costs some 10,000 lives a year through mining, transportation, and pollution. Despite this, Cohen says, 80 percent of the American public believes that coal burning is safer than nuclear power, and as a result, utilities are building coal plants rather than nuclear plants. "Every time this is done," he says, "many hundreds of innocent Americans are condemned to an early death."

Just how far the public has split with the experts was demonstrated by Slovic, Fischhoff, and Lichtenstein. They asked four groups of people—college students, members of the Eugene, Oregon, League of Women Voters, business professionals, and experts at risk assessment—to rate 30 technologies and activities in terms of "the risk to society of dying." The items included handguns, pesticides, food coloring, and nuclear power.

The groups' estimations were similar in some ways: motorcycles, smoking, and handguns were judged to be quite risky; power mowers and football were judged to be less so. But in some cases, the lay estimates were vastly different from those of the experts. The experts viewed surgery and swimming as riskier than the other groups did, and police work and mountain climbing as safer. The biggest difference was in the groups' assessment of nuclear power. The students and League of Women Voters rated it as number one in riskiness, the business people, eighth; the experts ranked it 20th, below electric power, railroads, and bicycling.

Slovic's results might be dismissed as just another example of lay people's inordinate fear of radiation. But it wasn't simply radiation phobia that put nuclear power at the top. One form of radiation, medical X rays, was thought to be far less risky by lay people than by the experts: the League of Women Voters rated it 22nd; the experts, seventh.

Slovic compared the results of the survey with known fatality statistics. He found that when he ranked the technologies and activities by the average number of deaths they cause per year, the ranking very closely matched that of the experts. When experts assess the risk of a technology, they are most concerned with how many people die from it in an average year.

Thinking that perhaps the lay groups did their ranking the same way but had estimated average fatalities inaccurately, Slovic asked them to estimate the average deaths from each activity and technology. Surprisingly, nuclear power, which was rated first among risks by most lay people, was rated last among fatality estimates.

When we think about risk, says Slovic, we are not only concerned that a technology has the potential to cause deaths. We also worry about more subtle aspects: How well do we understand the risk? How will it affect society? Could it wipe out an entire community? Make a particular area uninhabitable for a long time? Would it affect future generations or some members of society more than others?

Slovic and his colleagues found that when people were asked to apply these societal concerns to the risks of some 90 different activities and technologies, each took on a profile that was broader than a simple death statistic. Some items, like dynamite, were considered deadly, but also fairly controllable. Others, like microwave ovens, were thought to involve risks that were delayed in their effects and not well known, but were also voluntary and unlikely to cause catastrophes. The respondents overwhelmingly regarded the risks of nuclear power as involuntary, uncontrollable, unknown, inequitably distributed, likely to be fatal, potentially catastrophic, and evoking feelings of not just fear but dread. Automobiles, which kill far more people per year, evoked few of these concerns.

According to Slovic, we are also concerned about the inherent riskiness of assessing risks. Part of our worry about technologies such as nuclear power, toxic wastes, and genetic engineering, for example, stem from the knowledge that the assessments of these risks are not based as much on the experience of a proven track record as on scientific analysis which, like some scientific analyses, might be in error.

That's because scientists, while good at solving problems, are not always as good at determining the limits of their expertise. In 1950, 1955, 1963, and 1968, for example, scientists ran experiments trying to measure the mass of the electron. The mass estimates from each experiment differed widely. Though that might be expected in a difficult experiment, each group of scientists also estimated an upper and lower boundary indicating how much in error their values might be, and even *these* es-

timates didn't overlap. In another study, seven highly respected engineers were asked to predict at what height a particular embankment with a clay foundation would collapse and were told to include a margin of error large enough to have a 50-percent chance of containing the correct answer. None of the estimates, including the margins for error, contained the correct height.

Since many new technologies are understood by few people in the first place, says Fischhoff, the experts are left to assess the quality of their own judgments, which can lead to problems. "Many risk problems force experts to go beyond the limits of the available data," he says. "In doing so, they fall back on intuitive processes much like those of lay people and are capable of making the same types of mistakes."

The fact that the public is keenly aware that scientists can be wrong is at the root of the concern about the nuclear accident at Three Mile Island. Before the accident, scientists had said confidently that the chances of a serious reactor breakdown were quite remote. But when a potential disaster occurred relatively early in the history of nuclear power, even though the safety systems worked and the disaster never materialized, the mishap sent out a signal that the overall assessment of the risks of nuclear power might be in error.

Since we often put our fates in the hands of experts, we react strongly to signs that our faith has been misplaced. The largest aviation accident in history, for example, was the 1977 collision of two jumbo jets in Spain's Canary Islands, where 583 people were killed. But there was far less publicity and turmoil surrounding that crash than was generated by the 1979 crash of a DC-10 in Chicago, even though only half as many people were killed in that accident. This is because the Canary Island accident was caused by a simple human error in communications—something we are familiar with and can control. The DC-10 crash, on the other hand, occurred because an engine fell off a wing—a problem that could be generic to all DC-10s. "In a way, the DC-10 crash acted as a signal to people about a potential danger in the design and maintenance of this technology, which made a larger impact than the crash in the Canary Islands," says Slovic. "With the accident at Three Mile Island, the health and safety consequences were insignificant; no one was killed, and there is probably no latent cancer. But the costs to society were enormous. Because the accident was a signal of potential problems, the ripple effect shut down reactors all over the world at a cost of billions of dollars. That's an expensive signal."

The big question, says Slovic, is whether our worries and fears, which are sometimes the result of faulty logic and misinformation—but also stem from a broader concern for how risks affect society as a whole—should be considered when making decisions about risk. "The dilemma is that if you give extra weight to nonstatistical factors such as catastrophic potential, inequity, and dread, and therefore choose an alternative—coal-fired power plants, for example, over nuclear-powered plants—you may actually be harming more people," he says. "The crux of the problem is finding the proper way to look at risk. One person might believe that rational decisions should be based solely on death, injuries, and damage. Another might say there are other important, hard-to-quantify feelings and values that we need to consider when making a risk decision."

And because these feelings include concerns for society at large, we can add a different perspective to risk debates. The scientists are better at seeing the trees, perhaps, but maybe we're better at seeing the forest. "We come down real hard on the public because they seem uninformed and irrational," says Slovic. "But their behavior may tell us something important about the essential elements of a humane society. In a sense there is real wisdom in people's reactions."

This wisdom depends less on understanding the details of scientific risk assessment than understanding the limits of what that science can do. "People are often more scientific in watching the processes of science than scientists themselves," says Fischhoff. "If the public looks at us with a skeptical eye, maybe they know something we don't."

## QUESTIONS

1. What factors influence people's assessments of technological risks?

2. Given that many people will not voluntarily use car seat belts, should it be mandatory to use them?

3. Do you think that technological development will cause more harm or more good in the next few decades?

*Sandra Postel*
*Lester R. Brown*

# 57. Life, the Great Chemistry Experiment

*Industrialized societies offer their inhabitants many advantages, including a general standard of living that is the envy of people in less developed nations. But industrialism has its costs, and one of them is pollution. This pollution derives from many sources, such as manufacturing processes, the use of agricultural and other chemicals, and the disposal of waste products.*

*Until a few decades ago, few people would even have recognized the word "ecology." Today, we are becoming painfully aware that life on earth is part of an infinitely complex and finely balanced system comprising living organisms, inorganic matter, and energy. All life forms are interdependent, and all are dependent on the delicate natural environment that sustains them. But, as we have developed ever more sophisticated technologies for exploiting and transforming the natural environment, so we have increased our capacity to ravage the land, air, and water, and the multitude of life forms they contain. Some of our activities now threaten long-range and highly significant changes in the global temperature and atmosphere.*

*In this article, Sandra Postel and Lester R. Brown show how the complex chemistry of life may be endangered by the impact of modern industrial technologies.*

All humankind has a stake in the life-and-death game of agriculture. The rules of the game are governed by the growth patterns of crops and fairly predictable regimens of warmth and rain. For centuries, farmers have marched to their fertile fields, played the game with great skill, and most often won.

Changes in longstanding rules to which farmers have carefully adapted threaten not only their livelihoods but, ultimately, food security for the earth's hungry populations. We see hints of these effects during severe droughts, most dramatically in Africa in recent years and, to a lesser degree, in the southeastern United States last summer. Further shifts in agricultural conditions worldwide could generate unprecedented pressures on global food supplies.

Within the next fifty years, the earth's climate may change more than it has since agriculture began some 10,000 years ago. Human activities have caused a buildup in the atmosphere of chemical compounds that are known as "greenhouse gases." These gases let the sun's radiation pass through, but trap the longer-wavelength radiation emitted from the earth, which otherwise would escape into space. The anticipated result is a global warming and a worldwide shift in temperature and rainfall patterns. Crops in key food-producing regions will become vulnerable to heat waves, drought, and the loss of water for irrigation.

Scientists have long suspected that carbon dioxide ($CO_2$) plays a central role in regulating the earth's temperature. Since 1860, the combustion of fossil fuels (coal, oil, and natural gas), in power plants, home furnaces, factories, and automobiles, has released some 185 billion tons of carbon into the atmosphere. In addition, the clearing and burning of forests for cropland and pasture has contributed more than 100 billion tons. Since the early 1800s, the level of $CO_2$ has increased about 30 percent, and is still rising.

Recently, scientists have found new gases among the greenhouse gang of culprits. Methane and nitrous oxide (laughing gas) have also been increasing in the atmosphere as emissions from human activities have added to those from natural sources. And a family of synthetic chlorine compounds, used in such diverse consumer products as aerosol sprays, refrigerators, and air conditioners, could be second only to carbon dioxide in contributing to the greenhouse effect. Many scientists believe that, collectively, the climate-altering potentials of greenhouse gases other than $CO_2$ are now about as important as that of $CO_2$ alone.

The earth's climate will change gradually as the concentrations of greenhouse gases increase. Indeed, evidence exists that the warming has already begun. But climate modelers typically focus their predictions on what will happen from the equivalent of a doubling of carbon dioxide over preindustrial levels, which, taking into account all the greenhouse gases, could occur as early as the year 2030.

Most models agree that temperatures will rise everywhere, though by greater amounts in the temperate and polar regions than in the tropics. Since a warmer atmosphere can hold more moisture, average precipitation worldwide is expected to increase by 7 to 11 percent. In many regions, however, this additional rainfall would be offset by higher rates of evaporation, causing soil moisture—the natural water supply for crops—to decrease.

Recent model results indicate that large grain-producing regions of North America, the Soviet Union, and possibly, China could dry out during summertime. More than half of the world's cereal exports come from North America, and the United States alone accounts for more than two-thirds of total exports of corn. A drier average growing season, along with more frequent and severe heat waves and droughts, could lead to substantial crop losses in these major breadbaskets.

As a rule of thumb, for example, corn yields in the United States drop 10 percent for each day the crop is under severe stress during its silking and tasseling stage. Five days of severe temperature or moisture stress during this critical period would cut yields in half. With the anticipated climate change, such stressful conditions probably would occur frequently in the U.S. cornbelt.

While some regions suffer, prospects for expanding production could improve in others. Warmer and wetter conditions might increase rice production in India and much of Southeast Asia. The picture remains unclear for Africa. But reconstructions of the so-called Altithermal period some 4,500 to 8,000 years ago, when summertime temperatures were higher than at present, suggest that northern and eastern Africa could get more rainfall. If so, average flows of the Niger, Senegal, Volta, and Blue Nile rivers would increase, permitting an expansion of irrigation.

In northern latitudes, higher temperatures and milder winters might open vast tracts of land to cultivation. Agricultural production in Canada, northern Europe, and the Soviet Union might expand northward.

Unfortunately, shifting crop production to areas benefiting from climate change would not only be costly but would also have to overcome some serious constraints. Thin, nutrient-poor soils cover much of Northern Minnesota, Wisconsin, and Michigan, so a northward shift of the U.S. cornbelt in response to higher temperatures would result in a substantial drop in yield. Poor soils would also inhibit successful northward agricultural migrations in Canada, Scandinavia, and the Soviet Union. Centuries would be needed for more productive soils to form. While the present desert regions of North Africa were savannas suited for grazing during the Altithermal period, these lands also would require a long time to regain their former fertility.

Low-lying agricultural areas face the added threat of a substantial rise in sea level. Since water expands when heated, oceans will rise with the increase in global temperature. Warmer temperatures will also melt mountain glaciers and parts of polar ice sheets, transferring water from the land to the sea. By the middle of the next century, sea levels could rise as much as three feet, increasing risks of flooding in agricultural lowlands—where much of the world's rice is grown. Of particular concern are the heavily populated, fertile delta regions of the Ganges River in Bangladesh, the Indus in Pakistan, and the Chang Jiang (Yangtze) in China.

The productivity of major food crops will respond not only to changes in climate but directly to the higher concentration of $CO_2$ in the atmosphere. Carbon dioxide is a basic ingredient for photosynthesis, the process by which green plants transform solar energy into the chemical energy of carbohydrates. Experiments suggest that as long as water, nutrients, and other factors are not limited, every 1 percent rise in the $CO_2$ concentration may increase photosynthesis by 0.5 percent.

Adapting to climatic change will exact heavy costs from governments and farmers. The expensive irrigation systems supplying water to the 670 million acres of irrigated cropland worldwide were built for present climatic regimes. These irrigated lands account for only 18 percent of total cropland, yet they yield a third of the global harvest. Irrigated agriculture thus plays a disproportionately large role in meeting the world's food needs. Shifts in rainfall patterns could make existing irrigation systems—including reservoirs, canals, pumps, and wells—unnecessary in some regions, insufficient in others. Moreover, seasonal reductions in water supplies because of climatic change could seriously constrain irrigated agriculture, especially where competition for scarce water is already increasing.

A look at one key food-producing region—the western United States—highlights how costly climatic change could be. Some climate models suggest that much of this area could experience a reduction in rainfall, along with the rise in temperature, which would diminish the water supply. Assuming a 10 percent decrease in precipitation and a 3.5°F increase in temperature, supplies in each of seven western river basins would be reduced some 40 to 76 percent. Such reductions would create severe imbalances in regional water budgets. With no climatic change, only in the Lower Colorado region would water consumption exceed supply by the end of the century. With the assumed climatic change, however, consumption in the year 2000 would exceed the renewable supply in four regions, with local shortages probably occurring in the other three river basins.

Since agriculture is by far the biggest consumer of water, balancing regional water budgets would likely require that irrigation cease on a substantial share of cropland. This is happening now in portions of the Lower Colorado, where consumption already exceeds the renewable supply. Correcting the large imbalances resulting from such an altered climate could require that as many as 11.4 million acres be taken out of irrigation in these seven western U.S. regions—roughly one-third of the area currently irrigated.

A reduction of that magnitude would have high costs, measured either by the capital investments in obsolete dams, canals, and irrigation systems or by the replacement value of that irrigation infrastructure. Investment needs for expanding irrigation vary widely, but assuming expenses of $600 to $2,000 per acre, replacement costs could range from $7 billion to $23 billion in the United States alone. Worldwide, maintaining food security under the altered climate could require new irrigation systems with a global price tag of $200 billion.

The need for new drainage systems, flood control structures, cropping patterns, and crop varieties would greatly magnify the costs of adapting to a changed climate. According to some ballpark estimates, the annual cost of a greenhouse gas-induced warming of 4.5°F could amount to 3 percent of the world's gross economic output. Much of this expense would result from the loss of capital assets in agriculture. Poorer countries would have the most difficulty adapting, and as food production typically generates a relatively large share of their incomes, their people would suffer most.

Moreover, as climate expert William W. Kellogg points out, the need to adapt to climatic change will arise "against a backdrop of increased world population, increased demand for energy, and depletion in many places of soil, forests, and other natural resources." The disruptions created by a changing climate may thus bring new pockets of famine, losses of income, and the need for huge capital investments, which many countries will find difficult to afford.

Some change in the world's climate is already inevitable. Yet since carbon dioxide is the key variable in the climate equation, the magnitude of climatic change—and the pace at which it unfolds—will depend greatly on society's future use of coal, oil, and natural gas. Especially with the recent drop in oil prices, restraining carbon emissions will require investments in energy efficiency and alternative energy sources beyond what the market alone would induce. It will also demand a virtual cap on carbon emissions from industrial countries to allow for needed growth in energy use in the Third World.

Preserving forests and planting trees can also help minimize the threat of climatic change. The clearing and burning of tropical forests adds perhaps 20 percent to the amount of carbon released to the atmosphere each year from the burning of fossil fuels. Trees also remove carbon dioxide from the air during photosynthesis. Increasing global forest cover would thus help stabilize atmospheric $CO_2$ levels.

Averting a major change in climate is possible, but requires immediate action. No nation has yet taken steps explicitly geared toward limiting emissions of $CO_2$. Cooperation among governments is essential, since carbon emissions anywhere contribute to climatic change everywhere. But meaningful reductions could begin with concerted national measures by the world's three largest users of coal—China, the Soviet Union, and the United States.

More and more sick, dying, and dead trees are the most visible evidence of human-induced changes in the earth's chemistry. During the last several years, forest damage linked to air pollution and acid rain has spread rapidly throughout central and northern Europe.

In the autumn of 1983, West German officials galvanized both scientists and the citizenry with a startling finding: 34 percent of the nation's trees were yellowing, losing needles or leaves, or showing other signs of injury. The cause? Preliminary evidence pointed to air pollutants and acid rain. A more thorough survey in 1984 confirmed that tree disease was spreading. Foresters found that trees covering half of the nation's 18.2 million acres of woodlands were damaged, including two-thirds of the fabled Black Forest in the southwestern state of Baden Württemberg.

Spurred by West Germany's alarming discovery, other European nations assessed the health of their own forests. A sobering picture emerged.

Trees covering nearly 48 million acres in Europe—an area the size of Austria and East Germany combined (14 percent of Europe's total forested area)—now show signs of injury linked to air pollution or acid rain. The key symptoms for the conifers, the hardest hit, parallel those found in West Germany: yellowing of needles, casting off of older needles, and damage to the fine roots through which trees take up nutrients. In eight countries—Austria, Czechoslovakia, Finland, Luxembourg, the Netherlands, Poland, Switzerland, and West Germany—one-quarter to half the forested area is damaged.

National estimates often mask serious damage in specific regions. Total damage in Sweden is placed at about 4 percent, but an estimated 20 percent of the forested area in the south is affected. In 1984, foresters in France surveyed portions of the French Jura and Alsace-Lorraine, adjacent to West Germany's Black Forest, and found that more than a third of the trees were injured, at least 10 percent of them severely. In some heavily polluted regions of Eastern Europe, numerous trees are now in the last stages of decline. In Poland, for example, dead and dying trees cover 1 million areas, and trees with lesser damage occupy an additional 4.6 million acres.

The alpine regions of Austria, France, Italy, Switzerland, and West Germany exhibit the worst damage. Swiss officials worry about the increased risk of landslides and avalanches as dying trees are removed from forested hillsides. Already some villagers have been told to evacuate.

North Americans must travel to mountaintops in the eastern United States to see the kind of massive tree disease and death spreading throughout Europe. In the high-elevation forests, most red spruce trees are undergoing serious dieback—a progressive thinning from the outer tree crown inward. More subtle signs of ill health come from the discovery that pine trees in a broad region of the Southeast grew 20 to 30 percent less between 1972 and 1982 than between 1961 and 1972. In a November 1985 report, U.S. Forest Service analysts stated that the net annual growth of softwood timber in the Southeast "has peaked and turned downward after a long upward trend."

Although less well documented, declines in growth appear to have occurred throughout the Appalachians, extending north into New England. In written testimony presented to the U.S. Senate in February 1984, soil scientist Arthur H. Johnson noted that similar growth reductions preceded the "alarming incidences" of forest damage in Europe.

Hundreds of scientists in the affected countries continue to search for the cause of this unprecedented forest decline. Collectively, they offer a bewildering array of hypotheses, attesting to the difficulty of unraveling a mystery within a complex natural system. Most agree, however, that air pollutants—probably combined with natural factors, such as insects, cold, or drought—are a principal cause. Explanations focus on acid rain, sulfur dioxide, nitrogen compounds, heavy metals, and ozone, which singly or in combination cause damage through the foliage and forest soils.

Changes in soils may be irreversible for the near future. A severely damaged forest in Eastern Europe

shows the kinds of soil alterations that can take place. Large portions of the Erzgebirge, a mountain range northwest of Prague, Czechoslovakia, are now a wasteland. Near the industrial city of Most, where power plants burn high-sulfur coal, sulfur dioxide concentrations average much higher than in most other industrial areas, and thirteen times higher than in a seemingly undamaged rural forest about 100 miles to the southeast. Peak concentrations register several times higher than the average. The numerous dead and dying trees in this industrial region may thus be succumbing to the classic smoke injury known to occur near large sources of uncontrolled pollution.

Chemical measurements of runoff water from the Erzgebirge suggest that acidification has profoundly altered the soil's ability to support a forest. Czech geochemist Tomas Paces found that losses of the nutrients magnesium and calcium from the damaged forest were several times greater than from the undamaged rural forest. Runoff of aluminum, which normally remains bound up in soil minerals, was thirty-two times greater from the damaged forest. With the loss of calcium and other elements that can buffer incoming acidity, aluminum mobilizes to serve as the buffering agent. In soluble forms, this metal can be toxic to trees. Finally, outputs of nitrate exceeded those from the undamaged forest by a factor of twenty. Paces believes this reflects the damaged forest's inability to properly recycle nitrogen—a loss of basic ecosystem function.

Forests in the industrial regions of Eastern Europe have received extremely heavy pollutant loads during the last few decades. Few forests outside these regions have been drastically damaged. But the possibility of more widespread destruction from chemical stress may increase with time. Ecologist C. S. Holling of the University of British Columbia points out that natural systems may absorb stress for long periods so that change occurs very slowly. Eventually, however, systems may reach a stress point, and as "a jump event becomes increasingly likely and ultimately inevitable," forest ecosystems could collapse.

Substantial economic losses have already resulted from the existing level of pollution stress on forests. The Czechoslovakian Academy of Sciences estimates the cost of acid pollution at $1.5 billion annually, with forest damage accounting for much of the total. In West Germany, researchers at the Technical University of Berlin forecast that German forest industries will suffer direct losses averaging $1 billion annually through the year 2060. Healthy forests, in addition to supplying timber, protect the quality of streams and groundwater supplies, control soil erosion, and provide recreation. Adding in projected losses of these functions, the Berlin researchers estimate that the total cost of forest damage in West Germany over the next several decades will average $2.4 billion per year.

In Switzerland, forest damage threatens the tourist industry that underpins the economy of some Alpine cantons. In North America, sugar maple harvesters lament a drop in maple syrup production and visible deterioration of the sugar maple trees. With weather conditions or other natural factors unable to explain the sugar maple decline, acid rain and air pollution have emerged as probable causes.

In the United States, field and laboratory experiments, combined with the findings of reduced tree growth, strongly suggest that ozone is reducing the productivity of some commercial forest species. Ozone results when certain nitrogen and hydrocarbon pollutants, emitted largely by automobiles, mix in the presence of sunlight. In many rural areas of Europe and North America, summer ozone concentrations now measure two to three times higher than natural background levels.

Researchers at Cornell University subjected four tree species—white pine, hybrid poplar, sugar maple, and red oak—to a range of ozone concentrations typically found in the United States. In all four species, net photosynthesis, a measure of a tree's growth, decreased proportionately with increases in ozone. So even with no outward sign of damage, trees covering large regions are very likely losing vigor and growing slower. Growth reductions of even 1 to 2 percent per year amount to a large loss of timber over a tree's lifetime.

Chronic stress from a variety of chemical pollutants now places a substantial share of the industrial world's forests at risk. In just one year, forest damage in West Germany jumped from 34 percent to 50 percent. The damage increased only slightly during 1985 and 1986, perhaps because of weather conditions beneficial to the trees. Forest damage in all of Europe is now 14 percent, and growing. No one knows how many of the injured trees will eventually die or if and when forest damage will rapidly worsen. Whether the unexplained decline in growth of eastern United States forests portends a similar decline also remains unknown.

With many uncertainties and a variety of pollutants under suspicion, any effective action to protect forests has proved difficult. Most efforts so far have focused on single pollutants or technologies to control pollutants from specific sources. Some twenty-one nations are now committed to reducing their sulfur dioxide emissions by at least 30 percent within a decade. Austria, Sweden, and Switzerland recently enacted pollution control standards for automobiles roughly equal to those in the United States. New cars will likely employ catalytic converters to curb the nitrogen and hydrocarbon compounds that contribute to the formation of acid rain and ozone.

The oil price increases of the seventies were a largely unheralded boon for the environment. Higher prices led consumers and industries to use energy more efficiently, which in turn lowered the output of carbon, sulfur, and other fossil fuel pollutants. Without West Germany's 8 percent decline in total energy consumption between 1979 and 1984, air pollution damage to the nation's forests probably would be worse.

Despite improvements made during the last decade, enormous potential remains for increasing energy efficiency in the world economy. The existing world automobile fleet, for example, travels an average of eighteen miles per gallon of fuel. Test vehicles now under study can achieve three to five times greater fuel economy, reducing pollutant emissions commensurately. Setting progressively stricter standards could help achieve this technical potential far faster than will market incentives alone.

Similarly, great gains could be made by setting efficiency standards for common household electrical appliances. U.S. legislation that seems likely to become law in 1987 would require major appliances to be 15 to 25 percent more energy efficient by 1990 than they were in 1985. This measure alone would eliminate the need to build 20 to 25 large power plants, thereby restraining emissions of carbon dioxide, sulfur dioxide, and nitrogen oxides.

Forest health is inescapably linked to energy use. Any strategy that offers hope of saving the industrial world's forests must include rapid introduction of pollution control, concerted boosts in energy efficiency, and shifts from fossil fuels to less-polluting energy sources. Meanwhile, with each passing year of continued pollution stress, the cost of lost forest productivity mounts, as does the risk of forest decline and death.

The first case of environmental cancer turned up more than two centuries ago. In 1775, epidemiologist Percival Pott found high rates of scrotal cancer among British chimney sweeps and related the cause to their unusually high exposure to soot, a byproduct of combustion.

Since then, the health hazards of environmental pollutants have spread widely to the general population. The same fossil fuel pollutants that damage forests also harm people. In the United States alone, they may cause as many as 50,000 premature deaths each year, mostly through effects on the respiratory system.

Metals, including lead, cadmium, and mercury, have become a growing cause for concern. Released into the atmosphere through the combustion of fossil fuels, incineration, and other high-temperature processes, metals return to earth in concentrations 100 to 10,000 times greater than natural levels. If introduced into the body in large enough quantities, they can cause varying toxic effects, including cancer and damage to the liver, kidneys, and central nervous system.

More recently, the proliferation of synthetic chemicals applied to croplands, dispersed into the air, and disposed as waste on land has added new dimensions to environmental health risks. Some 70,000 chemicals are at present in everyday use, with between 500 and 1,000 new ones added to the list each year. Estimates of the share of cancer deaths they cause vary, but the most widely accepted range from 1 percent to as much as 10 percent. Because of the long lag time—often twenty to forty years—between exposure to a cancer-causing chemical and the appearance of the disease, the number of cancers induced by synthetic substances could increase markedly over the coming decades.

One family of synthetic chemicals, the chlorofluorocarbons (CFCs), pose some of the most far-reaching health risks because of their capacity to alter the chemistry of the atmosphere. In the early seventies, four decades after CFC production began, scientists began warning that these compounds could destroy the life-protecting layer of ozone in the upper atmosphere.

Ozone, a chemical that forms irritating urban smog in the lower atmosphere, performs a vital function in the upper atmosphere. It absorbs ultraviolet radiation from the sun, which if allowed to reach the earth would have many harmful effects, such as inducing skin cancer and damaging crops. Once aloft, the CFCs migrate to the upper atmosphere where the sun's intense rays break them down, releasing atoms of chlorine. This chlorine in turn drives a series of reactions that destroy ozone. Largely as a result of worldwide CFC emissions, stratospheric concentrations of chlorine are now more than twice natural levels.

Virtually all CFCs produced are eventually released to the atmosphere, so trends in production largely determine future effects on the ozone layer. Production of CFC-11 and CFC-12, the most worrisome members of the CFC family, rose steadily from the early thirties to the early seventies as demand grew for their use in aerosol sprays, air conditioners, refrigerators, and insulating foam products. Production dropped for several years after the United States and several other industrial countries banned or restricted aerosol uses of CFCs. Yet since 1982, worldwide production has again turned upward.

A recent assessment by the U.S. Environmental Protection Agency, though preliminary, warns that if current trends continue, an additional 40 million cases of skin cancer—800,000 of them leading to death—could strike U.S. residents over the next eighty-eight years. Increased exposure to ultraviolet radiation would also likely impair human immune systems, making people more vulner-

able to disease. More people would develop cataracts. Because greater amounts of radiation could increase the formation of smog, respiratory problems and other pollution-related health effects could also increase.

Concern about the pace and predictability of ozone depletion has heightened recently with the discovery of a "hole" in the ozone layer over Antarctica. There, ozone levels drop by about 40 percent each September and October, shortly after sunlight reappears following the continent's cold, dark winter. This finding took scientists by surprise, and they cannot yet explain why it occurs. Whether it portends a more-rapid-than-expected depletion of the ozone layer globally is a looming and urgent question.

International negotiations regarding CFCs are in progress but so far have not produced concrete results. A cost-effective first step would be a worldwide ban on using CFCs in aerosol products, which account for roughly one-third of annual CFC production globally. Such a ban actually proved beneficial to the U.S. economy, with available substitutes saving consumers an estimated $165 million in 1983 alone.

But even stronger action is needed to reduce the risks of ozone depletion. U.S. negotiators have proposed freezing global CFC emissions over the near-term, and then gradually phasing them out. This proposal would not only protect human health, but could ultimately preserve the habitability of the earth.—*Sandra Postel*

Our longstanding struggle to improve the human condition may founder as we enter uncharted territory. Our efforts to feed and enrich the lives of all humans have brought about global chemical changes, some of which may be irreversible. A frustrating paradox is emerging. The same efforts we employ to improve living standards are themselves beginning to threaten the health of the global economy. Everyday activities such as driving automobiles, producing food, and generating electricity are adversely affecting the earth's capacity to support continuously expanding human numbers.

A human population of 5 billion, expanding at 82 million per year, has combined with the dramatic power of industrial technologies to expand the scope of human-induced environmental change. We have inadvertently set in motion ecological experiments that involve the whole earth, and as yet we do not have the means to monitor the results.

A sustainable society satisfies its needs without diminishing the prospects of the next generation. By many measures, contemporary society fails to meet this criterion. Questions of ecological sustainability are arising on every continent. The scale of human activities has begun to threaten the habitability of the earth itself.

Nothing short of fundamental adjustments in population and energy policies will stave off the host of costly changes now unfolding.

The ozone depletion and pollution-induced forest damage described in the preceding pages are relatively recent discoveries. Yet the activities believed to have brought about these threats—the release of chlorofluorocarbons and fossil fuel pollutants—have been under way for decades. Taken by surprise, industrial societies may trap themselves into costly tasks of planetary maintenance—perhaps seeding clouds in attempts to trigger rainfall where it has diminished with climatic change or seeking means of protection from increased exposure to ultraviolet radiation or liming vast areas of land sterilized by acidification. While perhaps giving brief local relief, these efforts will be like applying bandaids to a profoundly sick patient.

Because environmental systems can reach thresholds beyond which change occurs rapidly and unpredictably, we need early warning systems that would alert society in time to avert disaster. Despite impressive progress, the scientific groundwork has yet to be laid for monitoring the earth's life-support systems. Meanwhile, the pace of change quickens.

We have crossed many of nature's thresholds in a short period of time. No one knows how the affected natural systems will respond, much less how changes in natural systems will in turn affect economic and political systems. We can be reasonably certain that deforestation will disrupt hydrologic cycles and that ozone depletion will induce more skin cancer. But beyond these first-order effects, scientists can provide little detail.

Any system pushed out of equilibrium behaves in unpredictable ways. Small external pressures may be sufficient to cause dramatic changes. Stresses may become self-reinforcing, rapidly increasing the system's instability.

The environmental problems of the chemical age stretch beyond the authority of existing political and social institutions. Matters of the global environment now warrant the kind of high-level attention that the global economy receives. World leaders historically have cooperated to preserve economic stability, even to the point of completely overhauling the international monetary system at the 1944 conference in Bretton Woods. They periodically hold summit meetings on international economic problems. Policymakers carefully track economic indicators to determine when adjustments—national or international—are required. Similar efforts are needed for the global environment, including the delineation and tracking of environmental indicators, along with mechanisms for making prompt adjustments when the environment is threatened.

Technological and demographic changes are leading us into the twenty-first century with political institutions inherited from the nineteenth. The need to comprehend our responsibility in time to exercise it successfully presses upon us. The values that guide the management of technology in modern societies have not been clearly articulated, and the need for cooperation is not yet widely recognized in a world where diplomacy remains tied to anachronistic definitions of national sovereignty. That we know so little about the consequences of our activities is humbling. That we have brought so much responsibility upon ourselves is sobering.

A sustainable future calls upon us to simultaneously arrest the carbon dioxide buildup, protect the ozone layer, restore forests, stop population growth, boost energy efficiency, and develop renewable energy sources. No generation has ever faced such a complex set of issues requiring immediate attention. Preceding generations have always been concerned about the future, but we are the first to be faced with decisions that will determine whether the earth our children will inherit will be habitable.—*Lester R. Brown*

## QUESTIONS

1. What are the basic principles of planetary ecology, and what are the possible implications of technologies that upset the ecological balance?

2. Is industrial development really progress? Is pollution simply part of the price we must pay for our way of life?

3. In situations where resource development and environmental conservation seem completely incompatible, which do you think should have priority?

David K. Shipler

# 58. The View from America

*The United States and the Soviet Union are the superpowers of the modern world. Like many other dominant powers in centuries gone by—such as Greece and Persia, Rome and Carthage, or England and Spain—they have conflicting interests and ideologies that have brought them into competition and even hostility. Unlike all previous powers, however, these two nations hold the fate of humanity in their hands. If the hostility between the superpowers ever came to full-scale war, the resulting nuclear holocaust would obliterate both societies and threaten the rest of the world as well. Under these circumstances, it would seem desirable for the peoples of each society to have a broad-based, well-informed view of the other.*

*Unhappily, that is not the case. The Soviet people undoubtedly have a distorted view of the United States, since their media are subject to heavy censorship and rigorous state control by a regime not noted for its truthfulness. The United States is a much more open society, but its schools and media provide the population with remarkably little information about the Soviet Union. The result, as opinion polls repeatedly show, is that Americans hold highly negative stereotypes of the Russians, while knowing very few hard facts about Soviet culture or society. Indeed, Americans and Russians—like the peoples of any hostile societies—tend to "demonize" one another, attributing all manner of unscrupulous deeds and motives to the other side.*

*In this article, David K. Shipler explores American perceptions of Russia and its people, and compares these views with his own experience of Soviet society.*

One day last summer, my family and I were wandering through a small museum in Concord, Mass., when we came to a diorama depicting the historic clash between British redcoats and American colonists at North Bridge. There, on a miniature landscape, toy soldiers faced each other across a tiny battlefield at the opening of the American Revolution. My 8-year-old son, Michael, pointed to one of the little redcoats that had been tipped over on its side. "Look," he said, "a dead Russian." Then he caught himself, laughed and shook his head at his slip. "I mean, *British* soldier."

After 11 years of living overseas, our family had returned to the United States only one year before, but Michael had quickly absorbed a view that has become as American as the shot heard 'round the world: The Russians are the enemy.

The concept has worked its way into our culture. The Russians have taken their place in film, advertising and popular literature beside the images of cruel Nazis and the earlier, sinister stereotypes of Chinese and Japanese. They are vilified by our Government leaders as militant aggressors devoted to conquering the world. Their reciprocal fears of us are usually ignored in the textbooks that introduce American teen-agers to world affairs.

And often, at a deeper level, we use the Russians to define ourselves. All nations have a way of demonizing their adversaries. And so do we, picturing our values as antitheses of the Russians'—our freedom, their slavery; our wealth, their poverty; our honesty, their deceit; our righteousness, their subversion; our peaceful intentions, their warlike militarism; our robust private enterprise, their stifling state socialism.

The Soviet Union has given us plenty of reason to think the worst, of course—as a brutal prosecutor of some of its own dissidents, a bully in Eastern Europe, a trainer of terrorists, an arms merchant in tense regions of the world, a nuclear power with a revolutionary ideology. Much Soviet behavior has been inimical to American interests and offensive to American beliefs.

But as I return now to my own society after a long absence that included four years in Moscow, I am struck by how incomplete our portrait of the Russians is, how much of a caricature we have drawn, how thoroughly the shadings and nuances and rich subtleties of Soviet society have escaped us.

The gaps in understanding were revealed in a telephone poll conducted by The New York Times of 1,277 adults across the country between Sept. 15 and 19.

For many Americans, images of Russia are dominated by the familiar events of political oppression and international tension. And because the Soviet system is undemocratic, giving the Russian people no real voice in selecting leaders or making policy, the people generally don't play a large role in our perceptions. We tend to imagine Russians as hostile to the regime that governs them—while overlooking the antidemocratic impulses that find deep roots among ordinary Soviet citizens.

The terrible reign of Stalin is fixed in our imaginations: his forced collectivization of Russian farmers, and particularly his madness in purging the Communist Party and sending millions of innocent people to prison camps and firing squads. Ultimately, this disillusioned even most of those Americans who had initially seen hope for human justice in Soviet socialism.

Moscow's actions after World War II crystallized our sense of the Soviet Union as an adversary. Communist parties were installed in Eastern Europe. West Berlin was blockaded in 1948. Missiles were sent to Cuba in 1962, then withdrawn only under an American ultimatum. Hungary was invaded in 1956, Czechoslovakia in 1968 and Afghanistan in 1979. The Helsinki accords of 1975 were violated as dissidents were arrested and most emigration was barred. Poland was induced to put down its free trade union, Solidarity, with martial law in 1981.

The record justifies our suspicion and outrage. But as a consequence, the political conflicts have overwhelmed our perceptions, obscuring the character of Soviet life. Most Americans rely on the news—and especially television news—which is shaped by momentary political events, not the longer-range, subtler elements of culture, tradition and attitude.

That kind of information is available in books, scholarly journals and the best newspapers, but it takes second place in the popular imagination to the daily drama of international politics. The easy news is all negative news, and for that you don't have to get up from your television set.

Indeed, news coverage of the Soviet Union, especially on television, tends to be dominated less by the knowledgeable correspondents in Moscow than by the frequent, scary pronouncements of officials in Washington on the Soviet threat. Important national perceptions can be shaped by a well-turned phrase or dramatic im-

age, even when the underlying facts are in doubt. Describing Soviet intentions, for example, President Reagan recently used a quotation that he ascribed to Lenin: "We will take Eastern Europe. We will organize the hordes of Asia. And then we will move into Latin America and we won't have to take the United States; it will fall into our outstretched hands like overripe fruit." It turned out to be a phony, contained in a 1958 book by Robert Welch of the John Birch Society.

There is a great paradox here. Although Soviet society is largely closed and only partially visible to us, our freedom enables us to learn much more than the Russians themselves know about Soviet history and current affairs. In an open society, the facts are available to anyone who wants to dig through the serious writing. But more immediate and ubiquitous sources of information are more easily distorted by political fads and insidious stereotypes.

The resulting misperceptions seem less a function of politics than of emotion, less rooted in the various positions Americans occupy along their political spectrum than in their mythologies about the nature and intentions of the Soviet Union. Indeed, as the recent Times poll showed, many misperceptions are held across political lines—by Republicans and Democrats, conservatives and liberals, voters for Ronald Reagan and for Walter Mondale. The profound ideological conflict between the two countries transcends the divisions of American politics.

It sometimes even affects personal behavior. Russians who visit the United States are generally received with the same courtesy Americans are offered in the Soviet Union. But some contacts have been laced with tension.

For the last two years, James E. Hill, who teaches high-school history in Claremont, Calif., has been conducting an informal experiment, putting on a Russian accent and giving the official Soviet viewpoint on a range of international issues, including the Soviet argument on behalf of peaceful coexistence with the United States. College audiences usually treat him well, but high-school students and adults often erupt in rage. "They say, 'We won't have peace with you unless you change and live like us,' " Hill reports. At Edgewood High School in West Covina, a suburb of Los Angeles, teachers walked out of his lectures. When he sat down in the faculty lunchroom, some teachers got up from the table and walked away; others moved to the far end.

When a class of Soviet diplomats' children was scheduled to visit the Arlington Middle School in the Poughkeepsie, N.Y., area, a few American youngsters on the morning buses were overheard planning to harass "the Commies," according to Jane Barley, a former teacher of Russian who supervises some of the language programs for the New York State Education Department. Perhaps their remarks were a variation of the slogans now seen on T-shirts: "Kill a Commie for Mommy." But the pupils involved were spoken to, and the visit occurred without incident.

At the Titusville Middle School in Poughkeepsie, Jane Barley said, a mother refused to let her son sign up for Russian language, arguing, "We would never let him study Russian. We're Christians."

The basic obstacle to understanding is lack of knowledge. Polls show that Americans are not very well-informed about other countries, and the Soviet Union is no exception. Of those interviewed in The Times survey, 51 percent said that they had no desire to visit the Soviet Union. Yet those of us who have returned from Moscow find intense curiosity about life there—enough to put books on the best-seller list and light up switchboards during talk shows on the subject. Many Americans also seem ready to have their stereotypes revised.

Russian-language study has never been very popular in the United States, and courses in Soviet studies have attracted relatively small enrollments. The number of public secondary-school students taking Russian swelled to a high of 26,716 in 1965—only two-tenths of 1 percent of the total student population—and dropped steadily thereafter to 5,702, or four one-hundredths of 1 percent, in 1982.

An opposite trend has been visible at the college level, with a rise from 1980 to 1983 of 26.7 percent in the number of students taking Russian. As Soviet-American tensions have grown, so has the interest in graduate study of Soviet affairs. The W. Averell Harriman Institute for Advanced Study of the Soviet Union at Columbia University had 182 applicants for the current academic year, up from 43 for 1980-81. The Russian Research Center at Harvard, which a decade ago received 30 to 50 applications for its masters program, saw 100 students apply for 15 places last year and 90 this year. At Middlebury College in Vermont, which has long enjoyed a fine reputation in Russian-language instruction, a new Soviet studies program has begun to attract significant numbers of undergraduates.

An average of more than 200 books and 2,500 articles a year are written by Americans about the Soviet Union. Some 40 full-time American correspondents reside in Moscow—one of the largest American press corps in the world. Legions of American academic experts sift the Soviet press, monitor Moscow television, talk with Soviet officials and publish learned analyses in scholarly journals. And yet little of this information filters down to the general public. Understanding is pockmarked with blank spots.

Of those polled in The Times survey, for example, 76 percent were unable to name Mikhail S. Gorbachev as the top Soviet leader. Historical knowledge was weak, especially in areas that weigh heavily on Russians' views of their relationship with us. Forty-four percent of the Americans surveyed did not know that the Soviet Union and the United States had fought on the same side in World War II; a smaller number within that group—28 percent of the whole sample—thought that the two countries had actually fought against each other. Only 42 percent knew that more Russians than Americans had died in the Second World War, and just 14 percent were aware that in 1918, the United States landed troops in northern and eastern Russia along with the British, French and Japanese to bolster anti-Bolshevik forces in the civil war that followed the 1917 Revolution.

Part of the fault can be found in an assortment of history textbooks used in junior and senior high schools. Some mention the American intervention in passing, although many ignore it entirely. In their account of World War II, many are almost mirror images of their Soviet counterparts, minimizing the Soviet role in combating Hitler's Germany just as Soviet books reduce the American role. Soviet texts place the Soviet Union at the center of the war, playing down the Pacific theater, portraying the battle of Stalingrad as the turning point, and castigating the United States for delaying its entry into the fighting, while the American books usually focus on the United States' role as decisive and the Normandy landing as the critical moment in the Allied effort.

*Freedom's Trail*, an American history text published by Houghton Mifflin, for example, passes quickly over the Soviet-German fighting: "In June 1941, Hitler attacked the Soviet Union. So the United States sent lend-lease supplies to help the Soviet Union fight Germany." The book mentions neither the battle of Stalingrad nor the extent of Soviet suffering. Only a note printed in the teacher's edition recalls that an estimated 20 million Soviet citizens died. *Exploring a Changing World*, a junior-high-school text published by the Globe Book Company, also gives America credit for much of the Soviet victory. "The Germans were very successful," it declares. "But with the help of the United States, the Soviets stopped the German armies." Stalingrad is recalled, but without reference to the heavy Soviet losses.

This parochialism surprises Russians who come here. "America is a rather isolated country in a way," observed Vasily Aksyonov, a dissident Soviet writer who immigrated to the United States five years ago. "I have even had to tell some people that Russia is located between China and Germany. They know that this is some terrifying power, but they don't know where."

Spy novels, films and advertisements reflect and reinforce stereotypes. Soviet spies in some thrillers are sympathetic individuals caught in the wheels of ruthless bureaucracy, and some films, such as "The Russians Are

Coming, The Russians Are Coming" of 1966 and the recent "Moscow on the Hudson" portray individual Russians in warm tones. But vicious and absurd caricatures of Russians have become standard fare in a current genre of commercials and films. These have had a major impact on American teen-agers, as I discovered when I went home to Chatham, N.J., the town where I grew up.

At Chatham High School, an upper-middle-class public school, I spoke with two groups of about 40 students each, one drawn from honors 11th- and 12th-grade history classes, the other consisting of sophomores and juniors at mixed levels.

I began by asking what words entered their minds when they thought of "Russians." The images came in a flood: Flight 007, Reds, Communists, vodka, not real, stubborn, nuclear war, cold, Siberia, gulag, trapped, nervous, programmed, strict, Olympic boycott, Berlin, Iron Curtain, K.G.B., enemy, Afghanistan, roulette, oppression, workers, regimented, hammer and sickle, chess, sports, defectors, strongwilled, wheat, propaganda, Socialist, Kremlin, long lines, absenteeism, Lenin, Cuba, Hitler, grain embargo, Marxism, Poland, terrorism, cold war. When I asked for more about the Russian people, they added: emotionless, ignorant, naïve, afraid, sadness, paranoid, ugly (later retracted by the boy who said it), alcoholics, gray, poor, strange, deprived, brainwashed, old-fashioned, spies, bravery, survival.

Most American prejudices were contained in these words, and they pervaded both the honors and nonhonors classes. A similar harshness emerged from The Times poll, whose respondents most often mentioned Communism, enemies, nuclear war, aggression, invasion, world domination and other threatening terms. Only 6 percent of those polled had positive thoughts about the Russians, ranging from "people like us" to "World War II allies" to sable, caviar and the like.

Even admirable traits are stained by political hostility. In polls since 1942, Americans have consistently labeled Russians "hard-working," and 56 percent of the Times survey's respondents thought Russians worked harder than Americans. While some explained that they were really criticizing the "lackadaisical" American worker, others held an exaggerated picture of gloom and hardship in the Soviet Union. Some thought, erroneously, that all Russians were assigned their jobs and worked in near servitude.

"I believe they really don't have much choice in their jobs or career," said a 35-year-old dragline operator for a strip-mining company in Pennsylvania. "I don't believe there is a situation there for vacations, holidays and leisure time," he added. "The Russians, in order to eat, have to perform a certain number of tasks for the Government. They are harder workers because they are forced to be."

A 34-year-old actress, college graduate and Reagan voter from St. Louis thought the Russians put in "way more hours" than Americans and that "they are allowed only one pair of shoes a year. I would not be very happy working for that one pair of shoes, knowing that's all I could have."

This is a dramatic misimpression of the Russians, whose habits on the job—with occasional exceptions—make the Soviet Union one of the world's greatest goof-off societies. Workers are virtually immune from dismissal, no matter how poorly they perform. The eight-hour day and the five-day week are normal features of Soviet life, as are holidays and vacations, of course. Long vacations and extra pay are offered as a way of attracting workers to the tough climate of Siberia. Given the country's labor shortage, low-skilled Russians have considerable latitude about the kind of job they take. Those with higher education are on narrower tracks, but with some free choice; they are usually able to select their areas of specialization before beginning their studies, and upon graduating from college are assigned three-year positions in their fields.

When a 1981 Roper Poll presented Americans with a choice of terms to describe Russians, practically every response was far off-target, in my experience. The Russian people were seen as aggressive and competitive, disciplined, insensitive and mean. Only 3 percent thought they were cheerful and fun-loving and had a sense of humor. Anyone who has lived in the Soviet Union would find these stereotypes utterly unrecognizable. To the extent that one can generalize about a nation more diverse than we care to realize, Russians are warm and compassionate, more complacent than competitive, more unruly in their souls than disciplined.

What may be happening here is that Americans, encouraged by their own films and advertising, are confusing politics with personality. You have to know Russians personally, and preferably in the cloistered privacy of their own apartments, to know the warmer side of them. A funny, nonsensical television commercial for Miller Lite beer, for example, shows a Soviet émigré extolling the virtue of America, which he says has parties everywhere. In the Soviet Union, he adds, you don't find the parties, the Party finds you.

This disparity between the public and private Russian came to the surface in Chatham High School, where one student called Russians "emotionless." When I asked him why, he gave an interesting answer. Watching Soviet athletes on television, he never noticed any expressions on their faces. "If they win, you expect them to be happy," he said. "Their athletes always look like they're upset all the time."

The comment drew objections from other students,

especially a couple who had met Soviet citizens personally. "I find it hard to stereotype such a large country as being emotionless," one boy declared. A girl in the class then spoke movingly about a visit to the Soviet Union with her father, who sang in the Yale Russian Chorus. She was only 10 at the time, but remembered visiting a Russian family at home. The experience remained deeply engraved in her feelings. "In their homes they're very emotional people," she said. "On the street they're just being careful. This facade of being so cold and so hard is just a facade."

That is precisely right, and it's a shame that Soviet authorities don't realize how much good they could do for American perceptions by opening up a little. Officialdom's suspicion of infectious foreign influence makes most Russians wary of inviting Americans home, so even tourists who travel briefly to Moscow often come away with an image of Russians in their public posture—cold, unfeeling and rude.

Others go too far in the other direction, making the wondrous discovery that the Soviet Union is a real country with real people who eat, sleep, brush their teeth and love their children. This can produce gushing, naïve declarations about how we really don't have any conflicts at all.

One Harvard student, participating in a recent PBS television discussion, delivered herself of a perfectly wide-eyed appreciation. "When I got a chance to go I was really excited by the fact that they are just people," she said, "and they walk in the street and they talk and act just like people, like us. There were times when you could have just limited contact with people, and you could get an old woman on the street to smile at you if you did something that she thought was good." Who can argue with her? The sun also rises over Moscow from time to time.

Our images of the Russian people as individuals reflect and reinforce the sense that Soviet society as a whole is bleak, regimented and wholly controlled from above. A recent television commercial for Royal Crown Cola, for example, begins with ranks of Soviet citizens in gray, Stalinesque tunics, their faces impassive as they stand in Red Square facing a stern leader who admonishes them to drink Coke and Pepsi. The scene then shifts to a cabin in the wintry countryside, where jovial Russians in old-fashioned Cossack costumes dance, sing and make merry with RC—until the door bursts open, two black-hatted secret policemen appear and the main reveler hides his RC Cola inside his coat.

The caricature of Soviet society as the ultimate in totalitarianism is widespread in American advertising, films and political cartoons. Even the film "Moscow on the Hudson," which compassionately portrays individual Russians, contains an absurd scene in which a Russian family sitting at home grows alarmed when the hero starts talking about American jazz and singing some tunes. "I know we'll get arrested for sure," one man says.

Similarly, an ad mailed out this autumn by Time-Life Books for a volume on the Soviet Union shows a full color picture of a uniformed Soviet schoolgirl holding an AK-47 assault rifle. The bold print declares: "Powerful. Defiant. Alert to every threat. . . ." Only in fine print is the girl identified as an honor guard at a war memorial. Inside, the blurb asks the reader to imagine himself as a Russian in Moscow, standing at a street corner and checking his impulse to curse at a speeding limousine as he notices a possible informer nearby. "No Party bigshot is worth a trip to Siberia." The ad invites the reader to discover "what life is *really* like inside a country where nothing—absolutely nothing—goes unnoticed under the unblinking gaze of the omnipotent state."

But life in the Soviet Union is not that way. Nor is it portrayed that way by the book itself, which is an excellent, fair-minded examination. The advertisement, in reinforcing the Stalinist image, ignores the extensive changes since Stalin's death in 1953. Although the structure of oppression remains intact, people do not disappear into Siberia for the relatively minor offenses of grumbling or telling political jokes; usually it takes an overt and deliberate act of dissent to provoke a political arrest, and lesser deviations mean lesser punishments, including the forfeit of material privileges, travel to the West and the like.

"It is not a totalitarian state," said Vasily Aksyonov, the dissident writer now living in Washington. "There is a second level full of confusion, full of idiocy, full of black markets, full of debauchery."

Soviet authorities reinforce the totalitarian image by persecuting highly visible, respected human-rights activists such as Andrei D. Sakharov and Anatoly B. Shcharansky, and by harassing and sometimes arresting Soviet Jews who want to study Hebrew, practice their Judaism or immigrate to Israel. The anti-Jewish oppression touches a powerful nerve in the United States, particularly for many American Jews whose parents or grandparents were born in Russia, came to this country and left their children and grandchildren with a legacy of gratitude and a sense of obligation. Rallies, newsletters and lobbying efforts on behalf of Soviet Jewry convey a justified sense of passion and outrage to large numbers of influential Americans.

For the most part, descriptions of Soviet life in American textbooks are frozen in the Stalinist era, when masses of Communist Party officials and others were arrested and shot capriciously. Few books update the picture, and when they do they are sometimes attacked by conservative groups who want them banned from schools for being too gentle with the Russians. One such text, used in Chatham, N.J.; Montgomery County, Md., and elsewhere is *Unfinished Journey: A World History* by Marvin Perry. In 1981 it was dropped from the Alabama State Board of Education's approved list mainly for its passages on evolution and organized religion, but also because it noted that "under Communist leadership the Soviet Union had been transformed into a modern nation in record time."

"Both sides have inundated their populations with malicious propaganda for a long time," said Stephen F. Cohen, a professor of Soviet politics and history at Princeton University. Among the resulting misperceptions he lists the notions that "the Soviet elite is utterly monolithic because all Communists think alike," that "every Soviet leader is strong," that "there is no real politics in the system—it is a kind of an administrative despotism." This last perceptual problem stems partly from the public struggle between dissidents and the state, which creates an appearance of politics while the real politics, the jockeying among constituencies for resources and priorities, takes place behind the closed doors of Soviet officialdom.

A final misperception holds that the regime has no legitimacy in the eyes of Soviet citizens. "Most Americans don't think of the Soviet system as having a social contract with its people," Cohen observed, citing the mistaken notion that a vast population of Russians detests its system and Government. Fifty-eight percent of those questioned in The Times survey thought Americans were more patriotic than Russians because, as one explained, "I don't think they are too proud of what they stand for, and their economy and life style is more of a grind."

In fact, as Americans who have lived in the Soviet Union have usually come to realize, a broad consensus seems to exist between the rulers and the ruled, one that transcends the widespread grumbling about shortages of goods and services, the acerbic political jokes, the yearning for material artifacts from the West. Despite their mediocre living standards Russians have a feeling of economic security, an appreciation for the cradle-to-grave welfare that distinguishes their system from what they are told is the chaotic uncertainty of life in the United States. The importance of this in Russian minds rarely seems to leave its mark on American perceptions. The characteristic is far from comforting, and may lead us to miscalculation if we assume that Russians form a captive nation yearning to be free.

In The Times poll, 49 percent of those surveyed thought the Communist Party would lose a free election in the Soviet Union while 40 percent thought it would win; 51 percent thought that most Russians disliked their

system and would prefer a democracy, while 35 percent believed that most preferred strong leadership and would not be attracted to democracy. Asked which they imagined the average Russian would choose, more consumer goods or more political freedom, 62 percent guessed more freedom and only 29 percent said more goods. After four years in the Soviet Union, my hunch is the opposite on each question; I came away convinced of the Russians' discomfort with weak leadership and of their aversion to the West's pluralistic array of political ideas.

That realization comes hard. It is a view of Russian political impulses that has only gradually and recently begun to gain acceptance among American academics, as Robert Kelley, a professor of history at the University of California at Santa Barbara, discovered upon his return from a semester of teaching at Moscow State University in 1979. When he described Russians' affinity for order and unanimity and their desire for a strong hand at the top, his colleagues "simply recoiled in disbelief," he recalled. "I remember being accused of being brainwashed when I said this at a faculty seminar. It seems to me that if I were coming back from Moscow now I wouldn't have the problem. People now are ready to accept this idea."

The academic world is as susceptible to fads as the population at large. It swings from one popular concept to the next. For many years following the launch of Sputnik in 1957, the Soviet Union seemed to have won the scientific and technological race with the United States. Soviet education seemed invincible, American schooling inferior. Now the coin has been flipped, and Soviet society is more widely seen as economically incompetent, technologically hopeless, gripped by imminent crisis and possible collapse. "Why?" asks Stephen Cohen, who has become a gadfly within his profession of Sovietology. "We hate the system and we want it to go away, and we know we can't make a war against it. So we want it to commit an act of self-abolition. It would solve our problems."

At a certain level, American antipathy toward the Soviet system satisfies our own need for a villain. And the villain is an abstraction, an all-purpose enemy that often has little to do with the Russians themselves. Thus it is in "Red Dawn," John Milius's World War III film that was popular briefly in the summer of 1984. The scenario plays to the wildest fears and fantasies in American society: An invasion force of Soviet, Cuban and Nicaraguan troops takes over the western part of the United States, shoots up a school, murders townspeople and herds men into a concentration camp. A few high-school students escape with guns into the mountains, where they organize themselves into a band of guerrillas called the Wolverines, attacking Soviet soldiers, convoys and bases in a satisfying orgy of violence that ultimately helps overcome the sinister occupiers.

Virtually all the Chatham students who had seen the film liked it, identified with the Wolverines and enjoyed the idea that a bunch of kids like them could kill a lot of Communists.

"It kind of made you feel good," one boy remarked. "You came out hating the Russians." Another boy added: "Americans went through Vietnam and suffered terrorist attacks. People are sick of America always being wrong. Americans are sick of that. They want the movies to kick their butts around." Only a few in the honors class criticized the film as absurd, scary and bloodthirsty.

The specter of a Soviet takeover will also be exploited by ABC television in a 16-hour miniseries called "Amerika" scheduled for broadcast during the 1986–87 season. Set a decade after the United States has fallen to the Russians without a fight, the program portrays a materially deprived and politically fearful America run by villainous Soviet agents. A K.G.B. colonel will be drawn as a sympathetic character saddened by America's departure from its own values.

But the damaging potential rests in the film's reliance on the debatable assumption that the Soviet Union is out to conquer us. Donald Wrye, the program's writer, producer and director, conceded that most experts his staff consulted "held the opinion that this could not happen." But his plan to sketch a United States as something akin to Vichy France under the Nazi occupation seems likely to encourage those Americans who like to see Soviet Communists behind every unwelcome opinion and development.

If the Russians began producing films and television shows about a conquest of the Soviet Union by the United States, we might rightly accuse them of whipping up hysteria, anti-American hatred and international tension. And we would have some reason to fear the effects on their population, as we ourselves might now worry about the influence of this genre of entertainment on young Americans.

The Chatham High School girl who thought of Hitler when the word Russians was mentioned explained that both regimes treated their people similarly—an idea formed from the images of Nazi-like Russians that appear increasingly in American films.

"Rambo: First Blood Part II," in which an American superfighter goes into Vietnam in search of American POW's, announces the arrival of Soviet officers with a closeup of their black jackboots. The Soviet interrogator, a Lieut. Col. Podovsky, speaks English with a German accent; his precise manner, erect posture and cool sadism make him a carbon copy of Hollywood's typical Nazi S.S. officer. The ruthless Russians torture Rambo with electric shocks, threaten to burn out an American pris-

oner's eye with a red-hot knife blade, shoot an escaping POW in the back. As Rambo's helicopter seems to spin out of control, there is a searing shot of the satisfied face of a Soviet pilot, set in a cold, malicious grin.

All this could be dismissed more easily if it did not have such an impact. When I asked one group of Chatham students who their heroes were, they listed Rambo and the Wolverines along with President Reagan, General Patton and the United States Marines.

Our confrontation with Soviet society is something of a confrontation with ourselves. Any thoughtful American who lives for a time in Moscow comes away with insights into his own fears about the darker sides of his political personality, questions about integrity, courage, principles, values. Some Americans who have read the chapters of my book on Soviet children learning hypocrisy and Soviet adults practicing political charades see aspects of American society there. At a seminar for Middlebury alumni last summer, several retired corporation executives said that they recognized the American business world in my descriptions of the Soviet drive for conformity.

We need an external villain to attack, an image, perhaps, of that villain we suspect lurks inside ourselves. The Russians fill the role conveniently, partly because they are in a real ideological conflict with us. At their cores, our two countries are both evangelical; each is possessed by what it conceives as the most righteous political and economic system in human history, and each is convinced that spreading its system would benefit all mankind. Each proselytizes out of its national interest, creating a mixture of ideological vision and military power that makes a potent chemistry.

Our images of Russia tend to define a certain intellectual orthodoxy in American Sovietology. Some on the political right, such as Polish born Richard E. Pipes, a professor of history at Harvard, see the consensus as "slightly left of center," as he put it. Others believe that academic debate about the Soviet Union is focused by the political climate of the moment, that as American attitudes have moved to the right, "the aperture of permissible discussion" has moved right as well, in the phrase of Michael McGwire, formerly a British naval attaché in Moscow and now a specialist in Soviet military affairs at the Brookings Institution in Washington. "It's like a spotlight," he said. "In Russia, you have a spotlight of permissible discussion, but it's fixed. In America, it swings."

Nevertheless, knowledge about the Soviet Union breeds neither affection nor unanimity among the American experts. They are fascinated by the Soviet system but rarely attracted to it. They argue among themselves about Soviet intentions and military capabilities, disagreeing on the most basic questions of whether Moscow is inherently aggressive or defensive in its motivations.

Many students and experts dislike the Soviet system. "That isn't necessarily bad," said Marshall D. Shulman, director of the Harriman Institute at Columbia. "If you train somebody who knows all the negative sides of it, he may be a better reporter, he may be a better negotiator than somebody who is pro-Soviet. The objective shouldn't be to make everybody pro-Soviet."

The penalty for straying beyond the beam in the United States is to be ignored, according to John Steinbruner, head of foreign policy studies at Brookings. "It is exceedingly difficult to get people to hear what you're saying if you're outside of that," he said. Being outside these days means arguing that the Soviet Government is complicated, makes decisions the way most organizations do—in a chaotic and disorganized way—and operates mostly defensively to hold onto what it has. The contrary assumption—that, despite its economic weaknesses, the Soviet Union is a logical, dedicated, expansionist enemy—"is the governing theology of the age, like the tenets of faith of the 14th century," Steinbruner declared. "It's easy to be an apostate."

There is a danger that if we accept our amalgam of images as the entire reality, we cannot deal with the real Russians; we can deal only with our own fears. Still, as I stood in my old high school, I saw a scattering of students in the honors classes whose questioning skepticism set them apart from the crowd. I had come back to my cloistered, homogeneous town wondering whether I would find the mirror image of a group of Moscow teenagers I once met. They were youngsters of the elite—well-scrubbed, patriotic leaders of Komsomol, the Communist Youth League—who thought their country was the font of all virtue and the United States the focus of evil. They were comforted by the certainty of simplicity, and they reminded me of my hometown, in which the world had seemed neatly divided into good guys and bad guys.

The only heroes the Soviet students could think of were Lenin and Che Guevara, and some of the Chatham youngsters were equally conformist. But the few questioning Chatham kids were quite different from those Komsomol kids in Moscow—and from most of their peers in Chatham—for their heroes included more than models of toughness. They mentioned Martin Luther King, John F. Kennedy, Bishop Desmond Tutu, Gandhi. They had a long list of wrongs to set right in the world, a more searching and self-critical list—poverty, crime, racism, hunger, the nuclear threat, and so on—than the Soviet students had given me. They were ready to learn.

## QUESTIONS

1. How do Americans view Russians, and why do they view them that way?

2. How would you characterize the Russians' opinions of Americans? Can you list ten adjectives that you think they might apply to the United States and its people?

3. How much do you know about the Soviet Union—its history, geography, economy, languages, peoples, political system, literature? Are you satisfied with your knowledge, or do you think you should know more?

*Thomas Powers*

# 59. Nuclear Winter and Nuclear Strategy

*Ever since the use of the atomic bomb in 1945, the world has lived in the shadow of a potential holocaust of almost unimaginable proportions. Today, the United States and the Soviet Union have thousands of missiles equipped with nuclear warheads aimed at each other's strategic targets, which in many cases include densely populated areas. These missiles represent enough firepower to destroy both societies hundreds of times over; indeed, they represent the equivalent of four tons of the explosive TNT for every person on the planet.*

*Scientists have actually proved to be surprisingly ignorant of the precise effects of nuclear weapons. For example, they did not realize in 1945 that a nuclear explosion would produce a burst of deadly direct radiation, followed by a rain of radioactive fallout that could contaminate the environment. When the surviving victims of the Hiroshima explosion developed radiation sickness, their plight was at first a mystery. And it was only a few years ago that scientists realized that a single high-altitude nuclear explosion could create an electromagnetic pulse capable of knocking out electronic circuits—including military ones—over an area half the size of the United States. In other words, the defensive systems that each side was relying on were much more vulnerable than either had suspected.*

*More recently, scientists have made a new discovery: even a relatively small nuclear war could generate so much smoke, soot, and dust that the sun's rays would be blocked out, causing a sharp drop in temperature. There is some debate about how or for how long temperatures would fall—but as Thomas Powers points out in this article, this new information has important implications for nuclear strategy.*

During the opening campaigns of the air war against Germany, it didn't take long for the British Bomber Command to realize that the right way to destroy a city is not to break it up with high explosives but to burn it. High-explosive (HE) bombs are purely local affairs. You've got to cube the blast power of the bomb in order to square the area destroyed. Not even a thousand British Lancaster and Halifax bombers, which was the size of the biggest of the fleets raiding Germany by the third year of the war, could carry enough high-explosive bombs to do more than sprinkle cities with holes of destruction. Bomb raids involving HE bombs were terrifying to live through but not very dangerous; casualties were generally few.

But fire is a living thing. Fire consumes and spreads. Fire attacks anything of organic origin the way disease attacks human bodies, and just as epidemics can flash through the crowds of cities, so fire finds a congenial host in the accumulated combustibles—the wood, the paper, and the fabric of cities. In March of 1942 Bomber Command attacked the medieval German city of Lübeck, figuring that its narrow streets of ancient timbered houses meant it would burn well. It did. As the war progressed, the British abandoned daylight attacks on specific industrial targets because too many planes were being shot down and it was too hard to drop bombs accurately. The price was high, the results paltry. So Bomber Command switched to nighttime raids on the sprawling industrial suburbs of German manufacturing centers. Darkness protected the bombers, cities were big enough to find at night, and their size meant that even a miss—and most bombs fell miles wide of the "target"—was still bound to hit *something*. The adoption of the "bomber stream" helped to concentrate the attack. The bombs were fused to explode not on impact but an instant later, which helped to break up buildings. The bomb-load mix was changed as well. A third of each plane's cargo was devoted to HE bombs, which broke windows, blew open doors, and splintered wood into matchsticks. The rest of the load consisted of incendiary bombs to set the wreckage afire.

But the art of burning cities did not approach full

flower until July of 1943, when successive raids on Hamburg brought something new into the world—the firestorm. The worst damage occurred on the night of July 27–28, when nearly 750 British bombers dropped 2,326 tons of bombs, about half of them incendiaries. For some reason the bomb patterns were unusually tight that night. A vast fire was ignited, producing temperatures estimated at nearly 1,000° centigrade at the center of the conflagration. Hurricane-force winds roared in from all sides to feed the fire. People abroad in the streets were actually sucked into the fire. Others were mired in molten asphalt, or they melted outside the steel blast doors of bunkers where they had—too late—sought refuge. When survivors inside opened the doors to emerge after the raid, they found pools of fat on the ground. In other shelters the heat was so intense that people were baked brown, leaving shriveled corpses the size of children, or they died of asphyxiation because the firestorm had sucked the air out of the shelter. A study by the United States Strategic Bombing Survey after the war found that the average number of deaths in an ordinary bombing run on an urban area was 1,850. In Hamburg the death toll was over 40,000. Whether this raid helped to win the war is hard to say. One reason for the attack on Hamburg was its importance as a submarine-building center. Some 400 U-boats were launched by the Hamburg yards during the war, about half before the raid and half after. But the Hamburg raid unnerved the German High Command and convinced Allied strategic-bombing enthusiasts that they had found the key to defeat of an enemy from the air.

As things turned out, creating a firestorm was no easy matter; everything had to work just so. But Bomber Command destroyed Dresden with another in February of 1945, and the Americans under General Curtis LeMay succeeded in creating the biggest of all in Tokyo the next month, when a roaring inferno destroyed sixteen square miles of the city and killed more than 80,000 people. In the late spring of 1945 General H. A. "Hap" Arnold asked LeMay how long he thought the war against Japan would last. LeMay said, "Give me thirty minutes." Then he called in one of his operations officers and did the numbers: so many Japanese cities left to burn, so many planes available to fly, so many flying days to do the job. When there were no more cities to burn, the war would be over. LeMay told Arnold, "The first of September." What was new about Hiroshima was not the firestorm—something well understood by that time—but the fact that its infernal horrors had been achieved by one bomb from one plane. This represented a quantum jump in military efficiency. When LeMay saw the Hiroshima photos a few days later, he told me recently, he realized that "we really had something extraordinary."

Burning cities were one enduring image to come out of the war. It obsessed military men for twenty years, but the general public caught the drift as well. I've often thought that this image had a lot to do with the rapid growth of the suburbs surrounding American cities in the 1950s. The message of Coventry, Hamburg, Berlin, Tokyo, and Hiroshima was hard to miss: War destroys cities. *Get out of the cities.* But my notion is a hard one to prove. Perhaps the growth of suburbia was only the doing of the automobile, or of cheap mortgages.

What is interesting now is something that was noticed only as a curiosity then—the vast pillars of smoke that rose over the burning cities and then diffused downwind, creating gorgeous sunsets for days thereafter. Color in the evening sky is a function of slanting sunlight shining through stuff in the air—clouds, dust, volcanic ash, the characteristic smoke and fumes of cities. In Cairo once, a friend and I watched the sun set over the Western Desert after a dust storm. The sky was stupendously aflame. On another occasion I took an air taxi down the length of Long Island toward New York City and watched the sun set through the yellow and purple and violet streaks of gunk suspended over the city. It seemed hard to believe that living creatures could breathe that livid stew. A lot of what we think of as nature is really the doing of man. One of the arguments raised against a plan to hide MX missiles among thousands of shelters in the deserts of Nevada and Utah was the dust that construction would stir up—thick enough at the Grand Canyon, hundreds of miles away, scientists said, that tourists often wouldn't be able to see one rim of the canyon from the other.

The general phenomenon is well known. Volcanoes pumping ash into the air can add a streak of color to sunsets thousands of miles away. In 1950 a gigantic fire burned over an area of 10,000 square kilometers of forest in Alberta, Canada. The trees, mostly conifers, were rich in tars and resins, which make oily black smoke. The pall covered about half the land area of the United States, spread across the Atlantic, was detected over Great Britain by aircraft as high as 35,000 feet, and actually reduced the amount of visible light reaching the ground in Western Europe. Smoke hangs well in the air, especially dark, sooty smoke. The particles are small. They absorb sunlight and heat up the surrounding air, which tends to linger aloft in a thick layer. Second World War bombers frequently returned to their bases covered with black soot picked up at altitudes of 20,000 or 30,000 feet. The smoke from the firestorm at Hiroshima, which burned five square miles of the city, was pushed high into the troposphere by the combined heat of the fires and the bomb's fireball. Survivors spoke of the awful darkness and the chill in the August air which accompanied the murk and the gloom. Water vapor condensed and fell back to earth as rain, black with the soot it picked up on the way down. A Japanese novelist, Masuji Ibuse, later wrote a fine novel called *Black Rain* about the bombing of Hiroshima. For him the black rain symbolized the ghastliness of what happened.

But to American officials and scientists who studied the bombing after the war, the black rain—an unexpected effect of the unique explosion—was nothing more than a curiosity. Scores of individuals contributed reports for the U.S. Strategic Bombing Survey account of the attacks on Hiroshima and Nagasaki, but the author of the account, Philip J. Farley, remembers no mention of smoke in the documents he collected. "I thought of the cloud in terms of the scenic effects," Farley said recently in his office at Stanford University, where he now teaches after a long government career spent mostly in the State Department. "Nobody was thinking [of side effects] except in terms of radiation."

Paul Nitze, one of the Survey's two vice-chairmen, took Farley to Japan in August to work on the Survey's study of the Pacific half of the war, and then, in November, assigned him to write the account of Hiroshima and Nagasaki. Farley never visited either city, but the reports he saw covered everything imaginable—heat and blast effects, radiation sickness, the durability of various types of construction, the hopeless task that had faced the city's firefighting services, and the like—except the smoke. The limits of the fire were mapped in great detail, but smoke was smoke. How much, where it went, how long it lingered in the air—none of that seemed to matter.

But now the question of smoke is very much on the minds of scientists and military men, for the simple reason that nuclear war would mean large numbers of burning cities, all pumping vast quantities of smoke into the air. Last December five scientists published a paper in *Science* magazine claiming that smoke from as few as a thousand fires in a hundred major cities could cast a sooty pall over the Northern Hemisphere thick and lingering enough to bring darkness at noon and radically cool the earth's surface for months, thereby triggering a climatic catastrophe—a "nuclear winter"—that would threaten many plant and animal species, including man, with extinction. The invention of nuclear weapons has brought dire warnings aplenty in the past few decades, but this one is on an altogether different scale. It's one thing to say that the United States and the Soviet Union would suffer beyond precedent in a nuclear war, even that a nuclear war "would destroy civilization as we know it." It's our civilization, after all; we built it, and perhaps that gives us the right to destroy it. But we are not our own fathers; we did not create the human race, much less the other forms of life that share the planet with us. A defense policy that threatens life itself on such a scale is simply too crazy to stand.

In a sense, the bad news about nuclear winter is *so* bad that it might even be taken as grounds for a perverse optimism. If we finally admit that we can't fight a nuclear war without destroying ourselves—*really* destroying ourselves—then perhaps the time has come to quit preparing to fight one. Even deterrence—preventing war through fear of the consequences—demands a credible threat. Can it be credible to threaten attacks on Soviet cities that would expose both nations—even without Soviet retaliation—to nuclear winter? Thus the problem of burning cities has introduced a wild card into the calculations of American (and presumably of Soviet) war planners.

Of course, many technical uncertainties remain. The authors of the nuclear-winter paper stopped short of claiming to know that a nuclear war would shroud the earth in a long, freezing night and kill everybody. Much scientific work remains to be done. But the preliminary findings are not encouraging; the prospect of smoke from hundreds of burning cities poses a real problem for defense planners. Even military men, normally skeptical of apocalyptic claims, are worried—especially the ones who draw up the plans for targeting nuclear weapons in the event of war. Some of the ones I've talked to—a retired admiral, for example, who was in charge of war planning for the Joint Chiefs of Staff (JCS) in the early 1970s— look rueful, smile ironically, and give vague waves of the hand and shakes of the head when they respond to claims that a thousand large fires in a hundred major cities could mean big trouble worldwide. The targeting experts know we're planning to do worse than that to the Russians. But if you take the cities out of the war plan, there's no plan left. It's an either/or proposition: either we stick to the plan and court ecological catastrophe, or we get rid of the plan and try to think of something else to do with the 9,500 strategic nuclear warheads in the American arsenal. What that might be is hard to imagine. Nuclear weapons are good for igniting fires over hundreds of square kilometers and obliterating downtowns. If cities are off limits, there's not much to use the weapons on. The public is having a hard time trying to grasp just how uncompromising the choice is, but the war planners got the point right away: if the smoke of burning cities is really a problem, then our current plans for fighting a nuclear war amount to literal suicide for the country that strikes first, even if there is no retaliation.

In the popular mind, at least, nuclear war has always meant the end of the world. Numerous public-opinion surveys have shown that the average American *expects* to die if there is a nuclear war; many even hope that they will die. Until recently military officials, and probably most scientists who take an interest in nuclear strategy, have not shared these apocalyptic fears. Indeed, one badge of the weapons fraternity has been a hardheaded knowledge of how bad nuclear war isn't. But ordinary citizens are difficult to reassure. They're convinced that we passed the point of overkill long ago, not just in rhetoric but in fact. Perhaps the toughest thing for the public to understand is why the military wants more nuclear weapons when "we've already got more than we need to kill everybody ten times over." Anyone who writes or speaks professionally about these matters hears this question again and again. The answer is that the world's nuclear arsenal of perhaps 50,000 weapons would certainly be big enough to kill everybody if people would gather together conveniently in exposed places, but not otherwise—or so the experts have thought. To "blow up the world" in the popular sense of the phrase would take far more nuclear weapons than we've got, probably even more than we could make. "There's just not enough fissionable material," Richard Turco, a scientist specializing in atmospheric studies at R & D Associates, in Marina del Rey, California, told me recently. Turco has been studying the effects of nuclear weapons on the atmosphere for years, and he was one of the five authors of the nuclear-winter paper—the phrase is Turco's coinage—published last December. Turco believes that a nuclear war could threaten man and many of his fellow creatures with utter disaster, but, like most technically minded men, he hates imprecision, and he is particularly irritated by popular fears that imagine disaster of the wrong sort. He once did some calculations to see what it would take to blow down all the world's buildings with blast waves, to ignite all the combustible materials on the surface of the earth with thermal pulse, or to expose everyone on earth to a dose of a thousand rads (units of radiation) within an eighteen-hour period. The first two would take about two million megatons of explosive power (that is, the equivalent of two trillion tons of TNT) and the third about a quarter of that amount. "Blowing up the world" in the literal sense is beyond us.

But there is more than one way to skin a cat. The late Herman Kahn, who made his reputation with a huge tome, published in 1960, titled *On Thermonuclear War,* speculated in that book on the feasibility of an ultimate deterrent, a "doomsday machine" that could destroy the planet in the event that the side in control of the trigger felt that it had been pushed into an untenable corner. Kahn could be something of an intellectual rascal; it amused him to carry rationality to extremes, outraging the tenderer hearts of traditional humanists. But also he had a serious purpose in mind. He felt that atomic weapons were a fact of modern life, and had to be considered rationally; they weren't something just to be brandished with wild threats of an apocalyptic *or else.* Kahn put the war plans of the late 1950s into that category. These plans were hard to execute but simple in theory—obliteration of the Soviet Union. In 1953 the Joint Chiefs of Staff approved a plan named Offtackle, devised by the Strategic

Air Command (SAC) under LeMay, which called for opening with attacks on Moscow (twenty bombs) and Leningrad (twelve) and then delivering the rest of the arsenal (about 900 weapons in all) to targets in other Soviet and East European cities. Another plan, named Reaper, adopted the following year, called for dropping 1,500 bombs on Soviet targets. Kahn thought this all-or-nothing approach was crazy, and he attacked it obliquely with his doomsday speculations.

The idea behind Kahn's proposal for a doomsday machine, dreamed up pretty much off the top of his head, was simple: pack the deepest hole that could be dug or found with thousands of megatons of nuclear weapons, thereby threatening to shatter the crust of the earth and literally break the planet apart. He concluded that such a project was feasible but dumb. It might blow up the world, all right, but it wouldn't deter, because the other side wouldn't believe anyone was crazy enough to trigger the machine. In a footnote, interestingly, Kahn wondered if we might not create a doomsday machine inadvertently. He decided not: the planet was too tough; you couldn't kill it without really trying.

Kahn worked for the Rand Corporation in 1960; he had high-level security clearances and was privy to a broad range of the nation's nuclear secrets. But like everyone else at the time, he failed to sense the ecological fragility of the earth; he overlooked the potential importance of the humblest of the side effects of nuclear war—the smoke of burning cities; and it never occurred to him that the United States had already built a doomsday machine and had been preparing since the approval of Reaper, in 1954, to use that machine, in complete ignorance of the possible result.

The threat to the world's climate that the smoke of burning cities poses was a long time sinking in. It was like Edgar Allan Poe's "Purloined Letter"—hidden in plain sight. One strand of discovery goes back to a 1980 theory that the mass extinctions of dinosaur species at the boundary of the Cretaceous and Tertiary periods, about 65 million years ago, were the doing of a large asteroid, perhaps six or seven miles in diameter, which slammed into the earth with tremendous impact. The dust and debris blown up into the atmosphere by the collision would have darkened the sky for months, cooling the surface of the earth and reducing ambient light—that is, the average visible light at the surface of the earth—below the level at which photosynthesis could keep green things alive. Each of these effects was lethal in its own right, but coming together they precipitated a downward spiral—a kind of unraveling of life systems a bit like an economic crash, in which the failure of one business or industry immediately threatens another, until all lie in ruins. The dinosaur-extinction theory was substantially revised over the following few years, but one point was established pretty thoroughly—junk in the upper atmosphere could have a significant darkening and cooling effect on the earth's surface.

A second strand of discovery began in 1971, when the *Mariner 9* space probe went into orbit around Mars and began transmitting photographs of the planet entirely surrounded by dust from a vast Martian storm. Carl Sagan, the well-known Cornell University astronomer, and other scientists monitoring the probe spent three months studying Martian dust storms, because there was nothing much else to do while they waited for the Martian atmosphere to clear. One thing they learned was that dust in the upper atmosphere tends to absorb sunlight and heat up, while the surface of the planet, in semidarkness, tends to cool down. The models they devised to describe the behavior of Martian dust storms seem to work equally well for the effects of volcanic eruptions on Earth.

The biggest of these, according to a study by the Smithsonian Institution, occurred in April of 1815, on the island of Sumbawa, in the Indonesian archipelago. Days of earth tremors and mighty rumbling like the sound of cannon culminated in a single tremendous explosion that blew off the top 4,200 feet of Mount Tambora and cast up some twenty-five cubic miles of earth and rock into the atmosphere—roughly a hundred times the stuff spewed up by Mount St. Helens or by the eruption of Vesuvius, which buried Herculaneum and Pompeii in A.D. 79. So dense was the dust, smoke, and ash in the air that the Tambora eruption was followed by three days of total darkness over an area 400 miles across. The volcano's plume carried debris into the stratosphere—the cold, rainless, slowly swirling blanket of thin air above the troposphere—where it circled the earth for a year or two before settling out. Scientists have estimated that the dust cloud generated by Tambora resulted in a cooling of the earth's surface that averaged about sixth tenths of one degree centigrade. That may not sound like much, but the result in New England has been remembered ever since as "the year there was no summer." Killing frosts in every month of the year in northern New England, and cold throughout the region, severely damaged crops and led to wheat prices so high that they weren't equaled for more than 150 years, until 1972. Similar weather in Europe caused outright famine in many areas, probably triggered a typhus epidemic that spread from Ireland to England, and may have contributed in a roundabout way to the arrival of cholera in Europe in the 1830s.

Another strand of discovery emerged in the early 1970s, when scientists demonstrated that the fluorocarbons used to provide the pressure in aerosol cans of everything from shaving cream to oven cleaner and deodorant could break down ozone. Ozone is only a minor component of the earth's atmosphere, but it is nevertheless important. A belt of the gas surrounds the planet and shields it from a good part of the sun's ultraviolet rays, mild doses of which cause sunburn, and strong, direct doses of which can cause skin cancer and blindness. The fluorocarbon controversy, typically, resulted in a broad range of scientific studies demonstrating that fluorocarbons do indeed drift into the upper atmosphere, where they break down ozone. Whether pressurized aerosol cans could release enough fluorocarbons to endanger the ozone layer was never conclusively established, but the controversy directed attention to another problem—the tendency of nuclear detonations in the megaton range to produce large quantities of nitrous oxides and to carry them up into the stratosphere, where, like fluorocarbons, they break down ozone. In 1975 the National Academy of Sciences published a major study titled *Long-term Worldwide Effects of Multiple Nuclear-Weapon Detonations*, which concluded that a major nuclear war would deplete the ozone layer, that this would increase the amount of ultraviolet light reaching the surface of the earth to a serious but not catastrophic degree, and that this effect would persist for several years before the ozone layer replenished itself naturally.

Throughout the 1970s the pieces were coming together: the controversy over dinosaur extinctions, the Martian-dust-storm studies, climatologists' increasingly sophisticated understanding of the effects of volcanic eruptions on weather, and the work by the National Academy of Sciences on ozone depletion prepared the way for illumination of the biggest light bulb of all—the realization that smoke, if there were enough of it, and if it reached high enough, had the capacity to plunge the globe into freezing darkness.

The first serious study of the smoke that would be generated by nuclear warfare, by Paul Crutzen, a West German scientist, and John Birks, an American, was published in a special issue of *Ambio*, the journal of Sweden's Royal Academy of Sciencies, in June of 1982. Crutzen and Birks assumed that a major nuclear war would ignite about five percent of the 20 million square kilometers of forest in the world's temperate regions. Their calculations showed that the smoke from these vast fires, like the dust generated by volcanic eruptions, but on a much greater scale, would threaten the climate through heating of the upper atmosphere and cooling of the earth's surface.

An early preprint of the *Ambio* article circulated among scientists at a meeting in Santa Barbara, California, in early 1982, where Richard Turco, who had worked on the ozone problem, read it. He started to crunch numbers on his own to see what would happen. Eventually he and four other scientists—Brian Toon, Thomas Ackerman,

James Pollack, and Carl Sagan—wrote a detailed, 127-page scientific paper called the Blue Book (the group were also the authors of the article published in *Science* last December; this was basically a condensed and corrected version of the Blue Book), and this was reviewed in detail by about a hundred scientists at a four-day meeting held in Cambridge, Massachusetts, in April of 1983. The Blue Book estimated the ozone and radiation effects of nuclear war along with the smoke problem, and went another step beyond the Crutzen and Birks study by accounting for the smoke from burning cities—a threat to the earth's climate much greater than forest fires, because there is more to burn in cities, and because the nature of the fires would help push smoke high into the atmosphere. By this time the nuclear-winter thesis was a subject of wide discussion throughout military and scientific circles in the United States. Technical objections were numerous, and every aspect of the paper's data base, methodology, climate modeling, and results was scrutinized rigorously at the Cambridge meeting. The TTAPS authors (the acronym is formed from the initials of their last names, and is pronounced as if there were only one T) were the first to admit that their work contained numerous uncertainties, but their science held up with sufficient "robustness" (scientific argot meaning that an answer to a question tends to come out the same even if you fiddle with the assumptions) to make any sober investigator recognize that this problem could not be lightly dismissed.

Available only in mimeographed form, the Blue Book makes hard reading for a layman. It is filled with the names of unfamiliar chemical compounds like peroxyacetyl nitrate, hard-to-imagine numbers like $10^9$, numerous technical terms like *entrainment* and *hygroscopic*, and mathematical symbols like $\sim$, $<$, $>$, $\phi$, and $\lesssim$. There are seventeen graphs, some of which have more ups and downs than a comb has teeth, and eighteen pages of references to more than 200 published scientific studies, which start with Aandahl, A. R., *Soils of the Great Plains*, and wind up with Yokoyama, I., "A Geophysical Interpretation of the 1883 Krakatoa Eruption." The Blue Book's authors studied several dozen imaginary nuclear wars, ranging from an all-out, 25,000-megaton exchange of the sort Herman Kahn used to refer to as a "spasm war," down to a relatively small (and improbable, as we shall see), 100-megaton war involving a thousand detonations entirely on cities. Keeping these wars straight as one reads is no easy task. The Blue Book frankly confesses, "The overall uncertainty in the present calculations is quite large. It arises from a lack of knowledge of the number, yields and types of nuclear bursts which might be detonated in a war, of the basic physical properties of nuclear dust and smoke, of the causes and characteristics of mass nuclear fires in cities and forests, and

of the response of the atmosphere to enormous particle injections."

Nevertheless, few readers would have difficulty in grasping the disquieting central message of the Blue Book. Nuclear weapons, especially when detonated in the air, produce an intense thermal pulse that can ignite fires simultaneously over vast areas. Any city attacked with nuclear weapons will burn, and many of these burning cities will generate firestorms whose gigantic smoke columns will carry soot particles into the upper atmosphere, where they might linger for months before settling out. The pall of smoke from burning cities would rapidly diffuse over the mid-latitudes of the Northern Hemisphere and might circulate into the tropical regions around the equator, which, for complex reasons, would be even more sensitive to changes in ambient light and temperature. Darkness at the earth's surface would bring a decline in mean annual temperatures of as much as 40° centigrade for months. If the war took place in spring or early summer, temperatures might fall well below zero throughout July, August, and September. For months it might be as dark at midday as it normally is on a moonlit night. The effects of this long, cold "night" on plant ecology—and everything that lives is ultimately dependent on the photosynthesis of plants—are hard to predict in detail but would almost certainly be catastrophic.

The science in the Blue Book may be complex, but it describes a simple mechanism. Think of the relief that comes on a hot, clear day in July when you pass from the brutal glare of the midday sun to the deep shade of a maple tree, or even a beach umbrella. Under normal conditions the heat absorbed from sunlight during the day escapes at night—but slowly, because the earth's atmosphere serves as a kind of blanket. The longer the night, the more heat escapes. In a "night" lasting months, heat would go on escaping and temperatures would go on dropping. In trying to calculate the smoke effects of a nuclear war, the first and most important question is: How many fires would be ignited? The answer is a military secret. It is contained in the war plans for targeting nuclear weapons which have been drawn up by military men in the United States and the Soviet Union.

The earliest and the most persistent criticisms of the nuclear-winter thesis have focused on scenarios—imaginary nuclear wars devised as a tool for predicting effects. When Richard Turco briefed his colleagues at R & D Associates on an early version of the Blue Book, some of them were quick to point out that he was trying to calculate the effects of wars that would never happen. One scenario, for example, describes a 100-megaton war in which 1,000 warheads of 100 kilotons each are detonated over 1,000 urban targets. Such a war would certainly produce a lot of smoke, but it is not anything we have to worry about. It contradicts too many principles of nuclear strategy, which call for wars of extreme caution or reckless extravagance—nothing in between. If American war planners elected to "limit" a war to 100 megatons, they would stay away from cities, which are generally targeted only in the final, all-out phases of war plans. If the planners decided to hit 1,000 urban targets (an attack virtually certain to bring an all-out response), they would use a lot more than 100 megatons and would target a lot of other things as well.

Academic defense analysts have often faulted the TTAPS study for worrying about the wrong sorts of wars, but the Pentagon has not joined them. When the TTAPS group presented its findings at a highly publicized conference in Washington, a year ago October, the response from the White House and the Pentagon was virtual silence. Many skeptical outsiders (including me, at first) interpreted this silence as indifference, as just one more bit of evidence, if any were needed, that the military was narrowly focused on its own obsessions—what the Russians had and what we had that could destroy what the Russians had. But in fact something deeper was at work. In early December the assistant secretary of Defense for atomic energy, Richard Wagner, arranged for a briefing of Pentagon officials on the nuclear-winter findings. One of those who took part was Michael May, a former director of the Lawrence Livermore National Laboratory, which, like Los Alamos, is mainly concerned with the design and development of nuclear weapons. May, who is still active at the Livermore Lab, and his colleagues—especially Michael MacCracken, an expert on climate—had already studied the nuclear-winter thesis in detail, and they told the assembled Pentagon officials that the problem was a serious one. Although they disagreed with some of the assumptions, they found no obvious faults in the science. The smoke of burning cities posed a serious threat to the earth's climate.

May has spent most of his life in weapons work. The Livermore Lab, founded largely through the efforts of Edward Teller, specialized early in advanced warheads and has designed perhaps half of those in the current American arsenal. The people who work at Livermore believe in deterrence, believe in making good weapons better, and believe that much public criticism of their work is based on misinformation and hysteria. If the nuclear-winter thesis had been full of holes, May and his colleagues would not have hesitated to say so. The briefing—which was gloomy not only from a broadly human but also from a narrow military point of view—resulted in the Pentagon's public silence and its private support for further research. The reason was simple: the nuclear-winter thesis, if valid, threatens to make nonsense of every notion the planners have managed to come up

with, in forty years of trying to devise a sensible way to fight a nuclear war.

Theories of how to fight a nuclear war come in two styles—one that is abstract and analytical, often referred to by professionals as metaphysics or theology, and another that is severely concrete and practical, called war planning. Most of what the public knows about these matters comes from listening in on the debates of theologians, who construct elaborate chains of "if–then" reasoning—if the enemy does X, then we do Y. The theologians are mainly concerned with demonstrating that nuclear weapons are safe to have, because they are too dangerous to use. Nuclear theology is a cottage industry providing gainful employment to many hundreds of academic defense specialists. A cynic might be forgiven for concluding that the Pentagon is willing to pay for so much theology to maintain a kind of smokescreen, behind which the real work is conducted by the war planners—the middle-ranking officers, mostly in the Air Force, who are responsible for the nuts-and-bolts details of running a nuclear war.

War planning is a very different sort of enterprise. Theologians talk about "an opponent" or "the enemy." War planners talk about the Russians. The planners begin with a courtly bow to deterrence—if we're ready, it won't happen—but that's the end of it. All the rest is deciding what to shoot at and when to shoot at it. The fundamental thing to grasp about war planning is that we *plan* to do what we *can* do.

For the past forty years the American nuclear arsenal has been in constant flux, becoming steadily more lethal through increases in the number of weapons, greater versatility in firing and retargeting, and improved accuracy. In the early plans weapons were targeted on the center of Moscow; now they might be targeted on the Ministry of Foreign Affairs, or on the main entrance to a blast shelter intended for top officials of GOSPLAN, the central Soviet economic-planning office, or on a point calculated to include three or more targets—say, a truck plant, a power station, and a local office of the KGB—within the lethal radius of a single warhead. As the weapons grow more numerous, the targets tend to divide, and the number of aiming points, or desired ground zeros (DGZs), always seems to be a jump ahead of the weapons available to attack them. Consider, for example, the problem facing planners who hope to cripple Soviet rail transport. With only a few weapons available for the task, they would limit targets to major switching yards. Given more weapons, the planners would add locomotive production plants and repair facilities to the list of targets. Eventually, with a big inventory of weapons available, minor bridges, rural sidings, telegraph offices, steel-rolling mills for the production of rails, and the central pension office for retired rail workers might all be included in the plan. The Harvard biochemist Paul Doty, long active as a consultant on defense issues, once asked the planners what was the smallest target on the list. The answer was an open field that might be used as a landing strip by returning Soviet bombers.

The dominant tone of the military mind is cautious. War may be hell, as General William Tecumseh Sherman characterized it, after cutting a swath of destruction through the South during the Civil War, but for the men who prepare to fight wars there is something worse than the horrors of battle: losing. From their point of view, too much is barely enough. Thus American planning for nuclear war—and no doubt Soviet planning as well—has always relied on overkill, an attempt to achieve certainty of result through overwhelming strength. General LeMay's theory of war was brutally simple. Back in 1953 he told Sam Cohen, a young defense consultant and weapons designer now best known for his invention of the neutron bomb, "I'll tell you what war is all about—you've got to kill people, and when you've killed enough they stop fighting." LeMay wanted the biggest warheads he could get. Eventually he loaded his planes with 20-megaton bombs, and his staff worked up plans for the virtual annihilation of the Soviet Union. A Navy captain who received a SAC briefing on war plans in early 1954 reported to a superior, "The final impression was that virtually all of Russia would be nothing but a smoking, radiating ruin at the end of two hours."

But it is still hard to say what LeMay's plans called for, because he wouldn't tell anybody—not the White House, not the Joint Chiefs of Staff, and certainly not Sam Cohen, who'd been sent out to SAC headquarters, in Omaha, to find that out, among other things. "This involves our secret war plans," LeMay told him. "I'm not going to tell you what they are." There is even some evidence that LeMay thought it was up to him to decide *when* to go to war.

But for all LeMay's secrecy the war plans were really very simple—hit 'em with everything we have. By 1960 we had a lot. In November of that year President Eisenhower sent a three-man team headed by his science adviser, George Kistiakowsky, to Offutt Air Force Base, in Omaha, to check up on the war plans being devised by the newly established Joint Strategic Target Planning Staff (JSTPS). Eisenhower was afraid that SAC was fiddling with the figures as a way of building pressure for more planes and bombs—for example, insisting that it would take several large nuclear weapons to destroy a hydroelectric dam with 100 percent certainty, when a single small one might do the job with 96 percent certainty. Kistiakowsky was accompanied by two young assistants, George Rathjens, a scientist now teaching at MIT, and Herbert Scoville, a former deputy director for science and technology at the CIA who is now a leading arms-control advocate.

The three men got a royal runaround at SAC headquarters from Air Force briefing officers under instructions to reveal as little as possible as slowly as possible. But they persisted, and eventually got a good idea of what was going into the first Single Integrated Operational Plan (SIOP). They were horrified to discover that the plan would almost entirely ignore the collateral effects of nuclear weapons. With few exceptions, SAC intended to destroy targets by blast pressure alone. If the prevailing winds on D-day were blowing from Leningrad toward Finland, then warheads targeted on the city would be fused to detonate in the air, to avoid the fallout characteristic of ground bursts, but that was about the only concession the JSTPS made to radioactivity. The tendency toward overkill was compounded by establishing a "very high certainty of kill against all these targets," according to Rathjens. That meant using more than one warhead, or warheads with very large yields, or both. The first SIOP, officially approved in December of 1960, called for an all-out attack on Russia with 4,000 weapons fired in "one flush"—everything we had.

The details of the SIOP have changed a great deal since 1960. The U.S. strategic arsenal now includes twice as many warheads, and many of them are extremely accurate. For our purpose here, one point is of overriding importance: all versions of the SIOP include plans for a society-destroying attack on Soviet "recovery targets"—the Soviet institutions that make Russia strong—and thousands of these targets are in Soviet cities.

We have always insisted that we do not plan to attack Soviet cities or the population per se, but the point is an academic one. Soviet cities are rich in targets—communions and transportation centers, offices of leading institutions of Soviet society like the Communist Party and the KGB, military command posts, blast shelters for the leadership, factories that make war materials, and so on. Even attacks on airfields—a staple of all war plans since the early 1950s—would threaten vast urban areas with fire. A 1978 study by the Arms Control and Disarmament Agency (ACDA) suggests the magnitude of the problem. In order to estimate the effectiveness of Soviet civil-defense planning (a subject of much contention in Washington at the time), ACDA outlined a typical American second strike, to follow a full-fledged Soviet counterforce attack on the United States (the purpose of which would be not destruction pure and simple but the elimination of things identified as the source of military and economic strength). Moscow alone would be struck with about sixty warheads, Leningrad with more than forty, the next eight largest cities with an average of thirteen warheads each. The next forty largest cities would receive an average of 14.4 warheads per million population and the 150 cities after that an average of 25.7 per million; 80 percent of all Soviet cities over 75,000 in population would be struck with nuclear weapons. All of these would burn. The United States could expect to suffer similar damage in return. Such attacks are integral to American theories of how to fight a nuclear war. "There's never been one of those plans that didn't have cities in it," William Kaufmann, a defense expert, says. "I don't care if it's the 1961 SIOP, or the '73 or the '78. The main difference now is that the set of non-urban targets has been expanded." At the Livermore Lab, Michael May said recently that he wasn't sure whether the nuclear-winter thesis would stand up, but that he very much doubted the war planners would be willing to leave cities out of the targeting line-up. "You can say, Don't shoot at the cities—that's fine," he said. "But are they [the Russians] going to leave all our airfields alone and let the B-52s and [midair-refueling] tankers land at them? Think of the aerospace targets in Los Angeles. Are they going to leave those alone even if they have the best of intentions for the Angelenos? It's not hard to come up with five hundred high-priority targets associated with cities, not hard at all."

If those targets are attacked, the cities will burn. If those targets are spared, we have no theory of how to fight a nuclear war. As a result the war planners are now faced with an extraordinary dilemma: either we stick to the theory and plan to run the risk of plunging the Northern Hemisphere into a nuclear winter triggered by the smoke of burning cities, or we abandon the theory and finally admit we simply cannot fight a war with nuclear weapons.

Not long ago a friend told me a story that he said had been told to him by someone who had heard it from a staff member on Jimmy Carter's National Security Council. It goes like this: When Carter and President-elect Ronald Reagan met after the election in 1980 to discuss the transition, Carter chose to use his time to tell Reagan what "pushing the button" would actually mean. According to the staffer, Carter really laid it out—the numbers of weapons and where they would go, the impossible difficulties involved in trying to keep track of the progress of the war, the excellent chance that the President would find himself aloft in his command plane with nowhere to land and nothing but static coming over the radios. The ghastliness sank in. When Reagan left the meeting, he was ashen and subdued. He finally *knew*.

It's an appealing story. I'm sure we all hope it's true, but it's almost certainly apocryphal. I've heard variants of it many times about other Presidents and high officials. I've come to think of these stories collectively as the Myth of the Frightened President. The drift of the stories is always the same: A man reaches high office, full of insouciant confidence. He gets "the briefing." He comes away sober and shaken. It's as if the collective unconscious of Washington, where these stories are mainly

told, needs to be reassured that the men at the top really understand the danger we face.

The evidence suggests that the reality is quite different. With the possible exception of Jimmy Carter, who had an enormous appetite for technical detail, no postwar American President has really understood precisely what we intend to do in the event of nuclear war.

Everything Eisenhower knew about the first SIOP came from George Kistiakowsky's ninety-minute briefing after his trip to Omaha in November of 1960. Four thousand targets in ninety minutes is pretty cursory. President Kennedy was urged to ask for a look at the SIOP early in his Administration, but the JCS discouraged him. They told him it was too technical—routes, refueling schedules, target coordinates, times on target, overlapping E-95 circles, and the like. Lyndon Johnson was bored by nuclear strategy and obsessed by Vietnam. According to people who were there, Richard Nixon's mind wandered when war plans were discussed. Admiral Elmo Zumwalt, the chief of naval operations during the Nixon Administration, describes in his memoirs a National Security Council briefing held shortly after Nixon had signed National Security Decision Memorandum 242, in January of 1974. This was the first of the so-called "war-fighting" documents that have marked a gradual sea change in American nuclear strategy over the past ten years. Before it was signed, the SIOP contained four basic war plans, or options, the smallest of which called for the use of 2,500 warheads. Afterward the JSTPS devised many new options, ranging from the delivery of a "few score" warheads on up to furious salvos intended to annihilate Soviet society—always the last stage of U.S. war plans. Many cities feel that the countervailing strategy adopted in 242 makes nuclear war more likely. Whether they are right is hard to say. But according to Zumwalt, Nixon had no idea what was implied by the new strategy.

Gerald Ford signed a similar document affecting strategy on his last day in office without—according to several National Security Council staffers—any clear idea of what he was doing. Carter was the exception: he drilled himself with frequent command-post exercises and fully grasped the importance of his own strategy document, Presidential Directive 59, which carried the war-fighting approach a step further and dwelt on the need for enhanced command, control, communications, and intelligence facilities to keep track of a war. Ronald Reagan represents a reversion to the traditional presidential approach: leaving the details to aides.

For the first ten years of its existence the JSTPS was pretty much on its own in coming up with a strategy on which to base its war plans. Guidance from the White House and the Pentagon was limited. Richard Garwin, who helped design the first hydrogen bombs and who has long been an adviser to the Air Force on targeting, told me not long ago that the men who picked targets used to read the public speeches of the President and his principal advisers for an idea of how to proceed. Since 1970 the war-planning process has been rationalized. Now it typically begins with a brief presidential document, perhaps ten pages in length—Nixon's was NSDM 242, Carter's was PD 59, Reagan's is National Security Decision Directive 13. With this as a guide the Office of the Secretary of Defense drafts a somewhat longer Nuclear Weapons Employment Policy (NUWEP), which is further elaborated by the office of the JCS and then forwarded to the JSTPS in Omaha for its twice-a-year revision of the SIOP.

When the revised plan is ready, officers from the JSTPS brief the staff of the Joint Chiefs, who brief the Joint Chiefs, who brief the secretary of Defense, who may or may not brief the President—but the extent of the briefing drops off sharply as it rises up through the Pentagon. Ninety minutes seems to be the outside limit at the upper levels. It is highly unlikely that anyone above the Joint Chiefs of Staff level really understands what is in the SIOP. According to many sources, there is no independent review of the SIOP at any stage in the planning process; the size of the U.S. arsenal provides the only limit to the size of a major projected war; and no one involved in drawing up the SIOP is authorized to consider the gross environmental effects of carrying out the plan. As a practical matter, if the nuclear-winter thesis is confirmed, then participation in the war-planning process, at all levels, will have to be broadened, current theories of how to fight a nuclear war will have to be jettisoned, and a whole new generation of weaponry, designed to implement a whole new strategy, will have to be developed and deployed. All of these things would be difficult, but none would be impossible. The military "solution" to the nuclear-winter problem is particularly clear—a much larger number of much smaller, extremely accurate weapons that would allow targets in cities to be destroyed without burning down the cities around them.

A Pentagon planner recently told William Arkin, a Washington journalist and defense specialist, "I wouldn't mind having twenty-five thousand Pershing IIs with forty-kiloton warheads, if they told me I had to have a hundred-megaton force." The nuclear-winter problem does not end the possibility of a big war with Russia, but it does push planners in a new direction, away from apocalypse. Nothing stands in the way of this change except habit, inertia, and the quite staggering cost in money of building a whole new arsenal.

The official response to the nuclear-winter problem has been reticence in public combined with funding for more study. Just about everybody, including the TTAPS authors, agrees that more study is required. The National Academy of Sciences is sponsoring a major new research effort, and other projects have been started at Livermore and Los Alamos and in the Pentagon's own Defense Nuclear Agency (DNA), which has been commissioning studies on the effects of nuclear weapons for years. The target planners in Omaha use DNA handbooks for estimating collateral damage, for example, but the current work is probably the first that will come up with guidelines for an overall limit—an admission that there is such a thing as a level of damage too great for the planet to handle.

"More study" will serve by way of response for a year or two, but what then? Pentagon officials are plainly worried about the nuclear-winter problem, and plainly at a loss over what to do about it. In conversation with officials at the nuts-and-bolts level one picks up interesting nuances of reaction: a wistful hope that "more study" will make the nuclear-winter problem go away, embarrassment at having overlooked it for nearly forty years, resentment that the peacenik doom-mongers might have been right all these years, even if they didn't know why they were. Above all, one finds frank dismay at what the nuclear-winter problem does to a defense policy heavily based on nuclear weapons. Being only human, officials are probably hoping to turn up uncertainties enough to justify more study forever, or at least until the next Administration. But to me, recognition of the nuclear-winter problem, awful as it is, seems a piece of immense good fortune at the eleventh hour, and a sign that Providence hasn't given up on us yet.

## QUESTIONS

1. Explain the implications that the "nuclear winter" scenario has for the superpower's reliance on nuclear weapons.

2. Using a sociological viewpoint, try to imagine what would happen to your society, or what was left of it, after an all-out nuclear war between the superpowers.

3. Do you think that the possession of nuclear weapons by the superpowers helps maintain world security, or do you think it undermines that security?